BUSINESS

BUSINESS

Barry L. Reece

Virginia Polytechnic Institute and State University

James P. O'Grady

St. Louis Community College
at Florissant Valley

Houghton Mifflin Company   Boston
Dallas   Geneva, Illinois
Lawrenceville, New Jersey   Palo Alto

To Vera, Lynne, Mark, Monique,
Michelle, and Colleen
Barry L. Reece

To Pattie, Pat, Mike, Dan,
and Tim — PTL
James P. O'Grady

PHOTOGRAPH CREDITS

Photo essays designed by Ann Schroeder

Business Views: Foreign Competition P. 1, © 1984 Jim Pickerell. P. 2: center, © Chip Peterson; top right, © Ellis Herwig/The Picture Cube. P. 3: top left, © 1981 Jim Pickerell; center, © James H. Simon/The Picture Cube. P. 4: top, © Paul Conklin; bottom, © Owen Franken/Stock Boston. P. 5: left, © Philip Jon Bailey/The Picture Cube; right, © Susan Van Etten. P. 6, © D. and J. Heaton/Uniphoto.

Business Views: The Changing Workplace P. 1, © James H. Simon/The Picture Cube. P. 2: center, © 1985 Martin Rogers/Stock Boston; top right, © Max Winter/Stock Boston. P. 3: center, © Paul Conklin; top right, © 1984 Richard Pasley/Stock Boston. P. 4: left, © 1984 Tom Tracy/The Image Bank; right, © Ann McQueen/Stock Boston. P. 5: top left, © 1983 Peter Menzel/Stock Boston; center, © 1985 Ron Blakeley/Uniphoto. P. 6, © Paul Conklin.

Business Views: The Changing Population P. 1, © David Woo/Stock Boston. P. 2: center, © Donald Dietz/Stock Boston; top right, © 1985 John Bowden/Uniphoto. P. 3: top left, © Bill Gallery/Stock Boston; center, © 1980 Jim Pickerell. P. 4: top, © Tony O'Brien/Stock Boston; bottom, © Paul Conklin. P. 5, © Raoul Hacke/Stock Boston. P. 6: left, © M. Messenger; right, © 1985 M. Tcherevkoff/The Image Bank.

Business Views: High Technology P. 1: top, © 1985 Balthazar Korab/Uniphoto; bottom, © Terry Qing/FPG International. P. 2, © 1985 Jim Pickerell. P. 3: center, © 1985 Jim Pickerell; top right, © Dick Luria/FPG International. P. 4: left, © 1985 Paul Katz/The Image Bank; right, © Michael Rizza/The Picture Cube. P. 5, © 1986 Susan Greenwood/Gamma-Liaison. P. 6: top, © 1985 Lou Jones/Uniphoto; bottom, © Stacy Pick/Uniphoto.

Business Views: The Global Economy P. 1, © 1985 Flip Chalfant/The Image Bank. P. 2: center, © Paul Conklin; bottom left, © Henryk T. Kaiser/Uniphoto; bottom right, © 1985 Robert Herko/The Image Bank. P. 3, © Susan Van Etten. P. 4: top, © 1986 Alvis Upitis/The Image Bank; bottom, © 1985 Gerhard Gscheidle/The Image Bank. P. 5, © Nicolas Sapieha/Stock Boston. P. 6: top, © 1985 Stacy Pick/Uniphoto; bottom, © 1986 Michael Melford/The Image Bank.

Business Views: The Future P. 1, © Don Carroll/The Image Bank. P. 2: center, © Lou Jones/Uniphoto; top right, © Charles Fell/Uniphoto. P. 3: top, © Susan Van Etten; bottom, © 1984 Lou Jones/Uniphoto. P. 4, © Carroll Seghers/Uniphoto. P. 5: top, © Susan Van Etten; bottom, © John Zoiner/Uniphoto. P. 6: center, © Susan Van Etten; top right, © 1980 Don Carroll/The Image Bank.

Chapter Openers P. 4, © Lou Jones; p. 32, © Dan Cornish/ESTO; p. 58, © 1985 Lou Jones; p. 86, © Al Fisher Photography; p. 122, © 1986 Jeff Smith; p. 150, © 1986 Jeff Smith; p. 176, © 1983 Jeff Smith; p. 210, © François Robert; p. 242, © 1983 Shelly Katz/Black Star; p. 272, © François Robert; p. 304, © 1985 Richard Howard; p. 328, courtesy of Burger King, a subsidiary of The Pillsbury Company; p. 354, courtesy of Staley Continental, Inc., Chicago; p. 382, © 1981 Tom Sobolik/Black Star; p. 416, © 1985 Richard Howard; p. 450, © Mark Joseph; p. 492, © David Burnett/Gamma-Liaison; p. 518, © 1981 Jeff Smith; p. 544, © 1986 Joel Gordon; p. 568, © 1985 Lou Jones; p. 604, © 1980 Dennis Brack/Black Star; p. 630, courtesy of NASA; and p. 656, © Robin Moyer/Gamma-Liaison.

Chapter 1 P. 7, © 1983 Nik Wheeler/Black Star; p. 11, courtesy of Carolina Power & Light Company; p. 15, The Granger Collection; p. 16, The Granger Collection; p. 21, The Granger Collection;

(continued after Glossary)

Cover photograph by Michel Tcherevkoff. Illustrations by Paul Metcalf. Bonnie Yousefian, line art editor.

Printed in the U.S.A.
Library of Congress Catalog Card Number: 86-81594
ISBN: 0-395-35694-6

BCDEFGHIJ-D-8987

CONTENTS

2

SOCIAL RESPONSIBILITY AND BUSINESS ETHICS

3

THE FORMS OF BUSINESS OWNERSHIP

4

**ENTREPRE-
NEURSHIP,
SMALL
BUSINESSES,
AND
FRANCHISES**

Part 2 **MANAGEMENT AND ORGANIZATION**   121

MANAGEMENT

5

ORGANIZATION

6

7

HUMAN RELATIONS IN BUSINESS

Part 3   HUMAN RESOURCES AND PRODUCTION   209

8

MANAGING
HUMAN
RESOURCES

9

**LABOR-
MANAGEMENT
RELATIONS**

OPERATIONS MANAGEMENT

10

Part 4 **MARKETING**

MARKETING MANAGEMENT

11

12

PRODUCT AND PRICING STRATEGIES

13

DISTRIBUTION STRATEGY

Contents

16

COMPUTERS AND MANAGEMENT INFORMATION SYSTEMS

Contents **xvii**

18
FINANCIAL MANAGEMENT

19
SECURITIES MARKETS

20

RISK MANAGEMENT AND INSURANCE

Part 7 BUSINESS AND ITS ENVIRONMENT 603

BUSINESS LAW

21

22

GOVERNMENT AND BUSINESS

23

INTERNATIONAL BUSINESS

PREFACE

The development of a comprehensive business text is not unlike the development of a new business enterprise. The starting point is to identify the needs of the market and then to develop a plan designed to satisfy those needs. BUSINESS was written to satisfy three basic needs of the introduction to business market. These basic needs focus on balance, clarity, and realism.

1. BUSINESS provides a *balanced* coverage of business fundamentals, trends, issues, principles, and practices. Large corporations make many important contributions to our business system, but students also need to become aware of the exciting developments taking place in the small business sector. One would expect a modern business text to focus on the contemporary scene, but not at the expense of ignoring important historical developments and future perspectives. The desire to achieve balance throughout the text influenced hundreds of decisions regarding content selection, depth of coverage, and examples used to illustrate key points.
2. *Clarity* of presentation has been emphasized throughout the text. We believe that presentation clarity is positively associated with student achievement. To achieve clarity, we avoided the use of vague terms and complex theoretical jargon. An abundance of illustrations and examples are used to clarify key concepts and ideas. Finally, every effort was made to eliminate unessential content that might distract the reader. Our aim has been to present the material in a non-technical, interesting, and readable style.

3. *Realism* in terms of appropriate real-world examples builds student interest in reading the text. Our goal has been to develop a book that students will enjoy reading. Every effort was made to select examples that are realistic to the wide range of students who enroll in introductory business courses.

With a focus on balance, clarity, and realism we established our objectives for BUSINESS. They were:

☐ To survey the basic concepts of business
☐ To build a vocabulary of key business terms
☐ To develop business decision-making skills
☐ To provide a background for further study
☐ To create an awareness of career opportunities in business

Achieving our objectives will mean that students will be prepared to enter the business world with objectives of their own.

The Text

BUSINESS will provide students with the opportunity to study the many dimensions of the American business system as well as help them to understand the relationship between business and the other elements of our modern society.

Organization

BUSINESS is organized along the lines that an entrepreneur would want to consider in the creation and management of a business entity. Part 1, "The Business System," provides the framework for studying

American business including its economic context, social responsibility, legal forms and small business considerations. Part 2, "Management and Organization," describes both processes and the human side of enterprise. Part 3, "Human Resources and Production," is concerned with personnel, labor-management and operations management. Part 4, "Marketing Management," considers the decisions on how a product is developed, what its packaging will look like, how it will be presented to end-users, what its price will be, how the product will be transported from its manufacturer to the next purchaser, and what types of promotion will be used to sell it. Part 5, "Information for Business Decision-Making," describes accounting, computers, and the collection, analysis and presentation of management data. Part 6, "Financial Information," focuses on money, our banking and credit system, financial management, the securities market, risk management and insurance. Part 7, "Business and Its Environment," deals with legal, regulatory and international trade.

The basic concepts of business are clearly presented in these seven parts. Each part is a self-contained unit and may be assigned in any sequence. In our presentation of the material we have tried to make the reader aware of opportunities in business and value of planning a business career. It is with a focus on planning for a career that we have included the Career Appendix — work in the 21st century by Dr. S. Norman Feingold, President of National Career and Counseling Services. This appendix will prove to be a valuable tool to those who choose to use it.

Presentation

Included in the plan for BUSINESS were special steps to assure that the design of the book would assist in the learning process. To be effective, a text must be inviting to the reader. It was with respect to this criterion that every aspect of the design of BUSINESS was evaluated. The art program is complementary as well as instructive. Photographs, tables, charts, and figures were either selected or created for the instructional and aesthetic value they bring to the book. The pedagogy is supportive without being obtrusive. Learning objectives, marginal notes, boxed inserts covering international, technological, and social issues, and two end-of-chapter cases support each chapter and help ensure comprehension of the material. Re-

view of each chapter is assisted by the chapter highlights, key vocabulary terms, review questions, and application exercises. Finally, a complete glossary and comprehensive index prove valuable items for reference and review.

A unique feature of BUSINESS is the inclusion of six "photo essays" that provide a business perspective on current issues affecting American business. *Business Views* present photographs and essays on timely issues that are changing the way we live our lives and the way we conduct our business. Changes in demographics, world economy, high technology, the work environment, and types of industries as well as questions about tomorrow have immediate and long-range effects on businesses large and small. These photo essays can be read at any time and as often as the reader wishes to reflect upon the big picture.

The Supporting Package

Student mastery is enhanced by the following enrichment materials:

□ *Study Guide* Written by Constantine G. Petrides, Borough of Manhattan Community College, this comprehensive study guide provides students with several options for reviewing and mastering the material. For each chapter of BUSINESS it contains a list of learning objectives, vocabulary mastery exercises, true/false, multiple choice, fill-in, and matching type questions.

□ *Business Microstudy* A microcomputer version of the study guide available for use with the most popular microcomputers.

□ *Entrepreneur* A computer simulation by Jerry Smith and Peggy Golden, both of the University of Louisville. This microcomputer simulation provides students with an introduction to the establishment and management of a new venture.

A battery of instructional support materials offer assistance for teaching and evaluation:

□ *Instructor's Manual* Includes suggestions for organizing the course, grading, and preparing lectures. The instructor's manual also provides a chapter overview, detailed lecture outline, and answers to in-text questions for each chapter as well as transparency masters, sample business papers, and film lists.

- *Lecture Bank* A floppy disk containing detailed lecture outlines offers instructors the option of personalizing their lectures or creating material for use in the classroom.
- *Test Bank* This manual contains over 2,200 exam questions of multiple choice and true/false format.
- *Microtest* A microcomputer version of the test bank.
- *Transparencies* A set of 100 acetate transparencies provide a variety of tables, line art, definitions, and photographs as additional lecture support.
- *GPA: Grade Performance Analyzer* A record keeping system for use with microcomputers.
- *Videotapes* Real-world situations are presented for classroom viewing and discussion.

Numerous colleagues have contributed to make BUSINESS possible. It has been improved by their advice, critiques, suggestions and recommendations. While recognizing our responsibility for the finished product, we gratefully acknowledge and thank the following reviewers:

David Aiken
  Hacking Technical College
Nikki Altman
  DeVry Institute of Technology
Toby Atkinson
  Brevard Community College
Gregory A. Bach
  University of North Dakota
Barbara Barrett
  St. Louis Community College At Meramec
Harvey R. Blessing
  Essex Community College
William J. Boeger
  St. Louis Community College at Florissant Valley
John S. Bowdidge
  Southwest Missouri State University
Robert Carrel
  Vincennes University
Jill Chown
  Mankato State University
J. Michael Cicero
  Highline Community College
Helen A. Corley
  Oxnard College

Lewis K. Cushing
  Illinois Valley Community College
Dexter Dalton
  St. Louis Community College at Meramec
Kathy Daruty
  Los Angeles Pierce College
John Egan
  Jersey City State College
Ruben C. Estrada
  Pima College, Downtown Campus
Roy Farris
  Southeast Missouri State University
Gilbert Fleming
  Guilford Technical Community College
Donald M. Freeman
  Pikes Peak Community College
William Friedman
  Fontbonne College
David Gennrich
  Waukesha County Technical Institute
Martin Gerber
  Kalamazoo Valley Community College
David K. Graf
  Northern Illinois University
Joseph Gray
  Nassau Community College
Janet M. Green
  San Bernadino Valley College
Glennon Grothaus
  St. Louis Community College at Meramec
Paul Hegele
  Elgin Community College, Fountain Square Campus

Sanford B. Helman
  Middlesex Community College
Nathan Himelstein
  Essex Community College
Louis Hoekstra
  Grand Rapids Jr. College
Paul F. Jenner
  Southwest Missouri State University
Owens Jensen
  North Dakota State School of Science
Gene Johnson
  Clark College
Ann Kane
  Rose State College
Steve Kirman
  Dyke College
Paul Londrigan
  C.S. Mott Community College
Patricia A. Long
  Tarrant County Jr. College
Gary Lyons
  East Texas State University
Donald D. Manning
  University of Northern Colorado
Allen D. Mason
  Stephens College
Robert Masters
  Fort Hays State University
James M. McHugh
  Forest Park Community College
Randall D. Mertz
  Mesa Community College
Nancy Meyer
  Northwestern Business College
James Mezsaros
  County College of Morris

William F. Motz, Jr.
  Lansing Community College
Mary K. Nelson
  University of Minnesota
Kenneth Papenfuss
  Ricks College
Dennis P. Pappas
  Columbus Technical Institute
Constantine G. Petrides
  Borough of Manhattan Community College
Raymond E. Polchow
  Muskingum Area Technical College
Richard Randolph
  Johnson County Community College
Robert Redick
  Lincoln Land Community College
John H. Rich
  Illinois State University
Gabe Sanders
  Jersey City State College
Paul D. Sanders
  West Valley College
Richard E. Schallert
  Black Hawk College
Dennis E. Schmitt
  Emporia State University
Robert W. Sexton
  Cuyahoga Community College
Dennis Shannon
  Belleville Area College
Jeffery D. Stauffer
  Ventura College
David Streifford
  St. Louis Community College at Forest Park
Jack L. Taylor
  Charles County Community College

Robert Wagley
Wright State University
George Wang
*St. Louis Community
College Meramec*
Bernard W. Weinrich
*St. Louis Community
College at Forest Park*

Mildred M. Whitted
*St. Louis Community
College at Forest Park*
William F. Wright
*Mt. Hood Community
College*

We would like to express our sincere thanks to Jane Sherman, Peter Kinder, and Brock Dethier for their contributions to this project.

BARRY L. REECE
JAMES P. O'GRADY

BUSINESS

I
THE BUSINESS SYSTEM

W. L. Gore and Associates is, without a doubt, one of America's most interesting companies. It was started by Bill Gore, an innovative person with a strong entrepreneurial spirit. The company's most famous product is Gore-Tex, a high-tech fabric used in the construction of boots and other outdoor apparel. Today, millions of people stay dry in the rain because of Gore-Tex clothing. W. L. Gore and Associates has not only achieved economic success, it has been recognized as a company with a strong social conscience. In Part I we will discuss how America's free market system fosters the development of new businesses. We will also discuss the evolution of social responsibility in an economic climate that emphasizes freedom and individualism. This section also reviews the various forms of business ownership and introduces entrepreneurship, the nature of small business, and franchising.

1

ECONOMIC FOUNDATIONS OF AMERICAN BUSINESS

Learning Objectives

After you have completed this chapter, you will be able to do the following:

- Define *economics* and explain the concepts of demand, supply, and equilibrium.

- Contrast the four forms of economic competition.

- Define *economic system* and categorize the types now in use.

- Outline the economic theories developed by Karl Marx.

- Explain the relationship between Adam Smith's views and those of the American founding fathers.

- Describe the ideology of our free-enterprise system.

- Trace our economic system's historical development.

- List the five factors that led to the restructuring of American business in the 1970s and 1980s.

Drinking is a hot topic in the Soviet Union, which has a problem with drunken workers. Many show up in no condition to work. And if they do work, they often injure themselves or others. If they do not, their absence leaves their manager short-handed. To reduce the demand for alcohol and cut back on drinking, the Russian government recently increased the price of liquor 40 percent and decreased the supply to its state-run stores, the only legal source of alcohol.

The American experience with controlling the consumption of liquor suggests that the result of the Russian effort is predictable. For instance, today in North Carolina there are counties where it is illegal to sell — but not to possess — liquor, and some who are unable to make a trip to another county buy illegally manufactured alcohol from bootleggers and illicit bars. Nearly ninety years of experience with consumption controls like high prices and "dry" counties have proven that these restrictions alone do not reduce alcohol abuse. The Soviet government has discovered for itself that price increases and restrictions on supply lead to bootlegging.

What are the lessons here? First, when the demand for something is greater than its supply, producers and suppliers will sense the possibility of making a **profit** — the excess of revenues over expenses. Even where the potential costs are great — the Soviet criminal code permits execution of certain classes of "economic" criminals — the potential profits may outweigh the risk. When they do, the supply of goods will increase. The second lesson is that a government's ability to legislate economic behavior is limited. Two very different societies operating under quite distinct political systems have tried to achieve the same goal through legislation and have both failed. Third, it follows that some aspects of basic economic behavior cross national and political boundaries.

This chapter takes a brief look at economics in general and at the work of Karl Marx and Adam Smith, the political economists whose writings have come to define the socialist and capitalist systems. We will then turn to the development of the American economic system.

THE ECONOMIC WORLD

We are a nation obsessed with business and economic news. We make decisions every day in both our private and business lives based on how the country is doing. President Calvin Coolidge summed it up when he said, "The business of America is business." If that is business, what is economics? And can economics be applied to ordinary business decisions?

Economics: A Definition

Economics is both the study of how individuals and society choose to employ resources that could have other uses in order to produce goods or services and also an analysis of how to distribute those goods and services for consumption to the various groups of people within the society.[1]

Economics Defined

The key word in this definition is **choose.** A company with a ton of steel can choose to turn it into either bayonets or ploughs. It must choose to **employ,** or

A garment factory in Hofei, China. *Manufacturers in communist countries do not have to pay much attention to competition or to consumer wants. Even though many decisions are made by the government, businesses still must produce goods for their society and someone must decide how those goods will be distributed.*

put to work, that metal and the labor required to change it into another form. Similarly, a company that makes cookware must decide whether it will manufacture and distribute pans for sale in gourmet shops or in supermarkets, for a specialty market or the mass market. Under normal circumstances, no one tells an American company to make bayonets or ploughs or to sell its pots to supermarkets rather than gourmet shops, but a company does not make such decisions simply on instinct.

In large part, society guides those decisions. Every society — without exception — must answer these three fundamental questions:

1. What goods and services will be produced?
2. How will they be produced?
3. For *whom* will they be produced?

A society's answers to these questions, combined with the method it uses to reach them, describe its **economic system:** how a society produces and distributes goods and services. In the United States, these questions are usually answered in the **marketplace,** the forum where individuals and businesses exchange money for goods and services. We have gotten ahead of ourselves, though. Before looking at the workings of economic systems, we must first see how the economic questions are framed.

FIGURE 1.1

A Demand Curve

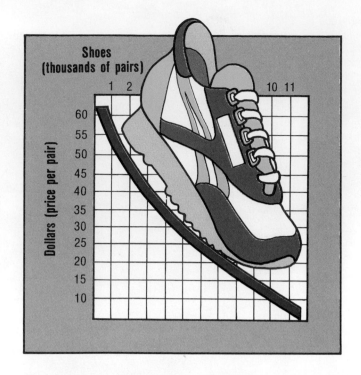

Demand, Supply, and Equilibrium

When economists study the three fundamental questions just listed, they deal with the concepts of demand and supply.

How Much Customers Will Buy   The willingness of purchasers to buy specific quantities of a good or service at a particular price and particular time is called **demand.** In other words, how much of something people will buy depends on its price when they want it.

Figure 1.1 graphs the demand for mid-quality running shoes on July 1. The vertical scale on the left lists prices at which a pair might sell. The horizontal scale on the bottom indicates what quantities the public might be expected to buy at each specific price in a range of prices. The line reflecting the relationship between each price and the quantities demanded is the **demand curve**. Not surprisingly, more people will buy shoes at ten dollars than at sixty dollars. Thus, the demand curve also shows the buyers for whom the manufacturer will produce the running shoes at each price.

Supply and Demand

What Sellers Will Provide   The willingness of sellers or producers to provide goods or services at a particular price and particular time is termed **supply.** In other words, how much of something people will sell or supply depends on its price when they can sell it.

Figure 1.2 graphs the supply of the running shoes that is available on July 1. The vertical scale lists specific prices within a range of prices at which the seller might sell the shoes. The horizontal scale indicates the number of pairs the seller might put on the market at each of those prices. The line reflecting the relationship between the price and the quantity is the **supply curve.** The higher the price,

FIGURE 1.2
Supply Curve

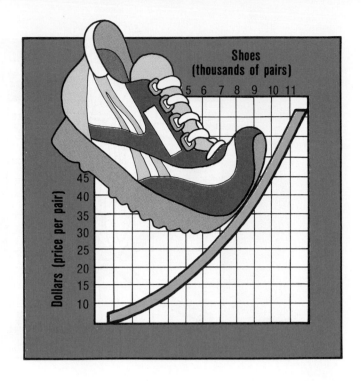

the more shoes the seller will be willing to sell. Thus, the supply curve also shows how many pairs of running shoes the manufacturer will produce at each price.

When Demand and Supply Meet   From your experience as a consumer, you know that demand and supply directly affect each other. A manufacturer will want to sell more shoes at fifty dollars than at twenty-five dollars, but the demand curve clearly indicates that fewer people will buy them at the higher price. By plotting the two curves on the same graph, we see that they meet at twenty-five dollars, the point marked E on Figure 1.3.

How Supply, Demand, and Equilibrium Are Related

The E on the graph marks the point of **equilibrium**, the location at which supply and demand are in balance. At that point the intentions of the seller and the buyers coincide. Figure 1.3 shows that at $50 per pair the manufacturer would supply 10,000 pairs, but the public would buy only 1,000. At $20 per pair, the maker would supply 4,500 pairs and the public would buy 7,500. Only at $25 per pair would supply equal demand. Thus, the point of equilibrium between supply and demand identifies the **market price** of goods or services, at least theoretically. There is another factor, however — competition — which affects the two curves and therefore the market price of the goods in question.

Competition and Markets

When two or more businesses offering similar goods or services go after the same customers, **competition** occurs. In our free-enterprise system, competition largely regulates the marketplace. Business must respond to customers' demands or else watch a competitor do so. On the other hand, businesses often survive

FIGURE 1.3

Equilibrium

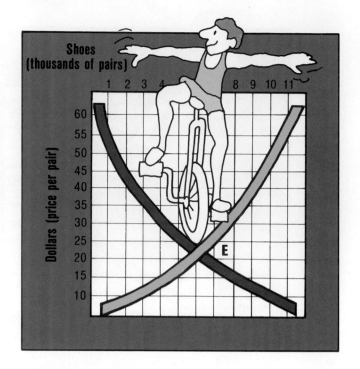

**Shoes
(thousands of pairs)**

Dollars (price per pair)

and expand if they can meet customers' needs at a price that customers are willing to pay. In our example of demand and supply, the manufacturer is not the only seller of mid-quality running shoes. Adidas, New Balance, Nike, Reebok, and a host of others compete for the same customers. What these companies do affects both the supply of and the demand for our manufacturer's shoes.

As Figure 1.4 illustrates, competition takes four general forms: pure competition, monopoly, monopolistic competition, and oligopoly. Very few, if any, examples of the polar extremes — pure competition and monopoly — exist. To one degree or another, all competition falls somewhere on the continuum between them.

Pure competition, or **"perfect competition,"** occurs when no single seller can control the price of a particular good or service. The classic example of pure competition occurs with a commodity, like wheat or corn, that has so many producers that no one of them can control its selling price. Another example might be hamburgers or pizzas in restaurants and take-out foods around a large university.

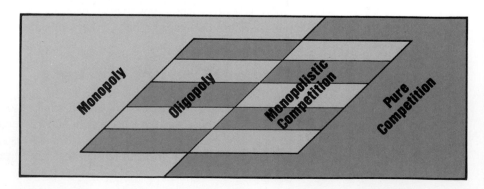

FIGURE 1.4

Competition Continuum

Some monopolies benefit consumers. *Carolina Power and Light Company is a monopoly, and that's all right with consumers. Legal, regulated monopolies can assure stability which the free market may not provide.*

Contemporary Economic Systems

A **monopoly** occurs when one company alone offers a particular good or service and therefore controls the market and price for it. The federal and state antitrust laws, which we will look at in detail in Chapter 22, are designed to promote pure competition. These laws prohibit activities like trying to create a monopoly that restrict competition. Nonetheless, the law and the Constitution permit the creation of certain types of monopolies. Public utilities like electric and gas companies have legal limited monopolies. And the Constitution permits the federal government to grant patents and copyrights, which are monopolies.

Despite such exceptions, the bias in our economic system is clearly against monopolies and in favor of pure competition. Between the competitive extremes are two other types, though, which we will now examine.

Monopolistic competition occurs when a relatively large number of sellers market similar but not identical products. These products are usually interchangeable. For example, blank audio or video cassettes are almost indistinguishable within the same grade, except to the expert. Yet Sony, Maxell, Scotch (3M), TDK, Realistic (Radio Shack), and others spend millions each year to convince you that they are better than their competitors.

Monopolistic competitors generally have some limited control over price. Although they can do little to discourage other companies from entering the market, they can exert influence over the retail outlets that sell their goods to consumers. For example, the producers of high-quality, prestige-priced stereo equipment might choose not to sell to the so-called deep discounters like Crazy Eddie, 47th Street Photo, Circuit City, or Silo.

The final type of competition is an **oligopoly,** a market dominated by a few large sellers, usually in industries that require huge initial investments in plant and equipment. An oligopoly can take one of two forms. In the first, a few sellers market products that are identical. The aluminum industry has this form. In the second, a few sellers sell products that differ somewhat from each other. The domestic and foreign auto makers compete in this fashion.

Competition and Economic Systems

Our society makes pure competition its ideal. To us, it answers the three fundamental questions of what, how, and for whom goods and services shall be produced. But a moment's thought tells us that **pure competition** really does not describe our economic system.

Figure 1.4 represents the poles of competition, monopoly and pure competition, like fence posts at the end of a run of wire. In the real world, the degree of competition — both within markets and within entire economic systems — lies somewhere between these posts.

Types of Economic Systems The American economic system is called a **free-enterprise** or **free market system** because at its heart lies the ideal of privately owned businesses competing freely. No other country has come as close to implementing this ideal, but even in the United States the government controls such portions of the economy as a large segment of the electric industry and an overwhelming portion of the water-supply. About three-quarters of United States economic activity depends on the **private sector,** the part of the economy not controlled by the government.

Marx, Mao, and Money

Ronald Reagan's 1984 trip to China focused Western attention on a phenomenon that may change the way people define economic and political ideologies. Mainland China, under Chairman Mao Tse-tung perhaps the most revolutionary and rigidly ideological communist state, is moving rapidly in the direction of capitalism. Chairman Deng is a pragmatist, and under his rule the Chinese are discovering the effectiveness of incentives, the backbone of free enterprise.

In China today, billboards which used to feature party slogans or pictures of Mao now blaze with more Western mottos: "Time is money! Efficiency is life!" 1600 foreign specialists work in China to help the economy. 128 American companies have offices in Peking. Factories that used to make tanks now turn out washing machines and refrigerators. Retail sales in 1983 reached $142 billion, up over 10 percent from the previous year's record total.

A slogan at the Chongqing Iron and Steel Works — "The more you work, the more you get" — captures the essence of the changing philosophy. In communist countries profits have traditionally been reserved for the state, and outstanding work performance was rewarded with government awards and commendations — not with money. But whether it's a basic human urge or just a "disease" brought in from the West, the desire on the part of individuals to improve their living conditions has profoundly affected China.

Under Deng, China seems eager to harness individual initiative and desires. Private restaurants serve gourmet food for $70 per person; incentives boosted agricultural production 25 percent and industrial output 80 percent in just three years in Sichuan province; farmers are encouraged to raise as much as they can on their own plots, and some become almost rich in the process. Four coast areas have been designated "special economic zones," where foreign investment and ideas are encouraged. These zones have become so successful that 14 more are planned.

Some American companies look eagerly toward China as one of the world's greatest largely untapped consumer markets, but many China experts are cautious. While trade between the two countries totaled about $7.5 billion

in 1985, seventy times what it was in 1972, that figure hasn't risen as quickly as some predicted because of a trade skirmish brought on by Washington's freezing of textile imports in 1982 and by China's retaliatory cutback in grain imports. The Chinese are wary of debt and opposed to trade deficits, and they aren't likely to be able to export enough to the U.S. in the near future to maintain a trade balance.

All these changes in China's economic life have brought changes in China's social and cultural life as well, many of them unwanted. Many Chinese are going to extremes to imitate white, Western looks: women are flocking to plastic surgeons to have their eyes and noses Westernized; sales of Western-style cosmetics and suits are booming. Many of Mao's supporters grumble, with reason, that Chinese today are becoming more interested in their own well-being than in that of the state. As one Peking student put it, "We've all become slick and sly."

The mixing of traditional Chinese culture with new ideas from the West often has disastrous results. China has begun to see the danger in its population explosion, and the state has enforced sanctions against families that have more than one child. This new emphasis has helped to revive old superstitions that a female baby is a sign of divine disfavor, and many baby girls have been drowned as a result. "Intellectuals" are still watched closely, books and plays still censured. And the gap between the poor and the newly "rich" is already causing discontent. The government has had to build a 50-mile fence around the most successful of the special economic zones to keep the less-privileged out.

Modern China has undergone a number of political and ideological shifts; and there's no telling what will happen when Deng dies. But for the moment, China provides fascinating insight into what happens when communism and capitalism mix.

Sources: Pico Iyer, "Capitalism in the Making," *Time*, Vol. 123, No. 18, April 30, 1984, 26–35. Larry Rohter, "Deng's Quiet Revolution," *Newsweek*, Vol. 103, No. 18, April 30, 1984, 40–49. "China's so-called capitalism," *Fortune*, Vol. 109, No. 11, May 28, 1984. Peter W. Bernstein, "Why Business Won't Follow Reagan to China," *Fortune*, Vol. 109, No. 10, May 14, 1984, 144.

At the other extreme, in countries like the Soviet Union and the Peoples Republic of China the part of the private sector that is legal is tiny and rigidly controlled. China, for example, has just allowed the formation of its first venture capital company, China Venturetech Investment Corp., but its executives may earn only a bureaucrat's salary, sixty dollars per month.[2] In Russia and China, the government owns or controls virtually all of the nation's land and industrial capacity. Because the government plays such a large role in determining what will be produced, who will produce it, and to whom the products will be distributed, these economic systems are called **planned economies** or **authoritarian socialist systems.**

Between these systems lie **mixed economies** or **democratic socialist systems,** economic systems in which there is both government and private ownership of businesses and resources. To varying degrees, Britain, France, and the Scandinavian countries have mixed economies. In such systems, the businesses that are central to the nation's economy are often government owned, like the steel industry in Sweden. Less critical industries like textile manufacturing tend to be dominated by private enterprise. Whatever the precise mix of government and private ownership, such economies feature high degrees of government economic planning.

One way of measuring the efficiency of an economic system is in terms of its **productivity**, the average output per worker per hour. In the United States, productivity increased at a rate of 3.6 percent per year between 1948 and 1973. However, changes in the make-up of the labor force, huge increases in energy costs, and a lag in research and development caused the rate of increase to drop to an average of 1.8 percent per year between 1973 and 1981.

If productivity measures the efficiency of an economy, a measure of what an economic system produces is its **gross national product (GNP),** which is the current market value of all final goods and services that a nation produces within a particular period. The GNP of the United States is about $4,000,000,000,000, an essentially meaningless number. What *is* meaningful — and of intense interest to government, business, and citizen alike — is the percentage changes that occur in the GNP from quarter to quarter and year to year. These changes indicate how well the economy is doing overall.

KARL MARX AND ADAM SMITH: TWO ECONOMISTS AND THEIR THEORIES

It is true that our free enterprise system does feature some elements of government ownership and control and that most planned economies contain some elements of market economies. All economic systems are by no means the same, however. In fact, the assumptions underlying the systems at the opposite ends of the economic spectrum are quite different. To see how and why they are different, let's examine the work of Karl Marx and Adam Smith, the economic theorists whose views are often used to define the two systems.

Planned economies rest on government-owned, government-run monopolies. Government planning and control in these systems is seen as a way to eliminate competition, because it is wasteful, and to ensure fairness of distribution among the population. It is believed that the people's wisdom expressed through their government determines what should be produced.

By contrast, free-enterprise systems do not place much confidence philosophically in government's ability to plan. Instead, they look to pure competition as the ideal. This goal is based on the collective pursuit of individual interests — whether as producer, seller, or consumer — which one defines for oneself. The marketplace brings together and focuses the various interests and sorts out the answers to the three fundamental questions. Guided as if by an invisible hand, persons in free-enterprise systems who pursue their own interests serve also the public interest.

These polar philosophical statements very loosely represent the views of today's followers of Karl Marx and Adam Smith. Note, however, that they have each influenced the other's followers profoundly. Marx's views have had considerable influence on countries with mixed and free-enterprise systems, and Smith's work has influential admirers in countries with planned economies. Because of the increasing importance of foreign trade, business people often deal with countries that have economic systems quite different from ours. Business students must therefore understand both men's philosophies and the views of their followers today.

As you study the great economists and the philosophical basis of our free-enterprise system, keep in mind the three fundamental questions given earlier that every economic system has to answer.

Karl Marx

Karl Marx and His Social Theories

More than half the world's population live under political systems that claim to be organized according to principles developed by Karl Marx (1818–1883). A great scholar and fierce political writer, Marx viewed history as a series of struggles between social classes. He foresaw conflict between the working class and the capitalist class for control over the **means of production**, the factories in which the workers toiled and the capital needed to organize and build the plants. Marx also advocated a **labor theory of value**, which holds that labor is what gives value to goods and services and labor therefore deserves to be rewarded for this production.

According to Marx, the working class would ultimately triumph. From that victory would emerge **communism**, a classless, propertyless society whose banners would read "From each according to his ability, to each according to his needs!"[3]

Socialism   Described by Marx as a forerunner of communism, **socialism** is an economic system in which the state owns the principal means of production but private property of some sort still exists. What distinguishes communism from socialism is the disappearance of private property and the state in the later stage, communism.

Marx's view of the process from socialism to communism by means of the class struggle was neither universally accepted in his own time nor today. In fact, many saw nonrevolutionary socialism as an end in itself. These so-called utopian socialists dreamed of ideal societies in which all worked according to their abilities and received what they needed. Today, in countries like Sweden, France, and Britain, Marxist and utopian socialists coexist. Their coexistence with parties advocating free enterprise has produced the mixed economic systems mentioned

Karl Marx

earlier. During this century, these countries and other have nationalized such major industries as airlines, steel, coal mining, and banking. Heavy taxation of profits usually accompanies the more serious efforts at socialist economies. These taxes are used to pay for government services, like health care, that free enterprise systems leave largely to the private sector.

A term often used to describe the mixed economies of Western Europe is *democratic socialism*. These countries have governments selected in free, open elections. Though their legal systems are often quite different from ours, they are designed to protect individual rights.

Communism In contrast, the authoritarian socialist systems, which we have been calling planned economies, lack democratic institutions and actively discourage their citizens from accumulating private property. Individual rights are rarely allowed to become an issue, because they are few when compared with the state's. In the United States we commonly refer to the authoritarian socialist systems as being communist because they look to Marx for ideological guidance. It should be noted, however, that none of these countries has approached, much less achieved, Marx's concept of pure communism.

Marx only hinted at what a socialist government might resemble. It was left for his principal Russian interpreters — Lenin, Trotsky, and Stalin — to create the authoritarian socialism we know today. As it has from the earliest days of communist rule, the Soviet Union relies on highly centralized long-range planning. The drive to control all economic activity has been accompanied by a similar urge to suppress all nonconforming political and social activity.

Adam Smith

Adam Smith

Three-quarters of a century before Marx published *The Communist Manifesto,* others had looked at history and reached very different conclusions from Marx's. On the one side of the Atlantic a group of American farmers, merchants, and ministers wrote the Declaration of Independence, in 1776. On the other side of that ocean, Adam Smith (1723–1790), an obscure Scottish professor and bureaucrat, published *The Wealth of Nations* in that same year. These two works laid the foundations of our political and economic system.

The Declaration of Independence   The fifty-six British subjects who signed the treasonous document called the Declaration of Independence asserted, in part, that

> We hold these Truths to be self-evident, that all Men are created equal, that they are endowed by their Creator with certain unalienable Rights, that among them are Life, Liberty, and the Pursuit of Happiness — That to secure these Rights, Governments are instituted among Men, deriving their just Powers from the Consent of the Governed. . . .

Note the relationship that is defined here between government and the governed: people create governments to protect their freedoms. The individual, not the state, stands at the center of our system.

The Wealth of Nations   It might be argued that with the publication of *The Wealth of Nations* Adam Smith did almost as much to assure the achievement of the Declaration's goals as did the American patriots.

Like Marx, Smith saw an order in history. **Natural laws** (unchanging laws in nature) governed economic life just as they controlled the physical world. Economic laws, which were as fixed as the law of gravity, operated through the marketplace. Finally, people acting in their own self-interest would, by transacting business normally in the marketplace, benefit mankind — if left alone. The key concept here is "if left alone," a warning directed at government intervention. The term used to describe this concept of marketplace nonregulation is **laissez faire,** a French phrase meaning roughly "to let people do as they choose."

The Views of Adam Smith and the Founding Fathers

The American patriots and Adam Smith thus reached a conclusion opposite that of Marx and his followers. The key to societal well-being was seen in guaranteeing the individual the maximum freedom of economic action. In self-interest lay the key to the wealth of nations. As Smith wrote:

> Every individual . . . neither intends to promote the public interest . . . he intends only his own gain, and he is in this, as in many other cases, led by an *invisible hand* to promote an end which was no part of his intention.[4]

HOW OUR SYSTEM WORKS

More than any other system, our free-enterprise marketplace approaches Adam Smith's ideal. Our economic system has never been a laissez faire one, though, and it could never be such a system.

The Free-Market System

A term often used to describe our economic structure is the **free-market system,** an economy based on the principle of voluntary association and exchange.[5] A market brings together those with goods or services to sell and those who wish to buy them. When you decide to buy a stereo in the free market, you go to any store of your choice that sells stereo equipment. No one forces you to buy a stereo from any one seller, much less associate with them. Your actions and theirs are voluntary.

In a free-market system, supply and demand define the price of goods and services. Competition is the ideal, and certainly it is the rule among stereo stores, camera shops, fast-food outlets, and most other types of businesses. The result is competitive prices. Wendy's hamburger prices cannot vary too much from Burger King's. If Wendy's prices are too low, they will lose potential profits, and if they are too high, they will lose potential sales.

The Ideology of Our Free-Enterprise System

A voluntary exchange follows when a price is agreed upon. That exchange should result in satisfaction to the buyer and profit to the seller. Figure 1.5 illustrates a completed transaction.

The Ideology of Free Enterprise

Our free-enterprise system really is an **ideology,** a set of aspirations or ideals on how society should function. These ideals are related to one another and come into contact in the free market.

FIGURE 1.5

How the Free Marketplace
Works

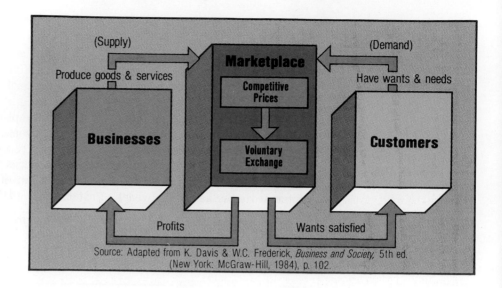

Source: Adapted from K. Davis & W.C. Frederick, *Business and Society*, 5th ed.
(New York: McGraw-Hill, 1984), p. 102.

Freedom and Individualism   The voluntary nature of the associations
and exchanges in the marketplace depends on individuals having the power and
freedom to make these choices for themselves without compulsion from the
state. Freedom and individualism are closely linked. It is difficult, for instance,
to imagine groups rather than individuals deciding whether to buy a certain type
of car. Individuals make these decisions; they are not made collectively. Both
the Declaration of Independence and the Constitution emphasize that our political
institutions exist to protect individuals, not vice versa.

Equality of Opportunity and Competition   "All Men are created
equal," asserts the Declaration of Independence. In the British Empire of 1776,
the accident of one's birth determined, at least initially, one's status in society.
To be born a lord or a lady, for instance, brought special privileges. Today we
interpret "all men" to mean "all people," regardless of their sex, race, color,
creed, or national origin — a notion no one who signed the Declaration would
likely have accepted. Still, both we and the signers would agree that equality
refers to equality of opportunity, the chance to make one's own fortune. Some
people are born richer than others, but those who are born poorer have the
opportunity to become rich. And those born rich have no guarantee that they
will keep their wealth and the privileges that come with it. Equal opportunity
thus gives rise to competition.

Natural Laws and Limited Government   Adam Smith believed that
government should not interfere with the natural laws governing the marketplace.
However much Smith disapproved of government interference, though, he had
no sympathy for private forms of it, either. For example, he repeatedly warned
of the dangers of monopolies and of conspiracies to control the marketplace. As
Smith used the term, laissez faire applies to both public and private interference
with the free market.

Adam Smith's ideal of a free marketplace proved over time to be incapable of
dealing with such problems as environmental pollution, workplace safety, and the
like. As we will see in Chapters 21, 22, and 23, government has had to step in
where competition dictated a result contrary to the common good.

3M: A Novel Company

The great diversity of American businesses often gets forgotten in discussions about "bottom lines" or marketing strategies. Someone with only a theoretical knowledge of American companies might think that they're structured more or less the same and that they develop products the same way. Current wisdom says that if you want a successful product, you need first to perform detailed market analysis, making sure that there are plenty of people who need the new product and that your entry into the market will be able to gain a significant share of that market. Then, with as much of the company's force as you can muster, you push your product to the top.

3M is a giant American company that rejects such wisdom and does things its own way. (If you don't know the company name, you know their Scotch brand tape or their Post-it notes, the best-selling office product in the world.) You can't argue with the company's track record. Started at the turn of the century, 3M has been growing at a healthy rate of about 10 percent a year, and it boasts of having 45,000 products on the market.

Yet 3M refuses to do things the traditional way. Rather than find a winner and stick with it, promoting it with all the company's resources, it prefers to make an array of products in 45 different, nearly independent divisions. Instead of hiring new executives from outside, the company looks to its own when it has an upper management position to fill. While other companies see a profitable product and copy it, 3M looks for niches no one else has bothered to fill.

The key to 3M's unique approach is its reliance on invention. It likes to create unique products that perfectly fill a need, even if only a limited number of people can use the product. It would rather make a little money on each of a great number of products than a lot from one big seller.

This unusual corporate philosophy started with the company's founders, who first made ordinary sandpaper. When some 3M people were inside an automobile factory making a sale, they noticed that workers choked from the dust produced by dry sandpaper, so the company developed a sandpaper that could be used wet.

The company has been spotting and filling small needs ever since. But they don't always identify a need before they have a new product. When one of the company's independent inventors comes up with a new product, the company will look until it finds a use for it. That happened with the Post-it adhesive and with a new kind of fabric the company developed in 1939 out of pressed, not woven, fabrics. Over the years a number of uses were proposed and dismissed. Finally, in the 1950s, the fabric found a home in surgical masks.

To keep its innovative products coming, the company uses a number of unusual corporate strategies. When a division gets large — over $100 million in sales — it is split in two so that market share will not become more important than innovation. The company reasons that the head of a huge enterprise won't care enough about the little products that have made the company famous. 3M likes to follow up "embryonic products" that open up new fields, like the surgical tape that didn't sell all that well but started the company's important health-care division. It shies away from making "me-too" products or battling big names in the marketplace. In the 1960s, it had the technology to compete with Kodak in the amateur film market, but chose instead to settle for making house-brand film for retailers like Sears.

To encourage innovation, the company insists that one-quarter of each division's sales must be derived from products that did not exist five years before. And every year it gives its own version of the Nobel prize to employees who have made the most important contributions to 3M technology.

3M's corporate structure, climate, and philosophy are no more "right" than are the more traditional approaches to American business. They do help to demonstrate, however, that there are many routes to corporate success in America, and that even if you've found a good thing like Scotch tape, you don't necessarily just have to stick with it.

Sources: Cathryn Jakobson, "High-Tech Vision," *Barron's*, May 28, 1984, 14. Lee Smith, "The Lures and Limits of Innovation," *Fortune*, October 20, 1980, 84. G. Bruce Knecht, "Three M's Unusual Strategy," *Dun's Business Month*, April 1983, 55.

The Work Ethic   When you are introducing yourself to someone at a party, after you exchange names the next thing you ask is usually, "What do you do?" In this country, as many commentators have noted, a person without a job lacks an identity. This conviction is a reflection of our strong **work ethic**, the generally held belief that work is good for both the individual and society. A recent study has revealed that leisure time dropped from over twenty-four hours per week in 1975 to just over seventeen in 1984.[6] In a society offering as many recreational opportunities as ours, something must motivate people to work instead of play. That motivating factor is often profit.

Private Property and Profit   Private property and the profits to be made from it are the foundations of our economic system. If private property did not exist, free markets could not exist. Since the time of Adam Smith, economists have described the ways in which people make money from their property in terms of three **factors of production**:

1. *Land:* real estate and all natural resources, including minerals, timber, and agricultural products.
2. *Labor:* the work supplied by humans.
3. *Capital:* the property, plant, and equipment required to produce goods.

One can earn rents or interest by leasing land or capital to others and wages by selling one's labor to others. Profits, though, come only from assembling the factors of production to create a **product**, any good or service that may be the subject of an exchange for money.

The person who assembles the necessary factors and applies enough creativity to generate a product or service is called an **entrepreneur** or **capitalist**. The compensation awarded a capitalist for the efforts and risk assumed in establishing or operating a venture is **profits**. Risk is the key element here, because simply assembling the factors of production is not enough. An entrepreneur is someone like Tom Monaghan, the man who after brushes with bankruptcy turned Domino's Pizza into the nation's fastest-growing franchise chain. The willingness to bet on one's own abilities to control the various factors of production to turn out products or services is what entrepreneurship is all about.

THE DEVELOPMENT OF OUR ECONOMIC SYSTEM

Since the Revolution, the face of American business has completely changed. We have passed from a primarily agricultural and natural-resource-based economy through industrialization to a service-oriented, information-based economy.

The Earliest Years

As early as the 1630s, American colonists residing in the richer, more established colonies lived as well as their European counterparts. Unlike their European cousins, however, the colonists achieved their standard of living largely by **barter**, trading goods for goods or services rather than for money. Throughout the

Industrialization in the nineteenth century. Textile workers in 1834 endured conditions that Americans would find unthinkable today. The rise of mills and factories did more than mechanize production. It changed the nature of American business and American family life.

colonial period, money in the form of gold or silver was in critically short supply. This shortage made accumulating the capital required for large-scale enterprises very difficult.

Before the start of the nineteenth century, most American businesses were small, owned either by individuals or partners who ran them. Between 1700 and 1776, only seven business corporations came into existence in the American colonies. By 1800 there were 335 corporations, over half of which had been created since 1796.[7]

The Industrial Revolution

The Industrial Revolution began in about 1750 in Great Britain and about 1800 in the United States. It had three distinct characteristics.

☐ Newly invented machines came to replace human labor.
☐ Work became centered in the factory, not the home.
☐ A division of labor in producing goods replaced the single artisan who had made a product from start to finish.

The Industrial Revolution was first the textile revolution. Cloth, when it could be bought, was extremely expensive. The process of making clothes — from converting raw cotton or wool into a dress, a shirt, or a pair of pants — was highly labor intensive. Factory production of cloth began in the late eighteenth century, and ready-to-wear apparel eventually appeared in the mid-nineteenth century. One of the earliest ready-to-wear producers was Levi Strauss. In the early 1850s, he invented blue jeans to sell to miners in the California gold rush.[8]

The History of Our Economic System — To the Civil War

The Growth of Industry Factories organized around the new machinery sprang up in New England. A surplus of cheap labor, abundant water power, and a growing concentration of capital made Massachusetts in particular an ideal location. Working conditions, hours, and pay in the mills were grim by today's standards but were often better than those on the farms the workers had left.

The principles that worked so well in producing textiles plainly applied to manufacturing many other goods. In Connecticut, Eli Whitney, who had made almost nothing on his cotton gin, did make money on mass-produced firearms. In Illinois, Cyrus McCormick invented a reaper for harvesting grain in 1834 and opened his first factory in 1847. A well-developed system of water travel and a rapidly growing rail system opened up most of the United States east of the Mississippi to the new manufacturing during the period before the Civil War.

The Civil War (1861–1865) marked a major turning point in America's business history. The North put over 2.2 million men in uniform, an unheard of number for that time, and mobilized its resources, developed transportation systems to move men and war supplies, and created new lines of communications. This genius for organization and for the production and transportation of goods and people characterized American business over the next several generations.

Within ten years after the war ended, the shape of industrial America had emerged. New immigrants, largely from Europe, kept wages low. The nation's expansion led to new products and transportation lines. Except for two major recessions, the times were generally prosperous. With the exceptions of the nine-month war with Spain in 1898 and World War I, the nation was mainly at peace until 1941.

The Production Era   The period from the Civil War until just after World War I might be characterized a production era. During this period, the demand for products exceeded many manufacturers' production abilities. Manufacturers thus focused on improving production capacity and efficiency and on lowering costs.

Production, regarded as the key to success, dominated all other business functions. In many industries, competition was limited because only a few firms were capable of consistent, efficient production. In these industries, marketing's main jobs were simply the taking and filling of orders. Other marketing activities were not required when firms with ample production capacity and robust product demand could sell all they could make.

The production era nurtured Thomas Edison, Alexander Graham Bell, and dozens of other innovative entrepreneurs who reshaped communications and transportation. Others built gigantic industrial empires. The names of many of their founders are still familiar: Philip Armour (meats); Frederick Weyerhaeuser (lumber); Eli Remington (arms); John D. Rockefeller (oil); Andrew Carnegie (steel); Gail Borden (dairy products); and Marshall Field (general merchandise).[9]

The ready availability of capital and the irresistible urge to generate ever-greater profits led men like Collis P. Huntington (1821–1900) to attempt to control entire business sectors. His career began when he helped found the Central Pacific Railroad, the western half of the first transcontinental rail line, completed in 1869. The construction of that government-subsidized line made his fortune. By the time of his death, he and his associates controlled most western rail transportation.

Reform and Regulation   The great transportation, industrial, and natural resource combinations of the late nineteenth and early twentieth centuries

FIGURE 1.6

Factors of Production and Their Rewards

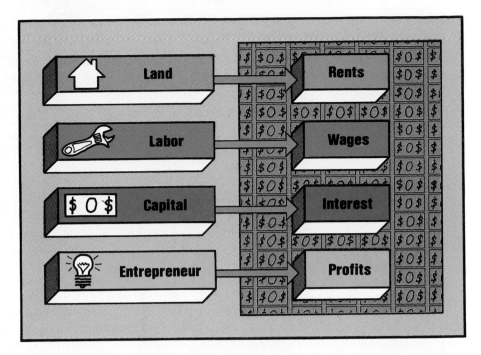

were known as trusts, a term that describes the unique business form adopted to avoid state corporation laws. Between 1890 and 1914, the states and the federal government enacted antitrust laws to free markets from the monopolists. (We will discuss these in more detail in Chapter 22.) These laws were the first serious attempt to impose any restriction on the practice of laissez faire. Other attempts, such as the creation in 1887 of the Interstate Commerce Commission to regulate transportation, failed, largely because of weak laws and ineffective or unsympathetic administrators.

The Great Depression of 1929–1939 began in the midst of several major business scandals, hundreds of bank failures, crashing prices on the major United States stock exchanges, and the onset of a global economic crisis. Those events also brought on an era of intense government activity in economic affairs.

In 1932, American voters elected Franklin D. Roosevelt president, but they did not give him a mandate to regulate the marketplace. The economic situation when he took office was so bad, however, that he and the country were willing to try anything. Banks and corporations selling stocks or bonds became closely regulated by new agencies like the Securities and Exchange Commission (discussed in chapters 18 and 19). With 25 percent unemployment, labor harmony became a major goal. As we will see in Chapter 9, Congress enacted several major labor laws, one of which created the National Labor Relations Board to oversee labor–management relations.

Our Economic History — The Depression

When World War II began in 1939, the country was just beginning to emerge from its decade-long economic depression. As the Civil War had proved, a modern war requires planning, organization, and control in all sectors. During the United States' participation in World War II (1941–1945), the government tightly controlled what was produced, bought, sold, earned, and developed. Every single sector of the economy experienced rationing of labor and resources and had to follow government plans.

Coke Keeps a "Classic"

The story of Coca-Cola may be the ultimate capitalist success story: from an obscure start grew an empire. In the past few years, Coke has also provided us with a highly publicized example of how the marketplace operates. As we saw old Coke die and then be reborn, we seemed to watch a classroom demonstration of the laws of supply and demand and the lessons of marketing. Indeed, some wonder if the lesson wasn't *too* perfect, and if Coke might have planned it all along.

In 1886 an Atlanta pharmacist, Dr. John S. Pemberton, mixed up a batch of a new "brain tonic" in the back yard of his home. The concoction contained lime juice, vanilla, cinnamon, caramel, and, for the first few years, cocaine extracts. Some of the other ingredients, and the formula used to mix them, are a closely guarded secret — the recipe that Pemberton wrote out on a sheet of paper still lies locked in an Atlanta bank vault.

In just under a century, the drink grew to become what some call "the most successful product in history," bringing in more than $3.5 billion in revenue around the world, leading the $25 billion soft drink industry, making the company rich enough to acquire other giants like Columbia Pictures.

In the face of such success, when Coca-Cola announced in April, 1985, that it was going to change the formula for its flavoring for the first time, the reaction of many people was, "Why mess with it?" There seemed to be two answers: competition and the discovery of a new formula.

Coke's main competitor, Pepsi, declared victory and a company holiday when Coke announced the change, and though Pepsi may not win the battle against the new Coke, the change certainly does reflect Coke's uneasiness with the growth of #2. While Coke still easily outsells Pepsi, both regular soft drinks have been losing ground to diet soft drinks, and Pepsi has surpassed Coke in take-home sales. Coke's overall market share has declined from 24.3 percent in 1980 to 21.8 percent in 1984.

How directly this competition influenced the big change, only Coke executives know for sure. Coke says the new formula was discovered by accident when chem-ists were experimenting with flavor combinations for diet Coke. Since the "accident," however, Coke has spent $4 million over four years in research on the new product, research that convinced the company that both taste experts and consumers preferred the new taste.

The rest of the story is well known. People liked their old Coke. In the first month of new Coke, 40,000 called the company to complain. Within a couple of months the dissatisfied minority became a majority; sales of new Coke dropped 15 percent in June. Company leaders held a series of emergency meetings, then, swallowing their pride, announced that old Coke would be brought back as "Coca-Cola Classic."

Although the sudden reversal was embarrassing, it may prove to be a lucky marketing move for the company. Some observers thought the "mistake" worked out so well for the company that it must have been planned, though Coke officials deny it. Six months after new Coke was introduced, it was preferred by only 4 percent of those in one survey, but the combined sales of the three Cokes (new, old, and cherry) had gained a couple of percentage points on Pepsi. If Classic Coke can continue to please loyal Coke drinkers while new Coke wins converts from Pepsi, the company will be in great shape. A 1 percent rise in market share would boost Coke's yearly revenues by a quarter of a billion dollars. But to many observers, a Pepsi ad said it all: "After 87 years of going it eyeball-to-eyeball, the other guy just blinked."

Sources: Eric Gelman, "Coke Tampers with Success," *Newsweek*, Vol. 105, No. 18, May 6, 1985, 50. "Coca-Cola's Stock Is No Sweeter — Yet," *Business Week*, No. 2895, May 20, 1985, 118. Jaclyn Fierman, "How Coke Decided a New Taste Was It," *Fortune*, Vol. 111, No. 11, May 27, 1985, 80. "Will Things Still Go Better with Coke?" *U.S. News & World Report*, Vol. 98, No. 17, May 6, 1985, 14. Scott Scredon, "New Coke Wins Round 1, But Can It Go the Distance?" *Business Week*, No. 2900, June 24, 1985, 48. Tom Morganthau, "Saying 'No' to New Coke," *Newsweek*, Vol. 105, No. 25, June 24, 1985, 32. John Koten and Scott Kilman, "How Coke's Decision to Offer 2 Colas Undid 4½ Years of Planning," *The Wall Street Journal*, Vol. 206, No. 10, July 15, 1985, 1. "Classic Comeback for an Old Champ," *U.S. News & World Report*, Vol. 99, No. 4, July 22, 1985, 12.

After the war, many controls were abolished or modified, but some remained in place. For twenty years after World War II ended, no nation experienced the level of prosperity that ours did. There were recurring complaints about over-regulation of business. However, it was hard to argue seriously with a low inflation rate, high employment, and an ever-increasing gross national product.

The Sales and Marketing Era

From the end of World War I to the beginning of the Korean War in 1950, production capacity was no longer a major problem. Now, instead, firms could not be sure of selling all they could produce. Many companies' marketing strategies consisted of producing all they could, then figuring out how to sell what they had. The result was close attention to advertising and to the hiring, training, and deploying of an effective sales force. Marketing's role thus began when there was product to sell. Sales personnel were expected to sell it, regardless of its quality or whether it met consumer needs.

The Evolution of Marketing Practices

The great post–World War II boom brought a new consumer attitude and forced firms to evolve new marketing approaches. For the first time, most American families had **discretionary income**, or more income than is required to obtain the necessities of life. They used their discretionary income to satisfy needs with different kinds of products and to acquire wants. For example, consumers who before could afford flour only for baking could now buy ready-made bread, cake mixes, Bisquick biscuit flour, or other flour-based products.

The implications of this change were immense. No longer could companies count on their sales forces alone to sell what was produced. Instead, they had to produce what customers wanted. Firms responded by introducing marketing at the beginning rather than the end of the production cycle and by integrating marketing into each phase of the business. Marketing assumed a more prominent role in product planning, pricing, product scheduling, and inventory control, as well as in distribution and servicing of the product.

Research became increasingly important. Marketers developed and improved their models to describe customer behavior. New-product planning grew increasingly sophisticated. Television advertising, branding strategy, and self-service dominated business thinking well into the 1970s.

The Rise of the Service and Information Sectors

Five harsh realities led to a fundamental restructuring of American business, starting in the mid-1970s:

□ The demise of the smokestack industries — steel, shipbuilding, coal, and the like — which had been our economy's backbone since the Civil War.
□ The shock of oil crises that demonstrated how vulnerable we were to foreign energy suppliers.
□ A loss of confidence that came with major recessions and staggering inflation.

A service economy. Today the production and distribution of services and information account for the largest segment of the American economy. This AT&T dispatch office is able to route phone calls across the nation in little more than the time it takes to dial a number. To maintain such complex service, AT&T relies on sophisticated equipment and a well-educated, highly trained work force.

☐ The astonishment at how easily foreign products could displace American goods in electronics and autos.

☐ A heightened consciousness of the problems of unemployment and underemployment as a new generation with great expectations joined the work force.

Five Factors That Led to a Restructuring of American Business

The New Industries Fortunately, one major effect of the shocks of the 1970s was to accelerate the growth of two sectors of our economy in which we were becoming world leaders: the service sector and the information sector. These sectors have close connections.

The **service sector** consists of businesses that perform work for others that does not involve producing goods. Education, for example, lies in the service sector, as do all the other professions. It is important to note, incidentally, that a person may provide a service that involves selling or creating a good. For example, a dentist may sell a patient a false tooth, but the character of the transaction is predominantly a service involving the fitting of the tooth.

A major element in the service sector consists of those who operate the new computer and information-processing technologies. The businesses that produce computers and related equipment and instructions are providing support for the information sector of our economy. Computers are essentially devices for the manipulation of information, like account information for banks and credit cards. That was one of their first and still most important functions.

Deregulation   In 1977, for the first time since Franklin D. Roosevelt, a president, Jimmy Carter, took seriously business's complaint about overregulation. He began intensive deregulation of the transportation and financial industries. His successor, Ronald Reagan, accelerated the deregulation process, particularly in those two areas. However, his dismantling of consumer, health and safety, and antitrust regulation has proven highly controversial, even among the businesses it was supposed to benefit.

WHY STUDY BUSINESS?

In reviewing this chapter, you will find that business is directly affected by political, legal, regulatory, societal, economic, and technological forces. Those factors define our social environment. The relationship between business and those forces runs two ways, however. Business affects our social environment, too. Consider the environmental laws relating to air and water pollution. When these laws were first enacted, many in the business community regarded them as being purely antibusiness. Today, business has not only recognized the benefits of environmental laws to their employees but has taken advantage of the opportunity to develop new technologies and services. Whole new industries have

Daily Publications	Weekly Publications	Biweekly Publications	Specialty Publications
Your local newspaper(s) *The Wall Street Journal*	*Business Week*	*Forbes* *Fortune*	Every field has its "trade" magazines or newspapers that address issues of particular concern to persons in that field. There are at least 5,000 such publications, ranging from *Aerospace Daily* to *American Carwash Review* to *Hospital Gift Shop Management* to *Pizza Today* to *Turkey World* to *Uniforms & Accessories Review*.

TABLE 1.1

Studying Business Outside the Classroom

The business scene changes every day. Businesspeople remain students all their lives. This table is a list of "must" reading for serious business students of all ages.

even developed, like solar energy and hazardous-waste treatment. Social, regulatory, and legal pressures on business have thus led to a response with a very positive economic effect.

This course is designed to give you an overview of the interrelationships between business and the social environment while introducing you to the various topics in the business curriculum. Table 1.1 lists a number of other sources of business information. You are beginning your study of business at an exciting time. The pace of technological and economic change is accelerating, creating many new opportunities and new types of jobs. Welcome to where the action is!

Chapter Highlights

1. Define economics and explain the concepts of demand, supply, and equilibrium.

Economics is the study of how individuals and society choose (1) to employ resources that could have other uses in order to produce goods or services and (2) to distribute those goods and services for consumption to various people and groups within the society. Demand is the willingness of purchasers to buy specific quantities of a good or a service at a particular price at a particular time. Supply refers to the willingness of sellers or producers to provide goods or services at a particular price at a particular time. Equilibrium is the point at which demand and supply are in balance.

2. Contrast the four forms of economic competition.

The four primary types of economic competition range along a continuum from pure competition at one end to monopoly at the other. Pure competition occurs when no

single seller can control the price of a single good or service. Monopolistic competition occurs when a relatively large number of sellers market similar but not identical products that are easily substituted for one another. An oligopoly is a market dominated by a few large sellers, who exert significant control over price and entry into the market. A monopoly refers to a market in which only one company offers a particular good or service. Public utilities are often regulated monopolies.

3. Define economic system and categorize the types now in use.

An economic system is the way a society organizes itself to answer three questions: (1) What goods and services will be produced? (2) How will they be produced? and (3) For whom will they be produced? Free enterprise systems emphasize the private sector, and economic questions are decided through the unhampered action of the marketplace. Planned economies or authoritarian socialist systems believe that government, not the marketplace, should make economic decisions. These systems emphasize government ownership and control. Between these systems lie mixed economies and democratic socialist systems, which rely on a mix of government and private ownership and control of businesses and resources.

4. Outline the economic theories developed by Karl Marx.

Karl Marx, a scholar and political writer who lived from 1818 to 1883, outlined the theory of communism. Marx advocated a labor theory of value, which holds that labor is what gives value to goods and services, and foresaw a struggle between the working class (whose labor received insufficient reward) and the capitalist classes (who controlled the means of production and received too much reward). While no country has achieved the pure communism outlined by Marx, many have developed socialist economies based on his ideas.

5. Explain the relationship between Adam Smith's views and those of the American founding fathers.

Both Adam Smith and the men who wrote the Declaration of Independence believed that individual freedom should lie at the center of both the economic and the political system. The key to societal well-being is to guarantee the individual the maximum freedom of economic action.

6. Describe the ideology of our free enterprise system.

The free enterprise system is based on Smith's belief that individuals, acting only in their own self-interest, are "led by an invisible hand" to promote the social good. Government must protect the individuals' rights to decide for themselves what economic action they will take. Our system also stresses the belief that all people should have the right to compete on an equal footing. Competition will benefit everyone. Natural laws — like the laws of supply and demand — should be allowed to operate in a free marketplace. Those who own property should be allowed to earn a profit from it. This chance to make a profit will assure that resources are used well.

7. Trace our economic system's historical development.

Colonial America was largely agrarian. The Industrial Revolution, which came to the United States in about 1800, brought factories to this country. Industrialization was spurred by the development of transportation systems, the needs of the Civil War, and the flow of immigrants to work in America's factories. From the time of the Civil War until just after World War I, businesses concentrated on improving production capacity to meet demand. During the sales era from the end of World War I until the early 1950s, the focus was on selling all that business could produce. The marketing concept evolved as business saw the need to assess consumers' wants and needs and use that information at all stages of product development and planning. Today American business is shifting out of manufacturing and into the service and information sectors.

8. List the five factors that led to the restructuring of American business in the 1970s and 1980s.

The five factors are the demise of the smokestack industries, the shock of the oil crises, the loss of confidence that accompanied severe recessions and staggering inflation, the success of foreign products in the American market, and a heightened consciousness of the problems of unemployment and underemployment.

Key Terms

Barter	Demand curve	Equilibrium	Gross National Product
Capital	Discretionary income	Factors of production	(GNP)
Capitalist	Economic system	Free-enterprise	Ideology
Communism	Economics	system	Labor theory of value
Competition	Entrepreneur or	Free-market system	Laissez faire
Demand	capitalist		

Market price	Monopoly	Private sector	Supply
Means of production	Natural laws	Productivity	Supply curve
Mixed economies or democratic socialist systems	Oligopoly	Profit	Work ethic
	Planned economies or authoritarian socialist systems	Pure competition	
Monopolistic competition		Service sector	
		Socialism	

Review Questions

1. What is the meaning of the term economics? What is an economic system?
2. Describe the concepts of supply, demand, and equilibrium.
3. List and describe the four general forms of economic competition.
4. Compare and contrast free market systems and authoritarian socialist systems.
5. How did Karl Marx distinguish between socialism and communism?
6. List and describe the three factors of production.
7. What are the three distinct characteristics of the Industrial Revolution?
8. Describe the Production Era. What are some of the positive outcomes of this period?
9. What factors motivated businesses to place greater emphasis on marketing practices during the Sales and Marketing Eras?
10. List and describe the five factors that have led to a restructuring of American business during the past two decades.

Application Exercises

1. In the early 1980s, American Telephone and Telegraph (AT&T) was the nation's largest regulated monopoly. This giant company owned the Bell Telephone system and other subsidiaries. In 1982, after many years of legal battles, AT&T's management signed a consent decree which required the firm to sever its relationship with each subsidiary that provides local phone service to consumers in specific geographic areas. The Justice Department took legal action because it believed AT&T was monopolizing the entire phone industry and stifling competition. In your opinion, was this action justified? Should AT&T have been allowed to continue in the role of a regulated monopoly? What has been the effect of the breakup of AT&T in your community?

2. Make a list of five business firms in your community that have been in operation for at least two years. The list should include several types of businesses. For each business, answer the following questions. Do the forces of supply and demand appear to have a strong influence on the prices charged for the firm's products and services? Would more competition result in lowering the prices of products and services offered by the firm?

Cases

1.1 Only in America

The story of Hebrew National Kosher Foods, Inc. is almost an allegory for American business in the late twentieth century. The firm was founded in 1928 by Isadore Pinckowitz, an immigrant Rumanian butcher, who peddled meats from a horse-drawn wagon in Manhattan. By the late 1960s, the firm had annual sales of over $15 million. At that time, the firm was being run by Leonard Pines, a son of the founder. (The family name was anglicized in 1950.)

During the 1960s there was a wave of corporate diversification through buyouts, and in 1968 Hebrew National was bought by Riviana Foods Inc. of Houston, for $13 million. Pines and his son Skip were hired to run the firm for its new owner. When other acquisitions did poorly, Riviana sought to squeeze maximum earnings from the firm, as a basis for further acquisitions.

Leonard Pines retired, and Skip took over the operation of Hebrew National. In 1978 Colgate-Palmolive Co. purchased Riviana for $170 million, to diversify its own product mix. But Colgate's management soon found that many of the products it had acquired through the Riviana purchase were not doing well. Hebrew National was put up for sale.

Skip Pines wanted desperately to buy back the firm. Father and son did buy back the firm for $13 million. Within a few years Hebrew National was the top kosher meat firm in New York, with annual revenues over $100 million and growing. By 1986 Skip and Leonard were able to pay off the money they had borrowed to buy the firm from Colgate.

Hebrew National is becoming a *diversified* regional family-owned business. Through buy-outs, Skip Pines has already added poultry and pickles to the firm's menu, and he is examining additional acquisitions. Moreover, Skip now plans to move most of Hebrew National out of its New York market and into Indiana — a state with lower taxes, lower wages, and fewer problems with unions.

Questions

1. Why would a large, successful soap company like Colgate-Palmolive want to own firms that operate in completely unrelated areas of business?
2. What effects might the purchase of small firms by larger firms have on competition and the free market system? When should such buyouts be allowed?

Source: For more information see *The New York Times*, August 8, 1986, p. B3; *Crain's New York Business Review*, January 27, 1986, p. 4; and *Forbes*, December 2, 1985, pp. 134–138.

1.2 Supply, Demand, and Silver

When the U.S. Government freed the dollar from the gold standard in the 1970s, the price of an ounce of gold rose quickly and steadily from $35 to over $500. The price of silver remained under $10 an ounce although silver is linked with gold in the minds of many people. Bunker and Herbert Hunt began buying silver bullion, in the expectation that the price would rise. They also bought silver futures. For the latter they borrowed heavily; to a great extent their loans were backed only by the silver futures.

The price of silver began to rise in 1979, slowly at first but then more quickly. By early 1980 it reached $50 per ounce. Estimates of the Hunts' silver holdings place their value at that time near $10 billion.

Then the bottom fell out. The price of silver plummeted to $11, rose briefly to $14, and then continued downward at a slower rate. The reason for the drop is not clear; obviously, the original price increases were not backed by real value. The Hunt brothers' silver and silver futures lost value, and the Hunts had to pay off their loans. A $1 billion shortfall was made up with a new ten-year loan, this one backed by one brother, two sisters, and their interest in the oil exploration firm.

The Hunt brothers lost most of their investment in silver, but not all of it. At the current price of about $6 per ounce, their 80 million ounces of bullion are worth about half a billion dollars. They paid between $7 and $12 per ounce for most of it.

Questions

1. Explain the increase in the price of silver in terms of supply, demand, and the expectations of buyers and sellers.
2. In what types of economies could the price of a commodity like silver change so dramatically?

Source: For more information see *Fortune*, April 1, 1985, pp. 26–30; *Newsweek*, March 11, 1985, pp. 62–63; and *Business Week*, March 11, 1985, pp. 84–86.

2

SOCIAL RESPONSIBILITY AND BUSINESS ETHICS

Learning Objectives

After you have completed this chapter, you will be able to do the following:

- Describe the meaning of social responsibility in a business context.
- List and describe the three dimensions of social responsibility.
- Outline and discuss the four classes of social responsibility strategies.
- Discuss some of the major arguments supporting a proactive social responsibility strategy.
- Describe the development and application of the social audit.
- Outline the ethical questions facing management.

On a June day in 1981, Eugene Lang stood on a podium in East Harlem in New York City. A self-made multimillionaire and president of Refac Technology Development Corporation, Lang was giving the commencement address at P.S. 121, which he had attended fifty years earlier. In the midst of his speech, he realized that he wanted to leave his audience with something more than the usual words of inspiration. He proceeded to tell the fifty-one graduating sixth-graders that if they completed high school he would pay for their college educations.

Five years later, at six other New York City grade-school graduations, other successful businesspeople pledged not only to put graduating classes through college but also to provide students with the tutoring and guidance needed to get them there. These people included Dianne B. Sullivan, the president of Miraflores Designs; Joseph H. Flom, a noted lawyer; Charles B. Benenson, the president of Beninson Realty Corp.; George Friedman, the president of Warner Cosmetics; Peter M. Flannigan, managing director of Dillon Read & Co.; and Paul Tudor Jones II, a successful commodities investor. Why did these six each promise what would cost them individually $250,000 and many hours of work? "New York has been incredibly good to me, and I love this city," Jones said. "For thirty-one years I've done nothing but think of myself, and this is my chance to pay back this community."[1]

The story of Eugene Lang and the six who followed him is a wonderful one, but it is not exceptional. People in business and businesses themselves make enormous contributions to the betterment of their communities. Just consider a few examples of the sort that could fill a book: sponsoring Little League teams, buying books for libraries, funding hospital rooms, providing labor for drug-abuse centers, and paying for alcohol-awareness programs. It is generally accepted that, from the largest to the smallest businesses, the firms and the people who own them have obligations to society. The great debate is over how they should fulfill their social obligations. This discussion has gone on for more than a century and is the focal point of this chapter.

THE PHILOSOPHICAL DEBATE

Business's obligation to consider the consequences of its decisions on society as a whole, for various groups within society, and for particular individuals is its **social responsibility.** Managers must consider whether the effects of an action will extend beyond positively affecting the company's financial returns. Social responsibility as a concept does not require that a business adopt a particular point of view or that it promote certain specified ends. For this reason, most definitions of social responsibility emphasize the means that a business chooses to employ rather than the ends it may seek to achieve.

Whether one believes that businesses have obligations to society beyond the minimal requirements imposed by law depends largely on whether one sees a business as just an economic organization created solely to increase the value of its owners' investments. If its only purpose is conceived of as that of making money for its owners, then its only obligation to society is to act within the law. As the influential economist Milton Friedman has written,

Finding new vehicles for social action. Ben Cohen figured how to run Ben & Jerry's and still do what he wanted to do for his employees and his community. The company offered its stock first to Vermonters, so the community could prosper along with the business. $500,000 from that stock offering was used to set up a charitable foundation, and 15 percent of Ben & Jerry's pretax profit goes into that foundation every year. Employees aren't left out either. Company policy mandates that no one can earn less than 20 percent of what top management earns.

[There] is one and only one social responsibility of business — to use its resources and engage in activities designed to increase its profits so long as it stays within the rules of the game, which is to say, engages in open and free competition without deception and fraud.[2]

Altruism, an unselfish concern for others' well-being, is the responsibility of government and of individuals acting on their own, according to this school of thought. Business should take care of business, believe Friedman and his followers.

THE NATURE OF SOCIAL RESPONSIBILITY

Three Dimensions of Social Responsibility

Milton Friedman's views do not represent the mainstream of current thinking on social responsibility. Today, the debate centers on the nature of business's responsibility to society, not on whether that responsibility exists. It is generally agreed that social responsibility has three dimensions:

☐ How a firm behaves as it pursues its goal of making profits
☐ What charitable efforts a firm undertakes that are not related to its normal business activities
☐ What positions a firm takes on issues of public policy that affect both business and society

The field within which a firm can act in fulfilling its social responsibility is defined by two boundaries: the minimum requirements for responsible social conduct expressed by laws, and the maximum boundaries permitted by its competitive economic position.[3]

TABLE 2.1

The Arguments For and Against Social Responsibility

In the debate over whether businesses have any responsibility to society beyond obeying the law and creating profits, these are the four main arguments for each side.

For	Against
1. Business is involved in social issues whether it wants to be or not.	1. Business's focus on profits already brings about the most efficient allocation of societal resources.
2. Business has the resources to deal with some of the most difficult problems that society confronts.	2. Business lacks the ability to pursue economic and social goals at the same time.
3. Business is a major beneficiary of every improvement in society.	3. Business has more than enough power over economic matters as it is.
4. Business invites government intervention, rather than avoiding it, when it fails to act on its own.	4. The public does not elect business managers, unlike its public officials. Managers are not accountable to the public, so they should not be asked to determine what society ought to do.

Voluntary Actions

Within this range, a business is free to define social responsibility in its own way. In other words, a business's actions in this arena are voluntary. For example, after a psychopath poisoned Extra-Strength Tylenol capsules, causing eight deaths, Johnson & Johnson, the maker of this aspirin substitute, immediately recalled 30 million bottles of it, at a cost of $100 million. Johnson & Johnson did not wait for an order from the Food & Drug Administration or a state agency. Rather, it did what it believed would best protect the public. The company received much praise — and customer loyalty — for its action. Most commentators failed to note, incidentally, that the company is also one of the largest corporate philanthropists.

By contrast, over a period of years the A. H. Robins Manufacturing Company disregarded mounting evidence that its Dalkon Shield birth-control device was causing serious health problems in users. When it was sued, it lied to the courts, hid documents, and defamed the individuals who had been its product's victims. The company finally recalled the defective product from the market, but it ended up in bankruptcy nevertheless.

Toward Greater Social Responsibility

Business has assumed ever-greater social responsibility in recent years. Some observers go so far as to claim that business can survive only by taking an aggressive role in social issues, especially since business in general is not held in particularly high regard by the public. At the beginning of the 1980s, some two-thirds of those surveyed in one poll felt that business was not sufficiently honest with the public. Because government and business have had a less adversarial relationship during the Reagan presidency, business may have a more positive image by now. Nonetheless, many businesspeople feel it necessary to develop strategies to involve business more deeply in the social issues confronting Americans. To understand why this is so, we must look at the historical development of the concept of social responsibility.

THE EVOLUTION OF THE CONCEPT OF SOCIAL RESPONSIBILITY

The Concept of Laissez Faire

The concept that business has social responsibility has evolved since the nation's founding. In Chapter 1, we saw that Adam Smith introduced the principle of laissez faire, a French term meaning "to let people do as they choose." To have a marketplace free of government interference was a radical break from the close regulation of trade and prices that had existed since medieval times. The concept of laissez faire dominated the social and political thinking of the next century and a half.

Caveat Emptor and the Nature of Contracts

Laissez faire found expression in the prevailing philosophy of the marketplace, **caveat emptor,** a Latin term meaning "let the buyer beware."

Responsibility for Products   Laissez faire suggested that the invisible hand that Adam Smith described as working through the marketplace would reward those who produced goods that the public wanted. Those who sold inferior or dangerous goods would fail. For the concept to work, however, some buyers had to receive shoddy goods or be maimed by dangerous products. (See Figure 2.1 on the following page.)

The concepts of laissez faire and caveat emptor also affected the courts' view of the nature of a **contract,** an agreement between two or more parties that the law will enforce. The courts of the time regarded contracts as being the product of bargaining in which each side protected its own interests. Thus, a contract between a retailer and a buyer for the sale of a product did not give the buyer the right to hold the manufacturer responsible for injuries from a defective product, because the manufacturer did not deal directly with the thousands of people, perhaps, who might have a claim against it. For example, someone named MacPhearson once bought a Buick. A defective wheel came off and MacPhearson was injured. The dealer was not at fault, because the manufacturer made the wheel. But the manufacturer was not responsible either, for it had not dealt with the buyer itself. MacPhearson could have protected himself only by carefully inspecting the car before buying it or by negotiating with the dealer for protection — or by not buying the car at all. Until 1916, this was the law in the United States. This notion did not entirely disappear until 1966.[4]

FIGURE 2.1
Laissez Faire

The effect of this narrow interpretation of the right to sue was to assign the defining of business's social responsibility to business. Anyone who insisted that society should have a say in the process was told that business's self-interest was the best protection the public could have. What ended the argument was not the question of responsibility for products but the one of the working conditions of employees.

Responsibility for Worker Safety   Implicit in the laissez-faire concept of contracts is another notion, that the parties to a contract are in an equal bargaining position. Because any two parties are free either to contract or not to contract, it was thought that legislatures and courts should not interfere with the parties' agreement. This view dominated the interpretation of employment contracts until the 1930s, and important aspects of it remain the law today.

Nineteenth-Century Working Conditions

Nineteenth-century working conditions were almost uniformly appalling. The standard work week exceeded sixty hours even until the 1930s, and paid vacations and health insurance were unknown. Efforts on the state level to improve working conditions largely failed. For instance, New York attempted to limit bakers' work weeks to sixty hours. The U.S. Supreme Court voided the statute, though, as unconstitutional interference with the right to contract. In effect, the courts refused to acknowledge the fundamentally unequal bargaining positions of employer and employee.

Again, the task of defining business's responsibility to society was assigned solely to business. Employers who wished to improve working conditions faced a hard choice. Any investment in better working conditions would put them at a competitive disadvantage, because their own costs would go up but their competitors' would not. Some employers nevertheless tried to improve their workers' lots, but most did not.

Pulling Out of South Africa

The relationship of the United States to South Africa has become the most important international social issue for many American businesses. For years, no American leaders have publicly supported the South African policy of apartheid, legally sanctioned racism which makes South Africa's 20 million blacks non-persons, subjugated in every way to the 4 million whites. Yet despite the country's political stand against apartheid, American companies have been eager to deal with South Africa. After years of living with this contradiction, in 1985 companies began responding to the increasing number of voices calling for the United States to separate itself completely from the racist South African government.

Most of these voices wish to influence South Africa through "divestment." They want universities, cities, and other big investors to "divest" their financial portfolios of companies and banks that do business with or invest in South Africa. Such divestment would be a radical move for many universities: demonstrators at the University of California at Berkeley called for a $1.7 billion divestment. Most worries that divestment would weaken institution portfolios have been put to rest by studies showing that since 1972 companies doing business with South Africa have fared worse on the stock market than those that steered clear of apartheid.

Cities and states have also taken a stand on apartheid. At least 7 states and 22 cities are participating in some kind of divestment program. A new law will keep New York City's money out of any bank that lends to South Africa. Mayor Tom Bradley of Los Angeles ordered that city's pension fund to get rid of $700 million invested in companies that are involved with South Africa.

Companies that want to continue to do business in South Africa are flocking to sign the Sullivan Principles, a set of guidelines drawn up by Philadelphia minister Leon Sullivan to insure that firms that do business with South Africa actively work to improve conditions for blacks. But Sullivan himself now says that his original guidelines don't go far enough — he wants U.S. companies to take public, political action to oppose apartheid.

Other companies, notably Goodyear and Mobil, refuse to be pressured out of South Africa. The Reagan administration has supported their views, although in 1986 it began to reconsider its stance. Reagan's policy is one of "constructive engagement." Its supporters argue that U.S. companies involved in South Africa — a third of the nation's largest corporations — can have a greater effect on apartheid if, rather than pull out, they stay in the country, provide good jobs for black workers, and generally work for change from the inside.

Divestment supporters say that "constructive engagement" has produced little or no change in South Africa and has allowed the racist government to continue with business as usual. They argue that American companies are reluctant to pull out because they have benefited for years by exploiting cheap black labor. But few protestors have illusions about divestment bringing quick change in South Africa's policies. Many of our allies are eager to take up the slack in the United States' trade with South Africa. West Germany is now South Africa's largest supplier of manufactured goods, Israel ships the country arms and is setting up companies in South Africa's black "homelands," and Taiwan has eagerly invested, once South Africa eased its policy of discriminating against Chinese.

So far, the South African government has responded defiantly to pressure from abroad. But if the raids into neighboring countries, the mass arrests, the killings of blacks in marches and in police custody, and the banning of black political groups continues, the pressure for change will continue to mount from both inside and outside. It is a situation that demands difficult moral decisions from America's business leaders.

Sources: Amy Wilentz, "Not a Black and White Issue," *Time*, Vol. 125, No. 24, June 17, 1985, 32. Mark Maremont, "Fire on Campus, Tremors in the Boardroom," *Business Week*, No. 2892, April 29, 1985, 98. William J. Holstein, "U.S. Companies Are Pulling Out — But Apartheid Is Likely to Stay," *Business Week*, No. 2900, June 24, 1985, 56. James Jones, "Why Botha's 'Reforms' May Be Doomed from the Start," *Business Week*, No. 2890, April 15, 1985, 65. Ed Magnuson, "The Issue Has Caught Fire," *Time*, Vol. 125, No. 22, June 3, 1985, 25.

The Coming of Regulation

Starting in the 1880s, public opinion began to favor the imposition of minimum standards of conduct on business by government. Under their **police powers**, the state and local governments' powers to protect the health, safety, and welfare of their citizens, governments started the long process of assuring safe and sanitary work places and residences.

For many the event that marked the end of the laissez-faire era in working conditions occurred in 1911. A twenty-minute fire on the ninth floor of the Triangle Shirtwaist Company building in New York City left 147 workers dead. The image of more than fifty young women leaping from windows to escape the flames came to haunt the public. Later revelations about blocked exits and generally unsafe conditions gave impetus to the gathering movement toward regulation of the work place.[5]

The Depression and the New Deal   The Depression of 1929–1939 shook Americans' confidence in the laissez-faire concept. By the time Franklin Roosevelt took office in 1933, one-quarter of the work force had no jobs and America's industrial output had fallen by 50 percent. Revolutions and dictatorships such as those afflicting Russia, Germany, and Italy seemed a real possibility in the United States.

Through programs like unemployment insurance, Social Security and federal bank deposit insurance, and various government regulations, Roosevelt and his fellow New Dealers hoped to protect Americans from capitalism's rough edges. The intense regulation of financial services, transportation, and energy dates to this period.

After Roosevelt replaced several of its members, the U.S. Supreme Court became much more favorably inclined toward laws regulating such working conditions as wages and hours. Roosevelt signed legislation enacting a national minimum wage and establishing the forty-hour work week as standard. Suddenly, business found itself with a set of governmental minimum standards of performance and even higher public expectations of performance.

World War II and a Period of Great Prosperity   Where the New Deal might eventually have taken the relationship between government and business and how a prolonged depression would have altered people's relationships with business remain unknown. World War II arrived, requiring the United States to pull itself together. It emerged from the war as the strongest and most prosperous nation the world had yet seen. The New Deal reforms had become generally accepted as business's social ground rules. The public and business agreed that these reforms represented in effect floors and that business's principal responsibility was to create jobs and prosperity. The prosperity was enormous enough to hide the inefficiencies and waste that regulation was forcing on all the transportation systems other than the automobile and on the financial-services industry.

The Civil Rights Movement

Perhaps the most important development in the period after World War II was the Civil Rights movement. It began in the South among blacks who demanded equal treatment under the laws. Their successes profoundly changed the nature of the work place. For example, in the 1960s Levi Strauss opened a plant in

Providing what many take for granted. *Business giving did not die out with the early industrialists. United Technologies, one of the 35 largest industrial companies in the world, and benefactor of United Technologies Hall at the University of Hartford earmarks more than 2 percent of its domestic pretax profit for its program of corporate giving. Many businesses carry on a long tradition of giving because they believe they have a duty to be good citizens and good neighbors.*

Virginia, for which it wanted to hire both blacks and whites. The white workers demanded separate restrooms and drinking fountains, with preferably a wall between white and black workers. Strauss refused these demands, which were not unreasonable by local standards, insisting upon an integrated facility because it felt that that was the right thing to do.[6]

The gains made by blacks led directly to the work place's being opened to other minorities, women, and the handicapped. By the late 1960s, equal opportunity had become a practical goal.

The Decade of Regulation: The 1970s

By the early 1970s, the postwar public confidence in business had eroded. A growing awareness of environmental pollution focused attention on businesses that could not or would not clean up their operations without being compelled to do so by the government. The Vietnam war, which began in earnest in 1965, put a spotlight on firms supplying war materials. One such company, Dow Chemical, attracted considerable attention because its defoliants had serious environmental as well as military consequences. The prevalence of occupational diseases like black lung among coal miners and brown lung among cotton-mill

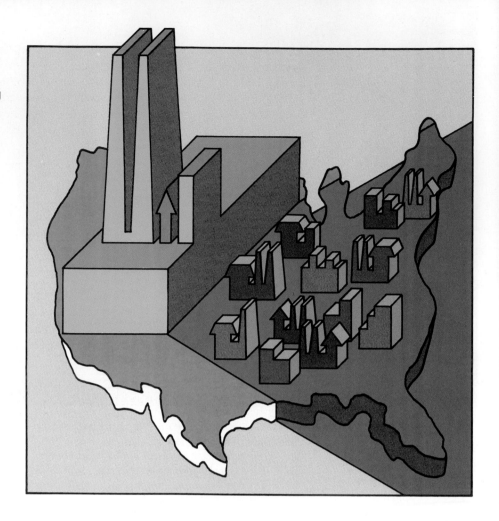

workers led to demands for more effective regulation of the work place. The great political scandals of the early 1970s centered largely on the role of corporations in both the national and international political processes. Finally, the consumer movement, led initially by Ralph Nader, drew public attention to the shoddy and sometimes dangerous quality of many products.

At all levels of government, the response to these unsettling events was a burst of regulation. Environmental laws and regulations came in a flood. Agencies like the Federal Election Commission, the Occupational Safety & Health Administration (OSHA), and the Consumer Product Safety Commission appeared seemingly overnight.

The Reaction to Regulation

A reaction against regulation also began in the mid-1970s. President Jimmy Carter initiated a series of deregulation programs that were aimed particularly at the energy, financial services, and transportation industries. These efforts were well under way by the end of his term in 1981.

The election of President Ronald Reagan was expected to bring an era of deregulation and what we describe as nonregulation in Chapter 22. Things did not work out quite as imagined, however. In fact, what surfaced instead was a general consensus in favor of regulation. One desirable effect of regulation is that it denies a cost advantage to those who do not act in a socially responsible manner. Also, it is hard to argue that pollution or hazardous goods benefit society. Although the pace of business regulation slowed greatly as the 1980s progressed, only small parts of the regulatory structure disappeared entirely.

SOCIAL RESPONSIBILITY STRATEGIES

Four Social Responsibility Strategies

Businesses may choose from among four classes of social responsibility strategies: reaction, defense, accommodation, or what is referred to as proaction.

The Reaction Strategy

A business follows a reaction strategy when it denies responsibility for something while at the same time it is developing an argument for continuing the status quo. For example, despite an increasing accident rate, the Ford Motor Company

FIGURE 2.3

Social Responsibilities Strategies Visualized

A Good Return on Principle

Can investors who don't want to support weapons manufacturing, nuclear power, or apartheid make money by investing in American companies without compromising their principles? Many enthusiastic supporters of capitalism would laugh at the question and assert that an investor's only concern should be profit. Those cynical about American capitalism might also scoff at the question, contending that simply by getting involved in Wall Street dealings, the investor becomes part of the system that exploits the world's resources and workers.

But now a growing number of voices are saying yes, it is possible to stand by your beliefs and still invest your money in American companies, without feeling like a hypocrite. A small industry has sprung up to cater to those who would like to be both ethical and rich, and according to Boston's Social Investment Forum, at least $40 billion is invested with social and moral issues in mind.

Those involved in the social investment industry tell stories of clients who were embarrassed to discover what their money was supporting. Amy Domini, co-author of *Ethical Investing*, gives as examples a church that was unwittingly benefiting from birth control, apartheid, and nuclear weapons, and her own mother, who devoted considerable time to fighting the nuclear arms race yet owned stock in companies that made nuclear weapons.

Keeping your money "clean" takes some work. Joan Bavaria, president of the Social Investment Forum, says, "If you don't specifically look for ways to keep your money away from these [morally unacceptable] issues, chances are extremely high that your stock, or your bank deposits, or your IRAs are going to foster at least one of them." Investors concerned about what their money is supporting can get information about companies' social responsibilities from a number of newsletters and data collection agencies. "Insight: The Advisory Letter for Concerned Investors" takes the positive approach of identifying companies to invest in; *Corporate Responsibility Monitor* keeps track of both positive and negative news items about companies.

The easiest and most popular way to make ethical investments, however, is to put money into one of a growing number of mutual funds that invest only in companies that meet their criteria. Pax World Fund has been operating successfully for 15 years avoiding any company connected with South Africa, liquor, gambling, weapons, or tobacco and favoring companies involved with food, housing, medicine, and transportation.

What surprises many Wall Street skeptics is not that such funds exist, but that they have been so successful. Calvert Social Investment Fund, which avoids companies connected with South Africa, defense contracts, nuclear power, liquor, tobacco, and gambling, returned almost 22 percent on investment for the 12 months ending in mid-1985, outperforming most other mutual funds and beating the Standard & Poor 500-stock index by two percentage points. Another "moral" mutual fund, Pioneer II, has gained 688 percent over the last ten years, as compared to the Standard & Poor gain of 254 percent.

Such gains do not surprise those involved in the social investment industry, who point out that people who invest in such companies don't have to worry as much about lawsuits by injured customers, takeovers of subsidiaries by hostile foreign governments, or disasters like Three Mile Island. Such investments are ultimately based on the belief that a company that's good for the world will be good for those who invest in it.

Few ethically oriented investors imagine that their money has made a difference in the policies of corporate America. For the moment, the greatest change is in the investors' consciences. Many people rest easier knowing that their money is not going to support the next generation of chemical warfare. If enough people feel that way, and enough of them put their money where their emotions are, ethically oriented investment could one day become a significant force on Wall Street.

Sources: Eleanor Johnson Tracy, "Noble Performance," *Fortune*, Vol. 111, No. 11, May 27, 1985, 27. Donald H. Dunn, "Investing with a Social Conscience," *Business Week*, No. 2894, May 13, 1985, 149. Terri Minsky, "Adding Morality to the Bottom Line," *The Boston Globe*, May 12, 1985, 77.

refused to admit that there was anything wrong with the fuel tank on its Pinto compacts. A. H. Robins, mentioned earlier, followed a reaction strategy, as did the Manville Corporation and the entire asbestos industry in the face of medical claims by asbestos workers, who believed that they suffered from asbestosis as a direct result of the working conditions to which they were subjected.

The Defense Strategy

The defense strategy involves the use of public relations, legal maneuvering, and whatever other means are necessary to avoid assuming additional obligations. This strategy, often coordinated by a trade association, is most often employed to avoid government regulation. For instance, the leading opponents of the regulation of offshore oil drilling operations are the American Petroleum Institute and the National Ocean Industries Association. The National Coal Association resists surface-mining regulation. A few individual companies, like Mobil Oil Company, have adopted this strategy. For some years, Mobil has bought advertising space in newspapers to present its views.

The Accommodation and Proaction Strategies

The accommodation and proaction strategies have in common a willingness to assume responsibility for their actions rather than to deny it. The difference between the two strategies lies in the motivation underlying the assumption of responsibility.

When a company assumes more social responsibility because of pressure from an interest group or the government, it adopts an accommodation strategy. If, for example, a company sets up stringent promotion goals for women and minorities under the threat of a lawsuit by its employees, it is using an accommodation strategy.

By contrast, a company like Sears, Roebuck and Company, which has had a long-standing policy of this type that it decided on without outside pressure,[7] is engaged in a proactive strategy. **Proactive** means in favor of action. A company adopts such a stance if it prefers to be involved in social issues. A good example is the Aetna Life & Casualty Co., which puts $30 million annually into social investments ranging from housing projects to minority-owned businesses.[8] Both General Motors and the Burroughs Corporation demonstrated their commitment to their headquarters city, Detroit, by redeveloping the areas around their offices instead of fleeing to safer, cleaner suburbs.

SOCIAL RESPONSIBILITY AND SELF-INTEREST

Some identify social responsibility with altruism and contrast it with self-interest. The issue is not, however, nearly so simple, and a strong argument can in fact be made that altruism and self-interest both dictate a proactive strategy.

Making the community a better place to live.
Companies like Detroit Edison try to serve their communities in many ways. Here linemen tell children how to avoid danger as part of the company's "Eyes and Ears" crime prevention program. The company also encourages its 11,000 employees to contribute to the United Way and other charitable organizations, helps to distribute food and clothing to those in need, and runs the largest private economic development effort in Michigan.

Altruism

Benefits of a Proactive Strategy

The benefits from a proactive strategy can be so significant that it is difficult to identify the decisions that are prompted solely by altruism except when an action can have no benefit whatsoever to the business. Luckily, virtue is rarely its own sole reward.

A recent survey of top management in U.S. corporations revealed high awareness of the need for, and benefits of, a proactive strategy. The overwhelming majority of those surveyed believed that social responsibility was in the best interests of the corporations they worked for. Approximately nine out of ten respondents agreed that society had come to expect more from business than simply the efficient production of goods and services. They also believed that the long-range success of business depends on recognizing that it is simply a part of society as a whole. Nearly eight out of ten managers surveyed believed that a company could not have a positive public image without establishing a reputation for social responsibility. Seven out of ten were convinced that socially responsible corporate behavior tends to discourage increased government regulation.

Given this widespread agreement on the positive nature of a commitment to social responsibility, it is not surprising that businesses have found many creative ways to fulfill what they perceive to be their obligations, such as the following:

□ Philanthropy
□ Community service
□ Community redevelopment
□ Employee development

| Reputation value | Publicity value | Recruiting & keeping personnel |

FIGURE 2.4

Enlightened Self Interest/ Altruism

Enlightened Self-interest

Every business faces choices that pit short-term gains — or the avoidance of losses — against its long-term interests. The conscious policy of pursuing long-term rather than short-term interests is termed enlightened self-interest.

An Argument Against Proactive Strategy

The chief argument against a proactive strategy is that a company that is increasing its expenditures that are not related to a narrowly focused business purpose may be doing good, but it is paying a price — out of its owners' pockets. Social responsibility is therefore seen as only a policy that costs money. Consider again the case of the Manville Corporation, though. It fought asbestosis claims for as long as it could, then entered into bankruptcy proceedings. When it emerges from them, its prebankruptcy shareholders will find their ownership interests reduced by over 80 percent. Would the shareholders have been better off if Manville had settled the litigation early on instead of fighting it? One can only speculate.

Maintaining a Good Reputation

Reputation Value Enlightened self-interest operates on several levels. At the highest level, it represents an understanding that nothing is more important to the long-term success of any business than its reputation. Unless a company is prepared to sacrifice its own immediate financial advantage to protect the public interest, it cannot expect the public to care about the company's long-term well-being.

Many companies encourage employees to take on community projects, like United Way campaigns, that cut into work time. Some businesses even allow employees to work full-time on a community project while on a paid leave of absence. The most noted program of this type is the Xerox Social Service Leave Program, which started in 1972. Qualified Xerox employees may apply for a six-month to one-year paid leave to work on a community-service program. Afterward, they are guaranteed their old job back or a similar one.[9]

Texaco takes another approach. Following natural disasters like hurricanes or floods, this oil company sends letters to its credit-card customers in the area

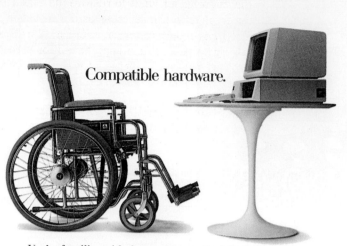

Compatible hardware.

You're familiar with the machine on the left. And with the machine on the right. You may be less familiar with how useful bringing them together can be.

Working with community groups around the country, IBM has helped start 31 training programs at centers where physically disabled people learn computer programming skills. At each center, a council of local business people ensures that the training meets current employer needs in the area—so the skills people learn help them get jobs.

More than 1,700 people have been trained and better than 80% are now working. They've found jobs in banks, insurance companies, hospitals, schools and government, for example.

Many of them have also found the independence that a job can provide. And the satisfaction every person gets from using his or her abilities.

And that's why companies that make computers, and employers that use them, should work together to make computers compatible. With everyone. IBM

Providing the right connection. For many people who want to work, physical handicaps present a major obstacle. IBM has helped put together training programs that teach computer programming to physically disabled individuals. More than 1,700 people have received training and over 80 percent of them have found jobs. IBM's advertising helps make business people aware of the programs.

that say, "We at Texaco are concerned that you or your family may have been personally affected by this unfortunate disaster and wish to cooperate if help is needed." They proceed to offer an extension on payment periods and a suspension of interest charges.[10]

Good Publicity and Recognition

Publicity Value   On another level, enlightened self-interest requires accurate calculation of the long-term benefits expected to be derived from the short-term costs of social responsibility. The corporate charitable contribution is the classic example of this. Its real benefit comes from the publicity and recognition that gifts attract. McDonald's, for instance, makes grants to the Public Broadcasting System to enable PBS to produce "Sesame Street." This contribution is acknowledged at the beginning of each episode. Families with small children — a prime McDonald's market — certainly know whose generosity is bringing them the program.

American Express has introduced "cause-related marketing," which is designed at once to create social benefits and to generate greater profits. During the campaign for funds to restore the Statue of Liberty, the firm pledged a penny for every American Express card transaction and a dollar for every new member. The three-month campaign raised $1.7 million for the Statue while boosting card use by 28 percent and applications for cards by 45 percent. American Express also has similar arrangements with nine countries' Olympic committees and fifty other causes in the United States.[11]

Recruiting and Keeping Personnel   Companies with strong reputations for their social commitments have a significantly easier time in recruiting

---

Profiting from Mistakes

For most companies, tangling with the Environmental Protection Agency is a worrisome task, and being caught contributing to a hazardous waste dump can be costly and can destroy a company's image. But when Westinghouse Electric Corp. agreed to the largest Superfund settlement ever in 1985, it set out to ensure stockholders that the company might actually gain from the situation. If the project works as planned it could lead companies to take a new approach to dealing with past mistakes.

From the 1950s through the early 1970s, Westinghouse dumped electrical capacitors containing polychlorinated biphenyls (PCBs) into landfills. The chemicals, which are suspected of causing cancer and other diseases, are now leaking out of the dump sites, contaminating nearby water, and endangering residents. The federal government established the Superfund and spent $1 million trying to contain the contamination before the EPA and Westinghouse agreed to the settlement. Under the agreement, Westinghouse will pay the EPA back that million, monitor groundwater near the sites for as long as 30 years, excavate contaminated sediments from nearby streams, and provide water to any resident whose well becomes contaminated with PCBs. Most importantly, within 15 years, Westinghouse will clean up 6 dumps near Bloomington, Indiana, by incinerating 650,000 cubic yards of contaminated soil.

The key to the settlement, and to Westinghouse's hopes to find a silver lining to its cloud, is the incineration. Often landfills have been cleaned up by removing contamination to another landfill, where the chemicals may become a problem in the future. Incineration destroys the chemicals entirely. The EPA estimated that the job would cost Westinghouse up to $100 million. Westinghouse puts the figure at closer to $20 million, and says it already has most of the technology to do the job.

The company purchased O'Connor Combuster Corp., a builder of municipal waste incinerators, in 1983 and has modified O'Connor's combustors so that they will burn hot enough to destroy the PCBs. Most toxic-chemical incinerators use fuels like natural gas to burn the chemicals, but Westinghouse plans to use municipal waste.

The company hopes that local cities will pay it to burn their waste, and that the incinerator will generate electricity that the company can sell. The incinerator should demonstrate the company's capacity to handle hazardous wastes, and Westinghouse hopes that the success of the project will convince other companies to buy its technology. If all these plans work out, other companies may begin exploring new ways of making the proper disposal of waste profitable. And Westinghouse may end up being glad that the EPA lit a fire under its plans to deal more effectively with hazardous waste.

Sources: Kenneth Dreyfack, "A Blessing in Disguise for Westinghouse," *Business Week*, No. 2897, June 3, 1985, 44. "Westinghouse Cleans Up," *Fortune*, Vol. 111, No. 13, June 24, 1985. "Westinghouse Set to Partially Clean Dump Site, U.S. Says," *The Wall Street Journal*, Vol. 202, No. 102, November 23, 1983, 18. Robert E. Taylor, "Westinghouse Will Clean Up Six Indiana Sites," *The Wall Street Journal*, May 21, 1985, 4.

---

and keeping personnel with similar interests. Firms with good records on hiring and promoting women and minorities tend to attract increasing numbers of qualified job applicants from these groups.

Businesses with a highly visible commitment to the communities in which they operate also tend to have better records in attracting and keeping personnel. Wang Laboratories has made its area of eastern Massachusetts a much better place to live through its generous donations to cultural affairs and its funding of Boston's Wang Center. Despite recent reversals in Wang's business fortunes, it retains a high reputation.

Many businesses have programs that pay part or all of an employee's tuition for courses taken outside of work hours. Such programs improve employee morale by demonstrating a firm's commitment to helping its personnel improve their chances of getting ahead. And tuition aid helps fill local college classrooms with committed students. Some businesses have taken these programs a step further by giving employees paid leaves of absence to complete their degrees or to obtain advanced training.

THE SOCIAL AUDIT

By law, every corporation that has more than five hundred shareholders and a value exceeding a certain minimal level must have its books audited. Shareholders and the investing public are thus provided with an accurate picture of the business's financial condition. Some people have applied this same concept to a business's interaction with society and encouraged a **social audit**, an annual assessment of a company's effects on society and the environment.

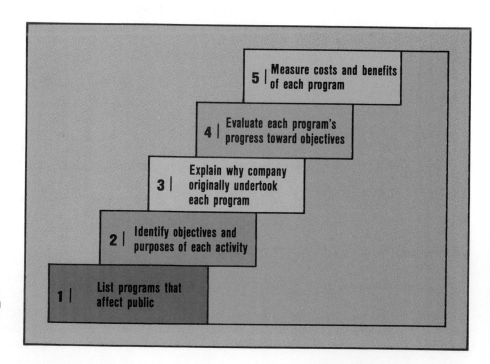

FIGURE 2.5

Five Steps Toward Creating an Ethical Environment

5 | Measure costs and benefits of each program

4 | Evaluate each program's progress toward objectives

3 | Explain why company originally undertook each program

2 | Identify objectives and purposes of each activity

1 | List programs that affect public

Setting social goals *Dart & Kraft sets well-defined social goals and uses its annual report to let investors and stockholders know how well it is meeting them. Long-range objectives call for 2 percent of domestic pretax income to be devoted to charitable giving. Kraft presented the land to the EPCOT Center as a showcase for crop management techniques. Here scientists work with grain sorghum, a major food crop in less developed areas of the world.*

Developing a Social Audit

A business would normally expect to perform a social audit annually, just as it issues an annual report. An accumulation of audits over the years would provide a good means of evaluating a company's long-term social contribution.

The Five-Step Process for Developing a Social Audit

A social audit requires a five-step process. First, the company must develop a list of all its programs that affect the public. The list might include such programs as pollution-control efforts, minority employment outreach programs, energy-conservation campaigns, work place safety awards, and charitable contributions. Second, the company must identify the objectives and purposes of each activity — what the company hopes to achieve and what society stands to gain. Third, the company should explain why it originally undertook each program. Fourth, it should evaluate each program's progress during the audit period in question. Finally, when it is possible to do so, the company should measure the costs and benefits of each program.

Objections to the Social-Audit Concept

A well-accepted body of accounting and legal standards governs financial audits. The standards for fiscal audits are objective and uniform across the whole range of American businesses. The basic problem with the social-audit concept is that no such body of standards exists for social criteria. Political, philosophical, and religious beliefs would all affect a social audit. Recall, for example, Milton Friedman's view of the entire concept of social responsibility. And consider, for example, whether, say, ServiceMaster Industries' express commitment to operate in accordance with Christian values[12] would be regarded in the same way by all who reviewed its social audit. In short, the objectivity required for a uniformly accepted social audit would be hard to come by.

The Future of the Social Audit

Few corporations have greeted the social-audit concept with enough enthusiasm actually to undertake one. If the social audit proves useful to the companies that are pioneering it, others will follow. It is worth noting that more than 90 percent of the nation's top five hundred corporations now include some disclosure of the social consequences of their activities in their annual reports. It thus seems likely that in the future a disclosure of the social consequences of corporate policy will in one form or another become a permanent part of businesses' reports to their owners and investors.

THE ETHICAL DIMENSION OF MANAGEMENT

What the law does not prohibit, a business can do, without fear of legal penalty. However, it does not follow that it is all right to do anything not forbidden by law. For instance, in most cases a person can ignore another's cry for help without threat of any legal penalty, but ignoring that cry is not morally right. And sometimes it is even not all right to do what the law commands. The founder of three hugely successful high-tech firms — Computervision Corporation, Automatix, Inc., and Cognition Corporation — is Phillipe Villers, who fled France just ahead of the German army in World War II. He has said: "As a young boy, I was

Table 2.2

General Dynamics Guidelines for Creating an Ethical Work Environment

In making complex ethical decisions, an employee should first determine what the facts of the situation are and where his responsibilities lie.

The employee should then try to think out the consequences of his course of action. Does the good it will do outweigh the bad?

☐ Which action best maximizes benefits to all parties, reduces harm, respects rights, and treats people fairly?
☐ Would I be comfortable explaining my decision to my family or on the "Today" show?
☐ Am I willing to make my decision become a general rule for the company?
☐ Will this decision look as good a month and a year from now as it does today?

Source: Adapted from "Developing Ethics Code Mom Would Be Proud Of," *St. Louis Post-Dispatch*, March 30, 1986, p. 8A.

very much aware of what the Nazis had done. Business men in Germany were able to keep their private sense of values separate. That is something I never could do, and I don't."[13]

Business Ethics

The study of moral, as contrasted with legal, obligations is called **ethics. Business ethics** is the study of the moral problems that confront members of business organizations and others who engage in business transactions. Business's role is to provide the goods and services that society requires, in the most efficient manner possible. In some cases this role conflicts with other important values. A common problem involves technological change. What should a company do with an excellent employee who cannot adapt to a new technology or who is made redundant by it? Sheer efficiency dictates termination, but loyalty to employees who have merited it may require another solution or a termination that is both gradual and generous.

The ethical dimension of management is not limited to a knowledge of the differences between right and wrong. It extends to choosing among different principles of moral obligations. In other words, ethical decisions may require choices between different alternatives that are each right in their own way. Ethical conduct is not learned by memorizing a handbook. A manager can fall back only on the knowledge that every action has ethical implications.

Encouraging Ethical Conduct

A Business's Commitment to Ethical Conduct

It is not enough for a company simply to encourage its employees to act ethically. Appropriate actions must accompany such statements. Top management can demonstrate its commitment to doing business ethically by starting companywide ethics-training programs. Many firms already have such programs. Some such corporations include the Cummins Engine Company, BankAmerica Corporation, the Avco Corporation, and the Prudential Insurance Company.[14] The defense industry particularly has emphasized these programs. The General Dynamics Corporation, the major defense contractor, has even established an "ethics hot line" that employees can call if confronted with ethical problems they can't resolve.[15] Another technique is to develop a corporate code of ethics, such as one the Dayton-Hudson Corporation has developed. Some corporations, and the federal government, have developed elaborate plans for protecting **whistle blowers,** employees who report unethical or illegal conduct to their superiors or a government agency.

BUSINESS ETHICS: A PERSPECTIVE

After a series of scandals involving its defense businesses, General Dynamics instituted an aggressive ethics program. The company asked Stanford University business professor Kirk O. Hanson, an expert on ethics, to help draw up suggestions for creating an ethical work environment. The company then circulated these guidelines, part of which are in Table 2.2, to its managers. [16]

One of the toughest dilemmas facing managers today may be how to communicate ethical values to their employees. General Dynamics gave its managers the suggestions in Table 2.3. Most companies do not try to teach their employees right from wrong, assuming that most people know the distinctions. Instead they try to encourage employees to do the right thing. General Dynamics has gone as far as appointing a corporate ethics director, who in turn has appointed ethics directors for many of the corporation's divisions. Thousands of its employees will then attend seminars designed to communicate the company's ethical standards. [17]

The question that sticks in many people's minds is how voluntary are the programs like General Dynamics'? Would the company have invested the necessary resources in these programs without the threat of the loss of government contracts for further violations? In short, is the program purely an accommodation strategy? Only the company's long-term performance will tell.

Table 2.3

General Dynamics Guidelines for Communicating Ethical Values

☐ Create an open environment in the work place that makes employees feel comfortable in bringing problems or ethical dilemmas to superiors.

☐ Be consistent and reward ethical behavior. For example, don't tell employees that you want an ethical environment at work and then issue an ultimatum — "The quarterly profit goals had better be reached, or else."

☐ Ask questions on value-related issues when visiting offices or factories.

☐ Include criteria in performance-evaluation systems that incorporate performance according to key ethical values.

☐ Prepare a statement of the values or "way" certain kinds of business problems should be handled.

☐ Use employee publications and other media to demonstrate and reinforce key values.

☐ Establish special ethics training or integrate such discussions into existing programs.

☐ Instruct by a good personal example.

Source: Adapted from "Developing Ethics Code Mom Would Be Proud of," *St. Louis Post-Dispatch.*

Chapter Highlights

1. Describe the meaning of social responsibility in a business context.

Social responsibility is business's obligation to consider the consequences of a decision for society as a whole, for various groups within society, and for particular individuals. This means that management must consider the effects of an action beyond whether it will positively affect the company's financial return.

2. List and describe the three dimensions of social responsibility.

It is generally agreed that social responsibility has three dimensions: (1) How a firm behaves as it pursues its goals of making profits; (2) what charitable efforts a firm undertakes that are not related to its normal business activities; and (3) what positions a firm takes on issues of public policy that affect both business and society.

3. Outline and discuss the four classes of social responsibility strategies.

Businesses may choose from among four classes of social responsibility strategies: reaction, defense, accommodation, and proaction. A business follows a *reaction strategy* when it denies responsibility for something while developing an argument for a continuation of the status quo. The *defense strategy* involves the use of public relations, legal maneuvering, and all other means necessary to avoid assuming additional obligations. *Accommodation* and *proaction* strategies have in common a willingness to assume responsibility rather than to deny it. The difference between the two lies in the motivation underlying the assumption of responsibility. A company that assumes greater social responsibility because of pressure from an interest group or a government agency, is adopting an *accommodation* strategy. When a company displays greater social responsibility without any pressure, it has adopted a *proactive* strategy.

4. Discuss some of the major arguments supporting a proactive social responsibility strategy.

A growing number of managers agree that society has come to expect more from business than simply the efficient production of goods and services. They feel the long-term success of the business depends, in part, on its public image. A positive public image builds consumer support for a company and its products. Managers also recognize that social responsibility tends to discourage increased government regulation. Companies with strong reputations for their social commitments find it significantly easier to recruit and keep personnel.

5. Describe the development and application of the social audit.

The social audit is an annual assessment of a company's effects on society and the environment. The audit involves a five-step process. Step one involves preparation of a list of all its programs that affect the public. The list might include such things as pollution control efforts or energy conservation campaigns. During step two the company identifies the objectives and purposes of each activity. Step three involves an explanation of why the company originally undertook each program. An on-going evaluation of each program's progress during the audit period is step four. Step five involves the assessment of costs and benefits of each program.

6. Outline the ethical questions facing management.

Every day management is faced with a series of ethical questions. These are concerned with treatment of personnel, safety in the work place, pollution control, minority employment, relations with customers, and a wide range of financial matters involving investors and the financial community.

Key Terms

Altruism	Contract	Proactive	Social responsibility
Business ethics	Ethics	Social audit	Whistle blowers
Caveat emptor	Police powers		

Review Questions

1. What is the meaning of social responsibility? Describe the three dimensions of social responsibility.
2. What was the influence of Adam Smith's principle of *laissez faire* on early business decisions regarding responsibility for products?
3. Why did the 1970s become the decade of regulation?
4. List and describe four classes of social responsibility strategies.
5. Why are more managers supporting a proactive strategy in terms of social responsibility?
6. What is meant by a policy of enlightened self-interest?
7. Describe the purpose of a social audit. What steps must be taken to complete a social audit?
8. What is business ethics? Why are many businesses adopting higher ethical standards today?
9. What are some of the ways a company can encourage ethical conduct among employees?
10. Compare and contrast the actions of Johnson & Johnson managers with the actions of managers working for A. H. Robins Manufacturing Company.

Application Exercises

1. Assume the role of Vice President of Marketing for a large bank. In the weeks ahead the bank will establish a telemarketing department that will be used to market two new services. One service will be a second mortgage loan plan for people who want to borrow money, using their home as collateral. The second service will be a special checking account that offers a higher interest rate. The staff of this new department will include a department manager, assistant department manager, and eight persons who will be involved in telephone sales. Prepare a series of guidelines that can be incorporated into a code of ethics for the department.
2. Review six to eight recent issues of the *Wall Street Journal* and identify those companies that are currently involved in some type of legal action. Compile a list of the legal problems and then try to determine which of these problems might have been avoided if the company had developed and initiated a social audit.

Cases

2.1 Proactive Banking in Chicago

Chicago's South Shore neighborhood is a community of 80,000 people, located 12 miles from downtown. It became primarily black and poor as middle-class whites moved to the suburbs during the 1960s. Businesses fled, and the neighborhood became a prime example of urban decay. Chicago's banks were fearful of lending money for investment in such a depressed area. They felt the risk of loss was too great. The banks' reluctance to invest in South Shore ensured continued deterioration.

In 1973, however, a group of investors decided to break the chain of circumstances that kept the neighborhood down. The investors (individuals, corporations, and charitable organizations) formed a holding company and purchased the South Shore Bank. Simply by maintaining the bank in the neighborhood, they had a positive effect. But they also began to provide loans for investors who were willing to purchase and rehabilitate multifamily residences there. Bank policy required rehabilitation; the goal was a better neighborhood, one that would attract long-term residents and increased investment. Although the bank did make some relatively unconventional loans, it was generally a conservative lender. Projects had to be financially sound, with a reasonable chance to be profitable. Borrowers have defaulted on less than 2 percent of mortgage loans, while the bank has financed the renovation of more than 200 apartment buildings.

The South Shore Bank was purchased for operation as a profit-making enterprise, and — except for one year — it has been exactly that. Its 1985 profit was $1 million, its highest ever. But just as important has been the change that has come about: Many people now consider the South Shore neighborhood a good place for themselves, their families, and their investments.

Questions

1. To what extent do you think altruism and self-interest were involved in the purchase and operation of the South Shore Bank? Explain.
2. Should South Shore Bank's rehabilitation concept be applied to other blighted urban neighborhoods? What might keep it from working in other areas?

For more information see *Money*, August 1986, p. 9; *The Boston Globe*, July 5, 1986, p. 26; and *Mother Jones*, June 1985, p. 24.

2.2 Cause-Related Marketing

Can a firm do better by doing good? Many large corporations are becoming involved in philanthropic projects as a profit-making strategy. One that has exhibited special expertise in this area is American Express (AmEx). In fact, it was AmEx that coined the current term for the concept: cause-related marketing. But a good number of firms have used the strategy.

The two major sponsors of the 1986 Hands Across America relief project were Citicorp and Coca-Cola, which together contributed $8 million — aside from what they spent on publicity. Coca-Cola participated to get back some of the goodwill it lost in 1985, with its New Coke/

Classic Coke misfire. But Citicorp was there to increase its national credit card business. The bank pledged to contribute one cent for each purchase charged to a Citicorp credit card, and $2 for every new card it issued, during three months preceding the event.

American Express was only a minor sponsor of Hands Across America. The firm paid $33,000 to sponsor one mile of desert in Arizona and New Mexico. But AmEx shrewdly chose the mile that had been billed as "the toughest mile in America" and, as a result, received extensive newspaper and television publicity.

The results of other AmEx cause-related marketing campaigns have been more tangible. Although AmEx was not an official sponsor of the Statue of Liberty restoration, it did run a three-month campaign in which it contributed to the project every time an American Express card was used or issued. During that period AmEx raised $1.7 million for the restoration, and its card usage rose by almost 30 percent.

Since 1981, when it began its cause-related marketing, American Express has sponsored sixty or so campaigns — mostly local and on its own. The Atlanta Arts Alliance campaign is typical. For two months in 1983, AmEx donated from five cents to $5 to the Alliance's fund drive whenever an Atlantan used or was issued a card. The Alliance earned about $60,000 from the campaign; AmEx earned a 20 percent increase in card usage in Atlanta over the period.

Cause-related marketing does benefit worthwhile causes, even while it benefits those who practice it. Most firms who use the strategy also contribute to charity.

Questions

1. Is cause-related marketing philanthropic? Society responsible? Is it ethical?
2. Does philanthropy constitute a large or small part of the social responsibility of business? Why? What might be more important?

For more information see *The New York Times*, July 6, 1986, p. F6; *Fortune*, June 9, 1986, pp. 71–80; and *Newsweek*, April 4, 1983, p. 62.

3

THE
FORMS
OF
BUSINESS
OWNERSHIP

Learning Objectives

After you have completed this chapter, you will be able to do the following:

■ Identify and describe three basic forms of business ownership.

■ Outline the advantages and disadvantages of the three forms of business organization.

■ Distinguish between general partnerships and limited partnerships.

■ Describe how a corporation Is organized and managed.

■ List and describe three other forms of business organization that exist for specialized purposes.

For twelve years, John and Donald Kielhafner jointly farmed their father's land near Cape Girardeau, Missouri. John eventually became dissatisfied with his share of the profits and sued Donald, claiming that he and Donald had orally agreed to be partners and to divide all profits equally. The evidence showed that the brothers had indeed farmed together and that they had in fact shared profits and expenses, though not always equally. However, they had maintained separate bank accounts and books and filed separate tax returns. On this basis, the court could not determine what the terms of the partnership agreement were, if there had really been a partnership, and left the brothers as they were.[1]

John made an all-too-common mistake: he failed to put his agreement with his brother in writing. Partnership agreements can be made orally, but when two or more persons are involved in a business their relationships should be defined in writing. An old proverb sums up this lesson: "Good fences make good neighbors." Without good boundaries, best friends — even brothers — can end up in court.

Partnerships are one of the three principal forms of business. The other two are sole proprietorships and corporations. Which form of business is best? The best business form is simply the one that fits. One form will not fit all businesses. What is good for General Motors is probably not good for Ma & Pa's Superette. The most that can be said about the best form is that as businesses grow, they tend to become corporations, if they are not already structured that way.

This chapter has two purposes. First, it describes the principal forms for business used in the United States. Second, it illustrates how those forms affect the people who work for or deal with businesses.

SOLE PROPRIETORSHIPS

The First Principal Form of Business: Sole Proprietorships

The form of business in which one individual (the **sole proprietor**) owns all the assets of the business and is alone responsible for its debts is a *sole proprietorship*. A sole proprietor may run almost any kind of business, from a dry cleaner to a movie theater to a computer store to an accounting practice. About the only industries that sole proprietors cannot enter are banking and, in most states, public utilities.

Sole proprietorships make up 70 percent of American businesses. As Figure 3.1 shows, however, they account for only a small share of business revenues or income. Many small businesses are not designed to grow beyond the size of business that their owners can manage by themselves. Others may have such a small market or such inadequate financing or limited management talent that they simply are not destined to grow. Table 3.1 shows some advantages and disadvantages of sole proprietorships. Still others may just be in their infancy. As a business grows, it comes to demand additional capital and more diverse managerial skills. At that point, many sole proprietorships change form, becoming either partnerships or, more likely, corporations.

Advantages of a Sole Proprietorship

Ask sole proprietors what they like most about their businesses and they will say, "Independence!" Sole proprietors have only themselves to answer to. Their

FIGURE 3.1

Business Revenues and Income

Source: *Statistical Abstract of the United States,*
(Washington, D.C.: U.S. Govt., 1986) p. 517, Table 874

judgments, good or bad, are their own responsibility. They can add a new product, hire a new employee, or relocate. Taking a vacation is easy, at least theoretically. Sole proprietors also have the advantage of secrecy. With no partners, shareholders, or government agencies requiring periodic reports, sole proprietors have only themselves to blame if a competitor learns of their product strategy, for example.

The Advantages and Disadvantages of Sole Proprietorships

Starting a sole proprietorship requires nothing more than simply going to work. No legal formalities are required. The same is true of closing a business. Many small businesses close by just canceling their answering services and closing their doors. If sole proprietorships succeed, the reward is all the profits, after taxes, from their enterprise. Sole proprietors pay taxes on profits as if their profits were wages. And they pay taxes in the year in which the profits are earned. If the sole proprietor can itemize deductions, like interest on a home mortgage, this treatment can be beneficial.

TABLE 3.1

The Advantages and Disadvantages of Sole Proprietorships

Advantages	Disadvantages
□ Owner has complete control and independence	□ Difficulty of raising capital
	□ Too much responsibility on one person
□ Owner keeps all profits	□ Succession problems: lack of a substitute or replacement in emergency
□ Secrecy	
□ Low start-up costs	□ Burden of tax reporting

Sole proprietors — a special breed. *Joan Venturino, owner of Bears to Go in California's Bay area, doesn't have to be all things to all people. Because she started with only one store, she needed to appeal to just a small segment of the population. She is her own boss and has the freedom to try out her own ideas. When she planned a bear reunion, well over 200 customers came from as far away as Missouri with bears they had purchased at Venturino's shop.*

Disadvantages of Sole Proprietorships

The main disadvantages of sole proprietorships stem from the fact that they are one-person shows.

Poor Management Skills Many sole proprietorships founder because of poor financial management. Sole proprietors often lack enough knowledge of bookkeeping to keep track of where they are, much less to project where they are going. Because of this weakness, banks are often unwilling to loan to them. Financial institutions are also reluctant to make loans where the collateral is simply an individual's capacity to make money. The sole proprietor alone is liable for his or her business debts, unless the proprietor can obtain a **surety** or **guarantor**, a person who promises to repay a debt if the debtor does not pay it. Parents do often **cosign** or guarantee student loans or car loans. It is considerably harder to convince someone to cosign business loans, however, because the amounts involved are usually so much greater. As a result, sole proprietorships often starve for lack of capital.

Taxes are also a major drawback to sole proprietorships. The burden of reporting to the numerous taxing authorities falls on the sole proprietor. If he or she takes on an employee, the burden of paperwork more than doubles, with the addition of reports and payments to local, state, and federal authorities. The attention that tax matters require often drains entrepreneurs of the energies that they could have used to produce more profits — and tax revenues. Hiring a good accountant is a key step for the sole proprietor.

Succession Because they are one-person operations, a business held as a sole proprietorship can be hurt or destroyed by death, illness, retirement, or even a vacation. In a recent article in *Inc.* magazine, Billye Ericksen-Desaiguador explained to an interviewer why she had devised a succession strategy for her company. "I saw the previous owner . . . get to the point where, at age 65, he was desperate. He had done nothing to prepare for his retirement, he had no succession plan . . . , and all his assets were in one place." Ericksen-Desaiguador was describing Capsco Sales, Inc., a Sunnyvale, California, distributor of electronic components, but the comment applies to many sole proprietorships.[2] Businesses with this structure die with the person, with potentially drastic effects on any survivors, unless the owner has carefully planned how to maintain a flow of earnings from the business or how to sell it.

The necessity of providing for succession is often a good reason for taking on a **partner** or co-owner of the business. An equally good reason is that offering an ownership interest to a key employee may keep that person when outside opportunities with ownership possibilities might develop. Employees are usually well aware of the risks that working for sole proprietorships pose for them.

THE PEOPLE WHO WORK FOR BUSINESSES

If a business is to grow, one person alone cannot expect to do all the buying, selling, hiring, government reporting, and bill paying. When a sole proprietor hires an employee or takes on a partner, the business becomes an organization. Much depends on how the relationships between the members of the organization are defined. For example, who will do the buying? Who will have responsibility for keeping the books? In Part 2, we will look at how task relationships like these develop in an organization.

Our concern here is the legal relationship between a business organization and someone working for the organization, specifically, the powers that this relationship gives the person to act on the organization's behalf. It is worth pausing to look at these relationships and powers, because they are the key to the definitions of all the business forms discussed in the remainder of this chapter.

Employees and Agents

The law divides people who work for a business into two categories: employees and agents. **Employee** has two meanings. First, it is a general term to describe anyone who works for a business but does not own it. Second, it is a technical term referring to a person who works for a business but does not have authority to make contracts on behalf of the business. Examples of this type of employee include counter clerks, machine operators, teachers, and secretaries. In this section, the term *employees* is used in this second sense.

An **agent** is, in the broadest sense, someone who has authority to represent another. The person that the agent represents is called the **principal**. A sole proprietor would be a principal if he or she were to hire an agent. The parties must agree both to create the relationship and to maintain it. **Authority** is the power and direction that a principal gives an agent to act on his or her behalf.

When you read about a baseball player's agent negotiating a contract for him, the player has given the agent the authority to act on his behalf. If the manager of a local Wendy's hires someone, the manager is acting as an agent for the owner of that restaurant.

Types of Agents   Agents are either general agents or special agents.

The Types of Agents

A **general agent** is a person hired by a principal to conduct a series of transactions over time. Most agents who work full time for a principal are general agents. The Wendy's manager in the example just given would be a general agent authorized to do whatever was necessary to keep the restaurant operating profitably. His or her responsibilities would include hiring, firing, and ordering food and supplies. A person dealing with a general agent is justified in assuming that the agent has all the powers of agents in similar positions.

A **special agent** is an agent for one transaction or a limited series of them. A principal defines a special agent's authority much more narrowly than a general agent's. Those who deal with special agents must ask what the limits of their authority are. Real estate agents, lawyers, accountants, and architects are typically hired as special agents.

Fiduciary Duties   The ability to act on a business's behalf is not the only thing that distinguishes an agent from an employee. An agent has duties beyond those that an ordinary employee has. These unique responsibilities are called **fiduciary duties** or **duties of trust**. The courts take violations of fiduciary duties very seriously. Fiduciary duties apply only to a person who acts on another's behalf. The principal fiduciary duties are listed in Table 3.2. It is important to note that all agents, including the following types, have these duties:

The Differences Between Employees and Agents

□ A partner in a business
□ A lawyer or accountant acting for a client
□ An officer of a corporation

A principal does not owe fiduciary duties to an agent, because the principal does not act on the agent's behalf. A principal has only the two duties to an agent listed in Table 3.2.

TABLE 3.2

The Duties of Agents and Principals

Agent's Fiduciary Duties	Principal's Duties to Agent
□ Obey lawful instructions	□ Pay the agent, if their contract calls for compensation
□ Account for money and property	
□ Use proper care and skill in carrying out assignments	□ Reimburse the agent's expenses and indemnify the agent's losses
□ Communicate information to the principal	
□ Be loyal to the principal	

ESOP: Fable or Future?

Nearly 10 million American workers in 7000 companies participate in employee stock ownership plans (ESOPs), earning a share in the company's stock with every paycheck. Thanks in part to tax law changes, the number of such plans is growing by 10 percent a year, and at the current rate 25 percent of American workers will own part of their companies by the turn of the century. Some see ESOPs as the wave of the future, the best way to motivate workers and distribute evenly the benefits of capitalism. Others see them as a Utopian idea gone sour. Anyone entering the work force should be aware of the two faces of these plans, for ESOPs are getting more and more workers involved in corporate ownership.

The ESOP idea was conceived in the 1950s by Louis Kelso, a San Francisco lawyer who founded an investment banking firm that still carries his name. Kelso felt that for capitalism to work well, workers had to become capitalists themselves, owners of their company's stock. In 1958 he helped employees of a West Coast newspaper take over their company using a loan backed by an existing stock bonus.

ESOPs have become more complicated and varied, but most of them are still arranged by Kelso's company, and most still share a number of features. Technically, the ESOP is a type of pension plan, not a simple profit-sharing plan. Employees gradually receive shares of the company in individual ESOP accounts. When employees leave the company, they can sell their stock.

Many ESOPs were set up to enable workers to buy out a failing company and save their jobs. In this decade alone, such plans have saved at least 50,000 jobs by allowing employees to take over more than 100 failing plants and companies. Studies have shown that companies in which workers own stock tend to grow faster than companies owned by outside investors.

Partly because of some success stories and partly because of the populist appeal of the ESOP idea, Congress has given such plans more and more tax breaks.

Aware of the tremendous tax advantages of these plans, a growing number of companies are creating them not to help workers but to avoid takeovers or simply to save money. Even Kelso's own company now promotes ESOPs as a way for management to control company stock and avoid takeovers, not primarily as an arrangement to benefit workers. Many agreements give employees stock, but not power — only 15 percent of ESOPs currently give workers voting rights for determining company policies. Often, the workers' interests are voiced by only one person, a trustee usually appointed by management rather than by the workers. Some companies have issued two different kinds of stock, one for workers and one for management, giving the management's lower-priced stock much greater growth potential and voting rights. Other companies have substituted ESOPs for existing pension plans without giving workers any say in the matter.

Such abuses may eventually destroy the image of the ESOP as a boon for all involved. The Justice Department has brought actions against some of the most unfair arrangements, and workers are learning not to accept blindly a proposal to give them "ownership" in a company. Even the best plans are a gamble for workers — instead of having their retirement money invested in a variety of companies, workers participating in an ESOP put all their eggs in one basket. If the company fails, they're out of luck. And as disputes at some worker-owned companies are demonstrating, ESOPs seem to ignore a fundamental split between management and workers. When some worker-owned companies make a profit, workers call for pay bonuses, while managers, looking towards the future, want to buy more machinery. It appears that ESOPs may be the arrangement of the future, but the stories about them must have more consistent happy endings before many of the nation's workers will sign on.

Sources: Carey W. English, "When Employees Run Their Own Steel Mill," *U.S. News & World Report*, Vol. 96, No. 18, May 7, 1984, 77–78. William Baldwin, "The Myths of Employee Ownership," *Forbes*, Vol. 133, No. 9, April 23, 1984, 108–111. John Hoerr, "ESOPs: Revolution or Ripoff?" *Business Week*, No. 2890, April 15, 1985, 94. "Uphill in West Virginia," *Forbes*, Vol. 135, No. 6, March 25, 1985, 12.

Agency and the Forms of Businesses

Partnerships and corporations operate only through agents. Each partner has general agency authority on behalf of the partnership unless the partners' powers are expressly limited by an agreement. A partner therefore owes the fiduciary duties of an agent to the partnership and his or her partners. It should be noted that partnership can employ agents who are not partners.

Suppose that two partners, Barb and Bill, run a gun shop, B & B Guns. If Barb places an order for ten .22-caliber rifles with a wholesaler with whom they regularly deal, she is presumed to be acting on behalf of the partnership. However, a partnership is nothing but an association of individuals, except in some very limited circumstances. What Barb has really done is to contract for certain goods on behalf of herself and Bill. As long as the partnership exists or as long as the people doing business with the partnership have reason to believe that a partner has the power to act on behalf of the partnership, a partner can bind his or her partners.

Because a corporation is not a human being, it can act only through agents. By law, corporate officers — the president, vice presidents, secretary, and treasurer — are general agents. The corporation's board of directors can appoint additional agents, such as purchasing agents. All corporate agents owe fiduciary duties to their principal, the corporation.

PARTNERSHIPS

The Second Principal Form of
Business: Partnerships

Federal law defines a **partnership** as "an association of two or more persons to carry on as co-owners of a business for profit."[3]

An Association of Co-owners

The Characteristics of
Partnerships

Voluntary Nature A partnership is an **association,** a voluntary organization of people with a common interest. Partnerships are characterized by **mutual agency,** the authority of each partner to act on behalf of the other partners and the partnership as a whole. An agency relationship is always voluntary, so there is no such thing as an involuntary partner.

It is not necessary, however, for a person to agree formally to be a partner. Not even a handshake is necessary. When two or more people act like partners by transacting business together and sharing the profits, the law will treat them as partners. Suppose that Alice and Barbara are independent real estate brokers who decide to share an office. Over time, they help each other on sales, cover calls for each other, and divide commissions on sales. The law will treat them as partners even though they may have no formal written or oral **partnership agreement,** a contract between two persons stating the terms on which they agree to be partners. (See Figure 3.2.)

Partnership Shares A partner is a co-owner of a partnership. **Co-owner** means joint owner, not equal owner. A partnership must have two or more co-owners. These co-owners may be either individuals or other businesses. If Alice

FIGURE 3.2

A Sample Partnership Agreement

and Barbara are partners, they are by definition co-owners of the partnership. They may agree that Alice owns 40 percent of the business and Barbara 60 percent, for instance. However, if there is not clear evidence of such an agreement, like a division of profits according to this formula, a court will presume their shares to be equal. This presumption is one reason a written partnership agreement is so important. In almost all states the law does not require one, though.

Another important presumption flows from the co-ownership concept: partners share both profits and losses. Courts treat people who share profits and losses as partners unless they can prove otherwise. Again, the partners may alter the

Combining skills for larger ventures. As businesses become more complex, one owner may not have the time or the skills to oversee every area. George Purnell's father retired from the business 23 years ago. Today Purnell and his partner Richard Jarvis have built Purnell-Jarvis into a giant organization that can easily handle large projects like this Maryland condominium complex.

profit and loss percentages by mutual agreement. For example, Alice and Barbara may choose to divide their profits equally but absorb their losses on a 40:60 basis.

Partnership Contributions   The ownership percentages in a partnership often depend on a partner's **capital contribution**, a partner's investment — whether in cash or property — in the business. For instance, one partner may contribute ten thousand dollars, another contribute inventory and a store, and a third his or her twenty years of experience in the trade. The law will presume the three to be equal partners and their contributions to the partnership to be of equal value. However, their partnership agreement might assign them 25, 50, and 25 percent interests, respectively, and value their contributions at $10,000, $20,000, and $0. Placing a value on partnership contributions can thus be seen to be extremely important. When a partnership terminates, after all its debts are paid the partners' contributions are repaid before the remaining assets are divided among the partners.

Partners' Liability   A partner, like a sole proprietor, generally has unlimited liability, which is a major disadvantage of the partnership form. A partner is legally responsible — **liable** — for any and all debts of the partnership. A creditor can force a single partner to pay an obligation of the partnership even though there might be other partners.

To Carry on a Business for Profit

In the definition given above of partnership, the phrases "to carry on" and "a business for profit" have very particular yet broad meanings.

A **general partnership**, the usual form of partnership and the one we have been describing, is an ongoing business involved in a series of transactions. Suppose that Anne, Bill, and Cheryl begin buying and subdividing land and reselling it for home lots. After they have sold some lots, they reinvest part of their profits in more land. They would be operating a partnership. On the other hand, if they had bought a farm together and were holding it as an investment, they would not be partners. They would have formed instead a **joint venture**, an association of individuals for a limited, specific, for-profit business purpose. The participants in a joint venture do not normally have mutual agency authority.

A nonprofit partnership is a legal impossibility. If two nonprofit organizations like the American Red Cross and the American Cancer Society, say, jointly founded a clinic, their relationship could not be a partnership.

Operating a Partnership

The Advantages of Partnerships

One of the great advantages of partnerships is that the partners share management responsibilities. Two heads are indeed often better than one, especially since, like sole proprietors, many partners lack management experience.

Another advantage to partnerships is the opportunity they offer for partners to specialize. For example, one partner in a car dealership might take charge of sales and car purchasing while the other supervises repairs and parts. In large accounting and law partnerships, specialties tend to be quite narrowly defined. The general rule is that the larger the partnership, the higher the degree of specialization. Specialization by partners usually brings with it less responsibility for each to manage the firm. In the large accounting and law partnerships, the

TABLE 3.3

The Advantages and Disadvantages of Partnerships

Advantages	Disadvantages
☐ Ease of formation	☐ Reliance on oral agreements
☐ Flexibility in assigning shares and responsibility	☐ Legal presumptions of equal shares and responsibilities
☐ Shared responsibility for management	☐ Individual liability for all partnership debts
☐ Opportunity to specialize	☐ Lack of total control by an individual over management decisions
☐ Ability to plan for succession	☐ Formal termination procedure

partners routinely vote to **delegate** (assign authority and responsibility for) day-to-day management to a **managing partner,** someone who has managerial skills.

The major disadvantages of operating a partnership are ones that partnerships share with corporations, particularly the small or closely held companies. Simply put, the problems are primarily those of human relations. The partners may come to disagree on the direction the firm should take, or they may begin to take different career paths. One partner may feel that he or she is carrying more of the load than are other partners. The range of potential causes for disagreement is almost limitless.

FIGURE 3.3

Sample Certificate of Limited Partnership

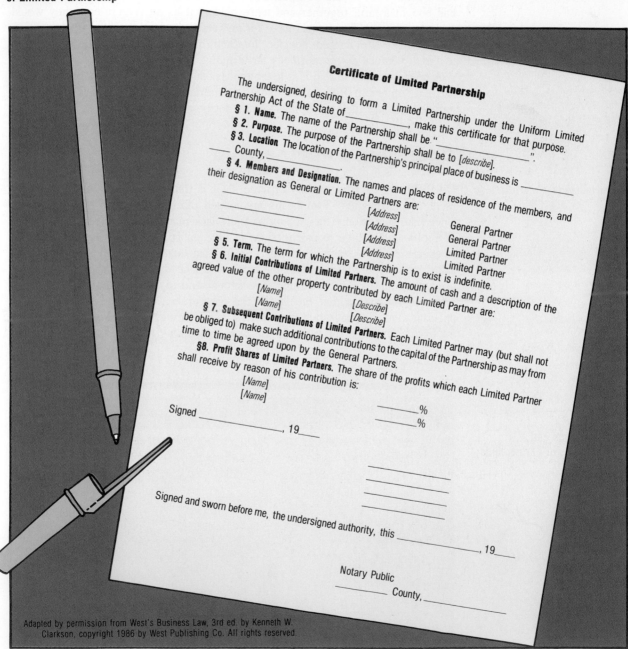

Certificate of Limited Partnership

The undersigned, desiring to form a Limited Partnership under the Uniform Limited Partnership Act of the State of _____, make this certificate for that purpose.

§ 1. Name. The name of the Partnership shall be "_____".

§ 2. Purpose. The purpose of the Partnership shall be to [*describe*].

§ 3. Location The location of the Partnership's principal place of business is _____ County, _____.

§ 4. Members and Designation. The names and places of residence of the members, and their designation as General or Limited Partners are:

_____	[*Address*]	General Partner
_____	[*Address*]	General Partner
_____	[*Address*]	Limited Partner
_____	[*Address*]	Limited Partner

§ 5. Term. The term for which the Partnership is to exist is indefinite.

§ 6. Initial Contributions of Limited Partners. The amount of cash and a description of the agreed value of the other property contributed by each Limited Partner are:

[*Name*]	
[*Name*]	[*Describe*]
	[*Describe*]

§ 7. Subsequent Contributions of Limited Partners. Each Limited Partner may (but shall not be obliged to) make such additional contributions to the capital of the Partnership as may from time to time be agreed upon by the General Partners.

§8. Profit Shares of Limited Partners. The share of the profits which each Limited Partner shall receive by reason of his contribution is:

[*Name*]	_____ %
[*Name*]	_____ %

Signed _____, 19___

_____
_____
_____
_____

Signed and sworn before me, the undersigned authority, this _____, 19___

Notary Public

_____ County, _____

Limited Partnerships

There is a form of business called the **limited partnership**, in which the general partners have essentially the same rights and liabilities as partners in a general partnership while the limited partners have virtually no management rights. In essence, **limited partners** are investors in a limited partnership whose liability is limited to the amount they invest. The number of limited partners in a particular partnership can range from one to thousands. The general partners, who often are corporations, manage the investments and normally receive both a fee and a percentage of the profits.

The main appeal of limited partnerships today is that the limited partners can use any losses the partnership generates to offset their own taxable income. The Internal Revenue Code actually encourages using this form of business for investments in real estate, capital equipment, and oil and gas production. The fact that limited partnership interests are extremely illiquid does not diminish their appeal in this respect.

Ending a Partnership

As compared with closing a sole proprietorship, ending a partnership is a complicated matter. It involves a three-stage operation: dissolution, winding up, and termination. At the point of closing a partnership, partners like the Kielhafner brothers, who were described at the beginning of this chapter, may regret the lack of a written partnership agreement.

TABLE 3.4

The Types of Partners

There are many terms used to describe a partner's relationship to the other partners in a general partnership. This table lists some of them. The key point to remember, however, is what makes a partner a partner: either mutual agency or sharing profits and losses — or both.

Silent Partner
A partner whose active involvement in the firm is not acknowledged publicly.

Dormant Partner
A partner who does not take an active role in the firm's management and whose participation is not known to the public.

Nominal Partner
A person who is not actually a partner but who with a partner's knowledge represents him- or herself as such. If a third party had reason to rely on such a representation, a nominal partner could obligate the partnership just like a real partner.

Junior Partner
A partner recently admitted to an existing partnership who usually makes a relatively small capital contribution, receives a minor share of the profits, and plays a small role in management.

Senior Partner
A partner of some tenure with a substantial investment in the firm, a significant share of the profits, and major responsibility for managerial decisions.

Business between family and friends. Like many partners, Cynthia and Lidia Perez are related. The sisters started Las Manitas, a small Mexican restaurant, with two long-time friends and ex-roommates, but Lidia and Cynthia bought out their partners, who were discouraged by the backbreaking work and long hours demanded by the business. It took over 2 years before the now popular restaurant turned a profit.

The Three Stages of Ending a Partnership

A **dissolution** is an act, like dying or saying "I quit," which indicates that a partner has ended the partnership relationship. The significance of a dissolution is that it forces the **winding up** — the liquidation of the partnership's assets, payment of its debts, repayment of the partners' capital contributions, and division of the remaining funds. A partnership agreement may establish a formula for dividing the firm's assets. If it does not, the law requires an equal division of them. During the winding up, the partnership must not engage in any new business. However, the partnership agreement may contain a provision allowing the remaining partners to buy out the departing one and continue the business without interruption.

The **termination** is simply recognition of the fact that the winding up is complete and the partnership has therefore ended. Until termination, the partners continue to owe fiduciary duties to one another and the partnership.

CORPORATIONS

The Third Principal Form of Business: Corporations

That form of business organization authorized by state law which comes into existence when the secretary of state of a state issues a certificate of incorporation is called a **corporation**. A **certificate of incorporation** or, as it is sometimes called, a **corporate charter,** is a document that a secretary of state issues certifying that a corporation has come into existence and is authorized to do business. For many purposes, a corporation is treated as an artificial person. It has the right to sue and be sued, to hold property, and, most importantly, its certificate of incorporation gives it a life of its own that does not depend on the lives of any of its owners.

The Key Characteristics of Corporations

Corporations have four fundamental characteristics that distinguish them from partnerships and sole proprietorships. These are:

1. A necessity of meeting certain formal requirements before a corporation can come into existence.
2. Unlimited life, independent of the lives of the corporation's owners and managers.
3. A separation of ownership and management.
4. A limitation on the financial liability of the firm's owners under certain circumstances.

The Four Fundamental Characteristics of Corporations

The First Fundamental Characteristic of Corporations

Requirements for Creation   A corporation cannot come into existence on a handshake the way a partnership can. In order to receive a certificate of incorporation, an **incorporator** must sign and file two copies of the proposed articles of incorporation with the secretary of state of that state. (Some states require two incorporators.) An incorporator can be anyone but is often the lawyer who represents those setting up the corporation. The incorporator's only functions are to sign and file the articles.

This section will discuss what the articles of incorporation should contain. Here, though, is a list of items that the law requires the articles to contain that we will *not* be discussing:

□ The corporation's name and address
□ The corporation's purposes, which may simply be described as "the transaction of any or all lawful business for which corporations may be incorporated"
□ The number, names, and addresses of the corporation's initial board of directors
□ The name and address of each incorporator
□ The number of shares of stock the corporation may issue as well as the classes of shares, if any, and their respective rights[4]

The secretary of state's office reviews the articles of incorporation to make sure that they are in the proper form. If they are and all filing fees have been paid, the secretary of state issues a certificate of incorporation.[5]

The Second Characteristic of Corporations

Unlimited Life   Unlike both a partnership and a sole proprietorship, a corporation has a life apart from the human beings who create it. It can remain alive as long as it pays the state an annual **franchise tax,** a fee for the privilege of doing business as a corporation. It is important to note, however, that just because a corporation can live forever does not mean that it will. Most corporations are small and, like partnerships, tend to die with their founders.

Citizens Energy: A Hybrid for the Future?

Every now and then someone comes along with a new kind of company, a hybrid that is hard to label but that grabs attention precisely because it's different. Joe Kennedy's Citizens Energy Corporation is one such company. Run like a lean, growing business, it gives its profits to the poor, mixing capitalism and socialism. It has done what many compassionate liberals dream of doing: it has supplied 200,000 low-income families with heating oil at one-third off market rates by skirting the big oil companies. Perhaps just as impressive to a fiscal conservative, the company has done its work without a cent of taxpayers' money.

As a business person, Kennedy provides a model for all who hear about him. He manages to be shrewd, smart, and big-hearted all at the same time. And though his company is set up primarily to benefit people in Massachusetts, where he grew up, it works because of unusual international business bonds, and it helps to build new bonds every year it's in operation.

Kennedy, the eldest son of Robert F. Kennedy and nephew of Ted, created the nation's first non-profit oil company in the late 1970s when he felt "the giant oil corporations are squeezing us." While watching a news report one night about huge oil company profits, a friend said to him, "I wonder what would happen if somebody gave all those billions back to the people?" Joe spent six months reading up on the idea and decided he could make it work.

The crucial step was finding the oil. The official OPEC price at the time was $31 a barrel, but OPEC members weren't supposed to deal with individual brokers. A small company like Kennedy's would normally have had to pay the spot market rate of $37 a barrel. However, Kennedy used his famous name and his skills as a negotiator and a "classic entrepreneur" to persuade Venezuela to sell him oil at the lower price. He also found a refiner who was willing to process the oil. From the many products made out of every barrel of oil, Kennedy would keep some of the heating oil and sell the rest. Using the profits from selling these products, Kennedy was able to sell his oil at bargain prices to the state of Massachusetts to distribute under its fuel assistance program. At first oil distributors grumbled about moving around oil from such an unorthodox source, but Kennedy persuaded them it would be good public relations.

Since then his company has delivered over 25 million gallons of heating oil, and Joe has constantly taken on new challenges. He has formed two subsidiaries: Citizen Conservation Corporation weatherizes the apartments of poor tenants, leading to savings of $300 per apartment, and Citizens Heat and Power modernizes the energy systems of schools, hospitals, and public buildings, saving hundreds of thousands in fuel costs.

As such work saves people money and helps break the dependence on foreign oil, it also creates thousands of jobs, one of the best ways to help the poor. True to his family's past, Joe believes passionately that government must help those who truly need it. But he also thinks that creative use of the free market system can do a lot for people without spending government money.

In his climb to prominence, Kennedy hasn't forgotten the good deal and the friendly international relations that allowed his company to get started. He has made one recent oil buy, from the Soviet Union, just to "open up a dialogue" between the two countries. And he has regularly taken 25 percent of his company's profits and invested them in projects like a solar water heating system in a Jamaican hospital, a demonstration project in biomass energy in Costa Rica, and a solar hot water heater and heat recovery system for a hospital in Venezuela.

Citizens Energy may not survive if Joe becomes a big political success, and it may be that it never could have worked in the first place without the magic of the Kennedy name. But it stands as a model of the good that can be done when people ignore the cynics, form international alliances, and develop companies that cut across the categories.

Sources: David Osborne, "Joe Kennedy Makes a Name for Himself," *Mother Jones*, Vol. 10, No. 3, April, 1985, 18. Fern Schumer Chapman, "Joe Kennedy, The Poor Man's Oil Tycoon," *Fortune*, July 23, 1984, 98. "More Hype Than Heat," *The New Republic*, December 30, 1985, 4.

Separation of Ownership from Management   A corporation's owners may work for it, but most do not, and certainly they are under no obligation to do so. The owners of a corporation are called **shareholders**, persons who own shares in a corporation. **Shares** are the units into which ownership of a corporation is divided. The articles of incorporation will specify whether there are to be five shares or 137 million (the number that Coca-Cola presently has)[6] or some other number. In theory, the ownership of a corporation is completely separate from the management of it. And in practice, in large corporations like General Electric, with its 462 million shares,[7] the two are indeed separate. However, in **closely held corporations**, firms with fifty or fewer shareholders, like the Pulitzer Publishing Company in St. Louis, with its 5,470.5 shares held by about 20 shareholders,[8] the owners or a faction of them manage the company.

The shares in most large corporations are **publicly traded**, meaning that they are bought and sold on stock exchanges. Shareholders can usually sell their ownership interests if and when they want to. This liquidity is one of the great advantages to owning the shares of publicly traded corporations. The shares of only ten thousand corporations are publicly traded, however. The interests that shareholders have in the remaining 3 million or so corporations are not nearly so liquid. In general, minority shareholders in corporations that are not publicly traded must be prepared to stick with the management that is in place whether they like it or not. Even so, unless the articles of incorporation or another agreement restrict the sale of shares, it is easier to transfer ownership in a corporation than in a partnership.

The corporation's separate existence means that it pays taxes as an entity in its own right. This separate taxation holds another enormous advantage for its shareholders. With a partnership, every dollar of net income is divided among the partners, and they must pay taxes on it. Even if the income is retained in the partnership for, say, new office equipment, the partners pay taxes on it in the year they earn it. This problem does not exist with corporations. Historically, corporations have paid taxes at a significantly lower rate than have their shareholders. More importantly, they can retain aftertax earnings and their shareholders do not pay taxes on them. Corporations are therefore superior to partnerships and sole proprietorships as a form for accumulating investment capital. It is worth noting, though, that when corporations do distribute their earnings to shareholders, those earnings are taxed again, as income to the shareholders.

Limited Shareholder Liability   The *Ltd.* at the end of the name of a corporation stands for "limited liability," which means to the British what *Inc.* means to us. It is not surprising that *Ltd.* came to mean "corporation." One of the corporation's key characteristics is the limitation of a shareholder's liability for a firm's obligations to the amount of his or her investment.

Limited liability is extremely important to the shareholders of a corporation faced with, say, responsibility for a large personal injury award. The shareholders in the Manville Corporation found themselves in that situation in recent litigation over asbestosis. Limited liability also protects shareholders when a company's debts have their source in contracts. However, the smaller the corporation, the less protection that limited liability offers on contractual debts. Because of the risk involved, financial institutions will often not make loans to small corporations unless one or more shareholders agree to cosign as individuals. By cosigning, the shareholders waive their limited liability in respect to that loan. Suppose that

Al, Barbara, Charlie, and Darlene are the four shareholders in the ABCD Corporation, which needs a $100,000 loan. The Last Resort National Bank agrees to make the loan — if the four shareholders cosign the note. If ABCD defaults, the bank may force any or all of the cosigning shareholders to pay the debt.

Types of Corporations

As Figure 3.4 shows, there are ten basic types of corporations.

Public, Quasi-Public, and Private   A **public corporation** is one set up by Congress or a state legislature for a specific public purpose. The Tennessee Valley Authority, the Student Loan Marketing Association, and many local school districts are examples of public corporations. A **quasi-public corporation** or **public utility** is one granted a monopoly by a government unit on providing certain kinds of services to the public. These companies usually provide electric, local telephone, water, or natural gas services in specifically defined areas. The vast majority of corporations are **private corporations,** however, meaning that private individuals or companies have organized them for some purpose other than for providing utility service.

Nonprofit and For Profit   A **nonprofit corporation** or **not-for-profit corporation** is an organization set up for charitable, educational, or fraternal purposes. The American Heart Association, most private colleges, and the Elks and Rotary clubs are nonprofit corporations. The focus throughout this book is on **for-profit corporations**. Their name describes them perfectly: they are created to make profits for their owners.

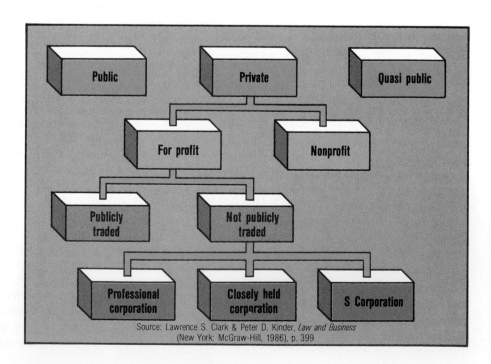

FIGURE 3.4

Types of Corporations

Source: Lawrence S. Clark & Peter D. Kinder, *Law and Business* (New York: McGraw-Hill, 1986), p. 399

Closely held corporations. John H. Johnson is president of Johnson Publishing Company, the Chicago publisher of Ebony *magazine and the largest black-owned business in the United States. His wife, Eunice, is secretary-treasurer of the corporation and director of Ebony* Fashion Fair. *His daughter, Linda Johnson Rice, is vice president and assistant to the publisher. The fact that Johnson Publishing is a closely held corporation has made it easier for Johnson to select and train his daughter as his successor.*

The Types of For-Profit Corporations

Publicly and Not Publicly Traded   For-profit corporations themselves fall into two general categories. The first, publicly traded corporations, was discussed earlier. (It should be noted that many quasi-public corporations are publicly traded, like Commonwealth Edison, which supplies electricity to the Chicago area.) The other category consists of the vast majority of corporations, those that are *not publicly traded*. This designation simply means that a corporation's stock is not traded on a stock exchange. The term does not necessarily reflect a company's size. For instance, Levi Strauss and Revlon, numbers 148 and 154 on the 1986 Fortune 500 list, are not publicly traded.[9]

Professional and Closely Held Corporations   Two types of corporations that are not publicly traded bear special mention. **Professional corporations,** the newest form of corporation, are firms whose shareholders offer such professional services as medical, legal, and engineering work. In some parts of the country professional corporations are rapidly replacing partnerships, because until recently the federal tax laws permitted corporations — but not partnerships — to set up highly advantageous pension and insurance plans.

We have already mentioned closely held corporations. Because of the small number of shareholders involved in them and because their shareholders tend to operate the corporation, some states' laws allow them to operate like a partnership. The principal advantage of this treatment is that it allows the corporation to dispense with having a **board of directors,** a group of individuals elected by the shareholders to oversee the operation of the corporation.

Subchapter S Corporations A corporation with thirty-five or fewer shareholders that elects under Subchapter S of the Internal Revenue Code to be treated for federal tax purposes essentially as a partnership is a **Subchapter S** or **S corporation**. This choice is the only thing that distinguishes a subchapter S corporation from other closely held corporations of the same size. By electing to have subchapter S status, the shareholders can use the corporation's losses to offset their income, something they could not do if the corporation was the taxpayer.

Classification of Corporations

A corporation is called a **domestic corporation** in the state in which it receives its articles of incorporation. It is a **foreign corporation** in any state other than the one in which it was incorporated. (States require foreign corporations to register with them if they wish to do business in them.) Finally, an American corporation that does business in a foreign country is called an **alien corporation**. For example, American Express is a domestic corporation of Delaware, a foreign corporation in California, and an alien corporation in Great Britain. Figure 3.5 illustrates these classifications.

Managing the Corporation

Logic suggests that since shareholders own the corporation, they should run it. That is not how a corporation works, though. Officers, elected by a board of directors, who in turn are elected by the shareholders, run the company.

FIGURE 3.5

Domestic, Foreign, and Alien Corporations

A corporation is called a domestic corporation in the state in which it received its articles of incorporation. It is a foreign corporation in any other state than the one in which it was incorporated. An American corporation which does business in a foreign country is called an alien corporation.

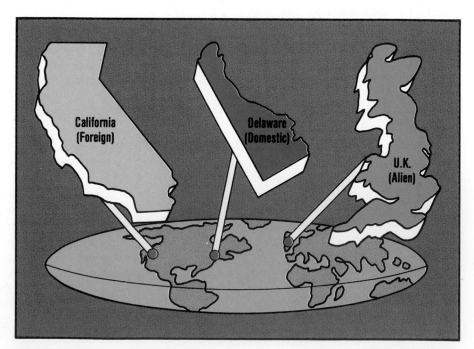

The Shareholders' Role Shareholders have only one function that relates to the management of their company: electing the board of directors. Apart from having a right to vote on certain extraordinary transactions, like selling the company or most of its assets, voting annually for directors is all they do. Shareholders are not corporate agents and therefore do not have fiduciary duties to the corporation.

BUSINESS TECHNOLOGY

The Heart of Health Care

America's system of health care is changing. More than 15 percent of America's hospitals operate for profit, and giant "supermed" integrated health care corporations are gobbling up traditional small, not-for-profit hospitals. Advertising has entered a business that once shunned it. Health maintenance organizations (HMOs) and walk-in clinics are becoming increasingly popular, and stocks of their parent organizations have found enthusiastic backers on Wall Street. In some cities, like San Francisco, one-third of the population now belongs to HMOs. Some experts estimate that if this trend continues, by the mid-1990s three-quarters of all Americans will be enrolled in "alternative delivery" health systems.

These changes are taking place partly in response to health care costs, which took off in the 1970s, partly as a way to insure doctors and hospitals a supply of patients. The oversupply of physicians in certain specialties in some parts of the country has made many doctors change their tune about health maintenance organizations. While a decade ago many doctors called HMOs "socialized medicine," now close to half of them are considering affiliating with an HMO. Insurance companies are buying hospitals, and hospital chains are setting up insurance plans, all looking for ways to provide an integrated health care plan, keep costs down, and make a profit in the $400 billion health care industry. Spearheading the changes is Humana, Inc., the people who sponsor the artificial heart implants.

Humana owns 87 hospitals and 200 walk-in health care centers, and they've enrolled 300,000 people in their prepaid health insurance, Humana Care Plus. To get people into their facilities and onto their insurance rolls, Humana needed advertising. So company chairman David A. Jones lured artificial heart pioneer William C. DeVries to Kentucky to work in Humana Hospital and promised to fund up to 100 artificial heart operations. The program is costly (about $200,000 per patient) but after DeVries performed Humana's first — and the world's second — artificial heart transplant in November 1984, the company had almost constant media exposure, as eager newspapers and television news programs told their audiences about the daily progress of Humana's latest artificial heart recipient. The technological marvel won the company more air time than it could possibly have afforded to buy.

The benefits of the artificial hearts for the company have been dramatic — enrollment in Humana's Care Plus more than doubled in the six months following Humana's first implant. Care Plus still trails giants like Maxicare Health Plans, which encourages joint ventures with physicians, and U.S. Health Care Systems, a Pennsylvania-based company that has become a Wall Street favorite as a result of predictions that it will grow at an annual rate of 35 to 40 percent for the next five years.

New twists to the business of America's health haven't yet made Americans any healthier. They do, however, change the way we relate to health care professionals, and the way those professionals interact with their insurers. If these changes work out ideally, most people may eventually feel that everyone involved with their health is working *together* to keep them healthy.

Sources: "The Hot and Healthy Glow of the HMOs," *Fortune*, Vol. 111, No. 8, April 15, 1985, 163. Kathleen Deveny, "Humana: Making the Most of Its Place in the Spotlight," *Business Week*, No. 2893, May 6, 1985, 68. Susan Dentzer, "Taking a Scalpel to Medicine," *Newsweek*, Vol. 105, No. 25, June 24, 1985, 56.

TABLE 3.5

Advantages and Disadvantages
of Corporations

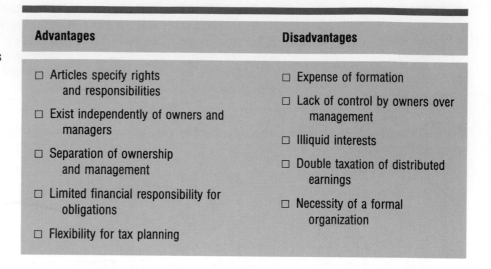

Advantages	Disadvantages
☐ Articles specify rights and responsibilities	☐ Expense of formation
☐ Exist independently of owners and managers	☐ Lack of control by owners over management
☐ Separation of ownership and management	☐ Illiquid interests
☐ Limited financial responsibility for obligations	☐ Double taxation of distributed earnings
☐ Flexibility for tax planning	☐ Necessity of a formal organization

The Board's Role The board of directors represents the interests of the shareholders. It sets general policy for the corporation and elects the company's top management. Although board members are not corporate agents, their duties to the corporation are fiduciary.

A board has to meet only once a year, but it is more likely to meet quarterly. The law requires that a board act by resolution after a formal vote. The secretary of the board records the votes in the meeting's **minutes** or records. These formalities emphasize the corporation's existence separate from its shareholders and board members. If the board fails to observe the formalities, it jeopardizes the shareholders' limited liability. The states that permit closely held corporations to do away with their boards have reasoned that such boards serve no purpose when the shareholders are essentially the management.

The relationship between the board and the management it elects is defined by the articles of incorporation and the corporation's **bylaws,** the rules adopted for the corporation's internal operations. In essence, the relationship is one of accountability.

Management's Role The board must elect **corporate officers**: a president, one or more vice presidents as specified in the bylaws, a secretary, and a treasurer.[10] A corporation must have officers, because they are its agents. A corporation is not a living person and could not transact business without agents. The board may appoint any other officers or agents that the bylaws permit. If the board wanted to appoint a board member to be a corporate agent for some purpose, it would have to adopt a resolution to that effect. No board member is automatically an agent of the corporation. Similarly, no shareholder is an agent of the corporation unless appointed by the board.

OTHER BUSINESS FORMS

A number of other business forms exist for relatively specialized purposes. These are listed on the following page.

"Now that you've all put in your two cents' worth, I should like to interject my fifty-one per cent controlling interest."

The Joint Venture

We have already mentioned one specialized business form, the joint venture. In essence, it is a partnership without mutual agency and without a continuing general business purpose. A joint venture has a single defined objective, though it may take years to achieve. The most common joint ventures are oil and gas development projects in which oil companies join to share the costs and risks of an exploratory well. But they are becoming increasingly common in areas marked by high entry costs. For example, Kodak and Cetus have joined forces to develop biotech diagnostic systems, while AT&T and Olivetti are working together to introduce AT&T's computers to Olivetti's European markets.*

Syndicates

A temporary association formed to carry out a specific, usually short-term investment is a **syndicate.** A syndicate resembles a joint venture, but rarely develops an administrative structure, as some joint ventures do. Syndicates are often formed to underwrite and distribute large issues of stocks and bonds, to purchase expensive real estate for resale, and to spread the risk of owning stallions and bulls.

Cooperatives

A corporation or association formed to perform services so its owners or members can make a profit — but without making any profit itself — is a **cooperative.** Some major examples of cooperatives are Ocean Spray, a cooperative formed by cranberry growers, and Land o' Lakes, a cooperative formed by Minnesota dairies to market their products. Cooperative members may be individuals or have any business form.

*"Corporate Odd Couples," *Business Week,* July 21, 1986, pp. 100–105.

The corporate giants. Most of the nation's largest businesses are publicly owned corporations whose shares are publicly traded on recognized stock exchanges.

BUSINESS FORMS: A PERSPECTIVE

Any time one tries to discuss a category that includes 17 million or so entities, one has to focus on common threads and characteristics and to avoid exceptions. And yet it is a safe bet that anyone who pays attention to the news has heard a lot more about conglomerates than about Subchapter S corporations, although there are a lot more of the latter than the former. A **conglomerate** is a corporation that owns several other corporations that are in different industries. A conglomerate makes **acquisitions,** purchases of other companies.

Many critics argue that conglomerates are dinosaurs that have grown so large that they will topple of their own weight. They reason that most conglomerates' acquisitions are made to build an empire rather than for sound business reasons. Certainly that appears to be happening with four of the conglomerate kings in the period from the 1960s through the 1980s: Dart & Kraft, Gulf + Western, Beatrice Foods, and ITT. All four have been selling individual companies — and sometimes whole divisions — that did not relate to a newly defined core of businesses.

Growth by acquisition today centers largely on **mergers**, the acquisition of companies in related businesses. As we will discuss in Chapter 22, mergers are either horizontal — the acquired company is a direct competitor — or vertical — the acquired company is in the same chain of supply. When Coca-Cola acquires one of its bottlers, the merger is vertical. If it had acquired Dr. Pepper, the merger would have been horizontal.

Whatever happens with the big acquisitions, opportunities abound in small businesses, as the next chapter reveals. It is fun to watch the dinosaurs battle themselves and the government, but for many it is more fun to make big money with ventures of their own.

Chapter Highlights

1. Identify and describe three basic forms of business ownership.

A *sole proprietorship* is a form of business in which one individual (the *sole proprietor*) owns all the assets of the business and is alone responsible for its debts. This form of business ownership makes up 70 percent of American businesses. A *partnership* is defined as an association of two or more persons who serve as co-owners of the business. A *corporation* is a form of business organization authorized by state law which comes into existence when a secretary of state issues a certificate of incorporation. To receive a certificate of incorporation, an *incorporator* must sign and file the proposed articles of incorporation with the secretary of state.

2. Outline the advantages and disadvantages of the three forms of business organization.

The major advantages of a sole proprietorship include ease of formation and dissolution, independence which gives the owner flexibility, and secrecy. Disadvantages include management limitations, unlimited financial liability, limited financial resources, and problems related to succession. Partnerships are also easy to form, provide expanded financial capability, and shared management responsibilities. Disadvantages of partnerships include the possibility of human conflict, unlimited financial liability, and complexity, of dissolution. The major advantages of corporations are limited financial capability, and the availability of specialized management expertise. The disadvantages include the difficulty of establishing the corporation, and legal restrictions.

3. Distinguish between general partnerships and limited partnerships.

A general partnership is an association of two or more persons who carry on as co-owners and all partners are liable for the debts of the business. A limited partnership is a form of business in which the general partners have essentially the same rights and liabilities as partners in a general partnership while the limited partners have few management rights and limited liability.

4. Describe how a corporation is organized and managed.

The first step in organizing a corporation is to obtain a certificate of incorporation from the secretary of state where the corporation will be incorporated. In most cases the legal papers are prepared and filed by an attorney who represents those setting up the corporation. Officers, elected by the board of directors who in turn are elected by the shareholders, manage the company.

5. List and describe three other forms of business organization that exist for specialized purposes.

A joint venture is essentially a partnership without mutual agency and without a continuing general business purpose. A joint venture has a single defined objective. A syndicate is a temporary association formed to carry out a specific, usually short-term investment. For example, a syndicate might be formed to purchase expensive real estate for resale. A cooperative is a corporation or an association formed to perform services so its owners or members can make a profit.

Key Terms

Acquisitions	Capital contribution	Corporate charter	Fiduciary duties or
Agency	Certificate of	Corporate officers	duties of trust
Agent	incorporation	Corporation	For-profit corporation
Alien corporation	Closely held	Cosign	Foreign corporation
Authority	corporation	Delegate	Franchise tax
Board of directors	Conglomerate	Dissolution	General agent
Bylaws	Cooperative	Domestic corporation	Incorporator

Joint venture
Limited partner
Limited partnership
Merger
Minutes
Mutual agency

Nonprofit corporation
or not-for-profit
corporation
Not publicly traded
Partnership agreement
Principal
Publicly traded

Quasi-public
corporation or
public utility
Shares
Shareholders
Sole proprietor
Sole proprietorship

Special agent
Subchapter S or
S corporation
Surety or guarantor
Syndicate
Termination

Review Questions

1. What is a sole proprietorship? Why is it the most commonly used form of business ownership?
2. What are the major advantages and disadvantages of sole proprietorships?
3. Define a partnership. What are the advantages and disadvantages of this form of business ownership?
4. The law divides people who work for a business into two categories: employees and agents. What is the difference between these two types of employees?
5. What is the difference between a general partnership and a limited partnership? Why are limited partnerships established?

6. What are the four characteristics that distinguish the corporation from other types of businesses?
7. Describe the day-to-day management of a typical corporation. What roles are assumed by shareholders, the board, and management?
8. What is a joint venture? Why are joint ventures formed?
9. What is a cooperative? What are its advantages? Can you identify a cooperative in your immediate area?
10. Describe a conglomerate. List at least three conglomerates that currently operate in the United States.

Application Exercises

1. You are currently interested in establishing the following types of businesses. What forms of business ownership would you consider?
   a. A frame shop that will offer professional picture framing.
   b. A real estate firm that will maintain residential and commercial divisions. In addition, a property management division will be established.
   c. A furniture manufacturing plant that will specialize in casual wood furniture.

2. For the past five years you have been the advertising director for a small chain of appliance stores. You plan and coordinate the advertising for all of the company's retail stores. Recently a friend who operates a successful graphic design agency contacted you and discussed the possibility of forming an advertising agency. He suggested the creation of a general partnership. Would this be the best form of business ownership? What are the major advantages of forming a general partnership? Disadvantages?

Cases

3.1 The T. Boone Pickens United Shareholders Association

Under the leadership of T. Boone Pickens, Jr., Mesa Petroleum Co. has invested heavily in oil companies, as well as in oil and gas reserves and producting oil fields. During the last three months of 1984, Mesa acquired almost 8 million shares of Phillips Petroleum Co. common stock in an attempt to gain control of that firm. The attempt at a "hostile takeover" caught that firm off guard. The Phillips board seemed to have no alternative but to bargain with Pickens for control of its company. An agreement was reached whereby Mesa would receive $53 per share for its Phillips stock, which it had acquired at an average price of about $43 per share. In addition, Phillips was to pay Mesa up to $25 million for expenses Mesa incurred in the takeover attempt.

In Mesa's 1984 annual report, Pickens explained to Mesa shareholders that takeovers were beneficial and that they were generally initiated by target-firm shareholders who were dissastisfied with management.

Pickens seems to be disturbed by a number of measures that directors have taken to protect their firms from takeover. Those measures have tended to weaken shareholders' voting rights and their control of the firms. Perhaps the most controversial is the issuing of several classes of common stock, with different voting rights. That tactic could be used to give increased voting power to majority shareholders or those who are part of the firm's management, so as to counteract votes in favor of a takeover.

Pickens plans to start a nationwide lobby to fight for shareholders' rights. His goals are secret stockholder voting in place of the present system in which corporate management mails, collects, checks, and counts the ballots.

Questions

1. How can shareholders control the actual operation of a corporation? What determines the amount of influence than an individual shareholder has?
2. How did Mesa's attempted takeovers affect shareholders of the target firms? How would successful takeovers likely have affected the managers of those firms?

For more information see *Business Week*, July 1986, pp. 64–65; *The New York Times*, July 4, 1986, pp. D1, D3; and *Moody's Industrial Manual*, 1985, vol. 2, pp. 3277–3285.

3.2 Agents and Athletes

Bob Woolf prefers to be called a sports attorney, but he and his colleagues are agents in the legal sense. Many are individuals, but there are also good-sized agent firms. Besides negotiating contracts, most manage the income earned by their clients. They usually collect paychecks, provide an allowance to the player, pay his or her bills, and invest the remainder. They handle the usually lucrative commercials and endorsements that star athletes tend to attract. Some handle personal matters as well. For their services, agents collect fees of 3 to 6 percent of the contract amount, around 5 percent of the funds they manage, and up to 20 percent of product endorsement income.

Many fine young amateur athletes must seek an agent if they hope to become professional athletes. The choice of *the* agent is a difficult decision that can affect the athlete's financial and professional future.

Johnny Dawkins, all-American basketball player from Duke University, played his last college game in the NCAA finals in March 1986. He would be a first-round choice in the coming NBA professional basketball draft. Duke University officials received and screened twenty-five requests to discuss agencies with Dawkins and three graduating teammates. Dawkins narrowed the field down to two — ProServ Inc. and Advantage International, both based in Washington, D.C.

Representatives of both firms flew to the Duke campus. Each gave a one-hour presentation, stressing its services, to Dawkins, his coach, and Duke officials. Then Dawkins and his coach spent a day in Washington, conferring with Advantage executives in the morning and ProServ's top official in the afternoon. They discussed details of fees and income potential and the quantity of representation each agent could provide. Dawkins eventually chose ProServ, primarily because Advantage had already signed two star players.

Dawkins was drafted and signed by the NBA's San Antonio Spurs. He was the team's first-round choice, and the tenth player to be chosen.

Questions

1. What type of agent is ProServ, relative to its client Johnny Dawkins? How are ProServ's specific duties determined?
2. Which of ProServ's fiduciary duties to Dawkins is (or are) the most important? Why?

For more information see *Business Week*, June 23, 1986, pp. 82, 87; *The Wall Street Journal*, April 2, 1986, p. 19; and *The Saturday Evening Post*, December 1985, pp. 18–22.

4

ENTREPRE-NEURSHIP, SMALL BUSINESSES, AND FRANCHISES

Learning Objectives

After you have completed this chapter, you will be able to do the following:

■ Describe the characteristics of an entrepreneur.

■ State the various definitions of *small business* and explain why there is more than one definition.

■ Discuss why certain fields attract small businesses.

■ Analyze why small businesses succeed and fail.

■ Describe the services of the Small Business Administration.

■ List the advantages and disadvantages of franchising.

■ Describe the protections offered by law to franchisees.

The Walden Book Company and B. Dalton Bookseller chains have taken the bookstore business by storm in recent years, but Michele Poire, owner of Odegard Books Saint Paul, is not running scared. In fact, she provides strong competition to these larger companies. This St. Paul entrepreneur has achieved success in the retail book business by offering personally tailored services that the big chains find difficult to match.

As an independent business person, she also has the freedom to act quickly when an opportunity exists. When she noted that the children's book section represented one of the fastest growing areas of her store, she decided to open the Red Balloon Bookshop which sells only children's books. Twice each week, there is a story hour for young children. When it ends, you can observe hordes of children leaving the store with complimentary red balloons in their hands.*

ENTREPRENEURS AND ENTREPRENEURSHIP

Michele Poire is an **entrepreneur,** a person who organizes, operates, and assumes the risk of a business venture in the hope of making a profit. In the past, the word *entrepreneur* described only those who created their own businesses. Today, the word applies to anyone who runs a business and who builds and innovates.[1] As Professor Nathaniel H. Leff describes it, "**Entrepreneurship** is the capacity for innovations, investment, and expansion in new markets, products, and techniques."[2] Normally, entrepreneurs are thought of in terms of being in small businesses, which will be our context here.

Millions of people decide each year to set out on their own. Some want independence, some look for large profits, and others hope to have some effect on society's ills. The same skills that enable one person to create a thriving business allow someone else to erect a community center, develop a civic orchestra, or establish a museum. Successful entrepreneurs possess the vision to identify needs and to develop ways to satisfy them. William L. Gore, the inventor of Gore-Tex fabrics and one of America's most innovative businesspeople, has expressed the entrepreneurial drive in his own way: "The creative, emotional urge that leads to the risk-taking and tremendous energies of entrepreneurs is a real factor in their accomplishments. Creative urges are widely present in humans and need only freedom and opportunity to be released."[3]

The Characteristics of an Entrepreneur

Entrepreneurs are a varied lot. It is extremely difficult to pigeonhole them or their goals for their businesses. Some want to become giants in their fields, whereas others want just a small, secure niche. Maryles Casto, for instance, parlayed a $3,000 investment in a tiny travel agency into a $30-million business — Casto Travel, headquartered in Santa Clara, California — which she is aggressively expanding.[4] Vince Hansen started his fresh juice business — Hansen Juices, Inc., in Los Angeles — on a shoestring, too. Hansen was a product of the Depression, however, and he did not want to grow at the price of going into debt. He has deliberately kept his business small and expanded only when he had the money in hand.[5] Table 4.1 compares the characteristics of the entrepreneur with those of the successful manager who works for someone else.

*Susan Bucksbaum, "A Nation of Shopkeepers," *Inc.*, November 1985, p. 69.

Dimension	Entrepreneur	Career Manager
Time Orientation	Medium to long (5–10 years).	Short to medium (monthly, quarterly, annual budgets and quotas; the next promotion).
Risk Taking	Moderate, calculated risks; will risk job security and net worth.	Lower risk taker; averse to making mistakes because of large company reward and penalty system; won't take the final plunge.
Tolerance of Uncertainty	High tolerance of ambiguity and uncertainty.	Lower tolerance of uncertainty.
Personal Standards	High — more oriented to internalized, self-imposed standards.	High — but more oriented to externalized standards of the organization; more responsive to organization's reward system and trappings, such as status, job titles.
Management Skills	No, or limited, formal management education; may have technical or scientific training if in a technical venture; knows a business well; may be former general manager with profit and loss responsibility.	More likely to have formal management education; broad knowledge and experience in managing people and resources.
Motivations	Highly goal oriented and achievement motivated, self-reliant and self-motivated.	More motivated by goals and rewards established by the organization; power motivated.

Source: Jeffrey A. Timmons, Leonard F. Smollen, and Alexander L. M. Dingee, Jr., *New Venture Creation — A Guide to Small Business Development.* Homewood, IL: Richard D. Irwin, 1977.

TABLE 4.1

The Entrepreneur and the Manager

Whatever their ultimate goals for their businesses, most entrepreneurs start small. McDonald's, after all, started with just one store and one set of golden arches. Today, McDonald's has over 8,900 restaurants, a figure more than twice the total number of fast-food restaurants in existence thirty-five years ago.[6] The McDonald's Corporation is now one of America's largest companies. Yet many of the people who own and run McDonald's restaurants are entrepreneurs. In the last section of this chapter we will examine the franchising system, which often makes for happy marriages between giant corporations and aggressive entrepreneurs. First, though, we must look at the nature of small businesses and how they operate.

THE NATURE OF SMALL BUSINESS

Small is a relative term. It implies the question, in comparison to what? Idaho Power, with a market value of $636 million, is small when compared to IBM, with its market value of $75.4 billion,[7] but Idaho Power is hardly small when compared with a neighborhood hair salon or a mom-and-pop grocery.

Focusing on a precisely defined market niche. Hood Sailmakers, Inc., of Marblehead, Massachusetts, makes custom racing and cruising sails. By concentrating on a small group of customers, the company can assure high quality and maintain its standards. Employing about 50 people and making good use of modern technology, the firm has sales of about $12 million a year — meeting the definition of a small business.

A Working Definition of Small Business

Let's define **small business** as any business that is independently owned and operated, is not dominant in its field, and does not employ more than five hundred persons. There is, in fact, no generally accepted definition of a small business. We can see why by looking at the elements of this definition.

Some commentators argue that franchised operations, like the National Video Stores outlets, are not true small businesses.[8] The franchiser, in this case National Video Stores, sets management standards that the store owner must observe. By this reasoning, the store owner — the franchisee — is not truly independent. We will see in the last section of this chapter why many franchisees argue that this assistance only reduces, but does not eliminate, the risk of entrepreneurship.

Depending on how *field* is defined, a small business fitting our definition could dominate its field. For example, a firm developing and marketing highly specialized software might dominate its particular **market niche,** the area in which it specializes or holds a special position. It could not dominate the software industry as a whole, however. The word *field* in the small-business definition should be understood in a broad sense.

For many people, describing as "small" a business that employs up to 499 employees flies in the face of common sense. Just to pay 500 employees only $100 per week for a year would mean that the company would have to earn $2.6 million just to meet the payroll. There is a good reason behind this element of our definition, though. The *Small Business Administration (SBA),* an agency of

Defining *Small Business*

the federal government that offers both managerial and financial assistance to small businesses, has adopted a basic definition of small business that parallels ours. Table 4.2 reveals that the SBA also uses additional standards to determine which businesses can receive its help. The SBA's services are described later in this chapter.

Other Definitions of Small Business

Other groups have defined *small business* somewhat differently. A White House conference on small business defined it essentially in terms of the number of employees. Four hundred employees or fewer designated a small business.

The Committee for Economic Development suggested that any business having more than two of the following criteria should be considered a small business:

☐ An independent management that often owned the business.
☐ A small number of individuals who were responsible for the capital contributions.
☐ A local orientation to the firm's business.
☐ A small market share when compared to its industry as a whole.[9]

Studies have shown that the public in general uses a very restrictive definition of *small business*. The average person uses the term to refer to an owner-managed business that employs only a handful of people, not more than, say, twenty or twenty-five.

TABLE 4.2

SBA Standards of Smallness for Selected Industries

Manufacturers	**Employing Fewer Than**
Petroleum refining	1,500 persons
Electronic computers	1,000
Macaroni and spaghetti	500
Wholesalers	**Employing Fewer Than**
Sporting goods	500 persons
Furniture	500
Paints and varnishes	500
Retailers	**Earning Sales of Less Than**
Grocery stores	$13.5 million a year
Automobile agencies	11.5
Restaurants	10.0
Services	**Earning Sales of Less Than**
Computer-related services	$12.5 million a year
Accounting services	4.0
Television repair	3.5

Source: "U.S. Small Business Administration: Small Business Size Standards," *Federal Register*, Vol. 49, No. 28 (Washington, D.C.: U.S. Government Printing Office, February 9, 1984), pp. 5024–5048.

The Economic Importance of Small Businesses

However *small business* is defined, one fact is not disputable: small businesses are critical to the soundness of our economy. In terms of numbers, small businesses dominate the U.S. economy. As Figure 4.1 indicates, businesses employing twenty or fewer persons account for nearly 95 percent of all businesses. And 99.9 percent of all businesses meet the five-hundred-employee criterion of our small-business definition.

Successful firms are built on innovation, which takes many forms. A common type of innovation involves applying an old idea to a new situation. For example, Lane Nemeth started her company, Discovery Toys, because she could not find an educational toy suitable to give a friend's one-year-old child as a present. Her idea was to sell quality toys through home demonstrations, just as Amway, Avon, and Tupperware sell their goods. In 1977, she started with a borrowed $25,000. Today, she has a sales force of twelve thousand and gross sales of more than $40 million.[10]

With the entrepreneur's energy, creativity, and innovative abilities come jobs for other people. One study found that firms with fewer than twenty employees created about 66 percent of the new jobs in this country between 1969 and 1976. In New England, the figure was 99 percent.[11] This high a percentage is not surprising in light of the booming high-tech industries in that region. Figure 4.1 compares the contributions of various sizes of businesses to the 2 million jobs created in 1985. Not surprisingly, companies with fewer than one hundred employees led the way.

Fields that Attract Small Business

Certain fields, such as retailing, services, and high technology, are more attractive to entrepreneurs than others. These fields tend to be easier to enter and require low initial financing. Also, it is easier to pick a market niche in these fields. (Chapter 11 discusses in more detail how to pick a niche.) New firms thus suffer less from heavy competition, at least in the early stages, than do more-established firms.

Retailing   One who acquires goods from manufacturers, producers, or wholesalers, then sells them to consumers is a **retailer.** Retailing has always attracted entrepreneurs. Any main street or shopping strip is lined with independent record stores, sporting goods shops, dress boutiques, drugstores, groceries, and hardware stores. Retailing particularly attracts entrepreneurs because it is so easy to gain experience and exposure in this field. Retailers always need sales help, and all but the smallest need many other types of employees, such as buyers or window dressers.

It is also relatively easy financially to open a store. The retailing entrepreneur does not have to make the heavy investment in equipment and distribution systems that a manufacturing business would require. All that the new retailer needs is a lease on store space, a minimal amount of merchandise, and enough capital to sustain the business through the always difficult start-up period. For example, in 1977 Julee Rosso and Sheila Lukins opened The Silver Palate, a 165-

FIGURE 4.1

U.S. Small Businesses by
Number of Employees

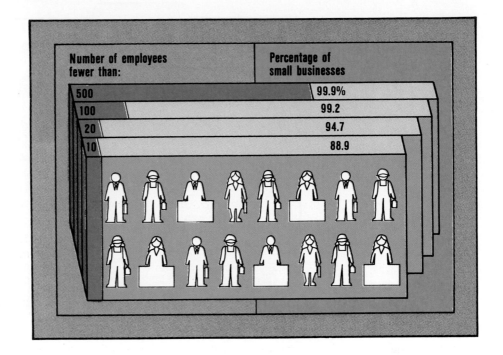

Number of employees fewer than:	Percentage of small businesses
500	99.9%
100	99.2
20	94.7
10	88.9

square-foot gourmet food shop featuring freshly cooked foods. This store serving New York's upper West Side attracted a large clientele of hard-working people who wanted to eat well at home but lacked time to cook. The partners were soon able to branch out into such high-profit ventures as catering and writing cookbooks.[12]

Why the Service and High-Tech Areas Attract Small Businesses

Services   The term **service** describes work that is done for others that does not involve the production of goods. Think about all the examples of service firms to be found on a main street, shopping strip, or in an office district: real estate and insurance and personnel agencies, barber shops, banks, computer repair shops, accounting firms, and many others.

Service industries attract entrepreneurs for much the same reasons as does retailing. And services also attract individuals whose skills are not ones normally needed by larger businesses, like beauticians, morticians, and jewelers.

High Technology   With its emphasis on emerging scientific advances, high technology seems an unlikely area to attract entrepreneurs. **High technology** is a broad term for the new and innovative types of businesses that depend heavily on advanced scientific and engineering knowledge. Yet it is precisely the people who have been able to identify innovations or new niches in the field of computers, biotechnology, genetic engineering, robotics, and a dozen other markets who have become today's high-tech giants. Many of them started out working in garages, basements, or kitchens.

Bill Gates of Microsoft began writing computer software in his teens. By the time he was thirty, he had become one of America's one hundred richest persons.[13] And although it requires more capital to develop hardware than software, there are many success stories relating to hardware. Apple Computers, for instance, began in a garage.

FIGURE 4.2

Who Creates the Jobs

Though there are exceptions — like IBM — to the rule, one would expect young, energetic companies to create more jobs than more mature companies.

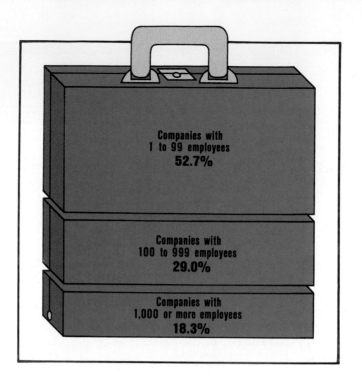

Companies with
1 to 99 employees
52.7%

Companies with
100 to 999 employees
29.0%

Companies with
1,000 or more employees
18.3%

OWNING A SMALL BUSINESS

An entrepreneur does not need an engineering degree to use new technology. Applying high-tech solutions in a stodgy business can lead to great success. Former Wall Street money manager Robert Waggoner bought Burrelle's Information Services, Inc., a one-hundred-year-old clipping service whose employees were still relying on razor blades and newspapers. Today, Burrelle's depends on computers and databases and is a high growth company. Waggoner is probably not typical of people who own small businesses — but only because there is no typical entrepreneur. However, Waggoner does share one particular characteristic with many small businesspeople: he bought into Burrelle's because he wanted to call his own shots. Independence is one of the great rewards of entrepreneurship.

The Rewards of Small Business Ownership

The desire to be one's own boss certainly is a major reason for going into business for one's self. During the last five years, entrepreneurs have created new corporations at a rate exceeding 575,000 per year.[14] That number does not, of course, include any of the other business forms discussed in Chapter 3.

Many people strike out on their own because they believe that they can do better for themselves than they could by remaining with their current employers. They often feel stuck on the corporate ladder, which is what happened to Janice Jones. She left a Wall Street house to found her own firm, Chartwell & Company, a $2-million venture that specializes in investing and financial consulting.[15]

People Who Start Small

How do you become an entrepreneur? "I bought a watering can," says Jean-Pierre La Tourette of Durham, New Hampshire. Pierre, as all his customers call him, graduated from the University of New Hampshire with a degree in Plant Science but without any immediate prospects for employment. He wanted to work with plants, but he didn't want to get an advanced degree and teach. Like all entrepreneurs, he started with an idea, a need. Local businesses, restaurants, and hotels were investing in more plants every month, and Pierre figured they could use someone to provide and care for those plants.

He was right. His plant care business, Flora Ventures, started with a single watering can. Gradually it took over his student apartment, then moved to a tiny shop. Now he has fifteen employees, a fleet of three sharply painted vans, and a large shop/storehouse with thousands of plants. If the business keeps expanding at the current rate, he may be a millionaire in another decade. But more important is the personal satisfaction Pierre gets out of "doing something better than anyone else."

According to people who study such things, most American entrepreneurs are motivated by the same forces that drive Pierre — they want to prove themselves right, they want to do one thing very well, and they want to work for themselves. Money, as one very successful California entrepreneur says, "is a great scorecard," but "not a main motivator." Like artists, most entrepreneurs can *envision*, see things that aren't there but that might be. Once they see something that really interests them, they tend to stick to that idea single-mindedly.

Such a person is Samuel Salter II, the U.S. Small Business Administration's 1984 Young Entrepreneur of the Year, who runs a corporation that handles more than $1 million a month in loans to small businesses. "I wanted to be J.R.," Salter said.

But many people who become successful entrepreneurs don't fit this mold. Some spend years apparently happy in other jobs before they discover how much they enjoy going out on their own. Some get Masters degrees in Business Administration. Others get Cs in Introduction to Business, or never go to college at all. Responding to this trend in the growth of small private companies, over 250 business and engineering schools now offer courses in starting a business, and a number of conference centers and companies offer training designed specifically for people who are trying to discover and develop an entrepreneurial spirit.

Many discover the spirit early. Samuel Kates of Massachusetts founded a business, Kandy Man, with his mother when he was a senior in high school. They make chocolate greeting cards and other edible items. In three years, their sales have risen from $2,500 to $17,500.

Others are interested in pursuing a cause as they succeed. Andora Freeman and Joy Ernst, for instance, run Toy Go Round, a toy-recycling center which they started to show children the benefits of conservation. They sell used toys inexpensively and give the former owners half of the money. They won't accept war toys like guns and G.I. Joe dolls. Although the two owners could make much more by compromising their beliefs, they pay themselves about $5000 a year and feel good about the effects they're having on children. Other entrepreneurs who make social conscience part of their business manage or invest in mutual funds that only support "socially responsible" firms. And some do very well. Tom Chappell is an environmentalist who tries to put nothing artificial or harmfull in his soap, shampoo, and toothpaste, and still sells $5 million of the products each year.

The 1980s seem to be the years of the entrepreneur. *Inc.* magazine was founded in 1979 to chronicle the world of entrepreneurs, and its pages are full of success stories. The computer revolution has lowered the age of entrepreneurship — some just into their teens have become big successes creating computer software. Many, of course, fail, and some fail time after time. But most return again to the challenge of finding an idea that works.

Sources: Sharon Nelton, "The People Who Take the Plunge," *Nation's Business*, Vol. 72, No. 6, June 1984, 22–26. Gordon M. Bock, "Capitalists Prosper on College Campuses," *U.S. News & World Report*, Vol. 96, No. 21, May 28, 1984, 77–78. Kim Foltz, "Doing Well by Doing Good," *Newsweek*, Vol. 103, No. 24, June 11, 1984, 62–63.

Tenant farming is a bigger operation than it once was. *Dick Oughton owns over 1,000 acres of prairie farmland in Illinois, and Forrest Woods, Jr., farms it. Oughton provides the land and buildings and pays the taxes, which were over $14,000 for 1985. Woods furnishes labor, fuel, and farm machinery. The machines alone are worth around $300,000. Owner and tenant split the $25,000 cost for seed, fertilizer, and chemicals and then split the crop. The farm, which grossed close to $400,000 in 1985, is a small business by all definitions.*

Entrepreneurs are sometimes persons who simply cannot work for someone else. More often, they just want the freedom to choose who they work with, the flexibility to pick where and when to work, and the option of working in a family setting. The development of the "electronic cottage," filled with computer, copying, telephone, and video equipment, has permitted many people to work at home. Only a few years ago, most of them would have needed the support that an office provides.

Historically, immigrants to the United States found that starting their own businesses was the best way to enter the American mainstream. This pattern

TABLE 4.3

The Rewards and Risks of Small-Business Ownership

Rewards	Risks
1. To gain control over your own destiny.	1. Uncertainty of income.
2. To reach your full potential.	2. Losing your entire invested capital.
3. To reap unlimited profits.	3. Quality of life until the business gets established.
4. To make a contribution to society.	4. Complete responsibility.

continues today among Hispanics, blacks, Asians, and women. For instance, according to the U.S. Census Bureau, the number of woman-owned businesses rose 329 percent, from 700,000 to 3 million, between 1979 and 1984.[16]

The Risks of Small-Business Ownership

Running a small business certainly is alluring, which is why so many people dream of it. Sad to say, though, of every ten small businesses formed, eight go out of business within the first ten years after they open their doors.[17] The financial risks of running a small business are very high, although, as Table 4.4 reveals, some businesses are considerably less risky than others.

TABLE 4.4

Relatively Low-Risk Small-Business Fields

Lowest failure rate	
Industry	**Failures per 100,000 in 1983**
Funeral services and crematoriums	10.9
Wholesale tobacco and tobacco products	22.6
Fuel and ice dealers	36.2
Laundry, cleaning and garment repair	38.0
Drugstores	39.7
Hotels	40.4
Wood products	44.7
Personal services (secretarial, consulting, etc.)	45.2
Beer and wine wholesalers	45.7
Service stations	46.2

Fields that grew the fastest	
Industry	**Increase in employment from October 1983 to October 1984**
Radio, TV and miscellaneous stores	20.8%
Computer and data-processing services	18.8
Inner-city highway transportation	18.8
Roofing and sheet-metal work	18.8
Masonry, stonework and plastering	16.3
Painting, paperhanging and decorating	14.7
Carpentry and flooring	14.5
Transportation services	14.0
Highway and street construction	13.9
Miscellaneous retail stores	13.8

Source: R. Greene, "Do You Really Want to Be Your Own Boss?" Reprinted by permission of *Forbes* magazine, October 21, 1985, p. 86. Forbes, Inc. 1985.

Even if the business keeps going, the odds are not in the entrepreneur's favor that he or she will have the next Ben & Jerry's Ice Cream Company, New England's leading premium ice-cream vendor. It is more likely that the business will produce a living for its owner, but not much more. And there are always worries about new equipment, expanding inventory, rent increases, or competition. Ben & Jerry's, for instance, found itself shut out of supermarkets as a result of competition from Häagen-Dazs, the original premium ice cream maker whose owners sold it to Pillsbury. It took a lawsuit to open the supermarket doors again.[18]

In addition to facing financial and psychological stresses, entrepreneurs tend to be victims of physical stress. The small businessperson often must be the owner, manager, sales force, shipping and receiving clerk, bookkeeper, and custodian. Sixteen-hour days quickly become standard, and vacations are rarely possible.

A key element in the definition of an entrepreneur is that he or she takes risks. If the potential rewards — whether financial or psychological — were not enormous, no one would go into a small business. A million or so people each year balance the risks and rewards of entrepreneurship and decide to become entrepreneurs. Our society rewards innovation and risk taking, if the entrepreneur can persist. Many creative persons succeed or fail not in their business concepts but rather in managing their businesses once they start.

The Keys to Success

Despite their failure rate, small businesses have some advantages over their larger competitors.

Flexibility   Small size can give a business's owners the flexibility to adapt to changing market demands. Small businesses usually have only one layer of management, the owners. Decisions therefore can — and should — be made and carried out quickly. By contrast, in larger firms decisions on even routine matters can take weeks, because they must pass through two or more management levels before an action is authorized. Some large companies have recognized this lesson and have eliminated certain layers of management. For instance, an aggressive young steel manufacturer, the Nucor Corporation, has only two levels of management between its mill workers and its chief executive officer.

Focus   Small firms can focus their efforts on a few key customers or on a precisely defined market niche. Large corporations, on the contrary, often must compete in the mass market or for large market segments. Firms like L. L. Bean, Inc., the outdoor wear cataloger, begin by identifying a niche, capturing a market, then gradually expanding their lines and customer base. Bean's originally specialized in hunting and fishing gear; today it is a major force in outdoor and casual clothing generally.

Reputation   Because of their capacity to focus on narrow niches, small firms can develop enviable reputations for quality and service. A good example is the Brookstone Company, with its unqualified returns policy that demonstrates a commitment to customer satisfaction.

FIGURE 4.3

Roads to Success — Paths to Failure

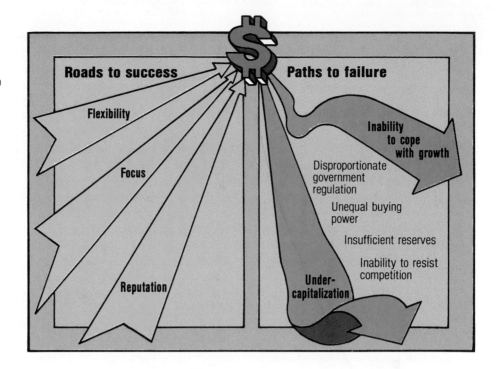

The Paths to Failure

Small businesses fail for dozens of reasons. A poor business concept, like offering refrigeration repair services above the Arctic Circle, will produce disaster nearly every time. Trying to expand a hobby into a business can work if a market niche genuinely exists, but all too often people start such a business without identifying a real need for the goods or services. Overoptimism is a great trap. Other notable causes of small-business failures include disproportionate burdens imposed by government regulation, insufficient reserves to withstand slow sales, and vulnerability to competition from larger companies. There are dozens more.

Two major paths to failure among small businesses deserve a closer look. These major problems are an inability to cope with growth and a lack of capital to continue the business.

Inability to Cope with Growth Sometimes, the very factors that are advantages to small business turn into serious disadvantages when the time comes for the firm to grow. Growth often requires the owner to give up a certain amount of direct authority. It is often hard for someone who has called all the shots thus far to give up control. Similarly, growth requires specialized management skills, in, say, credit analysis or promotion, which the founder may lack or just not have time to apply.

The small company's tendency to focus itself narrowly on a few customers or a single market niche can lead to disaster should those customers suffer a business downturn. During the auto industry's long recession in the 1970s and 1980s, the major auto makers saw their pool of suppliers shrink drastically. In order to maintain a healthy supply system, the auto makers now generally will not buy more than 40 percent of their requirements for a particular part from any single source.

Why Small Businesses Fail

From "Student" Magazine to Virgin Atlantic Airlines

In the sixties, Richard Branson, 15, left school, moved to London, and created a national student magazine called, simply, *Student*. To raise the $7000 needed for his first issue, Branson made a phone booth his office and sold ads to businesses he found in the yellow pages. It wasn't much, but Britain's most successful young entrepreneur had started his first business.

Gradually Branson moved on to the mail-order record business and then to recording and promoting rock groups. His break came when one of his performers, Mike Oldfield, had a huge hit with "Tubular Bells." From then on, almost everything seemed to go right.

Now, at age 35, Branson's Virgin Group is worth over 200 million dollars and employs over 1600 people. He records and publishes music by rock stars like Boy George, Phil Collins, and Julian Lennon. He owns Heaven, London's leading gay nightclub and emporium that generates over $500,000 profit yearly. And recently he earned headlines by starting his own airline, Virgin Atlantic. Virgin offers cut-rate fares from London to Newark, filling the gap left when Freddie Laker's airline stopped flying.

Despite the diversity of his ventures, Branson still relies on pleasing 15–35 year olds, although lately more and more of his young customers have come from outside Britain, particularly from the U.S. Virgin's rock musicians are still responsible for much of his success. They bring in money with which Branson can start other enterprises, and the company learned in the music world how to sell to its primary audience. Virgin's cable TV channel focuses on pop music, and one of Virgin's first films, *1984*, features music by the Eurythmics.

Branson's manner and attitude have had a lot to do with his success. He lets entertainers fly free if they perform on his planes. He appeared on TV in 1930s flying gear to promote his airline and in the bathtub to promote a newspaper. He clearly likes his work and has been reluctant to sell shares of his company publicly because he doesn't want to answer to a board of directors and follow more government regulations.

Of course to do so well, he has had to be a shrewd as well as an unusual businessman. He keeps overhead low by buying rather than making — his record company does not press its own records, and his airline started out by leasing just one plane. Neither he nor his rock groups flies first class, although he admits that he takes advantage of other airlines' policy of letting airline owners fly first class for free.

Perhaps that's why he has caught the public's attention in Great Britain, a country often accused of producing the most stodgy of business people. Maybe, deep inside their conservative suits, a lot of British executives would like to be like Richard Branson.

Sources: Jeffrey Robinson, "Virgin Group," *Barron's*, May 28, 1984, 26. "Freddie Laker II," *Fortune*, Vol. 109, No. 10, May 14, 1984, 7. "Britain's Richard Branson," *Dun's Business Month*, July 1985, 57. "What Size Virgin Does Richard Branson Want?" *The Economist*, November 24, 1984, 90.

Poorly managed growth probably affects a company's reputation more than anything else, at least initially. Products that do not arrive on time or goods that are poorly made can quickly destroy a company's reputation.

Undercapitalization   The quickest and most common way to fail in business is **undercapitalization**, the lack of sufficient funds to operate a business normally. More than 50 percent of small businesses fail within a year after they open, most often because they are undercapitalized. All too many entrepreneurs

FIGURE 4.4

Jewelry Stores' Percentages of a Year's Total Sales Month by Month

Jewelry stores have marked peaks in their sales. What types of retailers might have the opposite peaks or no peaks at all?

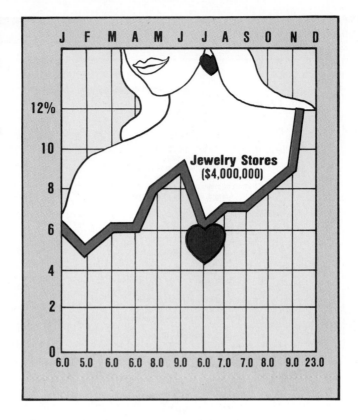

have thought that all they needed was enough money to get their doors open. They thought that the business could live on its cash flow after that. However, almost all businesses suffer from seasonal variations in sales when cash is tight, and very few businesses make money from the start.

Figure 4.4 charts the monthly sales figures for jewelry stores. A moment's thought reveals why jewelry sales peak in June and December. In May and June, jewelers sell class rings to students and engagement and wedding rings to the soon-to-be-married. December of course brings the holiday gift rush.

A key element of any successful **business plan,** a meticulous step-by-step statement of the rationale for a business and how it will achieve its goals, must be a strategy to acquire sufficient financing to keep the business going.

FINANCING THE SMALL BUSINESS

The Resources Available to Entrepreneurs

In the popular view, the entrepreneur is the person who invents the better widget or the way to sell it. A more accurate view might be that the successful entrepreneur is the one who obtains adequate financing to produce or market the better widget. We will discuss financing fully in Chapters 17 through 19.

Even a small retailer will probably need fifty thousand dollars to rent space, add necessary equipment and furnishings, buy an initial inventory, and use as

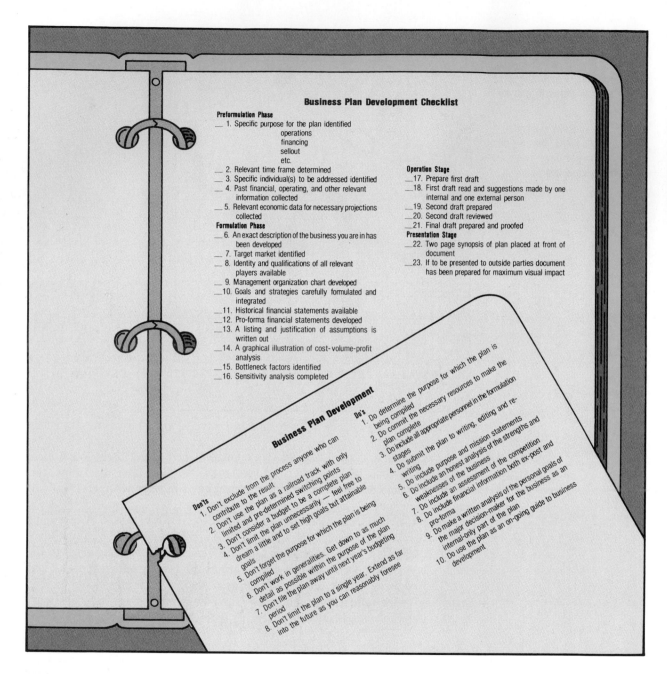

Business Plan Development Checklist

Preformulation Phase
___ 1. Specific purpose for the plan identified
         operations
         financing
         sellout
         etc.
___ 2. Relevant time frame determined
___ 3. Specific individual(s) to be addressed identified
___ 4. Past financial, operating, and other relevant information collected
___ 5. Relevant economic data for necessary projections collected

Formulation Phase
___ 6. An exact description of the business you are in has been developed
___ 7. Target market identified
___ 8. Identity and qualifications of all relevant players available
___ 9. Management organization chart developed
___ 10. Goals and strategies carefully formulated and integrated
___ 11. Historical financial statements available
___ 12. Pro-forma financial statements developed
___ 13. A listing and justification of assumptions is written out
___ 14. A graphical illustration of cost-volume-profit analysis
___ 15. Bottleneck factors identified
___ 16. Sensitivity analysis completed

Operation Stage
___ 17. Prepare first draft
___ 18. First draft read and suggestions made by one internal and one external person
___ 19. Second draft prepared
___ 20. Second draft reviewed
___ 21. Final draft prepared and proofed

Presentation Stage
___ 22. Two page synopsis of plan placed at front of document
___ 23. If to be presented to outside parties document has been prepared for maximum visual impact

Business Plan Development

Don'ts
1. Don't exclude from the process anyone who can contribute to the result
2. Don't use the plan as a railroad track with only limited and pre-determined switching points
3. Don't consider a budget to be a complete plan
4. Don't limit the plan unnecessarily — feel free to dream a little and to set high goals but attainable goals
5. Don't forget the purpose for which the plan is being compiled
6. Don't work in generalities. Get down to as much detail as possible within the purpose of the plan
7. Don't file the plan away until next year's budgeting period
8. Don't limit the plan to a single year. Extend as far into the future as you can reasonably foresee

Do's
1. Do determine the purpose for which the plan is being compiled
2. Do commit the necessary resources to make the plan complete
3. Do include all appropriate personnel in the formulation stages
4. Do submit the plan to writing, editing and re-writing
5. Do include purpose and mission statements
6. Do include an honest analysis of the strengths and weaknesses of the business
7. Do include an assessment of the competition
8. Do include financial information both ex-post and pro-forma
9. Do make a written analysis of the personal goals of the major decision-maker for the business as an internal-only part of the plan
10. Do use the plan as an on-going guide to business development

FIGURE 4.5

Developing a Business Plan

working capital, the money necessary to fund the business's regular operations. Ideally, the entrepreneur should put up a significant percentage of the necessary capital. Few new entrepreneurs have the entire amount, however. They must therefore look to other sources for additional financing. These sources include:

☐ The owner's resources
☐ Family and friends
☐ Financial institutions
☐ Vendors

Hard work and sufficient financing. These are the two ingredients that paved the way to success for Leeann Chin of Minneapolis. With $125,000 from friends, her own savings of $15,000, and an SBA loan of $165,000, Chin opened her first restaurant. Restaurants two and three were financed with $100,000 from the bank, $100,000 from cash flow, and the rest from developers. Chin was never afraid to ask for what she needed and to look at all possible sources of financing.

The Owner's Resources

The most important source of funds for any new business is its owner. Most people have more wealth than they realize. One form it often takes is **equity**, ownership interest, either in a home or accumulated value in a life-insurance policy or in a savings account.

Alternatively, the owner may have assets that could be used in the business and thereby become part of his or her equity in the firm. A computer, a typewriter, desks, and the like are common examples. The owner can also provide working capital for the business by reinvesting any profit back into the business or simply by not drawing a full salary.

Family and Friends

Entrepreneurs often look to family and friends as sources for loans or *capital,* assets that are exchanged for an ownership interest in a business. Family and friends are often hard put to turn down an entrepreneur in need of cash, but if the business goes bad, the emotional losses for all concerned may greatly exceed the money involved. As with any other serious transaction, anyone loaning a friend or family member money for a venture should state the agreement clearly in writing.

Despite their potential disadvantages, loans from family members are appealing to the entrepreneur. Usually, he or she can structure a favorable repayment schedule and even sometimes negotiate an interest rate below current banks'.

Financial Institutions

Inevitably, businesses must at some time borrow from a financial institution. As we will see in Chapter 17, savings and loans institutions, banks, trust companies, and investment companies are the major types of financial institutions.

Typically, entrepreneurs start shopping for financing in their local institutions. These sources know the environment in which the entrepreneur is operating. When Tidewater, Inc., of New Orleans decided to go into the business of servicing offshore oil-drilling platforms, it sought start-up financing from the Whitney National Bank in New Orleans. The bank not only made the loan but also granted the new company an extension when it could not make its first payment.[19] That is the kind of service that entrepreneurs look for from local institutions.

Start-up ventures sometimes borrow up to 75 percent of their needs, depending on a bank's evaluation of the venture's likelihood of success and of the entrepreneur's ability to repay the loan. The institution will often require the entrepreneur to give it a **security interest,** a financial interest in personal property or fixtures that secures the payment of a debt or obligation. The property securing the debt is called **collateral.** Collateral may consist of some of the new firm's assets, like its office equipment. Especially in the case of start-ups, the entrepreneur may have to offer some personal property as collateral, such as the entrepreneur's home. In a case like this the security is called a **mortgage,** a security interest in real property. If the entrepreneur or firm fails to repay the loan, the lending institution may eventually claim the collateral and sell it to recoup its loss.

Financial institutions can also grant a small business a **line of credit,** an agreement by which a financial institution promises to lend a business a predetermined sum on demand. A line of credit permits an entrepreneur to take quick advantage of opportunities that require a bank loan.

More Resources for Entrepreneurs

Trade Credit

Many suppliers will grant buyers financing in the form of **trade credit,** an agreement whereby the supplier sells goods or services to the buyer but does not require immediate payment. Sometimes, payment is not due for a specific period, such as thirty days. In other cases, payment is due in periodic installments.

Other Sources of Funding

Financial institutions are not the only sources for loans. Some community groups sponsor revolving loan funds to encourage the development of particular types of businesses. State and local agencies may guarantee loans, especially to minority businesspeople or for development in certain areas. The Small Business Administration offers four main financial assistance programs:

Corporate Angels and Gimmee Jimmy's

When we hear of entrepreneurs starting small and becoming successful using technology, we usually think of kids who tinker with computers or electronics for years until they come up with something new that other people will buy.

But for many American entrepreneurs, technology is a means, not an end, and the end itself may be neither money nor fame. Thousands of American business people are successful on their own terms by taking technology only as far as they need it.

Priscilla Blum, a pilot and recovered cancer patient, spends 50 hours a week using a computer and the sleek, fast jets of corporate America to reduce pain and save lives. Blum's Corporate Angel Network (CAN) arranges for corporate planes to give free rides to cancer patients who need to fly somewhere for treatment.

Almost 350 firms, including giants like American Express, AT&T, and General Foods, give their flying schedules to the CAN computer, which matches the flights and the patients' needs. The organization began in 1981, when it flew 24 patients, and in its first three years it flew over 300 patients more than 600,000 miles. Now it flies an average of 100 patients a month.

Corporations feel good about participating — they're just filling empty seats on their flights, and they get excellent publicity for it. Lee Robbins, director for Corning Glass Works, says "We've been offering this service for the community for 30 years, but CAN provides a screening operation we didn't have before." The service can accommodate only 20 to 30 percent of the cancer patients who request its help. Blum hopes one day to get almost all of the nation's 15,700 corporate aircraft to participate.

At their mother's urging, Jimmy Libman and his sister Ellen started Gimmee Jimmy's in 1983, using their family's oven and their mother's recipe for chocolate chip walnut cookies. Then, with money from their father and a loan from the Small Business Administration at a special rate for the handicapped, they built their own bakery.

The most important technology in Gimmee Jimmy's are the lights. The flashing blue strobe, which reflects off every wall so that everyone will see it, tells employees to look at the panel of lights. Green means a customer has walked into the West Orange, New Jersey, bakery. Orange signals a batch of cookies ready in the oven. Red means fire, and white alerts employees to respond to the odd telephone with a screen and a terminal. A bizarre way to communicate with employees? Not if, like Libman and 9 of his 12 employees, you're deaf. As Libman says, "We're totally high-tech deaf."

Now the company sells 1,000 pounds of cookies a week over the counter and to 50 retail food stores. In its first year, the company broke even, and its new agreement with Steve's Ice Cream stores should keep the lights blinking happily.

Sources: William H. Miller, "Corporate 'Angels' Give Cancer Patients a Lift," *Industry Week*, February 3, 1986, 37. Robert T. Grieves, "Corporate Angels of Mercy," *Time*, Vol. 123, No. 25, June 18, 1984, 63. Jaclyn Fierman, "Cookies by Deaf Bakers," *Fortune*, Vol. 111, No. 6, March 18, 1985, 62.

□ *Direct loans* Usually made only to businesses that do not qualify for loans from financial institutions.

□ *Guaranteed loans* Guaranteeing that a loan made by an institution to a qualified small business will be repaid.

□ *Participation loans* A mix of a guaranteed loan and a direct loan in which the SBA guarantees an institution's loan for part of the firm's needs and makes up the balance in a direct loan.

□ *Minority Enterprise Small Business Investment Companies (MESBICs)* Financing companies partially funded by the SBA that make loans to minority-run businesses.

Each year more than 150,000 entrepreneurs ask SCORE volunteers for help. Brenda Hauswirth began working with SCORE counselor Gordon Monkman soon after founding her business. Monkman, who had over 40 years' experience managing a large department store, helped Hauswirth develop a sound business plan. Although it took five years before Jewelry Designs by BreGé earned a profit, Hauswirth credits much of her success to Monkman's three years of consulting.

WHERE TO GO FOR HELP

The key role that small business plays in our economy and social fabric has resulted in many efforts to improve the entrepreneur's ability to compete.

Entrepreneurial Training Programs

Creativity and innovation, two keys to the entrepreneur's success, cannot be taught. What *is* being taught, in seminars and college classrooms from Harvard to the University of Washington, is management and financing techniques. As previously noted, these skills are crucial to a venture's success.

The Small Business Administration

When most people think of government help for small businesses, they think of the Small Business Administration. The SBA offers many types of management assistance to small businesses, including

☐ Counseling for firms in difficulty.
☐ Consulting on improving operations.
☐ Training for owner/managers and their employees.

Small Business Development Centers (SBDCs)   The SBA funds a number of small-business development centers, business clinics usually located on college campuses that are set up to provide counseling at no charge and training at only a nominal charge. These centers are often the SBA's principal means of providing direct management assistance where they exist.

Service Corps of Retired Executives (SCORE) and Active Corps of Executives (ACE)   SCORE and ACE are volunteer agencies funded by the SBA to provide advice for small firms. Both are comprised of experienced managers whose talents and experience the small firms could not ordinarily afford.

FRANCHISING

Many entrepreneurs choose to start a franchised operation in the hopes that they can avoid the pitfalls of starting a completely new business. For instance, many expect to receive management assistance from the **franchiser**, the company that sells the franchise. Franchises have their own unique types of risks, however, of which the **franchisee**, the person who buys a franchise, must beware.

The Franchise Relationship

A license to sell another's products or to use another's name in business, or both, is a **franchise**. In such a business relationship, the franchisee acquires the rights to a name, logo, certain methods of operation, national advertising, products, and other elements associated with the franchiser's business. Rent-a-Wreck and Lady Madonna, for example, are franchisers with well-known logos and national visibility.

Generally, the franchisee pays a flat fee to the franchiser for the franchise. Depending on the quality of the franchise, the initial fee can range from $5,000 to more than $500,000. In addition, the franchisee pays the franchiser a monthly or annual fee based on a percentage of sales or profits.

The Advantages and Disadvantages of Franchises

Franchises have unique characteristics that can either increase or decrease the entrepreneur's risks.

Advertising and Promotion   Most franchisers provide advertising and promotion for their entire system. The promotion might include nationally recognized logos like Wendy's freckle-faced girl or Midas Muffler's crowned logo. Many franchisers are not national, though, and their marketing help may be quite limited. For instance, Smokey Mountain Log Cabins, Inc., is a franchise of outlets for its prefabricated log cabins in Virginia, North and South Carolina, Mississippi, and Texas.[20]

A proven product, training, and financial requirements: three key ingredients in franchise success. Jim Buettner, training center manager for Mister Donut, teaches students from all over the world everything they need to know to operate a Mister Donut franchise successfully. That's no small task when you realize that Mister Donut has over 525 coffee and donut shops in the United States and 74 shops in 11 other countries (excluding Canada).

Management Assistance and Training Some franchisers offer their franchisees extensive management assistance and training. The older and more successful the franchiser, the better this help is likely to be. Some firms, like McDonald's, even have training centers for their franchisees.

As noted in the discussion of the definition of entrepreneur, some people question whether a franchisee is really an entrepreneur. They argue that the franchisee has a tendency to become too dependent on the franchiser for guidance on management decisions. The franchisee's success or failure also depends to a large extent on that of the franchiser. This dependence can be a distinct disadvantage if the franchiser runs into problems.

Central Purchasing and Product Consistency Many franchisers provide the supplies that franchisees need to do business. The hamburger chains usually sell the beef patties to their franchise stores. The advantages to the individual franchisee are assured supplies and uniform quality throughout the system, a major factor in customer decisions. The disadvantage to centralized purchasing may be prices that are higher than in the open market.

Some franchisers do not offer central purchasing or do not carefully monitor the quality of what franchisees buy. Product inconsistency in such systems can hurt franchisees badly.

The Disadvantages of
Franchising

Financial Requirements The sometimes stiff fees and capital requirements associated with franchises can be both an advantage and a disadvantage to the franchisee.

If properly administered, the fees and capital requirements of franchising assure the financial integrity of the franchiser and the system. Some franchisers, like Tubby's Sub Shops, also look for franchisees who will finance no more than 50 percent of their total investment, which in this case would be half of approximately $375,000.[21] Such capital requirements are probably the major reason that only 5 percent of start-up franchised outlets fail.[22]

FIGURE 4.6

Franchise Evaluation Form

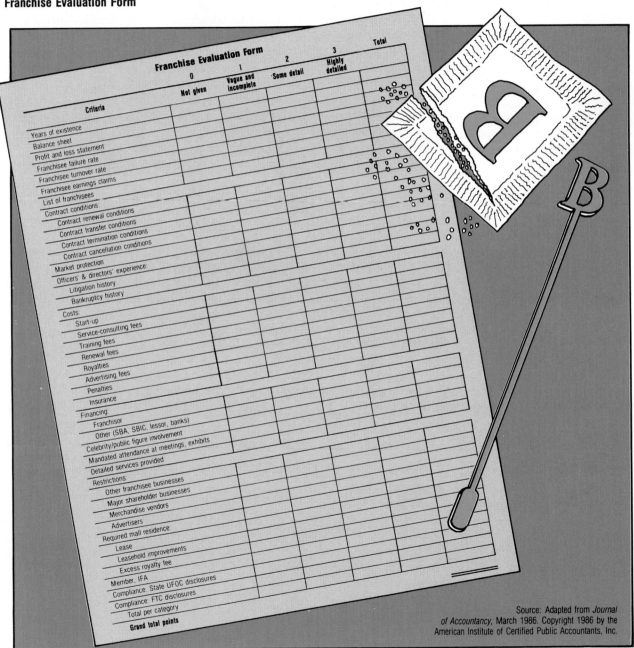

Source: Adapted from *Journal of Accountancy*, March 1986. Copyright 1986 by the American Institute of Certified Public Accountants, Inc.

If a system is not well run or its promotion is not effective, the franchise fees can become an insupportable burden. Computerland franchisees forced the franchiser to reduce its fees and to increase and improve its promotion when its national advertising campaigns proved unsuccessful.

Franchisee Protections

The earliest major franchisers were the automobile manufacturers and oil companies. Their retail dealers were, and still are, franchisees. In both industries, the franchisees are protected by federal laws from arbitrary terminations of their franchises.[23] Other types of franchisees may not be protected.

Legal Protections for Franchisees

The principal legal protections for franchisees are contained in the Federal Trade Commission's regulations. These stipulations require the franchiser to supply a prospective franchisee with a disclosure statement at least ten days before the franchisee signs a franchise agreement. The best protection, however, is an aggressive investigation of the franchiser and its competitors, the opportunities and risks in the particular franchise area, the terms of the franchise agreement, and all the other factors that go into a business plan.

SMALL BUSINESS: A PARTING LOOK

Small businesses are the heart of our economic and social system because of the great opportunities they offer and because they express the freedom that Americans have to make their own destinies. The risks are indeed great — but the opportunities for success, both financial and psychological, are greater.

The characteristics of the successful entrepreneur are rewarded in other business areas, too. Creativity, innovation, and willingness to take risks also characterize the most successful managers in large businesses and government.

Chapter Highlights

1. Describe the characteristics of an entrepreneur.

Entrepreneurs are a varied lot, but most successful entrepreneurs flourish in an atmosphere of moderate risk taking and are optimistic and energetic. Most entrepreneurs are very goal and achievement oriented.

2. State the various definitions of *small business* and explain why there is more than one definition.

As this text uses the term, a small business is independently owned and operated, is not dominant in its field, and does not employ more than five hundred persons. The Small Business Administration's definition, which is similar, classifies businesses by industry and sets different limits for each for the number of employees and amount of sales. A White House conference on small business limited small businesses to those that employ fewer than four hundred employees. The Committee for Economic Development included several other criteria: a small number of individuals responsible for capital contributions, a local orientation to the business, and a small market share when compared to its industry as a whole.

Because *small* is a relative term and because different industries make different demands in terms of initial investment costs to start up and also require an appropriate number of employees, no single definition has satisfied all groups.

3. Discuss why certain fields attract small businesses.

Retailing, services, and high technology are among the fields that are most attractive to small businesses. These fields tend to be fairly easy to enter, require less initial financing than other types of businesses, and allow firms to serve a smaller part of the market. In these fields it is relatively easy for the entrepreneur to parlay his or her own knowledge or skill into a successful business.

4. Analyze why small businesses succeed and fail.

Small businesses have some advantages over their larger competitors. Flexibility, the ability to focus their efforts on a few key customers or on a precisely defined market niche and the chance to develop a reputation for quality and service are some advantages small businesses have over their larger competitors.

Small businesses can fail for dozens of reasons. The inability to cope with growth and undercapitalization are major problems for small businesses. A poor business concept or failure to identify a real need for their goods or services, disproportionate burdens imposed by government regulation, insufficient reserves to withstand slow sales and vulnerability to competition from larger companies also contribute to the failure of a small business.

5. Describe the services of the Small Business Administration.

The Small Business Administration offers counseling, consulting, and training services. Small Business Development Centers (SBDCs), often located on college campuses, provide low-cost or free counseling and training and are one of the SBA's principal means of providing direct management assistance. The Service Core of Retired Executives (SCORE) and Active Core of Executives (ACE) provide assistance to individual businesses through the efforts of experienced volunteers. The SBA also offers some financial assistance to businesses that cannot obtain funding from other sources.

6. List the advantages and disadvantages of franchising.

Three of the most important advantages of franchising are the availability of a proven product and marketing plan, having the benefit of the franchiser's advertising and promotion program, management assistance and training, and the economies of central purchasing and control. Stiff financial requirements may prevent some potential franchisees from entering the business. Although this restriction may be viewed as a disadvantage, it does help entrepreneurs avoid some of the problems of undercapitalization. Lack of independence and control is often seen as a significant disadvantage of the franchise arrangement. The most important drawback, though, is that an individual franchisee's success or failure often hinges on the reputation of other franchisees and the performance of the franchiser.

7. Describe the protections offered by law to franchisees.

Investors have a right to receive a disclosure statement prepared by the franchiser and delivered at least ten business days before the individual may make a commitment to purchasing a franchise. Franchisers must provide a written explanation of all earnings claims. Franchisees have a right to obtain any promised refund as long as they meet all the conditions for obtaining it.

Key Terms

Active Core of Executives (ACE)	Entrepreneurship	Retailer	Small Business Administration (SBA)
Business plan	Equity	Security interest	
Capital	Franchise	Service Core of Retired Executives (SCORE)	Trade credit
Collateral	Franchisee		Undercapitalization
Entrepreneur	Franchiser		Working capital

Review Questions

1. Define *entrepreneur* and describe the characteristics associated with entrepreneurs.
2. Compare and contrast the various definitions of *small business*.
3. Which fields tend to attract small businesses most? Why? Explain.
4. What are the principal reasons for the high failure rate among small businesses?
5. Describe the potential advantages that small businesses have over their large competitors.
6. What are the potential advantages of owning a small firm? What are the disadvantages?
7. What types of financing do small entrepreneurs typically use? What are the pros and cons of each?
8. What types of financial assistance does the Small Business Administration (SBA) provide?
9. List the types of management assistance that the SBA offers.
10. Describe the franchising relationship.
11. What are the risks and benefits of buying a franchise?

Application Exercises

1. Make a list of 20 small business firms that opened approximately two years ago. Then place a check mark beside the name of each business that is no longer open. In your opinion, what are some of the reasons why these firms closed?
2. Assume you are planning to open a small convenience food store in your community. One option is to seek a franchise. A second option is to open your own store and purchase the merchandise from a wholesale food distributor. What are the advantages and disadvantages of each option?

Cases

4.1 The Master of Microsoft

Many people are familiar with the story of Steven Jobs and Steven Wozniak, who were in their twenties when they got the idea for a small personal computer, designed and built a prototype, and went on to found Apple Computer, Inc. But not many know that every Apple home computer contains an operating system invented by Bill Gates.

In 1975, Bill Gates was just your average super-intelligent college sophomore (he scored 800 on his math SATs), one who preferred computer hacking and poker to studying. As the result of a prank, Gates got himself into the position of having to adapt the BASIC computer language for the Altair kit computer. He did it in four weeks, and it worked the first time he tried it. Gates left school and, with a friend, formed the Microsoft Corpo-

ration to develop and sell software products.

Microsoft grew steadily as Gates developed one successful design after another. Perhaps his first important project was the operating system for IBM's proposed PC. Gates's design, the MS-DOS, is now the industry standard. Gates also helped design the first true portable computer for Radio Shack, and he designed the operating system that is used in a new Japanese computer. His firm's latest project is a compact disk that can hold any type of digital information.

Through it all, Bill Gates has remained at the head of his firm. He has exhibited not only technical wizardry, but marketing savvy and the ability to lead an organization that now boasts 1200 employees. Although he feels he needs the help of professional managers in such areas as finance and planning, Gates has never had to borrow from a bank. He began Microsoft with money he had already earned as a programming consultant, and he financed its expansion solely out of its earnings.

Microsoft went public in March 1986, and by June Gates's 40 percent share of the company was worth $390 million. Yet he still works sixty-hour weeks, although he now takes an occasional weekend off, and several days of vacation each year. Gates has no intention of leaving Microsoft, or even slowing down much — at least, not until he has helped place a computer on every desk and in every home in the United States.

Questions

1. Microsoft grew to become a $100-million-a-year business in just eleven years. How did Bill Gates avoid the major pitfalls of rapid business growth?
2. For what reasons might an entrepreneur want to restrict the growth of a firm like Microsoft — to keep it small? How might he or she attempt to do so? Would it be risky?

Sources: For more information see *Money*, July 1986, pp. 49–70; *Parade Magazine*, January 26, 1986, pp. 4–5; and *Inc.*, May 1985, pp. 57–67.

4.2 All in the Family

To many observers, the best run businesses in America are family businesses. Most family businesses by far are small ones, but many large firms are family empires. Family firms produce Levi's jeans, Schwinn bicycles, Johnson Wax products, Stroh's beer, and Mars candy bars. Descendants of the founders still run such corporations as Corning Glass, The New York Times Company, and McDonnell Douglas. Family businesses account for most jobs in the United States and for almost half the nation's production.

Some young people feel that they would be stifled if they entered the family business. Others believe the family business offers opportunities that would not otherwise be open to them, including the chance to one day own and run the firm. Many young women today feel that family firms offer more quality of opportunity than large publicly traded corporations. Many people in their twenties and thirties now join or rejoin family firms, after they have tried corporate life "on the outside."

Dan Jonkhoff of Traverse City, Michigan, never had any doubts about joining the family firm. At the age of 5 he astonished a kindergarten classroom full of parents by announcing that, when he grew up, he was going to be a funeral director. That isn't the usual kindergartner's ambition, but Jonkhoff's great-great-grandfather, great-grandfather, grandfather, and father were all funeral directors. Dan now runs a funeral parlor with his father in Traverse City.

Statistics reveal that only about one-third of all family businesses survive long enough to take in a second generation. And few of those continue to grow. Along the way, they face the same problems and challenges as other businesses — and some unique ones as well. Family problems tend to become business problems, and vice versa. Sibling rivalries may become power struggles, and the question of succession to the leadership position may intrude on the operation of the business. Unless such questions are resolved, the family business can become a battleground.

When his father died in 1980, Sam Sebastiani took over as head of Sebastiani Vineyards of California, the nation's eleventh largest winery. The elder Sebastiani had run the business almost single-handedly, with little input from others. Sam had to struggle to keep the business going. Although he was running the winery, Sam was neither head of the family nor the firm's major stockholder. Difficulties with his brother and sister spilled over into the business, and Sam became more and more distant from his mother — who held the controlling interest in the firm. She wanted an attentive son to help her through the loss of her husband; he acted the chief executive, communicating with her by memo or through intermediaries. Finally, after six years, Sam lost both his mother's support and his job. In a sense, he has also lost his family.

Questions

1. What might be some advantages of involving one's family in a new or growing small business? What might be some disadvantages?
2. Many observers feel that family businesses are most vulnerable during or soon after a change in leadership. Why should that be so? How can that vulnerability be avoided?

Sources: For more information, see *The New York Times*, June 11, 1986, pp. D1, D15; *The New York Times*, June 10, 1986, pp. D1, D26; and *Forbes*, October 21, 1985, pp. 86–96.

Foreign Competition

Not so long ago, American companies competed largely against each other. The United States' place in the world economy was secure. While much of Europe was rebuilding factories destroyed in World War II, U.S. manufacturing plants were cranking out goods in record numbers. The poor, unwesternized nations of the Third World bought American goods and sold their natural resources to American companies. They, too, provided no threat. All Ford really had to worry about was General Motors and Chrysler. Competition was seen as the sometimes ruthless heart of the American way of doing business. But it was mostly American competition, a family affair.

Now from the wharves in Baltimore to the docks of San Francisco, you'll see Toyotas and Mexican fabrics and Korean computer parts. In the first half of this decade, imports from China increased almost 200 percent, while those from South Korea, India, Taiwan, Singapore, and Brazil all more than doubled. On scores of products from cameras to anaesthesia machines, you have to look hard to find a "Made in America" label. Labor unions still point fingers at management when they strike or negotiate, but their real fear is the worker in Malaysia or Singapore whose daily pay wouldn't buy a dinner in Detroit.

America's economic relationship to its new competitors is a curious one, full of ironies. In half a century the Germans and Japanese have gone from our worst enemies to our friendly — and fierce — competitors. And they did it with our help. The huge factories that gave the U.S. its industrial prominence now keep American businesses tied to the technology of the past. Americans who used to believe that competition is always a good thing now find themselves asking the government to limit their competitors from abroad. In some cases the very technologies and philosophies that other countries borrowed from us have come back to make American competitors number two.

Generally foreign competition does work the way competition is supposed to — it brings down the price or improves the quality of goods or leads to a more efficient process or service. But suddenly American workers must compete with those making far less than they. A 1984 study by the U.S. Bureau of Labor Statistics found that pay for workers in South Korea, Taiwan, and Brazil averaged 12 percent of the pay of their U.S. counterparts.

Manufacturers must compete with companies whose countries may encourage the growth of their industries in ways that seem unfair to us. All that rebuilding taught some foreign business people lessons that many Americans are only now learning. And while the Third World countries still export a lot of raw material, they are *keeping* their greatest natural resource — their people — and doing work that used to be done in Dover, New Hampshire or Columbus, Ohio.

All this has been made possible by technology that continues to shrink the world. Sixty years ago, it wouldn't have mattered much if the Japanese could make a better radio or Brazilians would work cheaply — things so far away generally wouldn't affect Americans. But now a product from Hong Kong or Mexico can get to you almost as soon as one from Newark. And the money, minds, and information of the world are as close as a telephone or computer terminal.

So what has been happening to American business as a result of this competition from outside our borders? For one thing, fewer and fewer Americans are involved in what used to be thought of as the basic industries like autos and steel. We're becoming more a nation of people who serve or manage, getting goods to people but not making them ourselves.

From shoes to textiles to cars, the production jobs are going overseas, leaving a number of American industries and their workers calling for help to save their factories and skills. Some fear that the loss of too much manufacturing will threaten the future of the U.S. economy. Others see the changes as part of the constant evolution of American business, something that could have good consequences.

Many American companies, of course, have adapted to compete with their new rivals. Suddenly finding themselves playing a game of catch-up, American businesses have scrutinized their rivals, particularly the Japanese, to find the secrets that have helped them get ahead. What they have found is an emphasis on long-term goals, rather than short-term; on quality, rather than quantity; on making things right the first time; on involving workers in the decision-making process and using workers' ideas to improve production and efficiency; and on reducing the symbolic distance between executives and employees.

So now American business is relearning how to be competitive, to respond to the needs of customers and the strengths of workers, and to create quality goods that will stand up next to any. The American workplace is changing as labor and management start to work together against an outside threat. And many companies have decided that

PARKING FOR AMERICAN MADE VEHICLES ONLY

maintaining the health and welfare of their workers is good for the company.

Foreign competition has proved to be a boon for many American entrepreneurs. It has shaken up some industries, and when American giants flounder, entrepreneurs can often find an opening in the market. It has fostered a "Buy American" spirit that supports the growing home-made movement in America. Many New England residents have lost their jobs in textile mills partly as a result of foreign competition, but now some of those workers — and their children — are running knitting and weaving shops in small towns around the region.

The American companies that have handled the competition best are multinationals. A company that has subsidiaries in Mexico or South Korea can take advantage of the low labor rates to increase its profits. Such companies can, in effect, shop around the world for the place that will supply the most favorable conditions for a new factory. While this kind of global shopping keeps some American multinationals profitable, it further weakens the status of the American worker. Some critics of American trade policy say that it is time to start looking not at how foreign governments subsidize their industries, but at how unfair

and inhuman working conditions are making profits for American companies. American unions spent a century trying to rid the country of sweatshops and grossly exploitative working conditions, but now workers laboring in these same conditions are taking jobs away from the unions.

Every American has been touched by the effects of foreign competition, and some have lost their jobs to it. But most people whose jobs haven't been exported can look around them and count the good effects of the competition. Our cars and cameras work better and cost less — if you adjust for inflation — than they used to. Although management experts caution that we shouldn't just copy Japanese techniques, some of the management trends we've imported appear to make workers happier and to help production. Our bosses are becoming more likely to trade ideas with us than to scold us for parking in the executive lot.

Foreign competition will continue to scare those who can't react well to it. But American industries that do respond successfully will dominate the U.S. economy of the 21st century.

II

MANAGEMENT AND ORGANIZATION

Several years ago, United Technologies Corporation put an advertisement in the *Wall Street Journal* that featured a bold headline: LET'S GET RID OF MANAGEMENT. The main theme of the copy was that business leaders should stop managing and start leading. There is, of course, a difference between management and leadership. Good managers are able to do both. In Part II we will describe the process of management and distinguish between management and leadership. We will also discuss the organization process, or how managers group employees and distribute work for maximum efficiency. This section also focuses on the human side of enterprise. We then review the factors that influence worker performance and attitudes.

MANAGEMENT

5

Learning Objectives

After you have completed this chapter, you will be able to do the following:

■ Describe the management process and who and what it involves.

■ Explain what a management hierarchy represents and relate it to the three types of management skills.

■ Show how Henry Mintzberg's ten managerial roles can be divided into three main categories.

■ Describe the five steps in the managerial decision-making process.

■ Identify and define the five management functions.

■ Outline the five steps of the planning process.

■ Describe the four steps in the management-control process.

■ Define the term *corporate culture* and list the characteristics of one.

■ Identify the key concepts of the management excellence movement.

J ohn Teets, the chairman and chief executive officer of the Greyhound Corporation, can bench press 352 pounds at the age of fifty-two. Every morning he climbs the 314 steps to the nineteenth floor of the Greyhound Tower. It is Teets's style to make intense demands on himself and on those who work for Greyhound, a conglomerate with sales of $2.2 billion per year.

After high school, Teets went to work in a restaurant, a business that requires intense attention to detail. By the time he was twenty-nine, he was operating a highly successful complex of businesses, including a restaurant, an ice rink, and a shopping center. He then went to work for Greyhound for four years and reorganized its Post House Restaurants. After leaving Greyhound, he headed the Canteen Corporation at ITT, where he reported to the legendary manager Harold Geneen. From Geneen, Teets took the idea of gathering managers and publicly quizzing them on minute details of their operations. This technique not only demands that managers know their operations but that top management understand them, too.

THE MANAGEMENT PROCESS

When Teets took over Greyhound, he discovered that its bus subsidiary did not know which of its runs were profitable — it knew only in which states it made money. He insisted that the bus division spend $4 million to improve its accounting. Since then, Teets has pruned out the unprofitable bus operations. In fact, he has disposed of nearly half the businesses that Greyhound once had, while simultaneously boosting earnings to near-record levels and doubling the price of its stock in three years.

The discipline Teets imposed on Greyhound's operations is reflected in his treatment of subordinates. Like Geneen, Teets calls regular meetings of his top managers, at which they are expected to arrive fifteen minutes early. Latecomers find the doors locked and must wait until Teets allows them to be opened. They then have to walk to the front row, reserved for them. Unlike his former boss at ITT, however, Teets does not believe that Greyhound should be more important to himself or his employees than are their families. Teets gets to his office most days by seven o'clock and leaves by three-thirty. Employees who work late are not necessarily rewarded for it.

John Teets is a master manager. His personal life as well as his business practices reflect his commitment to putting his time and resources to their best possible use. Teets's techniques are not unique, however, nor are they the only ones he might have chosen. This chapter provides an introduction to the management processes common in businesses today.[1]

THE NATURE OF MANAGEMENT

The process of coordinating human, informational, physical, and financial resources to accomplish organizational goals is called **management**. A **manager** is thus a person who coordinates an organization's resources. Human resources is those people who actually make the organization's products or provide its services

FIGURE 5.1

The Management of Resources

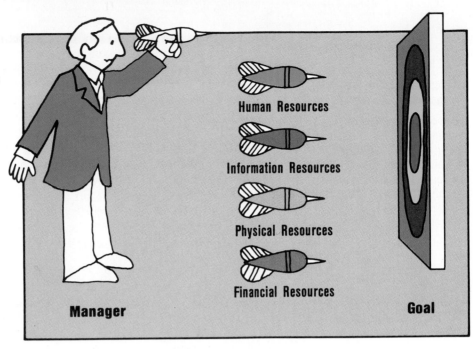

but also includes its other employees, as well as outside vendors and suppliers. Information resources comprises the knowledge and data necessary to the business, such as market research, legal advice, scientific or technical materials, and economic reports. **Physical resources** includes the business's tangible property, such as its raw materials, manufacturing machinery and facilities, office equipment, and real estate. Finally, a company's financial resources are its intangible property that may with more or less difficulty be converted into cash. Some examples might include bank accounts, accounts receivable, loans, stocks, and bonds. Table 5.1 shows where each of these resources is discussed in detail.

The Resources of Management

The Universality of Management Principles

The principles of management apply to all areas of human activity. In fact, some of America's great managers are not even in business as we commonly think of it. Cardinal Bernardin of Chicago runs an archdiocese that has thousands of employees, hundreds of educational institutions, and billions of dollars' worth of real estate. And for twenty years, Don Shula has put together football teams — first in Baltimore, then in Miami — and led them to division, league, and Super Bowl crowns. One could easily list thousands of nonbusiness entities, from hospitals to charities, prisons, and government agencies, that require management skills.

The Nature of Management

Whatever the organization and regardless of its size, its management must be able to identify and take control of its resources, set goals, and allocate the resources to meet these goals. John Teets, for example, set a 15 percent return on equity as the goal for each of Greyhound's operating units. Those that could not meet the goal, such as its meat-packing operations and some of its bus lines, were either sold or shut down.[2]

TABLE 5.1

Detailed Coverage of the Management of Resources

The specific resources of management are discussed in greater detail later in this text. Chapters in which different kinds of resources are covered are shown in this table.

Resources	Chapter	Example of Topics Covered
Human	5, 6, 7, 8, 9	Planning, organizing, motivation, employee selection, negotiation
Informational	11, 16, 19	Market research, cost of goods sold, computers, sales reports
Physical	10, 16	Production, computers
Financial	18, 19, 20, 21	Balance sheet, investment opportunities, insurance vehicles

The Management Hierarchy

The simplest organizations, like a small service station, have only one manager and one worker. A somewhat more complex example is the one represented in Figure 5.2. This organization is arranged as a **hierarchy**, an organization classified according to the rank or authority of the positions within it. At the top of the pyramid sits top management, the person or persons responsible for the entire operation. Beneath the top managers is middle management, and below that are the first line or supervisory managers. We will discuss their functions in concrete terms later.

The Management Hierarchy Defined

Normally, a person's position in the hierarchy indicates his or her status and responsibility in the organization: the higher in the higher hierarchy, the greater

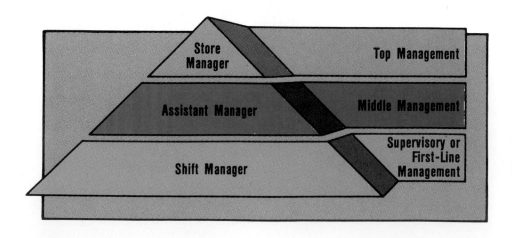

FIGURE 5.2

A Management Hierarchy

FIGURE 5.3

The Mix of Managerial Skills

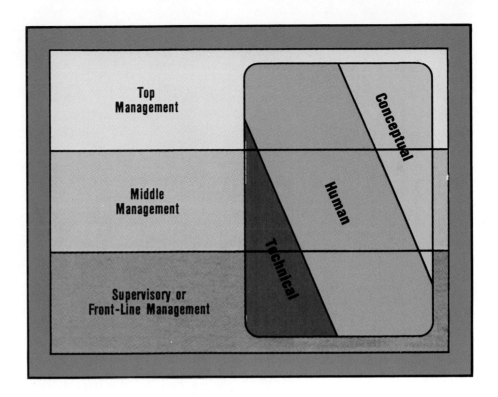

the status and the responsibility. But, this rule has notable exceptions. If a storeowner's mother works behind the counter, her status is likely to be considerably higher than anyone else's in that category.

Management Skills

The Three Types of Management Skills

A good manager needs three types of skills. First, he or she must have **human skills**, the ability to work with and for people, to communicate with others, and to understand others' needs. Second, a manager needs **technical skills**, the ability to use the tools, equipment, procedures, and techniques of a specialized field. Finally, a manager requires **conceptual skills**, the ability to understand all the organization's activities, how its various parts fit together, and how the organization relates to others. For example, a successful department head, such as a sales manager for an automobile manufacturer, must understand the relationship between sales, marketing, production, and manufacturing, among others.

All managers must have these three types of skills, but the mix of skills a particular manager requires varies with his or her rank in a hierarchy, as shown in Figure 5.3. Technical and human skills are most important in lower-level managers, for instance. The superintendent of a construction project needs good personal skills to deal with laborers as well as good technical skills to make certain that the construction is done right.

By contrast, a top manager must have excellent conceptual skills in order to manage an entire organization. Human skills are still important, but having strong technical skills becomes less and less critical as one moves up in the hierarchy. The middle manager needs a balanced mix of all three types of skills: human

Getting to the top. *Pam McAllister Johnson didn't set out to be one of the top women in publishing, but as a respected reporter and journalism professor she took the time to read the popular books on corporate life. When Gannett Co. Inc. spotted her as a professional with plenty of management potential, she was ready to seize the opportunity. As publisher of the* Ithaca Journal, *Johnson has gained national attention and influence.*

skills to work with people above and below in the hierarchy, technical skills to deal with day-to-day operational problems, and conceptual skills to manage the relationships between departments.[3]

Leadership

Successful management is largely a function of **leadership**, the ongoing process of influencing others' behavior toward certain goals. Leadership is not an off-the-shelf product. Rather, successful leaders possess unique mixtures of traits and skills that mix the ability to define and achieve work-related goals with strong interpersonal skills. Not all situations require the same mix of leadership skills. For example, a Marine Corps combat sergeant requires a considerably different blend of work-related and interpersonal skills than a print shop foreman.

Leadership does not occur in a vacuum. Once cannot lead unless others follow. Often people choose to follow because they believe that is the way to satisfy their own need for recognition or to gain a sense of accomplishment. A successful basketball coach, like the Boston Celtics' K.C. Jones, may routinely deflect media praise from his achievements to those of his players, who are therefore more willing to follow Jones's lead. The willingness to follow can also come from a sense of fear or terror. Between those two poles — personal satisfaction and terror — lie a variety of effective leadership styles. Management styles range from leadership by order to leadership by delegation. Again, styles from one end of the continuum work in particular situations. The greatest leaders know when to select a certain style to fit a particular situation and for particular people.

MANAGERIAL ROLES

The Ten Roles of a Manager

A manager, like an actor, must play many different roles. Unlike an actor, who plays one role and then moves on to another, however, a manager may play several roles in the same day and sometimes two or more at once. These roles often require different mixes of management skills. In a classic study, Henry Mintzberg identified ten managerial roles. These fall into three broad categories: interpersonal, informational, and decisional roles.[4]

Interpersonal Roles

The Three Main Categories of Managerial Roles

The roles that primarily require a manager to deal with people are the **interpersonal roles.** In the **figurehead role**, in which the manager engages in symbolic activities, he or she may have to appear at an awards ceremony or make a public presentation. As a **leader,** a manager directs the activities of certain employees, coordinates the work of others, sometimes hires and fires subordinates, does performance evaluations, and recommends employees for promotion. Finally, in the role of **liaison**, the manager serves as a communications link between people and groups. When Lee Iacocca, the head of Chrysler, presides at a press conference to announce next year's models, works with Chrysler's advertising agency, or testifies before a Congressional committee, he acts in various interpersonal roles.

Informational Roles

Informational roles are those roles that require a manager to gather and communicate information within the hierarchy and to the outside world. As a **disseminator,** a person who spreads information, a manager delivers information to subordinates. As a **monitor,** a manager who gathers information, he or she reports important changes, problems, and opportunities to higher levels in the hierarchy. The disseminator and monitor roles viewed together reveal why managers are an organization's vital communications links.

A manager's third informational role is that of **spokesperson**, a person who transmits information to outsiders for an organization. The spokesperson role may seem to overlap with the figurehead role, but there is a distinction. When the main purpose of a public appearance by a manager is to communicate information, he or she acts as a spokesperson. When the primary purpose is symbolic, he or she acts as a figurehead. Of course, a manager can fulfill the two roles at once. In his much praised appearances before the press following the Bhopal, India, chemical disaster, Union Carbide's Warren M. Anderson both spoke for the company and symbolized its commitment to the victims by his presence.

Decisional Roles

Roles that flow from and are based on a manager's interpersonal and informational roles are known as **decisional roles**. These roles center on solving problems and making choices. In an **entrepreneurial role**, a manager looks for and implements new ideas to make his or her group more effective. A marketing manager might, for instance, adopt a new promotional idea, or a production manager might accept a subordinate's suggestion for streamlining a manufacturing process.

As a problem solver a manager makes decisions to keep his or her group operating in the face of circumstances that are out of the ordinary. In this role, a manager might have to devise a way to keep parts coming into an assembly line despite a strike that has closed down a primary supplier.

A manager acting as a **resource allocator** decides how a group will use all the available resources. Managers rarely have all the resources they feel they need, so they must decide who gets additional clerical help, who must give up a computer terminal, what types of machines to buy, and dozens of similar issues. Of course, a manager does not make these decisions in a vacuum. Subordinates will provide input, whether wanted or not. The intensity of such discussions may be matched by those encountered in the manager's final role. As a **negotiator**, the manager acts as a company representative either in dealings externally with outside vendors or government agencies or internally in resolving disputes between subordinates. And, depending on the company, a manager may also have to perform this role in convincing another department to provide the support that his or her group needs for a project.

THE MANAGERIAL DECISION-MAKING PROCESS

As the preceding discussion of a manager's decisional roles implies, a **decision** is a choice of actions by means of which a manager seeks to achieve the organization's goals. Managers rarely make decisions based on mere inspiration. Most decisions come instead out of the process portrayed in Figure 5.4. This process has five important steps.

Step 1: Define the Problem

The first and most important step in decision making is to define the problem. In order to define a problem, a manager must have a **goal**, a condition he or she wishes to achieve in the end, and an understanding of the current situation. Recall that Greyhound's John Teets set an annual goal of a 15 percent return on equity for each of the company's subsidiaries. Stiff competition from low-cost bus companies and fare-cutting airlines kept the Greyhound bus companies from reaching that goal. Teets's problem thus became how to restructure the bus subsidiary to achieve the desired 15 percent return.

The Third Category of Managerial Roles

FIGURE 5-4

The Decision Making Process

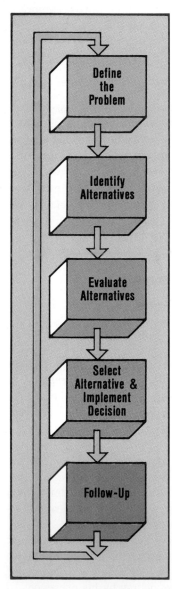

Step 2: Identify Alternatives

The second step in the managerial decision-making process is to identify alternatives. Clearly, these alternatives must be reasonable — there is no sense wasting time on useless solutions. Time and money always restrict the range of alternatives, but what is an impractical alternative at one time may become a practical one later. Managers should also decide how they will measure success. If they select measurement criteria at an early stage, managers will be more likely to be objective in determining at the end whether they have achieved their original goals. Returning to Greyhound's problems with its bus subsidiary, we may note that John Teets could identify several potential solutions: to prune unprofitable routes, close terminals, or cut labor costs.

INTERNATIONAL BUSINESS

Not Your Typical Business School

You wake at dawn to the sound of a giant drum or an irate instructor's voice; you rush to sweep your room or begin the day's rigorous calisthenics, or perhaps sing the national anthem while the flag is raised; you spend your day in constant stress, being yelled at by instructors or performing strenuous physical tasks. Sound like Marine Boot Camp? Or perhaps a sadistic 19th-century prep school?

Wrong. In fact, right now Japanese companies are paying up to $100 a day to send their employees to engage in such activities in training schools which have become known as "hell camps." The programs vary widely, but at the root of most is an idea related to the motivation behind groups like Outward Bound. Broken out of their routine, employees are forced to face new challenges. If all goes as planned, they discover something about themselves and come out better people. They may be chastized and humiliated along the way, but, advocates claim, participants become better, more productive workers. Working with teammates, they lose any sense of superiority and acquire the self-discipline which some feel is lacking in modern business.

Some camps stress traditional values: participants sit through lectures about the social structure and obligations of Japanese life, are encouraged to develop competitive and nationalistic fervor, and prove their physical machismo (90 percent of the participants are men) by swimming in a near-freezing river and parading through a village in loin cloths. Other camps stress humility and managerial skills and have participants role-play phone calls, give speeches, and finally sing the "Salaryman's Song" at the top of their lungs in a crowded city. Using a system that turns the Boy Scouts on their heads, they give participants "ribbons of shame" which the struggling employee can have removed only after passing rigorous tests in particular areas.

And the participants' reaction? Apparently most of them are positive about the experience, although the lessons learned in the stressful camp atmosphere can be quickly forgotten back in the relatively soft corporate world. But before you dismiss the idea as a crazy passing fad, consider how many management ideas we've imported from Japan recently. Rumor has it, some of the camps have plans to move to California.

Sources: Richard Phalon, "Hell Camp," *Forbes*, Vol. 133, No. 14, June 18, 1984. "Banzai!" *Time*, Vol. 121, No. 6, February 7, 1983, 50. "Executives Go Outward Bound," *Dun's Business Month*," Vol. 122, No. 1, July 1983, 56–58.

Management skills. While managers may be in the background on the shop floor, they still need to develop a good mix of skills. They must have good conceptual skills to formulate broad goals, such as Kellogg's commitment to quality; good technical skills to develop specifications for the product; and good communication skills to explain objectives and procedures to employees who actually monitor the production of Nutri-Grain cereal.

Step 3: Evaluate Alternatives

The Third Step in the Managerial Decision-making Process

Once a manager has identified the reasonable alternatives, he or she must evaluate them. An intelligent appraisal requires detailed information on each alternative. Then the manager evaluates each alternative, asking these questions about each alternative: Will an alternative solve the problem as defined? Could a potential solution to the problem jeopardize another organizational goal? Are the time and money available to implement the suggested alternative?

A manager's evaluation will often require projections and predictions. No method for forecasting the future is perfect, and the further into the future the predictions go, the greater will be the probability of error. The key to minimizing the possibility of error lies in having reliable data. Teets ordered Greyhound's bus subsidiary to spend $4 million on the accounting changes it would take to identify profitable routes. He forced its managers to develop the data to evaluate alternatives. Once the data were available, Teets evidently could see that, of the available alternatives, pruning routes and closing terminals were the easiest. Attacking labor costs meant taking on a strong union.

Step 4: Select an Alternative and Implement the Decision

After evaluating the various alternatives, a manager decides on one to put into action. Successful implementation demands a manager's full commitment: the willingness to devote his or her managerial skills and the group's resources to making the chosen course of action succeed. Managers may find their interpersonal skills tested by the need to motivate subordinates to support the decision. If subordinates believe that a manager may change the decision, they may not commit themselves fully to carrying it out, thus dooming it.

At Greyhound, the problem of meeting the new goal proved more difficult than just lack of support. Pruning unprofitable routes and eliminating terminals could not bring return on equity up to the 15 percent target. The next obvious place for cost cutting was labor. In bargaining with the Amalgamated Transit Union, Teets insisted on a 17 percent wage and benefit giveback. The union refused, and its 12,700 Greyhound workers went on strike. Within two weeks, the company had begun hiring replacements for the strikers and soon resumed limited service. After forty-seven days, the union agreed to a 15 percent giveback.

Step 5: Follow Up on Implementation

The final step in the decision-making process is to follow up on implementation. A manager must make certain that his or her group carries out the decision after the initial enthusiasm and thrust have ended. In other words, the manager must maintain the momentum. A manager must also monitor the results to determine whether the decision is having the planned effect. Monitoring measures the results against the goal. In Greyhound's case, the results were disappointing. Even with the givebacks, the bus lines lost money in the year following the strike. At the end of the year, Teets was looking for more terminals to close and was even considering franchising routes to other operators.

The final stage in decision making is thus very much like the first. If the results do not match the goal, the manager must reformulate the problem and begin the process anew.

TABLE 5.2

What a College Basketball Coach Manages

A big-time college basketball coach has to be an excellent manager. This table lists some of the resources that must be coordinated.

Human Resources	Information Resources	Physical Resources	Financial Resources
Players	Game plans	Players'	Budget from
Assistant	Scouting	equipment	college
coaches	reports	Training	
Equipment	Recruiting	equipment	
managers	reports	Fieldhouse	
Trainers	Player conditioning	facilities	
Clerical	reports	Offices	
staff			

FIGURE 5-5

Managerial Functions

A manager often carries out aspects of several functions at one time.

MANAGEMENT FUNCTIONS

As we have seen, management is the coordinating of resources to accomplish a goal or objective. Reaching the goal requires the manager to make decisions in order to plan, organize, staff, direct, and control. A manager often carries out aspects of several functions at one time. Still, for discussion purposes, we will separate these functions into the sequence pictured in Figure 5.5. As you look at the various management functions, keep in mind that a manager must be adept at all of them. Unlike, say, a basketball coach, who can always substitute a player, organizations rarely have the luxury of being able to shift managers to deal with particular situations. A manager must therefore be versatile.

Planning

The First Management Function

The process of determining the objectives of an organization, whether it is a large corporation, an individual department, or a small sole proprietorship, and deciding how to achieve them constitutes **planning**. As the Greyhound example has shown, the first step in planning is often the setting of a goal. Then managers map out how to reach it.

Interpersonal roles. Jim Schmitz, president of First Wisconsin — Waunakee, often starts his day at the local coffee shop where he talks to customers and townspeople on an informal basis. Although his bank is owned by a $5 billion bank holding company offering services in Europe, Asia, and South America as well as in the United States, an important part of his job involves communicating with people outside his organization.

For example, in the early 1980s the management of General Motors determined that in order to compete with Japanese automakers on price, GM had to reinvent the automobile-manufacturing process. Computers, robotics, and a new working relationship with the United Auto Workers were the key elements in this process. Planning for what is now GM's Saturn Corporation subsidiary began in 1984. By 1989, when the first car is scheduled to roll off new assembly lines, managers will have coordinated a wide range of functions including: designing and manufacturing robots, programing the computer systems, designing the car, constructing the new plants and assembly lines, arranging for delivery of parts, devising a marketing strategy, organizing a dealer network, and countless other tasks.

The Types of Planning   Planning takes a number of forms and occurs on several management levels. The type of planning that resulted in the birth of the Saturn project is called **strategic planning**, the determination of where an organization wants to go in the long run and how it plans to get there. Another type of planning, which will go into designing the new computer software, for instance, is called **tactical planning**, the coordination of activities designed to carry out the goals established by strategic planning. Finally, the type of planning used to assure sufficient staffing for the assembly line is called **operational planning**, the scheduling of an organization's day-to-day needs and designing how to meet them. In most large organizations, top management engages in strategic planning, middle management focuses on tactical planning, and supervisory personnel concentrate on operational planning.

The Planning Process   As Figure 5.6 reveals, planning is a multistep process. These stages, like the management functions, are rarely visible in isolation since most managers have several projects going at any given time. Some organizations do have a formal planning period, though, in which managers develop plans for the following year.

Step 1: Analyze the Environment   The first phase of planning is an **environmental analysis**, a study of conditions that might affect an organization. The political, legal, regulatory, technological, economic, and societal environment directly affect business. All firms, of whatever nature, should engage in environmental analysis on an ongoing basis. A large corporation might analyze foreign competition not only for threats to its existing product lines but also for oppor-

FIGURE 5.6

The Planning Process

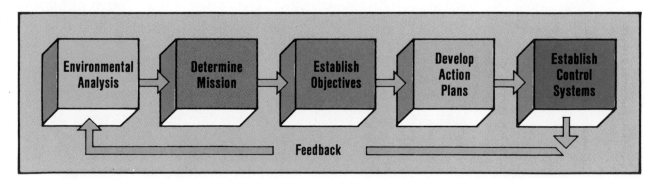

Environmental Analysis → Determine Mission → Establish Objectives → Develop Action Plans → Establish Control Systems

Feedback

Why Aren't Women Running Corporations?

Today about 25 percent of all managers are women. Yet women in all jobs still make less than two-thirds of what their full-time male counterparts make, a figure that hasn't changed much in 20 years. Only one woman, Katharine Graham of the Washington Post Company, heads a *Fortune* 500 company. Even more discouraging to women in business is that there are no women with reasonable expectations of soon rising to the top. Why are women so often stalled in their climb up the management ladder?

For reasons that researchers can't agree on, women tend to end up in lower-paying specialties, even women doctors. Some claim that women too often take safe, staff jobs rather than high-risk jobs that are more likely to result in more rapid promotions.

Almost all analysts agree that sex discrimination is still responsible for some of the problems women face in business, although these analysts differ sharply as to how much blame to place on this factor. While much of the overt discrimination of past years has disappeared, corporate managers still value traditionally male lifestyles, personality traits, and attitudes. As it is defined by many corporations, business is a male occupation.

Such attitudes are very hard to change because they are so deeply ingrained and because they can be held even by people who are very conscientious about being non-sexist. Most male managers have learned not to assume that a woman sitting at an office desk is a secretary, not to call women "girls," and not to expect some kind of sexual gratification from the new woman in the office. But when asked to choose someone for promotion, those managers most often look for people with traits very similar to their own — traits they share, generally, with other men.

This kind of perpetuation of certain traits and types is very hard to change, in part because it is usually done unconsciously, in part because of the double standard with which most people view women and men. Take, for instance, a particular character trait that most current executives feel is necessary for someone in an upper management position — aggressiveness. In our society,

men have traditionally been trained to be more aggressive than women, and the trait is valued highly.

Most people don't stop to ask themselves about the basis for such a deeply ingrained value system. We don't ask, for instance, whether an executive might be better off with less aggressiveness and with more traits traditionally considered female — the ability to listen well, to achieve compromise, to be sensitive to others' needs, or to make good intuitive judgments, for instance. Women who exhibit aggressiveness are often seen as "strident" or "pushy."

Help from above is important for anyone trying to climb the corporate ladder, and people tend to help those who are similar to themselves. Men often find it easier to criticize — and therefore improve — the performance of their male subordinates, while criticism of a female subordinate may go unsaid but be remembered at promotion time. A "mentor" can open many doors for a rising executive, but many men find it hard to play this kind of professional role with women managers.

Such subtle forms of discrimination tend to persist in part because a company often feels it has done its job once it has hired a woman and met legal requirements such as those in the Equal Employment Opportunity Act of 1972. Many companies don't realize that hiring a person is only the first step in treating that person fairly.

The problem of sex discrimination won't, it seems, go away on its own. As women's roles in the work force come to be more accepted in the eighties, gender issues create fewer confrontations and more cooperation between the sexes. But people who enter the work force thinking that all sexual inequalities have vanished often suffer a painful awakening.

Sources: "Why Do Women Earn Less Than Men?" *Changing Times*, Vol. 38, No. 4, April 1984, 10. Susan Fraker, "Why Women Aren't Getting to the Top," *Fortune*, Vol. 109, No. 8, April 16, 1984, 40. Lori B. Andrews, "The Lady Is a Boss," *Parents*, Vol. 59, No. 4, April 1984, 32. Melody Graulich, ed., *Closing the Revolving Door: The Retention of Women in Higher Education*, University of New Hampshire, Durham, NH, 1982.

Planning — a primary management function. *Philip E. Lippincott, chairman and chief executive officer of Scott Paper, assumes an active role in planning. Strategic planning, a responsibility of top management, allows an organization to set its direction and determine the paths it will follow to reach its goals. Scott's executives plan to maximize shareholder returns, develop human resources to their full potential, and deliver better value to customers.*

tunities to expand, either by beating the foreign firms to the punch or by providing more highly customized products or services to the domestic market.

Small businesses must monitor the environment even more closely than large ones, because they generally lack the large business's resources to survive a mistake. Small businesses should be on the lookout for new businesses moving into their locales, either as competitors or as new customers. If apartments for the elderly or new college facilities are built in a town, the mix of potential customers may change. If zoning regulations are up for review, businesses will want to make their views known to voters and politicians. If the state government is offering tax breaks to businesses that move into areas with high unemployment, a firm must know about the program in order to take advantage of it.

Step 2: Prepare a Mission Statement   In planning's second phase, managers define the organization's mission in a statement of the reason the organization exists. Many organizations have mission statements dating back to their founding. Over time, however, their missions probably change. For example, a small city's general hospital founded in the 1920s may have as its mission the providing of comprehensive health care to those in its community. Eventually, though, with greater levels of state regulation, increasing specialization, and the soaring costs of medical technology and malpractice insurance, that mission may no longer be possible.

Step 3: Set Objectives   After determining the organization's mission, managers next set its objectives or goals. Establishing objectives may be the most important phase of the planning process. Objectives serve as reference points for every decision maker and guide the organization's routine activities.

1. Loyalty is a two-way street.
2. The team always comes first.
3. Make plans.
4. The world changes — so should you.
5. Trust the people who work for you.
6. Keep it simple.

Source: Charles Stein, "The Lessons of Chairman Red," Reprinted courtesy of *The Boston Globe*, Dec. 17, 1985, pp. 29, 42.

To be meaningful, objectives must meet three requirements. An objective must first be measurable. It has to include something that can be evaluated. For example, a goal for a new commuter airline of a 17 percent market share within its first year of operation contains the measurable value of 17 percent. Second, an objective must have a time dimension, a date in the future by which the organization will either meet the objective or take its next measurement. In the airline example, the time dimension is one year. Finally, an objective must be extremely specific. Achieving a stated percentage of the market within a fixed period satisfies this requirement.

Step 4: Develop an Action Plan   The fourth step in planning is to develop action plans to accomplish the objectives. Plan development begins with the ranking of projects according to how they contribute to accomplishing one or more of the objectives. Those that rank highest should receive a greater portion of the resources to be allocated than those ranking lower. For example, when the Sperry Corporation decided to try to regain its position as a leader in computers, it allocated $2 billion to a five-year computer research program.[5] Action plans can result in shedding or altering the character of resources. An action plan could call for a significant reduction in a company's workforce or for the sale of an entire operating division. In developing plans, managers will use basically the same decision-making process previously outlined.

Step 5: Establish Control Systems   The final step in planning is to establish control systems that enable managers to measure what actually happened as opposed to what they planned. Establishing control systems is actually the fifth major management function (see Figure 5.5), to be discussed in detail below. For now, note that one of the main managerial functions, control, is an integral step in accomplishing another function, planning.

Organizing

The Second Management Function

Assigning to the appropriate position the tasks required to achieve the organization's objectives, along with the authority and responsibility for accomplishing those tasks, is the process of organizing. The broad tasks might be to staff the organization (the subject of Chapter 8), manufacture the product, sell it, account for the money paid for the product, and invest the proceeds. Clearly, management

New roles for women. As women make their way up the management hierarchy, they are taking on important interpersonal roles. They function as figureheads, as leaders, and as spokespersons. Sophia Collier, a 29-year-old founder of Soho Natural Soda, represents her company to the public. To advertisers like Fortune, *she represents an important class of new customers — women entrepreneurs and executives.*

will have to divide each of these broad tasks into many smaller jobs. The assigning of authority and responsibility for tasks often follows an organizational chart, such as the much-simplified example in Figure 5.2. We will take a close look at organizing in the next chapter.

Staffing

The Third Management Function

The process of locating, selecting, and assigning people to the tasks designed to achieve an organization's objectives is called **staffing**. Staffing is closely related to organizing. Managers must match the tasks that are assigned to certain positions with the right persons for the slots. Organizations often create new positions in order to accomplish new objectives. If no one already in the organization can do the task assigned to the position, management must hire and train a new employee. (Staffing and organizing are discussed in Chapters 6 and 8.)

Directing

The process of guiding, leading, persuading, influencing, and motivating people to accomplish an organization's objectives is known as **directing**. Organizations exist because people working together can accomplish more than they can as individuals working alone. Managers thus exist to direct the organization's activities toward its goals. Directing is a highly complex process not made any simpler by the fact that everyone who has a subordinate must do it, from the president of the United States to the manager of a convenience store. As we will see in Chapter 7, one technique will not serve all situations.

Controlling

The final management function is **controlling**, the process of measuring an organization's performance against its plans to determine whether its operations conform to its expectations. Control is a four-step process:

1. Establish measurable performance standards.
2. Measure actual performance.
3. Compare actual performance to performance standards.
4. Take corrective action, if necessary.

It is important to note that control includes not only the measures that managers may take to prevent breakdowns but also those they take to remedy breakdowns.

Step 1: Establish Measurable Performance Standards

The first step toward management control is to establish measurable performance standards to help an organization achieve the objectives set in the planning process. For example, a restaurant manager today may use a computer to track what sells and what does not. Over time, he or she can then set standards for waiters as to what they ought to sell in one shift. Standards do not always deal only with the bottom line, however. Quite often, for instance, restaurants establish employee dress codes, rules on cleanliness, and how servers and cashiers should deal with the public.

Step 2: Measure Actual Performance

Measuring actual performance may or may not be easy. In the case of the computerized restaurant, the manager can follow the night's orders almost as they are entered, a technique pioneered by McDonald's. Measuring performance can also be expensive and time consuming, though. A specialty metals company manufacturing parts for space vehicles will find the government's specifications to be quite precise. Determining whether a given part meets the specifications for it requires complex laboratory analysis and expensive, objective testing. In contrast, a manager's assessment of a restaurant's employees' dress, cleanliness, and courtesy can be quite subjective.

Step 3: Compare Actual Performance to Performance Standards

Once the actual performance has been measured, a manager should have little difficulty comparing it to the established standards. Of course, this is the critical step, because it determines whether corrective action is

Managing High-Tech's Apple

Even people who can't sink their teeth into bytes or bits often have a taste for the fortunes of Apple. Apple Computer, Inc., has always been the other guy in the computer business, the underdog, the non-conformist in a world that seems to take orders from IBM. But now the company that has been known for its quirky leaders and innovative products is being run more like a traditional "tight ship." The management style that wins out at Apple should provide a good indication of the way many other high-tech companies will be run for some time to come.

The founding of Apple, only a decade ago, has already taken on legendary status in the minds of many who have been affected by the computer revolution. At a time when computers took up whole rooms and the average household was as likely to have an aardvark as a computer, Apple's two founders, Steve Jobs and Steve Wozniak, created the personal computer in a garage. These men became models for a generation of computer hackers. Jobs was a college dropout who liked to experiment with electronics, mystical religions, and fruit diets. Young computer buffs cheered when he walked into university computer departments wearing blue jeans to receive the praise of older, suited professors. Wozniak, who was the true engineer while Jobs was the entrepreneur, earned fewer headlines, though he did put on a big rock concert, the Us Festival, in 1982.

The company was enormously successful in the early years of the computer era, and though IBM soon caught up and overtook Apple in personal computer market share, Apple was still the exciting company, the maverick. Jobs gradually took over greater control, and the company's continued brilliance was again displayed in the Macintosh. Apple has only sold a quarter as many Macintoshes as they had hoped to by this time, but it's a well-respected machine, the personal computer of choice for many people who work on mainframes.

By 1983, with computer sales leveling off, Steve Jobs began to look for a new president for Apple, someone who could help position Apple in the increasingly competitive market. Perhaps Jobs recognized his own weaknesses as a businessman and saw that to survive, a computer company would have to keep cranking out brilliant ideas *and* be well managed. As it turned out, by admitting that Apple needed a new style of leadership, Jobs was foretelling his own split from Apple.

The man Jobs actively recruited to run Apple was John Sculley, a very successful Pepsi executive who gave up the chance to become chairman of the soft drink giant to try to remake Apple. Apple under Sculley weathered a period that was difficult for the entire industry. Sculley closed three plants and laid off 20 percent of Apple's work force. He put a lot of the company's energy into transforming the Macintosh into a more attractive machine for large businesses. Drawing on his Pepsi experience, he established links with other computer companies and distributors to help get Apples into big corporations. And he adapted a market forecasting system from the soft-drink industry to calculate more exactly the demand for Apple's products and cut inventory problems.

The results of Sculley's reign have been mixed. Apple's share of the worldwide market dropped from almost 19 percent in 1983 to less than 11 percent in 1985. Sales have yet to take off. But Sculley's more disciplined company needs fewer sales to earn a profit. The operations breakeven point has dropped from $400 million to $325 million, and profits have been going up.

Most observers would agree that Apple is better run than it used to be. But the company can't stay profitable forever if its market share keeps dropping. The central question for Apple-watchers now is, can the company be made more successful primarily through better marketing and management techniques, or will it flounder without the periodic doses of brilliance that Jobs provided?

Sources: Janet Guyon and Erik Larson, "New Apple Chief Expected to Bring Marketing Expertise Gained at Pepsi," *The Wall Street Journal*, April 11, 1983, Sec. 2, 29. "Conflict, Conquest Mark Newsmakers" and "What Was Your First Job?" *Advertising Age*, Vol. 55, No. 1, January 2, 1984, 18. "Apple Reaches out for a Marketing Pro" and "Why Sculley Gave up the Pepsi Challenge," *Business Week*, No. 2787, April 25, 1983, 27.

required. Suppose that a restaurant manager's figures indicate that one waiter sells significantly fewer desserts than the restaurant's standard. The manager may then decide whether

☐ The waiter needs instruction on how to sell more desserts
☐ The dessert cart needs a more prominent location to attract customer attention
☐ The waiter is incompetent and should be replaced

Step 4: Take Corrective Action, if Necessary　Taking corrective action is the final control step. The comparison tools may tell the manager what needs corrective action, but he or she must have the will, resources, skills, and knowledge to do what is required. Sometimes a manager does not have what is required to correct a situation. Take, for instance, Dave DeBusschere, former general manager of the New York Knicks. This National Basketball Association Hall of Famer and successful league president was fired when his team failed to become a serious play-off contender. The team's shortcomings were obvious, but DeBusschere could do nothing about them, because the NBA's salary cap and his own conflict with his employers ruled out any personnel changes.

CONTEMPORARY TRENDS IN MANAGEMENT

"The choice for the presidency
was between Harry Melville and
myself. He was the best man
for the job, but I was the
best person."

In recent years, the books topping the business best-seller lists have dealt with successful management techniques. One reason is that no two groups of people are alike, and therefore no one set of management principles works all the time everywhere. A company's management techniques should respond to its changing environment. The penalty for failing to adjust to, say, changes in the nature of the work force may mean disaster in the work place. Many managers therefore constantly study techniques that have worked elsewhere, looking for effective ways of managing their human, informational, physical, and financial resources. Today, in management theory two concepts — both framed within the last fifteen years — dominate: corporate cultures and excellence.

Corporate Cultures

"A system of informal rules that spells out how people are to behave most of the time" describes the new concept of a **corporate culture**.[6] The two management consultants who developed this concept, Terrence E. Deal and Allen A. Kennedy, believe that the quality and strength of a corporation's culture determines its success or failure.

　A corporate culture has four essential elements: values, heroes, rites and rituals, and a cultural network. Values are the organization's basic beliefs that define the elements of success for it and its people. Heroes are the corporation's high achievers who personify its values and thereby set an example for others in the organization. Rites and rituals are the routine behavior patterns in the organization's daily life that are necessary for its success. For example, companies like Genentech and Advanced Micro Devices regularly schedule parties to develop a sense of community among employees who often operate alone or in small groups during the week.[7] Often, corporations make ceremonies out of their rites and rituals. Finally, the cultural network consists of informal communication channels within the organization that carry its values to everyone who works for the organization.

Deal and Kennedy suggest that having a strong corporate culture is the key to humanizing the work place. By describing what is expected of employees, strong cultures make people feel better about their work and give them a sense of belonging. As Deal and Kennedy point out, at the Xerox Corporation, the culture dictates hard work at a very fast pace. Managers there make decisions and take action quickly. In contrast, at General Electric, people work hard, too, but decisions and action come at a more thoughtful pace. Quite probably, a successful GE employee would find Xerox's culture stressful and frustrating. Speed and excitement are critical elements of Xerox's culture, however, as they are of many high-tech and biotech companies. The lesson is that a firm must develop its own unique culture — it cannot buy one off the shelf.

The Importance of Corporate Culture

For three reasons, as Deal and Kennedy see it, having a strong corporate culture will become increasingly important. First, the environment in which businesses operate is becoming increasingly complex. Second, the rate of technological, social, and environmental change is accelerating. Third, competition, which corporations must now define in global terms, is intensifying. Deal and Kennedy argue that these forces are leading to what they call atomized corporations: companies that consist of smaller, task-oriented organizations subject to more local control but connected to the parent organization by computerized links and by culture. They contend that success in this new world depends on the cultural ties that will come to bind small units together. Those ties require the evolution of values, heroes, rites and rituals, and a cultural network within the corporation.

Excellence

In the number-one best seller, *In Search of Excellence*, Thomas J. Peters and Robert H. Waterman, Jr., tried to identify the characteristics of the best-run corporations. Their eight principles of management excellence are listed in Table 5.4 on the following page.

The importance of the excellence concept lies in its identification of fundamental truths about management that fancier theories usually overlook. Peters and Waterman have not introduced anything new except the packaging. Take their first point, "a bias for action," for example. Peters and Waterman say that excellent managers tend to do *something* rather than to analyze a problem forever. Such managers often engage in "management by walking around" (MBWA). They keep themselves informed of what is happening and in touch with the people in the work place by walking around.

The Keys to Management Excellence

Like Kennedy and Deal, Peters and Waterman emphasize the human dimensions of management. Technological innovation has hidden the continued (and perhaps increased) importance of the human element in contemporary corporations. Peters and Waterman point out that giants like IBM, 3M, and Procter & Gamble have met this challenge. Despite their complexity, these large corporations still demand a simple organizational form and a lean staff. They focus on their people and customers and "stick to their knitting," the lines and products they know best. The bottom line seems clear: managers striving for excellence should make sure that they do the simple things well.

TABLE 5.4

The Eight Basics of Management Excellence

1. A bias for action
2. Closeness to the customer
3. Autonomy and entrepreneurship
4. Productivity through people
5. A hands-on, value-driven approach
6. A "stick to the knitting" view of the business
7. A simple organizational form and a lean staff
8. Simultaneous loose–tight management properties

Source: Adaptation of eight basic attributes from *In Search of Excellence: Lessons from America's Best Run Companies* by Thomas J. Peters and Robert H. Waterman, Jr. Copyright © 1982 Thomas J. Peters and Robert H. Waterman, Jr. Reprinted by permission of Harper & Roe, Publishers, Inc.

MANAGEMENT: A PERSPECTIVE

W. L. Gore & Associates, Inc., the maker of Gore-tex fibers for camping and outdoor wear, escaped the notice of Deal, Kennedy, Peters, and Waterman, although it has an extraordinary organizational structure. Gore has one of the strongest contemporary corporate cultures, and its commitment to management excellence may be unmatched.

Gore's founder and guiding presence was William L. Gore. As he explained to the authors of *The 100 Best Companies to Work for in America*, the company's organization has several key characteristics:

☐ No fixed or assigned authority
☐ Natural leadership defined by followership
☐ Person-to-person communication
☐ Sponsors, not bosses
☐ Objectives set by those who "must make them happen"
☐ Tasks and functions organized through commitments

Directing the people who make up an organization.

The organization of Gore & Associates centers on voluntary commitments rather than on a command structure. Everyone who works at Gore is called an associate. Each associate has a sponsor, who acts as his or her advocate and advisor. Associates who develop interests in other areas of Gore's operations are encouraged to pursue them. Decision making is by consensus. Only a company with an extremely strong corporate culture and a highly developed cultural network could succeed with this lack of structure.

Bill Gore came to one of his most important management inspirations during a routine walk around his rapidly growing plant. He suddenly realized that he did not know everyone's name — and if he did not, others would not either. Gore reasoned that when people become a crowd rather than individuals known to all their fellow workers, they become significantly less cooperative. As a result of this insight, since 1967, when Gore opened its second plant (there are now twenty), none has been allowed to grow beyond two hundred persons, despite the significant cost of maintaining so many facilities.

Bill Gore and John Teets probably have in common only three things: a willingness to work hard wherever and whenever required, the ability and willingness to lead, and the drive for success. Poles apart though they may be in management philosophy, Gore and Teets typify the excitement and creativity of business.

When someone suggested recently that Gore's determined drive for profits seemed incompatible with his more rarified ideas about human relationships, Gore said: "That's because there's something wrong with your education, sir. Actually making money is a creative activity. It means people are applauding you for making a good contribution. In fact, it gives us the freedom to be what we are."[8]

Chapter Highlights

1. Describe the management process and who and what it involves.

Management is the process of coordinating human, informational, physical, and financial resources to accomplish organizational goals. Managers are the people who coordinate the organization's employees and outside vendors and suppliers; the knowledge and data necessary to carry on the business; the organization's tangible plant, property, and equipment; and its financial resources so that the organization can achieve its objectives.

2. Explain what a management hierarchy represents and relate it to the three types of management skills.

The management hierarchy is a classification of the positions within an organization in terms of their rank or authority. Often depicted as a pyramid, the management hierarchy shows the position with the greatest rank and authority at the top and the various levels of positions ranked below it. A good manager must have human skills, technical skills, and conceptual skills. Top management must have excellent conceptual and human skills, with less need for strong technical skills. Middle managers need a good balance of all three types of skills. First-line managers need strong technical and human skills, with less need for conceptual skills.

3. Show how Henry Mintzberg's ten managerial roles can be divided into three main categories.

Mintzberg identified ten managerial roles, which can be categorized as interpersonal, informational, and decisional roles. Interpersonal roles include serving as figurehead, leader, and liaison. Informational roles consist of disseminator, monitor, and spokesperson. Decisional roles are identified as being those of the entrepreneur, problem solver, resource allocator, and negotiator.

4. Describe the five steps in the managerial decision-making process.

The managerial decision-making process has five steps: define the problem; identify alternatives; evaluate alternatives; select an alternative and implement the decision, and follow up on the decision to see if performance meets expectations. If the problem has not been solved, it must be redefined and the process begun again.

5. Identify and define the five management functions.

The five management functions are planning, organizing, staffing, directing, and controlling. Planning is the process of determining an organization's objectives. Organizing is the process of assigning to the appropriate position the tasks required to achieve an organization's objectives, along with the authority and responsibility for accomplishing those tasks. Staffing is the process of locating, selecting, and assigning people to the tasks designed to achieve the organization's objectives. Directing is the process of guiding, leading, persuading, influencing, and motivating people to accomplish the organization's objectives. Controlling is the process of measuring an organization's performance against its plans to make certain that actual operations conform to plans.

6. Outline the five-step planning process.

Planning is a process that begins with environmental analysis and ends with the establishment of a control system. First, all organizations must analyze the environment, that is, study the conditions in the marketplace and the world that might affect them. In the second step, management prepares a mission statement. This statement sets forth the organization's fundamental philosophy and the reason for its existence. Step three, probably the most important phase of the planning process, involves setting objectives — which must be measurable, specify a time frame, and be extremely specific. Fourth, once the objectives are set, managers must develop action plans to accomplish the objectives. The fifth step is to establish control systems. Feedback from the control system allows management to compare planned performance and actual performance.

7. Describe the four steps in the management-control process.

The management-control process begins with establishing measurable performance standards to help the organization achieve the objectives set in the planning process. The second step is to measure actual performance, which may be relatively easy or expensive and time consuming. In the third step, management compares actual performance to the performance standards established. The final step is to take any corrective action that may be called for.

8. Define the term *corporate culture* and list the characteristics of one.

A corporate culture is a system of informal rules that spells out how people are to behave most of the time. A corporate culture has four essential elements: values, heroes, rites and rituals, and a cultural network. Values are the organization's basic beliefs that define the elements of success for it and its people. Heroes are the corporation's high achievers who personify its values and thereby set an example for others in the organization. Rites and rituals are the routine behavior patterns in the organization's daily life that are necessary for its success. The cultural network consists of informal communication channels within the organization that carry its values to everyone who works for it.

9. Identify the key concepts of the management excellence movement.

The eight key concepts of the management excellence movement are:

1. A bias for action
2. Closeness to the customer
3. Autonomy and entrepreneurship
4. Productivity through people
5. A hands-on, value-driven approach
6. A "stick to the knitting" view of the business
7. A simple organizational form and a lean staff
8. Simultaneous loose–tight management properties

Key Terms

Conceptual skills
Controlling
Corporate culture
Decision
Directing

Environmental analysis
Goal
Human skills
Interpersonal role
Leadership

Management
Manager
Operational planning
Organizing
Planning

Staffing
Strategic planning
Tactical planning
Technical skills

Review Questions

1. What is management? Do managers of small organizations have anything in common with managers of large ones?
2. Describe the three types of skills needed by a good manager. Which of these skills are most important at the top of the management hierarchy?
3. Contrast and compare management informational roles and decisional roles.
4. Which of the five steps in the typical managerial decision-making process do you think is the most and least important? Why?
5. Identify and briefly explain the five management

functions. Why is it necessary for a manager to be adept at all of them?

6. Describe the process of staffing and explain why it is usually considered one of the primary management functions.

7. Explain the four steps involved in the control function.

8. How are the steps in the decision-making process similar to the managerial functions?

9. Briefly describe the term *corporate culture*. What are the four essential elements of culture in an organizational setting?

10. What are the eight major goals of management excellence?

Application Exercises

1. Several weeks ago you applied for the position of pool manager at a local community center. After two interviews, you were given the position. This three-month summer appointment will involve hiring and training of all personnel, updating pool regulations, contacting vendors who will supply food and soft drinks for the snack bar, developing work schedules, ordering pool supplies, and making other preparations for opening day. Throughout the summer you will manage day-to-day pool operations with the help of an assistant manager. You will maintain all payroll records.

   Review the five functions of management, then rate your potential for success in each area. In which of these areas will you be most effective? Least effective?

2. You are currently employed as a department manager at a department store. The store manager has sent you a memorandum regarding the need for a training program for new management trainees. In the final paragraph he says:

   Prior to development of this new program, I would like to receive your suggestions regarding content. What major topics should we emphasize?

   Prepare a memo outlining your suggestions. What should new trainees be able to do upon completion of this training program?

Cases

5.1 The New GM & H. Ross Perot

In 1980, General Motors Corporation (GM) lost $760 million — its first loss since 1921. Roger Smith, the firm's new board chairman, set out to determine why the firm was not competing effectively. What he found was that GM had become a bureaucratic dinosaur, complacent and mediocre. Smith then began a series of changes designed to move GM solidly into the twenty-first century.

Smith's first order of business was to regroup seven auto divisions and GM's Canadian subsidiary into two new divisions, each with its own management, engineering, production, and marketing personnel. Within each division, management has almost complete control of its own operations. Smith's objective was to end duplication, make management more accountable, and push decision-making down to lower management levels.

Smith also created the Saturn Corporation, an almost completely autonomous subsidiary, for the purpose of engineering and producing a new small car, using the latest managerial and technical innovation. Saturn officials expect to have a product available for the 1990 model year.

In 1984, GM acquired Electronic Data Systems (EDS), a very profitable computer software and systems service company. In purchasing EDS, GM acquired the expertise to integrate the auto firm's 200 telecommunications systems and data centers. But GM also "acquired" H. Ross Perot, who was EDS's founder and major stockholder, and is considered to be an excellent manager.

When GM's Roger Smith first contacted EDS's H. Ross Perot about a merger, Perot agreed to talk only because he thought he might pick up some business from GM. But after their talk, Perot decided a merger would be "fun." In the deal, GM got the second largest computer service organization. Perot retained managerial control of EDS and became GM,s largest shareholder. He also became its peskiest board member. Perot says he has always been a managerial irritant — the grain of sand that irritates the oyster enough to make the pearl.

Perot got into computers as an IBM salesman and soon became one of the best. Believing that U.S. firms knew they needed computers but not how to use them, Perot started EDS in 1962. His firm would show them how and, if necessary, do it for them. EDS grew quickly, through state and federal contracts, and its founder became a wealthy man.

Perot's managerial style seems to be both conservative and flamboyant. EDS has rigid dress and behavior codes that, for example, forbid alcohol at lunch and the wearing of tasseled shoes. Yet in 1979, Perot sent a team of executives, led by a former commando, to rescue two employees who were imprisoned in Tehran. (The book *On Wings of Eagles* was based on that mission.) Nowadays, he occasionally dons khaki pants, sport shirt, and baseball cap and wanders into a GM dealership, to see how customers are treated. He wants every customer to get the treatment he gets after he's recognized.

In 1985, one year after it acquired Perot's EDS, GM purchased Hughes Aircraft, which provided both technological know-how and diversification. Both EDS and Hughes are, like Saturn, highly autonomous.

Roger Smith is obviously planning for the long term. Even after spending almost $8 billion for EDS and Hughes, GM still has some $6 billion in cash to finance its transition from bureaucratic dinosaur to competitive tiger.

Questions

1. How has Smith made use of his firm's organizational resources in building the "new GM"?
2. How might the changes affect decision-making among GM's managers?
3. How important is managerial style — the way a person goes about performing the management functions? Explain.
4. Does Perot seem to believe in management excellence? How can you tell?

For more information see *The New York Times*, April 27, 1986, pp. F1, F8; *Business Week*, April 7, 1986, pp. 84–85; *The Economist*, October 12, 1985, pp. 35–38; and *Business Week*, June 11, 1984, pp. 43–44.

5.2 Rich Melman Eats at Ed's

On any given day, you might walk into Ed Debevic's Short Orders Deluxe, a dream diner on the corner of N. Wells and Ontario Streets in the heart of Chicago, and find Rich Melman, whose Lettuce Entertain You Enterprises Inc.,

a $40 million dollar Chicago-based restaurant holding company is one of the prime investors in Ed's. He'll be sitting in one of the naugahyde-covered booths, tasting the new atomic burger to make sure the subtle blend of jalapeno peppers and ground beef pleases his palate. On some visits he'll sit there, elbows on the formica table, and sample four or five different dishes. Rich Melman wants to keep tabs on his restaurant's products. He makes sure that Ed's delivers.

Ed's is the creation of Melman, his Lettuce Entertain You Enterprises, and Melman's friend Lee Cohn who runs Big Four, a restaurant business in Phoenix, Arizona. Collins Foods International, a publicly held company, which is also a major franchisor of Sizzler Steak Houses and Kentucky Fried Chicken restaurants, went in as a partner with Melman and Cohn and put up a good deal of the start-up money. The first Ed's opened in Phoenix in August 1984. The Chicago Ed's opened in November 1984. After meeting with astounding success, Ed's have opened in suburban Chicago and the Los Angeles area.

The concept of Ed's is simple. It's a diner replete with vintage rock-and-roll juke box, surly waitresses, an 11-foot Coke bottle in the valet parking lot beckoning passersby to "Eat at Ed's," and a wide assortment of classic diner fare ranging from meatloaf specials to jello cube garnishes on the chicken salad plate. The place oozes diner chic with its bowling machine, signs advising that "the more you tip, the nicer we are," and menu advisory: "If you're not served in 5 minutes, you'll get served in 8 or 9. Maybe 12 minutes. Relax."

Ed Debevic doesn't exist. Melman, along with Cohn and others, created him, gave him a history, and opened a restaurant with his moniker. "We have a sense of Ed," Melman told a reporter for the *Chicago Sun-Times*. With his classic hands-on management style, Melman never loses sight of that sense.

Prior to his success with Ed's, Melman had already built a reputation as a gutsy, albeit successful restaurateur in the Chicago market with restaurants like Lawrence of Oregano, R. J. Grunts, and Fritz That's It! His success has led larger, publicly held companies to seek him out for his management consulting services. One of those clients, in fact, was Collins Foods, who had sought his advice in its effort to take its Gino's East pizza restaurant into a national market.

Melman learned the ropes of restaurant management from the ground up. He's worked in restaurant or grocery stores since he was 13. After 3 years of college, he quit and went to work for his father in his Northwest Side deli. Melman put in 12-hour days to absorb everything he could about restaurant management. He went to seminars during his time off and hounded restaurant pros with countless questions.

With operations know-how firmly intact, Melman set his imagination to work. In 1971, he and Jerry Orzoff got together $47,000 and opened R. J. Grunts, à 60s style restaurant featuring waitresses in jeans, and a health-food-oriented menu. It was one of the first of its kind in the Midwest and met with rousing success.

By 1976 he was ready for a bigger challenge — bringing new life to the Pump Room, a Chicago landmark night club that had been losing money. Melman put in $780,000, and proved he could turn a profit at a "serious" restaurant.

At Ed's, Melman encourages creativity in his staff, as long as it fits within the structured service program. They are free to create their own personalities, tailor their costumes with buttons and plastic corsages, introduce themselves as "Hi, I'm Norma Jean, your waitress machine" — anything. as long as they fit into the "Ed's concept."

Since the cooks work in an area that is smack dab in the center of public view, they are part of the whole Ed's show, causing one of Ed's general managers to boast that overall the staff is a lot happier than in normal restaurants because everybody's part of the show. There's no front of the house (dining area), back of the house (kitchen) split.

Melman manages to get productivity from his people. In spite of the growing size of Lettuce Entertain You, his employees know who he is as a result of his involvement in the operations. He also treats them well. In fact, when any Lettuce Entertain You employee gets married or divorced, Melman will pay for up to three therapy sessions.

Melman also realizes his strengths. He knows the restaurant business hands down. But when it comes to numbers he has seasoned accountants handling the reigns, keeping his rampant creativity from costing the company too much in startup costs.

"The best thing I do," Melman has said, "is talk to customers and listen to them." He does not think business is an exact science; rather he believes it's instinct. He looks around to find out what his customers want and how to give it to them.

Melman believes that nothing he does is technically that hard to do, but it's hard to do it all right. He pays a lot of attention to detail. "I get real neurotic and keep jumping from area to area until we improve," he says. "My greatest strength is putting together a good team and knowing what I need."

Questions

1. How does Melman play the interpersonal, informational, and decisional managerial roles? Does he appear to be better at some roles than others? How?
2. Has Melman effectively coordinated the human, informational, physical, and financial resources necessary to accomplish his organizational goals? Explain.
3. How has Melman used human, technical, and conceptual skills to make Ed Debevic's Short Orders Deluxe a successful business?
4. Has Melman successfully employed a "bias for action"? Has he "stuck to his knitting"? Has he kept close to the customer? Does he exhibit simultaneous "loose-tight management properties"? Does he get productivity through people?

For more information see *America's New Breed of Entrepreneurs* (Acropolis Books, 1986), Jeffrey L. Seglin; *Business Week*, February 11, 1985, pp. 73–76; *Restaurant Business*, July 20, 1985, p. 124; *Nation's Restaurant News*, October 8, 1984, p. 103; and *Redbook*, January 1986, pp. 69–73.

ORGANIZATION

6

Learning Objectives

After you have completed this chapter, you will be able to do the following:

- Describe the elements of an organization.
- Define *organizational structure* and explain how that concept relates to an organization chart.
- Identify the reasons that the division of labor is the key concept in modern organizations.
- Define *departmentalization* and describe the four basic departmentalization models.
- Relate the concepts of authority, responsibility, and delegation.
- Discuss the function of policies and procedures.
- Explain the span of management concept.
- Identify the different qualities of centralized and decentralized structures.
- Contrast line-and-staff organizations with matrix organizations.
- Explain how informal patterns of organization meet the needs of workers and management.

t is the summer of 1988. You are in Seoul, South Korea, sitting in a glass-enclosed press box above the floor of a gymnasium. Beneath you, men and women with brightly colored uniforms bearing initials like USA or CCCP compete on parallel bars, rings, and mats for Olympic gold medals. At the edges of the floor, anxious coaches and trainers yell encouragement to the competitors or vent frustration at judges' scores. The thousands of people in the new seats cheer and groan as the athletes succeed or fail. In the excitement of the competition, it might not strike you that you are looking at an illustration of the principles that govern all organizations, whether they are Olympic teams or for-profit corporations.

WHAT IS AN ORGANIZATION?

"An **organization** is two or more people working together to achieve a common goal."[1] This simple definition contains a number of important elements.

The Elements of an Organization

An organization is founded on people; it cannot exist without them. It has a purpose that directs the efforts of the people within the organization toward a goal, though the goals of the individuals in the organization may be quite different. The organization deliberately structures its members' activities by dividing tasks among them and developing a system to coordinate them. Finally, an organization has a definable boundary that makes it clear who is included and who is excluded from it.

What Constitutes an Organization

Now think back on the Olympic gymnastics competition. Olympic teams are organizations consisting of more than two people. There are athletes, coaches, trainers, and others associated with each team. The whole team — an organization — has a purpose: winning the team championship for its country. However, each athlete may have winning an individual gold medal as his or her main goal. The team divides the duties of its nonathlete personnel so that each trainer, for example, has specific tasks, which the head coach coordinates. Finally, there is an identifiable boundary between the team and the rest of the world. A person either is a member or is not. No matter how ardent a team booster may be, he or she is not a team member.

The Olympics are, of course, not just athletic events. They are multibillion-dollar enterprises and, as the U.S. Olympic Committee proved with the Los Angeles Games in 1984, it is possible to make millions on them. No small reason

TABLE 6.1

The Elements of an Organization

All organizations have these characteristics.

- ☐ People
- ☐ A purpose
- ☐ Division of tasks
- ☐ A system to coordinate tasks
- ☐ A definable boundary with those outside it

The elements of an organization. *The Harlem Globetrotters, like all other teams, demonstrates the essential elements of an organization. The team is made up of people, it has a goal, it directs members' activities, and it has a boundary. Lynette Woodard knows about that boundary first hand. She wanted to play for the Globetrotters for years, but until 1984 the team wouldn't consider letting a woman try out.*

for the committee's success, where many others had failed, was the high degree of organizational skill that Olympic coordinator Peter Ueberroth and his staff brought to the challenge.

Organizational Structure

For 2 million years, humans have broken tasks down into subtasks to be performed in a structured fashion to accomplish an ultimate goal. Today's entrepreneur may be a sole proprietor employing no one, but he or she has to structure activities in order to succeed. When an entrepreneur considers taking on another person, the time has arrived for creating an **organizational structure**, a pattern of task groupings, reporting relationships, and authority in an organization.

Suppose that a student schedules a part-time job mowing lawns and doing garden work around her classes and social life. Jayne does large projects on weekends and small ones on weekdays, before or after classes. Jayne has thus divided her work into parts to manage her time better. Let's assume that after she graduates, Jayne's Lawn & Garden Service has more work than she can handle. If she wants the business to grow, she will need a helper. Before deciding on what type of person to hire, Jayne begins to organize. She divides her work

Organizational Structure Defined

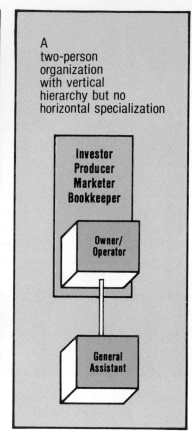
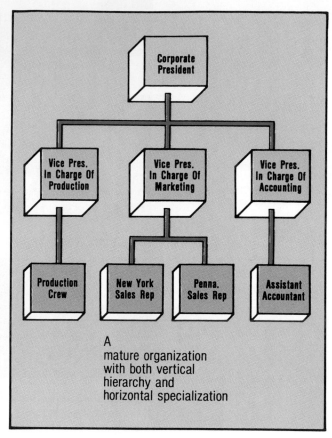

FIGURE 6.1

The Evolution of an Organization Chart

into four groups of tasks: mowing, edging and weeding, equipment maintenance, and clerical. While outlining these tasks, she considers whether and how to divide them with another person and how to relate to a new employee.

The Organization Chart

Usually, people describe a business in terms of an organization chart, a diagram of the positions and reporting relationships within an organization. As Figure 6.1 reveals, an organization chart consists of boxes linked by lines. Each box represents a particular job or function. In a simple organization chart like Part B of Figure 6.1, the two boxes represent very broadly defined positions. A general assistant essentially does whatever the owner-operator assigns.

How an Organization Chart Functions

As an organization matures, the boxes in the chart come to represent increasingly specific tasks. Part C of Figure 6.1 pictures a mature organization, in this case a corporation. The top box normally represents the president, the firm's top manager. Below the president comes a second level, made up of vice presidents, each of whom has specific responsibilities. Note that each vice president has responsibility for an operational area that the owner/operator held in parts A and B. Again, note how much more specific the vice presidents' tasks are, even on this hypothetical chart, than those of the general assistant in Part B. We will have more to say about the definition of tasks when we discuss the division of labor.

"Don't have me beeped. I'll have you beeped."

The lines that connect the boxes in an organization chart represent reporting relationships, the responsibility of a person to report information to his or her superior and vice versa. Lines connect the boxes representing all the positions that report to a manager to the box representing the manager. A series of levels of boxes connected by vertical lines comes to represent the **chain of command**, the organizational design to ensure the flow of communications toward authority, equals, and subordinates.[2]

An organization chart reveals an organization's skeletal structure much as an X-ray reveals human bone structure. A structure supports the organization's activities and identifies the connections among its parts. It is not the structure that does the work, however. Rather, the people represented by the positions on the chart give life to the organization through their work and enable it to meet its goals.

THE PRINCIPLES OF ORGANIZATIONAL DESIGN

The essence of structuring an organization lies in dividing labor into tasks to be performed and in regrouping them to achieve coordinated action. The need to balance these competing needs underlies the design of all organizations.

The Division of Labor

The concept of the division of labor is so much a part of our culture that it is difficult to realize that there is an alternative: everyone could try to do everything. Suppose that Jayne hires someone to do jobs on the east side of town for her Lawn & Garden Service while she works on the west. This arrangement would require two trucks, two complete sets of equipment, and two people with a full range of gardening skills. It is quite possible, though, that Jayne and her employee will have very different yet complementary skills. So an arrangement where everyone does everything would not seem to make the best use of Jayne's resources.

TABLE 6.2

The Division of Labor: The Pluses and Minuses

Advantages	Disadvantages
Efficient use of labor	Routine, repetitive jobs
Reduced training costs	Reduced job satisfaction
Increased standardization and output uniformity	Lower worker involvement and commitment
Increased expertise due to task repetition	Increased worker alienation

Source: Adapted from Ricky W. Griffin and Gregory Moorhead, *Organizational Behavior* (Boston: Houghton Mifflin Co., 1986), p. 550.

In fact, one of the major contributions of the Industrial Revolution was the realization that dividing work into smaller and smaller tasks increased productivity and profits dramatically. As early as 1776, Adam Smith noted how much more efficiently pins could be manufactured if managers assigned workers to individual parts of the process instead of having one worker produce a pin from start to finish.[3] The division of labor into particular tasks and specialization by workers were keys to the development of modern management. Part C of Figure 6.1 illustrates specialization as it functions in a modern corporation.

In manufacturing operations or the construction industry, where tools and equipment are a major expense, the division or specialization of labor minimizes the outlay needed for equipment by limiting the number of people working with it. Also, specialization makes those who work with tools and machinery more competent because of constant practice. An assembly line is the ultimate application of the division of labor.

One disadvantage to the division of labor is that finding temporary substitutes for ill or vacationing employees can sometimes be difficult. Far more importantly, workers can become bored with what they are doing. This tendency has led companies like Quad/Graphics, Inc., an innovative printing company, and North American Tool & Die to develop corporate work styles aimed at eliminating boredom.[4] In Chapter 7, we will look at some specific remedies for the problems of specialization.

Departmentalization

Departmentalization is the arranging of divided tasks into meaningful groups. As Figure 6.2 shows, there are four basic departmentalization methods:

☐ Departmentalization by function
☐ Departmentalization by product or service
☐ Departmentalization by customer
☐ Departmentalization by location

Departmentalization by function groups tasks according to the basic business functions with which they are associated. For example, a company might divide itself into marketing, finance, engineering, and production divisions. This arrangement allows people dealing with the same types of activities and issues to pool their skills and solve complex problems. General Electric, for instance, has a major-appliances department that produces its washers, dryers, and air conditioners. The instruction manuals that accompany GE's appliances include a customer-service 800 number for the large-appliance division. The other GE departments have their own customer-service mechanisms.

Departmentalization by product or service groups tasks according to the product or service with which they are involved. General Motors, for example, traditionally organized its auto-manufacturing divisions according to brand prestige, with Chevrolet in one division, Cadillac in another. In 1984, GM regrouped its divisions into a large-car division and one for small cars. Those working on a particular product or service coordinate their efforts. Their focus on output often leads to greater efficiency through a sense of teamwork.

Departmentalization by customer arranges employees according to the particular groups of customers they serve. This structure facilitates the development

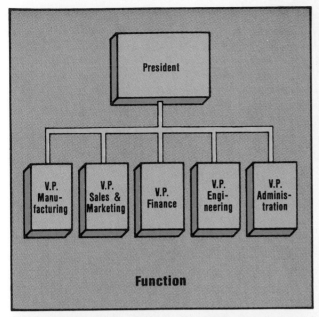

Function

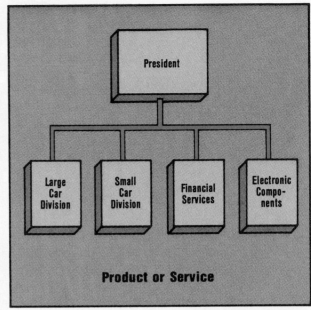

Product or Service

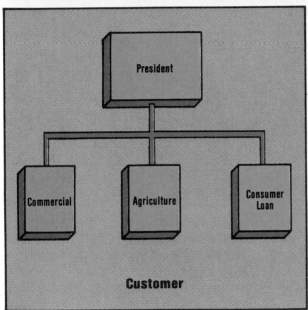

Customer

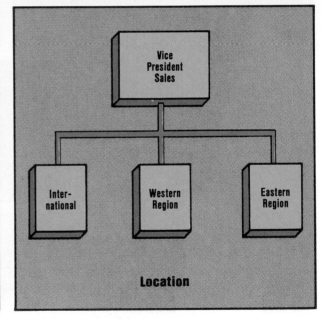

Location

FIGURE 6.2

Four Departmentalization Models

of extensive knowledge about customers and makes possible quick responses to their needs. Quite commonly, companies have industrial-products divisions and consumer-products divisions. Although the contents of a bottle of catsup or a jar of mustard on a grocery-store shelf may be identical in all respects to one marked "for restaurant use only," entirely different sales organizations are likely to sell the two types of containers. Full-service banks also organize, in part, by customer. One might have a commercial division to work with businesses, a consumer division to handle personal loans, and an agricultural section to deal with farm loans.

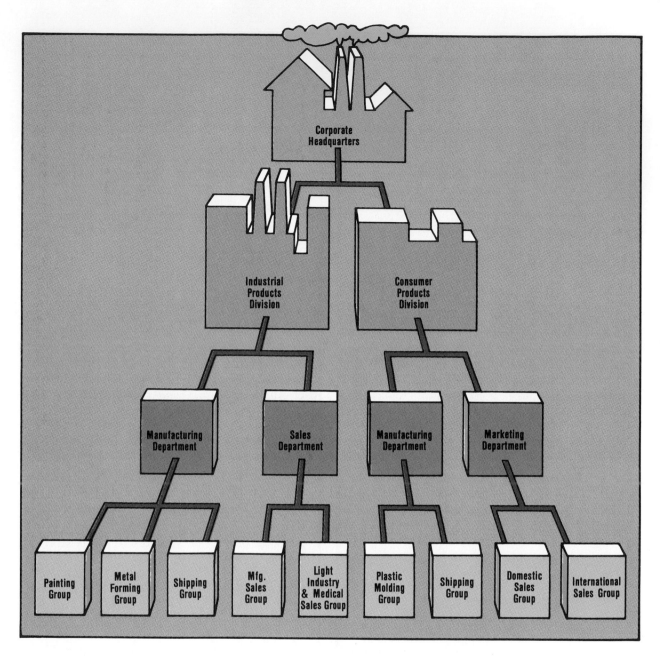

FIGURE 6.3

Multiple Bases of Departmentalization

Departmentalization by location arranges groups according to the physical location of people doing the tasks. A company will often divide its sales force into regional units to cover each potential market. In hospitals, the nursing staff is often divided into teams responsible for patient care on a particular floor or ward. Grouping by location facilitates communications considerably, because the lines are short and direct. When a company tries to cover large segments of the country with local offices, though, administrative costs and the logistical efforts needed may rise.

Multiple bases of departmentalization, as the term implies, is a mixture in one firm of two or more forms of departmentalization. Most large organizations, like the one shown in Figure 6.3, use at least two forms.

The Network Corporation

If you've ever been involved with a building construction project, you may have watched the work of a general contractor. The contractor may be, primarily, a carpenter, and may actually pound a few nails or cut some joists. But most of the time, the contractor works on the phone or oversees other workers at the construction site. The contractor hires surveyors, excavators, foundation pourers, drywall specialists, and painters. He or she also orders all the materials and makes sure they're delivered on time. An old-timer who built his own house might look at a modern contractor and say, "All that guy does is telephone." And that's precisely what many analysts, particularly foreigners, are saying about the latest evolution of the American corporation.

More and more American corporations are beginning to resemble the general contractor. Most, if not all, of a company's employees may be involved in contracting with various independent companies to develop, manufacture, distribute, or promote a product. Such companies become, in effect, communication centers that create and manage a *network* of relationships between other companies. Hence the name for this phenomenon — the network corporation.

The trend towards the network company began largely because of low foreign labor rates. American companies that used to manufacture their own products found they could make more money by buying certain manufactured goods from foreign suppliers, or by building their own factories in South Korea or Taiwan. By relying on Asian laborers, who often earn less than one-tenth as much as their American counterparts, the American company could pay the cost of shipping the product to the United States and still end up with an increased profit.

While international networks generally create profits for American companies in the short run, some industrial experts fear they spell trouble for the future of American business. Because they haven't invested in manufacturing plants, these companies aren't tied to selling the same product for long periods of time, and can therefore respond to trends and fads. But when a network company misreads a trend, as Nike did in 1985, it can end up with a lot of unsold merchandise — in Nike's case, 22 million pairs of shoes.

Even network companies that manage to guess right most of the time face a host of future problems. An Asian company that manufactures goods for an American corporation will soon develop expertise about those goods, and may come up with its own improvements in manufacturing. Then, with its products already selling on the American market under an American brand name, the foreign manufacturer can often start selling its own products, undercutting the price of the American competition. Taiwan's Kunnan Enterprises made tennis rackets for American companies for several years, and is now selling its own rackets in the U.S. Seiko of Japan made 20-inch color graphics display terminals for Tektronic Inc. for years and is now selling the terminals under its own name for 20 percent less than Tektronic charges.

On the other hand, network corporations often build strong, trusting relationships with foreign partners and suppliers. When the competition begins lowering its prices, Emerson Radio's management often works with its Asian suppliers to cut costs, and the company once even paid a supplier's payroll. Corporations that routinely work across national boundaries provide a major way for American business to break into markets like Japan's. And experts who aren't afraid of the effects of this new breed of corporation point out that American industrial output continues to rise, despite the predictions about the United States losing its manufacturing base. These optimists see the network companies simply as another face of the always-changing American corporation.

Everyone seems to agree that American companies will continue to become more international and to rely more on machines and less on human sweat. Whether that's a liberating prospect or a scary one depends, it seems, on your perspective.

Sources: John W. Wilson, "And Now, the Post-Industrial Corporation," *Business Week*, March 3, 1986, 64. Robert J. Samuelson, "Reported Death of US Industry Is Greatly Exaggerated," *American Banker*, June 19, 1985, 4. Thomas J. Bacher, "Multination Ventures Are a Fact of Life," *The New York Times*, April 6, 1986, Sec. 3, F2.

Line managers and line employees. *This maintenance worker and his supervisor at American Airline's Tulsa maintenance base are line employees. They have direct responsibility for their company's product.*

Authority, Responsibility, and Delegation

Effective coordination requires that the relationships among the people in an organization be clear to them. An employee may know the mechanics of his or her job and what the organization chart says about that job's relationship to others. Frequently, however, employees do not know exactly how far they can go in giving or taking directions to or from others. Organizations clarify these relationships through delegating authority and assigning responsibility.

Authority is a power granted by an organization to control the use of its resources, direct the actions of others, act on the organization's behalf, or perform all these functions.

By contrast, **responsibility** is a person's obligation to accomplish a task. A chief financial officer might assign responsibility to an accounting supervisor with words like "Finish this inventory by January 15." The chief financial officer has delegated, or assigned, the task. An employee who is to be held responsible for producing certain outcomes must have the authority to use the resources necessary to accomplish the task. In this case, the accounting supervisor would require authority to assign personnel to the project and to use the computers. **Delegation** is therefore the assignment of authority to perform a duty. As the late Richard E. Krafve of Raytheon Corporation has noted, however, "You can delegate authority, but you can never delegate responsibility for delegating a task to someone else. If you picked the right man, fine, but if you picked the wrong man, the responsibility is yours — not his."[5]

The Relationship of Authority, Responsibility, and Delegation

Delegated authority of course brings with it the duty to account for how it was exercised. **Accountability** is the mechanism that managers use to hold subordinates answerable for how they use their authority and live up to their responsibility. See Figure 6.4.

Most problems with delegation arise when individuals fail to delegate the authority needed to carry out an assignment. On the other hand, a person with responsibility for a particular task may not command the resources to accomplish it, or may simply have to go through so many hoops to obtain them that it deadens his or her enthusiasm. Many of the efforts to improve work styles focus on delegation. For example, at the Gromer Supermarket, Inc., in Elgin, Illinois, each department manager acts like an independent entrepreneur. This high degree of delegation contributes mightily to Gromer's profit margin of well over 2 percent in an industry where 1.5 percent is considered excellent.[6]

Policies and Procedures

An important means of achieving coordinated action is through policies and procedures. They are necessary features of almost any organization in which one person's or group's actions must mesh with another's. Policies and procedures may be as simple as deciding when a shop will be open or as complex as determining how an engineering and design until will account for the time its employees spend on projects. Policies and procedures should make interaction easier, define the scope of an organization's activities, clarify responsibilities, and simplify and make routine procedures uniform.

TABLE 6.3

Degrees of Delegation

Low	Low–Moderate	Moderate	High–Moderate	High
Investigate and report back	Investigate and recommend action	Investigate and advise on action planned	Investigate and take action; advise on action taken	Investigate and take action
Subordinate digs up relevant facts; superior uses those facts to identify decision alternatives, make decision, and take action	Subordinate digs up relevant facts and recommends alternative courses of action; superior makes decision and takes action	Subordinate digs up relevant facts and recommends a course of action; superior approves or disapproves action	Subordinate digs up relevant facts, makes decision, takes action, and advises superior about what took place	Subordinate digs up relevant facts, makes decision, and takes action without reporting back to superior

Source: Marion E. Haynes, "Delegation: There's More to It than Letting Someone Else Do It," *Supervisory Management* 25, January 1980, pp. 9–15, as adapted in Robert Kreitner, *Management*, 3rd ed. (Boston: Houghton Mifflin Co., 1986), p. 274.

FIGURE 6.4

The Delegation Process

Part 1
Assigning Responsibility

Part 2
Granting Authority

Part 3
Creating Accountability

For example, we will see in Chapter 8 that most companies have an employee performance-appraisal system on which the company bases raises, promotions, and other personnel decisions. Virtually all companies with such systems have detailed procedures as to how the appraisals are to be performed and ultimately used. A key element of a performance appraisal system is usually a standardized form used to evaluate all employees so that their work can be equitably compared.

The Span of Management

The number of people who report directly to a manager is that manager's **span of management**,[7] or spans of control, as they are sometimes called. Spans of management vary in size. Narrow spans consist of from two to four subordinates; moderate, from five to nine; and wide, ten or more.

The real question, however, is not how many people report to a manager but how many people he or she can manage effectively. The rule would appear to be that the more defined and limited the subordinates' tasks are, the wider the span may be. Conversely, the more complex and dispersed the subordinates' work is, the narrower the span should be. Of course, unquantifiable factors like the personalities of the individuals involved also play a role in determining an appropriate span of control.

Centralization and Decentralization

Perhaps the most common means of coordinating action is **centralization**, an organizational arrangement in which all decisions are passed along to top management before being implemented. Harold Geneen of ITT probably put the argument for centralization best:

> I don't believe in just ordering people to do things. You have to sort of grab an oar and row with them. My philosophy is to stay as close as possible to what's happening. If *I* can't solve something, how the hell can I expect my managers to?[8]

By contrast, **decentralization** is an arrangement in which decisions are pushed down the organization to the level where the functional expertise lies. At W. L. Gore & Associates, discussed in the last chapter, decisions are always made on the lowest possible level. In a centralized organization, the spans of management tend to be narrower than in decentralized organizations. Thus, centralized organizations with many layers and narrow spans of management are said to be tall; decentralized organizations with few layers and wide spans of management are termed flat. Figure 6.5 compares tall and flat organizations on a chart.

The Shape of Centralized and Decentralized Organizations

Because the same group makes all decisions in centralized organizations, they produce well-coordinated decisions, but the group may take a long time to reach a conclusion. It takes time to read and write reports, discuss issues, evaluate alternatives, and develop implementation strategies. The virtues of decentralization lie in its flexibility. Decisions that centralized organizations might agonize over tend to be made quickly at the level of the decentralized organization they affect the most. Decentralized organizations encourage their members to become generalists, not specialists, because they feature wide spans of management and informal communication networks. The chain of authority often shifts from problem to problem. Ideally, a coordination of efforts results from mutual adjustments made by all concerned. Benjamin Franklin, as he signed the Declaration of Independence, stated the principle that should guide decentralized organizations: "We must all hang together, or assuredly we shall all hang separately."

In general, decentralized organizational structures work better in smaller, younger, more entrepreneurial firms. Centralized structures usually characterize larger, more mature companies. There are many exceptions to this rule, however, such as Digital Equipment Corporation. And to varying degrees many companies incorporate aspects of both centralized and decentralized organizations.

FORMS OF ORGANIZATIONS

Organizations assume many structural forms, as described by tables of organization. This section examines the four main ones. Table 6.4 shows the advantages and disadvantages of these organizational forms.

The Organizational Breakdown That Led to the Challenger Tragedy

The 1986 Challenger tragedy may be history's most examined accident. For years scientists and journalists will be producing new theories about what went wrong. Clearly technical mistakes and human errors contributed to the explosion. But for people interested in business, the greatest lesson to be learned from the Challenger is what went wrong in the organization that put the Challenger into the air. The problems that plagued NASA are familiar to many people who have dealt with large bureaucracies.

Although outsiders may never know exactly who said what on that fateful day in January, it became clear almost immediately after the disaster that a number of people had known there were problems and did not want the Challenger to go up. Chief among them was Allan McDonald, head engineer at Cape Canaveral for the Morton Thiokol company which manufactured the booster rocket. McDonald was so worried about conditions that morning that he refused to give his approval to the launch. Yet his doubts were overruled, his concerns apparently never reached the ears of those who had final say about the launch, and a minute after liftoff his fears became horrible reality.

What happened that morning demonstrates one of the chief weaknesses of large organizations, especially ones with large bureaucracies: communication gets lost in its way up (or down) the organizational ladder. The organization that once symbolized what America can do at its best became instead a symbol of what happens when those at the top are isolated from those in touch with day-to-day operations.

The failure of information to percolate up through the organization has become one of the refrains of NASA's recent difficulties. NASA administrators have been publicly reprimanded for their handling of communication, and most observers agree that top brass attitudes had a lot to do with the Challenger disaster. From the first, the space program's administrators have been overly optimistic about the agency's ability to get the shuttle into the air cheaply and frequently. As late as 1983, NASA was predicting 21 shuttle launches in 1984 and 1985. Only 12 actually took place. Program administrators used such predictions to get money from Washington even while the engineers working on the shuttle knew that their figures were unrealistic.

In any organization, information that the boss doesn't want to hear moves up the corporate ladder slowly. All the way up the line of communication, people are likely to cover up or dispute information so they don't have to give their bosses bad news. Apparently such an information block occurred on the morning of January 28, and the information never reached the proper people.

On the day of the launch, NASA's uncertain leadership had already set the stage for a disaster. James Beggs, NASA's top administrator, was on a leave of absence to deal with charges related to his time as an executive at General Dynamics. His assistant, William R. Grahame, was in Washington during the launch. When the dispute about safety heated up on the morning of the launch, administrators at Marshall Space Flight Center made the decision at their own level — Level III in the organization — even though they could easily have involved higher officials from NASA. Perhaps if NASA had had a strong leader, Marshall would have felt compelled to clear the launch with the top.

The new NASA administration has searched for technical answers to Challenger's problems, but many observers hope NASA will continue to search for organizational answers too. To get back to the public successes and the high morale of the Apollo era, the big bureaucracy is going to have to act like an efficient matrix organization again, sharing with rather than competing with other parts of the organization, communicating with everyone involved, not just with immediate superiors.

Sources: Michael Brody, "NASA's Challenge: Ending Isolation at the Top," *Fortune*, May 12, 1986, 26. Seth Payne, "Challenger: 'Nothing Ends Here,'" *Business Week*, February 10, 1986, 24. Laurie McGinley and Frank E. James, "NASA's Shuttle Chief Is Seen Leaving His Position Sooner Than Expected," *The Wall Street Journal*, February 20, 1986, 2.

Form	Advantage	Disadvantage
Line	Simple and easy to understand Authority and responsibility clearly delegated Speedy decision making Direct Communication	Top management bogged down in operational decisions No specialization
Functional	Specialization Line Managers have time to manage Limited area of authority and responsibility	Responsible to more than one manager Possible overlapping authority and responsibility Possible breakdown in discipline
Line and Staff	Responsible to only one manager Availability of technical specialists	Possible conflict between line and staff Staff advice may be seen as order Increases firm's overhead costs
Matrix	Flexibility Specialization	Responsible to more than one manager Possible conflicts between project and function managers Difficulty in developing team spirit

TABLE 6.4

Advantages and Disadvantages of Organizational Forms

Line Organizations

The oldest and simplest organizational structure is the **line organization**, in which top management has total, direct control and each subordinate reports to a single supervisor.[9] The line concept evolved over time to refer to everyone involved in actually producing or distributing what a firm sells. The workers involved are called line employees, their managers line managers. Line managers have line authority, the power to make decisions that directly affect the firm's output. In a steel mill, for instance, the people who pour the molten steel are line employees, as are those who work on the shipping platform. The plant manager is a line manager.

The Four Main Forms of Structural Organization

Functional Organization

Early in this century, Frederick Taylor introduced the concept of scientific management at Bethlehem Steel. Taylor believed that the division of labor concept applied not just to the work of laborers and steel handlers but also to the responsibilities of managers. Based on that insight, he devised the **functional organization**, a system in which the various functions involved in supervising a worker are divided into separate tasks performed by specialists. A salesperson might report to a marketing boss who concentrated on planning sales strategies, a training boss concerned with training and development, a compensation boss who handled salaries, and any other bosses the organization might see fit.

Staff positions in an organization. *Staff employees provide important services, information, and expertise to an organization. Although trainers like Dorothy Johnson and Laraine Clarke at BankAmerica don't have direct authority over the managers they instruct, they play a vital role in the company's management development and executive leadership programs.*

The functional form of organization overcame some of the major deficiencies of the line form: too many responsibilities for each supervisor and too many areas in which a supervisor was expected to demonstrate expertise. In short, Taylor introduced specialization. Although the functional organization showed early promise, today's corporation is more likely to use the line-and-staff form described below. Nonetheless, Taylor's concept of management specialization has not just survived, it has flourished.

Line-and-Staff Organization

In a modern organization, many employees and managers, called **staff**, are not directly involved in producing or distributing the goods and services it sells. Yet they are crucial to the firm's success because they supply support, information, and advice to line personnel. Typical staff positions include those relating to personnel, marketing, food services, and bookkeeping. A staff position in one organization may of course be a line position in another. An accountant employed by Borden's would be a staff employee, but the same accountant working for a giant public accounting firm like Touche Ross would be a line employee. Determining whether a member of an organization is a line or a staff employee depends on the contribution of his or her job to the goods or services the organization sells.

Matrix-Structured Organization

An arrangement of information into a grid made up of rectangular boxes that can be read both horizontally and vertically is a **matrix**. A **matrix organizational structure** is one that combines horizontal and vertical lines of authority and also functional and product departments. This structure is sometimes referred to as **project management**, because it brings together personnel drawn from different departments to focus on a particular project. The matrix form probably first appeared in 1959 at the aerospace giant TRW.[10] It has since been used throughout high-tech industries.

The matrix form combines the common pool of technical specialists working together in the functional form with the special attention that only people assigned to a particular project can give to a specific product or problem. Project groups can be created by drawing on individuals permanently assigned to functional departments.

Companies often adopt a matrix structure when they come under extreme competitive pressures on significant projects and there is a limit to the resources they can devote to the project. Such situations require quick responses, something a matrix structure can provide. Project coordination in a matrix structure is better because instead of several functional managers being involved, there is only one project leader, who reports to the projects manager. Also, communication tends to be better, because those assigned to a project can discuss problems across functional lines as well as with others assigned to their home department. Members of a project team can be reassigned when it ends or as the need arises. Giants like General Motors, Monsanto, and the Chase Manhattan Bank are using this form of organization in selected areas of the company.

Matrix structures have their faults, however. The most serious is the dual reporting problem. Each employee has two supervisors: the supervisor in the functional department — say, accounting or engineering — and the project leader. Cooperation and communication between the two supervisors are the keys to

FIGURE 6.5

Tall and Flat Organizations

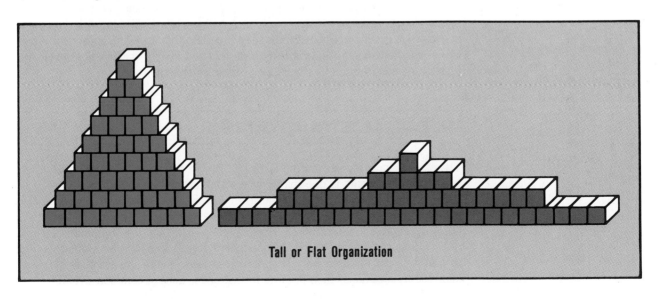

Tall or Flat Organization

Matrix structures work for big firms, too. Many people think of matrix structures in connection with high-tech, high-risk organizations. MCR, a big firm that has been around a long time, has found a way to make a matrix structure work for it.

keeping employees happy in matrix structures. Project managers in this structure sometimes find that the dual reporting problem limits their control over their teams. They must negotiate, persuade, and exchange favors with functional managers in order to get what they need, because they lack line authority. Firms like Texas Instruments and Citibank have adopted matrix organization forms but then abandoned them, often because of their complexity.

INFORMAL STRUCTURES

Thus far we have focused on the formal ways that organizations accomplish their goals. A **formal group** is one that exists within an organization because of management's decision to create it to perform certain tasks. Every organization also has its own ways of accomplishing the things outside the established structure. Such an organization is called an **informal group**, one that develops naturally as a result of people within an organization interacting.[11] People who lunch together or ride to work together become informal groups. Labor unions started out as informal organizations, then became formal ones, quite a common evolution.

Can an Un-organization Be a Technological Leader?

You've read about W. L. Gore & Associates and other innovative companies that have successfully avoided bureaucracies and standard organizational structures. Many people would be excited about working in Gore's loose, unconstricting atmosphere, but most wonder whether a company that employs hundreds of people "doing their own thing" can compete in the new technology marketplace against others that have complete, tightly structured divisions devoted to research and development. Can a company with very little formal structure stay alive in the fiercely competitive and quickly changing world of high technology? The history of Gore's technological innovations proves that it can.

Gore is an unusual, perhaps unique, organization. To keep its local workforces small enough so that everyone will know everyone else, Gore has to keep building new plants. To make up for the lack of traditional organizational structure, the company has created a more informal system of "sponsors" and "associates." A new employee accustomed to formal company structure would probably find the first few weeks at Gore difficult. The new employee would be encouraged to find interesting work, to create a niche or a project. For many people this kind of freedom can be unsettling.

Working at Gore can be frustrating if a sponsor isn't helpful. And the amount of individual freedom allows employees to make, and have to face, their own mistakes. But most Gore associates are willing to take on that responsibility in order to enjoy the freedom of being almost their own boss, and to have a chance to participate in the kind of technological innovation that has made Gore a household word among outdoor enthusiasts.

Bill Gore began his own business in 1958, on the kind of personal hunch for which his company became famous. He had been working for Du Pont with the polymer PTFE which most people now know as "Teflon." Du Pont wasn't interested in Gore's basement tinkerings with the polymer. So after Bill's son Bob helped spark a breakthrough that would allow the polymer to be used to coat computer cables, Bill and his wife, Vieve, started their own cable-making company.

Although the company was a success, the future didn't look particularly bright in the late 1960s when the wire and cable business began slowing down. Then Bob Gore, working alone on his own project, made the discovery that changed the company forever. He had a hunch that he could make PTFE more profitable if he could stretch it and introduce more air into it. Scientific studies said that what he wanted to do couldn't be done, and if he had had to get bureaucratic approval for his project, Bob might never have experimented, and most of the world would never have heard of Gore. For days he heated rods of PTFE and tried to pull them apart. Each time they snapped. Finally, in a moment of anger, he yanked a heated rod — and it stretched. Gore-Tex was born.

The use of Gore-Tex as a material to graft on human veins came about from a chance discussion between Bill Gore and a physician friend on a ski slope. Four years and thousands of grafts later, a problem arose with the grafts and the company had to show how it could respond in a crisis. Because Gore people don't have set areas of responsibility, the company was able to put many good minds on the problem immediately, and one came up with a solution. Now while millions of people stay dry in the rain because of Gore-Tex clothing, close to half a million walk about with Gore-Tex vascular grafts. And if Bob Gore has his way, some day millions more may be drinking sea water purified of salt by a film of Gore-Tex.

Companies like Gore have long since proved to their own satisfaction that it's not only possible but advantageous to run a growing, high-tech company without any traditional organizational structures. The big question for America's future managers is, will such companies remain mavericks, exceptions to the rule, or will other corporations develop with their own loose, innovative structures to fit their own purposes?

Sources: Lucien Rhodes, "The Un-Manager," *Inc.* Stanley W. Angrist, "Classless Capitalists," *Forbes*, May 9, 1983, 122. John Hoerr, "A Company Where Everybody Is the Boss," *Business Week*, April 15, 1985, 98.

Informal structures within formal organizations can become quite powerful. They are primarily powerful communications mechanisms. Nothing moves information faster than a **grapevine**, an informal, unofficial communications network within an organization. A grapevine satisfies social needs, clarifies orders from above, and functions as a safety valve, especially where upward communication lines are blocked. The grapevine can sway opinion and shape it on important organizational issues. Some managers have found that the extent to which their subordinates observe work rules and performance standards is largely determined by what the grapevine tells them that other employees are doing and what penalties management has imposed for noncompliance.

Grapevines are practically institutions at many firms, large and small. Other informal groups spring up from time to time, too. For example, when disaster strikes a business, employees commonly band together to help it through the rough times, even though what they are doing may not be found in their job descriptions. In short, creating an atmosphere in which positive, informal groups flourish can be as important as managing the formal organizational elements. As William B. Thurston, of GenRad, Inc., once noted with pride, "We probably have the most precise and exact grapevine in existence."[12]

ORGANIZATION: A PERSPECTIVE

One could argue that the dirtiest word in American English is bureaucrat, someone who works in a bureaucracy. A bureaucracy is commonly thought of as a government agency characterized by a diffusion of authority among numerous offices and an adherence to complex, inflexible rules which include a need to fill out all forms in triplicate.[13] However, bureaucracies are not unique to government. They typify almost all large organizations — and many smaller ones. Public and private colleges, churches, hospitals and public utilities are notorious for their bureaucracies, so are many large corporations, like Exxon, which employs 145,000 people.[14] Most large companies have from nine to thirteen levels of management.[15] Thus, **bureaucracy** is just another word to describe the administrative structure of a departmentalized, hierarchical organization.

Bureaucracies encourage the division of labor. By forcing employees to specialize, bureaucracies seek increased productivity. Ideally, they enhance efficiency by breaking tasks down into small units, thus making it easier to train people for them. A system of rules and procedures — the more specific, the better — defines employees' duties. Their actions are thus controlled and predictable. Every bureaucracy has a hierarchy of authority, which should result in increased efficiency. Every person reports to a single higher ranking individual. Finally, in an ideal bureaucracy, only technical competence and training should be used to determine selection and promotion. Favoritism of any sort should not therefore exist, and merit should be the sole criterion in employment decisions.

One can see why bureaucracies develop in corporations. Predictability and stability are great virtues, particularly when they lead to increased efficiency, but their cost can be high.

Innovation and creativity, two essential elements that make up the spirit

The informal organization. *These coworkers are sharing much more than a pizza. Informal groups give their members a sense of belonging to an organization and exert a strong influence on how much and how well each one works. They also share information, insights, advice, and office gossip. In fact, the grapevine is often the fastest way to speed information through an organization.*

required in successful entrepreneurs, can be stifled by bureaucracy. Because entrepreneurship relies heavily on an individual's creative innovations and sways from the systematic rules and procedures which are implicit in bureaucracy, it is no accident that the renewed emphasis on entrepreneurship in large corporations has led to renewed attacks on bureaucracy. Many of these innovations, such as those being implemented at companies using matrix management, are taking place at high-tech companies. Even old line businesses, however, have adapted entrepreneurship and other business methods that run directly counter to bureaucracies.

The clear trend in American corporations is toward flatter organizations. Not only have bureaucracies proven expensive, but today's more highly educated work force has shown little tolerance for them. At all levels, American workers are demonstrating a desire for independence and outlets for their creativity. Even in sectors that traditionally have been heavily unionized, like the auto industry, unions have made little headway in the last fifteen years.

America's success as a world competitor depends increasingly on its ability to innovate and respond quickly to challenges, so more of a premium will come to be placed on nonbureaucratic organizational forms.

Chapter Highlights

1. Describe the elements of an organization.

The three elements that characterize an organization are its people, its purpose, and a definable boundary that divides members from nonmembers.

2. Define *organizational structure* and explain how that concept relates to an organization chart.

An *organizational structure* is a pattern of task groupings, reporting relationships, and authority in an organization. An organization chart provides a graphic representation of how an organization is structured. Positions at the top of the chart have more power and authority than those lower on the chart. The lines joining boxes on an organization chart indicate reporting relationships.

3. Identify the reasons that the division of labor is the key concept in modern organizations.

The division of labor allows complex organizations to function by breaking tasks down into smaller segments that can be handled by one person or by members of a single department. It allows individuals to become expert in particular areas and also cuts down on the amount of equipment necessary to do a job. Once tasks grow beyond what one person can handle, applying the concepts of specialization and division of labor usually improves productivity more than it raises costs.

4. Define *departmentalization* and describe the four basic departmentalization models.

Departmentalization is the arranging of divided tasks into meaningful groups. Departments are generally organized by function, by product or service, by customer, or by location. In addition, many organizations use more than one basis for departmentalization.

5. Relate the concepts of *authority*, *responsibility*, and *delegation*.

Authority is the power to direct the use of an organization's resources. Responsibility is the obligation to accomplish some task. It is easy for a manager to assign responsibility for a task, but it may not be possible for an employee to carry out that responsibility unless the manager also delegates (turns over) the authority to control the resources necessary to get the job done.

6. Discuss the function of policies and procedures.

Policies and procedures make employee interaction easier, define the scope of an organization's activities, clarify responsibilities, and simplify and make routine procedures uniform.

7. Explain the importance of the concept of the span of management.

The span of management describes the number of people who report directly to a given manager. It is important that the span of management be appropriate to the manager's duties. When employees carry out complex and varied tasks and need intensive or frequent supervision, the span should be narrow. When employees perform simple and routine activities, needing only minimal guidance and individual attention, the span can be much wider.

8. Identify the different qualities of centralized and decentralized structures.

In a centralized organization, important decisions are passed along to the top of the management hierarchy. Top executives maintain strict control of subordinates as well as of any divisions or other businesses owned or managed by the organization. There are generally many layers of organization and narrow spans of management. Decentralized organizations are characterized by just the opposite traits. Decisions are generally made as far down the organization as possible, there tend to be few layers of management, and managers have broad spans of management.

9. Contrast line-and-staff organizations with matrix organizations.

In a line-and-staff organization, line managers have line authority, the power to make decisions that directly affect the firm's output. Staff managers, on the other hand, have specialized expertise. They advise and support the functions of many line managers and employees, but they do not have direct authority over or control of the organization's output. For example, members of the training staff may put together company manuals and instruction brochures that explain how certain jobs are to be performed. Members of the marketing department may develop an organization advertising campaign. But none of the staff in these departments would have the authority to decide how a product should be manufactured or what production equipment should be installed. They might advise line managers, but they could not ordinarily insist that their advice be followed.

In a matrix organization, tasks or projects are assigned to members of different departments who work together as a team or committee. In that way, expertise in many different areas — engineering, financial management, and marketing, for example — is available to the group as a whole. A major difference between the two forms of organization is that, in a line-and-staff organization, an employee reports to a single boss. In a matrix organi-

zation an employee normally reports to both a functional boss and a project or team leader.

10. Explain how informal patterns of organization meet the needs of workers and management.

Informal organizations can satisfy people's desire for good social relationships and help them to meet their psychological needs. In addition, the grapevine, often described as just a rumor mill, can clarify orders and serve as an important safety valve, especially if upward communication is otherwise blocked. The grapevine is tremendously powerful when it comes to shaping opinions and performance standards within an organization.

Key Terms

Accountability	Delegation	Line organization	Organizational
Authority	Departmentalization	Matrix	structure
Bureaucracy	Formal group	Matrix organizational	Project management
Centralization	Functional organization	structure	Responsibility
Chain of command	Grapevine	Organization	Span of management
Decentralization	Informal group		Staff

Review Questions

1. What is the difference between a large group of people in a movie theater and an organization?

2. What are the practical applications of an organizational chart?

3. If you were an auditor for a large accounting firm, would you hold a line or a staff position? Why?

4. Would you rather perform line-function or staff-function duties in an organization? Explain your reasons.

5. Why is it important that a large organization be structured but not so important for a small organization to be?

6. What difference would it make if the span of management were too large or too small?

7. If a manager can delegate authority, why can't he or she delegate responsibility to others?

8. List and describe the four basic departmentalization models.

9. Why do we always think of a bureaucracy as being inefficient, characterized by red tape and waiting in lines? Is this true at the school you attend? Why or why not?

10. Why aren't bureaucracies as efficient as they were originally designed to be?

11. Under what conditions is it better to have a bureaucratic structure?

12. What is a matrix structure? Why would an organization use this structure?

13. What factors contribute to an active grapevine within an organization?

14. What can top management do to manage the informal organization of a firm so that it does not become disruptive?

Application Exercises

1. Assume that you are the chief administrator of a medium-sized hospital. In recent months you have noticed that the informal organization has become very active. You have heard rumors that have greatly exaggerated the issues and problems in the hospital. What steps could you take to make the informal organization less active?

2. Draw an organization chart for the college or university you are currently attending. Include all administrative positions and departments. As you prepare the chart, be sure to distinguish between line and staff positions.

Cases

6.1 Nucor's Minimal Management

Nucor Corporation is one of a new breed of American steel companies — those that make steel in minimills. The traditional steelmaking operation begins with iron ore, which is refined in costly blast furnaces. Instead, the minimill starts with scrap steel, which needs only to be melted and then formed into various products. For minimills, those products are relatively small — for example, reinforcing rods for concrete rather than huge structural beams. Minimills generally, and Nucor in particular, make use of the latest technology to keep productivity up and costs down. As a result, Nucor's nonunion jworkers are twice as productive as those of the traditional steelmaking giants; their earnings are well above the industry average; and Nucor itself is highly profitable. More traditional steelmakers like U.S. Steel and Bethlehem have been losing ground to foreign steel firms, and losing money year after year. Many have tried to lower costs by asking their union workers to accept reduced wages and benefits.

Nucor's chairman and chief executive officer (CEO), F. Kenneth Iverson, believes that his firm is one of the lowest-cost steelmakers in the world. He attributes the firm's success to its cost-consciousness and its somewhat unusual management concepts. To start with, Iverson believes that if a firm is not productive, it is management — not the workers — that is at fault. So management compensation increases or decreases as productivity and profit rise or fall.

In keeping with the firm's emphasis on cost saving, managers are not treated to such "goodies" as company cars, jet planes, and company retreats. Everyone, including Iverson, travels economy class. Moreover, the corporation, its eighteen mills, and its 4000 employees are administered by a corporate staff of only sixteen people, housed in small offices in a nondescript building in Charlotte, N.C.

Iverson believes that the most important factor in business is the number of management layers between workers and the CEO. The more layers there are, the slower the decision-making process is, and the more difficult it is to communicate. Whereas traditional steelmaking firms may have as many as ten management levels, Nucor has only four: The foremen report to department heads, who report to general managers, who report to Iverson.

According to Iverson, Nucor's organizational structure requires a certain kind of manager — one who is willing and able to go into the plant, communicate directly with employees, and get them to work together as a team. Managers who are used to working through long command chains wouldn't make it at Nucor. He agrees that most organizations have the tendency to become increasingly more complex, almost as if they had a life of their own. "But," he says, "it's management's responsibility to fight that tendency."

Questions

1. Would you characterize Nucor as centralized or decentralized? As having a narrow, moderate, or wide span of management? How is Nucor most likely departmentalized?
2. From the description of Nucor and your answers to Question 1, draw as much of Nucor's organization chart as you can.
3. Do you think Nucor will have to add management levels if it grows? Why, or why not?

For more information see *Inc.*, April 1986, pp. 41–48; *U.S. News & World Report*, September 3, 1984, p. 57; and *Time*, January 24, 1984, p. 59.

6.2 The Importance of Organization

On January 28, 1986, the space shuttle Challenger exploded soon after takeoff from Kennedy Space Center, killing its crew of seven. An investigation of the disaster determined that the immediate cause was the cold-weather failure of synthetic rubber O-rings, used to seal the sections of Challenger's solid-fuel booster rocket. It seems likely that a contributing cause was management failure within the National Aeronautics and Space Administration (NASA). The investigating committee has recommended that astronauts become more involved in managing the shuttle program, especially where safety is involved.

NASA, the organization that administers the U.S. space flight program, has, in recent years, been beset by budget cuts and personnel reductions; by the problem of trying to reach overly ambitious space-flight goals; by occasional lack of cooperation and even jealousy among its several components (such as the Marshall, Kennedy, and Johnson Space Flight Centers); by the increasing isolation of NASA's leaders in Washington, D.C.; and by the temporary loss of its top executive, who was on a leave of absence. Probably no one of these managerial problems could have caused a breakdown of NASA's carefully structured system for handling last-minute flight decisions. But together they did.

Of late, NASA's top executives have had to spend much of their time lobbying Congress for funds. This has allowed them less time to keep tabs on and control their organization. NASA's component organizations, each concerned with its own part of the shuttle operation and its own budget and independence, seem to have found that situation agreeable. Staff cuts have helped to reduce the upward flow of information.

Six months before the Challenger launch, NASA executives were warned that the O-rings posed a safety threat. They were also told that the rings posed budget threat; it would cost perhaps $350 million to eliminate the problem. Lack of funding and personnel seems to have led officials to consider the O-rings as a long-term problem that could not be solved immediately. They may have felt reasonably safe in doing so, since the rings had already been given a special safety waiver. Waivers are required for all parts that do not meet NASA's fail-safe specification. However, the O-ring waiver was actually issued before the safety problem was discovered.

The Challenger flight had already been delayed twice due to cold weather. Just before the January 28 launch, Morton Thiokol's senior engineer at the launch site argued strongly for another delay. (Morton Thiokol is the firm that manufactured the booster rocket.) The engineer, Alan McDonald, refused to certify that the rocket was ready and safe for flight.

Some insiders believe that McDonald's argument and refusal should have been communicated to top NASA executives. Traditionally, the top administrator or his deputy is at every launch; however, for this launch the top executive was on leave and his deputy was in Washington. Instead, personnel from Marshall Space Center (which is responsible for NASA rocketry) communicated with executives at Morton Thiokol. They overrode McDonald, and the launch went ahead. Managers from Marshall maintain that a routine technical matter was involved, and that it was their responsibility.

Ironically, two of NASA's top executives were at the launch site. Both were plugged into a communications network that allows all personnel to hear what takes place during the countdown, and both had the authority to delay the launch. But the argument never came through on the network, and no one brought it to their attention.

Questions

1. How did each of NASA's problems contribute to the "organizational breakdown" that permitted the Challenger launch? How would you characterize that breakdown?
2. What type of organizational structure would minimize or eliminate the chance of such a breakdown? Why?

For more informatiion see *Newsweek*, June 23, 1986, pp. 66–68; *Fortune*, May 12, 1986, pp. 26–32; and *The Wall Street Journal*, March 18, 1986, p. 5.

7

HUMAN RELATIONS IN BUSINESS

Learning Objectives

When you have completed this chapter, you will be able to do the following:

■ Define human relations.

■ Explain what motivation is and describe the origins of the modern approach to it.

■ Describe Abraham Maslow's hierarchy of needs.

■ Describe Frederick Herzberg's motivation maintenance mode.

■ Explain the differences between Douglas McGregor's Theory X and Theory Y assumptions about what motivates people.

■ Describe some important internal and external motivators in the work place.

■ Describe three new strategies for involving employees in decision making.

■ Identify four types of alternative work patterns in use today and describe their prospects.

Delta is ready when you are." This familiar slogan of Delta Air Lines reflects its origin as a regional carrier specializing in frequent flights with good connections. By putting its travelers' needs first, Delta built itself into a national airline. It has now become the model for the industry, but its innovative scheduling does not alone account for its success.

A full-page ad placed in the major Atlanta newspaper by a Delta pilot on the eve of his retirement helps explain the airline's success. It said, in part, "[It] has been my privilege to work with the finest group of human beings that God ever created" in "an organization that has been exceedingly well managed."[1] That same year, Delta employees presented the airline with a $30-million gift — a new Boeing 767 jet.

Since its founding in 1929 as a crop-dusting operation, Delta has tried to maintain a family atmosphere. Delta's 36,800 employees are not laid off when business turns bad, and their benefits are quite good. The company has an open-door policy and encourages frank communications between all levels. It is no wonder that there is a love affair between Delta and its employees. In fact, Delta was ranked one of the 100 best companies to work for in a recent best seller.

Delta is not alone among American businesses in building a family atmosphere among its employees. Some, like Delta, have had the same philosophy since their founding. Others, from steel companies to hotels, have concluded that attention to the human side of their enterprises may lead to solutions to the contemporary challenges discussed in Chapters 1 and 2.

THE NATURE OF HUMAN RELATIONS IN BUSINESS

Most business organizations that survive for a long period maintain a balance between a concern for the success (growth or profit) and regard for their people. Modern businesses require the interaction of large numbers of individuals. Often, what appear to be policy, procedural, and organizational problems are really disguised conflicts between individuals. Better work relationships in contemporary businesses thus begin with an understanding of how people interact.

Human Relations Defined

In its broadest sense, **human relations** covers all the types of interactions among people: conflicts, cooperative efforts, and group relationships.[2] A human is a complex being. Each person is a unique mixture of emotional stability, physical fitness, mental alertness, self-image, morals, and values orientation. Some employers may wish that they could hire just the brain or the brawn of their workers, but they have no choice except to hire the entire person.[3] If the whole person can be improved, the firm will benefit. Thus, an increased understanding of human relations will help identify ways to improve employee and organizational effectiveness.

Morale

Human relations does not begin and end at the company's door. What goes on outside the work place affects what happens inside it. Good human relations in an organization usually means high **morale**, a state of psychological well-being based on such factors as a sense of organizational purpose and confidence in the

Openness, trust, and team spirit. *David Lowry, president of Data Design Associates, Inc., took his managers mountain climbing, white water rafting, and sky diving. Profits and productivity rose right along with feelings of trust and togetherness at this successful software developer. Building team spirit is an important ingredient in the human relations planning of many contemporary companies.*

future. Morale is the enthusiasm that workers display toward their jobs, their fellow employees, and their employers.

Consider the case of Nyloncraft, Inc., an Indiana plastics-molding company. By 1977, it had begun having horrendous absenteeism and turnover problems. Every job in the company turned over three times within the year. Management soundings and an employee survey revealed the source of the problem. The majority of Nyloncraft's employees were — and are — women, many of them single mothers. They could not find reliable child care. In 1981 Nyloncraft opened Indiana's first twenty-four hour child-care facility. Today, Nyloncraft's workers can worry less about their children's care and more about maintaining the company's reputation for consistently high quality production. Absenteeism now runs only 3 percent, with turnover at less than 6 percent per year. As Jim Wyllie, Nyloncraft's president, notes, "The only difference between us and every other injection-molding firm is the people."[4]

The emotional and physical health of individuals are closely linked. The quality of one's work, whether at a desk or on a plant floor, often relates directly to one's diet and physical fitness. The menus in the cafeterias of the Northwestern Mutual Life Insurance Company report how many calories each item contains.[5] The Adolph Coors Company invested $600,000 in a "wellness center," a health education and group exercise center in a former supermarket near its headquarters.[6] The Stride-Rite Corporation sought to improve the working environment by restricting smoking in its headquarters and four manufacturing plants.[7]

MOTIVATING WORKERS

The Nature of Motivation

One of the most important dimensions of effective human relations within an organization is **motivation**, the factors that cause people to behave in a certain way.[8] Put another way, motivation is what drives a person to accomplish a certain goal. In a work setting, motivation makes people want to work, but precisely what is it that motivates people? No question about human behavior is asked more often and is more difficult — or more important — to answer. For generations, managers have believed people to be primarily motivated by money. However, as Neil Simon, the playwright, has pointed out, "Money brings some happiness. But, after a certain point, it just brings more money."[9] Today, following sixty years of research, a growing number of organizations have come to assume that employee motivation centers on factors besides money.

The Hawthorne Studies

Researchers became more aware of the complex nature of motivation only in 1927. A Harvard University research team headed by Elton Mayo initiated a series of experiments in that year to determine relationships between changes in physical working conditions and employee productivity, which may be considered "the level of output of goods and services achieved by the resources of an organization."[10] Their research took place at Western Electric's Hawthorne plant outside Chicago, so these landmark reports are now simply referred to as the **Hawthorne studies**.

In one experiment, Mayo and his colleagues selected two groups of employees who did similar work under like conditions. The team increased the lighting for one group but kept it constant for the other. Productivity increased with the increase in lighting. To verify their results, the researchers began to dim the lights for the group being studied. To their surprise, productivity actually increased. Indeed, the workers reached one of their highest output levels when the light was quite dim. Some factor besides lighting was plainly influencing productivity.

When Mayo and his team began interviewing the employees, they quickly made two important discoveries. First, the attention focused on the test group made them feel important and appreciated. For the first time, they had gotten feedback on their job performance. Second, the way the experiments had been conducted had allowed the employees greater freedom from supervisory control. These circumstances had boosted their morale and motivation, so their productivity rose.

Wellness programs. *Jim Weidaw, director of employee relations at Plaskolite, Inc., can vouch for the value of wellness programs. Since beginning a wellness program and building this fitness center, Plaskolite has seen its insurance rates drop and employee satisfaction rise.*

The Origins of the Modern Approach to Motivation

The Hawthorne studies did not immediately convince managers that they should change their approach to motivating employees. Inevitably, the discovery that human factors, such as the need to be involved and the desire for feedback, affect productivity had a major impact. Managers began to consider motivation tools other than money and job security. Even more importantly, the Hawthorne studies led to an awareness of the average worker as a complex combination of needs, values, and attitudes. This recognition brought about the birth of the human-relations movement, whose principal assumption is that employees who are satisfied with their work are motivated to perform better than employees whose needs are unsatisfied.[11]

FIGURE 7-1

Maslow's Hierarchy of Needs

People have a number of different needs that each require some measure of satisfaction.

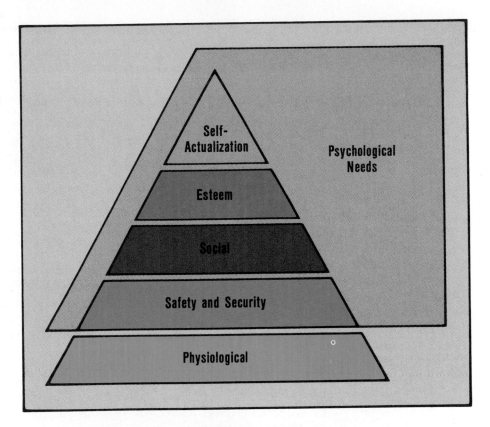

THE NATURE OF NEEDS

Motivation is, of course, a concept not limited to understanding the productivity of the work place. Rather, it is a term used to describe the force that prompts us to move toward the satisfaction of a **need**, something that disturbs our satisfied physical or psychological state.

After studying the relationship between needs and motivation, the psychologist Abraham H. Maslow concluded that

☐ People have a number of different needs that each require some measure of satisfaction.
☐ Only those needs that have not been substantially satisfied influence behavior. A satisfied need does not motivate.
☐ People tend to satisfy their basic human needs in a particular order, which Maslow called their **hierarchy of needs**.

As Figure 7.1 reveals, Maslow's hierarchy of needs looks like a pyramid. The following sections examine the blocks of which this pyramid is built.[12]

Physiological Needs

Abraham Maslow termed food, clothing, sleep, and shelter — the basic **physiological needs** — the "survival" or "lower order" needs. The satisfaction of these

Quality of Work Life

Long before robots appeared in American factories, many American businesses treated workers as if *they* were machines. Most companies had a strong hierarchy and strict authoritarian leadership. Those on the top made the decisions and passed them down the chain of command. The workers on the bottom were expected to follow the orders from above, even if those orders made the work unpleasant or cost the company money.

All that is changing now, as company after company adopts new programs to improve the "quality of work life." These programs give workers more control over their jobs and often let them participate in decision-making. They get companies involved in improving the physical and mental health of their workers. And they allow for restructuring of job positions and schedules.

Companies are making changes and instituting such programs not just to make workers happy. American business is learning that the quality of employees' work often depends on how employees feel about their jobs. Workers who feel they are irrelevant cogs in a machine are not likely to work as hard as those who feel that their work and their ideas are important to the company.

This commonsense idea has not won easy acceptance in American business, although researchers and theorists have been stressing the importance of job satisfaction for fifty years. Like many important business ideas of the last decade, the emphasis on quality of work life had to be imported from abroad. While American businesses felt strong and complacent after World War II, not eager to change the organizational structures and climate that had worked in the past, companies in the rebuilding countries of Europe and Asia desperately searched for ways to increase their output and efficiency in order to compete with the established American giants.

In Europe, a labor shortage and social changes leading to more democratic values added to the movement for change in the workplace. Businesspeople found that workers were happier and more productive if they could set their own hours to some extent, if they could work with management in making decisions and setting priorities, and if they could function in groups.

The changes at one company, Thorneburg Hosiery, give some idea of what's been going on throughout the country. When Thorneburg introduced a new line of expensive, innovative sports socks in 1980, sales more than tripled in a year to $2.7 million, and Jim Thorneburg envisioned the company growing to $100 million in sales. But he wasn't sure his employees were ready for that kind of growth or to produce the quality and quantity of socks needed for that growth.

So just before Christmas, Thorneburg called the first company-wide meeting and explained his new system. He told the company that each employee — not the employee's supervisor — would now be held accountable for his or her own work. Supervisors became "servants to the workers" instead of pressuring workers to perform. They asked, rather than ordered, when they wanted something done, and explained the reason for each task to the workers. Instead of punishing workers for discipline problems, they took the time to counsel and coach employees. Quality circles were formed in which employees could exchange ideas on how to improve their work and their working environment. These meetings also gave employees unused to so much responsibility a place to talk without worrying about ridicule.

Two years later, sales had risen to $7.5 million. More importantly, work quality was at a peak. Over 99 percent of the work turned out by the knitters group was "first quality" that could be sold to retailers, compared to an industry average of 90 percent.

Most surveys of companies that have undertaken quality of work life changes show consistent results. People are happier at their work and they're turning out more and better products. American business is finding out that quality of work life translates into quality of work.

Sources: Sharon Nelton, "Socking It to the Old Style," *Nation's Business*, May 1985, 63. Herman Gadon, "Making Sense of Quality of Work Life Programs," *Business Horizons*, January–February, 1984, 42. Paul D. Bush, "The Argument for Employee Participation," *Boston Globe*, November 12, 1985, 30.

physiological needs, what a human requires biologically to survive and function, comes first. In most work environments, basic needs rarely dominate. However, during periods of economic stress, like the prolonged recession of 1977–1985 in the western Pennsylvania steel industry, people take and keep jobs simply to put food on their tables.

Psychological Needs

Sometimes called **secondary needs**, the needs of the mind — **psychological needs** — are distinct from the needs of the body. Maslow believed that psychological needs, the pyramid's top layers, were of a higher order than physiological ones.

Safety and Security   The need for safety and security reflects a desire for order and predictability. Employees feel more secure when they know that they will not lose their jobs, they will be able to provide for their families, and they will have sufficient resources after retirement to be able to enjoy their lives. Organizations satisfy these needs, at least partly, by offering employees pension, profit sharing, and insurance programs. A few companies, like Johnson & Johnson Products, Inc., maintain a "no layoff" policy similar to that of Delta Air Lines. The Federal Express Corporation satisfies its employees' job security needs by providing a five-step Guaranteed Fair Treatment plan to ensure that employees with grievances can receive a hearing, if need be, from this cargo carrier's top officials.

Social   Social needs center on our desire for affection and approval from others. They include our wish for a sense of belonging to and identification with a group. To some extent, we satisfy our social needs by joining professional associations, religious groups, sports teams, or social clubs. The other members presumably share our interests, values, and goals.

For many, their jobs satisfy their social needs, and wise employers address that need. Mary Kay Cosmetics, Inc., in Dallas, takes several steps to be sure that its home office and manufacturing employees feel themselves part of the family. Within a month after being hired, employees meet with company chairperson Mary Kay Ash. On their birthdays, they receive a voucher for dinner for two. Everyone at Mary Kay eats in the same cafeteria. No titles appear on office doors, helping foster the attitude that there are no lower echelons at Mary Kay.[13]

Esteem   The next-to-the-top level of Maslow's hierarchy of needs is **esteem**, how a person is regarded by others and by himself or herself. Each of us needs to feel worthy in the eyes of others. From the satisfaction of this need, we gain a sense of competence, personal worth, and adequacy.

As Maslow uses the word, esteem includes self-esteem, how a person feels about himself or herself. The need for self-esteem cannot be overstated. The psychologist Arthur Witkin has written, "Perhaps the single most important thing is to be aware of a worker's need for self-esteem."[14] For most workers, even a passing word of praise or appreciation can be a strong motivator. Some companies have gone much further than that. At each Marriott Hotel, the staff picks an "employee of the month" whose picture is then prominently displayed. The employee also receives a gift.

Self-actualization   At the top of Maslow's hierarchy is self-actualization, which means self-fulfillment or the tapping of one's potential to one's own satisfaction. Few people do not wish to be better at what they do. The desire to be a better gardener, musician, carpenter, teacher, engineer, or salesperson is often triggered by the need for self-actualization. For nearly thirty years, Jack Lemmon made a name for himself as a light comedic actor. "The Odd Couple" and "Some Like It Hot" were two of his biggest hits. He then decided to test himself in dramas, including "The China Syndrome" and "Missing," for which he won the Academy Award for Best Actor. To much acclaim, Lemmon returned to the stage as the lead in what is commonly regarded as American drama's most difficult play, Eugene O'Neill's "Long Day's Journey into Night." At a time when many people might be expected to retire, Jack Lemmon made the critics reappraise him as a multidimensional actor.

The Hierarchy of Needs Today

Maslow based his theory about a hierarchy of needs on two observations. First, people satisfy their needs systematically, starting with the survival or physiological needs, then moving up the pyramid. Second, survival needs take priority over higher needs. We may say, however, that situations in life are not quite as precisely defined as Maslow made them appear. At any one time, a complex array of needs motivates an individual, and one activity may satisfy a number of them. Consider a business lunch, for example. You not only conduct business

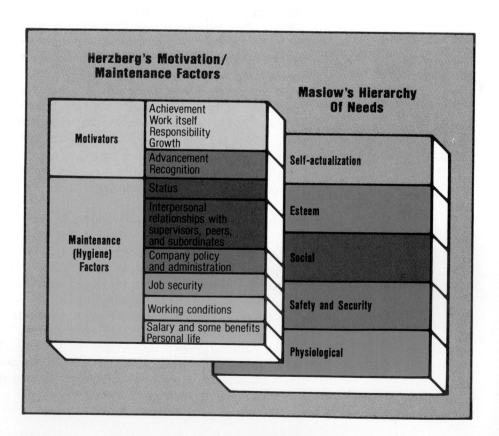

FIGURE 7-2

Abraham Maslow's and Frederick Herzberg's Models Compared

with your client but also satisfy the need for food and drink, and may well satisfy your social needs and fulfill your need for esteem as well.

To a great degree, American business has been able to satisfy its workers' survival needs — but it has not been so successful with their higher-order needs. This historic problem may become acute in the future because the generation now entering the work force has greater expectations than those that preceded it. These workers are better educated and want more from a job than just a paycheck and good fringe benefits. They are more apt to be motivated by the opportunity for participation in problem solving and decision making. Thus, the compensation they seek also includes meaningful work and recognition for what they do. These higher expectations place a considerable burden on management to develop a sophisticated understanding of human behavior.

FREDERICK HERZBERG'S MOTIVATION-MAINTENANCE MODEL

Frederick Herzberg, another psychologist, studied human behavior at work. He called his theory the **Motivation-Maintenance Model**.

Motivational factors are work-related experiences such as the following:

- ☐ Achievement
- ☐ Recognition
- ☐ Responsibility
- ☐ Advancement and growth
- ☐ The work itself

When these experiences are present, they tend to motivate employees to achieve higher production levels and to feel more committed to their jobs.

Maintenance (or **hygiene**) **factors** consist of the elements that form the work environment. They take their name from Herzberg's view that keeping these factors in good order is necessary to avoid the discontent that would reduce everyday levels of performance.[15] These factors include:

- ☐ Salaries and benefits
- ☐ Working conditions
- ☐ Relationships with superiors, coworkers, and subordinates
- ☐ Job security

Herzberg's Maintenance Factors vs. Motivational Factors

In short, maintenance factors are the basic benefits, rights, and conditions considered essential to any job. They are work place rewards that do not function as strong motivators. However, a reduction in their quality can create a level of dissatisfaction that may result in low productivity. At the least, a lack of maintenance factors hurts employee morale.

Motivational factors are those benefits above and beyond a job's maintenance factors. A regular paycheck certainly is a maintenance factor. Although wages are important and their reduction will lead to dissatisfaction, they are of low motivational value when they are present in adequate amounts. Both Herzberg and Maslow agree that the higher-order needs are more likely to motivate workers over the long run. A worker's sense of personal satisfaction in his or her work, an opportunity to grow on the job, and a feeling of being important seem to be lifelong motivating factors.

FIGURE 7-3

To illustrate how supervisors affect their relationships with subordinates, Douglas McGregor, a professor at Massachusetts Institute of Technology, developed two opposing models of management.

Theory X   Theory Y

DOUGLAS McGREGOR'S THEORY X AND THEORY Y

Supervisors and managers play key roles in motivating employees. The supervisors' overall management philosophies and attitudes toward their subordinates often determine the success of efforts to motivate employees and the way supervisors relate to their employees. To illustrate how supervisors affect their relationships with subordinates, Douglas McGregor, a professor at the Massachusetts Institute of Technology, developed two opposing models of management. He called them Theory X and Theory Y.[16] See Figure 7.3.

McGregor's **Theory X** holds that people really do not want to work and will avoid it if possible. To make people productive, it is necessary to push them, closely supervise them, and threaten them with some type of punishment. Because workers have little or no ambition, they prefer to avoid responsibility and will seek security above all.

Some have called this pessimistic theory a "carrot and stick" approach that combines rewards and punishments to motivate workers. In most cases, the reward is pay. Theory X managers and supervisors view employees as lazy, incompetent, and reluctant to accept responsibility, and they often treat employees with suspicion and little respect.

By contrast, McGregor's **Theory Y** holds that work is as natural to people as recreation and rest. Workers do not dislike work and, under the right conditions, will accept — in fact, seek out — responsibility. This theory says that employees do not want to be rigidly controlled or threatened with punishment. Instead, they look to work to satisfy many of their social, esteem, and self-actualization needs. It is up to the supervisor and the employer to provide an atmosphere in which they can do so.

Moog, Inc., a thirty-five-year-old heavy manufacturing company, typifies Theory Y management. Its three thousand employees do not punch time clocks but report their own time. Floor inspectors do not check every product; employees

Making High-Tech Offices for *People*

Technology's constant rapid changes mean that we use new machines in new environments before we have prepared ourselves for the human costs of adapting to the new technology. Most of us are so enthusiastic about the efficiency and perfection available with advanced technology that we don't stop to consider whether such enthusiasm might lead us to start looking for computer-like qualities in our friends and even to start treating the humans in our lives as though they were machines. Words like "technostress" and "technoanxiety" have been coined to describe the difficulties many people have in dealing with a world in which their co-workers and assistants may all be video monitors.

In response to such stresses, American businesses have begun to look more closely at interactions between people and technology. One of the greatest areas of interest is the office itself. Most businesses routinely treat new machines with the care appropriate to use with an expensive investment. But more and more companies are realizing that a good, long-term employee also represents a substantial investment. By one calculation, a company will put about $3 million into a $14,000-a-year worker over that worker's lifetime. Few companies would put a $3 million machine in a dusty, overheated corner. So a new breed of architects is promoting New Age Architecture and showing a new concern for how a building affects its occupants.

Over the last few years a revolution has quietly taken place in the attitudes of businesses towards their workers. In a recent survey by the American Society of Interior Designers, 99 percent of the executives at big American companies agreed that office design affects worker productivity. So now many companies are hunting not just for better personnel and better machines, but for better places to put them.

Some of the first changes have come in lighting. Many businesses have taken out the glaring, antiseptic lighting of the past, replacing it with softer, general lighting often supplemented by task-oriented lighting that can be directed by the worker. Natural light is being used whenever possible. Elements of solar design have found their way into business offices — windows are getting bigger and are placed more strategically, and skylights, open courtyards, and various kinds of sun spaces are being used to bring sunlight to everyone. Some architects are using a building's shape to achieve these ends. One corporate headquarters in South Carolina is just 65 feet across. Every office in the building gets two sets of windows, and energy costs are 50 percent lower than they would be in a traditional building of similar size.

This emphasis on natural light also helps provide workers with more outdoor views. Architects are moving away from the enclosed, sterile cubicles of the past and trying to give every office a view of nature, opening offices onto solar courts if not onto the outdoors. Recognizing that privacy is also important, designers have come up with long open offices punctuated by inner, closed offices with glass high on the walls to let light in.

Noise in these new offices is being controlled with carpeting and acoustical ceilings and partitions. And the problem of having to work where the machine is or near the electrical outlet is often combatted by designing buildings with "access floors." These half-foot-high spaces contain the room's wiring so that electricity and work stations can be moved where people want them, rather than people going where the work stations are.

In an effort to plan new buildings to be right for their workers from the start, architects now are involving the workers in the planning process, asking workers for a specific description of their needs and listening to what workers have to say about preliminary plans before starting to build. With more of such worker input and more attention to the elements of the workplace that affect workers, architects hope to make the building itself, not just the machines in it, "user-friendly."

Sources: Lois Friedland, "Where High Tech and Humans Meet," *SKY*, February 1985, 53. Erik Sandberg-Diment, "Waving to the Future from the Electronic Cottage," *The New York Times*, January 21, 1986, C3. Graig Brod, *Technostress* (Reading, Mass: Addison-Wesley, 1984), 14–21.

Theory X assumptions	1. People do not like work and try to avoid it.
	2. People do not like work, so managers have to control, direct, coerce, and threaten employees to get them to work toward organizational goals.
	3. People prefer to be directed, to avoid responsibility, to want security; they have little ambition.
Theory Y assumptions	1. People do not naturally dislike work; work is a natural part of their lives.
	2. People are internally motivated to reach objectives to which they are committed.
	3. People are committed to goals to the degree that they receive personal rewards when they reach their objectives.
	4. People will both seek and accept responsibility under favorable conditions.
	5. People have the capacity to be innovative in solving organizational problems.
	6. People are bright, but under most organizational conditions their potentials are underutilized.

Source: Ricky W. Griffin, *Management* (Boston: Houghton Mifflin Co., 1984), p. 47; Douglas McGregor, *The Human Side of Enterprise* (New York: McGraw-Hill Book Co., 1960), pp. 33–34, 47–48.

TABLE 7.1

McGregor's Theory X and Theory Y

check their own work. After ten years with the company, and every five years from then on, each employee gets an additional seven weeks of paid vacation. Moog's employees have responded by making its turnover rate less than 1 percent per year, and it has never had a work stoppage. Bill Moog, the company's founder and president, believed from the start that people "would be much more effectively motivated in an environment of trust, respect, positive rewards, and reinforcement than in an environment of coercion, punishment, and threats."[17]

THE DIMENSIONS OF MOTIVATION

Earlier in this chapter, we saw that motivation can be described as the drive to accomplish a particular goal. This definition suggests that in a work setting motivation is the result of rewards that a person receives while actually performing the job. These factors are the rewards known as internal motivators. However, rewards that are quite apart from what the job itself offers can provide their own motivation. These rewards are referred to as external motivators.

Internal Motivators

An intrinsic reward that occurs when a duty or task is performed is an internal motivator. In other words, it is the good feeling that one gets from doing something well.

Job Enrichment As Frederick Herzberg noted, work itself can be a motivational factor. For that reason, many companies have come to focus on the job itself as a motivator. After research found that work conditions can shape

MOTIVATIONAL SPEAKER

SHAPE UP OR SHIP OUT!

employee attitudes positively, many organizations started job enrichment programs, whose major goal is to make routine jobs more challenging and interesting by giving employees more independence and responsibility. Job enrichment can be as simple as giving a receptionist the responsibility for ordering supplies, or it can mean redesigning the work of an entire department. The Northwestern Mutual Life Insurance Company has reduced the drudgery associated with handling its overwhelming paperwork by redefining jobs. In the Milwaukee-based company's new-business department, sixty-four distinct job descriptions became six. Now the same number of people handle a variety of tasks, rather than just one each, so the work is less routine and more challenging. Maytag, the Corning Glass Works, IBM, and Motorola have also adopted job enrichment programs of one form or another.

The Three Types of Internal Motivation

Job Enlargement   A concept related to job enrichment is that of **job enlargement**, the adding to a worker's basic responsibilities of more responsibilities on the same skill and job level. A common means of job enlargement in manufacturing is to assign all the tasks involved in assembling a certain unit to one person rather than assigning one task to each of, say, five people.

Job Rotation   In a **job rotation** system, workers switch for a time from one job to another. Many companies use job rotation to give workers a more comprehensive view of the business or of production processes. The employee remains at a job long enough to become proficient in it before moving on to another job at the same level within the organization. Other companies use job rotation to alleviate stress, fatigue, or boredom. For example, many stores arrange to have an employee handle telephone calls from customers, a high-stress task, for no more than a few hours. The employee then works at a cash register or performs clerical tasks.

External Motivators

The most usual form in which external motivators appear is as rewards or other types of positive reinforcement provided to someone by another person. Reinforcement exerts a motivational force when a particular reward or reinforcement

Teamwork and customer satisfaction. *Bethlehem Steel employee teams look beyond their immediate jobs to get a picture of how products are eventually used and what customers really need. Visiting a General Motors plant gives workers at the Burns Harbor cold sheet mill division a better idea of what their jobs are all about.*

causes workers to respond in such a way that they increase the likelihood of their being rewarded in the same way again. In recent years, managers have tried many different types of external motivators to stimulate their subordinates' performance. Let us examine the more common ones.

Positive Reinforcement   A major component in productivity is employee satisfaction. Both Frederick Herzberg and Abraham Maslow cited the need for recognition and esteem as motivating forces. Demonstrations of appreciation for work well done can be cost-effective external motivators. A few sincere words of praise, an attractive plaque presented with ceremony to a loyal worker, or a letter of appreciation are common forms of **positive reinforcement**, actions following particular behavior that are designed to increase the likelihood of that behavior's being repeated. Positive reinforcement is perhaps the least expensive, most effective way to improve productivity and raise employee morale. As the authors of *The One Minute Manager* suggest, good managers try to "catch people doing something right!"[18] Employees who feel unappreciated often do not perform to the best of their abilities. In settings where supervisors emphasize what is wrong with employee performance, employees often become demoralized and defensive.

The Four Types of External Motivation

Management Expectations   The expectations of others can greatly influence people. Studies have shown that if teachers expect their students to be high achievers, the students often live up to those expectations. Other studies, on work-place motivation, have shown that the same principle applies to managers and workers. A manager's failure to be clear about his or her expectations can result in decreased motivation and increased frustration in an employee. Managers can motivate employees just by clearly communicating their expectations, letting their subordinates know what they want done, and when and how to do it. Managers can create an atmosphere in which their subordinates expect positive reinforcement and behave accordingly.[19] It is then up to the manager to monitor performance and provide positive feedback when it is merited.

Awards and Premiums Every year, American companies hand out about $8 billion in awards and premiums to their employees. These include color televisions, vacations, rings, pins, certificates, pens and pencils, and a host of other items. By giving these bonuses to employees, management intends them to get certain results. The principal goals are to

☐ Reduce absenteeism
☐ Improve sales
☐ Improve quality control
☐ Increase application of training program content
☐ Improve customer relations
☐ Reduce on-the-job accidents

This motivational technique dates back to at least the late 1800s when John H. Patterson, the founder of the National Cash Register Company (today's NCR), used a variety of award programs to motivate his sales force. Many businesses also use awards and premiums to stimulate suggestions for cost-saving practices. During the energy crisis of the late 1970s and early 1980s, the Gillette Company offered cash bonuses for useful ways to cut its electric and oil bills. In one remarkable case, a General Motors employee earned $30,000 in one year for his suggestions and had earned more than $70,000 for suggestions made over the years before that.[20] Some companies also offer merchandise awards, in addition to or in place of cash.

Award and premium programs are not without their critics. One concern is that they tend to merely "paper over" problems. For instance, a company that decides to offer trading stamps or other incentives to reduce absenteeism may overlook the bad working conditions or poor supervisors that are causing the problem. Such programs may also reinforce the wrong behavior. A salesperson set on winning a bonus trip to Hawaii or Bermuda may push a customer into buying a product that is not right for that person's needs. Despite these and other criticisms, however, the popularity of award and premium incentive programs continues to grow.

Financial Incentives Money is, of course, one of the most common sorts of external motivation. Although Herzberg and others regard cash as a maintenance — not a motivational — factor, one cannot overlook the power of financial incentives. An employee's pay often represents more than just money to that person. Pay levels also signify recognition and esteem. Employees commonly use the company pay scale to compare their worth and achievements with others. A host of corporations use financial incentives to boost productivity, improve quality, reduce operating expenses, improve attendance, or some combination of these goals. In the future, American businesses seem likely to experiment with a variety of "pay for performance" plans.

INVOLVING THE EMPLOYEE IN DECISION MAKING

The idea of bringing employees into the decision-making process in the work place is not new. The merits of increased worker involvement have been discussed for many years. In 1960, Walter Reuther, then president of the United Auto Workers, said, "I think in addition to earning your bread and butter that work ought to give you a sense of participation in the creative process."[21] Some companies have involved employees in decision making for years, but for the vast majority it is a new experience.

The Quality of Work Life Movement

The drive to achieve a better work-place environment for employees while increasing profitability for the employer is known as the **Quality of Work Life** (QWL) movement. Achieving its goals requires a process through which people become involved in creating an organization that achieves a satisfactory balance of business, human, and social needs.[22]

The key word in the QWL process is **involvement**, which brings employees, unions, and management closer together, for their mutual benefit. The QWL process also involves people in the day-to-day decision-making process on the job.[23] More than three thousand companies have QWL programs today, including IBM, General Motors, Sprague Electric, and Friendly Ice Cream. But even small firms can benefit from QWL. In the 1970s, John Simmons headed the World Bank's program to implement decentralized decision making. He became convinced that in QWL lay the key to revolutionizing American business. He left the World Bank to take over the firm his family had owned for generations, Simmons Construction Company. He immediately decided to practice what he preached by selling the firm to its employees. Simmons, who remained as chairman, proudly noted recently that under employee control, the company had "made more money in the last four years than it did in the previous fifteen."[24]

Theory Z

Three New Methods of Involving Employees in Decision Making

The QWL movement received a boost in 1981 from William G. Ouchi's best seller, *Theory Z.*[25] At the time he wrote, Japanese productivity was the highest in the world and productivity in the Western world had been declining for years. In **Theory Z**, Professor Ouchi outlined how American business could meet the challenges Japan poses. He provided new insights into the relationships between Japanese workers and their employers. He also made it clear that technological innovation was not the only reason for Japan's extraordinary success — employee involvement in a wide range of problem-solving and decision-making activities might be the key to their productivity. See Figure 7.4.

Since *Theory Z*'s publication, we have learned a great deal more about Japanese organizations. The Japanese emphasize lifetime employment, shared responsibility for making and implementing decisions, and a close working relationship

FIGURE 7-4

Theory Z

Professor William G. Ouchi of
Japan outlined how American
business could meet the
challenges Japan poses.

Theory Z

between management and the representatives of labor unions. Perhaps most importantly, Japanese organizations foster a climate of trust. Without trust, as many companies of the Theory X type have discovered, human relationships degenerate into conflict.

The bottom line, as QWL advocate John Simmons puts it, is quite clear: "High performance firms today are idea factories. They have learned how to generate, nurture and implement ideas and do it quickly. At Toyota, the average Japanese worker produces 44 ideas per year. Employee participation is the only way to do that, and the most cost effective way to do that."[26]

Quality Circles

One of the ways the Japanese have improved the quality of their products and increased their productivity is by organizing groups of workers into **quality circles**. These groups volunteer to meet regularly, often on a weekly basis, on company time to discuss ways to improve work procedures, eliminate defects, and perform their work more efficiently. The groups are usually small, commonly from six to eight people. Members receive special training that enables them to participate effectively. They share with management the results of their discussions.

The Third New Way of Involving
Employees in Decision Making

Over four hundred American companies have now adopted the quality circle idea or a variant of it. Mercury Marine was one of the first to try it. From the start, its program had these objectives:

☐ Improve quality
☐ Reduce waste
☐ Improve communications
☐ Develop group problem solving
☐ Increase work satisfaction[27]

Quality circles. *Employee involvement is important to Burlington Industries, Inc. This quality circle gets the data it needs to analyze company problems. After selecting a problem and making recommendations, workers get feedback from management. The process allows workers to refine their problem-solving abilities.*

Quality circles have the potential to improve communications throughout an organization. Management can learn the best ways to accomplish a task from the people who are actually doing it day in and day out. The very opportunity for communicating with higher levels in the organization encourages employees to contribute valuable ideas that often lead to significant cost savings.

ALTERNATIVE WORK PATTERNS

With better communications between workers and management has come clearer understanding of their respective needs. Particularly in the area of work scheduling, management now reacts more favorably to innovative proposals.

Flexitime

Some companies have adopted a policy of replacing traditional fixed work hours with a more flexible time (**flexitime**) schedule set by employees within the company's guidelines. Typically, companies using this policy divide the work day into two categories: core time and flexible time. During core time, typically 9:30 A.M. to 3:00 P.M., all employees must be at work. Flexible time is usually the three to three and a half hours on either side of the core time, as in Figure 7.6. Employees are free to choose when to arrive and leave during those periods, as long as they put in their required hours.

Second Thoughts About Japanese Management

The image of Japanese business in America has gone through tremendous changes. In the fifties, "Made in Japan" was the punch line for bad jokes, and Americans generally thought of Japanese industry as capable of making only souvenirs, trinkets, and poor imitations of American products. The Japanese got their revenge in the seventies, when Japanese exports of everything from cars to electronic goods to cameras became so popular in American markets that American producers clamored for protection. Having finally realized that Japanese business was onto something very important, American management experts began to search for the Japanese secret.

The result was a rash of articles about quality circles, worker loyalty, and "theory Z." According to these articles, the Japanese encourage a warm, cooperative relationship between workers and management. In "quality circle" meetings, managers listen to, and even encourage, worker suggestions about improving productivity and making work easier, believing that workers often know better than outside consultants how to improve production. Instead of staying behind their desks, Japanese managers get down on the production line with the workers, often dressing like employees. This spirit of cooperation helps raise productivity, cut absenteeism, and foster in workers intense loyalty to their company. Above all, the Japanese emphasize quality and mean it, as opposed to some American companies that talk about quality but are really interested in quantity and profits. Having identified such "secrets," many American companies and business schools rushed to imitate the Japanese models.

Recently, however, the Japanese model for management has been attacked from a number of different vantage points. Many wonder if we have jumped too quickly to imitate Japanese "secrets." Although the International Association of Quality Circles lists 2000 American companies among its members, one study found that 60 percent of the companies surveyed felt lukewarm at best about their quality circles. Ironically, only 10 percent of Japanese companies in the United States use them. Labor unions worry when the suggestions that arise from quality circles seem to threaten jobs, and some Japanese experts insist that American workers aren't properly educated or trained to handle this radical shift in labor-management relations.

According to management expert Peter Drucker, Japanese methods don't translate directly into American successes, in part because America has very different notions about competitiveness and cooperation. The Japanese tend to put national interest first and to seek common ground with opponents, rather than concentrate on short-term individual goals, as Americans often do. Most Japanese workers take for granted that what is good for the company is good for them. They are appalled by the bitter struggles of American labor and management.

Many companies still have difficulty dealing with American unions, and some have had to drop particular aspects of the Japanese model. In Japanese auto plants workers are often trained to do more than one job so they can move around and vary their routines. But Japanese companies have found that American workers tend to feel more comfortable doing just one task.

Whatever the conclusions future management experts draw, it seems clear that we will continue to watch closely what the Japanese do. The rest of the world envies their ability to produce quality goods inexpensively, and there's no question that they have much to teach us. But the greatest lesson we can learn from the Japanese may be that before we try to imitate foreign methods, we must look much more closely at the culture and contexts in which those methods evolved and function.

Sources: B. Bruce-Briggs, "The Dangerous Folly Called Theory Z," *Fortune*, Vol. 105, No. 10, May 17, 1982, 41. Peter F. Drucker, "Behind Japan's Success," *Harvard Business Review*, Vol. 59, No. 1, January-February 1981, 83–90. Jeremy Main, "The Trouble with Managing Japanese-Style," *Fortune*, Vol. 109, No. 7, April 2, 1984, 50–56. John Junkerman, "The Japanese Model," *The Progressive*, Vol. 47, No. 5, May 1983, 21. Carey W. English, "How Japanese Work Out as Bosses in U.S.," *U.S. News & World Report*, Vol. 98, No. 17, May 6, 1985, 75.

Flexitime   Job Sharing   Telecommuting

FIGURE 7-5

Alternative Work Patterns

Along with better communications between management and employees has come a better understanding of the other person's needs. Alternative work schedules are now growing in popularity in America.

Four Types of Alternative Work Patterns

Control Data Corporation introduced flexitime in the United States in 1972. Since then the Nestlé Food Corporation and the Occidental Life Insurance Company and others have adopted it. In Europe, about 40 percent of the Swiss work force, 30 percent of the West German, and 20 percent of the French take advantage of flexitime.[28]

Most studies of flexitime report there are benefits to both the organization and its workers. Employees can set their own work hours to avoid traffic tieups and other commuter problems. They adjust their work hours to match their own energy rhythms, which can help avoid stress and ultimate burnout. In addition, flexitime permits people to take care of personal business, such as banking or dealing with public agencies, during regular work days without taking a day off. From the companies' point of view, supervisors can make better use of their employees' time. Many companies report that flexitime has raised employee morale, reduced tardiness and absenteeism, and cut turnover rates.

The Compressed Work Week

Some companies have adopted a variant of flexitime, the **compressed work week**, a scheduling system that permits workers to vary the number of days they work from the traditional five — without changing the total number of hours worked. A compressed work week often permits workers to put in four ten-hour days instead of five eight-hour days. Workers at Electro Scientific Industries, Inc., in Portland, Oregon, not only have these options but may also work four 8.8-hour days and a half day on Friday.[29]

Job Sharing

A program in which two people share one job is known as **job sharing**. It is particularly popular among working mothers. One such mother took maternity

FIGURE 7-6

Flexitime

Typically, companies using
flexitime divide the work day
into two categories: core time
and flexible time.

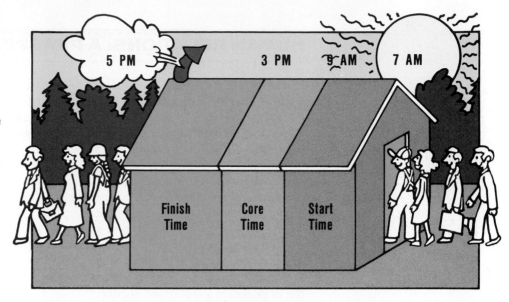

leave to have her baby, and faced a difficult decision when it ran out. She did not want to give up her career as a lawyer, but she also wanted to spend time with her child. Job sharing in a program sponsored by the New York State Department of Law where she worked allowed her to do both. She now works half time and receives half her normal pay.

Job sharing is likely to increase in the future. It will continue to appeal to mothers who work, but it will also benefit the increasing numbers of middle-aged persons who must take care of elderly family members. A recent study of employees at the Travelers Insurance Company in Hartford, Connecticut, revealed that 28 percent of the employees surveyed, all of whom were over thirty, spent an average of 10.2 hours per week caring for aged relatives and friends.[30]

Telecommuting

A growing number of Americans are **telecommuters**. According to Jack Nilles, the University of Southern California professor who coined the term,[31] these are persons "who work at home or in a satellite office and electronically transfer the information needed to do their job between home/satellite and headquarters."

The Fourth Type of Alternative
Work Pattern

Of course, some jobs, like sales, often center on activities outside the office, but telecommuting is substantially different from such traditional work. Within the next few years, about 5 million people will come to work at home two or three days each week. What is more, an even higher number could do so if they and their employers were willing. The technology is ready and waiting.

To date a number of companies have successfully experimented with telecommuting. The J. C. Penney Co., Inc., the American Express Company, and the Blue Cross and Blue Shield Association are among them. For the last several years, the New York Telephone Company has had a group of managers who worked at home. The company has noted significant gains in productivity among its telecommuters. Their jobs center primarily on writing training materials, screening employment applications, and financial forecasting.

HUMAN RELATIONS: A PERSPECTIVE

Managers are increasingly focusing on human relations in business. The job-creation statistics tell much of the story. Of the 9.8 million new jobs created between November 1982 and October 1985, 1.2 million were in manufacturing. Twice that number were in retail trade, but nearly three times that number — 3.1 million — were in business services. In fact, 7.7 million of the 9.8 million jobs created in this period were in the service sector.[32]

Karl Albrecht and Ron Zemke have pointed out in their best seller, *Service America*, that relationships in a service economy are more important than physical products. Restaurants, banks, hospitals, public utilities, colleges, airlines, and retail stores all have the problem of gaining — and retaining — their clients' and customers' patronage. Every service firm has, perhaps, thousands of "moments of truth," those critical incidents when customers come into direct contact with the organization. It is those moments when customers form their impressions of the organization's quality and service.[33]

Beyond this interaction between members of an organization and the public, managers have had to look carefully at the relationship between employees and their tasks and among the employees themselves. Managers have come to realize that productivity and job satisfaction increase when employees work as teams and can make decisions about how to perform their tasks. This emphasis exists in the service sector, where it is quite common to hear phrases like "the health care team."[34] The approach is becoming equally common on the manufacturing floor. However, the most important change of orientation is among managers themselves. As Crawford H. Greenewalt of Du Pont has noted: "Teams of laborers built the pyramids and teams of craftsmen the medieval cathedrals. Now, for the first time, however, management itself has become a team effort."[35]

Chapter Highlights

1. Define human relations.

Human relations include all the types of interactions among people: conflicts, cooperative efforts, and group relationships.

2. Explain what motivation is and describe the origins of the modern approach to it.

Motivation can be defined as the factors that cause a person to behave in a certain way or to accomplish a certain goal. The modern approach to the study of motivation began in 1927 with the Hawthorne studies by Elton Mayo and his colleagues at Western Electric.

3. Describe Abraham Maslow's hierarchy of needs.

Maslow proposed a theory of motivation based on a hierarchy of needs: physiological, safety and security, social, esteem, and self-actualization. Needs are generally satisfied systematically (that is, from the lowest to the highest), and only needs that have not been satisfied are motivators.

4. Describe Frederick Herzberg's motivation maintenance model.

According to Herzberg, needs can be divided into two primary categories: motivational factors and maintenance factors. Motivational factors, which cause workers to be more productive and to feel more committed to their jobs, include experiences of achievement, recognition, responsibility, advancement and growth, and inherent satisfaction in the work itself. Maintenance factors do not serve as motivators in themselves but lead to dissatisfaction when they are lacking. They include salaries and benefits, working conditions, interpersonal relationships, and job security.

5. Explain the differences between Douglas McGregor's Theory X and Theory Y.

Theory X states that people do not want to work and will avoid it if they can. They must be pushed, closely supervised, and threatened with punishment if they are to be productive. They have little ambition and seek security above all. Theory Y argues that work is as natural as rest and recreation and that workers will seek out responsibility on their own. Managers must provide an environment in which workers can satisfy their social, esteem, and self-actualization needs.

6. Describe some important internal and external motivators in the work place.

Internal motivators are the rewards that one gets from feelings inside oneself. Many companies today use the job itself as a motivator. People's feelings of reward and self-worth are enhanced through job enrichment (making routine jobs more challenging and interesting by giving employees more independence and responsibility), job enlargement (adding responsibilities at the same skill and job level), and job rotation (providing an opportunity for workers to perform a number of jobs at the same level). External motivators are rewards given to someone by another person. They include positive reinforcement, (good evaluations, praise), positive feedback about an employee's abilities and performance, awards and premiums, and financial incentives.

7. Describe three new strategies for involving employees in decision making.

The quality of work life (QWL) movement focuses on bringing employees, unions, and management closer together for their mutual benefit and attempts to decentralize decision making, thus fostering a sense of involvement throughout the organization. William G. Ouchi expanded upon this idea in *Theory Z*, which attempted to explain the reasons for Japan's extraordinary business success. Ouchi pointed out that Japanese organizations are based on trust, an expectation of lifetime employment, shared responsibility, and a close relationship between management and unions. Theory Z organizations try to promote such attitudes here. Quality circles are another idea adopted from the Japanese. Small groups of workers meet to discuss ways to improve work procedures, promote quality, and increase efficiency. Members generally receive special training. Quality circles can improve communications throughout an organization and lead to significant cost savings.

8. Identify the four types of alternative work patterns in use today and describe their prospects.

Four common alternative work patterns are flexitime, the compressed work week, job sharing, and telecommuting. Flexitime has been widely adopted and has been found to benefit both the organization and its workers. The compressed work week, in which employees work the same number of total hours per week but vary the number of work days, has not been as widely adopted. Job sharing, in which two people share a single job, is likely to increase in the future. As the number of working women with young children or middle-aged people with elderly family members increases, the attractiveness of job sharing will doubtless rise. Telecommuting (working at home or in a satellite location and transferring information to the main office electronically) will become even easier and more affordable.

Key Terms

External motivator	Job enrichment	Motivation	Quality of Work Life
Flexitime	programs	Motivational factors	(QWL) movement
Hawthorne studies	Job rotation	Need	Secondary needs
Hierarchy of needs	Job sharing	Physiological needs	Telecommuters
Human relations	Maintenance (hygiene)	Psychological needs	Theory X and
Involvement	factors	Quality circles	Theory Y
Job enlargement	Morale		Theory Z

Review Questions

1. Define human relations.
2. What is the relationship between high morale and human relations in an organization?
3. What was the most important finding by researchers involved in the Hawthorne studies? If the study were to be duplicated today, would the findings be different?
4. Briefly describe Abraham Maslow's hierarchy of needs. How are a person's needs related to his or her motivation?
5. Is it possible to achieve self-actualization in the modern work place? Explain your answer.
6. Briefly describe Frederick Herzberg's motivation-maintenance model. Explain the difference between maintenance (hygiene) factors and motivational factors.
7. Compare Douglas McGregor's Theory X and Theory Y. Why is it important for modern managers to study these two motivational theories?
8. What is the difference between internal and external motivation? Give examples of each.
9. Describe the terms *job enrichment* and *job enlargement*. Give examples of each.
10. What are some of the principal goals of award and premium programs?
11. Describe the Quality of Work Life (QWL) movement. In what ways has Theory Z contributed to the QWL movement?

Application Exercises

1. Within the next week, talk to three persons who hold supervisory or management positions. Ask them which is the bigger challenge in their business careers: people problems or technical problems. If time permits, discuss the problems with them in detail, and record their responses in writing.
2. Many organizations throughout America experience high rates of employee turnover. In many retail businesses the turnover rate is 60 percent annually. In some service industries, such as fast foods, the turnover rate is 90 percent annually. What external rewards might be used to reduce turnover and increase worker productivity?

Cases

7.1 UPS: Doing It Their Way

United Parcel Service (UPS) believes that its employees should give the firm a fair day's work for a fair day's pay. The package delivery firm seems willing to give more than a fair day's pay. Its drivers earn about $1 more per hour than drivers at any other trucking company. But in return, UPS expects maximum output from its employees.

Since the 1920s, the firm's industrial engineers have been studying every detail of every task performed by most UPS employees. From their studies have come time and motion standards that govern how those tasks are performed and how long they should take. Drivers, for example, are expected to walk to a customer's door at a speed of exactly three feet per second. They are told to knock as soon as they get there, rather than waste time looking for a doorbell.

Work engineers are continually riding with drivers, timing everything from stops at traffic lights, to waits at customers' doorways, to stairway climbs, to coffee breaks. And they are not averse to pointing out the occasional inefficiency — as when a driver handles a package more than once. In addition, supervisors ride with the "least best" drivers, noting how they work and constantly correcting them until their work is up to standard.

The work standards extend to package sorters at UPS depots as well. Each sorter is expected to handle 1,124 packages every hour, reading the Zip code on each one and then placing it on a conveyor belt. One mistake is allowed every 2,500 packages.

The object of all this work engineering is efficiency — and UPS has been called one of the most efficient companies anywhere. It is also a highly profitable company. Most drivers take the regimentation in stride; many show pride in meeting the UPS standards each day. Others, however, feel that they are constantly being pushed, that it is impossible for them to relax at work. UPS officials claim that the standards provide accountability. And, they say, employees who work according to UPS standards should feel less tired at the end of the day.

UPS's human relations techniques have served the firm well so far. But they are about to be put to a double test. UPS recently invested more than $2 billion on airplanes with which to enter the overnight air delivery market, boasting rates about half those of more established overnight carriers.

Questions

1. Discuss UPS's relations with its drivers in terms of the Maslow, Herzberg, and McGregor motivation models.
2. What might UPS gain, and what might it lose, by involving its drivers in workplace decision making?

Source: For more information, see *The Wall Street Journal*, April 22, 1986, pp. 1, 23; *New England Business*, April 21, 1986, pp. 57–64; and *Newsweek*, February 7, 1983, pp. 55–56.

7.2 Work Life at Steelcase

Eighty-eight percent of the people working at Steelcase Inc., a Grand Rapids, Michigan, manufacturer of office furniture, were working there ten years ago. Seventy-two percent of its employees were there fifteen years ago. Many are second- and third-generation employees. The firm receives about 30,000 unsolicited job requests each year, but hires according to a somewhat unique policy. Twenty percent of new employees are recruited from minorities, families in hardship, and some former employees. The remaining 80 percent must be sponsored by current employees. And because so many friends and relatives are sponsored whenever the company requests applications, applicants are considered according to the seniority of the sponsor.

Why the clamor for jobs at Steelcase? Average factory workers' earnings at the firm are about 20 percent higher than the regional average, the company contributes 15 percent to a profit sharing plan, and has both bonus and incentive programs, along with a wide range of employee benefits.

And there's a lot more besides:

☐ The firm is developing robots to perform the most tedious manufacturing operations. The final assembly line has been replaced with assembly benches where pairs of workers do complete assembly. The newer system requires more employee training but involves much less drudgery.

☐ Steelcase designs and builds all new machinery in-house. The firm continually solicits input from the person who will be operating each machine, and when it is delivered to the work area it bears a plate with that employee's name on it.

☐ The firm's incentive plan, by which employees have added as much as 80 percent to their paychecks, is run on the honor system. Employees keep track of their own incentive bonuses.

In return, Steelcase demands the best from its employees. The firm has a reputation for quality and for meeting promised delivery dates, and employees must work toward both goals. Quality is checked first by the workers themselves, then by supervisors. Work that it not up to standard must be redone

Steelcase also has a formal system for taking disciplinary action. Various infractions result in the assessing of points; for example, an employee who is late without an excuse gets 10 points, and infractions such as careless workmanship, theft, drinking during working hours, and insubordination are worth up to 120 points. A worker who accumulates 160 points is summarily dismissed — but along the way, he or she will have been counseled at least once concerning the problem. Many of those who lose their jobs are eventually rehired — and most of them remain.

One thing Steelcase does not have to demand from its employees is loyalty; that develops naturally. Since it was founded in 1912, the firm has never had a work stoppage, and 96 percent of its shipments (valued at over $1 billion per year, from twenty-one plants) arrive on time. Steelcase seems to practice what *Inc.* magazine has called *workstyle*, and which might best be characterized as a concern for the quality of work life. Obviously, most people are quick to respond to that concern.

Questions

1. Evaluate Steelcase Inc.'s attention to employee wants as listed in Table 7.1, and its concern for the quality of work life generally.
2. Is Steelcase too demanding of employees in some ways? Explain.
3. Does Steelcase's approach to employee relations increase or decrease the work and responsibility of management? Why?

Sources: For more information see *Inc.*, January 1986, pp. 45–54; *Management Review*, November 1985, pp. 46–51; and *Forbes*, October 7, 1985, pp. 90–99.

The American working environment is undergoing a quiet revolution, partly in response to new ideas and competition from overseas. The relationships between worker and manager and manager and company have changed. Labor unions are losing ground as workers and management reach uneasy alliances, trying to keep jobs from moving overseas. Robots and computers continue to scare some and to replace others, but most workers have learned to live with — sometimes even love — their high-tech tools. And more employers are accepting the idea that the health and well-being of their employees affect their performance and productivity.

Many of the changes in the American work place, particularly in American factories, have come about in large measure because of the success of Japanese industry. American manufacturers were motivated to change their work places because they had to do something to improve efficiency. So they have set out to discover the secret to Japanese success, the holy grail of American management. The Japanese seem to get a lot of ideas, work, and loyalty from their workers. From the Japanese, American companies have learned to use quality circles, groups of workers who get together to trade ideas on how they can improve the quality of their work. Following the Japanese model, many U.S. companies are encouraging their workers to participate more in decision making.

Some workers are participating by becoming owners through employee stock ownership plans. Most such plans were originally set up to give workers a chance to revive a dying company that management had given up on. Employee-owned companies like Weirton Steel have been very successful, reviving profits, keeping jobs from moving overseas, and motivating workers with the feeling that they're working for themselves. However, the tax advantages of the plans have led some companies to give workers a share in owning the company solely as a way to benefit management.

Struggling companies have also resorted to a relatively new kind of wage agreement, the two-tier contract, which establishes two different pay scales for exactly the same work. Current workers are generally kept on the higher pay scale but new recruits may make only half as much as the people they work next to. Such agreements allow unions

The Changing Work Place

and current workers to save face — and money — by not giving away any current benefits. But in the long run such plans create a lower class of worker and undercut the rights and benefits that workers have fought for over the last century.

Another new variation on the relationships in the work place is worker leasing. Operating mostly in the West and Southwest, and serving mostly small businesses, employee-leasing firms provide employees with benefit and pension packages and lease companies the number of workers they need, when they need them. Because they don't have to keep track of things like employee pension plans, employers can reduce administrative paperwork. One owner of a meat-packing company fired all of his workers, including himself, and instantly rehired them from a leasing company, thus greatly simplifying his life. Employees who want to change jobs like the arrangement because they can change employers without losing benefits. So far only about two dozen worker-leasing firms are involved, but these firms are growing quickly.

Some companies are redesigning buildings, offices, and machines. Some are converting old buildings, making factories into restaurants, condominiums, and boutiques. Others are building high-tech offices, giving workers more natural light and more control over the physical setup of desks, computers, and machines. They're buying company

exercycles and setting up lunchtime volleyball and jogging programs. Some enroll employees in health plans and take preventive health care to heart. Companies are now more likely than ever to offer employees drug or alcohol counseling. And either in response to local laws or just to keep their employees happy, many are now prohibiting on-the-job smoking.

In response to employees' desires for more control over their work time, many businesses have instituted flextime plans. Under most such plans, employees must be at work for certain core hours at midday, but they have the option of either coming early in the morning or staying late in the afternoon to put in the remainder of their hours. Flextime allows employees time to run errands during business hours and makes scheduling easier for two-worker families.

Although these plans give workers more responsibility and control, other trends show that a certain degree of trust seems to be ebbing out of the American work place. More and more companies are screening employees with drug tests, lie detector tests, and psychological tests. The results of all such tests have been challenged as inaccurate, misleading, and unfair. Often such testing blurs the fine line between a company's looking out for its best interests and invasion of privacy. Many workers wonder why companies have suddenly involved themselves in police

work. But for now the practice seems to be on the rise, and the question of whether or not to submit to such tests faces many people entering the work force.

There are considerably more women in the work force than there were a decade or two ago. The barriers which excluded women from some positions are slowly breaking down, although women still have a very difficult time making it to the top of big corporations. In the past decade the issue of sexual harassment on the job has received a lot of attention, and women have established their right to a fully equal status in the work place. The government has dropped its support of most affirmative action programs and their future is in doubt, but many businesses have grown accustomed to them and have recognized the benefits of hiring some women and minority workers. For years American executives have generally been white and male, with bosses picking men like themselves to move up the corporate ladder. But the employees in the offices of the future are likely to be a more heterogeneous group.

The movement of more women out of homes and into the work force has spawned a host of other changes. Day care centers have become big businesses, looking after the children of two-career couples. Pregnant women are staying on the job much longer than they used to, and mothers are more often bringing their children into the office. Men, too are adapting to the changes, and many fathers are — slowly — learning to take on more of the parenting and homemaking roles that have been traditionally left to women.

Fast becoming a standard item in virtually every type of American work place is the computer. You see them on secretaries' desks, at the "Pay Here" tables of flea markets, and on the school principal's desk. Computers — and especially their mechanical extensions, robots — have replaced some workers and have changed the work habits of millions more. Typically, people given computers as tools to improve their work have overcome initial fear and anxiety and become grateful for their ability to eliminate busy work and for their potential to help out with virtually every process that involves numbers and words.

Of course the new ideas from Japan have caught on in only a minority of American businesses and may not affect the overall work force for some time to come. Many people worry that budget cuts in the Occupational Safety and Health Administration and the current administration's "hands off" policy have led many employers to think less about worker safety. But with America's industrial leaders spreading the word that a happy and healthy worker is a better, more productive worker, the movement to improve the American work place should continue to pick up momentum.

III

HUMAN RESOURCES AND PRODUCTION

John Naisbitt and others who have carefully studied the American business scene say that human capital has replaced dollar capital as the strategic resource. To develop this resource, American companies are spending $30 billion each year on training and education programs. And a growing number of union bargaining agreements contain components for the education and training of workers who need retraining. In Part III we examine the broad field of human resource management, including labor-management relations. Operations management, the process of coordinating the production of goods and services with all the activities associated with production, is also discussed in this section.

8

MANAGING HUMAN RESOURCES

Learning Objectives

After you have completed this chapter, you will be able to do the following:

■ Explain what human resource management is and describe the factors that have contributed to its importance.

■ Explain the human resource planning process.

■ List the steps in the employment process.

■ Identify the primary purposes of performance appraisals and describe three appraisal techniques.

■ Describe several training methods and development methods.

■ Explain how compensation systems achieve their three primary purposes.

Why do companies like Polaroid, the Southland Corporation, IBM, and AT&T underwrite day-care programs for their employees' children?[1] And why do companies like Procter & Gamble and Pacific National Bank offer from three to six months' unpaid paternity leave to new fathers?[2] It is probably impossible to point to a company's financial statements and show that such programs have increased its revenues. Nevertheless, these benefits create a positive working environment while raising worker productivity. They therefore affect the bottom line.

Human resources require careful management, as does any other resource. In this chapter, you will begin exploring the management techniques that successful businesses use to attract, keep, and develop productive employees.

THE GROWTH OF HUMAN RESOURCE MANAGEMENT

What Human Resource Development Is

The last two decades have seen a marked change in **human resource development**, those activities involved in acquiring, developing, and using people effectively in a business. The three key words used to describe the field reflect the changes in it. Until the mid-1960s, the people involved in human resource work were usually called personnel managers. Their duties normally centered on hiring, keeping employment records, attending to minor medical benefits problems, and organizing company teams and outings. Since then, dramatic changes have occurred in our society and in the make-up of the work force. Figure 8.1 shows some dramatic changes in the work force. From the standpoint of human resource development, the most important of these factors are

☐ The entry of minorities into skilled jobs and the professions.
☐ An enormous increase in the number of women in the work place.
☐ An increasingly better educated population.

The Legal Environment

Beginning in the 1960s, government action accelerated the changes in the social attitudes that have altered the American work force. Collectively, these federal, state, and local regulations are known as the **antidiscrimination laws**, since they forbid treating people differently — particularly in employment and housing — because of their not being the "right" religion, color, sex, race, age, or national origin. Table 8.1 lists the major federal antidiscrimination laws, regulations, and executive orders.

Factors in the Development of Human Resources

The Civil Rights Act of 1964 The law foremost in the minds of those responsible for human resources development is the **Civil Rights Act of 1964**, which is commonly referred to as **Title VII**, after its key section. That part declares it to be illegal to discriminate in employment against any individual in respect to his or her compensation as well as the terms and conditions or privileges of employment because of that individual's race, color, religion, sex, or national origin.

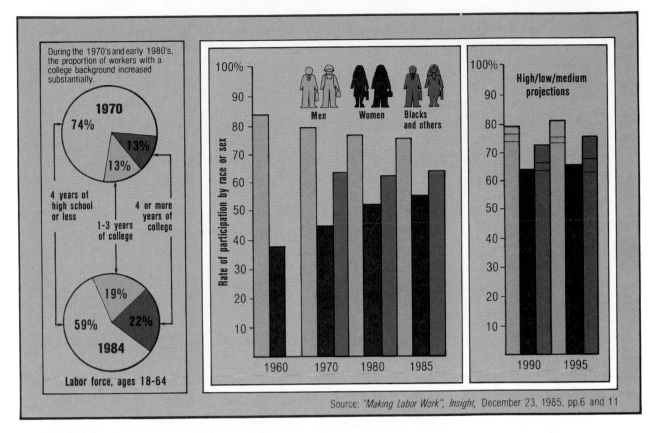

During the 1970's and early 1980's, the proportion of workers with a college background increased substantially.

1970

74%

13%

13%

4 years of high school or less

4 or more years of college

1-3 years of college

19%

59%

22%

1984

Labor force, ages 18-64

Rate of participation by race or sex

100%

90

80

70

60

50

40

30

20

10

Men

Women

Blacks and others

1960   1970   1980   1985

100%

90

80

70

60

50

40

30

20

10

High/low/medium projections

1990   1995

Source: *"Making Labor Work", Insight,* December 23, 1985, pp.6 and 11

FIGURE 8-1

Dramatic Changes in the Work Force

In recent years dramatic changes in our society and in the make-up of the work force have occurred.

How Antidiscrimination Laws Have Affected Human Resource Development

In 1972, Congress revised or amended *Title VII* of the Civil Rights Act by means of the **Equal Employment Opportunity Act**. This act created the **Equal Employment Opportunity Commission (EEOC)**, which enforces the employment-related aspects of the antidiscrimination laws. This independent board consists of five members appointed by the president. The EEOC's staff of attorneys and investigators evaluates complaints of discrimination. If a complaint appears to be valid, the staff first attempts to work out a settlement with the employer. If this effort fails, the staff seeks the commission's permission to file a lawsuit against the employer.

Enforcement of the antidiscrimination laws is not limited to the EEOC. All the states, many localities, and individuals themselves can enforce these laws.

Affirmative Action Programs Beginning with the Civil Rights Act of 1964, many federal provisions have required employers to develop **affirmative action programs**. These programs consist of written plans to hire, train, and promote minority workers and women. A plan typically states a program's goals, the steps to achieve them, and timetables that the employer has committed itself to follow.

Not all employers must develop affirmative action programs. Certain federal contractors and subcontractors do have to develop them in order to obtain government contracts. And courts will sometimes order employers to develop affirmative action programs to correct an employer's past pattern of discrimination.

Fair Labor Standards Act (1938)	Regulates child labor; establishes minimum wage; regulates overtime pay for nonmanagerial workers.
Equal Pay Act (1963)	Prohibits wage discrimination on the basis of sex for jobs with "substantially equal" duties.
Civil Rights Act, Title VII (1964) **Equal Employment Opportunity Act (1972)** **Affirmative Action Programs**	As discussed in text.
Executive Orders 11246 and 11375 (1965–1967)	Prohibits discrimination by contractors and subcontractors for the federal government; requires preparation of affirmative action plans for achieving equal employment opportunity.
Age Discrimination in Employment Act (1967)	Forbids discrimination in compensation, terms and conditions of employment, or privileges on account of age; applies to employees between the ages of forty and seventy; forbids forced retirement under seventy.
Occupational Safety and Health Act (1970)	Requires federal government to establish health and safety standards and to conduct inspections.
Vocational Rehabilitation Act (1973–1974)	Requires federal contractors and subcontractors to take affirmative steps to hire the handicapped.
Employee Retirement Income Security Act (1974)	Regulates pension plans so covered employees receive their pensions.
Pregnancy Discrimination Act (1978)	Requires pregnant employees to be treated as all other employees for the determination of benefits.
Uniform Guidelines on Employee Selection Procedures (1978)	Establishes criteria for federal agencies to use in judging the compliance of federal contractors and subcontractors with antidiscrimination laws.
EEOC Sexual Harassment Guidelines (1980)	Prohibits sexual harassment that affects decisions about employment conditions, promotions, and raises.

Dramatic changes in the work force. *Chiyoko Winters, Esther Fernandez, and Victoria Acosta install electrical wiring in Lockheed's advanced antisubmarine warfare aircraft. When Fernandez began work as a bench assembler 24 years ago, there were few women in jobs like the one she has now. Today there are three women in her crew of electricians, and her 27-year-old daughter is following the same career path. Lockheed provided the training and promotion that allowed Fernandez to move into what was once considered a man's job.*

Responsibility for Human Resource Management

The responsibility for who handles human resource management in a firm depends on the business's size. In smaller firms, the owner and the other managers perform these functions. Then, as firms grow, they develop a need for human resource professionals. A recent survey found an average of one professional for every hundred employees.[3]

In large businesses, a human resource department and other managers in the organization generally share the responsibilities. In some companies, operating management plays an active role in all hiring decisions. In others it simply takes a final look at the human resource department's candidate. All companies should treat their human resources as carefully as they do their other resources — by planning for their acquisition and use.

HUMAN RESOURCE PLANNING

Not long ago, the Chrysler Corporation and Mitsubishi Motors Corporation announced that they would jointly build a 1.7-million-square-foot production facility in central Illinois, for which they would hire twenty-five hundred new workers.[4] A few months earlier, AT&T had announced a major cost reduction effort in its Information Systems Group, which would result in layoffs for twenty-four thousand employees, one-third of them being managers.[5] These two unrelated events demonstrate the need for **human resource planning**, the systematic process of forecasting the future demand for employees and estimating the supply available to meet that demand. Employees represent a substantial investment, and their deployment and redeployment require as much planning as for other assets.

The Three Main Steps in the Human Resource Planning Process

Forecasting Demand

The First Step in Human Resource Planning

Human resource planners consider both the internal and the external factors when forecasting a firm's demand for workers. The internal factors include possible shifts in goods or services, planned expansions or contractions in operations, purchases of new equipment, and likely personnel changes such as retirements and leaves of absence. Suppose that the K mart Corporation plans to open twenty-five new stores during the next two years. Twenty-five store managers and assistant managers alone must be hired, just for the new stores. Also, K mart will have to find replacements for the managers it expects to lose by **attrition**, the normal loss of employees from retirement, job changes, death, and the like.

Perhaps the most important external factor to consider in planning for workers is the state of the nation's economy. Rising or falling interest rates, for example, can affect a firm's demand for human resources. Other important external factors include government regulations, technological changes, and the level of competition a firm faces.

Estimating the Supply of Workers

The Second Step in Human Resource Planning

Among the most important external factors affecting the supply of workers are the number of high school or college graduates available, existing patterns of worker mobility and migration, general economic conditions (especially the unemployment level), and the overall characteristics of the labor force that the firm can tap. For example, over the next two decades the work force will age considerably as the baby boom generation grows older. Workers can no longer be forced to retire until they are seventy, so there will be fewer openings for younger workers.

Forecasting the supply of workers available from within a company requires the firm to estimate how many current workers may move into anticipated vacancies. In making this estimate, the human resources department must evaluate the worker's current performance and potential for satisfactorily performing the new job. The department must also assess production schedules and budgets,

*"Offhand, I'd say you're just the type
we're looking for."*

Equal Employment Opportunity goals, and possible relocations, plant closings, turnover and absenteeism rates, and transfers within the firm. One method of making this evaluation is to use a **skills inventory**, a data bank containing each employee's employment history, skills, interests, and performance that can be used to match personnel with new jobs or to select candidates for promotion, transfer, or added responsibilities. If these data are stored in a computer, finding the right employee for a job can often be relatively simple.

Planning to Meet Needs

The Third Step in Human Resource Planning

After the human resources specialists have forecasted the demand and supply of personnel, they develop a plan to assure a work force appropriate for the firm. If they anticipate a greater demand than the supply available, their plan will focus on attracting new employees. If, on the other hand, they see supply exceeding demand, they will plan for a reduction of the work force. Many firms hope to deal with work-force reductions through attrition, but attrition takes time — layoffs are much quicker.

Job Analysis

Hiring, training, and evaluating employees is a lot easier when both the employer and the prospective employee know precisely what a job entails. This information should come from a **job analysis**, a systematic study of an employee's duties, tasks, and work environment. Among the questions a job analysis addresses are

Job Analysis Defined

☐ What are the actual job activities?
☐ What equipment is used on the job?
☐ What specific job behaviors are required?
☐ What are the working conditions under which the job is performed?
☐ What interaction with other employees and superiors is required?
☐ Does the job require the employee to supervise others?

Recruiting. *It's not easy to find the best employees — or to convince them that yours is the right company. Large companies can advertise for employees in magazines and newspapers, and a few even use television and radio. By using media like* His-panic Times, *AT&T hopes to attract a wide variety of quali-fied applicants.*

A job analyst may gather this information by observing the worker on the job site, interviewing the employee, having the person fill out a questionnaire, or using a combination of these methods.

After determining what a job involves, the job analyst identifies the knowledge, skills, and abilities required to perform it successfully. Then the analyst prepares two documents, a job description and a job specification.

Job Description Defined

A **job description** is a written summary of the duties, tasks, and responsibilities associated with a job. The first part of a job description, the identification section, states the job title, the department in which the job is located, and the supervisor to whom the applicant would report. The second part, the general summary, briefly describes the job. The specific duties section, the third area, describes what those functions are.

Job Specification Defined

A **job specification** lists the key qualifications a person needs to perform a job successfully. Human resource professionals classify qualifications into knowledge, skills, and abilities. Some of the factors considered are education or training, experience, specific work skills, mental or physical abilities, and personal abilities. Suppose that the Levi Strauss Company wanted to hire an individual to supervise its physical fitness program for pregnant workers. The qualifications for this position might include a master's degree in health and physical education, two years' work experience in a physical fitness facility, certain teaching skills, and the ability to interact well with people.

Educating America's Employees

Most companies routinely pay for new employees' on-the-job training. Very few people come from school or another job knowing exactly how to operate a company's machines or to manage a company's chain of command. But for more and more companies, on-the-job training has become less important than on-the-job schooling, as businesses take over many of the tasks traditionally assigned to high schools and colleges.

Educational programs run in, by, or for businesses are much more extensive than most people would guess. While $60 billion are spent annually on colleges and universities, corporations spend over $40 billion a year to educate close to 8 million employees.

This corporate education takes two different forms: one supplements what employees learned in schools and colleges, while the other tries to make up for what they should have learned but didn't. The Institute of Textile Technology is an example of the former. Thirty-five textile companies support the Institute, which graduates masters of science who have learned management techniques and the latest high-tech manufacturing skills. The program takes two years, combines work and study, and is as rigorous as many university graduate programs, though it is more directly industry-related.

At the other end of the educational scale are programs like the one at New York Telephone, where about 500 employees a year participate in classes focusing on basic math and language skills. The program, which has the seemingly modest goal of raising employees' skills to the ninth or tenth grade level, cost the company about $300,000 in 1985.

Many companies — about three-quarters of those in one survey — sponsor this kind of remedial program because they find that employees often can't handle the simplest kinds of tasks with words or numbers. Such gaps in employees' skills can be costly for a company. Executives tell horror stories of the employee who sent out a check for $2200 rather than $22 because the employee didn't understand the decimal point, or the worker whose inability to use a ruler cost a company $700 worth of material.

Many companies use extensive testing and interviews to avoid putting functional illiterates on the payrolls, often screening out a depressingly high proportion of their applicants. But when a company finds that one of its employees lacks a basic skill, it generally costs the company less to provide remedial training than to repeat the lengthy hiring process.

Opinions vary about the quality and long-range usefulness of the 12 million courses paid for by businesses. Because corporations are willing to put time and money into the programs, they can provide students with modern equipment and expert instructors. But sometimes, as one educator put it, "technology drive[s] the educational process rather than the other way around." Many companies televise university lectures yet their employees can't participate in discussions unless they have expensive teleconferences.

Traditional educators worry that businesses put too much emphasis on teaching employees to correct a particular kind of problem or to prepare for a particular task. Such training often doesn't provide employees with a solid educational background or a theoretical understanding of their specialty. Educators argue that while corporate education might be useful to an employee immediately, preparing the employee to deal with the latest technical innovation, a good university education helps employees for the rest of their lives. A traditional college education should enable employees to move up and conquer new kinds of tasks and challenges. It should prepare them to deal with the next technical innovation, so they don't have to be continually re-trained. But until the standard educational system can live up to such ideals, most companies will continue their involvement in the business of education.

Sources: Ezra Bowen, "Schooling for Survival," *Time,* Vol. 125, No. 6, February 11, 1985, 74. Carey W. English, "As Businesses Turn Offices into Classrooms," *U.S. News & World Report,* Vol. 98, No. 12, April 1, 1985, 70. "How Business Is Joining the Fight Against Functional Illiteracy," *Business Week,* No. 2838, April 16, 1984, 94.

Application Interview Employment Tests

FIGURE 8-2

The Employment Process

To prospective applicants, the steps in the employment process look like a series of hurdles that must be cleared before a candidate is selected.

The Steps in the Employment Process

THE EMPLOYMENT PROCESS

The procedure by which a firm matches its hiring needs resources is the **employment process**. It includes **recru** attracting qualified people to apply for jobs; **selection**, the priate candidates; and **orientation**, the systematic introdu to their new organization, job, and coworkers. Figure 8.2 of the employment process. At any point in this proce determine that its needs and the job applicant's do no application. The applicant may also withdraw at any poir

Recruiting

The objective of recruiting is to attract a pool of qualifi to choose the most appropriate person for a particular j only as many candidates as there are jobs, the employ on the other hand, the efforts to recruit result in a delu may waste time weeding them out. There is in fact an size pool of applicants.

When companies have openings above the entry le to hire from within, but all occasionally have to hir applications, firms rely on job postings, advertising, p agement recruiters. Other good sources include lo unions, government agencies, and current or former

*"Offhand, I'd say you're just the type
we're looking for."*

Equal Employment Opportunity goals, and possible relocations, plant closings, turnover and absenteeism rates, and transfers within the firm. One method of making this evaluation is to use a **skills inventory**, a data bank containing each employee's employment history, skills, interests, and performance that can be used to match personnel with new jobs or to select candidates for promotion, transfer, or added responsibilities. If these data are stored in a computer, finding the right employee for a job can often be relatively simple.

Planning to Meet Needs

The Third Step in Human Resource Planning

After the human resources specialists have forecasted the demand and supply of personnel, they develop a plan to assure a work force appropriate for the firm. If they anticipate a greater demand than the supply available, their plan will focus on attracting new employees. If, on the other hand, they see supply exceeding demand, they will plan for a reduction of the work force. Many firms hope to deal with work-force reductions through attrition, but attrition takes time — layoffs are much quicker.

Job Analysis

Job Analysis Defined

Hiring, training, and evaluating employees is a lot easier when both the employer and the prospective employee know precisely what a job entails. This information should come from a **job analysis**, a systematic study of an employee's duties, tasks, and work environment. Among the questions a job analysis addresses are

☐ What are the actual job activities?
☐ What equipment is used on the job?
☐ What specific job behaviors are required?
☐ What are the working conditions under which the job is performed?
☐ What interaction with other employees and superiors is required?
☐ Does the job require the employee to supervise others?

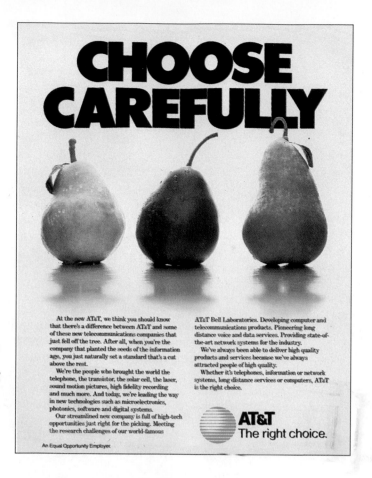

At the new AT&T, we think you should know that there's a difference between AT&T and some of these new telecommunications companies that just fell off the tree. After all, when you're the company that planted the seeds of the information age, you just naturally set a standard that's a cut above the rest.

We're the people who brought the world the telephone, the transistor, the solar cell, the laser, sound motion pictures, high fidelity recording and much more. And today, we're leading the way in new technologies such as microelectronics, photonics, software and digital systems.

Our streamlined new company is full of high-tech opportunities just right for the picking. Meeting the research challenges of our world-famous

AT&T Bell Laboratories. Developing computer and telecommunications products. Pioneering long distance voice and data services. Providing state-of-the-art network systems for the industry.

We've always been able to deliver high quality products and services because we've always attracted people of high quality.

Whether it's telephones, information or network systems, long distance services or computers, AT&T is the right choice.

AT&T
The right choice.

An Equal Opportunity Employer

Recruiting. *It's not easy to find the best employees — or to convince them that yours is the right company. Large companies can advertise for employees in magazines and newspapers, and a few even use television and radio. By using media like His-panic Times, AT&T hopes to attract a wide variety of quali-fied applicants.*

A job analyst may gather this information by observing the worker on the job site, interviewing the employee, having the person fill out a questionnaire, or using a combination of these methods.

After determining what a job involves, the job analyst identifies the knowledge, skills, and abilities required to perform it successfully. Then the analyst prepares two documents, a job description and a job specification.

Job Description Defined

A **job description** is a written summary of the duties, tasks, and responsibilities associated with a job. The first part of a job description, the identification section, states the job title, the department in which the job is located, and the supervisor to whom the applicant would report. The second part, the general summary, briefly describes the job. The specific duties section, the third area, describes what those functions are.

Job Specification Defined

A **job specification** lists the key qualifications a person needs to perform a job successfully. Human resource professionals classify qualifications into knowledge, skills, and abilities. Some of the factors considered are education or training, experience, specific work skills, mental or physical abilities, and personal abilities. Suppose that the Levi Strauss Company wanted to hire an individual to supervise its physical fitness program for pregnant workers. The qualifications for this position might include a master's degree in health and physical education, two years' work experience in a physical fitness facility, certain teaching skills, and the ability to interact well with people.

Educating America's Employees

Most companies routinely pay for new employees' on-the-job training. Very few people come from school or another job knowing exactly how to operate a company's machines or to manage a company's chain of command. But for more and more companies, on-the-job training has become less important than on-the-job schooling, as businesses take over many of the tasks traditionally assigned to high schools and colleges.

Educational programs run in, by, or for businesses are much more extensive than most people would guess. While $60 billion are spent annually on colleges and universities, corporations spend over $40 billion a year to educate close to 8 million employees.

This corporate education takes two different forms: one supplements what employees learned in schools and colleges, while the other tries to make up for what they should have learned but didn't. The Institute of Textile Technology is an example of the former. Thirty-five textile companies support the Institute, which graduates masters of science who have learned management techniques and the latest high-tech manufacturing skills. The program takes two years, combines work and study, and is as rigorous as many university graduate programs, though it is more directly industry-related.

At the other end of the educational scale are programs like the one at New York Telephone, where about 500 employees a year participate in classes focusing on basic math and language skills. The program, which has the seemingly modest goal of raising employees' skills to the ninth or tenth grade level, cost the company about $300,000 in 1985.

Many companies — about three-quarters of those in one survey — sponsor this kind of remedial program because they find that employees often can't handle the simplest kinds of tasks with words or numbers. Such gaps in employees' skills can be costly for a company. Executives tell horror stories of the employee who sent out a check for $2200 rather than $22 because the employee didn't understand the decimal point, or the worker whose inability to use a ruler cost a company $700 worth of material.

Many companies use extensive testing and interviews to avoid putting functional illiterates on the payrolls, often screening out a depressingly high proportion of their applicants. But when a company finds that one of its employees lacks a basic skill, it generally costs the company less to provide remedial training than to repeat the lengthy hiring process.

Opinions vary about the quality and long-range usefulness of the 12 million courses paid for by businesses. Because corporations are willing to put time and money into the programs, they can provide students with modern equipment and expert instructors. But sometimes, as one educator put it, "technology drive[s] the educational process rather than the other way around." Many companies televise university lectures yet their employees can't participate in discussions unless they have expensive teleconferences.

Traditional educators worry that businesses put too much emphasis on teaching employees to correct a particular kind of problem or to prepare for a particular task. Such training often doesn't provide employees with a solid educational background or a theoretical understanding of their specialty. Educators argue that while corporate education might be useful to an employee immediately, preparing the employee to deal with the latest technical innovation, a good university education helps employees for the rest of their lives. A traditional college education should enable employees to move up and conquer new kinds of tasks and challenges. It should prepare them to deal with the next technical innovation, so they don't have to be continually re-trained. But until the standard educational system can live up to such ideals, most companies will continue their involvement in the business of education.

Sources: Ezra Bowen, "Schooling for Survival," *Time*, Vol. 125, No. 6, February 11, 1985, 74. Carey W. English, "As Businesses Turn Offices into Classrooms," *U.S. News & World Report*, Vol. 98, No. 12, April 1, 1985, 70. "How Business Is Joining the Fight Against Functional Illiteracy," *Business Week*, No. 2838, April 16, 1984, 94.

Sources of Employees   Possible Rejection

Application   Interview   Employment Tests   Background Investigations

FIGURE 8-2

The Employment Process

To prospective applicants, the steps in the employment process look like a series of hurdles that must be cleared before a candidate is selected.

The Steps in the Employment Process

THE EMPLOYMENT PROCESS

The procedure by which a firm matches its hiring needs with the available human resources is the **employment process**. It includes **recruitment**, the process of attracting qualified people to apply for jobs; **selection**, the identification of appropriate candidates; and **orientation**, the systematic introduction of new employees to their new organization, job, and coworkers. Figure 8.2 illustrates the sequence of the employment process. At any point in this procedure, the employer may determine that its needs and the job applicant's do not match and reject the application. The applicant may also withdraw at any point.

Recruiting

The objective of recruiting is to attract a pool of qualified applicants from which to choose the most appropriate person for a particular job. If recruiting produces only as many candidates as there are jobs, the employer cannot be selective. If, on the other hand, the efforts to recruit result in a deluge of applicants, the firm may waste time weeding them out. There is in fact an art to recruiting the right-size pool of applicants.

When companies have openings above the entry level, many of them prefer to hire from within, but all occasionally have to hire from outside. To solicit applications, firms rely on job postings, advertising, personnel agencies, or management recruiters. Other good sources include local schools and colleges, unions, government agencies, and current or former workers.

Acceptance

Physical Examination · Selective Interview · Orientation · Employment · Training and Development

Selection

The Seven Steps in the Actual Hiring Process

Employment Application As the first step in the hiring process, candidates usually must complete an employment application. Figure 8.3 is a typical job application. See following two pages. An employment application serves three purposes. First, it records the candidate's interest in the firm. Second, it provides a profile of the candidate, which the human resources department can use to determine whether the applicant is qualified for the job and therefore merits interviewing. And third, it becomes the basis of the successful applicant's employment records.

FIGURE 8-3

Typical Job Application

(See following two pages.)

An employer must draft its employment application so that it avoids questions that might lead to charges of illegal discrimination. Some questions that on the surface seem proper could still result in discrimination. For example, "Have you ever been arrested?" seems neutral. However, many people are arrested for crimes yet are not prosecuted, much less convicted. Of course, an employer may ask whether a person has been convicted. It is important to note that if an employer cannot include a question on an application form, it cannot ask the question at any point in the employment process.

The Second Step in the Hiring Process

Initial Interview An initial interview should determine whether an applicant meets the firm's minimum qualifications for the jobs it has open. The interview should cover the type of work the applicant wants, his or her pay expectations, and possible starting dates.

The Types of Employment Tests — The Third Step in Hiring

Employment Tests Many firms require applicants to take **employment tests**, standardized tests of various types designed to help an employer predict whether a job applicant will perform successfully. The most widely administered

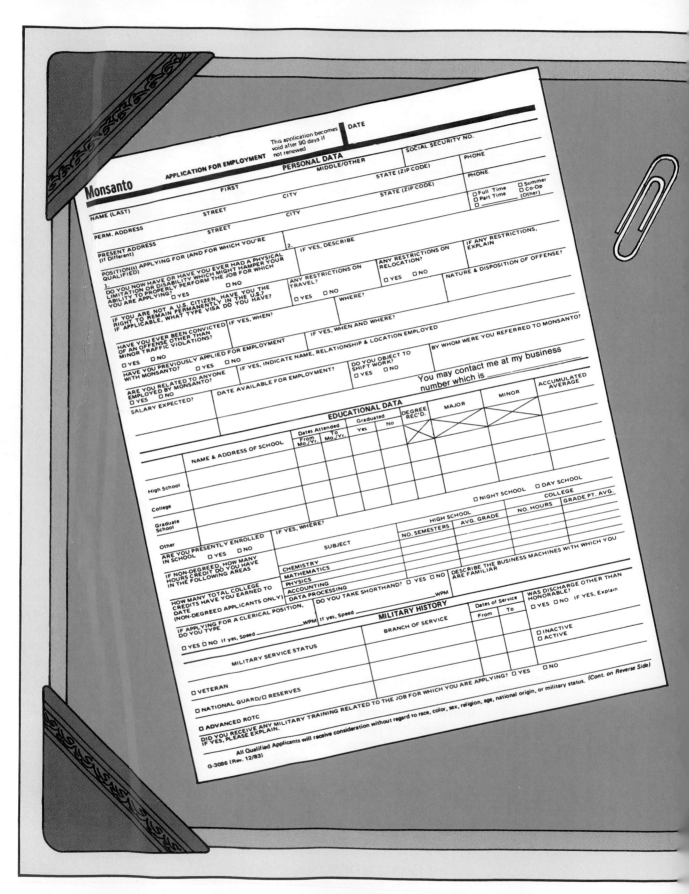

Monsanto

APPLICATION FOR EMPLOYMENT

This application becomes void after 90 days if not renewed

DATE

PERSONAL DATA

NAME (LAST)   FIRST   MIDDLE/OTHER   SOCIAL SECURITY NO.

PERM. ADDRESS   STREET   CITY   STATE (ZIP CODE)   PHONE

PRESENT ADDRESS (If Different)   STREET   CITY   STATE (ZIP CODE)   PHONE

☐ Full Time ☐ Part Time ☐   ☐ Summer ☐ Co-Op (Other)

POSITION(s) APPLYING FOR (AND FOR WHICH YOU'RE QUALIFIED)

1.   2.

DO YOU NOW HAVE OR HAVE YOU EVER HAD A PHYSICAL LIMITATION OR DISABILITY WHICH MIGHT HAMPER YOUR ABILITY TO PROPERLY PERFORM THE JOB FOR WHICH YOU ARE APPLYING? ☐ YES ☐ NO   IF YES, DESCRIBE

ANY RESTRICTIONS ON TRAVEL? ☐ YES ☐ NO

ANY RESTRICTIONS ON RELOCATION? ☐ YES ☐ NO

IF ANY RESTRICTIONS, EXPLAIN

IF YOU ARE NOT A U.S. CITIZEN, HAVE YOU THE RIGHT TO REMAIN PERMANENTLY IN THE U.S.? IF APPLICABLE, WHAT TYPE VISA DO YOU HAVE?   WHERE?

HAVE YOU EVER BEEN CONVICTED OF AN OFFENSE OTHER THAN MINOR TRAFFIC VIOLATIONS? ☐ YES ☐ NO   IF YES, WHEN?

NATURE & DISPOSITION OF OFFENSE?

HAVE YOU PREVIOUSLY APPLIED FOR EMPLOYMENT WITH MONSANTO? ☐ YES ☐ NO   IF YES, WHEN AND WHERE?

ARE YOU RELATED TO ANYONE EMPLOYED BY MONSANTO? ☐ YES ☐ NO   IF YES, INDICATE NAME, RELATIONSHIP & LOCATION EMPLOYED

DO YOU OBJECT TO SHIFT WORK? ☐ YES ☐ NO

BY WHOM WERE YOU REFERRED TO MONSANTO?

You may contact me at my business number which is _____

SALARY EXPECTED?   DATE AVAILABLE FOR EMPLOYMENT?

EDUCATIONAL DATA

	NAME & ADDRESS OF SCHOOL	Dates Attended From Mo./Yr.	To Mo./Yr.	Graduated Yes	No	DEGREE REC'D.	MAJOR	MINOR	ACCUMULATED AVERAGE
High School									
College									
Graduate School									
Other									

ARE YOU PRESENTLY ENROLLED IN SCHOOL ☐ YES ☐ NO   IF YES, WHERE?

☐ NIGHT SCHOOL ☐ DAY SCHOOL

SUBJECT

	HIGH SCHOOL NO. SEMESTERS	AVG. GRADE	COLLEGE NO. HOURS	GRADE PT. AVG.

IF NON-DEGREE, HOW MANY HOURS CREDIT DO YOU HAVE IN THE FOLLOWING AREAS

CHEMISTRY
MATHEMATICS
PHYSICS
ACCOUNTING
DATA PROCESSING

HOW MANY TOTAL COLLEGE CREDITS HAVE YOU EARNED TO DATE (NON-DEGREE APPLICANTS ONLY)

DO YOU TAKE SHORTHAND? ☐ YES ☐ NO   WPM

DESCRIBE THE BUSINESS MACHINES WITH WHICH YOU ARE FAMILIAR

IF APPLYING FOR A CLERICAL POSITION, DO YOU TYPE _____ WPM If yes, Speed

☐ YES ☐ NO If yes, Speed

MILITARY HISTORY

MILITARY SERVICE STATUS   BRANCH OF SERVICE

Dates of Service From	To

☐ INACTIVE
☐ ACTIVE

WAS DISCHARGE OTHER THAN HONORABLE? ☐ YES ☐ NO IF YES, Explain

☐ VETERAN

☐ NATIONAL GUARD/☐ RESERVES

☐ ADVANCED ROTC

DID YOU RECEIVE ANY MILITARY TRAINING RELATED TO THE JOB FOR WHICH YOU ARE APPLYING? ☐ YES ☐ NO
IF YES, PLEASE EXPLAIN.

All Qualified Applicants will receive consideration without regard to race, color, sex, religion, age, national origin, or military status. *(Cont. on Reverse Side)*

G-3086 (Rev. 12/83)

EMPLOYMENT HISTORY

LIST BELOW, BEGINNING WITH YOUR MOST RECENT, ALL PRESENT AND PAST EMPLOYMENT

NAME OF EMPLOYER	IMMEDIATE SUPERVISOR
LOCATION EMPLOYED	YOUR JOB OR TITLE

DATES EMPLOYED From - Mo./Yr.	To - Mo./Yr.	STARTING WAGE OR SALARY	PRESENT/FINAL WAGE OR SALARY	IF STILL EMPLOYED, MAY WE CONTACT YOUR PRESENT EMPLOYER? ☐ YES ☐ NO

REASON(S) FOR LEAVING

DESCRIBE YOUR DUTIES

NAME OF EMPLOYER	IMMEDIATE SUPERVISOR
LOCATION EMPLOYED	YOUR JOB OR TITLE

DATES EMPLOYED From - Mo./Yr.	To - Mo./Yr.	STARTING WAGE OR SALARY	PRESENT/FINAL WAGE OR SALARY	

REASON(S) FOR LEAVING

DESCRIBE YOUR DUTIES

NAME OF EMPLOYER	IMMEDIATE SUPERVISOR
LOCATION EMPLOYED	YOUR JOB OR TITLE

DATES EMPLOYED From - Mo./Yr.	To - Mo./Yr.	STARTING WAGE OR SALARY	PRESENT/FINAL WAGE OR SALARY	

REASON(S) FOR LEAVING

DESCRIBE YOUR DUTIES

(IF MORE SPACE IS NEEDED FOR PRIOR EMPLOYMENT, PLEASE USE A SEPARATE BLANK PAGE)

DO YOU HAVE TRADE SECRET AND/OR NON COMPETITIVE OBLIGATIONS WITH PRESENT OR PREVIOUS EMPLOYERS? ☐ YES ☐ NO

PERSONAL REFERENCES	Name	Address	Occupation
1.			
2.			
3.			

PLEASE READ CAREFULLY BEFORE SIGNING:

I certify that the information on this form is true and correct to the best of my knowledge. I understand that willfully withholding information or making false statements in this application may be used as the basis for dismissal. I also authorize Monsanto Company to verify these statements through former employers and any other individuals who can testify to my ability and character, and I release Monsanto Company from any liability in connection with any such verifications or attempts to verify. If employment is offered to me, I agree to submit to periodic physical examinations at the Company's request, sign an employment contract if required, and abide by the policies, rules and regulations of Monsanto Company.

SIGNATURE	DATE

Internal Sources	
Job posting and bidding	Promotion or transfer from within. Vacancy notices posted throughout the facility, giving employees a set time to apply; union rules often require this procedure before job can be offered to outsiders.
Current employees	Pass the word to family members, friends, etc.
Past employees	Also refer candidates; sometimes willing to return themselves.

External Sources	
School recruiting	Type of school approached varies with candidates required; e.g., high schools for minimal-skill jobs; technical schools for computer programers; colleges for professional and managerial candidates.
Public (state) employment agencies	Try to match employer's stated requirements with job seekers who are referred; no charge to either the employer or the job seeker.
Private employment agencies	Use same matching process as the state but charge 10 to 20 percent of first-year's salary for this service; usually — but not always — employer pays fee.
Advertising	Newspaper help wanted or display ads for nonprofessional positions are most common; journal and magazine ads for professionals; radio and TV where labor is in great demand.
Temporary-help agencies	Supply, on short notice, a broad range of nonprofessional help on a day-to-day basis; some provide low-level professionals.
Labor unions	Especially in construction, unions establish a labor pool from which workers are drawn to meet employers' needs.

TABLE 8.2

Sources of Employees

The human resources department's greatest challenge is to provide a qualified pool of candidates for every job opening. It must draw on many sources for these applicants. This table charts the most significant sources.

type of psychological tests is **intelligence tests**, standardized tests that measure such general mental abilities as reasoning, comprehension, verbal fluency, memory, spatial relations, and numerical ability. Intelligence tests are better at predicting success for skilled workers, clerks, and managers than for salespeople or unskilled workers. However, they are of limited value even in predicting job success in those categories and, worse, they tend to discriminate against minorities.[6]

An **aptitude test** measures whether a person has the "capacity or latent ability to learn a given job if given adequate training."[7] In contrast, an **achievement test** measures what a candidate can do and whether the candidate has the knowledge or skill necessary in a certain position. For instance, firms usually give typing tests to clerical applicants.

People who are really interested in a job often perform better on tests than those who have more basic abilities but less specific interest in an opening. Firms thus sometimes administer **interest tests**, standardized tests that measure an individual's likes and dislikes. Some interest tests are designed to predict success in specific occupations. Others measure more general interest in such areas as, for example, mechanical, scientific, or social service work.[8]

A **personality test** assesses a candidate's mental make-up. Although a few businesses still use these once common tests, most have now abandoned them. The consensus is that personality tests do not in fact measure how well people might do on a job. Among those still using personality tests are financial services and insurance companies, because these tests seem to indicate whether an applicant has service and people skills, the critical abilities in these competitive industries. Many companies that give workers a say in their management rely on personality tests to determine whether an applicant can function well with others. However, unions sometimes have a different view of personality tests. They have a tendency to believe that companies look for personal traits indicating that applicants would not be likely to join unions and that as a result companies do not hire candidates who might.[9]

Some companies rely on less common, less generally accepted tests. Lowes, Inc., a large home-center chain in the Southeast, is one of a growing number of firms using honesty tests to predict reliability. And a few firms use handwriting analyses to screen job candidates.

The Fourth Step in Hiring

Background Investigations To protect themselves against falsified resumes and lies on employment applications, employers often perform background checks on candidates who reach the final stages of the selection process. These investigations can be as simple as checking references or as detailed as verifying all of the candidate's claims.

References are usually the starting point in any background investigation. However, they are not always valuable to an employer. Financial references have little relevance to job performance, and personal references are usually not worth much, since no one would deliberately refer a potential employer to someone who would give negative information. Information from previous employers is more valuable. Immediate supervisors especially have had the opportunity to observe the candidate's behavior and performance. Employers seldom want academic references for candidates who have been working for some years. They are quite helpful, though, when an applicant is about to graduate and has only part-time or summer work experience.

The Fifth Step in Hiring

Physical Examinations Some firms require candidates to take physical examinations. Either the company doctor or a doctor approved by the employer performs the examinations, which the firm pays for. Where jobs require heavy lifting or other major forms of exertion, physicals are a must. Also, firms hiring for food-service positions must have prospective employees tested for communicable diseases like tuberculosis.

Some firms use preemployment physicals to protect themselves against insurance or worker's-compensation claims for conditions employees had before taking the job. Not long ago, an insurer ran an ad featuring a picture of a high-school football player being carried off the field on a stretcher. The caption urged employers to insure with that company because its recordkeeping would eliminate claims for injuries that might not be made until years later.

The Sixth Step in Hiring

Selection Interviews Selection interviews are in much more depth than initial interviews. They typically come after the employer has all the information it wants on the candidate. The interviewer can as a result probe an applicant's personality and give him or her an opportunity to explain or elaborate on information in the application. The interviewer should also tell the applicant more

Coping Overseas

For many Americans transferring to work overseas, the problems begin long before the first business transaction in the new country. Americans often grow up thinking that their ways of doing things, from setting a dinner table to conducting a business meeting, are not only the *right* ways but the *only* ways. A business person with this attitude is not likely to succeed in a foreign country, even if that person's other skills are impressive. An international businessperson must be able to see the world the way people from other cultures see it. As American businesses become increasingly international, more and more companies are looking for people who can learn a new language and understand a new culture.

Few Americans go to foreign countries with the intent of ignoring the traditions and rituals of their host countries, yet many do just that. People going overseas should be trained to understand what culture is and to be sensitive to cultural variations. Then they need to study the particular culture they're going to. If a new manager doesn't realize that everyone in the host country eats lunch at 11 am, he or she will have a difficult first day when everyone walks off the job an hour "early."

Elements of a person's personality and talents that seem to have nothing to do with business may be crucial in that person's success as an overseas manager. Some people adapt easily to changes in time zone; others don't. Some people develop particularly effective strategies for getting used to a new culture, like getting lost in the middle of a city and wandering around for an afternoon. Many companies like to send overseas only people who have already proven themselves in the United States. Successful American managers will be more likely to succeed overseas. And they will have an easier time fitting back into the work force when they return to the United States.

Once on the job, the new manager in a foreign country must be ready to use a variety of management and human resource skills to deal successfully with both cultures. Such managers should make clear their assumptions — about their work and about the people they're working with — and their goals. Non-Americans may be working diligently, but if they're aiming towards goals that the American company doesn't share, the American manager is going to be upset. Americans need to be particularly willing to encourage the airing of grievances from non-American employees. Bringing the foreign workers into the decision-making process can help insure that the decision insults no one and works effectively.

Such joint decision making often shows American managers that the process of understanding another culture works both ways. Americans may conscientiously study a new culture, but then forget that foreign workers need to be introduced to the ways of American business as well. The process of give-and-take between cultures is necessary for an international company to function effectively, and the ability to make that process work will be earning jobs for many American business people in the next decade.

Sources: Elizabeth M. Fowler, "New Skills Sought in Executives," *The New York Times*, December 17, 1985, D24. Bernice Cramer, "Training a Bicultural Team," *Training*, November 1985, 39. "How Do You Ensure Success of Managers Going Abroad?" *Training and Development Journal*, December 1985, 22.

about the company and the particular position. The success of the employment process may well depend on how clearly the interviewer and the applicant understand each other on the terms and conditions of the job. The candidate should thus ask questions in the same vein as the interviewer.

The number of selection interviews a candidate will have depends on the nature of the position. A candidate for, say, a retail sales position will have probably only one interview, probably with the sales manager. By contrast, a candidate for an entry-level auditing position with a major accounting firm can expect several selection interviews. One may be with a human resources professional, the others with potential coworkers and supervisors.

The Three Types of Selection Interviews

Selection interviews are of three types. The first and most common is the **structured interview**, in which the interviewer asks a series of prepared questions based on the job specifications. This type is also known as a guided, directed, or patterned interview. Its structured nature protects against untrained interviewers by ensuring that the same questions are put to all interviewees. The second type is the **unstructured interview**, in which the interviewer does not have a firmly set structure for the interview and the interviewee does most of the talking. This format is more common in grievance, counseling, and exit interviews.

The third type of selection interview is the **stress interview**, in which the interviewer deliberately annoys, embarrasses, or frustrates the applicant to determine his or her reaction. Businesses use stress interviews for positions that are primarily managerial, particularly in customer and employee relations, where it is important to remain calm and in control under pressure.

The Final Step in Hiring

Selection Decision   Usually, the human resources department and the manager filling the position make the selection decision cooperatively. A joint decision improves their chances for making a good choice. Such a decision brings to bear the expertise both of employment professionals and of the person for whom the new employee will work.

Orientation

Soon after a new employee joins a firm, he or she should receive an **orientation**, the process of introducing new employees to their new organization and job. Commonly, during the orientation the human resources representative covers background like the company's history, organizational structure, product or service lines, and key managers. Other topics may include the company's employee policies and procedures like sick leave and vacations, the availability of health and life insurance, and safety regulations.

Because the new employee's major source of information about the new work environment will come from the orientation session, it is critically important that the company's expectations and demands be fully explained. The new employee's supervisor should detail the requirements of the position and how it relates in a larger way to what the company does. Other topics the supervisor should cover include the policies on coffee breaks and lunch hours, the physical layout of the work area, and the nature of the new employee's on-the-job relationships with other employees.

LIFE ON THE JOB

We have already seen that planning for work-force needs affects current as well as new employees. Planning routinely calls for filling new openings from within, except at the entry level. To fill openings internally, the company must have already identified prospective in-house candidates and prepared them for advancement. The key element in this process is the performance appraisal.

Performance Appraisal

The Primary Purposes of Performance Appraisal

Once hired, employees must perform to the employer's satisfaction. Most organizations of any real size conduct some type of **performance appraisal**, a formal assessment of how well employees are doing their jobs, then communicate the results of the assessment to the employees. One study revealed that 84 percent of the companies surveyed had an appraisal system for office employees, whereas 54 percent had one for production workers.[10]

Performance appraisals serve two kinds of purposes. First, they help evaluate employees, including determining eligibility for pay raises and promotion and deciding which employees to retain. Second, they have the development purpose of being future oriented and being aimed at improving the employee's career potential.

Techniques Because an employee's immediate supervisor is in the best position to observe the employee, he or she usually conducts the performance appraisal. In some companies, however, the employees do self-appraisals, which the supervisor then reviews with them. In a few companies, coworkers review each other's performance.

The employee performance-appraisal technique based on objectives established jointly by the employee and his or her supervisor is called **management by objectives (MBO)**. The employee's progress is reviewed periodically during the course of the period for which the goals were set. Some organizations use MBO primarily as a planning technique.

Performance-Appraisal Techniques

Companies can choose from a variety of measurements for their appraisals. The most frequently used is the graphic-rating scale, which focuses on the employee's specific behaviors as they relate to job performance. See Figure 8.4. Another method, the **rank-order technique** of performance appraisal, requires the supervisor to rank all employees under his or her supervision from the best to the worst on a global performance scale. This simple technique becomes quite difficult to use with large numbers of employees.

Performance appraisals are an empty exercise if the employer does not communicate the results to the employee. In most cases, the immediate supervisor conducts the postappraisal interview. This supervisor should tell the employee the results of the appraisal, encourage the employee to continue his or her positive behavior, and plan for future improvement as well as explain salary or promotion decisions.

Training and Development Programs

Among a human resources department's primary responsibilities are setting up and monitoring training and development programs.

Types of Learning Training addresses current needs, because **training** consists of "learning activities designed to improve current job performance. Its objectives can be stated in specific behavioral terms." By contrast, **development** consists of "learning activities that increase the competence and ability of employees to progress with the organization as it changes and grows." The objec-

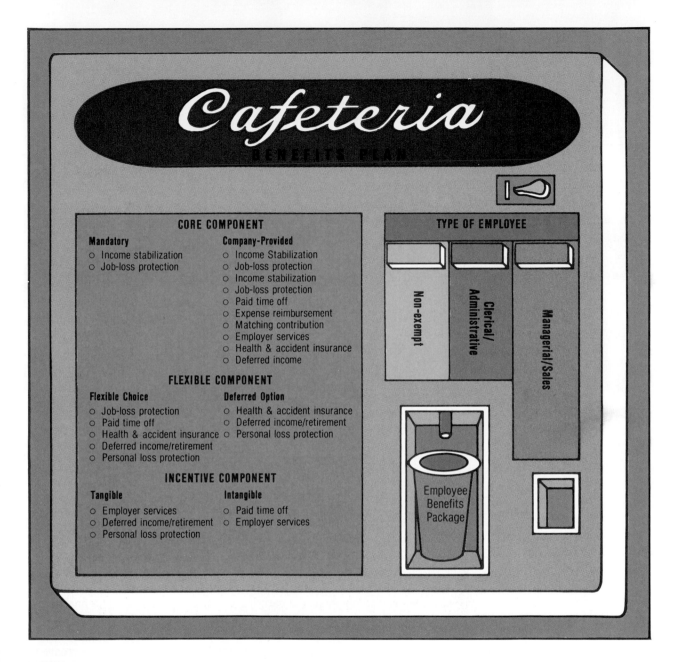

CORE COMPONENT

Mandatory
- Income stabilization
- Job-loss protection

Company-Provided
- Income Stabilization
- Job-loss protection
- Income stabilization
- Job-loss protection
- Paid time off
- Expense reimbursement
- Matching contribution
- Employer services
- Health & accident insurance
- Deferred income

FLEXIBLE COMPONENT

Flexible Choice
- Job-loss protection
- Paid time off
- Health & accident insurance
- Deferred income/retirement
- Personal loss protection

Deferred Option
- Health & accident insurance
- Deferred income/retirement
- Personal loss protection

INCENTIVE COMPONENT

Tangible
- Employer services
- Deferred income/retirement
- Personal loss protection

Intangible
- Paid time off
- Employer services

TYPE OF EMPLOYEE

Non-exempt

Clerical/Administrative

Managerial/Sales

Employee Benefits Package

FIGURE 8-4

Flexible Benefits Cafeteria

Because individuals have different benefit needs, some employers have established flexible benefit programs which permit employees to choose from an array of benefit programs.

tives of development cannot be stated in specific behavioral terms, because the firm cannot know what the job's requirements will be in the future. Thus, development addresses predicted needs. Many training and development programs contain as well a third element: **education**, which is the learning activities that prepare an employee for a higher position in the organization. Education may have no immediate or long-term benefits. Rather, it addresses possible future needs.[11]

The Program The first step in establishing a training and development program is to assess the company's general needs and specific objectives. For

Training. *Businesses can't deliver top-quality service without capable employees. In today's fast-changing environment, training is a vital element in getting and keeping a
qualified work force. As part of its effort to provide consistent, reliable service, Firestone
Tire & Rubber Company provides training for over 2,000 mechanics each year at five
regional and approximately 40 satellite training centers.*

instance, an insurance company might need claims-processing clerks able to deal
with six claims per hour at an error rate of less than 1 percent. Once the
objectives are established, human resources personnel can design programs to
achieve the objectives. This task requires the careful selection of appropriate
training and development methods. These techniques are outlined in Table 8.3.
Next comes implementation, the carrying out of the programs. The final step is
evaluation of the program to determine whether it has met its objectives.

**Training and Development
Techniques**

Good training and development programs represent commitments to effective
human resource management. Even if a firm lacks the resources to create its
own program, it can hire specialists to develop one for them. In recent years,
American businesses have spent at least $60 billion per year on training, edu-
cation, and development.[12]

Assessment Centers and Training Centers   One technique for
identifying potential supervisors and managers among employees is the **assessment center**, which carries out "a process in which individuals have the opportunity
to participate in a series of situations which resemble what they might be called
on to do in an actual job. They are observed in situational or simulation exercises
. . . while assessors who are well trained in observation and documentation
methodology evaluate their performance."[13] Companies like AT&T and Mont-

gomery Ward use assessment centers not only to identify candidates for promotion but also to evaluate the candidates' developmental needs.[14]

Many large corporations run their own training centers. These companies have chosen to fund in-house educational programs so that they can control the content and quality of their programs. Among the most notable of these firms are Walt Disney, Aetna Life & Casualty, J. P. Morgan, and Western Electric. IBM claims that all of its 400,000 employees receive at least ten hours of customized in-house training each year, at a total cost of $1.5 billion.[15] In-house training programs are not limited to those of corporate giants, however. For instance, Mrs. Fields' Cookies operates what it calls Cookie College.

TABLE 8.3

Training and Development Methods

Training Methods	
On-the-job training	The most common method today, in which the worker learns the job, often informally, on the job site under the direction of either an immediate supervisor or an experienced worker. Tends to stress actual production as soon as possible.
Apprentice training (apprenticeship)	A program aimed at producing a skilled, certified worker within a certain period; requires the apprentice to reach certain proficiency levels.
Vestibule training	A costly training method that occurs in a separate area equipped like the actual work site. Its advantage over on-the-job training is its emphasis on developing the trainee's skills.
Computer-assisted instruction (CAI)	A training method in which trainees learn at their own pace through interaction with a special computer program.
Development Methods	
On-the-job coaching	A development method in which employees receive regular instruction and feedback from their immediate supervisors.
Mentoring	More personal than coaching, a one-on-one developmental relationship between senior and junior employees. The mentor, the leader, assists the junior employee to build a network within the firm.
Job rotation	Moves trainees from one position to another to expose them to a wide range of tasks from which they gain understanding of the total organization and of how the various parts work together.
Multipurpose Approaches	
Conferences and workshops	The most common off-the-job development programs, varying widely in length from half a day to a week or longer. Often use *case studies*, which require trainees to evaluate situations that have actually occurred in business organizations, and *role playing*, which requires trainees to resolve a situation in which they play the parts of the people who were actually involved.

Promotion, Transfer, and Discharge

Aside from compensation (discussed in the next section), the reality of an employee's business life might be summed up in terms of three concepts: promotions, transfers, and separations. A **promotion** is an advancement granted to an employee to a higher position, greater responsibility, or more prestige. An increase in salary often accompanies a promotion. Organizations promote on the basis of performance, seniority, or both. Union contracts usually require promotion on the basis of **seniority**, the length of employment with a particular employer in relation to the time that all the other employees in the unit have worked for the employer. For example, in a unionized steel mill all union members have the right to bid on a job, but the job will usually go to the bidder who has worked there the longest.

Sometimes a promotion includes a **transfer**, a shift from one job to another in an organization that may or may not require a change in the employee's place of work. Transfers can also be horizontal changes that do not involve a promotion.

Separation is the ending of the employment relationship. One form of separation is quitting, an employee's voluntary leaving of a job. Retirement (discussed below) is a form of separation. So, too, are **layoffs**, separations caused by the employer's lack of work, which may become permanent. A **discharge** or **termination** is a permanent separation initiated by the employer, usually for cause, such as absenteeism or poor job performance.

COMPENSATION AND BENEFITS

Employees work for **compensation**, the money or benefits or both for which an employee exchanges work.

The Purposes of a Compensation System

The Three Purposes of a Compensation System

A business's compensation system has three main purposes: attracting qualified employees; retaining those employees; and motivating higher levels of performance from them. A firm achieves each of these goals through the various aspects of the compensation system.

Attracting Qualified Employees A company's ability to attract qualified employees depends in part on how its general level of pay compares with that of other firms competing for the same type of employee. The average pay for a particular position among comparable firms is called the **going rate**. Businesses do not want their pay scale to vary much from the going rate. A company that sets, say, entry-level credit supervisors' salaries at $18,000 when the going rate is $21,500 will not attract as many qualified applicants as its competitors. To determine what the going rate is, companies consult a **wage/salary survey**, a review of pay rates at companies within comparable industries in a particular region. Thus, a retail clothing chain centered in the New York metropolitan area might look at credit supervisors' wages at consumer electronics outlets in and

Directors of High-Tech Personnel

Managers in charge of fitting people into a company can have a tremendous effect on how well that company functions. Many companies have dropped the old idea that a good manager can run any kind of business. They are now recognizing that some are great startup entrepreneurs, while others show their skills best by keeping an old company from bankruptcy. Lately, a third major element, technology, has made the relationship between employee and company into a triangle of employee-company-technology. By helping to make this triangle work successfully, the human resource manager makes sure the company gets the most out of its people *and* its machines.

The introduction of new computers or other high-tech machines into a business may eliminate some jobs, but it seldom eliminates the need for workers altogether. In fact, those who work with the new technology often have a tremendous effect on how efficiently the technology is used. They may think up new applications for the technology.

Managers involved with personnel and training can affect many different parts of the process that brings people and machines together. If such managers are successful, the people working with the technology will see it as a tool, something given them to help them do their jobs better. If all the resources are not well managed, workers are likely to feel distanced because of the technology, and this distancing leads to boredom, apathy, and poor work performance.

The personnel manager will often play a role even in the planning stages of bringing new technology into a company. In analyzing the human dimensions of the technological change, such a manager will need to look first at what the job *now* requires, and what those requirements will be once the change has taken place. Related to such analysis is the question of whether the company should train current employees to use the new technology or hire people specifically to run new machines.

Next, the manager will look at the fit between human and technological abilities. What parts of the task is the machine best at, and what parts seem to be for humans only? How will the machine affect departmental structure or relations between workers? Should the workers whose jobs are being affected have a say in how the technology is used? Is there a best way to train workers on the new system?

A manager's answers to such questions can help determine which particular kind of software, for instance, a company purchases, as well as what kinds of people the company will hire. Beyond that, the manager tries to affect the introduction of the technology to make people feel it is complementing their skills, not replacing them.

In a typical example of an unsuccessful introduction of new technology, United Biscuits purchased a computer mixer to do the jobs previously performed by doughmen. In the process it alienated some of its best workers. The company built a new control room for the machine and staffed it with new workers. The doughmen lost their important role in the process and began performing simple housekeeping roles like telling the control room when to start the machine. Management soon noticed that the doughmen had become careless and irresponsible, seeing no connection between their jobs and the product.

Human resource experts recommended that the doughmen should be more involved with the new machine. Instead of separating the functions of doughman and operator, the company should combine the two and not shut the operations in a new room. That way, the doughmen could use their expertise to control the machine's operation.

Back at the dawn of the computer revolution, many people worried that new technology would take the humanity out of work, and we'd all be left mindlessly punching buttons. In fact, technology often does just the opposite, eliminating the mindless work and giving much more power to the human mind to make changes.

Sources: David Boddy and David Buchanan, "New Technology with a Human Face," *Personnel Management*, Vol. 17, No. 4, April 1985, 28. N. R. Kleinfield, "A Human Resource at Allied Corporation," *The New York Times*, June 6, 1982. Herbert E. Neyers, "Personnel Directors Are the New Corporate Heroes," *Fortune*, February 1976, 84.

around New York. Data from Dallas or Los Angeles would be of little use. A business, a consulting firm, a human resources trade association, or a government group might take or commission the survey.

Retaining Employees   Hiring an employee is expensive, so retaining productive employees is a key goal of compensation systems. Keeping workers is primarily a function of maintaining a fair **pay structure**, the relationship among the rates of pay for various jobs within the company. Employees dissatisfied with a pay structure often look for new jobs.

The relative importance of jobs to the company determines their rates of pay. For instance, a defense contractor would pay a research engineer more than a bookkeeper, but an engineer makes less than the vice president of the division in which he or she works.

Types of Compensation

A compensation system includes base pay, incentives, and benefits. A good system motivates effective performance by establishing fair individual rates of compensation and by effectively linking performance to compensation.

Base pay refers to the basic wages or salaries that workers receive. For example, a job description stating a wage of $7.50 per hour, $300 per week, or $1,200 per month states the position's base pay. **Incentives** refers to bonuses and other plans designed to encourage employees to produce work beyond the minimum acceptable levels. Incentives take many forms, including cash bonuses, options to buy stock, and gifts. **Benefits** are services that employees receive that are paid for by the employer, like health insurance, pensions, and vacations.

Bases of Compensation

Employers can choose among three bases of compensation: time, productivity, or a combination of the two.

Wages *vs.* Salaries

Time   Employees paid on the basis of the time they work may receive **wages**, compensation usually calculated according to the number of hours an employee actually worked. Employees covered by the Fair Labor Standards Act who work more than forty hours in a given week must receive overtime pay. That rate is normally one and a half times the usual hourly rate. Thus, an employee whose wages are four dollars per hour who works forty-four hours in a week will receive six dollars per hour for the four hours of overtime. In contrast, **salary** is compensation calculated usually on a weekly, monthly, or yearly basis and not normally related to the number of hours actually worked. The Fair Labor Standards Act exempts many salaried employees from its overtime pay provisions.

Two Key Incentive Systems

Productivity   Compensation systems that pay employees according to their productivity are called **incentive systems**. We are able to discuss only the two most important of the many incentive systems. A **piece-rate system** is an incentive system that compensates a worker according to the number of units of a product he or she produces. The employer determines wages by multiplying the number of units produced times the piece rate for one unit. The other main incentive system is the **commission basis**, in which sales employees receive either a fixed amount or a percentage of the value of the sales they make. The commission system in effect gives employees a double incentive. On the one hand, if they do not sell anything, they get no pay. On the other, there usually is no upper limit on what they can earn.

Time and Productivity   Perhaps the most common compensation systems combine the time and productivity criteria. The weight given each element depends on both the company and the job.

Many firms pay their employees a **bonus**, a payment beyond the employees' base pay or commissions. Often, only upper management receives bonuses, but some firms distribute them to all employees after a successful year. Companies calculate bonuses usually on either a lump sum or a percentage of salary basis. Anaheim Custom Extruders, a plastic tubing manufacturer, assigns 28 percent of its profits to a bonus pool, which it then distributes in proportion to the employees' base salaries. This company is built on incentives. At the end of each shift, supervisors hand out fifteen and twenty-five-dollar cash bonuses and six packs of beer or soda to workers who make their productivity goals.[16]

A **profit-sharing program** distributes a set portion of a company's profits to its employees, according to a standard formula. For example, a firm might set aside 15 percent of its profits for distribution to its employees, based on a formula related to their salaries. Ryan Transfer in Green Bay, Wisconsin, offers a variant on profit sharing. Employees who choose to participate divide 40 percent of the company's gross sales with management, up to and including the president, instead of receiving wages.

Employee Benefits

An employee receives benefits as a reward for being a member of the organization, not for job performance. Benefits are called indirect compensation, because they are not paid to the employee in cash. Nonetheless, benefits are not cheap. Recent data indicate that the cost of benefits, both those required by law and those that companies give voluntarily, amounts to an additional 36.6 cents for every payroll dollar. The average employee receives $7,582 in benefits per year.[17]

Benefits Required by Law   The federal program designed to provide employees with a safety net of retirement income, survivor's benefits, and the like is **Social Security**. Both employers and employees pay taxes into this fund. In 1986, the tax was 7.15 percent on the first $42,000 in wages. **Workers' compensation** is a program established under state law to provide compensation for workers who suffer on-the-job injuries. All employers above a certain size must participate in the program. The compensation takes the form of reimbursement for medical expenses and of cash payments to the worker for the period of the disability. Every state has some form of workers' compensation program. **Unemployment compensation** is a state program, sometimes supplemented by federal funds, that for a set period pays allowances to workers who are out of work and actively looking for a job. To fund the system, employers pay a tax calculated as a percentage of their employees' earnings.

Employee Benefits Required by Law

Child Care at Campbell Soup. *Although company-sponsored child care centers are old hat to a few companies like Campbell Soup, most business leaders are just beginning to appreciate the significance of this kind of benefit. With over 60 percent of all new jobs going to women, it's not surprising that providing good child care is one way to attract a qualified work force and hold down employee turnover.*

Voluntary Benefits Employers voluntarily provide employee benefits, depending on their perceptions of their workers' needs. Voluntary benefits vary widely from company to company. Among those commonly offered are

- □ Life insurance
- □ Health insurance
- □ Pensions
- □ Recreation programs
- □ Financial counseling

- □ Health/fitness programs
- □ Tuition reimbursement
- □ Child care
- □ Drug/alcohol treatment

Voluntary Employee Benefits

From the end of World War II until the late 1970s, employers routinely added benefits to their compensation packages, particularly in contracts negotiated with organized labor, because benefits seemed cheaper than additional wages. That perception changed, however, when health-care costs skyrocketed. Despite efforts by employers and insurers to control costs, group health premiums nearly doubled in the first half of the 1980s, to almost $90 billion per year. Employers like the General Motors Corporation and Dresser Industries have instituted checks on the need for surgery to control costs. The Quaker Oats Company pays bonuses to its employees if they keep health-care costs under the company's budget for the year.[18]

Because individuals have different benefits needs, some employers have established **flexible-benefit programs** (also known as **cafeteria-style benefit programs**), which permit employees to choose from an array of benefit programs, up to a preset limit. See Figure 8.5. The employee's choices are like those of a person entering a cafeteria with just a five-dollar bill. The person may select whatever

CP F 8472
APPRENTICE PERFORMANCE RATING - Training Section, Industrial Relations Department

CLOCK NUMBER	DEPARTMENT	JOB CLASSIFICATION
NAME	DATE OF LAST RATING	DATE OF THIS RATING
DATE STARTED ON JOB		

TO THE RATER: This rating will represent your appraisal of the trainee's actual performance on his present job or in related classroom work. The value of it depends upon the impartiality and sound judgment you use. You should keep in mind both the interest of the company and the personal interests of the individual, when making the rating.

TO HELP YOU MAKE A CAREFUL ANALYSIS, THE FOLLOWING SUGGESTIONS ARE OFFERED:
1. Consider only one factor at a time. Do not let your rating in one trait influence your rating of another.
2. Base your judgment on the requirements of the job and his performance in it as compared to others doing similar work.
3. Carefully read the description of each trait and specifications for each grade before making your entry, then check the space which most nearly describes your opinion.
4. Upon completion, review and check your rating.
5. Make any comments in provided space which you believe will furnish additional information concerning trainee.

PERFORMANCE RATING

PERFORMANCE FACTORS	Does not meet job requirements	Partially meets job requirements	Meets job requirements	Exceeds job requirements	Far exceeds job requirements
	Consistently unsatisfactory	Occasionally unsatisfactory	Consistently satisfactory	Sometimes superior	Consistently superior
QUALITY OF WORK: Accuracy, skill, thoroughness, neatness	☐ Consistently below requirements	☐ Frequently below requirements	☐ Usually meets requirements	☐ Frequently exceeds requirements	☐ Consistently exceeds requirements
QUANTITY OF WORK: Output; consider not only regular duties, but also how promptly he completes "extra" or rush assignments	☐ Requires constant supervision	☐ Needs occasional follow-up	☐ Ordinarily can be counted on	☐ Needs very little supervision	☐ Completely trustworthy in job requirements
DEPENDABILITY: Follows instructions, good safety habits, initiative, punctuality and attendance	☐ Seldom works with or assists others; indifferent	☐ Frequently uncooperative; too critical of others	☐ Generally works well with others; normal interest	☐ Eagerness often displayed; a good team worker	☐ Extraordinary interest; inspires others to work
ATTITUDES: Toward company, job and fellow workers; cooperation	☐	☐	☐	☐	☐

COMMENTS:

DEPARTMENT SUPERVISOR

CLASSROOM SUPERVISOR

FIGURE 8-5
Graphic Rating Appraisal Form

he or she wants, as long as the total cost does not exceed five dollars. The American Can Company, for example, allows its employees to design their own benefits, drawing from five benefit areas: medical insurance, life insurance, disability insurance, vacations, and retirement programs. A healthy, unmarried woman in her twenties can thus create a very different mix of benefits from that of a chronically ill married man in his sixties.

Pensions and ERISA It is important to note that companies do not have to provide pensions for their retiring employees. However, if a company does provide a pension plan, it must follow detailed rules established by the federal

Employee Retirement Income Security Act (ERISA), enacted in 1974. ERISA was designed to correct serious abuses in private pension plans that had led to the denial of benefits to thousands of people who believed themselves eligible. Many plans had loopholes artfully drawn to allow companies not to pay even their employees with thirty or forty years' service. In one famous case a company went out of business, leaving a bankrupt pension fund and hundreds of workers without pensions.

ERISA specifies how an employer must handle pension funds. It also describes when and how a worker becomes entitled to benefits under a private pension plan. Even if a company does go out of business, its pensions may be paid through the Pension Benefit Guarantee Corporation, which insures pension funds in much the same way the Federal Deposit Insurance Corporation insures bank savings accounts.

TODAY'S HUMAN RESOURCES CHALLENGES

At no other time in history has business faced so many and so complex human resources challenges as it does today. It is worth noting a few more of them.

☐ How to establish and maintain equal employment opportunities for women and minority group members.

☐ How to cope with the increasingly complex legal requirements relating to employee compensation and benefit plans.

☐ What to do about the skyrocketing costs of health care, which directly affect the cost of medical insurance.

☐ How to set up equitable rates of pay to reflect employees' comparable worth to the firm.

☐ What businesses can use to motivate employees when labor-market conditions dictate that entry-level salaries must nearly match those being paid to senior employees in the same job classification.

☐ How to motivate new hires in a two-tier system who will never achieve the base pay of senior employees in the same job classification.

☐ Seek out solutions to stem on-the-job use of alcohol and drugs.

Chapter Highlights

1. Explain what human resource management is and describe the factors that have contributed to its importance.

Human resource management encompasses the activities involved in acquiring, developing, and using people in a business. The work force has changed dramatically over the last two decades. Three changes in particular have raised the importance of human resource managers in a firm: the entry of minorities into skilled jobs and the pro-

fessions, an enormous increase in the number of women in the workplace, and an increasingly better educated population.

2. Explain the human resource planning process.

The human resource planning process consists of several stages: forecasting demand, estimating the supply, and planning to meet the needs. In order to plan effectively, businesses must engage in job analysis, the systematic study of an employee's duties, tasks, and work environment. After studying a job, job analysts prepare a job description — which is a written summary of the duties, tasks, and responsibilities associated with a job — and a job specification — a list of the key qualifications a person needs to perform a job successfully.

3. List the steps in the employment process.

The three steps in the employment process are recruitment, the process of attracting qualified people to apply for jobs; selection, the process of identifying appropriate candidates; and orientation, the process of introducing new employees to the organization and the job.

4. Identify the primary purposes of performance appraisals and describe three appraisal techniques.

Performance appraisals, the formal assessment of how well employees are doing their jobs and the communication of the results of the assessment to the employees, serve two kinds of purposes: evaluation purposes and development purposes. Their evaluation purposes include determining eligibility for pay raises and promotion and deciding which employees to retain. Their development purposes are future-oriented and are aimed at improving the employee's career potential.

5. Describe several training methods and development methods.

On-the-job training methods include apprenticeships; vestibule training, which takes place in separate training areas equipped like the actual work site; and computer-assisted instructions, which lets employees proceed through programmed materials at their own pace. Commonly used on-the-job development methods include coaching, in which employees receive regular instruction and feedback from their immediate supervisors, and mentoring, in which a senior employee assists a junior employee to build a network within the firm and to develop a successful career there. Conferences and workshops are common multipurpose, off-site approaches.

6. Explain how compensation systems achieve their three primary purposes.

A business's compensation system has three main purposes: attracting qualified employees; retaining those employees; and motivating higher levels of performance from them. When a firm pays the going rate or better, it is likely to attract employees. Retaining employees is primarily a function of maintaining a fair pay structure. Incentive systems that involve bonuses, pay that is tied to productivity, and/or profit-sharing plans serve to motivate employees to perform better.

Key Terms

Achievement test
Affirmative action
  programs
Antidiscrimination laws
Assessment center
Attrition
Base pay
Benefits
Cafeteria-style benefit
  programs
Case studies
Civil Rights Act of
  1964 (Title VII)
Commission basis
Compensation

Development
Discharge (termination)
Employee Retirement
  Income Security Act
  (ERISA)
Employment process
Employment test
Equal Employment
  Opportunity Act
Equal Employment
  Opportunity
  Commission (EEOC)
Flexible-benefit
  programs

Going rate
Human resource
  development
Human resource
  planning
Incentive systems
Incentives
Job specification
Management by
  objectives (MBO)
Mentoring
Orientation
Pay structure
Piece-rate system

Profit-sharing program
Promotion
Rank-order technique
Seniority
Skills inventory
Stress interview
Structured interview
Title VII, Civil Rights
  Act, amended
Training
Unemployment
  compensation
Wage/salary survey
Workers' compensation

Review Questions

1. What are the three steps in the human resource planning process? Explain them.
2. Define the following terms: *job analysis, job description,* and *job specification.*
3. Describe four major sources of potential employees.
4. What are the steps in the employment process? Explain each step.
5. What is an orientation? How does it work?
6. Explain the purposes of performance appraisals and describe three appraisal techniques.
7. Explain the difference between training and development.
8. Describe three training methods and three development methods.
9. Explain the three purposes of a compensation system.
10. What are the two ways of paying employees on the basis of time? Distinguish between them.
11. What are the two main types of incentive programs and how do they work?
12. Identify three employee benefits required by law. What are four employee benefits often voluntarily offered by employers?

Application Exercises

1. Recently you assumed the management duties at a shoe store in a large metropolitan area. This store has a history of high employee turnover and low morale. These problems have had a negative impact on profits of the business. To correct these problems, you have decided to improve the employee selection and screening process. Briefly describe the steps that might be taken to identify capable employees. How would you screen applicants?
2. In recent weeks you have applied for several part-time positions. One position is with a small manufacturing plant. The starting wage is $5.30 and you will be able to work from 20 to 25 hours each week. The other position is with a small manufacturing plant that uses a piece-rate compensation system. The hours will be the same, but the potential for higher hourly earnings exists. At the present time, the average hourly pay earned by employees is $5.90. Which position would be most appealing to you? What are some of the major advantages and disadvantages of each compensation plan from your standpoint? From the employer's standpoint?

Cases

8.1 Stockholders in Every Store

Publix Super Markets Inc. owns and operates more than 300 food stores in Florida with average annual sales of about $12 million per store. For years the chain has had to compete primarily with Winn-Dixie supermarkets (over 400 units), but now new competition is entering from all sides. Lucky Stores, A&P, Pueblo International food warehouse markets, Safeway, and Pantry Pride, have either opened their first outlets in Florida or expanded operations in that fast-growing sunbelt state.

Mark Hollis, the president of Publix, does not see this influx of competition as a threat. "As long as people appreciate service and value," he says, "there's a market for Publix." And, in fact, throughout the half-century it has been in existence, the firm has attempted to provide friendly and pleasant shopping for its customers. It does this by making Publix a pleasant place to work.

To begin with, Publix is wholly owned by employees. About 12,000 of its 35,000 full- and part-time employees own Publix stock, which is traded only among employees. Ownership tends to give rise to enthusiasm and dedication, both of which are fostered by management; according to the Publix company handbook, they bring both enjoyment on the job and promotion to positions of greater responsibility.

Good pay and very good voluntary benefits help maintain an unusual *esprit de corps* in the Publix work force. Even employees who work approximately half-time are eligible for profit-sharing and retirement benefits. And all full-time employees receive bonuses based on individual store performance. In return, the firm expects employees to dress, work, and behave according to guidelines detailed in the Publix handbook.

Publix is the second-largest supermarket chain in Florida and one of the most profitable grocery chains in the country. Yet it was the last major chain to open on Sundays. It finally did, only because many of its customers wanted to shop on Sunday. According to Hollis, the firm had stayed closed on Sundays to give its employees the traditional day of rest. Little wonder, then, that Publix was recently chosen as one of the 100 best employers in America.

Questions

1. Why might Publix management pay particular attention to employee recruiting and selection? To employee training and appraisal?
2. Besides employee ownership, what other Publix policies foster employee enthusiasm and dedication? What do you think is the effect of the employee dress and behavior codes?

Sources: For more information see *Management Review*, August 1985, p. 43; *Progressive Grocer*, January 1985, pp. 55–58; Robert Levering, Milton Moskowitz, and Michael Katz, *The 100 Best Companies to Work for in America* (Reading, Mass.: Addison-Wesley, 1984)

8.2 Training to Survive

New employees learn about Orlando's Walt Disney World in classrooms located deep beneath the Magic Kingdom. They learn that Disney World's product is happiness; that spotless grounds and neat, well-groomed employees are important to guests and, therefore, to Walt Disney World; and that the appearance of grounds and employees is continually checked. They learn their way around Disney World, and they learn to perform their jobs "The Disney Way."

Au Bon Pain Co., a $30-million-per-year chain of gourmet food stores provides several levels of learning for its employees. Among them are:

☐ A six-week store operator training program
☐ An equipment management program, which trains store managers in the repair of in-store equipment

☐ A program that provides one or two years of corporate staff experience to senior-level store employees
☐ A management skills program for all employees

Au Bon Pain management decided to institute its learning programs to solve one of the problems of extremely rapid growth: The firm could not find enough qualified employees to fill the jobs that were becoming available.

JMT Electronics & Controls Inc., a distributor of electrical and electronic components, has only twenty-eight employees. Recently, when its main business shifted from television tubes to control systems, sales began to fluctuate heavily. JMT went to an outside consultant for help. The consultant arranged a three-day seminar for JMT sales people, designed to teach them how to discover and satisfy their customers' needs. The results were so good that JMT purchased a second seminar six months later, and is now planning a third.

Firm after firm is discovering that in-house training and development are a necessity — and the learning they provide seems to be increasingly more formal. About twenty firms, including Wang Laboratories and J. P. Morgan, now award academic degrees. (Morgan's program is an abbreviated MBA curriculum in which students focus on economics and finance.) A number, like IBM, maintain separate college-like campuses for learning programs.

Altogether, America's large and small firms spend tens of billions of dollars annually on employee learning. The reasons for spending that much money on training and development seem as varied as the firms that spend it and the programs they spend it on. But perhaps those reasons all boil down to one: They spend it to survive.

Questions

1. Characterize each of the learning programs mentioned above according to type: training, development, or education.
2. Why might a firm like Wang or J. P. Morgan operate its own educational facility, rather than send employees to a college or university?
3. What benefits are provided by employee learning programs, other than that of having well-training workers?

Sources: For more information see *The Boston Globe*, March 7, 1986, pp. 10–11; *Inc.*, March 1986, pp. 119–122; and *The Boston Globe*, March 4, 1986, pp. 41, 51.

9

LABOR— MANAGEMENT RELATIONS

Learning Objectives

After you have completed this chapter, you will be able to do the following:

- Describe the role of Samuel Gompers in the development of the American labor movement.

- Identify the antitrust acts that affected the labor movement's effort to organize American industry.

- List the key features of the National Labor Relations Act, the Taft-Hartley Act, and the Landrum-Griffin Act.

- List the steps in the organizing process and summarize each.

- Identify the subjects that may be and may not be discussed in collective bargaining.

- Describe the stages of a grievance proceeding.

- Define *givebacks* and discuss the effects of this concept on bargaining in the 1980s.

- Analyze the phases of collective bargaining.

- Identify the weapons each side in collective bargaining has to force an agreement.

The Pontiac Fiero was one of General Motors's bright spots during the grim early 1980s. Japanese competition had cut deeply into GM's sales. Low sales also meant fewer jobs for the members of the United Auto Workers (UAW). As GM developed the Fiero, it involved the UAW in planning the conversion of an old plant to produce the new model. Management and union representatives even went to Japan to study quality control and production techniques.

The plan that GM and the UAW jointly developed called for unprecedented cooperation between unionized workers and management. The status distinctions between management and labor, like wearing ties and having reserved spaces in heated garages, disappeared. Teams of employees and managers were to meet weekly to resolve quality and production issues. In short, labor and management would have to work together very closely. They did, and the Fiero's success is history. More importantly, they achieved their objective: "To provide an environment for employee involvement, an atmosphere of trust, of mutual respect and human dignity, so that we may achieve our common goals of high quality, mutual success, job security, and effective community relationships."[1]

This chapter's focus is on **unions**, organizations like the UAW through which employees combine their strength to advance their common interests. Relations are not always harmonious between management and **organized labor**, workers represented by unions. In fact, when most people think of labor–management relations, what comes to mind is often harsh words and bitter strikes. But as GM and the UAW are proving, traditional foes can work together to meet challenges not dreamed of when unions first succeeded in organizing American industry.

THE EARLY UNION MOVEMENT

In 1787, representatives of the thirteen original states met in Philadelphia and drafted our Constitution. Five years later, a small group of Philadelphia shoemakers formed the first union. When they went on strike, their employers quickly crushed the union — with the help of local authorities. This pattern persisted for the next 140 years.

The First Organizing Efforts: 1830—1865

Conditions in the mid-nineteenth century work place were so awful as to be simply unimaginable to people today. The noise, dirt, lack of sanitary facilities, poor ventilation, and absence of fire exits would not be tolerated in any modern work place. As the Industrial Revolution progressed, workers increasingly looked to unions as a way to bring pressure to bear on unresponsive management and government.

Although the union movement gradually gained strength from the 1830s through the 1850s, it could claim few successes. Tailors in New York City and women cotton-mill workers in Lowell, Massachusetts, made up two of the unions beaten in this period. Some sense, though, of the justice of the early unions' causes comes from their principal demands in the late 1830s: for free public education and a ten-hour work day, six days a week.[2]

The Emergence of Strong Unions: 1865—1914

The Civil War marked the beginning both of modern warfare and of the modern industrial economy. It marked as well a turning point for the labor movement. The victorious North had organized its population, industrial production, and financial resources during the war years to a degree that had never been seen before anywhere. This momentum did not ease after the war ended. The railroads, for example, carried it forward. By 1869, when the first transcontinental rail line was completed, the railroads employed tens of thousands of both skilled and unskilled workers.

The Knights of Labor   The year 1869 also saw the founding of the **Knights of Labor**. The Knights' goal was to organize all workers, regardless of their skills or industry, into one organization. In 1885, the Knights won organized labor's first two great successes, through strikes against the Missouri Pacific Railroad. The issues were pay cuts and the railroad's discrimination against members of the Knights in hiring and promotion. In the next year, membership in the Knights soared from 100,000 to 700,000. The Knights' successes were short-lived, however. On May 6, 1886, someone threw a bomb during an anarchist rally in Chicago, leaving seven policemen dead. The Knights were blamed and could not recover their original momentum, even though the charges were never proved.

Labor unions have always been vulnerable to charges of being the tools of radicals. Today, in France and England, Marxists and Communists dominate several large labor unions. For the most part, American unions bear little resemblance to their European counterparts. The work of one man, Samuel Gompers, is the main reason that American unions focus on their members' material needs rather than on political philosophies.

The Role of Samuel Gompers in Developing Unions

Samuel Gompers   Gompers understood the inherent weakness of organizations that tried to represent all types of workers in all industries, the way the Knights of Labor and its radical offshoot, the International Workers of the World (the "Wobblies") had attempted to do so. American workers and industry were much too diversified to be capable of being organized in one all-encompassing union.

In 1881, Gompers founded the **American Federation of Labor** (AFL), an umbrella organization for craft unions. A **trade** or **craft union** is a union made up of skilled workers of the same or related vocations. Over the next four decades Gompers built the AFL into the nation's most important labor organization. More importantly, he established the political and social philosophy that guides unions even today. That philosophy, **business unionism**, emphasizes that American unions exist primarily for the economic improvement of their workers, not to engage in a class struggle to alter the American form of government or to promote socialism.[3] Indeed, Gompers once declared, "I want to tell you Socialists that I have studied your philosophy; read your works on economics. . . . Economically, you are unsound; socially, you are wrong; industrially, you are an impossibility."[4]

What Gompers wanted was **collective bargaining** — negotiation of the terms and conditions of employment between management and an organization representing employees. He believed collective bargaining to be the only way that workers could gain enough strength to negotiate effectively with management for labor's proper share of the capitalist pie.

The First Major Antitrust Act

The Sherman Act   Ironically, the legislation originally designed to curb large companies' abuses of the market system, the **Sherman Antitrust Act** (1890), became business's main tool against unions. Typically, when a union began to organize a company, the firm would seek an **injunction**, a court order forbidding certain actions. The companies claimed, often successfully, that organizing employees to bargain collectively with employers had the effect of restraining trade and therefore violated the Sherman Act.

For forty-two years, Gompers and organized labor fought to neutralize this unintended result of the Sherman Act. What Gompers wanted from the federal government was impartiality. He felt that labor should be free to negotiate with management without government's interference.

THE MODERN ERA: REGULATION OF LABOR RELATIONS

Ten years before his death in 1924, Gompers got part of what he wanted. However, within ten years after his death it had become clear that government neutrality could not alone create an atmosphere in which labor and management could coexist.

The Era of Government Neutrality: 1914–1932

The Amended Sherman Act

In 1914, Congress adopted the Clayton Act, which amended the Sherman Act. In it Congress declared that

> [the] labor of a human being is not a commodity or article of commerce. Nothing in the antitrust laws shall be construed to forbid the existence and operation of labor . . . organizations.[5]

Despite this language, the Supreme Court regularly interpreted the new law to let employers continue using injunctions to block organizing. It was eighteen years more before Congress, in the Norris-LaGuardia Act of 1932, effectively removed that obstacle to unionization.

The Rise of Industrial Unions   The removal of antitrust restrictions did not swell the AFL's rolls. Most major crafts were already unionized, so union organizers shifted their focus to the mass of unskilled workers being recruited for America's major industries: steel, mining, and autos. The Utility Workers, the United Rubber Workers, the Amalgamated Clothing and Textile Workers,

John L. Lewis — A giant in the union movement. *After walking out of the AFL, Lewis led the battle to organize unskilled workers in the nation's basic industries. By 1940, the CIO could claim more members than the AFL. Nevertheless, only 28 percent of all American nonfarm workers were union members.*

the Oil, Chemical and Atomic Workers International, and other unions like them are **industrial unions**, unions whose membership includes all the workers in an industry, regardless of the tasks they perform.

The distinction between craft and trade unions on the one hand and industrial unions on the other is an important one. When the New York Knicks are going to play the Los Angeles Lakers in Madison Square Garden, members of the electricians' craft or trade union work on the lighting, members of the plumbers' union fix clogged sinks, members of the carpenters' union make any last-minute adjustments to the movable seating, and members of the NBA Players Association actually play the game. They are all members of craft or trade unions. When a new Corvette rolls off a General Motors assembly line, however, every one of the thousands of parts in that car was installed, assembled, adjusted, and inspected by members of just one industrial union: the United Auto Workers.

The leading figure in the industrial union movement was the United Mine Workers' president John L. Lewis. In 1935, Lewis founded the **Congress of Industrial Organizations (CIO)**, an umbrella organization for industrial unions. Several years earlier, it had become clear that the government neutrality established by the Clayton Act would never make a reality of Gompers's ideal of having labor and management negotiate their differences. Bloody organizing strikes, especially in coal and steel, and the onset of the Great Depression in 1929 convinced the public that Congress would have to act.

The Era of Legislation: 1932—1959

Between 1932 and 1959, the peak period in union membership and strength, Congress enacted several major labor laws. Table 9.1 identifies their key provisions as well as those of some other related statutes.

Statutes	Major Provisions
Clayton Act (1914)	Declared union activity not subject to the antitrust laws.
Railway Labor Act (1926)	Designed to keep interstate commerce flowing despite labor difficulties. (1) Governs railroad and airline collective bargaining; (2) Created National Mediation Board to conduct union elections and resolve disputes between labor and management.
Norris-LaGuardia Act (1932)	(1) Outlawed contracts under which management could fire a worker if he or she joined a union; (2) Prohibited federal courts from issuing injunctions against lawful union activities, including picketing and strikes.
National Labor Relations Act (Wagner Act) (1934)	(1) Created National Labor Relations Board (NLRB); (2) Prohibited unfair labor practices; (3) Guaranteed employees the right to join and participate in unions.
Taft-Hartley Act (1947)	(1) Outlawed unfair labor practices by unions; (2) Abolished the closed shop; (3) Permitted states to enact right-to-work laws; (4) Allowed president to order 80-day "cooling off" period in disputes of national importance; (5) Created the Federal Mediation and Conciliation Service, to assist parties in resolving disputes.
Landrum-Griffin Act (1959)	(1) Gave the Secretary of Labor powers to monitor and control union corruption; (2) Serves as bill of rights for union members.

Source: Adapted from R. N. Corley, et al., *The Legal Environment of Business*, 6th ed. (New York: copyright © 1984 by McGraw-Hill Book Co.), p. 246. Reprinted by permission.

TABLE 9.1

Federal Laws Governing Labor–Management Relations

The Key Provisions of the National Labor Relations Act

The National Labor Relations Act (NLRA)   The **National Labor Relations Act** of 1935, popularly called the **Wagner Act**, made labor–management relations a federal matter and established the National Labor Relations Board (NLRB) to regulate them. Called "labor's Magna Carta," the act makes it unlawful for an employer to interfere with its employees' rights to form, join, and participate in a union or for management to try to subvert the union itself. The NLRA forbids employers to discriminate against workers who join a union or to retaliate against those who file charges of **unfair labor practices**, violations of the laws that the NLRB enforces. In addition, it compels an employer whose employees select a specific union as their exclusive bargaining agent to bargain with that union.

The **National Labor Relations Board (NLRB)**, a five-member board appointed by the president to carry out the federal labor laws, has two major responsibilities. First, it supervises elections in which employees decide whether to be represented by a union. Second, it determines the validity of charges that an employer or a union has committed some unfair labor practice.

Not surprisingly, the Wagner Act boosted union membership dramatically, from 3 million in 1933 to 9 million in 1940. By 1945, unions claimed almost 15 million members.[6]

The Taft-Hartley Labor Act   While World War II raged abroad, labor and management agreed on peace at home. However, when peace came abroad, workers tried to make up for the minimal raises granted during the war.

The **Taft-Hartley Act** reflected the public's wish to blunt union drives for more

The Bias Battle Goes On

The issues of hiring discrimination, affirmative action, and seniority rights often put labor in conflict with management and sometimes turn one group of workers against another. In one important case that pitted worker against worker, the Supreme Court in 1984 ruled that seniority privileges should win out over affirmative action goals when the two clash.

The decision came as the result of a major battle between forces in American society. Seniority rules are firmly entrenched in American labor. Yet for the last decade or so, federal courts have sided with plans that give preference to minority workers in an attempt to undo years of racial discrimination. Some such plans call for companies to make sure that a certain percentage of the workers they hire come from a specific group, or require that the ratio of whites to blacks or men to women in a company's work force reach a certain level.

The 1984 decision grew out of a conflict in Memphis over which firefighters should be laid off when the city's budget shrank. A job-discrimination law suit filed by Carl Stotts, a black District Fire Chief, had resulted in the hiring of 18 black firefighters. But during budget cutting the next year, 15 were fired. These firings followed the union's seniority rules, which stated that the first to get laid off would be those who had been most recently employed — "last hired, first fired." But the black recruits appealed and at first won.

The Supreme Court ruled that Title VII of the 1964 Civil Rights Act protects seniority rules unless those rules discriminate. Justice Byron White wrote that "It is inappropriate to deny an innocent employee the benefits of his seniority in order to provide a remedy" in such a case. "Mere membership in the disadvantaged class is insufficient to warrant a seniority award," the Court declared. Only "those who have been actual victims of illegal discrimination" have rights to such awards. The three justices who disagreed with White's opinion contended that "race-conscious relief" could be granted under the 1964 Civil Rights Act.

In the wake of the ruling, changes quickly became visible. The Justice Department, which had been eager to fight against "reverse discrimination," reviewed hundreds of affirmative action plans to see if they violated seniority rights. Just a few days after the ruling, the government moved to reverse a court order in Cincinnati that barred police from using seniority as a basis for laying off minority officers.

Yet an aide to Denver's mayor Federico Pena expressed a widespread reaction to the Reagan administration's move to dismantle quota plans: "We're not dismantling anything — we're forging ahead." Many cities have come to accept affirmative action goals and to appreciate the benefits of hiring more women and non-whites. Eleanor Holmes Norton, former chief of the federal Equal Employment Opportunity Commission, says "there would be a real morale problem if companies jumped on the Reagan bandwagon." The National Association of Manufacturers endorsed affirmative action in a May, 1985 vote; a personnel director at Ford says "Businesses decided that affirmative action is the right thing to do."

The battle is far from over. The number of race and sex bias complaints rises every year, and the Reagan administration's support of reverse-bias cases has already led to changes in hiring and firing rules. The Justice Department's new attitude seems to be separating those people and businesses who really believed in affirmative action from those who merely went along with hiring rules out of fear. Many of the latter are now slipping back into their old practices. But the idea that the traditional victims of prejudice should get a break in hiring is far from dead, and it will be affecting labor-management relations for years to come.

Sources: Steve Curwood, "Furor Over Quota Issue Grows," *The Boston Globe*, June 24, 1984, A21. Ted Gest, "Seniority vs. Minorities — Impact of Court Ruling," *U.S. News & World Report*, Vol. 96, No. 25, June 25, 1984, 22. Aric Press, "A Right Turn on Race?" *Newsweek*, Vol. 103, No. 26, June 25, 1984, 29. "Much Ado About a Shift to the Right," *Time*, Vol. 123, No. 26, June 25, 1984, p. 63. Daniel B. Moskowitz, "Battling Another Bias in Business Lending," *Business Week*, No. 2896, May 27, 1985, 68. Ted Gest, "Why Drive on Job Bias Is Still Going Strong," *U.S. News & World Report*, Vol. 98, No. 23, June 17, 1985, 67.

Union members on parade. *These members of a local union which is part of the AFL-CIO, demonstrate their spirit and solidarity by presenting a united front in this local parade.*

The Key Features of the Taft-Hartley Act

The Five Types of Union Shops

wages, benefits, and — most importantly — power. The Taft-Hartley provisions that labor most bitterly resented abolished the closed shop and authorized the states to enact **right-to-work laws,** which outlaw union shops. A **shop** is simply a work place. There are five types of shop. A **closed shop** is one that requires workers to belong to the union before they can be hired. A **union shop** is one in which workers do not have to be union members when hired but must later join, usually within thirty days. An **agency shop** is one in which employees may choose not to join the union. However, since they receive the benefits of the union's bargaining on their behalf, the employer deducts from their pay a sum equal to the union's dues and pays that to the union. In a **maintenance shop**, an employee who joins a union must remain in it only so long as he or she works in that bargaining unit.

Finally, an **open shop** is one in which union membership is not a condition of employment. It is this type of shop that most right-to-work laws require. The union shop is the principal means by which unions protect their status in the work place. For this reason, unions have rightly regarded right-to-work laws as direct threats to their existence. Today, twenty-four states have right-to-work laws.

The Taft-Hartley Act also imposed on labor the requirements that the Wagner Act had imposed on management. For example, it requires unions to bargain in good faith, as discussed later.

Union membership continued to grow until the early 1950s, when it peaked both in numbers and in percentage of the work force. Total union membership has declined almost continuously since then. See Figure 9.1. Nonetheless, the AFL and CIO, which merged in 1955, still form the largest union organization in the world. Only the Teamsters and the National Education Association are not affiliated with it.

The Key Features of the Landrum-Griffin Act

The Landrum-Griffin Act   In many organizations, corruption accompanies growth and power. Labor unions have been no exception to this trend. For instance, various congressional hearings and trials have exposed racketeering in the Teamsters Union. The 1954 Academy Award–winning movie *On the Waterfront* accurately portrayed intimidation, bribery, theft, and even murder in the dockworkers' unions. As a result of revelations like these, in 1959 Congress enacted the **Landrum-Griffin Act**. This act's bill of rights for union members guarantees them the right to vote in union elections, speak at union meetings, receive union financial reports, and be treated like other members.

Only a few unions suffered the same ills as the Teamsters and dockworkers. Unions and their leaders accomplished much good during the mid-century period. John L. Lewis of the United Mine Workers redefined the benefits, like health care and pensions, that workers should receive. Walter Reuther of the United Auto Workers played a key role in the social movements of the 1950s and 1960s. And George Meany, head of the AFL-CIO, played a critical role in the effort to keep European unions noncommunist.

FIGURE 9-1

Union Share of the Work Force

Union membership continued to grow until the early 1950s, when it peaked both in numbers and in percentage of the work force. Total union membership has declined almost continuously since then.

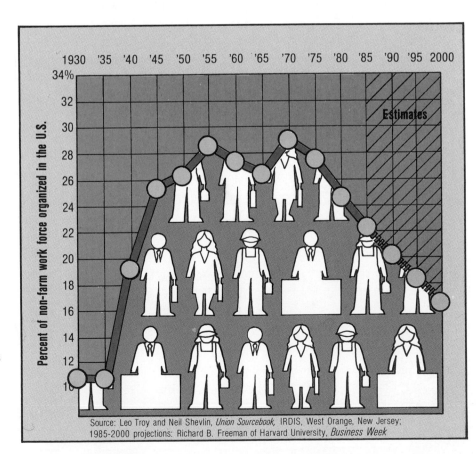

Source: Leo Troy and Neil Shevlin, *Union Sourcebook*, IRDIS, West Orange, New Jersey; 1985-2000 projections: Richard B. Freeman of Harvard University, *Business Week*

UNIONS TODAY AND TOMORROW

Unions continue to play an important — but changed — role in American life. Nonunion operations have reduced the number of workers in the trades on which Samuel Gompers built the AFL. Membership in industrial unions, the foundation of the CIO, has dropped as jobs have gone overseas. Membership dropped 27 percent in the United Auto Workers and 42 percent in the Steelworkers during the 1970s.[7]

The Emerging Service Sector

Demographic Trends Affecting Organized Labor

The shape of the American work force has changed. As Figure 9.2 indicates, workers are shifting into the service sector of the economy. Office workers, hotel and restaurant employees, and civil servants — teachers, police, and government workers — are service workers. Today, for example, more people work at McDonald's restaurants than for General Motors. The unions that are growing are those that represent service workers.

Women and minorities tend to dominate service unions. Service jobs often require fewer skills and are less well paid than those in the trades or heavy industry. As more jobs are lost in traditionally male-dominated fields, more white men are likely to join these unions.

FIGURE 9-2

Changes in the U.S. Job Market

The shape of the American work force has changed. Workers are shifting into the service sector of the economy.

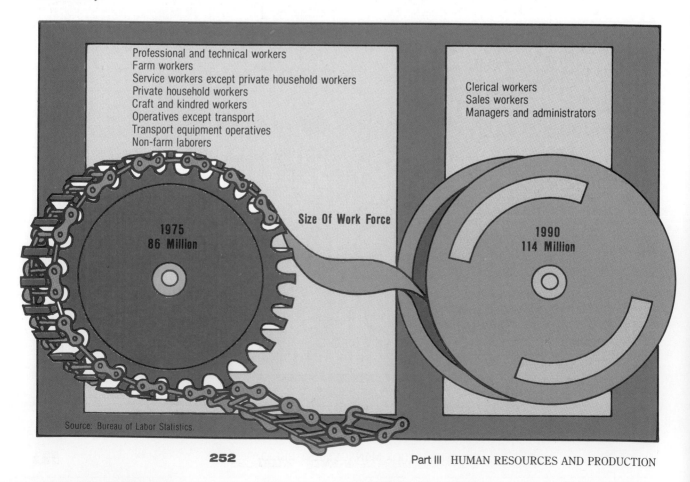

Professional and technical workers
Farm workers
Service workers except private household workers
Private household workers
Craft and kindred workers
Operatives except transport
Transport equipment operatives
Non-farm laborers

Clerical workers
Sales workers
Managers and administrators

Size Of Work Force

1975
86 Million

1990
114 Million

Source: Bureau of Labor Statistics.

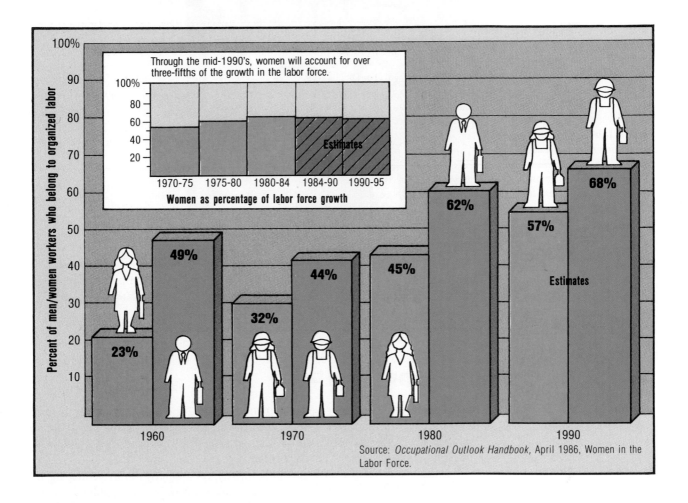

Through the mid-1990's, women will account for over three-fifths of the growth in the labor force.

Women as percentage of labor force growth

1970-75 1975-80 1980-84 1984-90 1990-95

Estimates

1960: 23% 49%
1970: 32% 44%
1980: 45% 62%
1990: 57% 68%

Estimates

Source: *Occupational Outlook Handbook*, April 1986, Women in the Labor Force.

FIGURE 9-3

Women in the Work Place

The number of women in the work place has increased dramatically from 1960 to 1990. The Civil Rights Act of 1964 is a major reason for this increase.

Growing Numbers of Women and Minorities

Overall, the number of women in the work place has increased dramatically, as seen in Figure 9.3. A major reason for this increase is the Civil Rights Act of 1964, discussed in Chapter 8.

That law has also led to a greater number of minority group members entering the unionized work force. Today, blacks make up 15 percent of the 17.4 million unionized workers. Not surprisingly, some of the bitterest organizing battles in recent years have centered on groups of workers dominated by minorities.

THE UNIONIZATION PROCESS

Unions thrive when workers believe that employers are not treating them fairly. Workers join and support unions because unions increase their power in bargaining for wages and benefits, because they encourage greater job stability and predictability, and because they protect workers from arbitrary firings or demotions. This section describes the process by which a work place becomes unionized.

When labor and management combine forces. *Mergers and acquisitions are becoming more and more frequent, and unions are likely to play a larger role in management contests. When Jack H. Brown lost his job as president of Stater Bros. supermarkets, two of the chain's unions — the Teamsters and the United Food and Commercial Workers — joined in the fight to reinstate him.*

The Organizing Drive

The First Step in the Organizing Process

Either the workers themselves or a union may take the necessary steps toward unionization, which are collectively called the **organizing drive**. Sometimes a union may already represent some workers at the same firm. At other times the union may represent workers at similar firms.

Normally, the union makes its initial moves very quietly, to avoid tipping its hand to management. Then the union gradually becomes more public about its efforts. In some cases, unions are quite creative in their attempts to win workers. For instance, the Amalgamated Clothing & Textile Workers offered employees at the Hanes Corporation a simple cardboard slide rule so that they could calculate their earnings under Hanes's extremely complicated compensation system. [8]

Once the organizing drive has gained what the union feels to be sufficient strength, the union requests that management recognize it as the workers' representative. The request is almost never granted. Typically, when the union requests recognition, it tells management that more than 30 percent of the workers have signed **authorization cards**, forms signed by employees that either authorize the union to represent them or to request a representation election (discussed next), or both.

The Representation Election

The Second Step in the Organizing Process

If the employer refuses to recognize the union, the union uses the cards to support a petition filed with the National Labor Relations Board to hold a **representation election**, an election to determine whether a union will represent a particular group of workers. After receiving the petition, the NLRB meets with the union and the employer. It tries to gain the parties' agreement on the date,

Buss 1301 Class Schedule

Instructor: Steve Wolfe

SESSION

ACTIVITY

1st MAR 20   Orientation and Chapter 1

2nd MAR 22   Chapters 2 and 3

3rd MAR 27   Chapters 4 and 5

4th MAR 29   Chapters 6 and 7

5th APR 3   TEST - Chapters 1 thru 7
                 Chapter 8

6th APR 5   Chapters 9 and 10

7th APR 10   Chapters 11 and 12

8th APR 12   Chapters 13 and 14

9th APR 17   TEST - Chapters 8 thru 14

10th APR 19	Chapters 16 and 17
11th APR 24	Chapters 18 and 19
12th APR 26	Chapter 20
13th MAY 1	TEST - Chapters 15 thru 20 Chapter 21
14th MAY 3	Chapters 22 and 23
15th MAY 8	TEST - Chapters 21 thru 23 REVIEW
16th MAY 10	FINAL EXAM

time, and place of the election; the form of the ballot; and a definition of the bargaining unit. If the parties can be led to agree on all these issues, the NLRB holds a **consent election**, a representation election agreed on by union and management. If the parties disagree on even one of these points, it is up to the NLRB to decide whether to hold an election.

First, the NLRB judges whether the workers seeking the election make up an appropriate **bargaining unit**, a group of employees who share common interests in wages and working conditions and have common skills. The parties may hotly contest this issue. The union will want the bargaining unit defined broadly enough to contain the greatest number of employees favoring unionization. The company will of course want the opposite. Once the NLRB has defined the bargaining unit, it must determine whether at least 30 percent of the unit's employees are interested in union representation. Normally, the authorization cards provide a ready answer.

Before a representation election can take place, each side presents its case to the workers. There are some restrictions on what can be said and done. For example, management cannot either directly or indirectly threaten workers with the loss of their jobs if they vote for the union. The workers vote by secret ballot during working hours at the job site.

Representation elections can involve more than one issue on the ballot. The workers may have two or more unions to choose from, as well as "no union." If no one choice receives a majority, the NLRB stages a run-off election between the top two choices in the first one. If the majority of voters choose to be represented by a union, the NLRB certifies that union as representing all workers in the bargaining unit for the purposes of collective bargaining.

THE SUBJECTS OF COLLECTIVE BARGAINING

Parties may negotiate on any subject that a federal or state law does not forbid them to. In other words, they can agree on discussing any topic that does not involve breaking the law. For instance, the Sheet Metal Workers could negotiate a wage agreement with a construction company — but the agreement could not waive time and a half for overtime work. The **Fair Labor Standards Act**, also known as the minimum wage law or the wages and hours law, requires it.

The Taft-Hartley Act requires that labor and management negotiate about wages, benefits, hours, and working conditions. Each of these mandatory subjects for collective bargaining is discussed in turn. There are also voluntary subjects for collective bargaining, such as any subjects that the parties might bargain about that are neither illegal nor mandatory. These topics usually fall under the heading of management rights or union rights.

What May and May Not Be Discussed in Collective Bargaining

The Respective Rights of Management and Union

In a collective bargaining agreement, management will want to retain as much control as it can over the conduct of employees on the job. It will also want to reserve the right to control the type and pace of production. For example,

Two-Tier Contracts

Of all the recent effects of low foreign labor rates, none has been more feared by American workers than the loss of American blue-collar jobs. Many American companies have taken their factories overseas, lured by the prospect of getting 6 or 8 foreign workers for the same wages they'd pay one American. The amount of investment capital and jobs moving out of the country has spelled trouble for some industries and especially for union workers. With efficient modern transportation and communication, shipping a product from Brazil or Singapore isn't that large a burden if the company can save money by not hiring local American union workers.

That was the situation General Motors' Packard Electric Division faced in 1984. At its Warren, Ohio plant, Packard paid semi-skilled workers $22 an hour (including benefits) to bundle wires into harnesses. At that rate, the workers could not compete with those in Packard's Mexican plants where Packard paid less than $3 an hour. The company had already moved out 5000 jobs since 1973 and threatened never to hire in the area again. Desperate to save jobs and their community, union members accepted a relatively new and controversial form of labor agreement — the two-tier contract.

Packard kept current workers on at their current pay-scale, guaranteeing them jobs until retirement. But it began to pay new workers only $9 an hour including benefits, less than half what the top-tier workers made. The contract contained a number of innovative benefits for the workers, and the job guarantee looked good to the workers voting on the contract. But basically it was an attempt by the union to save jobs.

Packard isn't the only company to recognize the pos-sible savings and negotiate such a contract recently. Under a contract signed by American Airlines and the Allied Pilots Association new entry-level pilots make $18,000 a year, as opposed to $36,000 under the old contract.

Many such contracts were ratified during the recent recession when labor was plentiful and executives could convince union negotiators that the company simply could not survive with labor rates at the current levels. From the labor standpoint, a two-tier contract often looks better than wage concessions and givebacks.

A number of problems can arise from this sort of arrangement. The two tiers create a lower class of workers who may earn 1/2 or 1/3 as much as someone doing the same job who was hired a few months earlier. Under the provisions of the Packard agreement, which calls for new employees' pay to catch up gradually to that of long-term employees, there will eventually be people on nine different pay scales working side by side at the factory. The contracts give the companies incentives to let more experienced workers go, so that a higher percentage of the workforce will be drawing the lower wage. No doubt some of the second-tier workers will feel bitter towards their union or their company, and some may sue. But so far a number of companies — from Boeing to Safeway Stores to Dow Chemical — have been able to convince union negotiators to accept a two-tier contract as the only way American plants can compete with foreign ones.

Sources: Steven Flax, "Pay Cuts Before the Job Even Starts," *Fortune*, Vol. 109, No. 1, January 9, 1984, 75. "The Revolutionary Wage Deal at GM's Packard Electric," *Business Week*, August 29, 1983, 54. John Hoerr, "A Pioneering Pact Promises Jobs for Life," *Business Week*, December 31, 1984, 48.

management will want to control the scheduling of overtime so that it can respond quickly to fluctuations in demand for its products. Paying overtime is always cheaper than hiring new workers, so management will want a small permanent work force. The union will want employees to be able to refuse overtime so that they can choose between leisure time and overtime. Unions have historically argued also that every person has a right to a job, and unions are committed to creating permanent jobs.

The rights that concern the union most include control over the definition of the bargaining unit, the scope of the employer's recognition of its right to negotiate on behalf of the bargaining unit, the duration and renewal schedule of the collective bargaining agreement, and the way in which jobs are to be assigned. For example, one of the hottest issues in recent years between New York's transit management and the Amalgamated Transit Union involved the contracting out of repair work on subway cars and buses to companies whose workers were not ATU members. Other unions have made the issue of part-time nonunion workers a major collective bargaining point.

Management protects its rights by inserting a clause in collective bargaining agreements saying that it retains any rights that it has not expressly given up.

Wages and Benefits

The Four Standard Areas of Collective Bargaining

Under normal circumstances, wages and benefits are the most important subjects of collective bargaining.

Base Wages and COLAs   The **base wage rate**, the minimum paid per hour to any worker in the bargaining unit, is the basis upon which everything else is calculated. Until quite recently, contracts routinely called for **cost of living adjustments (COLAs)**, changes to the base wage rate (up to an established maximum) to reflect increases in the inflation rate for the preceding quarter or year. COLAs were designed to ensure that inflation did not reduce real wages. A contract might call for an annual COLA of up to 3 percent, assuming that the inflation rate, usually measured by the government's **Consumer Price Index**, equaled or exceeded 3 percent. However, as inflation increased and productivity declined in the decade from 1975 to 1985, the reduction of COLAs became a key management objective in collective bargaining.

Wage Differentials and Incentives   Some contracts call for a **seniority differential**, an incremental pay increase determined by the length of the worker's service with the employer. This differential is usually defined in terms of years worked. Contracts involving employers who operate on other than a strictly nine-to-five, Monday-through-Friday basis often call for a **shift differential**, an incremental pay increase for working specified time periods. The increase is for working at times that other workers do not want to work. The graveyard shift, from 11:00 P.M. to 7:00 A.M. almost always carries the highest shift differential.

As we discussed in the last two chapters, employers often pay premiums for above-average productivity. **Incentive rate formulas** are pay increments awarded for increased productivity. These formulas are not always tied to the base wage rate. Unions traditionally oppose incentive rates because they resemble **piecework rates** that pay employees according to what they produce, not by the time they work. In the past, when employers used this pay method they often adjusted upward the output requirements and reduced the piece rate. For that reason, machine quotas and speeds are hot issues when labor and management are negotiating incentive rates.

Benefits and Health Insurance Of course, direct wages paid to workers are not the employer's only costs. Benefits make up a significant component of those costs, as seen in Chapter 8. Two of the most expensive benefits are pensions and health insurance. In both cases, the employer makes payments to specific funds, not directly to the employee.

In the case of pension funds negotiated by unions, the company pays in a sum equal to a percentage of each worker's wages. Upon retirement, the employee receives a monthly check for the rest of his or her life, if the system works as it is supposed to. As we saw in Chapter 8, it does not always work that way.

As the cost of health care has soared, so have employers' contributions to their employees' health-care plans. Today, for instance, General Motors spends $2.1 billion for employee health benefits.[9]

Hours

The Second Standard Bargaining Area

As already noted, the hours that employees work are the subject of federal and state laws and also of collective bargaining agreements. The issues related to hours go well beyond questions of shift differentials and the length of the work week. They also include paid vacation time, unpaid leave, maternity/paternity leave, paid holidays, breaks, and rest periods.

Working Conditions

The Third Main Bargaining Area

Virtually all collective bargaining agreements deal with the question of working conditions. **Working conditions** is a catch-all term to describe all aspects of the relationship between employer and employee that are not related to the area of compensation. Coal miners, for example, engage in some of the most routinely dangerous work in American industry. Like anyone else, a coal miner wants to take home the maximum pay. From their earliest collective bargaining agreements, however, the United Mine Workers have emphasized safety.

There are other working conditions typically covered in collective bargaining agreements. Some of them are

☐ Shift assignments: Will management, or employees (using seniority), determine who works which shifts?
☐ Work schedules: What periods of the day will shifts fall into?
☐ Work rules: What will be the rules of the work place, and how much say will the union have in them?

Job Security

The Fourth Standard Area in Collective Bargaining

There are two components to job security: the right to employment and the right to receive unemployment compensation when work is not available.

The **right to employment** refers to the methods by which promotions, transfers, and layoffs are determined within a bargaining unit. For the most part, unions have insisted that all three factors be determined on the basis of **seniority**, a system in which the order of hiring determines the order of promotions, layoffs, rehirings, and the exercise of all other employment rights. For the employer, seniority means that the most experienced — and most highly paid — workers are the last to be laid off. For the worker, seniority gives more security. It is, of course, easier for younger workers to find a new job or trade than for older ones. Still, in the face of widespread plant shutdowns, as in the steel industry, seniority is of little value.

Workers who are laid off are entitled to **unemployment compensation**, payments from a pool created by employer contributions and required by state law to be made for a certain period to laid-off workers. Some collective bargaining agreements also require the employer to make supplemental payments to laid-off workers. For instance, under the United Auto Workers program, when big layoffs hit the auto industry in the early 1980s, some workers received for a time almost 95 percent of their normal wages, paid from a combination of government benefits and employer contributions.

The Grievance Process

A **grievance** is an employee complaint about wages, hours, working conditions, or disciplinary action for which the collective bargaining agreement provides a procedure to resolve it. The procedure both assures the just resolution of employee complaints and identifies recurrent problems in a work place. It is the primary means for seeing that management lives up to the collective bargaining agreement.

The Stages in a Grievance Proceeding

Discussions Between Management and Union   Normally, an employee starts the grievance process by taking a complaint to the **shop steward**, a union member elected to represent the other members employed in a particular work unit in their day-to-day dealings with the employer. An employee might complain to the shop steward if, for example, he or she thought the foreman had filed inaccurate performance reports or if he or she had been fired

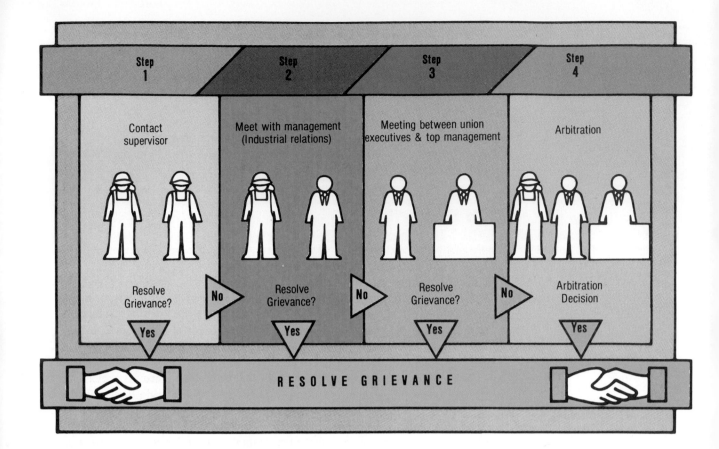

Step 1 — Contact supervisor — Resolve Grievance? — Yes / No

Step 2 — Meet with management (Industrial relations) — Resolve Grievance? — Yes / No

Step 3 — Meeting between union executives & top management — Resolve Grievance? — Yes / No

Step 4 — Arbitration — Arbitration Decision — Yes

RESOLVE GRIEVANCE

FIGURE 9-4

A Typical Grievance Procedure

The procedure to resolve an employee complaint about wages, hours, working conditions, or disciplinary action is called a grievance procedure.

for fighting in the lunchroom. The shop steward would then take the matter up with the employee's supervisor.

If the supervisor decided not to reconsider the action or reduce the punishment, the grievance might go to the union's **chief steward**, an elected union official for the employee's department or plant who represents the members in grievances and oversees the execution of the collective bargaining agreement. The chief steward meets with the employer's department head.

A grievance that goes beyond the chief steward becomes the subject of negotiations between the company's human resources director and the union's **grievance committee**, a union committee that meets with management to resolve matters relating to the contract that the stewards are unable to resolve. It may include officers of the local union, the union's **business representative** or **business agent** (a person employed by a union to represent it in matters with management), and the chief steward.

Arbitration   The final stage in most grievance procedures is **arbitration**, the submission of a dispute to a neutral third party, an **arbitrator**, who makes a decision binding on the parties who submitted the matter. There are two principal sources for arbitrators: the American Arbitration Association, a private group; and the Federal Mediation and Conciliation Service, an agency created by the Taft-Hartley Act that maintains a list of arbitrators. Arbitration works rather like a court trial, but it is less formal. The arbitrator's decision is usually final.

Organizing the service sector. Unions made their biggest gains in the skilled trades and basic industries, but they have been less successful in the service sector of the economy. If unions are to halt their decline, they will have to convince service workers of the benefits of union membership.

Givebacks

Someone once asked Samuel Gompers what labor wanted. His reply could not have been clearer: "More, more, and more!"[10] After World War II, unionized workers grew used to wage increases, benefit expansions, and more-advantageous working conditions in every new contract. In recent years, though, several trades and industries have slumped in the face of foreign competition and advancing technology, and others have virtually disappeared. In 1917, for example, 180,000 coal miners worked in anthracite pits. In 1985, they numbered only 3,000.[11]

Givebacks and Their Effect on Current Bargaining

Today, almost every collective bargaining agenda lists **givebacks**, a union's foregoing of wages or benefits or working conditions won in earlier collective bargaining. Up to 40 percent of the contracts negotiated in recent years have contained givebacks. Many of them have been negotiated in an atmosphere of joint management and labor concern for the future of their industries and jobs. Some, like those that Greyhound won from its bus drivers, as discussed in Chapter 5, came after long strikes.

Workers in steel, coal, meatpacking, airlines, and nonferrous metals, to list just a sampling of industries, have agreed to wage and benefit cuts. Perhaps more importantly, unions have agreed to changes in work rules. Such givebacks enabled Firestone Tire & Rubber to boost productivity 10 percent and Jones & Laughlin Steel to reduce the man-hours required to produce a ton of steel from six to three and a half.[12] When the United Auto Workers became convinced that sacrifices by its members might ultimately save their jobs, it agreed to contracts with the Big Three American automakers (GM, Ford, and Chrysler) in which

☐ Wages were frozen.
☐ Nine paid holidays were given up.
☐ Wage increases created by COLAs were deferred for eighteen months.
☐ Management obtained new power to discipline workers for excessive absenteeism.
☐ Management gained greater discretion in organizing production.

Givebacks often have a significant price to the employer. General Motors, for instance, agreed not to close several plants it had planned to, created a profit-sharing plan for union workers, guaranteed income to any employee with ten years' seniority who was laid off, and promised to lay off supervisors in proportion to unionized workers. Chrysler had to agree to put the president of the United Auto Workers on its board of directors.

THE COLLECTIVE BARGAINING PROCESS

In the last section, we examined some topics that a collective bargaining agreement usually addresses. Now let's go back a step and look at how the parties actually reach an agreement.

The Taft-Hartley Act requires that labor and management "meet at reasonable times and confer in good faith with respect to wages, hours and other conditions of employment." This description is a good definition of the collective bargaining process itself.

Preparations for Bargaining

The First Phase of Collective Bargaining

Before negotiations start, both sides spend substantial energy preparing.

Union officials begin their preparation by determining what the members want and then drawing up a set of demands. Next they assemble information to support these demands, like data on wage rates at the company's competitors. Issues relating to working conditions, like production quotas, also require documentation. At the same time that union officials are preparing their demands, they publicize and explain what they are doing. Not only must the union's negotiating team reach an agreement with management, it must also convince its own members of the rightness of its strategy and of the justice of the final contract package.

Management generally prefers to respond to proposals from labor rather than to offer proposals itself, to avoid tipping its hand. Management tries to anticipate the union's demands and to have ready an appropriate response to every union demand.

Management's principal concern is cost. It will therefore develop detailed statistical summaries and formulas to take into the negotiating sessions that will permit its negotiating team to estimate costs quickly. These summaries typically categorize employees by age, sex, seniority, and job classification. If the union asks for changes in, say, paid vacation time or health insurance coverage, management can plug these demands into formulas and quickly calculate their costs.

Negotiating Teams

The Second Bargaining Phase: Selecting Negotiators

Each side in the collective bargaining process is represented by a negotiating team. On the union side, the relationship between the local and its national union determines who is on its negotiating team and what it negotiates. This relationship can take one of four forms.

A Futuristic Union Pact?

General Motors' Saturn car, expected in 1990, generated publicity long before construction began for its manufacturing complex. Many hope that the Saturn will be America's answer to the flood of imported cars that has caused headaches in Detroit and deficits in Washington for years. The Saturn factory is revolutionary, dominated by electronics and robots, GM's response to the renowned Japanese auto production facilities. But the car may have its greatest effects on the union and the workers that are putting it together, for the union pact on which the Saturn project is founded is like no other before it.

As GM envisions it, this is how the Saturn system will work: A buyer will select features, options, and colors on a computer in the dealer's showroom, while the dealer, on another computer, arranges for financing from a GM affiliate. On the assembly line, the Saturn frame destined for the buyer will send off radio messages to other computers and robots, asking for particular tires, engine parts, and body paint. When the Saturn rolls off the line, it will send a message to the dealer to alert the customer. Because each car will be built as it is ordered, GM will have almost no inventory of parts or cars, so they won't wind up with warehouses filled with cigarette lighters or purple car bodies.

GM expects this new production method to save about $2000 per car over current methods, and to employ only one-quarter as many people, a fact that makes the United Auto Workers nervous.

When the labor agreement was announced in 1985, GM heralded it as "a milestone and leap forward." For the first time the United Auto Workers at a GM plant were to become "full partners" in decisions made about the Saturn. Management and labor agreed to make decisions by consensus, and both parties have the ability to block a potential decision.

The gap between labor and management has been narrowed under the agreement in other ways as well. No longer will executives park in reserved spaces or eat in their own cafeteria. Workers will earn salaries, not hourly wages, and won't have to punch time clocks. Individuals will not be as restricted to specific tasks as they are in most auto plants. Instead, teams will work on particular projects and interact with other teams. The company promised to fill at least 80 percent of the 6000 jobs at the Saturn plant with workers now at GM or laid off from GM plants. And the company agreed to guarantee these workers job security.

Some union activists saw the agreement as giving up much that unions had gained during years of bargaining with the auto makers. They worried that the agreement would weaken the union itself. The workers hired from outside the current GM work force will not have job security, creating what some call a "lower class" within the union. Shop stewards will lose much of their power under a new grievance procedure.

Speaking about the agreement, UAW president Owen Bieber sounded alternately proud and apologetic. While praising the cooperation and relative equality between the company and the union, he also seemed to admit that the union *had* to reach an agreement. Union leaders know that the difference between American and foreign auto workers' pay accounts for a significant part of the greater expense of American cars. And the Union can see that if the technology at the Saturn factory really represents the future of American auto making, any job in an auto plant will be harder and harder to get, no matter what the pay.

Bieber was eager to point out that the contract affected only Saturn workers, but the Big Three are all interested in using some of its provisions in future contracts. Union activists may be right that the Saturn technology and the contract that goes with it represent a major defeat for traditional unions in their battle with management. A more optimistic view, however, sees the Saturn agreement as the first of a new breed of industrial agreements that will recognize the mutual goals of labor and management and involve both in setting the policies to reach those goals.

Sources: Sharon Cohen, "'Milestone' Accord for GM, Union," *The Boston Globe*, July 27, 1985, 1. Micheline Maynard, "A Labor Deal that Clears Way for GM's Saturn," *U.S. News & World Report*, Vol. 99, No. 6, August 5, 1985, 22. Tom Nicholson, "Saturn Gets a Launching Pad," *Newsweek*, August 5, 1985, 42.

1. **National negotiation**. The national union negotiates wages and benefits on an industry- or company-wide basis and the local unions negotiate working conditions. The United Auto Workers uses this type of negotiation system.
2. **Pattern bargaining**. The local unions in a single company or industry negotiate on their own under the supervision of the national union.
3. **Council bargaining**. Several locals join to negotiate together.
4. **Independent bargaining**. The local negotiates for itself, without any help from the national or any other local unions.

Regardless of which structure applies, the local union selects its own negotiating team, usually at a meeting of the local's membership. The team is often made up of a combination of the local's officers and regular members.

On the management side, its team consists usually of the human resources director or labor relations director and the plant managers and superintendents whose departments are involved in the negotiations.

The Bargaining

The Actual Bargaining Process

Since the 1930s, collective bargaining negotiations have followed a well-defined pattern. Some significant variations in the pattern have appeared since the late 1970s, however.

As noted earlier, management traditionally has preferred to respond to union demands rather than to propose its own initiatives. Recently, though, companies in such fiercely competitive industries as airlines, copper, and rubber have begun to make demands themselves. And unions have had to give back benefits won in past collective bargaining, to keep their companies afloat.

The early bargaining sessions often proceed slowly, sometimes bogging down in disputes over procedural issues. The serious bargaining begins with the noneconomic issues, like management rights or the form that union recognition is to take. The parties usually agree, however, that nothing is to be considered settled until both parties have agreed on the whole contract. Each side agrees to accept some of the other's points and drop some of its own demands.

When they have resolved all the noneconomic issues, the negotiating teams turn to wages and benefits. Now bargaining becomes intense. The two sides make concessions, labor perhaps trimming its wage demands in exchange for concessions on benefits. The negotiators exchange proposals and counterproposals until each knows how far the other will go.

At that point, if the sides are not too far apart they often split the differences and agree on a contract. If the gap is too large, the union may strike. However, under normal circumstances both sides have options for bridging an impasse, which they will examine carefully before giving up on the negotiating process.

Selling the Contract The collective bargaining process does not end when the teams reach agreement. The contract must have the strong support of both negotiating teams, because both teams' constituents must ratify it.

Management's team must convince senior management that it should sign the contract. Normally, this amounts to a formality. And though it rarely happens, the union's membership can vote to reject the contract. The union must therefore

FIGURE 9-5

**The Collective Bargaining
Agreement's Functions**

All collective bargaining
agreements deal with the
question of working conditions.

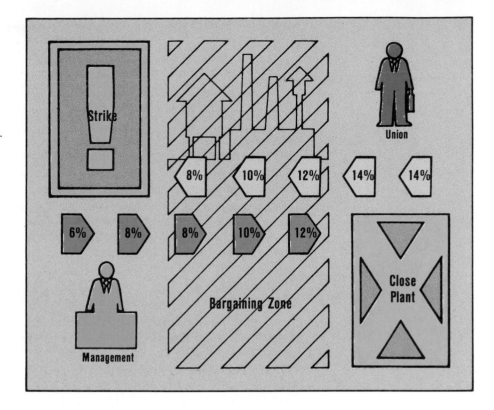

conduct an intensive education campaign to sell the contract to its members. If a majority of the members voting agree to support the contract, the collective bargaining process is at an end, until it is time to negotiate a new contract.

Mediation, Arbitration, and Factfinding

**The Final Phase in Collective
Bargaining: The Resolution of
Differences**

When the negotiating teams cannot resolve their differences they sometimes resort to **mediation**, the process in which an impartial third party, a **mediator**, helps the parties settle their unresolved issues. The mediator suggests nonbinding alternatives for their consideration. The Federal Mediation and Conciliation Service will supply mediators, as will some states. In some cases, the parties draw up lists of acceptable mediators themselves. Regardless of how a mediator becomes involved, the goal is the same: to avoid work stoppages.

Mediation should not be confused with arbitration. An arbitrator makes decisions that bind the parties. Some state laws require binding arbitration when a public-sector employer like a city, county, or state-government unit cannot reach agreement with certain types of workers. These laws most often affect teachers, police, and fire fighters. Binding-arbitration laws are often highly controversial, because arbitrators have tended over the years to make decisions without regard for their overall impact on an employer's budget.

Another device commonly used in public-sector (but not private-sector) bargaining is **factfinding**, the process by which an outside factfinder narrows the isues that are before the negotiating parties.

When the Parties Cannot Agree

Collective Bargaining: Ultimate Weapons

Unions and management both have weapons to force the other side to meet its terms. If they did not, collective bargaining could not take place.

For their part, unions can threaten either strikes or picketing. And management has the options of lockouts, injunctions, or bringing in strikebreakers.

Strikes When a union, in an effort to put economic pressure on management, calls on its members not to work, a **strike** occurs. Strikes are usually characterized by **picketing**, the patroling of the entrances to an employer's facilities by members of a labor union often carrying signs to inform other employees and the public that a strike is in progress and to persuade them not to enter.

The law imposes significant restraints on how unions are allowed to conduct strikes. For instance, unions may not throw up mass picket lines, nor may pickets block entrances to an employer's facility. Employers can get injunctions in state courts limiting both the number and the placement of pickets.

Lockouts One of the techniques management has to put economic pressure on a union is to close its doors to the unionized workers, a procedure known as a **lockout**. As a weapon, the lockout is a two-edged sword. The workers lose wages, but management also loses production — and therefore profits. Lockouts were more common earlier, when an industry or groups of companies typically negotiated contracts with unions together. Until the 1970s, for instance, all the New York City newspapers bargained together so that a strike against one closed them all. Lockouts are now rare.

Legal Restraints A party that wants to modify or end a contract must give the other at least sixty days' notice before the effective date of the proposed modification or termination. If a strike or lockout takes place before the end of that period, the party taking the action commits an unfair labor practice. Before a strike or a lockout can occur, the side taking the action must give the other notice.

A union has unique legal restraints on it during a strike or lockout. It cannot stage a **secondary boycott**, a refusal to work for, purchase from, or handle the products of another company with which the union has no dispute in order to force that company to stop doing business with the company with which the union does have a dispute. Suppose that the printers strike a certain newspaper. The union may not organize a boycott of the paper's newsprint supplier, for example, in order to pressure the paper to settle. In contrast, a union is allowed to organize a **primary boycott**, an action by a union to try to persuade others not to deal with an employer against whom it has a grievance. Boycotts organized by the United Farm Workers against produce grown on nonunion farms had some successes in the 1970s and 1980s.

Strikebreakers Persons hired to replace striking employees, either in an effort to force the union to come to terms or to destroy its effectiveness by minimizing the strike's effect on the employer's operations, are referred to as **strikebreakers** or **scabs**. In 1981, the Professional Air Traffic Controllers Organization (PATCO) went on strike, severely disrupting air travel. The government

Labor strikes — a last resort. *While the government protects workers' right to strike, it places many restrictions on how strikes may be carried out. In the bitter strike at Hormel, the National Guard had to be called in to protect both the strikers and those who chose to cross the picket lines.*

immediately moved to replace the strikers with new employees and never settled with the union. The major reason against hiring strikebreakers is that it forever poisons relations between union and management. Strikebreakers are thus an ultimate weapon.

The PATCO strike involved special circumstances. The government exercised its rights as an employer confronted by an **economic strike**, a strike called because of failure to reach agreement on wages and benefits. In such a case, the employer can hire strikebreakers and need not rehire the strikers even if the strike ends. However, if a strike is over something other than economic issues, the employer commits an unfair labor practice by bringing in strikebreakers.

LABOR—MANAGEMENT RELATIONS: A PERSPECTIVE

The labor movement had fallen on hard days by the 1980s. Unions like the United Auto Workers, used to organizing successes, found themselves rejected by workers in new plants like Honda's Marysville, Ohio, facility. Other unions, like the flight attendants', found themselves in the position of having to admit defeat after long strikes when their employers kept operations going with strikebreakers. Still other unions found themselves forced to accept givebacks and layoffs.

Some commentators have predicted a continued decline for labor unions, based on current trends. Whether that in fact happens will depend not only on the unions themselves but in large part on how management treats its workers. Unions have traditionally based their appeal on an "us versus them" perception, saying workers were overworked, undercompensated, and generally unappreciated. Should management allow such perceptions to flourish, unions will no doubt appear. Much depends on management's learning and implementing the lessons that the automakers have learned the hard way. Cooperation is a two-way street, and if any trend appears certain, it is for the continued need of management and labor to work together.

Chapter Highlights

1. Describe the role of Samuel Gompers in the development of the American labor movement.

In 1881, Samuel Gompers founded the American Federation of Labor, an umbrella organization for craft unions. Over the next four decades he built the AFL into the nation's most important labor organization and established the philosophy of business unionism. This philosophy holds that American unions exist primarily for the economic improvement of workers, not to engage in a class struggle to alter the American form of government or to promote socialism.

2. Identify the antitrust acts that affected the labor movement's effort to organize American industry.

Three antitrust acts significantly affected labor's effort to organize American industry. They were the Sherman Antitrust Act, the Clayton Act, and the Norris-LaGuardia Act of 1932.

3. List the key features of the National Labor Relations Act, the Taft-Hartley Act, and the Landrum-Griffin Act.

The National Labor Relations Act, also known as the Wagner Act, made labor–management relations a federal matter and established the National Labor Relations Board to regulate them. The act made it unlawful for an employer to interfere with its employees' rights to form, join, and participate in a union or to try to subvert the union itself. The Taft-Hartley Act abolished the closed shop and authorized states to enact right-to-work laws, which outlaw union shops. The Landrum-Griffin Act guarantees union members the right to vote in union elections, speak at union meetings, receive union financial reports, and be treated like other members.

4. List the steps in the organizing process and summarize each.

The organizing process begins with the organizing drive, the union's first attempt to gain worker support. If enough workers have signed authorization cards and if management refuses to recognize the union, then the union files a petition with the NLRB to hold a representation election. If the union and the employer agree on the date, time, and place of the election, the form of the ballot, and the definition of the bargaining unit, a consent election is held. If they do not agree, the NLRB decides whether the workers seeking an election make up an appropriate bargaining unit and whether 30 percent of the workers want an election. Each side presents its case to the workers before a representation election is held.

5. Identify the subjects which may and may not be discussed in collective bargaining.

Unions and management may negotiate on any subject a federal or state law does not forbid them to. They must negotiate about wages, benefits, hours, and working conditions.

6. Describe the stages of a grievance proceeding.

A grievance is an employee complaint about wages, hours, working conditions, or disciplinary action for which the collective bargaining agreement provides a procedure for resolution. An employee starts the grievance process by taking a complaint to the shop steward. If the shop steward and the employee's supervisor cannot resolve the matter, it goes to the chief steward. It can then go to the company's human resources director and the union's grievance committee. The final stage in most grievance procedures is arbitration. The arbitrator's decision is usually final.

7. Define givebacks and discuss the effects of this concept of bargaining in the 1980s.

Givebacks are a union's foregoing of wages or benefits or working conditions won in earlier collective bargaining agreements. As America's basic industries slumped or disappeared, unions were willing to give up benefits they had won in previous negotiations in order to prevent their employer from going bankrupt or closing down facilities. It is likely that unions will continue to show flexibility on work rules and other changes as long as it seems their jobs might otherwise disappear.

8. Analyze the phases of collective bargaining.

Collective bargaining has three primary phases: preparations, negotiations, and selling the contract. If agreement cannot be reached, the process moves on to mediation, arbitration, or factfinding. During the first phase, unions assemble information and draw up their demands. Management tries to anticipate the union's demands and ready its response. During negotiations each side hammers out areas of agreement. Each side agrees to accept some of the other side's points and to drop some of its own demands. Once the teams have agreed, the union must convince its members to vote to support the contract. When the sides cannot agree, they can seek help from impartial outsiders — either mediators, arbitrators, or fact finders.

9. Identify the weapons each side in collective bargaining has to force an agreement.

Management and unions each have weapons they can use to force an agreement. Unions rely on strikes and picketing. These tactics not only do economic damage to the employer, they also publicize the union's position. Management can turn to lockouts and to strikebreakers.

Key Terms

Agency shop	Consent election	Lockout	Primary boycott
American Federation of Labor (AFL)	Consumer Price Index	Maintenance shop	Representation election
Arbitration	Cost of living adjustments (COLAs)	Mediation	Right to employment
Arbitrator		Mediator	Right-to-work laws
Authorization cards	Council bargaining	National Labor Relations Act (NLRA) (the Wagner Act)	Secondary boycott
Bargaining unit	Economic strike		Sherman Antitrust Act
Base wage rate	Fair Labor Standards Act		Shift differential
Business representative (business agent)	Givebacks	National Labor Relations Board (NLRB)	Shop
	Grievance		Strike
	Grievance committee		Strikebreakers (scabs)
Business unionism	Incentive rate formulas	National negotiation	Taft-Hartley Labor Act
Chief steward	Independent bargaining	Open shop	Trade or craft union
Closed shop	Injunction	Organized labor	Unemployment compensation
Collective bargaining	Knights of Labor	Organizing drive	
Congress of Industrial Organizations (CIO)	Landrum-Griffin Act	Pattern bargaining	Unfair labor practices
		Piece-work rates	Union shop
			Unions

Review Questions

1. Briefly describe the labor movement from 1865 to 1914. What were some of the most significant events?
2. What influence did the National Labor Relations Act (the Wagner Act) have on the American labor movement? What affect did the Taft-Hartley Act have on the labor movement?
3. What are some of the major factors that motivate workers to join and support unions?
4. When a labor union decides to initiate an organization drive, what steps does it follow?
5. What are some of the most common subjects of collective bargaining? What are the mandatory subjects? Voluntary subjects?
6. From the employees' standpoint, what are the advantages of a seniority system? Disadvantages?
7. Describe the major steps in the collective bargaining process.
8. What are the major contributions of the mediator?
9. Discuss the bargaining issues that have surfaced in the past decade. Why are strikes and lockouts less common today?
10. In what ways does mediation differ from arbitration?

Application Exercises

1. Contact a person who is a member of a union representing service workers. Conduct an interview and obtain answers to the following questions:
   a. What are the major subjects of collective bargaining between labor and management?
   b. What issues are most difficult for negotiators to agree on?
2. Review selected issues of *Fortune, Business Week,* and *Nations Business* published during the past six weeks. Identify the contemporary issues and problems facing organized labor.

Cases

9.1 Work-Investment

Lynn Williams, president of the United Steelworkers of America, won his 1985 campaign for the union's presidency because of his abilities as a politician, negotiator, and strategist.

He brought a new twist to the latest contract talks with steelmaking companies. Two large steel firms had already gone bankrupt; other firms in the ailing steel industry were near the brink. The steelmakers were sure to ask for wage and benefits concessions.

Williams was willing to negotiate givebacks to save jobs, but he wanted the givebacks to be treated as investments that union steelworkers would make in the firms that employed them. He felt that union employees should ben-efit if a steel producer became profitable after a giveback; moreover, they should have an investor's say in company matters. Williams was concerned that firms which survived because of givebacks would not then farm out work to nonunion contractors.

Potential investors need sound investment advice, so Williams retained an investment banking firm, Lazard Freres. Any steel company that expected to discuss a giveback had to open its books to Lazard and to union accountants. They verified that the firm was in trouble, advised the union on how it could help, and provided advice regarding the "return" that steelworkers should expect for their investment.

Williams negotiated "investments" with firm after firm. At LTV Steel, the union gave up $3.15 an hour in wages and benefits; at Bethlehem Steel the figure was $1.97. The return on their investment was a profit-sharing plan that will pay back every penny of the giveback — either in cash or in stock. In addition, the new contracts limit the amount of work that can be subcontracted.

Questions

1. What did each side give up and/or gain in Williams' "investment" contracts?
2. Do the contract terms seem fair to the union, to management, and to the steel company stockholders?

For more information see *Fortune*, August 4, 1986, pp. 154–157; *Business Week*, April 18, 1986, pp. 221–222; and *The Wall Street Journal*, January 16, 1986, p. E12.

9.2 Complexity at Simplex

In 1983, in *Belknap* v. *Hale*, the U.S. Supreme Court heard a case involving a unionized employer, striking union workers, and nonunion employees who had been hired as permanent replacements for the strikers. Both sides in the strike eventually filed charges of unfair labor practices with the NLRB. However, those charges were dropped and the striking union members returned to work as part of a settlement negotiated by the NLRB's regional director. The replacement workers were discharged to make room for the returning strikers; they sued Belknap Inc. for breach of contract and misrepresentation. The NLRB maintained that federal labor laws required the workers to be reinstated, and that federal law takes precedence over state law; thus, the laid-off workers could not sue.

Three years after the *Belknap* decision, union workers at Simplex Wire and Cable Co. in New Hampshire began to picket their employer. The union claimed that its workers had been locked out of Simplex after their contract had expired; union workers maintained that they had been willing to continue at their jobs until a new contract was signed. The state of New Hampshire agreed that the union had been locked out, and began to pay unemployment benefits to the strikers.

Simplex officials maintained that they had not locked out their union employees and were considering an appeal of the state's decision. Meanwhile, Simplex began to advertise for, and hire, replacements for the strikers. The NLRB agreed with Simplex, ruling that there had been no illegal lockout. The union appealed that ruling but consented to a meeting with Simplex officials and a federal mediator. That meeting has not yet taken place.

Questions

1. Suppose the meeting is successful, Simplex and the union agree on a new contract, and the NLRB does not change its ruling regarding the lockout. What group of workers will lose its jobs? Why? Can that group sue for breach of contract and misrepresentation?
2. Answer Question 1 again, this time assuming the NLRB changes its lockout ruling as a result of the appeal. What effect would the New Hampshire ruling have on the suit?

For more information see *Foster's Daily Democrat*, October 28, 1986, pp. 1, 11: *Foster's Daily Democrat*, September 20, 1986, pp. 1, 17; and *Journal of Commerce*, July 1, 1983, p. 5A.

10

OPERATIONS MANAGEMENT

Learning Objectives

After you have completed this chapter, you will be able to do the following:

- Define *operations management* and describe the elements that go into it.
- Classify the types of production processes.
- Describe the steps that go into planning an operation.
- List the steps in the PERT process for scheduling production control.
- Identify the criteria that go into a facilities location decision.
- Describe the principal considerations In designing the layout of production facilities.
- Describe the relationship between computers and robots.
- Identify the key elements involved in implementing an operational plan.

Not long ago, Gulf States Utilities of Beaumont, Texas, faced an unpleasant problem. This public utility produces electricity in natural gas–fired generating stations. Gulf States has been squeezed by the costs of a new nuclear plant, a faltering economy and angry customers who have beaten back its bids for higher electrical rates. A highly favorable contract with their natural gas supplier was about to expire, and Gulf States knew it would now have to buy gas at a significantly higher price. This rate increase would have to be passed on to the consumers. Gulf States wanted to avoid "rate shock" among its customers, but it could not decide on an appropriate strategy.

Gulf States hired a consultant to help them solve their problem. They assembled a group of local residents to find out what they knew about electricity. The residents were asked to outline a sixth-grade level booklet on how electricity reaches their homes. The results were quite surprising. Gulf States realized that most people did not understand how natural gas was generated or that the utility did not own the gas. Gulf States used the results of the research to develop an ad campaign that took consumers through the process of the purchase of gas to the generation of electricity.

Gulf States' ads explained what the consumers were paying the utility for. Through this educational campaign they came to understand that they were paying Gulf States to transform natural gas into electricity, then to deliver the electricity to their homes and businesses. The consumers realized that they were paying for goods — the electricity — and Gulf States' services — the transmission of electricity.

Every business provides a product or a service or both. Customers, like the Gulf States' consumers, pay for the value added by transforming raw materials into finished products or the convenience of the service provided, among other things. Many people believe that the key to improved national competitiveness in world markets lies in **operations**, all activities associated with the production of goods and services. Even the nation's leading business schools, which long focused on strategic planning, have now begun to recognize the importance of what happens where the goods and services are produced.[1] This chapter describes how businesses manage the production of what they sell.

PRODUCTS AND OPERATIONS MANAGEMENT

From Chapter 5 you may recall that management is the process of coordinating human, informational, physical, and financial resources to accomplish an organization's goal. The goal this chapter discusses is that of **production**, the process of transforming resources into the goods or services that an organization sells. A **product** is thus a good, a service, or a combination of goods and services that an organization sells. People normally associate the term *product* with a tangible good like a typewriter, but the sense of this word also includes the concept of an intangible service like a checking account, or a combination of the two, like a restaurant meal, which is both prepared and served.

One way that production occurs is through **manufacturing**, the management of the resources necessary to convert raw materials into finished goods. A furniture maker, for example, might buy cherry wood, a raw material. The company's workers would then apply tools and their skills to the raw material in order to turn it into, say, rocking chairs. It is this process of transforming wood into rockers that is manufacturing.

However, manufacturing is only a part of the larger concept we have called operations. When you see a doctor in a clinic during a checkup, this examination is a service. The bill the clinic sends you is associated with the production of its service. Billing is a part of the clinic's operation. The process of coordinating the production of goods and services with all the activities associated with production is called **operations management**.

Operations Management Defined and Described

THE TRANSFORMATION PROCESS

The key concept in production is **transformation,** the conversion of input (resources) into output (goods or services). For example, AT&T takes plastic and electromechanical parts and transforms them through design, manufacturing, and assembly into telephones. Other common synonyms for transformation are *conversion* or *creation.*[2] Figure 10.1 is an example of a transformation system.

FIGURE 10.1

A Transformation System

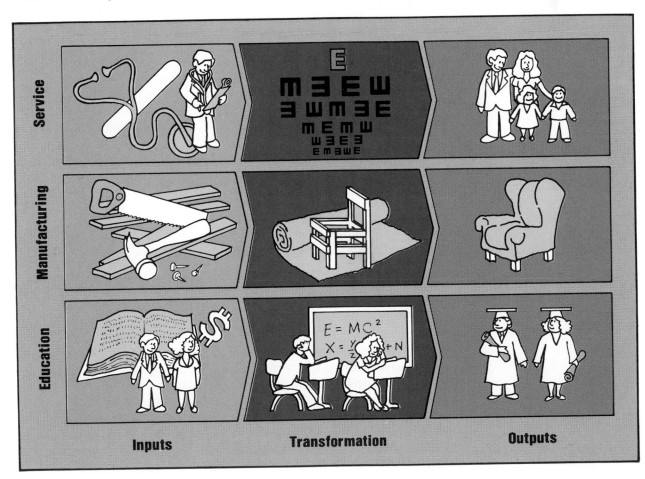

The transformation process. How does Moore's transform raw onions into gourmet onion rings enjoyed by restaurant customers throughout the U.S.? Up-to-date production and food storage facilities are one factor in the firm's high productivity. Another is the care given by people like Lori Jilek, a packer for Moore's. Quality and efficiency are two primary concerns of operations management.

All these terms — *transformation, conversion,* and *creation* — imply physical changes, but today they also include the changing of resources into services. For instance, an educational institution takes its primary input — enrolled students, faculty, and facilities — and produces graduates.

Division of Labor and Specialization

We saw in Chapter 6 that modern organizations are based on the related concepts of division of labor and specialization. It is hard to conceive of a productive system today that would not rely on these concepts. From fast-food restaurants to automobile assembly lines, tasks are divided and workers specialized.

A Classification of Production Processes

Production processes are classified according to the variety and quantity of goods produced under them. In general, the greater the quantity and the less the variety of goods produced, the more structured the process is.[3]

The Types of Production Processes

Production to Order and Production to Stock   All production organizations are either production-to-order systems or production-to-stock systems. A **production-to-order system** produces only what customers or clients demand, as the order comes in. Catering services or custom upholstery shops would be examples of production-to-order systems. A **production-to-stock system** produces goods to be held in inventory. The automobile industry is a classic example of production to stock. One of the most closely watched barometers of economic health is the national inventory of new cars.

Continuous-Flow System   The production-to-stock process that produces large quantities of a single standardized product is called the **continuous-flow system** or **continuous-process system**. Industries using continuous-flow systems are capital intensive and are often highly automated.

Mass Production or Assembly-Line Production   The production-to-stock process that produces large quantities of a small number of products is **mass production** or **assembly-line production**. The auto industry was the one that brought these terms into our everyday vocabulary. Originally, the variation in products was tiny. Today, in contrast, some claim that part of Detroit's disadvantage in competing with Japan lies in the hundreds of different equipment configurations that can be provided on an American car.

Batch Processing or Intermittent Processing   The system of production called *batch processing* or *intermittent processing* is a production-to-stock system that generates lower quantities of goods than a mass-production system. However, this system is likely to use processes similar or identical to those in mass-production systems. A restaurant uses this method when the cook prepares salads, then biscuits, and then soup.

Further Production Processes

Job-Shop Processing or Job-Order Processing   The production-to-order process in which the producer makes a quantity of goods to the customer's satisfaction is the *job-shop processing* or *job-order processing* system. Such shops produce a far greater variety of types of goods than the three production systems we have just discussed, but the quantities they produce are quite small by comparison. Individually tailored clothes and custom-built houses are produced this way.

Project Processing   The production-to-order system in which the manufacturer produces a one-of-a-kind item is *project processing*. Production of such relatively unique products as telecommunications satellites or nuclear power plants is usually on a project basis.

PLANNING AN OPERATION

A firm's vision of itself and of its future dictates the kind of operation it should develop. Operations planning begins with strategic planning. Once a firm's senior management has adopted a strategy, its middle management can develop the tactics to carry it out while its line management will develop operational plans to execute the tactics.

The Strategic Decision

The Steps in Planning an Operation

In the last decade, no strategic decision has been more analyzed than IBM's to enter the highly competitive personal computer (PC) market. Although this statement may seem odd, in the late 1970s the PC field belonged to Apple and Commodore. The other personal computer makers were nonetheless acutely aware that this highly active market sector was virtually the only one in which IBM did not have an entry.

Until its PC model, IBM took great pride in developing and manufacturing its own unique machines. All IBM product development was structured to occur in a centralized, integrated environment under the direct supervision of top management. IBM did many things differently in producing its personal computer, not the least of which was to set up what amounted to an independent subsidiary to develop the PC.

INTERNATIONAL BUSINESS

Just in Time for Harley-Davidson

Back when James Dean was alive, Marlon Brando was young, and Elvis Presley looked good in black leather, a "Harley" was about the only motorcycle to own. Owners of Harley-Davidson "Hogs" proudly displayed their company's name on shirts and belt buckles long before such personal advertisement became popular. But then came "Little Hondas" riding on the Beach Boys' hit song of the sixties. Harley-Davidson watched in horror as Honda was joined by Kawasaki and Suzuki in the little motorbike market, then as all three began building bigger and bigger bikes until they challenged Harley in the heavyweight category (over 900 cc). Harley's market share slipped to 30 percent in 1980, customer complaints about quality kept rising, AMF got ready to sell the company, and many people thought the Hog was dead. Then a new group of owners brought some lessons back from across the Pacific and made the company competitive again.

The secret to Japanese manufacturing superiority is the just-in-time (JIT) system. Harley-Davidson calls its version "materials as needed"; IBM boasts "continuous flow manufacturing"; and Motorola now follows the "inventory productivity process." They're all based on the same principles.

The just-in-time approach, as the name implies, involves getting the right materials to the right places just when they are needed. Such an approach virtually eliminates inventory and the capital that a company has locked up in that inventory sitting in warehouses. To reach just-in-time goals requires major adjustments for most American firms.

One of the first changes that Harley-Davidson made in 1980 was to stabilize its production schedule so that it made the same mixture of products each day. The company finds it can get just what it needs from suppliers at just the right time if it asks for the same supplies every day. The stabilized production mix also helped the company cut set-up times, which are down by almost 75 percent in 4 years.

The just-in-time approach has a ripple effect throughout an industry. Harley's suppliers must prove their quality and efficiency, and they in turn ask for the same from their suppliers. One change imported from Japan to help the suppliers is that JIT manufacturers tend to saddle their suppliers with fewer specifications, giving them more ability to produce their own design within a given set of guidelines.

Using JIT at one of its plants, Hewlett Packard was able to cut inventories by 75 percent, improve quality by 60 percent, and cut manufacturing time in half for one of its major products. Xerox, taking a lesson from its Japanese partner, Fuji-Xerox, reduced the reject rate at one of its copier-making plants from 5000 parts-per-million to 1300 ppm in only a year. And at Harley-Davidson, a motorcycle frame that used to take 72 days now gets made in 2. At that rate, the Hog may some day be able to reverse the motorcycle invasion.

Sources: Ernest Raia, "Just-in-time USA," *Purchasing*, February 13, 1986, 48. "The Hog Is Back," *Purchasing*, February 13, 1986, 58. "No Inspection, Please!" *Purchasing*, February 13, 1986, 56. Joshua Hyatt, "The Japanese Must Be Laughing Now," *Inc.*, January 1986, 18. Richard C. Walleigh, "What's Your Excuse for Not Using JIT?" *Harvard Business Review*, March-April 1986, 38.

The Make-or-Buy Decision

Once a firm decides to develop a certain new product, it must decide whether it is to be a manufacturer or a packager of that product. In other words, should it make the product or just buy it from other companies and merely put its own label on the package?

Such a decision has an impact not just on the one company but on the entire nation. Over the last twenty years, increasing numbers of American corporations have abandoned manufacturing operations in favor either of buying products from other vendors — usually foreign ones — or manufacturing goods abroad themselves. "Own markets, not manufacturing"[4] is their motto. Videocassette recorders bearing American brand names like RCA are made only in Japan and Korea. And half of Motorola's manufacturing jobs will have moved overseas within the next five years.[5] This flight from domestic manufacturing led *Business Week* to call American firms that "import components or products from low-wage countries, slap their own names on them, and sell them in America" **hollow corporations**.[6] IBM's PC went a similar route. About 73 percent of its parts, including the keyboard, video monitor, and disk drives, for instance, were manufactured abroad, but the "brains," like the microprocessors made by the Intel Corporation, were American, as was the final assembly.

The Nature of the Business

The make-or-buy decision relates to the fundamental question what is the nature of a given business? Many writers have hailed IBM's development of the PC as exhibiting marketing genius, and so it did. IBM must have carefully weighed the cost of making the PC against the cost of buying its components. However, it seems likely that IBM's principal tactical consideration was ultimately its understanding of its basic business: selling and servicing, as opposed to manufacturing, business equipment. Its choice has proven a brilliant one. Here is an example of what the authors of *In Search of Excellence* would call "sticking to your knitting."

High-Tech versus Low-Tech Decisions

In some business sectors, companies may have a choice between high-tech and low-tech manufacturing methods. For example, a company manufacturing pianos can choose between applying modern production techniques to the pianos' parts and final assembly or constructing its pianos the way they were made a century ago. Steinway has chosen the older method, which is why it takes thirteen months to produce a Steinway piano. Similarly, Cordwainers, in Deerfield, New Hampshire, makes its shoes by hand to fit the pattern of each customer's feet. These customers are willing to wait six weeks or more for delivery and pay at least two hundred dollars for a pair of shoes.

The 1960s marked the beginning of a renewed interest in crafts. Despite a continuation of that trend, it has proven difficult for artisans to provide sufficient quality and uniqueness to overcome the price differential favoring machine-made goods, which are often imported.

"Unless I'm misinterpreting the signs, gentlemen, we are approaching the end of the golden age of shoddy merchandise."

Production Planning and Control

The management function called **production planning and control** involves the scheduling of operations relating to the production of goods or services. Its goals include:

☐ High-quality production
☐ High productivity of human and physical resources
☐ Low operating costs
☐ Customer satisfaction

For example, a job shop can achieve high productivity and minimize operating costs by reducing the number of **setups**, modifications of a process or a machine to meet the specifications for a new order, that it must do. Scheduling jobs together that have similar requirements can reduce setup costs and delays.[7]

Product Planning Production and marketing departments should work together to develop products that meet the market's requirements. These decisions are generally tactical ones made in the context of a strategy outlined by top management. In a new company the production and marketing departments may of course consist of one person, the entrepreneur.

Planning a service operation has much in common with planning a manufacturing operation. The emphasis on quality may be higher in service, and certainly the planning of a service operation must center on the personnel who will perform the services. In making high-quality chocolates, for instance, a confectioner like

Planning and facilities location. *Planning is a tremendously complex undertaking. Not even the sources of material remain constant. In 1974 Alcoa produced only 14 percent of its can body sheet from recycled aluminum beverage cans. By 1984 that figure had risen to 58 percent. Ore deposits no longer dictate the location of facilities. Raw materials are brought in by truckers like Tom Kimbrough and carefully examined by supervisors like Don Dossett (rear).*

The Steps in the PERT Process

Mother Myrick's, in Manchester, Vermont, must control the quality of its product from the creation of the recipe through the sale to the consumer.[8] Likewise, a financial planner must train his or her employees to produce clean, precise work for presentation to clients.

Scheduling Techniques The function of production control that sets the time for and duration of tasks is called **scheduling.** Its goal is to bring people and materials together at the right moment in the right place so that resources will be used efficiently. Scheduling is never simple. Ensuring that workers have the thousands of parts required to build a Piper Cub — when they need them — requires great organization. Making appointments requires both organization and tact for a busy hair stylist, since such a business is built on customer relations.

One of the most popular scheduling techniques for production control is known as **Program Evaluation and Review Technique (PERT)**. (See Figure 10.2.) The PERT process's first step is to identify all the major activities required to complete a project. The completion of all such activities is called an **event.** For example, in building an apartment house, laying the foundation and putting on the roof are activities that become events when completed.

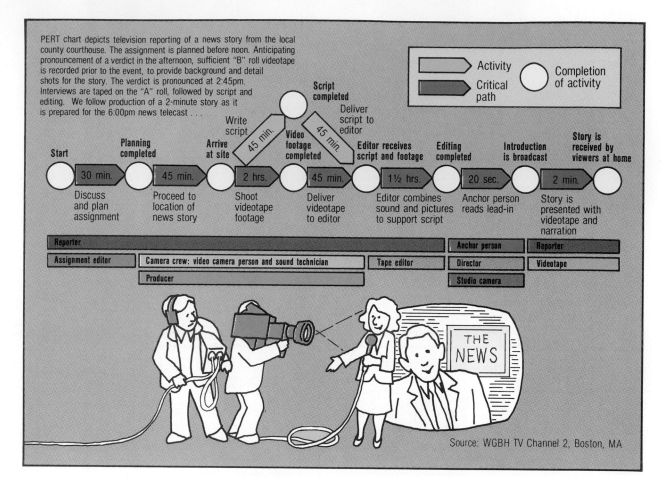

PERT chart depicts television reporting of a news story from the local county courthouse. The assignment is planned before noon. Anticipating pronouncement of a verdict in the afternoon, sufficient "B" roll videotape is recorded prior to the event, to provide background and detail shots for the story. The verdict is pronounced at 2:45pm. Interviews are taped on the "A" roll, followed by script and editing. We follow production of a 2-minute story as it is prepared for the 6:00pm news telecast . . .

Activity
Critical path
Completion of activity

Start — 30 min. — **Planning completed** — 45 min. — **Arrive at site** — 2 hrs. — **Video footage completed** — 45 min. — **Editor receives script and footage** — 1½ hrs. — **Editing completed** — 20 sec. — **Introduction is broadcast** — 2 min. — **Story is received by viewers at home**

Write script — 45 min. — **Script completed** — 45 min. — Deliver script to editor

Discuss and plan assignment | Proceed to location of news story | Shoot videotape footage | Deliver videotape to editor | Editor combines sound and pictures to support script | Anchor person reads lead-in | Story is presented with videotape and narration

Reporter | Anchor person | Reporter
Assignment editor | Camera crew: video camera person and sound technician | Tape editor | Director | Videotape
Producer | Studio camera

Source: WGBH TV Channel 2, Boston, MA

FIGURE 10.2

PERT

The second step in the PERT process is to arrange the events into a sequence so as to separate the events that can happen simultaneously from those that must occur sequentially. For instance, a roof can go on before the basement's concrete floor is poured, but the wiring cannot go in before the walls are up.

The PERT process's third step requires estimating the time it will take to complete each event. The planners then total the time required for each **path**, a series of sequential events in the production process. The path with the longest total time from start to finish is called the **critical path**. If any of the activities on the critical path lag, the project almost certainly cannot be completed on time.

Facilities Location

A large corporation that needs to develop a new facility faces three basic decisions regarding where to locate the new establishment:

1. In what part of what nation should it locate?
2. In what community should it locate?
3. On what site within the community should it locate?

The smaller the firm, the more likely it is to begin with the second or third question. Even so, every business faces the same decision criteria in choosing a location:

☐ Proximity to raw materials and/or markets
☐ Availability of qualified personnel
☐ Availability of appropriate transportation
☐ Affordability and availability of energy
☐ Attractive government inducements
☐ Favorable local regulations and taxes
☐ Congenial general living conditions in the area

These factors will have different weights in each firm's decision. For instance, when Borden's moved its headquarters from New York City to Columbus, Ohio, an important consideration was Columbus's reputation as a good place to raise a family. When Honda located its first U.S. plant fifty miles northwest of Columbus in Marysville, the key factors were favorable state taxes and the ready availability of all three major types of ground transportation.

Proximity to Raw Materials and/or Markets Virtually every type of business must locate its facilities close to either a source of raw materials or a key market or both. The ideal is of course to be located close to both, but that is often impossible. The Adolf Coors Company decided to locate its first eastern brewery in Virginia, because the water quality there matched that in Coors's home state of Colorado and because the plant would be near its new markets. Of course, the company still had to transport grain and hops to Virginia.

When raw materials are large, bulky, or heavy, a manufacturer usually locates its operation near the source of such materials, to avoid high transportation costs. If, however, the cost of transporting raw materials is only a minimal part of the cost of production, firms tend to locate near markets.

Availability of Qualified Personnel All firms obviously require qualified personnel to operate them. The nature of the jobs determines whether the availability of qualified personnel will be a determining factor in the decision about where to locate a facility.

Appropriate Transportation A firm must have appropriate transportation facilities, including parking, for receiving its raw materials or for receiving customers and clients. These facilities must be able to handle both the firm's finished products and departing customers or clients. Finally, the firm's employees must have appropriate transportation facilities available to them to reach work comfortably and conveniently.

Affordability and Availability of Energy The price and availability of the energy needed for production often plays a key role in site selection. For instance, the process of manufacturing aluminum requires enormous quantities of electricity. It is thus not surprising that the aluminum industry has concentrated in areas like that served by the Bonneville Power Authority in the Pacific northwest. The federal government originally established these public corporations to supply low-cost hydroelectric power in their service regions to attract jobs.

Availability of personnel. What does a business do when the people who want its service are in one place and the people who are looking for entry-level jobs are somewhere else? This Darien, Connecticut, McDonald's hires buses to transport teenage workers from the Bronx. The situation was so bad in nearby Stamford, that one in five companies surveyed there considered moving in 1985.

Government Inducements   Other government inducements to locate in particular areas include a possible tax forgiveness for a certain period, industrial revenue bonds to finance a project at very low cost to the business, and the construction of necessary water and sewer hookups and facilities. Governments often use these inducements to lure businesses into blighted areas or to train minorities.

Government also has a broad range of powers that it can use to either hinder or promote a business in choosing a particular site. For instance, within localities, **zoning regulations** specify the uses to which land and the buildings on it can be put. The local zoning authority may at its discretion grant **variances** from the regulations in order to permit a business to use land for its own purposes.

THE LAYOUT OF PRODUCTION FACILITIES

Very early in the stage of planning for a new facility, management must decide on the new plant's **layout**, the physical arrangement of an operational facility.

Design Considerations

The design of a facility's layout should maximize the efficient use of a firm's human and physical resources. However, no operation can be designed with just these considerations in mind. For instance, management must also take into account such limitations as state and federal safety requirements.

Manufacturing Operations Manufacturers want a layout that will promote the smooth flow of materials within a plant. Raw material must enter the plant at an appropriate point for easy input into the manufacturing process. The process of transforming raw materials into salable goods should move smoothly, without bottlenecks, to the moment the finished products leave the facility.

An operations-management team has a number of layout models from which to choose. A **process layout** groups machinery or activities according to their

The Pursuit of Quality

Observant television viewers may have noticed a change in the focus of many TV ads in the past few years, particularly ads for cars. "Quality is job 1," says Ford, and other companies echo the message. While Detroit hasn't given up on selling you sleek, sexy, fast cars, the Big Three automakers — and other manufacturers around the country — are now trying very hard to convince people that their products are made well and will last. American companies have come at last to realize that quality sells.

But for many American manufacturers, quality has not been "job 1" in the last few decades. Most businesses don't worry about defects unless the percentage of problem products goes above a certain level. Companies tend to think about quality when customers or retailers return an unusually high number of products in a given month. Then the company might investigate the problem, fix it, and not worry about quality again.

Japanese manufacturers have largely rejected this way of thinking, emphasizing instead continuous quality improvements, working towards error-free production. Their emphasis on quality has made their goods respected world-wide and has helped to make Japan such a formidable economic power. But we don't have to turn to Japan to learn about quality; for the last 20 years, America has had its own self-appointed quality guru, Philip Crosby.

Crosby started preaching his message while working at ITT as a quality control executive in the 1960s. "They used to think I was a madman," he says, but his 1979 book, *Quality Is Free,* has sold nearly a million copies. One of his favorite sayings is, "We've got to get out of fixing." He wants American business to abandon the idea of fixing things once they leave the factory, and to start making things right the first time. He points out the many ways defects cost a company — in work that must be scrapped or reworked, in inspection, and in liability and warranty headaches.

Studies show that inspection systems — America's traditional last defense against defects — don't work. U.S. firms already have at least 3 times as many inspectors as do Japanese manufacturers, but they produce five times as many defective parts. Crosby and others look for ways to *prevent* defects, not fix them.

Virtually every new manufacturing technique you'll read about emphasizes quality as a major goal. The "just-in-time" approach in particular demands high quality. The entire manufacturing process may have to stop if a component part delivered to the factory just-in-time is defective. Therefore just-in-time manufacturers insist on high-quality parts and tend to have a much closer relationship with their suppliers than do other companies.

Robots, automated assembly lines, and the computerized factory are all attempts by manufacturers to make products not just more cheaply, but better. In general, they seem to work — company after company reports a dramatic decrease in defects after switching to new manufacturing technologies. But the real winner in this pursuit is the consumer. We can worry less now about getting stuck buying a "lemon," and in a few years we may be able to approach a purchase with the feeling that "Made in America" means "made well."

Sources: Gary Slutsker, "They Thought I Was a Madman," *Forbes*, May 19, 1986, 100. Craig R. Waters, "Improved! New! Manufacturing," *Inc.*, January 1986, 73. Ernest Raia, "Just-in-time USA," *Purchasing*, February 13, 1986, 48.

purposes. In a pipe factory, for instance, all the machines that put threads on household water pipes would be placed together. Normally, small operations with differentiated product mixes, like job shops, use process layouts. In a **product layout**, though, the equipment arrangement relates to the sequence of operations performed in manufacturing a product. Product layouts are most commonly used in assembly-line operations.

In both process and product layouts, the raw material or product moves from one processing stage to the next. In contrast, a **fixed-position layout** is an operational arrangement in which workers and equipment come to the product, instead of the usual arrangement. Commercial and military aircraft are made this way, as are medium to large ships.

Nonmanufacturing Operations Even nonmanufacturing facilities must address the layout question. Retailers, for example, carefully control the flow of customers through the display areas and into checkout lines. And the design and location of work stations can make or break a service business like a restaurant, computer-repair operation, or accounting office. In service operations, a **consumer-oriented layout** is an operational layout designed to make easy the customer's interactions with the firm's services. Banks introduced the familiar roped waiting lines for tellers in order to end customers' frustration if they happened to pick a slow-moving line. Grocery stores instituted express-checkout lines for the same reason.

Design Techniques Designing operational layouts that work is an art but also requires art, as well. Simple one-dimensional diagrams of the process are a sufficient starting point, but two-dimensional maps are essential for proper planning. Indeed, a scale model or even three-dimensional drawings are often necessary to make a design come to life. Computer-assisted design programs can assist in developing the overall design.

Capacity The rate at which an operation can produce output over a given period is called its **capacity**. Appropriate capacity concerns the facility planners, who must forecast demand. The capacity problem is generally more acute for service companies than for manufacturing concerns. A manufacturing company can compensate for too little capacity by building up inventory during slack periods or adding extra shifts. Such service businesses as restaurants usually do not have these options, however. Overcapacity in the form of empty seats has driven bus companies, passenger train lines, and airlines into bankruptcy over the years.

Some decisions about capacity have nothing to do with the demand for a company's goods or services. As we saw in Chapter 5, for instance, Bill Gore of W. L. Gore & Associates has deliberately kept the size of each of his plants to under two hundred employees in order to maintain the company's uniquely successful corporate culture.

Mass Production, Computers, and Robotics

One of the hottest topics in operations management is the factory of the future, which will incorporate recent developments in computers and mechanization. Applying technological breakthroughs to operations has proven far more difficult than anyone originally imagined, however.

Production layout. Modern, automated production facilities can move material smoothly and efficiently through the transformation process. This system of insulating and winding machines replaces numerous separate machines and manual operations in GE's DeKalb, Illinois, motor plant. But modern facilities carry a high price tag. GE will spend over $290 million upgrading 17 motor plants around the world.

Automation and Computer-Assisted Design/Computer-Assisted Manufacturing (CAD/CAM)

When the term first entered our language, **automation** referred to the substitution of mechanical for human labor. The word still carries that meaning, but the development of so-called smart machines has broadened its meaning to include the replacement of human sensory applications, too. For example, Allen-Bradley, a manufacturer of controls for electric motors, has designed an assembly line that can read bar codes so that it can produce unique controls without stopping for retooling.[9]

Robots and Computer-Integrated Manufacturing (CIM)

A **robot** is a reprogramable machine capable of performing a variety of tasks requiring programed manipulations of tools and materials. Some believe robots to be the key to recapturing world markets for manufactured goods, because they perform routine, repetitive tasks thousands of times without a mistake.

The Relationship Between Computers and Robots

The great benefit of robots to manufacturers lies not in having them replace human labor but in their vastly improving product quality. Robots most fully achieve this upgrading as an element of **computer-integrated manufacturing (CIM)**, CAD, and CAM linked together in a system that manages data flow while at the same time directing the movement and processing of material. The resulting combination of lower labor costs and greater quality control may reduce a factory's typical breakeven point from 60 to 65 percent of capacity to as little as 25 to 30 percent. Besides the Big 3 U.S. auto makers and IBM, many job shops have also decided to adopt CIM systems.[10]

IMPLEMENTING THE PLAN

Many of the decisions we have been discussing, like deciding on a plant's capacity, are made just once. By the time the facility is built and the necessary equipment installed, the management should have in place plans for running it. The quality of the planning will of course not matter if the plan is not implemented appropriately. Effective planning is a never-ending process of communication, evaluation, and reevaluation.

The key to successful implementation is **control**, the process of measuring an organization's performance against its plans to make certain that the actual operations conform with the plans. In short, "control is assuring that desired results are attained."[11]

Operational Planning

The scheduling of an organization's day-to-day needs and the designing of how to meet them is **operational planning.** In a sense, all operational planning supports one key decision: the amount of output the facility is desired to generate over a particular planning period. For example, management must decide how many workers to hire and train according to the number needed to achieve the desired output. Similarly, the output target determines the quantity of raw materials that will have to be ordered.

Inventory Control

The First Element in an Operational Plan

Inventory is a general term to describe certain classes of goods that are assets to a business. There are two classes of inventories, indirect and direct. **Indirect inventories** are the supplies a business uses that are not purchased with the intention of reselling them. The ribbons used in an office typewriter or antifreeze for a company truck fall into this class. **Direct inventory**, in manufacturing, includes raw materials, work in process (whatever stage of production it is in), and finished products. In retail and service operations, direct inventory includes all goods bought for resale. Controlling the costs and flow of direct inventory is a major concern for an operations manager.[12]

Indirect inventory is not a major focus of operations management, but direct inventory is. In this chapter, when we refer to inventory we mean direct inventory.

The Costs of Inventory   The basic objective of inventory control is to balance two types of costs. **Carrying costs** are expenses incurred because an item is held in inventory. Among many others, carrying costs include taxes, storage charges, insurance, maintenance, and spoilage. **Ordering costs** are expenses incurred whenever a business places an order for inventory goods with a vendor. They include not only all the vendor's charges but also the costs associated with receiving and processing the order and the cost of any delays in production caused by not receiving the goods promptly.

Good suppliers make the difference. Purchasing is never easy, but restaurant owners George Germon and Johanne Killeen know that they can't serve great meals without great ingredients. They are willing to pay for the freshest and the finest supplies. Germon and Killeen demand top quality, but they treat their suppliers with the respect they deserve. The restaurant can't succeed without them.

Management's goal is to achieve a minimum total inventory cost and to balance the two carrying and ordering costs. Achieving this goal requires two separate actions. First, management must minimize the controllable inventory costs, like spoilage. Second, it must balance the irreducible costs against each other.

To accomplish these two goals, the Japanese developed the so-called **just-in-time inventory system**, an ordering system that aims to have inventory arrive on the premises just moments before it must enter the transformation process. These systems have a very narrow margin of error and therefore require close cooperation between the supplier and the manufacturer. Various U.S. companies are now beginning to adopt just-in-time systems. All the auto makers and other manufacturers like Allen-Bradley are now using just-in-time inventory systems, at least in parts of their manufacturing operations.

Inventory costs are as big a problem for service operations as for manufacturing. For instance, the cost of keeping every conceivable part in stock would bankrupt a small appliance shop. Likewise, a restaurant cannot afford to throw out large quantities of unsold food regularly.

Materials Requirements Planning (MRP)

The Second Element in an Operational Plan

The computerized technique used to plan and control manufacturing inventories is called **materials requirements planning (MRP).** MRP's purpose is to ensure that a manufacturer has available the necessary materials and components in the right

Manufacturing with Computers

Computers have affected manufacturing technology perhaps more than they have changed any other branch of business. Advocates of high-tech manufacturing say they've already seen the future of manufacturing and have called it "computer-integrated manufacturing" (CIM).

The idea behind computer-integrated manufacturing is to automate all the functions of a factory and connect them with computers. Such a factory can turn out flawless products, cheaply and relatively quickly, even if each product is completely different from the previous one.

At the first step in the CIM factory, a designer creates a new product with a computer-aided system, then passes the design information on to a computer-aided engineering system which makes sure the design will work and can be made economically. The engineering system sends its information to the automated storage and retrieval system which picks up materials and tools and delivers them with an automated guided vehicle. The computer-aided manufacturing system sends electronic instructions for making the product to automated equipment like computer-controlled machine tools and robotic assembly stations. The information from all these systems is constantly available to computerized management systems keeping track of the consumption of parts and materials, scheduling, and planning. Eventually buyers and suppliers may make bids on the same electronic network and sign electronic contracts.

One major advantage of this kind of computerized manufacturing is flexibility. At a CIM plant, economies of scale are virtually eliminated: the factory can make the first copy of a product almost as cheaply as it can make the hundredth.

The computerized factory also cuts labor and inventory costs. By eliminating much of the assembly-line labor of traditional factories, computerized manufacturing can turn out products inexpensively and therefore undercut a company's desire to save on labor costs by building a plant overseas. And because of CIM's flexibility, computerized factories can take the just-in-time approach to its logical extreme, virtually eliminating inventory.

Managements at some companies that could use CIM have been slow to accept the new technology. Many companies have already sharply cut their labor costs and must justify the computerized factory in terms of the speed, flexibility, and improved quality available with CIM. And there is still some resistance, especially among workers, to the concept of "robots" on the factory floor, although most who actually work with the new computerized machines find that they're just another sophisticated tool.

The movement is clearly towards the automated factory, and at the moment the United States holds an edge over its foreign rivals in CIM. The manufacturing challenge for the next decade is making sure that edge doesn't slip away.

Sources: Richard Brandt and Otis Port, "How Automation Could Save the Day," *Business Week*, March 3, 1986, 72. Carol Fey, "Working with Robots: The Real Story," *Training*, March 1986, 49. Craig R. Waters, "Improved! New! Manufacturing," *Inc.*, January 1986, 73.

---

quantities and at the right time so that it can complete its finished products according to the master schedule. At the operational level, management uses MRP to plan production on a short-term basis.

The enormous improvements in both computer hardware and software over the last decade have turned MRP's goals into reality for many firms. MRP has reduced inventory investment, improved work flow, reduced shortages of materials and components, and achieved more reliable delivery schedules. In addition, materials requirements planning has led to better communications and improved integration of support functions.[13]

Quality control is serious business. *The scene at Goodyear Tire's test facility near Fort Walton Beach, Florida, can be quite a surprise. Building a giant climatic laboratory was about the only way Goodyear could evaluate snow tires in Florida.*

Purchasing

The Third Feature of an Operational Plan

The operational function by which a business obtains the goods and services it requires is **purchasing.** Purchasing's objective is to ensure that a firm has the right materials at the right price at the right place at the right time. To do so requires good suppliers. A purchasing manager will try to identify several qualified suppliers for each item the firm needs. In this way, he or she can force suppliers to compete on price, quality, and reliability.

Small differences in pricing can turn into large sums over a long period. Quality is always a consideration, but getting the highest quality is not. A purchasing manager needs to be as specific as possible about the quality necessary for the product. Finally, the supplier's reliability is a critical factor in operational planning, because the probability of on-time delivery must be factored into the purchasing department's **lead time,** the period that elapses between the time of placing an order and its receipt.

Quality Control

The Final Aspect of an Operational Plan

The operations management function meant to ensure that output meets the planning standards is **quality control.** A successful quality control program results in the production of goods and services of a specified uniform quality — not necessarily of the highest quality. The goal is consistency.

The most common quality control technique is **inspection**, "the determination, sometimes by testing, of whether . . . an input or output conforms to organizational standards of quality."[14] We should note that those with responsibility for inspection are not responsible for correcting the failings that caused the defective production. Rather, it is their job to make sure that substandard products go no further and to call attention to irregular production processes. Quite often, inspectors simply cannot check every single product. Quality control must therefore often rely on statistical analyses of random samples.

OPERATIONS MANAGEMENT: A PERSPECTIVE

Quality control is by no means a new concept. For those who sell food in areas with large Jewish populations, it involves following rules of purity established as long ago as three thousand years. During Passover, in particular, Jewish law forbids Jews to eat *chometz*, any grain or grain product exposed to water to the point that leavening has begun. This restriction extends to any food made with *chometz*. For food processors, the problems of eliminating *chometz* are enormous. Some, like Dairylea Farms, in Syracuse, New York, eliminate the corn-based additives blended with the vitamins that are added to their milk and substitute a palm-oil or cotton-seed-oil base. Other food processors halt production altogether for a few days before they begin preparing food for Passover, then clean their plants and equipment with extra-special care.

A rabbi from a *kasruth* or dietary board will inspect the plant to make sure that it satisfies Jewish law. Rabbis are even lowered into grain silos at bakers. If the facility passes inspection, it may label its foods *kosher* or *kosher for Passover*, depending on whether the plant satisfies the dietary laws all year round. Companies like Coca-Cola, Pepsi-Cola, and Beatrice Foods plan each year to ensure that their regular customers do not have to go without their products during the eight-day observance. As we will see in the next unit, "Marketing," such commitments to meeting customers' needs can be expected to be rewarded in the marketplace.[15]

Chapter Highlights

1. Define operations management and describe the elements that go into it.

Operations management is the process of coordinating the production of goods or services and all of the activities associated with production. It requires the management of people and machinery to convert materials and resources into finished products.

2. Classify the types of production processes.

Production processes are classified according to the variety and quantity of goods produced. The continuous-flow system or continuous-process system is a production-to-stock process that produces large quantities of single standardized product. Mass production or assembly line production is a production-to-stock process that produces large quantities of a small number of products. Batch processing or intermittent processing is a production-to-stock system that generates lower quantities of goods than a mass production system but may use similar or identical processes. Job shop processing or job order processing is a production-to-order process in which the producer makes a quantity of goods to the customer's satisfaction. Project processing is a production-to-order system in which the manufacturer produces a one-of-a-kind item.

3. Describe the steps that go into planning an operation.

Once a firm decides to develop a new product, it must decide whether to make the product or buy the product from other companies and just put its label on it. An increasing number of American corporations have abandoned manufacturing operations in favor of buying products from other vendors. If a company decides to produce its own product, it may be able to choose between low-tech and high-tech manufacturing methods. High-tech industries make greater use of modern production techniques such as automation and the use of robots. Planning the operation also includes decisions related to production planning and control. Production planning and control is a management function involving the scheduling of operations relating to the production of goods or services. Its goals include high quality production and low operating costs.

4. List the steps in the PERT process for scheduling production control.

One of the most popular scheduling techniques for production control is the program evaluation and review technique (PERT). The PERT process's first step is the identification of all the major activities required to complete a project. The second step is to arrange the events into a sequence in order to identify which events can happen simultaneously and which must occur sequentially. The third step requires the estimation of the time it will take to complete each activity.

5. Identify the criteria that go into a facilities location decision.

The factors that must be considered in selecting a facilities location include proximity to raw materials or markets; availability of personnel; availability of appropriate transportation; cost and availability of energy; government inducements; the favorability of local regulations and taxes; and general living conditions in the area.

6. Describe the principal considerations in designing the layout of production facilities.

Layout refers to the physical arrangement of an operational facility. The design of a facility's layout should maximize the efficient use of human and physical resources. An operations management team has a number of layout models from which to choose. A process layout groups machinery or activities according to their purposes. In a product layout, the equipment arrangement relates to a sequence of operations performed in manufacturing a product. In both of these layouts, the raw material or product moves from processing stage to processing stage. In contrast, a fixed-position layout is an operational arrangement in which workers and equipment come to the product.

7. Describe the relationship between computers and robots.

A robot is a reprogramable machine capable of performing a variety of tasks requiring programed manipulations of tools and materials. These machines are designed to perform routine, repetitive tasks thousands of times without a mistake. Robots are sometimes part of Computer-Integrated Manufacturing (CIM), a system that manages data flow while directing the movement and processing of material. Firms that use CIM and similar systems seek lower labor costs and greater quality control.

8. Identify the key elements involved in implementing an operational plan.

Operational planning is scheduling an organization's day-to-day needs and designing how to meet them. Inventory control is one of the key elements of the operational plan. The basic objective of inventory control is to balance two types of costs: carrying costs and ordering costs. To achieve these two goals, many companies are using the just-in-time inventory system. Material requirements planning (MRP), a computerized technique used in planning and controlling manufacturing inventories, helps ensure that the firm has available the materials and components in the right quantities and at the right time. Purchasing, the operational function by which a business obtains the goods and services it requires, is another element of operational planning. The final element of operational planning is quality control. Quality control ensures that output meets the planned standards.

Key Terms

Automation
Capacity
Carrying costs
Computer-integrated
    manufacturing (CIM)
Consumer-oriented
    layout
Continuous flow
    system or
    continuous process
    system

Critical path
Direct inventory
Fixed-position layout
Indirect inventory
Inventory
Just-in-time inventory
    system
Layout
Lead time
Materials requirements
    planning (MRP)

Operational planning
Operations
Operations
    management
Ordering costs
Path
Process layout
Product layout
Production
Production planning
    and control

Program Evaluation
    and Review
    Technique (PERT)
Purchasing
Quality control
Setups
Transformation
Variances
Zoning regulations

Review Questions

1. Define the term operations management. What are some of the activities that would be involved in operations management?
2. Distinguish between production to order and production to stock production systems.
3. Many firms must decide whether to be a manufacturer or a packager. What are some of the reasons a firm might make its own product? What are the advantages of buying a product from another company?
4. Steinway pianos and Cordwainers shoes are still constructed with a great deal of hand labor. What factors appear to contribute to the success of these two companies?
5. List and describe three types of transformation processes.

6. List five criteria to be used in choosing a location for a plant that will manufacture baseball bats. Explain why each of these criteria is important.
7. Explain the difference between process layout and product layout production designs.
8. What does *automation* mean? What role do robots play in the automation of some production facilities?
9. List and describe the two major types of cost of inventory which must be considered by management.
10. Describe Materials Requirements Planning (MRP). What are the benefits of this strategy for firms involved in production?

Application Exercises

1. Quality control is an important operations management function. What quality control techniques would be appropriate for the following firms:
   a. dairy
   b. hospital
   c. building contractor
   d. bank

2. Assume you have decided to begin production of a simple three-shelf bookcase to be made of fine wood. You would like to produce at least five book cases each day. Decide whether you would use a process layout or a product layout in your production area. Prepare a sketch of the layout you select.

Cases

10.1 No More Railroad Blues

After World War II, the American railroad industry was dying. Because of low productivity and high costs, carrier after carrier went into bankruptcy. But now the industry is alive and vigorous, as a result of mergers, recent deregulation, new and reasonable work rules, and heavy investment. The result has been a productivity increase of over 600 percent. The U.S. government-owned Conrail system is now profitable and will soon be sold to private interests. Several railroads are healthy enough to compete for freight business earlier lost to the trucking industry.

One of these is the Union Pacific System. Deregulation permitted railroads to abandon unprofitable routes and to set realistic and competitive rates for their services. Under government regulation, freight hauling rates were rigidly structured. Now, railroads can set their own rates, perhaps offering a one-time low rate that is attractive enough to fill an otherwise empty train while covering the variable cost of running it.

The negotiated reduction of featherbedding, the requirement that certain workers be retained even when they are no longer needed, has increased productivity. The locomotive fireman (steam boiler attendant) is a classic example; until recently, railroad workers' unions demanded that train crews include firemen, even though steam boilers have been replaced by diesel engines. Now the unions are allowing the elimination of the fireman's position through attrition.

Union Pacific has financed what may be the most productive innovation of all — the TCS (transportation control system), a computerized management system that, among other things, assigns cars and a routing to each customer's shipment, controls the movement and switching of cars throughout the 22,000-mile Union Pacific system, reports on the status of cars and trains, and computes freight rates and bills. The TCS can also be queried about expected traffic at each freight yard over the next half day to several days, and it routes empty cars to where they will be needed next. An early trial of the system, on a single busy route, showed a solid gain in reliability, an increase in the volume of freight handled, and a *decrease* in the number of train-miles traveled to move that volume.

Questions

1. Describe and classify Union Pacific's transformation process.
2. How have Union Pacific's changes increased productivity?

For more information see *Forbes*, June 30, 1986, pp. 86–90; *Railway Age*, January 1986, pp. 39–40∠d *The Wall Street Journal*, January 13, 1986, p. 16.

10.2 Handling High Technology

Two of America's big three automakers — Ford and General Motors — have rushed headlong into high-tech automation and computerization with almost predictable results. An automobile assembly plant that begins operations almost a year later than planned. A vision-equipped robot that smashes windshields against car bodies while installing them, because it lacks the proper depth perception. Brand new assembly equipment that won't work until the auto parts it installs are redesigned. These are some of the problems that are keeping production down at new "state-of-the-art" plants. Officials at both firms optimistically feel certain that once the bugs are removed, the new plants will produce vehicles of higher quality at lower cost and provide needed operational flexibility.

Officials at Chrysler, on the other hand, admit to only an occasional unexpected problem; they say that their newly automated plants started on schedule and are producing more vehicles per day than expected. They attribute this success to an effective combination of high tech and heavy-industry know-how, the computer simulation of all new technology, more than a million hours of worker training, and a production technique called "in-line sequencing."

In-line sequencing means that the whole line shuts down if any car is not built right. Once a vehicle is placed on the assembly line, it retains its position until it leaves the line as a finished vehicle. There are no repair bays along the line, where problem vehicles can be moved and worked on. When there is a problem of any magnitude, the entire plant must cease operation.

In-line sequencing produces tremendous pressure to get everything right the first time. That's how the system was designed, according to Chrysler's chief of manufacturing. And that's how it seems to be working.

Questions

1. What factors might account for the difference between Chrysler's experience with high-tech plants and that of Ford and General Motors?
2. Which areas of operations management, other than production, are affected by the use of in-line sequencing? How is each affected?

For more information see *The New York Times*, May 18, 1986, p. F6; *The Wall Street Journal*, May 13, 1986, pp. 1, 10; and *Consumers Digest*, March/April 1985, pp. 47–49.

The United States is no longer young. We have recently celebrated some important anniversaries marking 200 years since the signing of the Declaration of Independence and 100 years since the building of the Statue of Liberty. The country that once felt inferior to Europe because it lacked history and tradition now has cities old enough to have gone through an entire cycle of growth, prominence, decay, and rebirth. Many of the industries that made millionaires and provided the country's economic muscle are dying from the effects of outmoded technology and foreign competition, and they're being replaced by industries that didn't even exist ten or fifteen years ago. Perhaps most important for those who sell to America's populace, 1986 marked the 40th year since the start of the baby boom.

Americans born since the end of the Second World War have grown up in a youth-oriented culture. Many probably feel that America is simply fascinated with young people and always has been. But in fact the country responds, like a big consumer products company, to changing demographics, catering to the largest group in the population. It is not simply coincidence that the fifties and early sixties — when baby boomers were kids — was the heyday of Walt Disney and cartoons, while the late sixties and early seventies — when baby boomers were in their teens and twenties — were times of radical change and protest.

In the last fifteen years, as most of the population bulge settled into careers, bought houses, and became more conservative politically, the taste of the nation as a whole changed too. In what some call the era of selfishness, best sellers and talk shows focused not on how to change the world, but on how to reduce your waistline, make a million before age 40, and "be your own best friend." Someone coined the term "yuppie" to describe Young Urban Professionals who had the money to buy BMWs and windsurfers and condominiums and who gave little thought to anything beyond themselves.

Consumer products aimed for this young, affluent, and health-oriented group have been among the big sellers for the last decade. To entertain the baby boomers, VCRs, compact disk players, and "walkmen" were created and sold like mad. To keep them fit, running shoes went

The Changing Population

through a revolution in technology and style, exercise machines came out of smelly gym basements and into spotless high-tech health clubs, and sweatclothes became ubiquitous, high-fashion apparel.

With the postwar population bulge reaching child-bearing age, the nation's attention began to turn to marriage and babies. Along with the political turn to conservative, religious candidates came a return to traditional big weddings. Caring for babies became a huge industry, with day care centers springing up all over to help working parents cope with two careers and raising a family. Suddenly there were high-fashion baby carriages, and scores of action figures promoted by Saturday morning cartoons appeared to amuse the new generation of kids.

Now that the first baby boomers have turned 40, the focus of much of America's media and marketing attention has turned to the needs and desires of those who are beyond the ages of bearing children and buying boom boxes. Suddenly America's slick magazines have discovered that women over 40 — and even over 50 — can be attractive. Products are being developed and advertised not just to give you the slim body of traditional bathing-suited models, but to keep you healthy into old age by cutting down on your salt and cholesterol and giving you more calcium.

With an eye to the future and the year that the bulge in America's population starts to retire, companies are now courting the elderly. Hotels and airlines provide them with discounts, car dealers recognize them as the best market for their most profitable models, catalogues cater solely to the needs of the elderly. Even television sitcoms have begun to focus on older people leading active lives, breaking the old stereotypes that allowed older actors to appear only in denture commercials.

The graying of America involves the movement as well as the aging of its populace. Across the Northeast, the huge brick or stone factory buildings that once turned out shoes and fabrics for the rest of the country now stand idle, as Americans buy their clothes and footwear from the Far East. In the Middle Atlantic and Midwest states, steel mills and automobile factories struggle to stay open. The heavy capital investment that these industries made in their plants and machinery have come back to haunt them, as foreign companies with newer machinery and less expensive labor change more quickly to produce new goods and improve quality.

These two factors — the aging of the American populace and the outmoding of heavy industries — together with rising energy costs have led to a major shift in where Americans live and work. During the 1970s, the number of jobs rose only slightly in the Northeast and North Central states, while the South saw 20 percent growth and the

West 24 percent. The populations of the sunbelt states — from Florida to California — grow steadily with people leaving New York, Pennsylvania, and Michigan.

Such trends can be deceiving, however, and may be short-lived. Texas, which experienced a tremendous growth in jobs and population in the 1970s, is now faced with high unemployment and low real estate occupancy as a result of the oil glut. Wyoming's job market grew by 37 percent between 1973 and 1983, then fell between 1983 and 1984. The rampant population growth in the Southwest is sucking water supplies dry at an alarming rate, and the desert climate that draws many older people to Tucson and Phoenix may begin to limit future growth. Even states that are losing jobs may not be bad places to look for work, because the number of young people entering the work force is falling so rapidly. There were 3.5 million new workers in 1977, compared to 1.5 million in 1984.

The Eastern states have not simply stood by and watched the mass exodus. From Baltimore to Boston, cities are cleaning up their downtown districts, turning factories into shops, and attracting tourists with historical sites and ambience that Los Angeles can't match. High-tech companies have been successfully wooed to replace the old manufacturers by states like New Hampshire, with no sales or income tax, and Massachusetts. Now certain parts of the Northeast are growing as quickly as Florida.

The aging in the populace also affects education. Administrators of schools and colleges look at the population dropoff after the baby boomers and wonder who will fill the classrooms for the next decade. Many colleges are finding that one answer is to bring older people back to school, and adult education enrollments in some parts of the country are soaring.

So from manufacturers to employers to educators, people around the country are finding that the future is symbolized as much by the gray hair of age as it is by the bright eyes of youth. And, as many older people will quickly point out, it's about time. The cult of youth that has gripped America for three decades has tended to ignore the value of older people, often treating them as stereotypes and hiding them away in retirement communities and nursing homes. Now many companies have dropped mandatory retirement rules and are learning to make use of older workers' expertise. Programs have sprung up around the country that link successful, retired business people with new business ventures that can use a guiding hand and good advice. Maybe the graying of America will lead to a new valuing of Americans with experience.

IV MARKETING

Every year sees the introduction of thousands of new products to the marketplace. Some products generate millions in profits each year. The movie "Gone With the Wind" (1939) and Tide soap (1946) have produced phenomenal profits every year since their introduction. By contrast, the DeLorean automobile may have cost investors $500 million.

Most products are neither skyrocketing successes nor fabulous flops. What makes them profitable or causes them to disappear quickly often has less to do with the merits of the idea behind the product than with how the new product was marketed. *Marketing* is a broad term whose meaning includes the decisions on how a product is developed, what its packaging will look like, how it will be presented to end-users, what its price will be, how the product will be transported from its manufacturer to the next purchaser, and what types of promotion will be used to sell it. This unit explores these and other marketing issues.

11
MARKETING MANAGEMENT

Learning Objectives

After you have completed this chapter, you will be able to do the following:

- Define marketing and describe the functions it performs.
- Outline the evolution of marketing.
- Identify and describe the elements of the marketing mix.
- Identify and contrast the four basic types of utilities.
- Explain the relationship between market segmentation and target markets and describe how marketers identify target markets.
- Describe the key elements of consumer behavior.
- Explain the importance of market information and market research.
- Distinguish between consumer products and industrial products.
- Evaluate the costs and benefits of marketing.

Suppose your company has developed "Whoosh!," a one-minute, biotech, no muss–no fuss oven cleaner. All the user has to do is to pop the top, stick it in the oven, close the door, wait one minute (two if the broiler is very dirty), open the door, remove the can, and the whole job is done.

Your advertising agency has asked you to approve a massive campaign to introduce Whoosh! to the public. This plan features full-page ads in every major women's magazine and saturation of the daytime television schedule. When your in-house marketing staff heard about the proposal, however, they bombarded your office with objections. The agency has targeted the wrong media, they insisted. The people who really need Whoosh! are not going to hear about it.

What should you do? The answer is to find a new ad agency. The people who might buy an oven cleaner that really takes no effort — primarily those who work during the day — have little time for kitchen chores. Singles certainly would be a prime target. Married women with jobs, which includes over 50 percent of all women under age sixty-five, would be another. For your company, a crucial subcategory of working women would be the working women with children. Over 65 percent of mothers with children between six and seventeen are employed, as are almost 50 percent of those with children under six.

Men are also primary targets for convenience products. The number of men living alone has risen more than 110 percent, to over 7.4 million, since 1970. A recent study shows that men spend 42 percent of all the food-shopping dollars. It is no wonder that Procter & Gamble runs some male-oriented Charmin television ads, General Foods' Post cereals and Nestlé Foods Corp. advertise in *Esquire,* and Campbell's Swanson division has two-page spreads for Le Menu frozen dinners in *Playboy.*[1]

Thirty or even twenty years ago your ad agency's strategy would have been the norm. The nature of our society has changed markedly, however, and what used to be easy marketing decisions are now so challenging that our time is often called the era of marketing.

WHAT IS MARKETING?

Marketing Defined

Marketing is the process of planning and executing the conception, pricing, promotion, and distribution of ideas, goods, and services to create exchanges that satisfy individual and organizational objectives.[2] In the past, marketing dealt only with those business activities that moved goods and services from producers to consumers or end-users. Although marketing continues to fulfill that function, today it focuses on nonbusiness, intangible services, and marketing activities for persons and organizations.

Marketing Functions

Approximately 33 percent of the American civilian work force have jobs in marketing. About 50 percent of every buyer's dollar goes for marketing costs.[3] With so many jobs and that much money involved, it is plain that marketing takes in an extremely broad spectrum of functions, even more perhaps than the wide-ranging definition above suggests. As Figure 11.1 illustrates, at some point in

FIGURE 11-1

Eight Basic Functions of Marketing

Marketing takes in an extremely broad range of functions beginning with the producer and ending with the consumers or end users.

the chain beginning with the producer and ending with the consumer or end-user marketing performs eight basic functions. Who performs them is not critical at this time; what is important is to remember that all eight are performed by someone, and cannot be omitted.

Selling   Selling is marketing's most visible and identifiable function. It makes possible the **exchange process**, the transfer of money or its equivalent for goods, services, or labor. Some firms, like American Telephone & Telegraph (AT&T), make goods for their own use or consumption, but the overwhelming majority of firms sell their goods to someone else. After all, firms generate their revenue by selling.

The Functions of Marketing

Financing   Someone must finance products from the time they are completed until a customer pays for them. Sometimes even after it sells the product, the manufacturer will continue to finance the goods through the extension of **trade credit**, a commercial buyer's open account arrangements with suppliers of goods or services.[4] For example, General Motors extends credit to its dealers and auto buyers through its credit organization, General Motors Acceptance Corp. (GMAC). **Marketers**, the people who work in marketing, are often heavily involved in credit decisions because the availability of credit often influences a customer's decision to buy.

Satisfying needs. *Vernon Johnson and Rod Flakes, two industrial marketing specialists at Digital Equipment Corp., know it's not enough to understand their company's product. They have to understand the customer as well. Marketing smarts and a technical background have helped Johnson develop successful marketing strategies and explain them to the company's sales force. Then the sales force can tell customers how Ethernet works and show how it can improve their businesses.*

Collecting and Analyzing Market Information   Market information has become a key factor in decision making in all segments of firms. Accurate, timely market information that is intelligently analyzed greatly increases the probability that the firm will deliver products buyers want, when and where they want them, at a price they are willing to pay. Marketing activity often starts when a product is little more than a concept, because firms recognize that they have a better chance to develop a successful product if they know what the end-user wants. McDonald's conducts extensive research before adding a new sandwich to its menu. Marketers generally obtain this information through surveys and other market-testing strategies.

Transporting   To facilitate the flow of products to ultimate purchasers, most businesses that produce goods have created extensive **channels of distribution**, a group of intermediaries or middlemen that direct products to customers. **Intermediaries**, or **middlemen**, are firms between the manufacturer and the ultimate user that take title or directly assist others to take title to goods. For example, Singer sells its sewing machines through its own stores, while Campbell Soups are distributed through wholesalers and retailers. When marketers are choosing a mode of transportation, they weigh such factors as speed, cost, and security.

Storing   Products often do not pass directly from production to a consumer. Often, products are stored first for a while at the factory where they are produced and later in wholesaler or retailer warehouses such as those owned by IGA or Safeway.

Grading and Standardization These marketing tasks are related but not identical. The American Marketing Association has defined both terms. **Grading** is the assignment of "predetermined standards of quality classifications to individual units or lots of a commodity."[5] When you buy meat or butter at a supermarket, it bears a United States Department of Agriculture (USDA) grade. Coal is also graded. **Standardization** is "the determination of basic limits or grade ranges in the form of uniform specifications to which particular manufactured goods may conform and uniform classes into which the products of agriculture and [mineral extraction] industries may or must be sorted or assigned."[6]

Buying Many firms buy goods that they then resell with little or no processing. Good buying decisions result in products that are easily resold. When Lucky Stores buys a truckload of one-pound cans of Maxwell House Coffee from General Foods, it will have to do little more than put a price on the outside of the cans and place them on the shelves.

Assuming Risks Manufacturing goods or buying them and owning them until they are sold sometimes involves considerable risk. The risk may take many forms. Obsolescence, spoilage, or fashion changes are just a few of them. For example, Sears must buy their Christmas merchandise during the summer at the latest and take delivery well before Thanksgiving. As a result, retailers not uncommonly bear the risk of spoilage on these Christmas goods for three months. If the goods do not sell, Sears bears the loss.

THE EVOLUTION OF MARKETING

Marketing's eight functions are constants, but the emphasis that marketers have given each function has changed over time. In this country, we can identify three distinct eras in marketing. See Figure 11.2.

The Production Era: From 1860 to 1920

The production era in marketing came at the same time as America's first great burst of industrial growth. From the Civil War until just after World War I, demand exceeded many manufacturers' ability to produce their goods. They therefore rightly regarded improving their production capacity and efficiency and lowering their costs as their keys to success. In many industries, the marketer's main jobs were simply the taking and filling of orders. The other activities of marketing were not required when firms with robust product demand could sell all they could make.

The Sales Era: From 1920 to 1950

In the period from the end of World War I to the beginning of the Korean War, the scope of marketing broadened greatly. Production capacity was no longer a major problem. Consistent, high-quality output had become commonplace. In the sales era, firms could no longer be sure of selling all they could produce.

FIGURE 11-2

The Evolution of Marketing

While marketing's eight functions are constants, the emphasis marketers have given each function has changed over time.

Successful firms recognized the need to pay attention to advertising and to the hiring, training, and deployment of an effective sales force. A common view was that "good advertising and a fast-talking sales force can sell anything." During this period marketers came to realize that they needed accurate information about the marketplace. This recognition led to the development of systematic market research, which permitted the effective planning of advertising and sales campaigns at an early point in the production process.

The Marketing Era: From 1950 to the Present

The marketing era that began with the great post–World War II economic boom has continued to the present. The great economic historians have referred to America in the 1950s as "the affluent society." For the first time, most American families had **discretionary income**, more income than what is required to obtain the necessities of life. They used this extra income to satisfy their needs with different kinds of products and to acquire goods and services wanted. For example, consumers who before could afford only to bake with flour now bought Wonder bread, Betty Crocker mixes, Bisquick, and other flour-based products.

The Marketing Concept Marketers now had to learn how to satisfy wants as well as needs. An excerpt from the 1952 General Electric annual report describes how this 1950s' leader in marketing was meeting this challenge.

> In 1952 your Company's operating managers were presented with an advanced concept of marketing. . . . This, in simple terms, would introduce the marketing man at the beginning rather than the end of the production cycle and would integrate marketing into each phase of the business. Thus marketing, through its studies and research, would establish for the engineer, the designer and the manufacturing man what the customer wants in a given product, what price he is willing to pay, and where and when it will be wanted. Marketing would have authority in product planning, product scheduling and inventory control, as well as the sales distribution and servicing of the product.[7]

Thus, as early as 1952, firms like General Electric had begun to look toward what is now called the **marketing concept**, the idea that "the ultimate purpose of every business should be to satisfy the customer."[8]

The Marketing Concept's Four Pillars This operating philosophy rests on four pillars. See Figure 11.3. It is . . .

☐ oriented toward the customer
☐ backed by integrated marketing
☐ aimed at generating customer satisfaction
☐ achievement of its organizational goals

These terms are critical to an understanding of the marketing concept.

Firms with a **customer orientation** base their marketing decisions on their customers' wants. For example, a consumer-oriented auto-sound manufacturer like Delco would not bring out a product line of radios simply because it had the technical capacity to make a radio. It would instead make its decision following an analysis of the potential demand for such a product.

FIGURE 11-3

The Four Pillars of Marketing

The marketing concept rests
on four pillars: customer
orientation; integrated marketing;
customer satisfaction; and
achieving organizational goals.

Integrated marketing plays a key role in maintaining a customer orientation. This concept views marketing as the job of everyone in the company because each employee can influence the firm's ability to gain and retain customers. Firms like Wal-mart Stores, Inc., and Publix Supermarkets have been built on this concept. In companies adopting an integrated marketing approach, marketers make sure that the customers' needs and the firm's response mesh. They deal with customers and interpret their needs to the company. The Vermont Castings wood-stove company supplies probably the ultimate example of integrated marketing. Every summer it gives an old-fashioned New England picnic for its customers, eleven thousand of whom are likely to show up. The management corresponds with its consumers directly, and with every stove comes a lifetime subscription to *Vermont Castings Owners' News.*[9] Such devices encourage the kind of two-way communication on which successful marketing depends.

Firms that can deliver **customer satisfaction** have a greater chance for long-run survival than those that do not. Customers buy products and services because of the satisfaction they receive from them. Firms must therefore remove any potential dissatisfaction that might be associated with what they sell. For instance, sport fans hate to stand in line except for the hottest contests, so minimizing the ticket line wait is every team's goal. Consequently, teams such as the Boston Celtics and Los Angeles Rams begin to promote ticket sales well in advance of the season and at a variety of locations.

In reality, the marketing concept's first three pillars — customer orientation, integrated marketing, and customer satisfaction — are a means of achieving the fourth — the firm's **organizational goals**, its long-range objectives. Of course, the key goals are survival and profitability. The firm may emphasize other goals as well, among them commitments to environmental quality, equal opportunity for all, and worker participation in decision making.

Marketing Today

Having examined the history of marketing as a succession of periods, we can now see that there are companies still practicing the philosophy of these eras.

Another Life for the Big Cat

Many Americans used to think of Jaguar, the British auto maker, as an English version of Mercedes-Benz, manufacturer of stylish, expensive, high-quality cars. Despite their scarcity, or perhaps because of it, everyone knew what a Jaguar looked like, and they were firmly established as a clear sign of success. Americans were, therefore, surprised when, at the beginning of the decade, Jaguar looked like it might follow its sister companies, MG and Triumph, in going out of business. Management analysts have been even more surprised by the company's turnaround since then. The story of how Jaguar survived provides a number of lessons in management.

In 1980, Jaguar was producing fewer than 14,000 cars a year, down from 32,000 in 1974, and was losing $1.5 million a week. Sales in the U.S. bottomed out at 3,000 a year, down from a high of 7,000 in 1976. BL, formerly British Leyland, the parent company of Jaguar, Rover, Triumph, and MG, was in the process of closing down its MG and Triumph plants, and many expected it to soon close down Jaguar as well. Production problems were so bad that the company actually skipped a model year. The company's reputation had tumbled since its heyday, to the point where Jaguar quality and service had become a joke in America.

The head of the team that turned Jaguar around was John Egan, brought in from Massey-Ferguson. His first moves were to focus on sales in the U.S. as being the company's only hope, to assure dealers that the company would not sell MGs and Triumphs to liquidators, which would have destroyed many dealers, and to face the company's quality problem head on. In a week-long series of meetings with dealers around the country, he admitted that Jaguar had had quality problems, and he listed 250 problem areas, from steering gear leaks to peeling paint, that he intended to correct. Dealers were impressed and encouraged.

Back at the factory, Egan made sure that everyone was aware of how much depended on improvements in quality and output. He used a range of management techniques — including quality circles and late-night management meetings — to get everyone involved and enthusiastic.

After cutting the workforce by 30 percent and investing in advanced technology, the company instituted productivity bonuses and gave each worker Jaguar shares.

Such enthusiasm became one of the main reasons for the company's rebound. By the end of 1981, problems at the factory had been corrected to the extent that the company felt confident about inviting 85 American dealers over to tour the plant. The dealers were impressed, and the final dinner closed with the dealers pledging to sell 9000 cars — as many as the factory could turn out for the U.S. — in 1982.

These energized dealers went back to America and began making changes of their own. They provided their own money for cooperative advertising. They heralded the return of Jaguar to the American racing circuit, a move calculated to show that the company was not about to go bankrupt. When Jaguars won four races in a year, people began again to be proud to say that they worked for Jaguar. Most importantly, the dealers steered through a legal and financial minefield in an all-out effort to make up for past quality problems and ensure that customers' complaints received prompt, helpful attention. To cap off their emphasis on quality, the company doubled its warranty period to two years.

The company's success is easy to measure. It is now selling seven times as many cars in the U.S. as it was in 1980. Perhaps more importantly, a respected surveyor of customer opinions now ranks Jaguar among the top five in customer satisfaction, when it used to be off the low end of the scale. All this was accomplished not with a big influx of cash nor with a new product, but with a different management attitude. By admitting past mistakes, dealing with problems head on, and getting employees at all levels involved, John Egan and team gave the Jaguar a new life.

Sources: Michael H. Dale, "How We Rebuilt Jaguar in the U.S.," *Fortune*, April 28, 1986, 110. Thomas N. Troxell, Jr., "In Gear Again," *Barron's*, February 3, 1986, 51. David Fairlamb, "Comeback of a Class Car," *Dun's Business Month*, November 1985, 64.

Service as the key to customer satisfaction. *The Marketing Era saw businesses begin to focus on customers. Research to determine consumers' wants, needs, and perceptions was one way to provide more satisfaction. Better service was another. Today the service element is a major consideration in the purchase decision for all kinds of products.*

For instance, in the mid-1980s Douglas Aircraft Company, the commercial aviation division of McDonnell Douglas Corporation, found it could no longer count on airlines to buy for cash what it produced. When sales of its aircraft were at a particularly low point, Douglas came up with the idea of financing its customers' purchases just the way General Motors finances cars through its General Motors Acceptance Corporation (GMAC). Even that innovation was not enough, though, and it has accepted blocks of tickets and even hams in exchange for its jets. Despite the progress Douglas has made, its vice-president for marketing once said, "When it comes to marketing, we are in the Stone Age."[10] That is quite an admission, even if exaggerated, from a company on the leading edge of aerospace technology. However, it is one that many high-tech companies *should* make, because many of them continue to act as if they were in the production era of their business rather than the marketing era. This attitude does much to explain the many business failures in the private sector.

THE FOUR P'S AND THE CONCEPT OF UTILITY

The Elements of the
Marketing Mix

One can look at marketing from either the seller's or the buyer's perspective. Students of marketing have long used the Four P's to summarize the seller's activities and the concept of utility to explain the buyer's actions.

The Marketing Mix

The marketer's major tools that summarize the seller's activities are those called the Four P's:

□ Product strategy
□ Price strategy
□ Place (distribution) strategy
□ Promotion strategy

The Four P's are the variables that marketers can control, unlike the variables in the marketing environment, such as the country's economic condition or the overall demand for what their industry produces.

The recipe that marketers develop for putting these elements together becomes their marketing campaign. The blend varies for each product, so the combination of the Four P's in any strategy is called the **marketing mix**. In the following chapters, we will examine the Four P's in detail. Here we will just sketch each.

Product Strategy   Product strategy calls for much more than just deciding to make a product. Among the crucial issues a manufacturer must face are:

□ Product quality
□ Product features
□ Number of models, sizes, styles, and so on
□ Branding
□ Packaging
□ Labeling

Price Strategy   The major pricing decision is whether to assign a price above, below, or about even with the competitors'. Of course, a firm must consider other factors too, such as product cost, consumer demand, and the need to offer discounts.

Place (Distribution) Strategy   In designing a distribution strategy, a manufacturer focuses primarily on selecting the marketing intermediaries such as wholesalers and retailers. For example, a manufacturer like Black & Decker who sells to Lowe's Companies, Inc., which operates nearly three hundred retail home-center stores, ships to one of Lowe's large distribution centers. There, Lowe's organizes shipments for its stores using its own trucks. Figure 11.4 shows a typical channel of distribution.

FIGURE 11-4

Channel of Distribution

The figure illustrates a single channel of distribution which a consumer products firm might use.

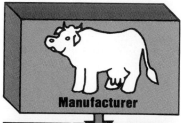
Manufacturer

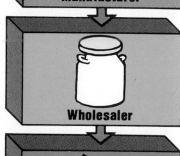
Wholesaler

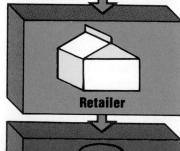
Retailer

Consumer

Promotion Strategy A promotion strategy centers on transmitting information to potential customers. The major forms of promotion are advertising, personal selling, sales promotion, and publicity.

Customer Satisfaction

The Utility of Goods and Services

The purpose of marketing is to "create exchanges that satisfy individual and organizational objectives," according to one definition. The satisfaction that goods and services yield to their buyers is called their **utility**. A purchaser receives satisfaction when the product is in the right form, which is created in the production phase, is available in the right place and at the right time, and provides the satisfaction promised or anticipated from its use. If a product lacks any of these utilities, a potential purchaser probably will not buy it. Marketing bears substantial responsibility for creating each of these utilities.

Form Utility Although production creates much of a product's form utility, marketing influences its form by determining what kinds of products and product attributes the market demands and transmitting that information to production. Suppose that market researchers for a soft-drink company determine that cola drinkers want a softer, sweeter taste than their company's main cola. Their discovery might lead to a new product, as it did at Coca-Cola when it brought out New Coke.

The Four Basic Utilities

Place Utility Marketing has the primary responsibility for creating place utility by arranging for appropriate outlets for the product. Columbia Records, for example, distributes its records and tapes to a variety of outlets, ranging from discounters like Gold Circle Stores to record stores like Strawberry's to mail-order companies like the Columbia Record Club. In contrast, a specialty steel company may itself be the only outlet for its own products.

Time Utility Marketing must also insure time utility by supplying customers with the product when they want it. Marketing's job is to make certain that outlets carry sufficient inventories. Seasonal timing is important, for instance. In most parts of the country, lawn-care products have a limited selling season. Stocking stores with Scott's Turf Builder or grass seed in November makes little sense. At the other extreme, the demand for animal food products continues year-round.

Possession Utility Finally, marketing is responsible for possession utility. It must arrange for the transfer of ownership or title to the goods. In many cases the transfer is no more complicated than putting coins in a vending machine, pressing a button, and retrieving a can or a candy bar. In other cases, the exchange can be quite complicated, as in buying a major item like a home or a car. The real-estate developer or car dealer who simplifies the process for the customer by arranging financing and performing other such services stands a good chance of making the sale.

FIGURE 11-5

Target Market

Target marketing is choosing the particular markets on which marketers will focus their marketing activities.

IDENTIFYING MARKETS

A **market** is a group of people or firms who currently demand or might potentially require a product or service and who have the ability, willingness, and authority to buy it. (See Figure 11.5.) The identification of markets is a critical marketing function because it defines the objects of the company's marketing efforts. Stated broadly, a market might consist of teen-agers or retirees, working women or minorities. More likely, it will be described in terms of "single females from seventeen to twenty-five."

Marketing to Specific Groups

Very few firms can afford to market their products to all consumers or all businesses in the United States. At the same time, few firms would want to, because it is a rare product that is acceptable to all consumers. Until the end of World War II, Coca-Cola was such a product. But today Coca-Cola offers consumers several variations on its original cola formula as well as noncola drinks

Selling to the "New Old"

Marketers have long been interested in the tastes and buying habits of baby boomers. American businesses have been eager to fill the needs and meet the desires of those born in the twenty years after World War II. As the biggest bulge in the American population has grown older, different industries have benefited from the group's buying habits. But now many perceptive marketers have turned their attention to a different group that has been with us for a long time — the baby boomers' parents, the "new old."

Many Americans still retain images of the elderly as being poor and forgotten, barely scraping by on Social Security and Medicare. Unfortunately this description still fits the lives of some, particularly elderly single women, one-sixth of whom live in poverty. But it does not apply to the majority of the over-50 generation.

This group is not particularly large, but it matured and worked in prosperous times. Many of the "new old" came of age during the Second World War and established their careers during the post-war boom when the standard of living rose more than 150 percent. They bought houses — now largely paid for — with low-rate mortgages. They were covered by private pension plans made generous by companies feeling prosperous. And their futures became even brighter when, in 1972, Congress boosted Social Security benefits and protected retirees against cost of living increases by tying future benefit increases to inflation.

For years these workers saved their money or invested it in their houses and their children. Now, for many, all that saving has begun to pay off. The children are grown, the house paid for, and many in what are now called "mature households" find that they have amassed a considerable nest egg.

About one-quarter of all Americans are over 50, and they have about half of the nation's disposable income. A generation ago, the over-50 crowd were known as big savers, salting away about 15 percent of their income. Now the typical mature household spends most of its income, more than $800 billion a year, on goods and services. Income from financial holdings of over-65-year-olds rose 70 percent in the first half of this decade, and the overall wealth of the average American household now peaks when the members are nearing retirement age.

The tremendous buying power of the new old has begun to intrigue marketing experts around the country. But the group is not necessarily easy to target. Many older people don't like to be reminded of their age and are therefore likely to reject products and sales pitches directed at the elderly. Advertisers have found that commercials need to feature characters who look 5 to 15 years younger than the intended audience. One advertising executive said of using the elderly in ads, "it's easier to sell with just about any other image."

Companies that haven't been able to reach the senior age group with traditional mass-marketing techniques have developed a variety of special approaches. Sears, Roebuck, & Co., the nation's largest retailer, has enrolled over 400,000 members in its Mature Outlook Club, started in 1984. For a small yearly membership fee, club members get discounts of up to 25 percent on a variety of Sears's goods and services, from garden tools to financial advice. Airlines and hotels are trying to lure older customers with special deals: for $2300 a year, a 65-year-old can fly around the country on Eastern and stay in Hilton hotels.

Those who are catering to the elderly don't need to worry about this newly discovered market suddenly disappearing. Companies that are testing and perfecting their marketing techniques now can expect to profit for a long time to come, for by the turn of the century, baby boomers will be starting to retire, and 76 million Americans will be over 49.

Sources: Peter Petre, "Marketers Mine for Gold in the Old," *Fortune*, March 31, 1986, 70. Paul B. Brown, "Last Year It Was Yuppies — This Year It's Their Parents," *Business Week*, March 10, 1986, 68. Joan Berger, "'The New Old': Where the Economic Action Is," *Business Week*, November 25, 1985, 138.

like Minute Maid Orange Juice. Most firms must choose specific groups of customers on which to focus their marketing efforts.

Market Segmentation   The total market can be subdivided, in a process called market segmentation, into smaller groups of consumers based on identifiable common characteristics or segmentation variables. See Figure 11.6.

Segmentation variables are usually classified under four headings. **Geographic variables** include regions, counties, cities, and climate areas. The most likely purchasers of snow blowers, for instance, are suburban and rural residents in the snow belt. **Demographic variables** include age, sex, family size, income, occupation, education, religion, race, nationality, and social class. Families with children under three are likely to buy diapers; families with children in college are not. **Behavioral variables** include lifestyle, personality, product-usage rate, and loyalty. An average Ford Escort owner and an average Porsche 911 Carrera owner respond quite differently to the cost of auto accessories. **Benefit variables** include economy, convenience, and prestige. A two-career couple is more likely to buy convenience foods, like Stouffer's frozen entrees, than couples in which one partner does not have an outside job.

The Four Market Segmentation Variables

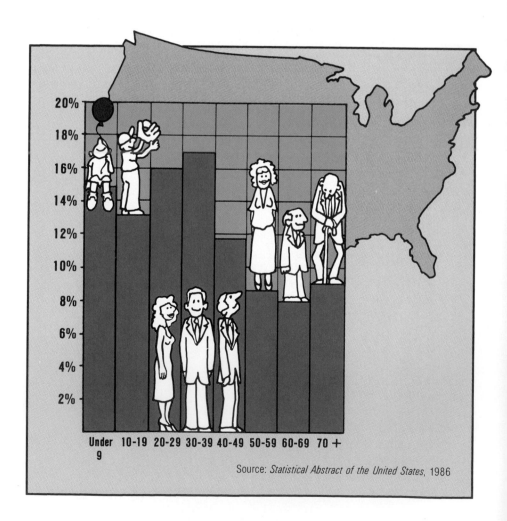

FIGURE 11-6

Market Segmentation

Market segmentation involves dividing the total market into smaller groups of consumers based on identifiable common characteristics called segmentation variables.

Source: *Statistical Abstract of the United States,* 1986

Differentiated marketing can mean a lot of different ads. *Coca-Cola used to be aimed at everyone. Not any more. Not only does the company sell several kinds of soft drinks, but its advertising campaigns are aimed at specific markets. This ad, targeted at Spanish-speaking consumers, will run in regions that have sizable Hispanic populations.*

The Key Elements of Consumer Behavior

Target Marketing   Once marketers have identified several market segments, they are ready to launch the process of **target marketing**, choosing the particular markets on which they will focus their marketing activities.

To qualify as a target market, a segment must be measurable. If marketers cannot measure the number of potential buyers and their income levels, for example, they may not know whether the market segment is worth pursuing. The segments must also be accessible by the firm's marketing program. Advertising in *South Florida Home & Garden* magazine would not reach a main market for New England winter vacations. Even if the advertising reaches the right segment, however, the advertiser must have the capability of delivering its products or services. If zoning laws prohibit fast-food restaurants in a certain section of a city, it does not matter how many residents might potentially patronize a Wendy's in that area. Finally, the target segments must be large enough to be potentially profitable.

Marketers choose from three principal types of strategies in developing target markets. The first, **undifferentiated marketing**, really does not qualify as target marketing because it consists of a single strategy aimed at the total market. **Differentiated marketing** consists of individualized appeals aimed at particular market segments. The pain reliever market can be subdivided into customers who do or do not want aspirin. Consequently we have Bayer Aspirin and Tylenol. **Concentrated marketing** consists of a single strategy aimed at one specific market segment. Maximum Strength Tylenol is targeted at people who seek fast relief of sinus headache and congestion.

Consumer Behavior

Most effective marketing decisions are based on a thorough knowledge of consumer behavior. Gaining that knowledge requires marketers to find out how and why consumers make buying decisions. Just knowing what products are selling today and to whom is not enough — marketers have to predict tomorrow.

Although sociologists and psychologists still have much to learn about consumer behavior, a wealth of knowledge does exist to guide marketers. For example, researchers have identified two categories of primary buying motives. **Rational buying motives** include the desire for dependability, durability, efficiency, financial gain, and economy. Commercial banks rely on rational buying motives in their promotions. **Emotional buying motives** include the wish for social approval, a desire to be different, and a need to be free of fear. Quite often, consumers make purchases based on a combination of rational and emotional motives. Marketers must determine the most relevant motives for their products, incorporate into the product the features that appeal to those motives, and focus their promotional strategies on appeals to those motives. Toothpaste ads often appeal to both rational and emotional motives. Many consumers want clean teeth so they can avoid seeing the dentist, and also want to be popular and attractive.

Market Data

Marketers must have timely marketing information on a variety of issues such as consumer behavior, market characteristics, competitors' activities, potential substitute products, and other environmental factors. Interpreting and, when necessary, adding to the vast array of data that marketers need requires a marketing information system and marketing research.

Marketing Information Systems A **marketing information system (MIS)** is a combination of people, equipment, and procedures organized to gather, process, and disperse information needed for making marketing decisions.

The sophistication of a firm's MIS will depend on the size of the firm and its management's perception of the importance of marketing information in its overall decision making. A large firm may have a mainframe computer dedicated to its MIS, but smaller firms often do not even have a structured MIS. Their MIS may be in random file folders or in someone's head. With the availability of powerful, low-cost personal computers, small firms can now afford to develop MISs that large firms could not have had thirty years ago.

Wrangler Womenswear, a division of Blue Bell, Inc., recently outfitted its entire sales force with portable computers. Sales representatives can place orders, update data files, and transmit memoranda and letters by telephone from the road. Better yet, the computer gives them instant access to home-office files. Now salespeople can give customers "while you wait" information about pricing and style and quantity availability. Thus, Wrangler's hundred sales representatives can avoid the annoying situation of taking an order and then, weeks later, having to tell less-than-thrilled customers that what they wanted is unavailable.[11]

Market Research When a firm's MIS does not contain the necessary information, its decision makers may have to initiate **market research**, the systematic gathering and analyzing of data on a particular marketing problem. The topics of market research might range from whether customers perceive a beer to taste great or to be less filling to sophisticated psychological evaluations of an advertising campaign's effectiveness.

A market research project involves five distinct steps:

☐ Defining the problem
☐ Developing a hypothesis
☐ Collecting data
☐ Interpreting the findings
☐ Reporting the findings

Data comes either from primary sources, an interview with a potential customer, or secondary sources, like published reports and library materials. Researchers should start with internal secondary sources, data the firm already has. This information is usually readily available and inexpensive. Gathering new information from outside the firm is a last resort because it is time consuming, difficult, and expensive.

The Importance of Marketing Information Systems

Finding out what people want. Market researchers are an important element in Campbell Soup Company's business. Knowing what people need and want has helped the firm maintain the popularity of its old brands and develop new products for today's lifestyles. Here a market researcher conducts a survey at a supermarket.

CONSUMER AND INDUSTRIAL MARKETS

Most of what we are discussing applies to both consumer and industrial markets. However, the two markets are different enough to consider separately.

The Invention Is Just the Beginning

Americans have long loved inventors and inventions. However, we often don't hear about the difficulty inventors had producing or benefiting from their inventions, or about the thousands of brilliant ideas that never left the inventor's lab because the inventor had no knack for business or publicity.

That's something that Kevin Keating learned the hard way. Kevin got his great idea while selling light-socket diodes for his brother's company. Because they transform alternating current into direct current, which is easier on the bulb's filament, the diodes extend the life of the light bulb and reduce the power it consumes. Unfortunately they also cut the light output of the bulb and can create shock and fire hazards. Kevin's idea: build the diode into the bulb, where it won't create a hazard.

Sure that he had a great idea, Keating enlisted a mechanical engineer to design the bulb and a business expert to create a business plan. Convinced the idea was feasible, he began a long search for someone to make the bulbs and for money to get the business going. Two years after his idea, and with all the elements assembled, Keating thought he was ready.

His product looked attractive. The bulb cost about seven times as much as a conventional bulb, but lasted about 60 times as long. It did produce less light per watt, making it somewhat less of a bargain, but it seemed the answer to every maintenance worker who dreamed of some way to avoid having to climb long ladders, risking life and limb to change a bulb in a chandelier or a vaulted ceiling every couple of months. DioLight's first bulb was made for exit signs which are supposed to burn 24 hours a day and therefore use up a lot of conventional bulbs.

But the bulb didn't sell. At first the company tried approaching people who would use the bulbs themselves and benefit from them directly. The response of many building managers and restaurant owners was skepticism. They were wary of paying $6 for a bulb from a company they'd never heard of, and they thought if the idea really worked, GE would have come up with it. DioLight was only a little more successful at selling directly to big corporations, who generally buy such things from a distributor. Initially the DioLight sales force didn't approach the distributors directly because they figured that distributors would buy only from the major light bulb manufacturers. Perceptive distributors would certainly see that selling one DioLight bulb might lose them sales of 60 conventional bulbs. But the company did offer distributors a much higher per-bulb profit, and the company's first big break came when three New York distributors ordered 15,000 bulbs.

The company might still be floundering along from one such sale to the next if it hadn't realized that even if people weren't ready to *buy* the bulb, they would probably be ready to *read* or *hear* about it. Keating began sending out press releases. A small story in the *Detroit Free Press* caught the eye of a correspondent for the Cable News Network, who did a feature on the company that aired at the time of the Republican National Convention. That story got the snowball rolling, and soon Keating was being interviewed by radio stations and featured in articles from *Newsweek* to *High Technology*.

The company still has less than a 1 percent share of the light bulb market, but it's selling more than half a million bulbs a year and getting more customers every day. It has tried to keep the public's attention by calling its bulb "Forever" and guaranteeing it for eternity. "With that kind of product, it's all just marketing," scoffs a competitor. And in fact another company has been making a 20,000-hour light bulb for 15 years without getting the kind of national attention that DioLight now has. But, as Kevin Keating learned, "just" marketing is no small matter. Realizing that the idea is only the first step, and capitalizing on the public's love of inventions and gimmicks helped Keating turn what could have been just another good idea into something that really shines.

Sources: Tom Richman, "How Do You Sell a Light Bulb That Never Burns Out?" *Inc.*, March 1986, 90. N. R. Kleinfield, "An Eternal Light in Every Socket," *New York Times*, March 16, 1986, F11. Glen Macnow, "A Bright Idea That Makes Waves," *Nation's Business*, November 1985, 79.

"Excuse me, Ma'am, could you please tell me if Spurt is a toothpaste, a detergent, or a breakfast cereal?"

Customers in the consumer market purchase goods and services for their own personal use or for the use of someone in their household. Anything you take off the shelf and put in your grocery cart is a consumer good. Customers in industrial markets purchase goods and services to use in the manufacture of other products. The steel that went into your grocery cart was an industrial product. Since the reasons for buying are different in each major market, marketers must adopt individual strategies to attract buyers in each.

Consumer Products

Goods and services purchased in the consumer market are **consumer products**. Consumer goods are classified into three categories, each of which requires a distinct marketing strategy based on the effort consumers are likely to be willing to exert to find the product.

Convenience Goods Products that consumers purchase frequently, generally at low prices, and for which they are willing to spend only a minimum of effort in completing the exchange are **convenience goods**. Milk, bread, newspapers, soft drinks, and chewing gum are common examples. The marketers of convenience goods must, therefore, maintain competitive prices, distribute their products through many retail outlets, and center their promotional efforts on constant reminders to shoppers.

Shopping Goods Typical **shopping goods** are purchased infrequently, have a relatively high unit price, and are bought only after comparison with other product alternatives. For example, homeowners needing a new lawnmower generally visit several stores to learn what features are available and to find the machine they want at an appropriate price. The may also consider the availability of service where they buy.

Specialty Goods Products for which consumers develop a strong preference and loyalty are called **specialty goods**. Generally, price is not a major consideration in the decision to buy these goods. Consumers are willing to spend a great deal of effort to locate them. For example, some consumers may buy only Curtis Mathes Corporation televisions and will search their area until they locate a dealer.

Industrial Products

An **industrial product**, as noted earlier, is one that is used in the production of another good or service. Essentially, any product not for personal or household consumption is an industrial product. The electronic control in a production robot is an industrial product, as is the label on an audio cassette.

Industrial products. Industrial products are used to produce another good or service. They can be raw materials, component parts, or goods and services used to run the business. Long-distance phone service is purchased by consumers and by businesses, but the needs of the two markets are often very different.

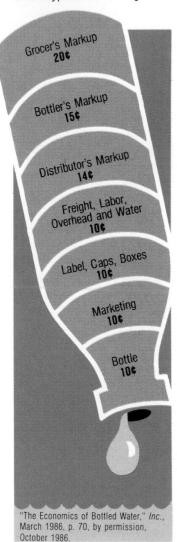

FIGURE 11-7

Bottled Water

Today bottled waters sell at the rate of a billion gallons per year. This figure shows where the $.89 a typical liter costs goes.

Grocer's Markup
20¢

Bottler's Markup
15¢

Distributor's Markup
14¢

Freight, Labor, Overhead and Water
10¢

Label, Caps, Boxes
10¢

Marketing
10¢

Bottle
10¢

"The Economics of Bottled Water," *Inc.*, March 1986, p. 70, by permission, October 1986.

Unique Market Features The industrial market is different from the consumer market in several ways. Perhaps the most important distinction is that the demand for industrial products is **derived demand**; that is, the demand for them is caused by the demand for other products. For example, the demand for American car radios depends largely on the number of automobiles American auto assemblers produce. As Toyota captures a larger share of car sales, American firms that make car radios sell fewer of them.

Industrial markets are also more concentrated than consumer markets — there are fewer firms than people. Also, there are concentrations of similar types of manufacturing in particular localities. The two most famous areas today are the high-tech concentrations on Route 128 around Boston and in the so-called Silicon Valley outside San Francisco. Of course, industrial products are also usually ordered in far larger quantities and in far larger dollar amounts than are consumer products. For that reason and because of both the buyer's and the seller's corporate bureaucracies, the purchasing process for industrial markets is considerably more complex — and more carefully planned.

Overlap It is important to note that a specific product can, under different circumstances, be both a consumer and an industrial good. For instance, a video cassette recorder bought for home use is a consumer good, whereas an identical recorder bought to show training tapes to Toys "Я" Us employees is an industrial product.

MARKETING'S COSTS AND BENEFITS

Justifying marketing costs requires an evaluation of marketing's benefits. In conclusion, let's look at two major costs of marketing: distribution and promotion.

As we have seen, middlemen operate the channels of distribution. In periods of escalating prices, people often claim that eliminating middlemen would reduce the final price of goods. However, the middleman significantly reduces the costs and time involved in the transactions. As the number of transactions increases, the advantages of using a middleman increase dramatically as we will see in Chapter 13.

As already noted, these transactions also provide information to the firms involved about what their customers and consumers generally want. Promoting the product can result in a larger number of customers learning of the product. When customers use the product regularly, the product unit cost is reduced, allowing a lower price for each customer. Take, for instance, the bottled-water industry. In the mid-1970s, only "health nuts" bought it, and then they bought mineral water. Today, bottled waters sell at the rate of a billion gallons per year. That is a lot of Perrier, Poland Springs, Polar seltzer water, and the like. Figure 11.7 shows where the $.89 typical cost for a liter goes. In this chapter, we have looked at many of the factors that account for the markups: product development, market analysis, and inventory carrying charges, among others. In the chapters that follow, we will look intensively at additional aspects of pricing and at the other costs listed on the bottle.

Chapter Highlights

1. Define marketing and describe the functions it performs.

Marketing is the process of planning and executing the conception, pricing, promotion, and distribution of ideas, goods, and services to create exchanges that satisfy individual and organizational objectives. Marketing performs eight basic functions: selling, financing, collecting and analyzing market information, transporting, storing, grading and standardization, buying, and assuming risks.

2. Outline the evolution of marketing.

The production era (from 1860 to 1920) was characterized by an excess of demand over supply. The marketer's main jobs were taking and filling orders. During the sales era (from 1920 to 1950), the primary focus of marketing was on advertising and selling. During the marketing era, which began in the early 1950s, the focus shifted to the marketing concept, which has as its central premise the idea that the ultimate purpose of every business should be providing customer satisfaction. The marketing concept is characterized by a consumer orientation backed by integrated marketing aimed at generating customer satisfaction as the key to achieving organizational goals.

3. Identify and characterize the elements of the marketing mix.

The four elements of the marketing mix are strategies to deal with product, price, place, and promotion. Product strategy involves decisions about quality, features, number of styles and sizes, branding, and packaging. Price strategy deals with how a seller will price his product in relation to market and demand. Place strategy concerns the distribution of a good or service. Producers and marketing intermediaries must develop a marketing channel, decide who will sell the product to the end-user, and determine how the product will move along the channel. Promotion strategy centers on advertising, personal selling, sales promotion, and publicity.

4. Identify and contrast the four basic types of utilities.

The four utilities are: form, place, time, and possession. Form utility, e.g., design, color, or size, means that what is offered is what the customer wants, place utility means that a product is where a buyer wants it, time utility means that the product is available when the buyer wants it, and possession utility focuses on the ease with which ownership can be transferred.

5. Explain the relationship between market segmentation and target markets and describe how marketers identify target markets.

Market segmentation is the process of dividing a large market into smaller groups at which a marketing program can be aimed. Market segments must be measurable, accessible, and substantial. They are generally classified according to their geographic, demographic, behavioral, and benefit variables.

6. Describe the key elements of consumer behavior and buying motives.

Consumer decisions are generally based on rational buying motives (which include the desire for dependability, durability, efficiency, financial gain, and the like) and emotional buying motives (the desire for such things as social approval, the wish to be different, and freedom from fear). Most purchase decisions are based on a combination of rational and emotional buying motives.

7. Explain the importance of market information and market research.

Marketing information and marketing research are key elements in the marketing concept. Only by keeping abreast of consumer wants and needs can marketers hope to deliver what the consumer wants — when, where, and how the consumer wants it.

8. Distinguish between consumer products and industrial products.

Consumer products are goods and services purchased in the consumer market for personal use or for the use of someone in the buyer's household. An industrial product is a good or service used to produce another good or service. Some items can be either a consumer or an industrial product, depending on its final use.

9. Evaluate the costs and benefits of marketing.

Marketing costs claim about half the buyer's dollar, but the services that marketing provides are essential. Marketing increases the efficiency of the exchange process, raises consumer satisfaction, and leads to the development of products that satisfy consumer wants and needs.

Key Terms

Behavioral variables
Benefit variables
Concentrated
  marketing
Convenience goods
Customer orientation
Demographic variables
Derived demand
Differentiated
  marketing
Discretionary income

Emotional buying
  motives
Facilitating agent
Four P's
Geographic variables
Grading
Industrial product
Integrated Marketing
Intermediaries
Market

Market research
Market segmentation
Marketers
Marketing
Marketing concept
Marketing information
  system (MIS)
Marketing mix
Middlemen
Organizational goals

Rational buying
  motives
Shopping goods
Specialty goods
Standardization
Target marketing
Trade credit
Undifferentiated
  marketing
Utility

Review Questions

1. What is marketing? What major functions does marketing perform? Analyze each of them.
2. What are the elements of the marketing mix? Define each element.
3. Define *utility*. Describe the four basic types of utilities.
4. What is a market?
5. Define *market segmentation*. By what criteria do marketers segment markets?
6. How do marketers target markets? What are the characteristics of the three types of target marketing?
7. Why is a knowledge of consumer behavior important?
8. Distinguish rational from emotional buying motives.
9. List the benefits of a marketing information system.
10. What are the benefits of market research? Describe the process by which market research is conducted.
11. Distinguish consumer products from industrial products.
12. Characterize each of the classifications of consumer goods.
13. What is the key characteristic of an industrial market?
14. Identify the principal marketing eras and specify the main characteristics of each.
15. What is a marketing concept? How is it implemented?

Application Exercises

1. Recently you were selected to serve as chairperson of the promotion committee for a celebrity golf tournament. The tournament will match several well-known celebrities from your state against the best local golfers. Tickets will sell for $25 per person and your goal is to attract a large gallery of fans. All proceeds will be given to a local charity. As you develop a promotion plan, what segmentation variables would be most important? What buying motives would you appeal to?
2. Develop a marketing plan for a new lawn care service that will be offered to residents of a three-county area. As you prepare this plan, consider these questions:
   a. What market information will be needed?
   b. How will you collect appropriate market information?

Cases

11.1 Marketing for Hospitals

Traditionally, hospital administrators have considered marketing (which they equated with advertising) to be unnecessary and somehow inappropriate to their profession. But in the late 1970s they began to turn to advertising as a means of dealing with rising costs, increasing competition, and empty beds. These first efforts were decidedly unsuccessful in attracting patients. Hospitals began to advertise before they knew what they had to advertise.

Now, however, many hospitals are doing at least some basic market research. They are also attempting to expand existing services and develop new services to accommodate their markets. Their new offerings range from home health care for elderly outpatients to valet parking and room service for more affluent inpatients. One large obstetrics hospital has opened a downtown maternity clothing store, where it also holds classes for prospective parents. Hospital officials see the store as a natural extension of their patient services.

Hospitals still have the problem of deciding where to direct their marketing efforts: to physicians, who usually choose a hospital for their patients; to patients, who receive the hospital's "product"; to insurance firms, which usually pay for it; or to some combination of the three.

Questions

1. Has the marketing concept finally penetrated the health care industry? Explain.
2. To whom should hospitals market their services; why?

Sources: For more information see *Hospitals,* June 5, 1986, pp. 50–55 and 66–67; *Marketing & Media Decisions,* April 1986, pp. 96–101; and *Healthcare Financial Management,* May 1984, pp. 62.

11.2 Not Just Desserts

Since 1921, Reuben Mattus's family had produced hand-turned ice cream for local consumption. Theirs was one of dozens of small firms vying for distribution in New York City's neighborhoods. By the time Reuben took over the business, the competition was fierce; it got worse in the 1950s, when the large ice cream manufacturers began to use their economic power to drive small local firms out of supermarkets.

Mattus decided he'd had enough of that kind of competition, and he searched for something that would get him out of it. What he came up with, in 1960, was the first of the so-called "super-premium" ice creams — twice as rich as mass-produced ice cream, and made with only natural ingredients.

Because he believed that the Danish made superior ice cream, Mattus made up a danish-sounding name for his product: Häagen-Dazs. He also gave it a high price betting that there were plenty of people who would pay more for a quality product with a foreign-sounding name.

He was right. At first he had trouble getting local supermarkets to carry Häagen-Dazs, because they didn't believe people would pay the price. Mattus refused to advertise his product, because he didn't trust advertising. But his persistence and a higher-than-usual markup convinced some supermarkets to carry it, and word-of-mouth advertising convinced the rest. Competitors soon followed Mattus's lead; the market for super-premium ice cream now is estimated at $2 billion annually, and growing by about 25 percent each year.

Questions

1. How did Reuben Mattus identify the market for Häagen-Dazs ice cream? How did he satisfy that market?
2. Describe and evaluate the Häagen-Dazs marketing mix.

Sources: For more information see *Business Week,* June 30, 1986, pp. 60–61; *Marketing & Media Decisions,* June 1986, pp. 38–46; *The New Yorker,* July 8, 1985, pp. 31–45; and *Fortune,* March 9,

12

PRODUCT AND PRICING STRATEGIES

Learning Objectives

After you have completed this chapter, you will be able to do the following:

■ Describe the new-product development process.

■ Explain the product life cycle concept.

■ Identify the functions of branding, packaging, and labeling.

■ Describe the role of pricing in the marketing mix.

■ List the potential pricing objectives for a product.

■ Describe the principal pricing methods.

■ Identify the pricing strategies available for both new products and those already on the market.

To many people in the business world, Mercedes-Benz represents the ultimate example of a company that has developed effective product and pricing strategies. First, let's look at the product. Many automotive journalists and historians believe that Mercedes-Benz automobiles are the best engineered cars in the world. Owners of these expensive cars do not disagree. Owner loyalty to the marque remains extremely high in markets throughout the world. Secondly, let's look at sales. For all practical purposes, the company sells every car that rolls off the production line. In America, consumers pay anywhere from $25,000 to $60,000 for the privilege of driving the car adorned by the three-pointed star. Many years ago the company made a decision to adopt a *prestige pricing* policy for exports to America. This psychological pricing strategy will be discussed later in this chapter.

PRODUCT STRATEGY

A **product** is a good, a service, an idea, or any combination of the three that may be the subject of an exchange.

When you stop at an Exxon station, the gas you buy is a *good*, a tangible item of personal property. (The name *Exxon* as it appears on the pump is a type of intangible personal property called a **trademark**, a legally protected name or design used to identify a product.) Signs announcing a special on Exxon batteries are part of a nationwide advertising campaign that an agency sold Exxon. An advertising campaign is an **idea** — a concept, a philosophy, an image, or an issue.[1] Suppose you ask the mechanic on duty to check a knock in your engine. The mechanic spends fifteen minutes adjusting your spark plugs and charges you $10. That work is a **service**, the performing of labor or duties by one person at another's request. Had the mechanic installed new spark plugs, he or she would have sold you both a service — installing the plugs — and goods — the plugs.

Developing New Products

The Need for New Products

Successful firms must maintain a line of products that meets their customers' needs and wants. Firms that do not continually improve what they sell find their products replaced with their competitors'. The standardized TV dinners of the 1950s lost much supermarket space to frozen entrees aimed at specific market segments: Budget Gourmet dinners for the value conscious, Lean Cuisine for the weight conscious, and Armour Dinner Classics for the status conscious.

Markets are rarely static, and businesses cannot be either. A well-planned **new-product development process**, the six-step procedure for testing, developing, and selling a product (see Figure 12.1), reduces the risk of falling behind the competition. It also holds out the promise of achieving a competitive advantage.

Phase 1: Idea Generation

The New-Product Development Process

In the present context, an idea is the starting point of the new-product development process. An idea is just a product concept that does not have a concrete

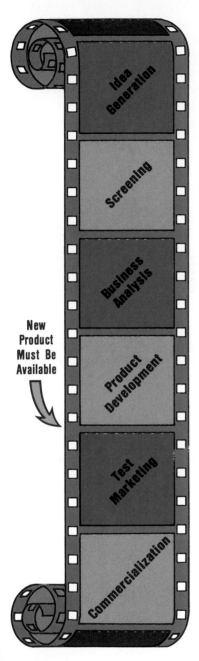

FIGURE 12-1

The New Product Development Process

A well-planned new product development process, the six step process for testing, developing, and selling a product reduces the risks of falling behind the competition.

New Product Must Be Available

form. Businesses should develop a logical strategy for generating as many product ideas as possible. Even the most illogical sounding idea, like contact lenses for chickens, may bring big payoffs. It is hard to believe that such a product made money for its inventor, Robert Garrison. The lenses stop the birds from pecking each other. Contact lenses not only save chicken farmers the cost of debeaking their birds but also increase the productivity of the flocks.[2]

Firms should encourage suggestions for new products. Excellent ideas can come from customers, salespeople, secretaries, janitors, competitors, and others. The more ideas a firm can generate, the better the chances are that one can be commercialized, the final stage of new-product development. As one study indicates, it takes approximately seven ideas to generate one commercial success, which is a substantial improvement over the 1968 rate of one out of every fifty-eight ideas.[3] And it can be a long time between the birth of an idea and its commercialization — five years in the case of a new car model, for instance.[4]

Phase 2: Screening

In the screening phase of the new-product development process, a firm sifts the good ideas from the bad. Companies should develop decision criteria to eliminate ideas that have little promise, do not relate to customer satisfaction, or do not fit their objectives or resources.

Phase 3: Business Analysis

In the business analysis phase, the firm studies the proposed product's potential costs and revenues. It also closely examines how the new product will mesh with existing products, pricing policies, distribution channels, and promotional resources. Researchers may solicit potential customers' reactions to the idea. The business analysis phase can thus be seen as a continuation of the screening phase. Only the criteria used are more precise. For example, Frito Lay's O'Grady Potato Chips required that the company buy bigger cutters and sort its potatoes, so the chip would have a unique texture and taste.

Phase 4: Product Development

A firm can take an idea through the first three phases without actually producing anything. In the product-development phase, however, the firm begins to give the idea real form. Researchers will develop and test prototypes against the customer's needs and wants and the company's ability to engineer and manufacture the product. Product development may require up to 40 percent of the time it takes to turn an idea into a commercial product.

Many firms and inventors make the mistake of skipping the screening and business analysis stages and begin their new-product development process at this point. They do not take advantage of the opportunities offered by the earlier phases to focus on what customers want and need. Without question, this failure leads to the introduction of products that have no profitable commercial future.

Turning ideas into reality. Research and development often requires highly trained specialists and sophisticated equipment. This scientist at Memorex is using a high-power electron microscope to analyze magnetic recording materials. Memorex, a division of Burroughs Corp., also makes floppy disks. Research is a particularly important function in high-tech companies.

Phase 5: Test Marketing

Once the product is ready from a business and engineering standpoint, the company may begin limited production. The manufactured product is then sold in **test markets**. Sales are carefully audited in order to gain an insight into the behavior of the entire market. Among the most popular test markets for consumer products are Columbus, Ohio; Peoria, Illinois; and San Diego, California. The test-marketing results can lead to product or packaging refinements. The Adolf Coors Company's test marketing of its light beer revealed that consumers confused light Coors with regular Coors because of their similar labels. So when Coors officially introduced its new beer, Coors Light came in distinctive "silver bullet" cans.

Prolonged test marketing is a danger. The Procter & Gamble Company, which historically has intensively test marketed products, should have cut short its eighteen-month test marketing of Duncan Hines crisp and chewy chocolate chip cookies. By the time this product went national, Nabisco Brands, Inc., and the Keebler Co., Inc., had established competing products.[5] Some products are not test marketed at all, however, because their manufacturers believe they would lose a competitive advantage by revealing their products too early.

Phase 6: Commercialization

Only a very few products reach the final phase, commercialization. If the results of the test marketing are positive, the firm will then introduce the product to the entire market. A good introductory marketing program can make all the difference. When Coca-Cola introduced Diet Coke, it rented Radio City Music Hall and had well-known actors and actresses endorse the new product. Many feel that diet Coke captured a greater market share than it would have without this spectacular introduction. Still, it is unlikely that Diet Coke would have shared the fate of seven out of ten new products: failure.[6]

THE PRODUCT LIFE CYCLE

Another key marketing concept, the product life cycle, highlights the importance of a good introduction for the product.

The Basic Stages

The **product life cycle** assumes that products have lives with four identifiable stages: introduction, growth, maturity, and decline. As Figure 12.2 illustrates, a product's sales or revenues determine its life cycle. The length of each stage can vary dramatically from product to product. For example, Procter & Gamble's Ivory Soap has been in its mature phase for almost a century. By contrast, the mature phase of the Osborne computer, the first successful portable, lasted less than a year.

As you study the product life cycle, keep in mind that it is just a convenient way to classify where products are today and what happened to others in the past. Ivory Soap and the Osborne computer prove that the product life cycle is

FIGURE 12-2

The Product Life Cycle

The product life cycle assumes products have lives with four identifiable stages: introduction, growth, maturity, and decline.

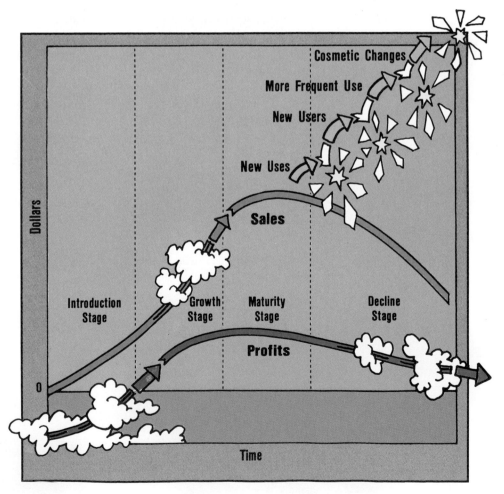

not a tool for predicting the future. In 1879, would Harley Procter, the brand's creator, have predicted Ivory would still be a top seller in the 1980s? In 1979, would anyone have predicted that Osborne Computer would be out of business by 1984?

The Four Stages of the Product Life Cycle

The Introduction Stage In the **introduction stage** of the product life cycle, the product is first brought to market. The introduction period varies in length from product to product. As might be expected, the major characteristic of this period is low sales and high costs per unit. High fixed costs continue until the sales volume picks up. The initial expenses associated with arranging appropriate channels of distribution can be quite high. Promotion costs are also quite high, both in terms of the number of dollars spent and as a percentage of sales. All these factors keep profits in this stage low or nonexistent.

The Growth Stage This stage begins when sales start to increase rapidly and ends when sales begin to level off. During the **growth stage**, early buyers

Choosing a promotion strategy. Sometimes a product appeals to a customer's dreams. By featuring real musicians in its ads, Yamaha hoped that its product and today's musical stars would be linked in the minds of potential customers. The company's ads could feed young player's dreams; Yamaha dealers could supply the facts about each guitar.

The Perils of Packaging

Until a few years ago, most people who created new ways to package goods worried about whether a new container would make the product stand out and attract customers, whether it would keep the product in good condition, and whether it would save the company time or money. Then, in 1982, the business of packaging changed, probably forever. Seven people in the Chicago area died from taking Tylenol capsules contaminated with cyanide. Suddenly, the key word in the packaging world became "safety."

The activity that followed the Chicago deaths resulted in the bewildering and sometimes frustrating variety of tamper-resistant packages that continue to be manufactured and improved today. Such a variety has evolved because industry and government experts agree that no one is likely to come up with a package so perfect that it will foil even the most clever and deranged tamperers. Unable to develop a truly "tamper-proof" container, manufacturers keep experimenting with ways to make packages more tamper-resistant.

Johnson & Johnson, the manufacturers of Tylenol, came up with a three-part seal on its packages of Tylenol capsules. The flaps of the outer box were glued together, a plastic seal was put around the top of the bottle itself, and a foil seal was placed across the mouth of the bottle.

Johnson & Johnson's effort to recapture worried consumers worked in 1982. Tylenol regained its place in the market — about one in every three people looking for minor pain relief would buy it. Other companies came up with their own packaging, the scare gradually died away, and some manufacturers even began promoting their improved packages as a reason to buy their product.

Then, in February 1986, a young woman from New York died from the cyanide in a capsule of Tylenol she had taken. A few days later a similarly contaminated Tylenol bottle was found in a different store near the victim's home. Johnson & Johnson was faced with another crisis. In 1982 the company had rewon public confidence by trying to appear open and honest about the tampering and by agreeing to give consumers new, tamper-resistant bottles of Tylenol in exchange for their old ones.

In 1986 the company used many of the same tactics to reassure consumers. But after a week of agonizing about how to save a product that brought in almost half a billion dollars a year, Johnson & Johnson's management decided to change not the outer packaging, but the form of the Tylenol itself. It ended production of capsules and tried to persuade capsule lovers — about 30 percent of Tylenol consumers — to switch to "caplets." These hybrids of tablets and capsules had already been attracting 22 percent of all Tylenol customers. But Johnson & Johnson worried that people who preferred capsules would switch to products of competitors who had not followed J & J's lead into caplets.

It will be some years before Johnson & Johnson knows whether it made the right decision — to change the packaging of the smallest unit of its product rather than of whole bottles. But while the pharmaceutical giant waits and hopes, other companies are learning from Johnson & Johnson's crisis, trying to make their products even safer before they, too, encounter a problem.

Manufacturers who didn't want to give up capsules have developed ways of sealing the capsules so they can't be reopened without being destroyed. Most vacuum-packed products now come with pop-up lids to alert consumers if the container has already been opened. And foods that aren't vacuum-packed like mayonnaise and peanut butter have begun appearing with their own plastic neck seals.

Perhaps some creative entrepreneur of the future will come up with the perfect container, and packaging experts will go back to worrying about how to make their products more eye-catching. But for now, many of the most creative minds in one branch of American industry will spend much of their time trying to outwit a few demented people.

Sources: Bill Powell, "The Tylenol Rescue," *Newsweek*, March 3, 1986, 52. Cindy Skrzycki, "Tampering with Buyers' Confidence," *U.S. News & World Report*, March 3, 1986, 46. Michael Waldholz, "For Tylenol's Manufacturer, the Dilemma Is to Be Aggressive — but Not Appear Pushy," *Wall Street Journal*, February 20, 1986, 27.

repurchase the product and new ones enter the market. Distributors begin to seek out the product, so distribution expenses decline. As more and more potential purchasers become aware of the product, the firm may be able to reduce promotion expenditures. Because sales are increasing, promotion expenses as a percentage of sales have probably already declined significantly. In fact, the marketing costs of generating sales should generally decline. These factors should lead to decreasing fixed costs per unit and thus to greater profits.

In this stage, demand sometimes overwhelms manufacturers, who may find that they simply cannot produce what the stores can sell. For some months after they were introduced, both the Chrysler Caravan and the Ford Taurus/Mercury Sable caused this problem for their manufacturers. To a lesser degree, 3M could not initially meet demand for its "Post-it" message pads.

Strong demand for a new product may not seem like much of a problem, but when competitors sense a profit to be made they look for ways to enter the market. A business with a successful new product should prepare for competition during the growth stage by developing a **product differentiation strategy**, a program designed to give a product distinctive characteristics that can serve as competitive advantages over similar products in the maturity stage of the product life cycle. A never-ending flow of variations, such as Classic Coke, Diet Coke, and Cherry Coke has kept the Coca-Cola Co. on top of the soft drink market.

The Maturity Stage   The **maturity stage** of the product life cycle begins when sales start to level off and ends when they eventually begin to decline. During the maturity stage, sales are fairly high. They peak sharply or remain relatively stable for a long time. Competition can become intense as firms fight to keep their products alive. When this occurs, promotion expenses will increase and prices often decline. This combination puts the squeeze on profits, and marginal producers will begin leaving the market. However, the stage can be very profitable for those companies that remain.

The Decline Stage   The **decline stage** of the product life cycle begins when sales begin to decrease and normally ends with the firm abandoning the product. Decreasing sales lead to decreasing profits and eventually to losses. If the firm cannot devise a way to revive sales, it drops the product. Decline and termination are not inevitable, however. Creative businesspeople can revive dying products. For instance, Miller's, a saddlery in New York City, does a good trade in buggy whips! Thus, the product life cycle cannot be used as a forecasting tool. Instead, it is a valuable lens through which a company can study the shift in demand for a product and the marketing strategies proposed for it.

Extending a Product's Life

The real value of the product life cycle concept is as a planning tool. Managers can view their products in view of where they appear in this cycle and adjust their strategies accordingly. Most importantly, they can use the product life cycle as a means to identify when it is time to look at ways to extend a product's life. A firm's survival will often enough depend on extending a major product's life. And even when extending a product's life is not so critical, it is often less expensive, less risky, and less time consuming to do so than to develop an entirely new product. After all, existing products usually have a base of loyal customers. Keeping them is better than going through the whole product-development process and the introduction and growth stages for a brand-new product.

How to Rejuvenate Fading Products

New Uses Most products start their lives intended for one particular use, but many products have more than one potential use. Marketers can put their minds to devising new uses, but those currently purchasing a product are a more likely source of ideas. For example, it was a consumer who came up with the idea of using baking soda as a refrigerator freshener. The need to identify new uses for products is a major reason for having a marketing information system that taps those who have direct contacts with purchasers.

New Users Companies can sometimes find new customers for their products. A new promotional theme or new product features may be the key here. For example, Bounty added all-white microwave-safe towels. Another source of new users may be market segments that had not previously seemed promising. Pellon made its name selling nonwoven fabrics as garment interfacing for home sewers and apparel manufacturers. Today it is successfully marketing the same type of material to computer software floppy disk manufacturers as a protective lining to go inside a diskette's cover.

Finding new uses. *What do you do when the baby boomers are grown and fewer little girls are dancing? Danskin, a manufacturer of ballet tights and leotards, faced just that problem. They jumped on the fitness bandwagon and convinced women and teens that quality, color, and style were important for exercise and casual clothing. Their market grew by leaps and bounds.*

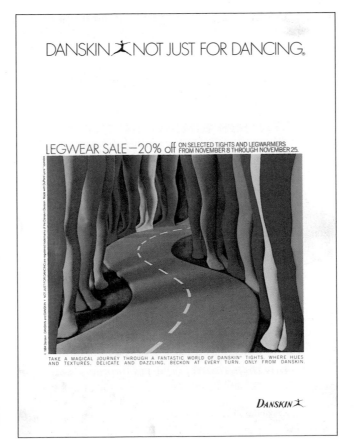

More Frequent Use Another way to revive a declining product is to encourage more frequent use, user in greater quantities, or the need for back-up units. Head & Shoulders shampoo, for instance, recommends two applications per washing, and Johnson & Johnson Baby Shampoo advertises that it is mild enough to use every day. Manufacturers of smoke alarms, telephones, and personal computers have used variations of these strategies. The American Express Company's "Don't leave home without it!" campaign persuaded card holders to use their Amex cards more often.

Cosmetic Changes An alteration in a product that has little or no effect on its basic function is a **cosmetic change**. New packaging, colors, styles, sizes, and the like can boost sales without requiring fundamental changes in the product. Makers of household products often stimulate sales by advertising products as "new and improved," even though little may have changed save in appearance and packaging. For generations, auto makers have extended their vehicles' product life cycles by making minor changes to exterior and interior appearances without changing what was hidden from view.

BRANDING

Lee Iacocca made his name at Ford in the mid-1960s with an idea for a car designed to appeal to the baby boomers just then reaching their twenties. His concept would have been less brilliant had it not been tied to a name and symbol that captured the spirit of the car: a Mustang at full gallop. The distinctive styling, the name, and the symbol worked together to create a product uniquely satisfying to the needs of a well-defined market segment.

Names and Symbols

Mustang is a **brand**: a name, term, symbol, design, or any combination of these elements used to identify a specific product and distinguish it from its competition. Technically, *Mustang* is a **brand name**, that part of a brand that can be spoken. The running horse is a **brand symbol**, a graphic portrayal of an element that identifies a product or firm. A brand symbol does not have to represent the words in the brand name. Coca-Cola's classic narrow-waisted bottle design is a brand symbol.

Types of Brands

When a manufacturer owns a brand, it is referred to as a **national brand** or a **manufacturer's brand**. Del Monte and Heinz are both national brands. A **private label brand** is one owned by a retailer or wholesaler. Many supermarket chains, including A&P Food Stores and Stop & Shop Companies, Inc., feature private brands.

Infringement The law protects certain brand names and symbols from **infringement** or violation. When you see the symbol ® at the end of a brand name or ™ beside a symbol, it tells you that the name or symbol is a **trademark** registered with the U.S. Patent and Trademark Office.

Registration gives the owner exclusive property rights to the trademark. Ralph

WE'RE BEATRICE

WE'RE BEATRICE

WE'RE BEATRICE

THE DAY THEY FINALLY TOOK OVER

Lauren has successfully sued clothing manufacturers who used symbols like his polo player on their clothes. And the Federal Trade Commission has forced clothes bearing imitation Izod alligators off the market. Even when a brand name or symbol is registered, its owner must protect the trademark from becoming a **generic term**, one that has passed into common, everyday language. Examples of trademarks that became generic terms include aspirin, zipper, linoleum, and kleenex. To avoid this fate, Xerox has mounted advertising campaigns designed to keep people from using *xerox* as a synonym for *photocopy*.

Brand Strategies

The Functions of Branding

Many consumers buy brand-name products to assure themselves of consistent quality. One can of Campbell's Chunky Vegetable Soup will vary little from another. Companies develop brands because customers are willing to pay higher prices to satisfy brand preferences. Pepperidge Farm cookies, Skippy peanut butter, and Planters peanuts have all developed a loyal following of customers. However, to secure consumer loyalty, manufacturers must promote their brands (discussed in Chapter 14) and must control the quality and consistency of their products.

Generics   Businesses have a wide range of branding strategies to choose from. At one extreme is what might be called the no-brand strategy. Many companies do not use brands, preferring to sell generic or unbranded goods.

Family or Blanket Brands   For some firms in some industries, the benefits of branding outweigh the costs of creating and protecting brand names and symbols. Some adopt a **family brand** or **blanket brand** strategy, an approach based on the use of one brand name for all of a firm's products. The General Electric Company, Canon U.S.A., Inc., the Mobil Oil Company, the Eastman Kodak Company, the Campbell Soup Company, and the H. J. Heinz Co. use this strategy. The major advantage to a family-brand strategy is that promotion of one product benefits every product bearing the same brand name because it heightens name recognition. The big disadvantage is that poor quality in one product can hurt all the other products sold under the same name.

Individual brand strategy.
You might not realize at first glance that all these brands are owned by Campbell Soup Company. One of the major reasons for using an individual brand strategy is to keep consumers' unhappiness with one brand from affecting their reactions to other brands offered by the same company.

Individual Brands Some firms use an **individual brand strategy**, an approach that calls for a different brand name for each product. The Lever Brothers Company, the Beatrice Companies, Inc., and the Colgate-Palmolive Company generally use an individual-brand strategy for their products. Clearly, the major disadvantage to this strategy lies in the expense of launching each new brand. On the other hand, how many consumers can list, say, all the flops from the General Foods Corporation? When asked to think of a toothpaste associated with Colgate-Palmolive, how many would remember Cue, which was a product failure? The main advantage of the individual-brands strategy is obviously that one or even a series of failures will probably not affect the other, successful brands. Another major advantage is that the company can effectively target products to particular market segments.

Some firms use a modified version of the individual-brand strategy in which the firm name is always tied to the individual brand name. For instance, *Kellogg's* always precedes the name of one of its cereal brands, like Kellogg's Rice Krispies or Kellogg's Corn Flakes. Sears, Roebuck, and Company uses a variation of the Kellogg's model. It has multiple family names, including Kenmore, Arnie, Cheryl Tiegs, Craftsman, and several others.

PACKAGING

The development of a container and a graphic design for a product are called **packaging**. The functions of packaging are to preserve, protect, promote, and provide utility.

The Functions of Packaging

A package may serve to prevent spoilage or damage. Where the product is food, like potato chips or cookies, this function can be critical. The package may also prevent harm to intended or unintended users. Child-resistant caps and safety seals on patent medicines belong in this category, as do pop seal tops on bottled juices. However, even a manufacturer's best efforts may not deter a serious killer. Johnson & Johnson (J & J) promptly removed from the market all Super-Strength Tylenol capsules after someone put cyanide in some bottles. After devising a tamper-resistant package, they reintroduced the product — only to have history repeat itself. This time, however, J & J decided to abandon capsules (itself a type of packaging) for caplets. The distinctiveness of the container also serves as a basis for promotion.

Good packaging can make product use and reuse easy. A well-designed spout on a bottle of soy sauce or a comfortable handle on a container of cooking oil can make an enormous difference in consumer satisfaction. Stonyfield Farm Yogurt and other manufacturers emphasize that their containers can be reused for different purposes. Some packages are biodegradable or recyclable. As manufacturers become increasingly aware of the societal impact of their packaging, more firms are likely to adopt such containers.

LABELING

A **label** is that part of the package or product that contains information. **Labeling** is therefore the presentation of information on a package or product. A package's basic function is, of course, to hold the product. Its total function may involve considerably more than that, however. The label may also transmit useful information to the purchaser and promote the product. Typically, a label contains the brand name and symbols, the size and contents of the package, directions for use, safety precautions, and the universal product code and symbol. A label may state the product's ingredients, warn of its hazards, and give antidote instructions in case it is used improperly. Under federal law, garment labels must state:

The Functions of Labeling

☐ The manufacturer's name
☐ The country in which the garment was made
☐ The fabric content
☐ Cleaning instructions

The label on processed foods must state their ingredients, in order of their abundance. Any nutritional claims must also appear on the label.

Packaging and Promotion

A well-designed package can serve an invaluable promotion function. It gives the customer the brand name and symbol, but more importantly it creates an image for the product. Just compare any black-and-white package containing a generic dishwasher detergent with the green-and-gold Cascade package. Some packages are particularly designed to be convenient for the retailer. Items like

The Death of the American-Made Car?

Since the oil crisis of the early 1970s, American automobile manufacturers, once among the strongest companies in the world, have been struggling to stay on top. The Big Three (General Motors, Ford, and Chrysler) weren't ready to meet the sudden demand for small cars when "miles per gallon" became the most important term in many car buyers' minds. The federal bailout of Chrysler, relaxed pollution standards, a drop in gas prices, and a return of interest in big cars have helped American car makers in the past few years. But the latest developments in international auto manufacturing suggest that the day may soon come when very few people in the United States will be able to say they're driving a totally American car.

One major source of worry for the Big Three is ever-increasing foreign competition. At least 27 companies now compete for the market once dominated by U.S. manufacturers and a handful of imports. Two of the most important new entrants are Yugoslavia's Zastava and South Korea's Hyundai Motor Corp. Zastava already makes the most popular car in Yugoslavia and is selling its cars in America through big, established dealers to ease customer fears about parts and servicing problems. Although Hyundai has been making cars for only a decade, it is a huge company with a long history of manufacturing heavy industrial equipment.

Detroit finds these new companies particularly threatening because they are attacking the U.S. market in its most vulnerable spot, at the low end of the price scale. Since Volkswagen stopped bringing its Beetle to America, no manufacturer has dominated the low end of the car market. People looking for an inexpensive first car often go to Toyota or Datsun showrooms, but because of import quotas Japanese auto manufacturers have been concentrating on higher-priced models that bring in higher profits.

With more competition and more new "mini" cars to worry about, American auto makers haven't been idle. But they've been slowly removing the "Made in America" stamp from their own models, gradually conceding that a small car made in America of American parts can't compete in quality and price with imports. Chevrolet introduced the first mini car, the three-cylinder Sprint, to the American market, and it has been a success, selling for less than the Japanese competition. The trouble is, the car is made by Suzuki Motor Co. of Japan. Chevrolet is just the importer.

Similar blurring of the line between "domestic" and "import" exists throughout the industry. Both the "domestic" Chevrolet Nova (made in California by a joint Toyota-GM venture) and the "import" Honda Accord (made in Ohio) contain about 50 percent American parts. In 1988 the Big Three plan to buy 440,000 cars from U.S.-based Japanese plants and twice that number made in foreign plants. As a result of these kinds of trends, analysts expect that Detroit will lose almost one-third of its auto-making capacity in the next five years.

Detroit has been hoping that it can learn new technology from the Japanese and put it to use building American cars. Such hope led to the development of GM's much-heralded Saturn, which is expected to roll off the super-automated assembly line in 1990. But already GM is admitting that the car will be more expensive than planned, and in the years before 1990 Japanese manufacturers will probably introduce four times as many new models as will American companies. Perhaps too late, American auto makers are learning that the secret to Japanese success may not be technology as much as management practices and an ability to foresee and produce what people will want to buy.

No one is forecasting the demise of the Big Three any time soon. In good years Detroit still makes a lot of money off of big cars, and automakers are finding that they can turn a profit on small cars if they buy them rather than make them. But if you want to buy an all-American car, don't just look at the logo on the front. And don't be surprised if, when you open the hood, you find parts made or assembled in a dozen different countries. The era of the truly international car is upon us.

Sources: Thomas Moore, "Maxi Hopes Ride on New Mini Cars," *Fortune*, January 20, 1986, 57. William J. Hampton, "Downsizing Detroit: The Big Three's Strategy for Survival," *Business Week*, April 14, 1986. Eric Gelman, "Wheels of the Future," *Newsweek*, Vol. 105, No. 24, June 17, 1985, 64.

Form and function. *Packages must not only attract consumers' attention, they must also protect contents and users while selling the product. Brockway, a leading producer of containers, can provide its customers with glass, plastic, metal, or combination products.*

kitchen accessories and shoelaces come in packages adapted for hanging on racks. Such packaging significantly improves their chances of winning the fight for supermarket and discount-store shelf space. Other packages are designed to prevent shoplifting. Cassette tapes come in large packages for that reason.

THE ROLE OF PRICING

Pricing is a critical element in the marketing mix. It is also an important consideration in each phase of the product-development process and in each stage of the product life cycle. And pricing may play a determining role in screening new product ideas and in test marketing products.

Allocation of Resources

Pricing helps allocate markets between firms. The prices a firm assigns its products have a direct relation to the revenue the firm generates. Setting a product's price may be a firm's most complicated and important decision. Too high a price will negatively affect sales. For example, when Apple Computer,

Inc., priced its Lisa at $10,000, it effectively eliminated a large part of the new model's market. A product may not sell at all if its price exceeds what the target market is willing or able to pay. Conversely, too low a price may prevent the firm from recapturing its development costs or may starve it into bankruptcy.

A product's price also helps consumers allocate their resources. Consumers compare the price of a product and its perceived value to them. When the value is less than the price, they are likely to drop that item from consideration. A consumer may decide to pay more for a Corvette than for a Thunderbird because of the greater satisfaction he or she anticipates.

Pricing Objectives

Setting prices is not a simple process. As with any critical decision, the pricing decision should be made deliberately and systematically. The first step in the pricing decision is to determine the firm's objectives. The most common ones are profit maximization, target return on investment, market share, status quo, and survival.

Profit Maximization   Many firms try to set their prices to maximize their profits, but it is very hard to determine just what price will precisely do that. Profit maximizers aim for a price as high as possible without causing a disproportionate reduction in unit sales. Suppose Ford Motor Co. increases its prices by 20 percent and its unit sales decrease by only 15 percent. In that case, its profits should increase. But if unit sales decrease by 25 percent, lower profits will likely result. Unfortunately, no computer program exists to strike this balance. Experimentation is the only way to reach it.

Target Return on Investment   Many firms set their prices based on a target return on investment. The firm has analyzed its other investment opportunities for its money and determined that in order to justify its investment in the product, it must receive a certain return. The company may then determine — based on what it could get by putting its money in, say, a bank — that it needs a 25 percent return on every dollar it puts into a new product. In other words, if its investment were $1 million, it would need a $250,000 profit to reach its target. That figure would dictate the price per unit.

Market Share   In some instances, a firm will set a market-share objective. Management may decide that the strategic advantages of an increased market share outweigh a temporary reduction in profits in order to get there. Suppose General Motors has a 20 percent share of the world automobile market and wants 25 percent. It may lower prices until it achieves its goal, then raise prices. This strategy has its risks, as the airlines periodically prove. When one competitor lowers prices, others follow suit so that none make money until prices go up again. A variant of this strategy, popular among banks and national auto-rental firms like Hertz and Avis, calls for giving away goods like luggage with each new account or rental.

Status Quo   Many firms follow what is called status-quo pricing, a strategy that might also be called "follow the leader" pricing. When a leading firm in an industry raises prices, the other firms follow suit. For generations, the U.S.

FIGURE 12-3

A Demand Curve

FIGURE 12-4

A Supply Curve

FIGURE 12-5

Equilibrium

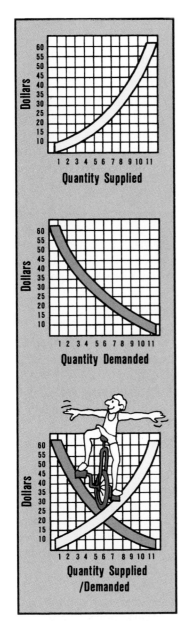

Steel Corporation filled the leader's role in the steel industry and the industry maintained pricing uniformity and steady profits. However, when competition arrived in the form of European, Japanese, and Korean steel, our steel industry pricing practices were altered.

Survival   A survival pricing objective is generally short run in nature and is often aimed at generating enough cash to pay current or past-due bills. Distress sales are an extreme type of survival tactic designed to generate enough cash to keep the business going for a few more days or weeks. One of the biggest such distress sales took place in 1982 when Braniff, Inc., dropped its ticket prices shortly before declaring bankruptcy.

PRICING METHODS

The pricing method a firm chooses should generate a price consistent with its pricing objectives. Firms have four basic methods to choose from: economic theory–based pricing, cost-based pricing, demand-based pricing, or competition-based pricing.

Economic Theory—based Pricing

Economic theory–based pricing applies the principles of supply, demand, and equilibrium. **Demand** refers to the willingness of purchasers to buy specific quantities of a good or service at a particular price at a particular time (see Figure 12.3). **Supply** refers to the willingness of sellers or producers to provide goods or services at a particular price and particular time. In other words, how much of something people will sell depends on its price when they can sell it (see Figure 12.4).

Demand and supply directly affect each other. By plotting their curves on the same graph, we see that they cross at the point marked *E* on Figure 12.5. The *E* marks the point of **equilibrium**, the point at which demand and supply are in balance. It is there that the intentions of the seller and buyers coincide. The point of equilibrium between supply and demand identifies the **market price** of goods or services.

Economic theory–based pricing is critically important not only as a pricing method itself but also as the basis for the three other principal methods. It is, however, extremely hard to apply. First, constructing supply and demand curves that go beyond a narrow range of prices is very difficult. Second, supply and demand curves apply only to a particular period of time. The amount of goods demanded at a certain price can change over time, for example.

Cost-based Pricing

Many firms use a **cost-based pricing** approach. The cost of producing or purchasing a good serves as the starting point. The firm then adds to the product's cost a predetermined percentage of the cost called a **markup**. The formula is:

$$\text{Cost} + (\text{Cost} \times \text{Markup percentage}) = \text{Price}$$

The markup must be sufficient to cover any additional costs (overhead) and provide an adequate profit. Suppose a wholesaler buys a General Electric radio for $20 and applies a markup percentage of 60 percent of cost. The calculation would be:

$$\$20 + (\$20 \times 60\%) = \text{Price}$$
$$\$20 + \$12 = \text{Price}$$
$$\$32 = \text{Price}$$

When discussing the markup percentage, it is extremely important to indicate whether the calculation is based on cost or on the selling price. Here is an example:

$$\text{Markup as a percentage of cost} = \frac{\text{amount added to cost}}{\text{cost}} = \frac{12}{20} = 60\%$$

$$\text{Markup as a percentage of selling price} = \frac{\text{amount added to cost}}{\text{selling price}} = \frac{12}{32} = 38\%$$

Simplicity is the main appeal of cost-based pricing. Otherwise this method has its problems, especially in determining the appropriate markup percentage. That percentage should produce a price appropriate for the firm's profit objectives, market demand, and competition. Some firms defeat the markup's purpose by not altering their percentage in light of current economic or business conditions.

Demand-based Pricing

The focus of **demand-based pricing** is on **breakeven analysis**, a method used to determine the demand or sales volume required at a given price for the firm to break even. See Figure 12.6. The formula for determining a breakeven point is:

$$\frac{\text{Fixed costs}}{(\text{Price} - \text{variable cost per unit})} = \text{Breakeven point}$$

In this formula, **fixed costs** are costs that do not vary with the level of output or production. **Variable costs** are costs that depend on the number of units produced. **Total costs** represent the sum of the fixed and variable costs.

Suppose that a business expects a product to sell for $100. The total fixed costs are $12,000 and variable costs per unit are $40. The calculation would be:

$$\frac{\text{Fixed costs}}{(\text{Price} - \text{variable cost per unit})} = \frac{\$12,000}{(\$100 - 40)} = 200 \text{ units} = \text{Breakeven point}$$

If management believes they can sell more than 200 units at $100, that might be the appropriate price. But if management estimate sales to be less than 200 units, they probably should recalculate the breakeven point using a lower price per unit.

Competition-based Pricing

Some firms, particularly in retailing and in fields where they market products similar to their competitors', use **competition-based pricing**, pricing based on competitive price levels. After determining the prices charged by the competition,

FIGURE 12-6

Breakeven Analysis

A breakeven analysis is a
method used to determine
the demand or sales volume
required at a given price for
a firm to break even.

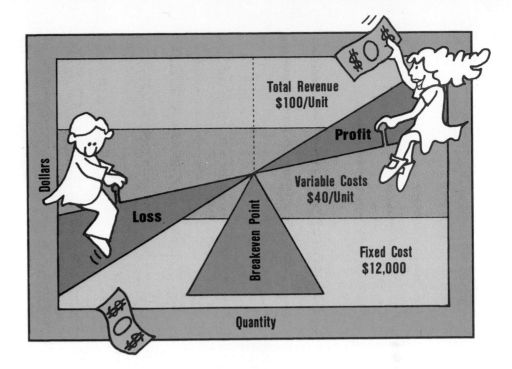

management has three options: it can price higher than, lower than, or the same as its competitors. Businesses like this method because it is simple and unlikely to set off price wars. Its major flaw is that the price settled on is not necessarily related to a particular firm's objectives. It also assumes that the firm's marketing costs and mix are the same as its competitors'.

PRICING STRATEGIES

The price set for goods or services must be adjusted to a firm's overall pricing strategy, regardless of which pricing method it uses. A number of pricing strategies exist, and it is not at all uncommon for a firm to be using several of them at once, even for the same product.

New-Product Pricing Strategies

The pricing strategy for a new product must be consistent with the overall marketing strategy for the product. The choices here are either a skimming strategy or a penetration strategy.

A **skimming price strategy** involves charging a high price when the product is first introduced. This technique takes its name from the notion of skimming the cream from the top of unhomogenized milk. This strategy works only when a sufficient number of customers are not particularly price sensitive. Early purchasers of innovative electronic equipment fall into this category, like those who paid $1,000 for the first compact-disk players. A successful skimming strategy permits a firm to recover the costs of product development relatively quickly. After a time, the firm may consider lowering the price or even withdrawing from the market as new competitors, sensing a profit to be made, enter it.

Two Methods of Pricing New
Products

Price can be crucial. *Economic theory says that more people will want a product at a lower price than at a higher price. Yugo is betting that there is still a high demand for low-priced cars in America. It's a tactic that can backfire, however. Calculators and digital watches were high-price, high-prestige items until price competition pulled down profits and drove many producers from the market.*

A **penetration pricing strategy** calls for introducing a new product at a low price, to attain a strong grip on a sizable market share. The combination of low prices and an entrenched competitor can discourage other firms from entering the market. When a business anticipates product growth over the long term or when product-development costs are extremely high, this strategy may be the best. Commodore VIC-20 was originally priced at $299, compared to $600 for the Atari 400 and $500 for the Texas Instruments 9914A. Over 1.5 million VIC-20s were sold in the first two years, while the two competitors were forced out of the market.

Psychological Pricing Strategies

Many of the more specifically targeted pricing strategies are based on consumer behavior. These psychological strategies often influence the product's image.

The Four Types of
Psychological Pricing

Odd/even pricing is one of the most popular psychological pricing strategies. "Odd" prices, which end in an odd number (usually nine), are meant to give the customer the impression of low prices and convey the idea that the firm has cut prices to the last possible penny. Even prices are meant to give the opposite impression. They are usually stated in round dollar amounts, which are thought to give the consumer a sense of prestige. In theory, a bargain hunter should be attracted to an $89.99 price and the prestige buyer to a $90.00 price. Researchers have not been able either to prove or disprove the concept behind the odd/even pricing theory.

Multiple-unit pricing is the practice of providing discounts for purchases of two or more units. The idea here is to sell a greater total amount by convincing the customer to buy more at one time. It works best for retailers, like grocers, who can price Del Monte green beans at "two for $1."

Prestige pricing involves setting a very high price on an item to give an impression of high quality. Rolex watches and Porsches carry prestige prices. Prestige pricing is directly related to the familiar customer attitude that "you get

---

The Electronic Catalogue

How would you like to do most of your Christmas shopping sitting in one place, not walking a marathon in the mall or standing in line while the checkout trainee figures out the register buttons? You can do such shopping from a catalogue, but catalogues have their drawbacks — you get a limited amount of information about a limited number of products.

Now one of the country's leading catalogue printers, R.R. Donnelley & Sons Co., has set out to perfect catalogue shopping. It has created the Electronistore.

This new kind of "store" consists of a 19-inch color video monitor, a videodisc player, a stereo system, a touch-sensitive screen, a credit card reader, a microcomputer, and a printer, all housed in a kiosk set up in a shopping center. The customer sits in the kiosk and is welcomed by an electronic "shopping hostess" who provides step-by-step instructions.

The shopper inserts a credit card into a slot, then presses the touch-sensitive screen to view the first general category of products. The shopper looking for a dishwasher might press "household appliances," then "dishwashers" and would be presented with an array of products on the monitor. Interested in one unit but wanting more information, the customer can press "details." If the price and the product look right, the customer puts the item on a "shopping list." When the shopper is finished, the Electronistore displays the entire shopping list, asks for credit card and delivery information, and gives the customer a receipt.

The company has been working on the Electronistore concept since 1981 and introduced the product in late 1984. By 1985 it was generating $250 million of business, a figure the company expects to rise to $17 billion by 1990.

The new concept also has a number of advantages from a retailer's point of view. Price and product information can be changed daily, if necessary. The kiosk can expand shopping hours and product selection without adding costs for more salespeople or floor space.

Retailing experts see the kiosk as another step towards electronic home shopping. For years people have been predicting that eventually we will do most of our shopping from home using a special computer terminal. But for now, the terminals are very expensive, and most of us are more likely to be able to afford driving to the nearest Electronistore kiosk.

You may not find the Electronistore in your local mall for a few years, but if Donnelley has its way, this new method of shopping will catch on as quickly as did catalogue shopping. The kiosks are sure to attract many people interested just in trying them out. Most customers surveyed enjoyed the experience. Imagine having a department store's entire inventory with you in a booth and letting your fingers do the shopping!

Sources: "Electronistore Debuts," *Marketing News*, Vol. 19, No. 11, May 24, 1985. Steven Radwell, "In-Store Computer Lets Fingers Do the Shopping," *Daily News Record*, November 30, 1984, 4. "Electronic Shopping," *Fortune*, December 24, 1984, 9.

---

what you pay for." To marketers, this saying states the **price–quality relationship**, which is that a high price implies high quality. If customers lack any other cues to a product's quality, they will judge it by its price.

Price lining is a pricing strategy used primarily by retailers in which the firm selects a limited number of key prices or **price points** for certain classes of products. For example, a department store might price all its Arrow dress shirts according to a $17.50–$20–$25–$30 scheme, regardless of how much they cost at wholesale. In other words, the store would not apply a fixed markup to them.

PRODUCT AND PRICE: A PERSPECTIVE

For three generations of consumers, General Electric was the preferred brand when it came to small appliances: irons, toasters, toaster ovens, coffee makers, and the like. One survey asked consumers to list small-appliance makers. General Electric appeared on 92 percent of the lists, Sunbeam 41 percent, and Black & Decker 12 percent. The irony was that GE had sold its small-appliance division to Black & Decker some months before.

Under the terms of the two companies' May 1984 agreement, Black & Decker could use GE's name in connection with its small appliances for three years. Except in the case of irons, a fiercely competitive market, Black & Decker chose instead to relaunch the products under its own name. Black & Decker was gambling that it could take the products marketed under the best-known blanket brand in the small-appliance business and succeed with them under its own name.

Black & Decker's new rivals — Hamilton Beach, Proctor-Silex, Norelco, Sunbeam, and others — took advantage of the situation by aggressively promoting their products. Because profit margins in the $8.3 billion-per-year small-appliance industry are less than 5 percent of sales and because of the $300 million it spent to acquire the GE division, Black & Decker has to keep its prices up. It must persuade consumers to buy Black & Decker–brand products based on a product's features, not on its price.[6]

Black & Decker has clearly changed the product and price aspects of its marketing mix. It has also changed how it puts products in the hands of retailers and budgeted an industry record $100 million for advertising, so it has also altered the place and promotion elements. In the next two chapters, we will look at these last two of the Four P's.

Chapter Highlights

1. Describe the new-product development process.

The new-product development process consists of six phases: idea generation, screening, business analysis, product development, test marketing, and commercialization. This process depends on marketing information from the very first stage.

2. Explain the product life cycle concept.

The product life cycle concept assumes that products have lives with four identifiable stages: introduction, growth, maturity, and decline. There are no hard-and-fast rules as to how long any stage will take for a particular product, and marketers can extend the life of a product by finding new uses, new users, promoting its more frequent use, or making cosmetic changes in the product. The concept is most valuable as a planning tool because it allows a company to monitor shifts in demand for its products and develop appropriate responses.

3. Identify the functions of branding, packaging, and labeling.

Branding identifies a product and distinguishes it from its competition. Brands help consumers assure themselves of consistent quality and allow companies to develop loyal customers. Packaging may prevent spoilage or damage, protect against injury, promote safety, or make a product easier to use. Packaging also serves a promotion function by creating an image for a product and making the product easy to recognize. Labeling, the part of the package that contains information, informs the consumer what the product is and how it should be used.

4. Describe the role of pricing in the marketing mix.

Pricing helps firms allocate resources because a product's price is directly related to the revenue it is expected to generate. Pricing helps consumers allocate their resources by allowing them to compare the price of a product and the satisfaction anticipated from it. Price also provides some clues about quality. High prices are assumed to accompany high quality.

5. List the potential pricing objectives for a product.

The potential pricing objectives for a product are profit maximization, target return on investment, market share, status quo, and survival.

6. Describe the principal pricing methods.

There are four basic pricing methods. Economic theory–based pricing seeks to apply the principles of supply and demand to identify the equilibrium point and market price. Cost-based pricing adds a predetermined percentage to the cost of a product. Demand-based pricing relies on breakeven analysis to find out how many units of a product must be sold at a particular price to cover the cost of producing and selling the product. Competition-based pricing uses the prices charged by competitors as a starting point. A business can then charge more than, less than, or the same as its competitors.

7. Identify the pricing strategies available for both new products and those already on the market.

Businesses use skimming or penetration pricing strategies for new products. For established products, firms generally rely on one of several psychological pricing strategies: odd/even pricing, multiple-unit pricing, or prestige pricing.

Key Terms

Blanket brand	Equilibrium	Manufacturer's brand	Private brand
Brand	Family brand	Market price	Product differentiation
Brand name	Fixed costs	Markup	strategy
Brand symbol	Generic term	Maturity stage	Product life cycle
Competition-based	Good	Multiple-unit pricing	Service
pricing	Growth stage	National brand	Skimming price
Cosmetic change	Idea	Odd/even pricing	strategy
Cost-based pricing	Individual brand	Prestige pricing	Supply
Decline stage	strategy	Price points	Test markets
Demand	Introduction stage	Price–quality	Trademark
Demand-based pricing	Infringement	relationship	Variable costs
Economic theory–	Label		
based pricing	Labeling		

Review Questions

1. What are the basic steps in the new-product development process? Describe each briefly.
2. What is the product life cycle concept? For what purposes may it be used?
3. Identify the stages of the product life cycle and discuss each.
4. Describe the major means to extend the product life cycle.
5. The terms *brand, brand name, brand symbol,* and *trademark* describe related concepts. What are the relationships among these concepts?
6. List the major benefits of branding.
7. Describe the potential functions of packaging. How does labeling relate to packaging?
8. What is the role of pricing in marketing?
9. Define the range of a firm's possible pricing objectives for a product.
10. Identify the major pricing methods. How is each different from the others?
11. What are the main new-product pricing strategies? Create examples showing how each type works.
12. Describe the main psychological pricing strategies.

Application Exercises

1. For many years people living in your community have raved about your mother's chocolate brownies. A typical comment made by friends and relatives is: "If you marketed these brownies nationwide, you could make a fortune." Let's assume that the brownies are quite good and appear to have wide appeal in the marketplace. What steps in the new product development process would be most important if a decision is made to market this product nationwide? What steps would you take to properly package and label this product?

2. Two years ago you purchased a small copy center in a college town with a population of 25,000. Most of your current customers include students and faculty members from the college. Recently the store next door was vacated and the space is available to you. You are considering expansion of your business to include a wide range of professional services such as typing resumes, legal documents, business letters, theses, and dissertations. If the expansion takes place, decisions must be made regarding a price for each of the services. Which pricing method would you use to develop a price list?

Cases

12.1 P&G Turns the Tide

For decades, Procter & Gamble (P&G) had pursued the same successful marketing strategy: Develop a superior product, test it fully, promote it widely, and sell it at a premium price that reflects its higher quality. In the early 1980s the consumer goods giant, whose products include Crest toothpaste, Tide detergent, Bounty paper towels, and Pampers disposable diapers, seemed to abandon that approach. Instead, P&G presented consumers with new products that have been characterized as hastily con-

ceived, mediocre, and "copycat" offerings. Consumers were not impressed. Wholesalers and retailers began to devote less shelf space to P&G products and more to competing products. P&G's brands lost market share, its new products did poorly, and revenues and earnings dropped drastically.

Now, however, P&G has gone back to its old strategy. The firm has developed and marketed several new products that are obviously superior, and is promoting these products heavily.

Tide, P&G's powdered detergent, has been (and remains) the number one seller. However, the market for liquid detergents has been growing since they were introduced and now accounts for about 25 percent of detergent sales. Although liquids don't clean nearly as well as powders, many consumers prefer them because they are easier to handle and use. P&G had marketed two so-so liquid detergents but they found little consumer acceptance.

Then P&G announced Liquid Tide, a new liquid laundry detergent. According to the firm, Liquid Tide is the first liquid detergent that cleans well enough to bear the Tide name, and is far superior to any other liquid on the market. It contains twelve cleaning agents, rather than the usual six, and a new molecule that traps dirt in the wash water. P&G packaged Liquid tide in a plastic bottle with a cap that doubles as a no-mess measuring cup; when the cap is replaced after use, excess liquid drains back *into* the bottle. One industry observer has noted that consumers are even more enthusiastic about the bottle than about the detergent.

P&G has made similar advances in its new Ultra Pampers and Tartar Control Crest. These marketing changes seem to have turned things around completely: P&G's market share has gone up in all three product areas; supermarket shelves are well stocked with P&G products; and earnings are on the rise.

Questions

1. P&G has generally shied away from family branding. Why did the firm use that strategy for all three new products?
2. What method would you have used to set the price of Liquid Tide, and why?
3. What functions does the Liquid Tide container perform for the product, the consumer, and P&G?

Sources: For more information, see *Fortune*, August 4, 1986, pp. 130–134; *Business Week*, July 15, 1985, pp. 130–134; and Fortune, February 4, 1985, pp. 30–33.

12.2 Honda and the Big Guys

In the 1970s, inflation and the gasoline crunch created a huge demand for small, fuel-efficient cars. Many U.S. consumers purchased Japanese imports. Sales of American cars dropped sharply, and American auto manufacturers were hurting. In 1980, under the threat of formal import restrictions, the Japanese agreed to "voluntarily"

limit auto exports to the United States for three years. Although the quota has been raised several times since the first agreement expired, the idea of an informal import limit has been retained.

Demand for Japanese imports has remained high, even though Detroit was able to regroup and produce its own fuel-efficient cars. To make the most of their quota, Japanese auto makers have been sending their highest priced models, to the United States. As a result, their profits have soared.

Japan's Honda Motor Co. began as a motorcycle producer, later added subcompact autos to its product mix, and in 1983 became the fourth largest Japanese auto maker. Honda's management felt that the firm could sell well beyond its quota of cars in the United States. For that reason, and to help reduce protectionist friction between Japan and the United States, Honda opened an auto production plant in Marysville, Ohio. Output from that plant has prompted Honda of America to assert that it is now the fourth largest auto manufacturer in the United States.

Honda is also building a line of cars which it has entered in the latest automobile sweepstakes — the luxury/sport/performance car market. Americans are by now accustomed to high prices on Japanese cars. However, Honda management worried that the firm's reputation for low-priced subcompacts would make it difficult for them to sell cars in the $20,000 range. For that reason, Honda is selling its new entry through an entirely separate division, under the Acura brand. Management expects the new line to affect the sales of European imports well before it cuts into sales of American luxury cars. By that time, the Acura may, itself, be an American-made car.

Questions

1. What product and pricing strategies have Japanese auto makers used since the voluntary import quota was imposed?
2. What does Honda gain from producing cars in the United States, given that cars cost more to produce here than in Japan?

Sources: For more information see *Barron's*, December 2, 1985, pp. 13, 48–49; *Business Week*, December 9, 1985, pp. 114, 118; *Forbes*, September 10, 1984, pp. 41–48; and *Fortune*, February 20, 1984, pp. 104–108.

13

DISTRIBUTION STRATEGY

Learning Objectives

After you have completed this chapter, you will be able to do the following:

- Define the term marketing intermediaries.
- Describe the basic channels of distribution for consumer and industrial products.
- Distinguish between intensive, selective, and exclusive distribution strategies.
- List the two main types of wholesalers and identify their functions.
- Specify the services wholesalers provide to producers and retailers.
- List the main types of retailers and identify their functions.
- Describe the organization of a physical distribution system.
- Identify the principal modes of transportation for goods and discuss their advantages and disadvantages.
- Explain the difference between a public warehouse and a private warehouse.

Suppose you are a manufacturer who has just developed the Asparagus Bed doll, with the potential of becoming next year's toy sensation. Your company, which has annual sales of $5 million, is typical of the toy industry, in which only 3 percent of the companies have sales exceeding $150 million and 80 percent have sales under $20 million. Your small sales force is presently marketing primarily to the large toy chains, like Kay-Bee Toy & Hobby Shops, Inc. (585 stores), Toys 'R' Us, Inc. (241 stores), and Circus World Toy Stores, Inc. (189 stores). You fear your Asparagus Bed dolls will not reach many of the discounters and specialty stores that sell enormous quantities of toys each Christmas. What can you do to ensure the market coverage you want?

What you need is a sales force, but you probably cannot invest the time and money to hire and train them. Instead, you should look for a firm that has a sales force who will go to work for you. You need to look for an intermediary, a wholesaler, who can reach the retailers your sales force cannot. In reality, you would probably look for several wholesalers who would give you the geographical and store spread you want.

Now let's look at this problem from another perspective. Suppose you want to open a warehouse-type toy store that would compete with Toys 'R' Us. However, Toys 'R' Us stocks eighteen thousand types of toys.[1] How are you going to stock your store? Again, intermediaries — wholesalers — can provide the buyers you could not afford to hire, and they will also keep tabs on industry trends and arrange transportation of the goods to your store.

The issue is the availability of products. In the first instance, you as a producer are trying to make the Asparagus Bed doll available to retailers. In the second, you as a store are trying to make sure that stock is available for your shelves. Availability of a product is the key concept in place utility, the third of the marketing mix's Four P's discussed in Chapter 12. For a product to deliver satisfaction, it must be somewhere the purchaser can buy it. This chapter focuses on how products reach their ultimate user or consumer.

CHANNELS OF DISTRIBUTION

To facilitate the flow of products to their ultimate purchasers, most businesses that produce goods have created extensive **channels of distribution**, paths or routes composed of marketing intermediaries or middlemen that direct products to customers. A channel of distribution, which is sometimes called a **marketing channel** or **distribution channel**, always begins with a producer and ends with a consumer or end-user. Between them, a number of different types of firms may handle the goods.

Wholesalers and retailers are the main types of marketing intermediaries. They are found in the channels of distribution for both consumer and industrial products.

The Roles of Intermediaries

Figure 13.1 shows that channels of distribution commonly contain **marketing intermediaries** or **middlemen**, firms between the manufacturer and the ultimate

FIGURE 13-1

Channels of Distribution for Consumer Products

To facilitate the flow of their products to their ultimate purchasers, most businesses which produce goods have created extensive channels of distribution.

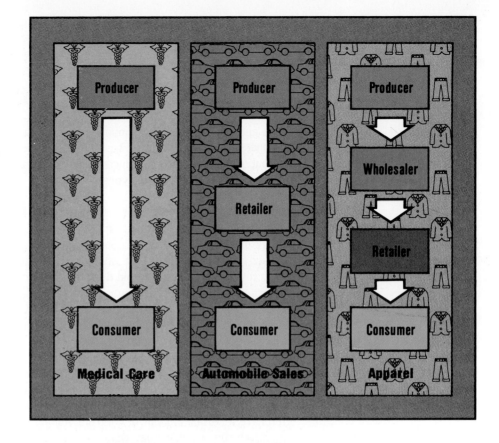

Marketing Intermediaries Defined

user or consumer that take title to the goods. Facilitating organizations directly assist others to take title to goods or that assist in physically moving or storing goods while they are in the channel. For example, Pierre Cardin might ship goods by Emery Worldwide to the May Company department stores, which could need them for a special promotion. The May Company as a retailer, is an intermediary between Pierre Cardin and the ultimate consumer. Emery is a facilitating organization assisting in the title exchange by physically moving the goods.

Marketing intermediaries simplify the process of getting products to consumers and industrial end-users. As Figure 13.2 demonstrates, marketing intermediaries can reduce the size of the sales force a producer must maintain and cut the number of sales calls.

Merchants An intermediary — a wholesaler, distributor, or retailer — who takes title to goods and resells them is a **merchant**. Often, merchants pay for goods from the proceeds of their resale. Intermediaries of this type typically take delivery of products, hold them ready for resale, divide large shipments into lot sizes acceptable to their customers, and distribute the products to the next point in the channel of distribution.

Merchants as Intermediaries

Merchants always take **title**, the right to own property that usually (but not always) comes with physical possession of tangible personal property or real property. A better way to think of title is as the right to sell or otherwise transfer property, whether or not the seller has actual possession of the property or has paid for it.

Agents and Brokers   In contrast to merchants, an **agent** or **broker** is an intermediary who receives a commission for bringing together buyers and sellers for the purpose of negotiating an exchange but never takes title to property.[2]

Channels for Consumer Products

Goods and services bought by individuals for their personal or household use are **consumer products**. Figure 13.1 shows the three basic types of channels of distribution for consumer products. It is important to keep in mind that there are many variations on these types.

The First Distribution Channel for Consumer Products

Producer to Consumer   Channel A in Figure 13.1 runs directly from the producer to the consumer. Virtually all services, from haircuts to tax preparation, use Type A channels. Some producers sell their goods directly, and exclusively, to the public. One of the best known of these is Avon Products, Inc.'s, cosmetics, which are sold door to door. Some firms use Type A channels as part of their overall distribution system for goods. Most of the major oil companies, like the Atlantic Richfield Company (Arco) and Standard Oil Company of Indiana (Amoco Oil Company), own some retail outlets — service stations, in their cases — through which they sell their products. Similarly, many of the better known franchisers, like Wendy's International, Inc., own and operate outlets, too.

The principal reason producers want direct channels of distribution is to maintain control over the distribution of their products. Marketing intermediaries often have a certain amount of control over matters such as pricing and promotion, which the producer may want to limit or eliminate. A Type A channel also lets producers maintain closer ties to consumers. Direct dealings with consumers can lead to insights about their needs and wants. Finally, this type of channel cuts out the profit that marketing intermediaries must make. Nevertheless, a marketing intermediary's functions often involve resources and expertise that the producer may not have. Intermediaries may well perform their functions more economically than can the producer.

The Second Distribution Channel for Consumer Products

Producer to Retailer to Consumer   In Channel B in Figure 13.1, the product moves from producer to retailer to consumer. A **retailer** is a merchant who sells products or services or both to the ultimate consumer. Supermarkets, like Ralphs Grocery Company, and discount stores, like Venture Stores, Inc., are retailers. Merle Norman Cosmetics, Inc., unlike Avon, makes its own cosmetics, which it then sells to consumers through twenty-five hundred franchised Merle Norman Studios.

Many producers use Type B channels because these lines are relatively short and make possible a wider range of distribution than do Type A channels. They also facilitate the movement of bulky, perishable, and fashion-sensitive goods.

The Third Distribution Channel for Consumer Products

Producer to Wholesaler to Retailer to Consumer   Most consumer goods pass through the Type C channel shown in Figure 13.1: from producer to wholesaler to retailer to consumer. A **wholesaler** is a business or individual who buys and resells products to other merchants such as retailers and other wholesalers and larger industrial users, but not to consumers.

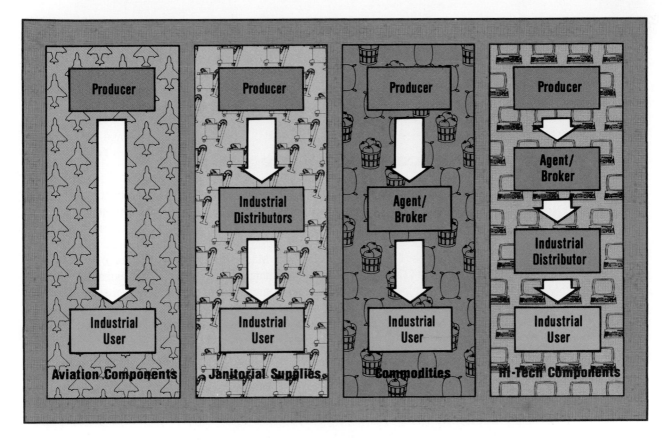

Aviation Components	Janitorial Supplies	Commodities	Hi-Tech Components
Producer	Producer	Producer	Producer
	Industrial Distributors	Agent/ Broker	Agent/ Broker
			Industrial Distributor
Industrial User	Industrial User	Industrial User	Industrial User

FIGURE 13-2

Channels of Distribution for Industrial Products

Producers are likely to use Type C channels when a large number of retailers carry their products. Most electronic equipment, canned goods, office supplies, and hardware passes through such channels. The use of wholesalers may also make it easier for producers to reach different market segments. For example, a hammer manufacturer may deal with one group of wholesalers that serves hardware retailers and another that serves discount and department stores.

Channels for Industrial Products

Figure 13.2 illustrates the primary channels of distribution for industrial products.

Producer to Industrial User Channel D, the direct channel to the ultimate purchaser, is the most commonly used one for industrial products. Producers using this channel often sell large, costly items requiring custom installation. For instance, the Boeing Company markets airliners directly to carriers like Japan Air Lines. The General Electric Company markets turbines for electricity-generating stations directly to utilities. Type D channels require producers to maintain their own sales forces and generally to provide users with after-sale services, such as delivery, setup, and maintenance. Quite often, the company promising the best performance on these services gets the sale.

The Basic Distribution Channels for Industrial Products

Producer to Distributor to Industrial User Standardized goods that are somewhat lower priced normally pass through Type E channels. For instance, Northland Industrial Trucks, a distributor, sells and services forklifts, trucks, and other industrial equipment. Janitorial supplies also move through Type E channels to cleaning services. Table 13.1 summarizes the ways in which various middlemen relate to the ultimate seller of a product.

Vertical Channel Integration

The combination of two or more entities within the channel stretching from the producer to the consumer or end-user is called **vertical-channel integration**. Vertical-channel integration occurs when a firm either acquires another firm in its channel or sets up a division to carry out other channel functions. Some oil companies, like the Sun Refining & Marketing Company (Sunoco), or Texas Oil Company (Texaco) perform all the channel functions from the extraction of crude oil to pumping gasoline into consumers' cars. Such arrangements are called **corporate vertical-marketing systems**.

In an **administered marketing system**, one channel member dominates all the others in its channel or channels. Sears is a well-known example of a channel leader, the dominant entity in a distribution channel. It buys in such large quantities that it sets the standards for producers and other intermediaries within its channels. In a **contractual vertical-marketing system**, a contractual relationship formalizes the dominance of the channel leader. Many franchise systems operate in this way.

MARKET COVERAGE

A producer should base its choice of a particular channel of distribution on the **market coverage** — the number and types of outlets — it wants for its products. This choice depends, of course, on the producer's marketing objectives, marketing strategies, and resources.

Patterns of Market Coverage

The Three Basic Distribution Strategies

A producer can choose from three basic patterns of market coverage: intensive, selective, and exclusive distribution. Producers often adopt one type of market coverage for one product and another for a different one. They may also vary their coverage for one product from, say, region to region, depending on what strategy seems to work in a given area.

Intensive Distribution The way to take advantage of virtually all the available retail outlets is with an **intensive distribution strategy**. A producer uses such a technique to saturate the market and guarantee purchasers that its brand will be available wherever they are. Cigarette companies, candy manufacturers,

Type of middleman	Functions
Full-service merchants	Assemble, collect, and store goods; provide fast delivery, extend trade credit, and furnish market information. These services appeal especially to small- and medium-sized retailers.
Limited-service merchants	Charge less and provide fewer services than the full-service merchant wholesaler; generally do not grant credit or offer delivery service. Offer only fast-moving items; may do business by mail only.
Rack jobbers	Supply mainly nonfood items to supermarkets, set up displays, maintain merchandise assortment, and receive payment only on goods actually sold, thereby guaranteeing a markup of an agreed-upon percentage to the outlet.
Brokers	Receive a commission for bringing retail buyers and suppliers together; do not handle merchandise or take title to goods. Handle only a few lines, mainly grocery specialties, dry goods, fruits, vegetables, drugs, and hardware. Represent customers.
Commission agents	Similar to broker, except that they handle merchandise, but they do not take title to it. Supply mainly large retailers with dry goods, grocery specialties, and fruits and vegetables. Represent seller/producer.
Manufacturers' representatives	Render services similar to those of a salesperson. Restricted to a limited territory and have limited authority to negotiate price and terms of sale; sell only part of the client's output.
Selling agents	Similar to manufacturers' representatives except that selling agents are responsible for disposing of the entire output of the client.
Auctioneer	Places products on display and sells to the highest bidder. Used mainly to sell livestock and fruits and vegetables to small restaurants, large chains, or other wholesalers.

Source: Adapted from Raymond A. Marquardt, James C. Makens, and Robert G. Roe, *Retail Management,* 2nd ed. (The Dryden Press, 1979). Copyright © The Dryden Press, a division of Holt, Rinehart & Winston.

TABLE 13.1

Characteristics of Middlemen Serving Retailers

and soft-drink bottlers typically use this strategy because consumers will readily substitute other products for their particular ones if they are not available. It is virtually impossible to achieve saturation without relying on intermediaries, so intensive distribution gives producers very little control over retailers.

Selective Distribution An approach that centers on a moderate proportion of the retailers likely to carry a particular product in a given market area is called a **selective distribution strategy**. In this system, a producer carefully evaluates each potential outlet for its ability to market the product successfully. Producers of shopping goods such as clothing, furniture, and major appliances often adopt this strategy, which works well for products that consumers will seek out. A shopper who wants a Cuisinart food processor will make an effort to locate a store carrying the brand. Quite often, producers adopting a selective distribution strategy offer training for retailers as well as service facilities and promotional support.

Exclusive Distribution Another distribution arrangement, called an **exclusive distribution strategy**, relies on a single retail outlet or a very few retail outlets in a market area. This strategy is most appropriate for specialty items for which consumers will gladly search, like Rolls-Royce automobiles. In return for guaranteed sales rights within a specified region, retailers often allow producers to maintain a high degree of control over the product's marketing, especially its pricing. In turn, producers generally provide a good deal of promotional and other assistance.

Choosing a Retail Strategy

"No copy machines, no video games, no 24-hour banking . . . You won't see me here again."

Producers select a retail strategy based on their products and their target markets. Some products, such as an ordinary candy bar or brand of cigarettes, for instance, require an intensive distribution strategy to be successful. However, for shopping goods or specialty goods, products for which a consumer will search, the most important retail strategy is the target market. The manufacturer must identify the segmentation variables (discussed in Chapter 11) that characterize its market, then identify the outlets that cater to the markets the variables describe. Many considerations come into play. Does the product appeal to residents of only one region? To what age and income levels does it appeal? What types of stores does the target market frequent — shops in malls, or downtown boutiques? Is service a major consideration? If so, to what types of retailers does the target market look when it buys products like computers that have a high potential for requiring service?

Successful retailers carefully plan their stores to appeal to particular target markets. They try to create a specific image and spark a particular emotional response among potential customers. The variables that go into designing retail stores are called **atmospherics**. For example, what type of sales help do customers want? Are they looking for fashion consultants, or for someone who can write up a sale? The effects of atmospherics on consumer buying are studied intently.

MARKETING INTERMEDIARIES: WHOLESALERS

Types of Wholesalers

Wholesalers are those infamous middlemen whose profits so many people talk about eliminating. As we have already seen, however, wholesalers play an important role in making channels of distribution efficient. Like retailers, all wholesalers do not fit into a single mold. Each offers a different mix of services, but it is possible to divide them into two main groups. **Full-service wholesalers** offer the widest variety of services to their customers, including maintaining inventories, gathering and interpreting market information, extending credit, distributing goods, and promotional activities. **Limited-service wholesalers** offer a narrower range of services than do full-service wholesalers, and they often tend to specialize.

An industrial channel of distribution: producer to distributor to industrial user. *Flying Foods International, Inc., buys exotic foods from around the world and sells them to creative chefs in New York's trendier restaurants. After working for a couple of weeks at a restaurant supply import company, Walter F. Martin II, Paul Moriates, and Andy Udelson spotted a market no one else was supplying. Making $120,000 on sales of $4.48 million after only three years, Flying Foods hoped to hit sales of $5.75 million during 1985.*

Wholesalers' Services to Producers

Wholesalers perform many functions that the producer would otherwise have to perform.

Sales   The wholesaler's sales force represents the producer to retailers. Obviously, if a producer had to maintain a sales force to call on retailers, its cost of sales would be much higher.

Inventory   Most wholesalers maintain warehouses in which to store merchandise. If producers had to maintain and store inventories of finished products, their costs would rise dramatically. And when a wholesaler performs the inventory function, it bears the risk of damage, theft, and obsolescence of the goods.

The Services of Wholesalers to Producers

Coloring Classics

Hollywood likes to stick with proven winners. The success of the first "Rocky" led to Rocky II, III, and IV. Rather than risk millions on an untried script, producers remake former hits like "The Postman Always Rings Twice" and "Heaven Can Wait." Or they take an unusual box-office winner like "Animal House" and develop it into a formula, a type that can be made over and over with new names and characters. Now a couple of companies have taken this trend to its logical extreme — they're re-releasing classic black-and-white films, this time in color.

To transform the old black and white into something today's video junkies will accept, a "colorist," an art director, and a computer work on the old negatives, frame by frame. First an electronic scanner breaks each frame into 525,000 separate dots which are stored in the computer. The art director selects a specific color for every object on the screen in a given scene — using up to 30 different colors at once. Then, with a digital graphics tablet and an electronic palette, the colorist handpaints each object, following the art director's instructions, as though painting-by-numbers. Because fewer than 4 percent of the dots change from one frame to the next, the computer can keep track of objects and color subsequent frames for a scene. During this process, the companies sometimes restore the negative itself and the soundtrack. And they try to be faithful to the original, getting the color of, for example, W. C. Field's nose just the right shade of red.

As you can imagine, coloring a movie negative frame by frame is an expensive business. It takes about 4 hours and about $2000 for each minute of film. But, as one enthusiastic executive involved in the process puts it, "How else can you make a proven classic movie for a couple hundred dollars?"

Once the process is complete, the new/old movie is released for pay television, broadcast syndication, video-cassettes, and foreign markets. The first color-converted movie to be broadcast nationally was Twentieth-Century Fox's "Miracle on 34th Street." The conversion cost $200,000, but two television airings brought the company five times that much, as well as ratings as good as those from a first-run movie.

One of the two leaders in the field, Colorization, Inc., has converted an old Cary Grant film, "Topper," and a Laurel and Hardy classic, "Way Out West." Its chief competitor, Color Systems Technology, Inc., is working on "Yankee Doodle Dandy" and Disney's "The Absent-Minded Professor," and plans to color 18 Shirley Temple films for Fox. Already, fans of classic television shows have enjoyed episodes of "The Twilight Zone" with colors the show's creator, Rod Serling, never envisioned.

Lovers of the black-and-white art form will no doubt reject this attempt to improve upon what was great already. Some modern directors like Woody Allen still aren't convinced that color always makes a better film. There are still some copyright problems to be dealt with. And today's young moviegoers may not be convinced to watch old films they've never heard of even if they are in color. But to companies with huge black-and-white film libraries, the new technology is the next best thing to bringing Bogart or Chaplin back from the grave to make one more film.

Sources: Eric Schmuckler, "Play It Again, Sam . . . in Color," *Forbes*, February 10, 1986, 117. Philip Elmer-DeWitt, "Play It Again, This Time in Color," *Time*, October 8, 1984, 83. Daniel P. Widener, "Color Systems Technology Inc.," *Fortune*, March 3, 1986, 45.

FIGURE 13-3

Distribution With and Without Wholesaler

On first thought, one might think adding a wholesaler to a channel of distribution would complicate matters. From this figure, it is easy to see the opposite is true.

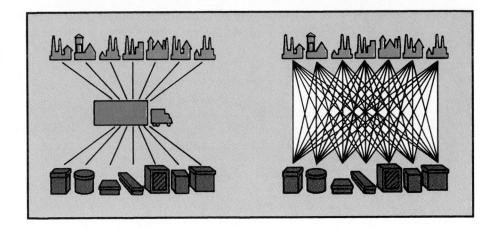

Credit   Wholesalers reduce producers' risks by extending credit to retailers.

Promotion   By assisting retailers with promotions and helping with their expense, the wholesaler does some of the producer's promotion for it and confers considerable savings on it.

Market Information   Obviously, in order to manufacture goods that customers want, producers must know what their wants are. Wholesalers, who deal with many retailers, can serve as conduits for this information.

Wholesalers' Services to Retailers

Wholesalers also provide a number of critically important services to retailers. Without them, retailers would find the cost of doing business considerably higher.

The Services of Wholesalers to Retailers

Buying   The major service that wholesalers provide retailers is buying. Without wholesalers, retailers would have to deal with hosts of producers directly, instead of working through a far smaller number of wholesalers.

Promotion   Wholesalers may provide window displays and end-of-aisle racks for specials or even designate employees to work with the retailer during special promotions. They may also offer cooperative advertising allowances, making advertising a joint venture between wholesaler and retailer.

Market Information   Retailers often find wholesalers to be unique, informal sources of market information because they deal both with producers and other retailers. Wholesalers know from other retailers what products are moving well and from producers what products are on their way.

Financial Assistance   The extension of **trade credit** is the most common way in which wholesalers grant financial assistance to retailers. We have already noted some other ways in which wholesalers provide retailers with services they would otherwise have to pay for or forego.

Inventory One of the most important services a wholesaler provides retailers is the inventory function. The wholesaler maintains a large inventory from which a retailer may purchase small quantities. Because the wholesaler bears the cost of maintaining the inventory, retailers can offer a larger selection of goods than they could if that burden fell on them.

MARKETING INTERMEDIARIES: RETAILERS

Retailers sell goods or services — or both — to consumers. Retailers vary in size from the "mom and pop" store to the giant stores operated by major chains like the R. H. Macy Company, Inc., and Albertson's, Inc. Nonstore retailing, discussed later, may take place in people's homes or at a vending machine or in the stands at a football game, and is also big business.

In-Store Retailers

Retail stores are categorized according to their operational structure. **Independent retailers** are often sole proprietorships or partnerships. **Chain stores** are groups of retail outlets under common (usually corporate) ownership and management. In-store retailers can also be categorized by the type of store they run, which we will examine next.

Types of In-Store Retailers

Department Stores A retail outlet that carries a diverse assortment of merchandise grouped into departments is a **department store**. Typically, department stores, like the Carter Hawley Hale Stores, Inc., are quite large and may

It's not business as usual in America's supermarkets. Retailing is a fast-changing field these days and stores work hard to keep ahead of the competition. There was a time when supermarkets sold food, cleaning products, a few health and beauty aids, and not much else. Not any more. This shopper can rent a video cassette while she buys food for her family's dinner.

offer everything from clothes to home furnishings to tools and major appliances, luggage, and books under one roof. Department stores also usually offer services — for example, appliance repair, delivery, and gift wrapping — as part of their marketing strategy. Credit often plays a key role in marketing; most department stores offer their own charge cards. Department stores like John Wanamaker's, Macy's, and Gimbels got their start in the mid-1800s in the central business districts of major cities. Today, at least one department store anchors nearly every major suburban shopping mall, and most department stores are chain stores.

Discount and Off-Price Stores

Retail outlets that compete primarily on the basis of price are called **discount stores**. They offer low prices, accept lower markups or margins, and generate their profits through rapid turnover of merchandise and careful cost control. Often, cost control takes the form of fewer customer services and low-rent locations. The K mart Corporation, Wal-mart Stores, Inc., and Target are well-known discount chains. Some discounters are now offering better services and improving the atmosphere in stores, which means, of course, higher prices to consumers. These retailers have become more like department stores.

An **off-price retailer** carries high-quality, name-brand merchandise priced usually 20 to 70 percent lower than department stores. These retailers buy goods at below wholesale prices, usually by purchasing "irregulars," excess stock, or off-season inventory.

Types of Mass Merchandisers

Catalog Showrooms   There is a special type of discount store called a **catalog showroom** in which only one unit of each product the store carries is on display. The customer selects the product he or she wants and it is brought to a pickup area from an adjacent warehouse. This arrangement minimizes the floor space required for display and lessens the opportunities for shoplifting and accidental damage to goods. These retail outlets are growing in popularity. Among the better known are the Service Merchandise Company, Inc., McDade & Company, Inc., and the Best Products Company, Inc.

Specialty Stores   Stores carrying a limited line of merchandise, such as records and tapes, computers, bridal gowns, or auto parts, are known as **specialty stores**. Most specialty stores are small, focus on local markets, and are managed by their owners. Rather than competing with larger retailers on the basis of price, they compete with specialized knowledge and personal service. A few offer merchandise not sold by their larger competitors, such as the King's Collar in Philadelphia, whose owner, Nancy Gold, designs and makes custom shirts.[3] Specialty stores have flourished in recent years. Between 1977 and 1982, a period of consistently poor economic news — specialty store sales grew 56 percent, one and one-half times the rate for department and variety stores.[4]

Variety Stores   A relatively small store that offers a wide range of small, inexpensive items is a **variety store**. Long known as "five and tens," the amounts the Woolworth Company charged a century ago when variety stores were a great retailing innovation, they are a dying breed. Discount stores now offer a larger selection of merchandise at competitive prices.

TABLE 13.2

America's Largest Retailing
Companies

Rank 1985	1984	Company	Sales $ Thousands
1	1	Sears Roebuck (Chicago)	40,715,300
2	2	K mart (Troy, Mich.)	22,420,002
3	3	Safeway Stores (Oakland, Calif.)	19,650,542
4	4	Kroger (Cincinnati)	17,123,531
5	6	American Stores (Salt Lake City)	13,889,528
6	5	J.C. Penney (New York)	13,747,000
7	7	Southland (Dallas)	12,719,241
8	8	Federated Department Stores (Cincinnati)	9,978,027
9	9	Lucky Stores (Dublin, Calif.)	9,382,282
10	11	Dayton Hudson (Minneapolis)	8,793,372
11	10	Household International (Prospect Heights, Ill.)	8,685,500
12	13	Wal-mart Stores (Bentonville, Ark.)	8,580,910
13	12	Winn-Dixie Stores (Jacksonville, Fla.)	7,774,480
14	15	F.W. Woolworth (New York)	5,958,000
15	16	BATUS (Louisville)	5,881,408
16	17	Great Atlantic & Pacific Tea (Montvale, N.J.)	5,878,286
17	14	Montgomery Ward (Chicago)	5,388,000
18	21	Supermarkets General (Woodbridge, N.J.)	5,122,633
19	18	May Department Stores (St. Louis)	5,079,900
20	19	Albertson's (Boise)	5,060,265
21	20	Melville (Harrison, N.Y.)	4,805,380

Source: "The 50 Largest U.S. Retailing Companies," June 10, 1985, *Fortune* magazine. © 1985 Time Inc. All rights reserved.

Food and Related Retailers

Supermarkets   The familiar large food stores known as **supermarkets** offer relatively low prices and carry many nationally recognized brands displayed in various departments, most of which are self-service. They principally sell food, but more and more supermarkets have moved into carrying nonfood items, like flowers, housewares, books, and drugs, because extremely stiff competition has led to very low profit margins on food — often 1 or 2 percent. The Kroger Company and Safeway Stores, Inc., are two of the leading supermarket chains.

Superstores and Hypermarkets   Supermarkets evolved into **superstores** and **hypermarkets**. They are large stores offering a broad selection of food, specialty food, and nonfood items. They often include a flower shop, a pharmacy, a delicatessen, a bakery, and a cafe. Some have electronic teller services connecting them to a bank.

Warehouse Stores   A discount or off-price food store that offers approximately the same merchandise as supermarkets but has virtually no ambience or services is called a **warehouse store**. Heartland Food Warehouses in New England not only have the customer bag the groceries but charge for bags if he or she fails to bring enough. Still, many customers find the lower prices worth the effort.

FIGURE 13-4

Wheel of Retailing

Retailing and retailers evolve over time. The concept of wheeling of retailing describes the effect of new competitors' innovations in a retail market.

High prices and markups, many services, expensive surroundings

Low prices and markups, few services, austere surroundings

Among the leading warehouse chains are Edwards Food Warehouse, Warehouse Foods, and the Pic n Save Corporation.

Convenience Stores Food stores called **convenience stores** are considerably smaller than supermarkets and offer a limited range of staples and snack foods at prices considerably higher than those at supermarkets. These stores charge premium prices because they are open from eighteen to twenty-four hours a day, seven days a week. The leading convenience stores are Open Pantry Food Marts, Inc., Seven-Eleven Convenience Food Stores (Southland Stores), and Stop n Go (National Convenience Stores).

Nonstore Retailers

Retailers who do not operate in conventional store facilities are **nonstore retailers**. They include in-home retailers, mail-order houses, and vending machines.

In-Home Retailers Someone who sells directly to customers in their homes is an **in-home retailer**. If the retailer books an order, the merchandise is generally delivered quite soon after the sale. Among the leaders in this field are World Book, Inc., for encyclopedias, Avon, and Electrolux vacuum cleaners. Decorating Den, a nationally franchised consulting service, brings designing vans to homes so consumers can choose from paint and drapery samples, carpet squares, and everything else a consumer needs to make home redecorating decisions.[5]

They're Not Just "Sneakers" Anymore

Reebok is a company with an identity problem — the kind of problem most companies wish they had. Many different groups of people think that Reebok shoes are just for them. Reebok has British roots, yet its shoes sell mostly in America. The company is a former subsidiary of the world's oldest athletic-shoe maker, Foster, yet to most Americans it's the new kid on the block, the fad shoe of the 1980s. Until 1979, the company made running shoes for top runners by hand, and most Americans first saw the name on aerobics shoes, introduced in 1983. Yet competitors call the Reebok "a women's fashion shoe." As long as such identity confusion keeps paying off, Reebok probably doesn't care what people call their shoes.

And the shoes have been paying off enormously well. Sales and profits have been increasing five- or six-fold every year, and in just a few years the company has grown to challenge Nike's top spot in the American athletic shoe market. Reeboks' popularity has caused a flurry of activity among competitors trying to match the shoes' looks and soft, supple feel.

Reebok's chief executive, Paul Fireman, attributes much of the company's success to one of the basic rules of marketing: find out what people want and give it to them. Reebok entered the market just as athletic shoes were becoming fashionable to wear anywhere, not just in a gym or on a track. Analysts estimate that 70 percent of basketball and aerobics shoes are now used primarily for street wear. The company recognized that people wanted fashionable good looks and comfort in their sneakers, and it produced striking shoes in a variety of colors and models made out of the softest leather most people had ever put on their feet.

By getting women interested in athletic shoes, Reebok tapped an enormous market that traditionally had resisted paying $40 for sneakers. Apparently many women liked being able to wear their aerobics shoes all day, feeling stylish and comfortable. Soon the company found that it was drawing business away from makers of conventional casual shoes as well as from athletic shoe manufacturers. Once Reeboks became chic to wear anywhere, the fad took off. Although the company spends more than $10 million on advertisements, its best publicity comes unsolicited from stars. Mick Jagger wore Reeboks on his music video "Dancin' in the Street." Bruce Springsteen and Lionel Richie have also worn them on-screen. And Cybill Shepherd appeared in orange Reeboks with a high fashion black dress at the Emmy awards.

Of course any company riding the wave of a fad has to worry about that wave crashing. Competitors' soft-leather shoes may soon eat into Reebok's business. And the supple leather itself can sometimes be a problem, tearing away from the rubber soles, leading an unusually large number of customers to return defective shoes. Reebok so far has been unsuccessful at selling its shoes on the Continent, and its new clothing line has yet to catch on. But as long as Reeboks manage to be different things to different people, the company should continue to do well even if aerobics becomes passé.

Sources: Lynn Langway, "Doing the Reebok Be-Bop," *Newsweek*, Vol. 105, No. 24, June 17, 1985, 79. Jeffrey A. Trachtenberg, "Reebok Madness," *Forbes*, Vol. 136, No. 1, July 1, 1985, 84. Lois Therrien, "Reeboks: How Far Can a Fad Run?" *Business Week*, February 24, 1986, 89.

A relatively new form of in-home retailing is "party sales." Sales representatives recruit a cooperative customer to put on a party so that the sales person can show his or her merchandise to several customers at once. The Tupperware Division of Dart & Kraft, Mary Kay Cosmetics, Inc., and Sarah Coventry, Inc., successfully use this approach.

Types of Nonstore Retailing

Mail-Order Retailers   A retailer who issues a catalog from which consumers can choose items and place their orders by mail or telephone is a **mail-order retailer**. Such retailers generally offer competitive prices, a relatively wide selection of goods, and, most importantly, convenience for busy customers. A few catalog retailers even offer prestige products and charge premium prices. For some mail-order retailers, catalog sales are their only source of revenue. For others, like L. L. Bean, Inc., Cabela's, and Bass Pro Shops, a comparatively small portion of their receipts comes from in-store sales. For the most famous mail order retailer, Sears, Roebuck and Company, catalog sales now make up only a small (though critical) portion of its revenues.

Vending Machines   When a customer inserts the appropriate amount of money, a credit card, or a code into a **vending machine**, an electromechanical device dispenses something. Vending machines offer place utility in locations where it is impractical to operate a retail outlet. They supply soft drinks and snacks. However, vending machines have recently come into use also as providers of necessities for travelers, such as toothbrushes, combs, and even airline tickets and banking services, among other things. Vending machines do have a downside — they are expensive to operate and maintain — but the vending-machine business is growing, because their convenience makes them profitable.

Mail order retailing. L.L. Bean is one of the best-known mail order companies in America. L.L. Bean sells casual clothing and outdoor goods to many consumers who want quality and convenience.

The Wheel of Retailing

One method of describing the evolution of retailing and retailers over time is called the **wheel of retailing**. This concept describes the effect of new competitors' innovations in a retail market.

A new retail entrant gets the wheel moving when it recognizes a void in the market, usually at the low end of the price spectrum. The innovator challenges the established retailers by offering lower prices, cutting service and ambience, minimizing expenses, and accepting a lower profit margin. However, as the new competitor matures, it upgrades merchandise, adds services, improves the store's appearance, and increases its promotional expenses — all in the quest for still-higher profits. In the end, the former innovator joins the ranks of higher margined, higher priced, mature retailers. Then it in turn becomes vulnerable to innovators filling the low-price void.

How Innovation Affects the Retail Market

Supermarkets, for example, have moved up the wheel of retailing. When they first appeared, they were usually self-service operations located in buildings with limited aesthetic appeal, like old warehouses. Over time, supermarkets evolved into the typically attractive modern market that offers many services. This progress up the wheel has caused supermarket prices to increase enough to encourage a new form of food retailing, the warehouse store.

Another classic example of the wheel of retailing at work is Detroit's vulnerability to low-priced imports, first from Japan and Germany and now from Korea

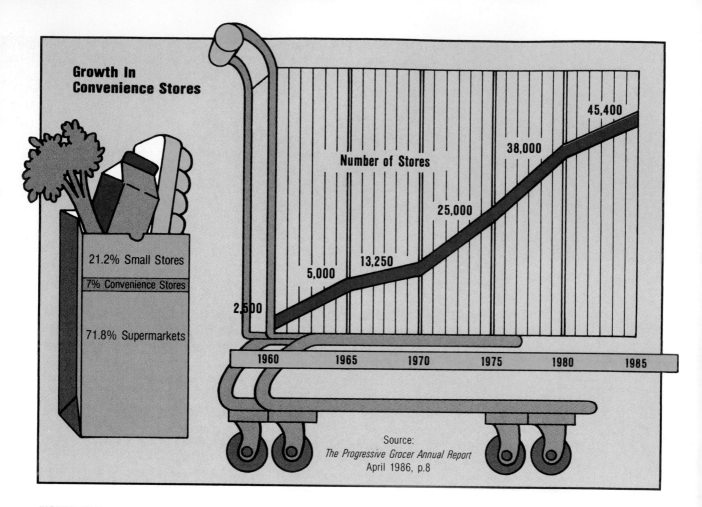

Growth In Convenience Stores

21.2% Small Stores

7% Convenience Stores

71.8% Supermarkets

Number of Stores

2,500

5,000

13,250

25,000

38,000

45,400

1960　1965　1970　1975　1980　1985

Source:
The Progressive Grocer Annual Report
April 1986, p.8

FIGURE 13-5

Where consumers spend their food dollars and the growth of convenience stores.

and Yugoslavia. In fact, the Japanese had largely vacated the low end of the car market in favor of higher margined models. The wheel works even in the fast-food business. John Jay Hooker has started Hooker's Hamburgers, a no-frills operation emphasizing a low-priced 99-cent hamburger and fast service for drive-through customers. (However, Hooker's last attempt to introduce competition to a fast food market — Minnie Pearl's Fried Chicken franchises — ended in one of the 1970s' most spectacular bankruptcies.)[6]

PHYSICAL DISTRIBUTION

Try to visualize all the products you bought in the last month. Did you ever ask yourself how they came to be where you bought them? One reason the American quality of life is so high is our ability to bring products from across the nation and around the world into outlets in the most remote parts of the country. This process of moving goods is called **physical distribution**. "Moving goods" brings to mind transportation, a most important part of physical distribution, but there are other critical aspects of physical distribution as well. These steps include materials handling, order processing, and inventory control.

A corporation's view of itself. When Emery says it aims to deliver information, packages, and cargo any weight, any size, anywhere, it means it. Determined to grow as a company and to provide its employees with career growth opportunities, Emery now offers a truly global transportation service.

Transportation

The process of actually moving goods from one location to another is called **transportation**. Note, incidentally, that the transportation of goods and the passage of title to goods are entirely separate concepts. There is no necessary connection between the physical movement of goods and a change in ownership. For instance, a grain dealer may buy 100,000 bushels of wheat stored in an elevator and resell the wheat without moving it.

Transportation Factors

Before a product reaches its ultimate user or consumer, at each point in the channel of distribution someone must make a decision as to how it will reach the next point. The producer, for instance, must decide how it will reach a wholesaler. Several factors affect the transportation decision, not the least of which is cost. However, other factors may outweigh cost alone, such as the recipient's timely need for the goods. It is no coincidence that the U.S. Postal Service leaped into the already crowded overnight-delivery field with its Express Mail service and competed quite effectively on price. The perishability of goods may also dictate particular modes of transportation. Freshly cut tulips from Holland must be flown to Minneapolis because even the fastest boat met by the fastest train could not outrace their deterioration.

Types of Carriers Firms that offer transportation services are called **carriers**. A **private carrier** is a carrier owned and operated by a shipper. For instance, some oil companies operate private carriers to distribute gasoline to service stations. A **common carrier** is a firm that offers transportation services to **The Organization of a Physical Distribution System** the public. Allied Van Lines is a common carrier. A **freight forwarder** is a common carrier that will often lease space from other carriers and combine small individual shipments into economical lot sizes. Emery Worldwide is a freight forwarder. A **contract carrier** provides service to one shipper or a limited number of shippers. Carriers provide transportation in all the categories compared and listed in Table 13.3.

You only have to turn it on. Actually pipelines are a little more complicated than that, but they're still one of the cheapest and easiest ways to transport certain types of products. While pipeline construction is expensive and complex, once the equipment is in place it needs relatively little attention and can reach a wide geographic area. Tennessee Gas operates within a 26-state marketing area.

The Five Principal Modes of Transportation

Railroads Railroads carry more total freight than any other transportation mode. For many large or bulky products, rail transport is the least expensive option that meets minimum speed requirements. Railroads do not reach all areas, however, nor are they generally able to move goods door to door.

Trucks Virtually no product escapes being transported by truck at some stage. Often goods are shipped by rail to a central distribution point, then by truck to retailers or smaller distribution centers. In the 1950s innovative railroaders came up with the idea of "piggy back" service. Loaded trailers were placed on modified flat cars for shipment to central distribution facilities. There they were offloaded, hooked to tractors, and pulled to retailers or end-users. Piggybacking combined the energy efficiency and lower costs of rail transport with the convenience of truck delivery.

Water Barges and cargo ships are the least expensive means of transporting goods. Their disadvantage is their relative slowness. Water transport is ideally suited for bulky nonperishable goods like iron ore, coal, grain, and motor vehicles. Barges and ships can also offer piggyback service connecting with road or rail transport.

Air Air transport is the fastest and most expensive means of transporting goods. For that reason, air carriers typically transport only items of high value or goods that are highly perishable or are needed immediately. The General

TABLE 13.3

Comparing Modes of
Transportation

	Rail	Truck	Water	Air	Pipeline
Speed	fair	good	poor	best	worst
Cost	moderate	high	low	highest	lowest
Locations served	many	most	few	moderate	fewest
On-time dependability	fair	good	poor	worst	best
Frequency	low	high	lowest	fair	highest

Source: Evans & Berman, *Marketing*, 2nd ed. (New York: Macmillan, 1985), Figure 12-9.

Motors Corporation is flying the bodies for its $50,000 Cadillac Allante from Turin, Italy, to Detroit at a cost of $2,500 to $2,800 per car. The time that would be lost and the capital tied up during the month it would take GM to transport the bodies by boat justifies this expense for them.[7] It is possible that with all the entrants into this field — from United Parcel Service to Purolator Courier Corporation to the Flying Tiger Line, Inc. — air prices will decline, but not to the level of trucks.

Pipelines Pipelines can carry only certain types of products, like natural gas and oil. They have very high fixed costs but low variable costs. In other words, they cost a lot to build but not a lot to maintain and operate. When they are in heavy use, their total cost per measure moved can be quite low.

Warehousing

The set of activities designed to ensure that goods are available when they are needed is known as **warehousing**. This process is not simply one of storing goods in a building called a warehouse. Among the activities of warehousing are:

- ☐ Receiving the goods
- ☐ Identifying the goods
- ☐ Sorting the goods
- ☐ Holding the goods
- ☐ Assembling shipments
- ☐ Dispatching shipments

Each of these activities requires recordkeeping so that the goods are always easily retrievable. Recordkeeping is also important because goods are often sold or used as security for a loan by transferring the **warehouse receipt**, the record that a public warehouseman gives a person who is storing goods. A **public warehouse** is a storage building that can be used by the general public to store goods for a fee. A **private warehouse** is one owned by a firm that has sole access to it. Maintaining a private warehouse can be expensive, especially if the firm does not use all the space.

Materials Handling

The physical handling of items during transportation and warehousing is called **materials handling**. Efficient, effective materials handling is critically important to any business selling goods because of its potential effects on customer satisfaction and on costs from breakage or spoilage. Almost everyone has at some time bought a product that proved to be damaged when its carton was opened. Quite often, such damage results from the misuse or careless use of materials-handling devices, like forklifts. One way to reduce the likelihood of damage to goods is to minimize the number of times a product is handled. Good warehouse organization can help do this. Putting smaller units together to form a larger load — say, a pallet load or a truckload — also keeps handling to a minimum.

Order Processing

The physical distribution activity known as **order processing** has as its purpose the receiving and filling of customers' orders. Fast, accurate order processing can be a major advantage for a firm. Regardless of whether they are intermediaries of some sort or end-users or consumers, customers want their orders filled quickly and without errors.

Inventory Control

The purpose of **inventory control** is to develop and maintain levels and assortments of products appropriate for a firm's target markets. If a firm holds too many items in inventory, it will have unduly high carrying costs. On the other hand, if the firm carries too low an inventory, it risks running out of certain merchandise and losing sales. Inventory control's goal is to balance these risks.

The advent of the inexpensive microcomputer has given firms almost total control over their inventories, if they choose to take advantage of the technology. The computer can tell them both how much they have in inventory and how much it is costing to carry it. However, even the best computer equipment cannot make up for incorrect data entry, shoplifting, and pilfering. It can help find out what happened more easily and enable the firm to act to halt the losses.

DISTRIBUTION: A PERSPECTIVE

Talking to some people about inventory control or methods of transporting goods makes their eyes glaze over. "Dull stuff! When it gets to be a problem, then I'll think about it." In the last ten years, however, the physical distribution of goods has become a hot topic not just among penny-conscious managers but also among aggressive entrepreneurs.

Manufacturers, particularly in the auto industry, have noted the benefits that Japanese producers have reaped from **just-in-time inventory systems**, programs designed to ensure a continuous flow of manufacturing input from suppliers while

Computers have changed the way warehouses do business. CFS Continental has 17 full-line distribution centers. Each center handles approximately 10,000 products for food-service customers. Up-to-the-minute technology allows these centers to track their inventory, move product efficiently, and give their customers the kind of information and service they expect.

The Inventory-Control Function

Outlet for Frustrated Shoppers

More than 10,000 buses a year journey to Reading, Pennsylvania, from as far away as Washington, D.C. — 138 miles. Reading isn't a transportation center, and the people don't come to look at historical sites or Amish buggies. They come to find bargains and vent their frustration with overpriced goods at retail stores. They come to shop the outlets.

Shopping at factory outlet stores has been called a "sport" and an "obsession" for some people. Bargain-minded shoppers plan entire vacations around visiting various outlets, and tourist areas like Freeport, Maine have become modernized meccas because of their outlet stores.

For years, some companies sold their products — often seconds or damaged items — directly to the public at a discount. These traditional factory outlets usually occupied a dusty corner of the factory building itself, and customers often had to hunt for matching shoes or find the right size themselves. During the 1970s, however, such outlets began to gain popularity and to outgrow their musty quarters, moving into separate, more pleasant buildings. Manufacturers began to see the outlets as places to move a lot of merchandise without high overhead.

But it wasn't until the 1980s that outlets really caught on, along with the latest phenomenon, the factory outlet mall. In 1980, there were 60 such malls around the country; now there are over six times that number. Sales from factory outlets reached $10 billion in 1985, rising at a 17 percent rate, almost six times the rate of growth of overall retail sales.

Of the outlets' appeal, a retailing consultant says, "Customers get self-esteem not so much from buying status merchandise but from buying status merchandise at a discount." At discounts of up to 50 percent below standard retail prices, shoppers can buy Dansk housewares, Bass shoes, and Calvin Klein clothing. In an outlet mall a clever shopper can buy a year's supply of wedding and Christmas gifts without having to repeat a brand name.

One visitor to Reading, "the Factory Outlet Capital of the U.S.A.," spent $573 in outlets, then went home (210 miles away) to price the same items in local stores. She saved over $700. On a good weekend 40,000 cars cram the parking lot outside Ceasar's Bay Bazaar in Brooklyn, a former Korvettes building that houses 360 individual booths. In Southern California, you can sign up for Tours About Town which will take you to the garment district and give you tips on where the bargains are. In other parts of the country, recently published guidebooks provide the names and locations of the best outlets.

Many outlet stores now stock first-quality, popular merchandise rather than the outmoded seconds that used to fill their shelves. They hold prices down by keeping overhead low. Many outlet malls are not in prime location, high-rent areas, and while most outlet stores are now brighter, neater, and more spacious than were the original outlets, they still lack many of the touches that make standard retail stores classier and costlier.

Not everyone is pleased by the boom in outlet sales. Some retailers don't like to compete with outlets and blame manufacturers for undercutting their own retail sales. Other retailers don't worry about losing business, certain that their selection and service will keep customers heading to them rather than to the outlets.

No matter how they feel about it, retailers are going to have to get used to competing with outlet malls, which have altered the way Americans shop and even the way they plan and take vacations. After you've spent a couple of days in Disney World and Epcot center, what do you do with the rest of your time in Orlando? Go to Belz Factory Outlet Mall, of course. You may not find a bargain you like, but if you do, you'll save enough money to pay for part of the trip.

Sources: Lois Therrien, "The Wholesale Success of Factory Outlet Malls," *Business Week*, February 3, 1986, 92. Diane McWhorter, "Designer Outlets Transform a Town," *The New York Times*, February 13, 1986, c1. "Cut Rate Fever," *Time*, October 4, 1982, 59. "Render, Therefore, Unto Ceasar's Bay," *Chain Store Executive*, March 1983, 97.

at the same time minimizing the amount of goods held in inventory. Just-in-time systems rely on sophisticated warehousing, materials handling, order processing, and inventory control at both ends of the industrial channels of distribution.

Just-in-time inventory systems require fast, reliable transportation systems. The everyday requirements of many businesses in our fast-paced world place demands on our transportation systems that were inconceivable fifteen years ago. Only a few insightful people like Federal Express's Fred Smith foresaw those demands. In 1965, under pressure to produce an undergraduate economics term paper, Smith came up with the basic outline of what would become Federal's unique distribution network (he got a C grade). Following three years in the Marines and after developing a highly successful airplane brokerage business, Smith launched Federal Express at the age of twenty-eight.[8] Today it is hard to imagine our transportation system without Federal Express and its many competitors.

When products are in transit or in storage, time is certainly money. More than one historian has attributed our economic system's success to our willingness to innovate in transportation. With space shuttles, new generations of jet aircraft, innovative approaches to material handling, a reinvigorated rail system, and thousands of less obvious innovations, we are in the midst of another distribution revolution. Its end is not yet in sight.

Chapter Highlights

1. Define the term *marketing intermediaries*.

Marketing intermediaries are firms between the producer and the ultimate user or consumer that take title or directly assist others to take title to goods or that assist in physically moving or storing goods. These are commonly wholesalers, agents or brokers, distributors, or retailers and any firms that handle the physical distribution of products.

2. Describe the basic channels of distribution for consumer and industrial products.

Consumer products use one of three channels (see Figure 13.1): (A) producer to consumer, (B) producer to retailer to consumer, or (C) producer to wholesaler to retailer to consumer. Industrial products use one of four channels: (D) producer to industrial user, (E) producer to distributor to industrial user, (F) producer to agent/broker to industrial user, or (G) producer to agent/broker to distributor to industrial user.

3. Distinguish between intensive, selective, and exclusive distribution strategies.

Intensive distribution is a strategy that attempts to place a product in all available retail outlets. With selective distribution, a moderate proportion of retail outlets carry a particular product in a given market. Some producers use exclusive distribution, in which a single retailer carries the product in a given retail area.

4. List two main types of wholesalers and identify their functions.

Full-service merchant wholesalers take title to goods and offer the largest variety of services. Limited-service merchant wholesalers take title to goods but offer fewer services. However, they tend to specialize in the services they do offer. Agents and brokers receive a commission for bringing together buyers and sellers; they do not take title to goods. These intermediaries help to move products more efficiently through the distribution channel.

5. Specify the services wholesalers provide to producers and retailers.

Wholesalers commonly provide the following services to retailers: buying, promoting products, gathering and interpreting market information, extending credit, and maintaining inventory.

6. List the main types of retailers and identify their functions.

In-store retailers include department, discount, off-price, and specialty stores; catalog showrooms; variety stores; supermarkets; superstores and hypermarkets; warehouse stores; and convenience stores. Nonstore retailers include in-home retailers, mail-order retailers, and vending machines.

7. Describe the organization of a physical distribution system.

Physical distribution involves transportation (the physical movement of goods), warehousing (including receiving, identifying, sorting, and holding goods, and assembling and dispatching shipments), materials handling (the physical handling of items during transportation and warehousing), order processing (the activities connected with receiving and filling customers' orders), and inventory control (the procedures necessary to develop and maintain desired levels and assortments of products).

8. Identify the five principal modes of transportation for goods and discuss their advantages and disadvantages.

Of the five principal modes of transportation for goods, railroads are often the least expensive, but they may not be available for a given location and can only rarely provide door-to-door service. Trucks are moderately inexpensive, moderately fast, and offer high accessibility. They are often piggybacked on trains to combine the efficiency and low cost of rail with the convenience of trucks. Cargo ships or barges are the least expensive mode of transportation, but they are quite slow. Air transport is generally the fastest and most expensive way to transport goods. Pipelines are expensive to build and can carry only certain types of products but are inexpensive to operate.

9. Explain the difference between a public warehouse and a private warehouse.

A public warehouse can be used by the general public to store goods for a fee. A private warehouse is owned and maintained by a specific firm for its own use.

Key Terms

Administered marketing system
Agent (broker)
Atmospherics
Carriers
Catalog showroom
Chain stores
Channels of distribution
Common carrier
Contract carrier
Contractual vertical-marketing system
Convenience stores
Corporate vertical-marketing system
Department store

Discount store
Distribution channel
Exclusive distribution strategy
Freight forwarder
Full-service wholesaler
Hypermarket (superstore)
Independent retailer
Intensive distribution strategy
Inventory control
Just-in-time inventory systems
Limited-service wholesaler

Mail-order retailer
Market coverage
Marketing channel
Marketing intermediaries (middlemen)
Materials handling
Merchant
Middlemen
Nonstore retailer
Off-price retailer
Order processing
Physical distribution
Private carrier
Public warehouse
Retailer

Selective distribution strategy
Specialty store
Supermarket
Superstore
Title
Transportation
Variety store
Vending machine
Vertical-channel integration
Warehouse receipt
Warehouse store
Warehousing
Wheel of retailing
Wholesaler

Review Questions

1. Provide an overview of the channels of distribution.
2. List, then discuss, the three basic degrees of market coverage.
3. Describe the four basic consumer channels of distribution.
4. Identify the main industrial channels of distribution and define their functions.
5. How do consumer channels differ from industrial channels?
6. What roles do marketing intermediaries play?
7. List the services that wholesalers provide to producers and retailers.
8. Distinguish wholesalers from retailers.
9. Identify the principal types of industrial channel intermediaries and describe their roles.
10. What are the principal types of in-store retailers and how are they different from each other?
11. Specify the major types of nonstore retailing.
12. Describe the role of physical distribution in the marketing process.

Application Exercises

1. During a recent vacation in Ireland you became acquainted with a line of very high quality Irish sweaters for men and women. At the present time these products are not available to consumers in America. Describe at least three channels of distribution that might be used to direct these products to consumers. Which channel do you feel would be most effective?

2. Identify at least two wholesale firms that provide services to retailers in your community. What services to producers do these firms provide? What services to retailers do they provide? In your opinion, are these wholesalers fulfilling an important marketing function?

Cases

13.1 Spiegel's "Store in Print"

The Direct Marketing Association estimates that the number of mail-order catalogs sent to consumers has been increasing by an average of 20 percent each year. Some 10 billion were sent in 1985 alone — more than forty catalogs for every man, woman, and child in the United States.

The proliferation of catalogs has paralleled a boom in mail-order purchasing, which seems to fit the busy lifestyles of many Americans. But that boom has also brought increased competition and, with it, the demise of a number of established catalogs. The Montgomery Ward catalog, which had been published for 113 years was discontinued in 1985.

One catalog that did not go under is that of Spiegel, Inc., the nation's third largest mail-order retailer. Instead, the Spiegel catalog went through a total changeover. Until the early 1980s, Spiegel featured low-priced general mer-

chandise, targeted primarily to low-income customers. But those customers were being lost to discount stores like K mart and Zayre. Sales were holding at about $300 million annually, but profits were slim.

In 1981, under new ownership and management, Spiegel completely revamped its marketing approach. Rather than a low-priced mail-order retailer, Spiegel would become a "fine department store in print." Its target market would be comprised of busy working women, who were willing to buy more expensive items but didn't have the time to shop for them. To satisfy that market, Spiegel rewrote its catalog from front to back. The new and elegant catalog featured designer fashions by Evan Picone, Liz Claiborne, and Pierre Cardin. In place of hand tools, it featured home computers. And instead of low price, it featured fashion, quality, and a guarantee of satisfaction. To complete the transition, Spiegel redirected its mailing lists and advertising toward working women.

Two years later, Spiegel began to publish specialty

catalogs, directed toward smaller market segments and featuring such things as furs, gourmet Kitchenware, and hard-to-find sizes. The firm now publishes more than thirty of them.

The result of Spiegel's changeover: a new look, new and expanding markets, increasing sales (and profits) year after year since 1981, and the expectation of a $1 billion sales year by 1988 at the latest.

Questions

1. Describe the distribution channel that includes Spiegel, Inc.
2. What functions do catalogs perform for a mail-order retailer like Spiegel Inc.?
3. In what ways did (or didn't) Spiegel take atmospherics into account in its changeover?

For more information see *Forbes*, August 11, 1986, p. 112; *The Wall Street Journal*, January 19, 1986, p. 19; and *Forbes*, July 4, 1983, pp. 138–139.

13.2 Absolutely, Positively Innovative

Fred Smith believes that innovation is important to a firm's survival, and he should know. It was his innovation — Federal Express Corporation — that began the multi-billion-dollar overnight delivery industry. Smith says the key to innovation is the willingness to examine a problem from every possible angle, and to continue doing so until a solution is found. His formula also includes a bit of intuition, proper timing, the willingness to take a risk on the solution, and the ability to stick with that solution.

Smith's problem was to provide fast, reliable delivery of small packages throughout the United States. His solution was to pick up the packages by truck, fly them to a single central "hub" where they would be sorted and rerouted, and then fly them to their destinations — all overnight — for truck delivery the next day. Smith risked

$76 million on his solution (including $4 million of his own). His ability to stick with his solution was tested immediately, because Federal Express shipped a total of seventeen packages in its first night of operation. Today, the firm moves half a million parcels each night.

When traffic managers and purchasing managers balked at the higher prices necessitated by air delivery, Smith tried a new strategy. He had his sales reps call on administrative people, including executive secretaries, and had them stress Federal's·speed and reliability: Here was a way they could get themselves out of a time bind, for a relatively small extra cost. It was only a small step from there to Federal's "absolutely, positively . . . overnight."

All Federal Express representatives take a Distribution Problem Solving Course; the course prepares them to help customers find the best way to move goods within a defined time period, and at reduced cost. And to ensure reliability, Federal is working on a radar system that allows pilots to "see" through fog that might otherwise close airports down.

Federal's latest major innovation is ZapMail — an electronic transmission service for almost any kind of document. Federal can pick up a document, transmit a copy across the country, and deliver the copy in under two hours. ZapMail has had an unexpectedly slow start, but Smith feels that the timing is right and the service is needed. He intends to stick with it until it "flies."

Questions

1. Because Federal Express markets a service, it is essentially restricted to a single type of distribution channel. What is that channel? What characteristics of services make it mandatory to use that channel?
2. In what ways could the consistent use of overnight delivery affect the other parts of a firm's physical distribution system?

For more information see *Inc.*, October 1986, pp. 35–50; and *Inbound Logistics*, January 1986, pp. 11–13 and 15–17.

CITIZEN WATCH
2:57:02
CITIZEN WATCH

FINISH NEW YORK CITY

izen Watch ★ The Runner ★ New York Telephone ★ Rudin Fa

14
PROMOTION STRATEGY

Learning Objectives

After you have completed this chapter, you will be able to do the following:

- Define promotion and describe two major promotional objectives.
- Identify at least two promotional strategies.
- List the elements of the promotional mix.
- Define advertising and identify the three principal types of advertising.
- Weigh the advantages and disadvantages of the principal advertising media.
- List the six steps in the selling process.
- Describe the four major types of sales positions.
- Define sales promotion and identify the principal means involved.
- Distinguish between publicity and public relations.

When Paul Newman sped across the finish line in 1985 at the Road Atlanta race course, the man who gave him the checkered flag was not following a movie script. The sixty-year-old actor, producer, and professional driver had not only driven his Nissan 300ZX Turbo to victory but had clinched the National Sports Car Club of America's GT-1 Division championship. As pleased as Newman was, the representatives of the Nissan Motor Corporation were even more so. Nissan had invested hundreds of thousands of dollars in the car and in related promotional activities. The combination of a victory in a prestigious race, a photogenic celebrity driver, and a championship meant enormous opportunities for promotion and the prospect of a significant boost to Nissan's sales.

Promotion is an activity not limited to for-profit businesses. An ever-growing number of nonprofit corporations are developing their own unique promotional mixes. Hospitals, civic orchestras, convention centers, colleges and universities, and local arts councils are among the more familiar examples. Like for-profit businesses, the nonprofits face the problem of gaining and retaining the patronage of those who might benefit from their services. Although this chapter focuses on the planning of promotions and on the elements of the marketing mix in the context of for-profit companies, keep in mind that the same principles apply to nonprofit organizations.

THE NATURE OF PROMOTION

Promotion Defined

For most consumers, promotion is the most visible of marketing's Four P's: Price, Product, Place, and Promotion. **Promotion** describes the communications that an entity uses to inform, persuade, or remind a target market about its product, its services, its message, or itself.

Promotional Objectives

Businesses use promotion not just to increase sales but also to manage sales. They use promotion to increase sales of specific products, increase sales at a particular time, or even decrease sales or demand temporarily.

Two Major Promotional Objectives

Some firms may want to build up sales of a new product or of an established one that is generating high profits. Some companies design their promotional strategies to increase a product's market share, whereas others use promotion to differentiate their product by establishing its market niche. Another firm may hope to increase sales of its products at off-peak periods. For instance, big city hotels may advertise sharply reduced rates for weekend tourists to fill the rooms that business travelers demand during the week. And turkey breeders have successfully extended the demand for what was once only holiday fare. Today supermarkets carry turkeys all year-round. Finally, when manufacturers cannot meet the demand for a new product, they should use promotion to maintain customer good will. The computer industry has frequently used this strategy when long-promised machines or software is late.

FIGURE 14-1

Push-Pull Strategy

A push strategy is directed at selling goods or services directly to the next entity down the channel of distribution. The pull strategy attempts to develop consumer demand for a product or a service primarily through advertising or sales promotion.

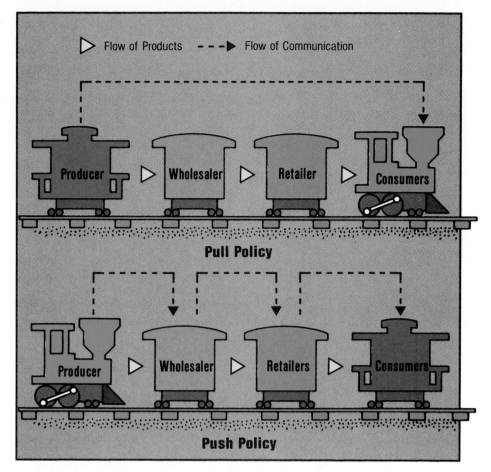

Flow of Products   - - -▶ Flow of Communication

Producer ▷ Wholesaler ▷ Retailer ▷ Consumers

Pull Policy

Producer ▷ Wholesaler ▷ Retailers ▷ Consumers

Push Policy

Promotional Strategies

Effective promotion requires careful planning. In most larger corporations, the marketing manager or the vice president for marketing oversees and coordinates promotional activities. Promotional planning begins with the need to make a choice between two distinct promotional strategies: push or pull.

A **push strategy** is directed at selling goods or services directly to the next intermediary in the channels of distribution, which we discussed in the last chapter. The success of a push strategy depends largely on the effectiveness of an organization's sales force. It is often appropriate for low-volume, high-value items like mainframe computers or construction equipment where buyers tend to rely on salespeople to answer questions and suggest appropriate options. It can also work for low-value consumer goods.

Frito-Lay, Inc., relies on a push strategy. This snack-food manufacturer's whole organization is committed to providing a 99.5 percent service level to its ten-thousand-person sales force, who in turn make over four hundred thousand sales calls to retail accounts per week. To achieve it, Frito-Lay does things that lose money in the short run to keep stores stocked with fresh products. Sending a truck to restock a store with a few thirty-dollar cartons of potato chips can cost several hundred dollars. Braving extraordinary weather to deliver a box of potato chips or helping a store owner clean up after a hurricane, as Frito-Lay

Two Promotional Strategies

sales representatives have done, do not pay an immediate return either. Store owners remember this dedication to service, however, which may explain how Frito-Lay has captured 70 percent of the potato chip, tortilla chip, and corn chip market in some parts of the country.[1]

The other approach, the **pull strategy**, promotes a product or service directly to the consumer, primarily through advertising or sales promotion. A pull strategy is most effective with high-volume, low-value products like laundry soap or chewing gum. When the Procter & Gamble Company developed its improved Crest toothpaste, it promoted the new product by sending sample tubes to consumers across the country. Procter & Gamble's objective was to encourage the ultimate consumers to ask their retailers for the new product. The retailers would then order the improved Crest from the next intermediary up the channel of distribution. In another market, the recording industry uses videos developed for television to stimulate consumer demand from retailers. They order records and tapes from wholesalers, who in turn order them from the record companies.

The push and pull strategies are, of course, not mutually exclusive, and firms often use both at the same time. For example, Pella Windows & Doors, which manufactures a high-quality product, has developed a strong distribution network of home-center stores, lumberyards, and other businesses catering to builders and home owners. At the same time, it advertises in magazines like *Southern Living*, *Yankee*, and *McCall's* to build interest among ultimate consumers.

The Promotional Mix

Promotional activities fall into four categories:

The Elements in the
Promotional Mix

☐ Advertising
☐ Personal selling
☐ Sales promotion
☐ Publicity and public relations

The way a firm combines these elements in its promotion strategy is called its **promotional mix**. We will examine each element in the following sections.

ADVERTISING

Advertising Defined

The American Marketing Association (AMA) defines **advertising** as "any paid form of nonpersonal presentation and promotion of ideas, goods, or services by an identified sponsor."[2] The AMA used **nonpersonal** in this context so that the term **advertising** would not include the face-to-face contact that characterizes personal selling. The word *paid* similarly excludes publicity, which is not bought.

Advertising Objectives

In their planning processes, businesses must decide what they want their advertising campaigns to accomplish. One objective might be to provide the consumer with product information. **Informative advertising**, which performs this function, is generally used to build demand for new products or to let consumers

FIGURE 14-2

The Promotional Mix

A firm's combination of four categories — advertising, personal selling, sales promotion, publicity and public relations — in its promotion strategy is called its promotional mix.

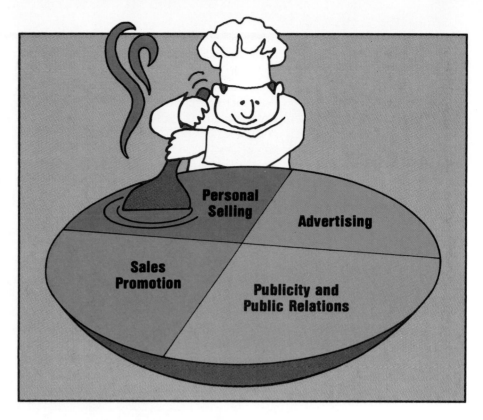

The Three Principal Types of Advertising

know about improvements to mature products. When Ford launched the Mercury Sable, it had to promote a totally new car. Informative advertisements described the Sable's suspension, fuel system, and instrumentation to help consumers distinguish this new product from its competitors.

Another objective in an advertising campaign may be to persuade the customer to take some action. Firms use **persuasive advertising** to influence the target market's beliefs, attitudes, or behavior. Almost all sale ads on television or in newspapers are designed to persuade. Another objective of promotion may be to remind the target market about something. **Reminder** or **reinforcement advertising** does just that. The "thank you for not smoking" campaigns deliberately recall past persuasive antismoking campaigns because most people, smokers and nonsmokers alike, are convinced of tobacco's dangers. Reinforcement advertising is also used to reassure consumers about choices they have already made.[3]

Types of Advertising

Advertising can be classified into three broad categories:

☐ Selective or brand advertising
☐ Primary demand or generic advertising
☐ Institutional advertising

Selective or Brand Advertising The most common type of advertising is **selective** or **brand advertising**, promotion materials designed to encourage a consumer to buy a certain brand of product and thereby build customer pa-

The Advertiser's New Best Friend

Let's say you're Jerry Wilson, owner of Soloflex, Inc., which makes $850 exercise machines. How do you get the most sales out of your advertising dollar? Television time is very expensive, especially when you're trying to reach the small, select group of people interested in serious home exercise. Print media are cheaper, but they can't show the action machine in action, and only about 10 percent of those who look at Soloflex's printed brochure buy the product. What you really need is a way to show the select group of potential buyers your machine in action. The solution? Make a videocassette.

Soloflex did just that, spending $150,000 to produce its 22-minute "video brochures" which cost $6.50 each to make and mail. The company sends the cassettes free — an expensive freebee — to prospective buyers. But the response has been worth it. Almost half of those who get the cassette end up buying a machine.

Using videocassettes to sell and promote products is a relatively new concept, and one that may play a much larger role in the future as more and more households purchase videocassette players. As an executive for a leading ad agency put it, "These advertisers are at the starting line in a tremendous race." The possibilities seem endless.

Like Soloflex, some companies send their cassettes to prospective customers, though a few, like Air France, ask the prospects to return or buy the cassettes after a given number of days. Others, like Glenmore Distilleries Co., take a somewhat more subtle route, making videocassettes that are sold in video stores. Glenmore makes "Mr. Boston Official Video Bartender's Guide" that shows how to mix exotic drinks. Not incidentally, the drinks feature a lot of Glenmore's products.

A number of companies use videocassettes as part of a coordinated sales presentation. Portable desktop play-back units have made such presentations easy and profitable. American Saw & Manufacturing has created 30 videotapes over the last five years, some in Spanish. With its own in-house production facility, the company can produce at low cost a tape specifically tailored for a particular kind of presentation.

Interested in rafting down the Grand Canyon but curious to know what it really looks like? Outdoors Unlimited, a leading river trip company, has the solution. For $15 it will send you a 15-minute videocassette of whitewater action filmed in the Canyon with the aid of the company's guides. The company hopes the film will help you get your feet wet about going rafting.

Those in the business of making feature-length videocassettes have also found new ways to plug products. Hollywood studios put promotional "trailers" for other films at the ends of movie videocassettes. Coca-Cola has taken the idea one step further, putting a Coke commercial at the beginning of the foreign cassette versions of "Ghostbusters," a movie produced by a Coke subsidiary.

Cuisinart has come up with what may be the ultimate way to profit from the videocassette technology. For $19.95, it sells a 30-minute tape on how to use a food processor. The tapes and machines appear in the same store displays. The tape itself is profitable, and according to the company, it boosts Cuisinart sales. With such payoffs, videocassettes may eventually become as important an advertising medium as newspapers or television.

Sources: Edward C. Baig, "Pushing Products via Videocassettes," *Fortune*, April 28, 1986. "Grand Canyon Video Now Available," *OU News*, Spring 1986. "Home Video: The Newest Boom in Entertainment," *Business Week*, April 2, 1984, 66. Steven Mintz, "Marketers Choose Their Weapons," *Sales & Marketing Management*, January 16, 1984, 70.

If this is how you think of Coleman, you're missing the boat.

Skeeter® Bass Boats. No other bass boat has caught more fishermen.

Coleman® Canoes. Number one in America, possibly the world.

MasterCraft® Ski Boats. No one makes them better. No one makes more.

Holder® Sailboats. The fastest selling small sailboat in America.

With over 75% of the market, the Hobie Cat® Catamaran is the Big Kahuna.

Coleman sells a lot of things besides lanterns.
Coleman made its name selling camping gear, and some people don't realize how big the company has grown. Coleman's advertising promotes individual brands like the Hobie Cat and Master Craft ski boats, but the corporate connection can't be missed. The same ad builds brand and company recognition.

tronage. The largest share of all the money spent on advertising goes to convince consumers to buy one brand — Pirelli tires or Bose speakers or Post Natural Raisin Bran, or some other brand — instead of its competitors.

For major marketers, like the McDonald's Corporation, advertising's cost effectiveness makes it an excellent way to tell people about its new products, like the McD.L.T., and to rekindle interest in Quarter Pounders and McNuggets. H & R Block, Inc., advertises its services on national television during the first four months of each year when people are focusing on their income-tax returns. Although H & R Block spends millions on advertising, its cost per person reached is actually quite low.

Many companies have found that turning their trademark into a familiar logo or symbol can make it a powerful advertising tool. Virtually everyone recognizes the yellow-on-red Eastman Kodak Company emblem or the cocked arm holding a mallet on Arm & Hammer products. Some companies, like Coca-Cola U.S.A. and the Harley-Davidson Motor Company, Inc., have even made a lucrative sideline out of licensing their logos for use on sportswear, boots, boats, and many other products.[4]

Can you recognize
America's favorite diet food?

Potatoes. America's Favorite Vegetable.

As lifestyles change, so do ads. America used to be a meat-and-potatoes nation. Today, with health and slimness on everybody's mind, some old standbys have fallen by the wayside. The Potato Board sought the help of Ketchum Communications, a San Francisco advertising agency, for ideas on how to promote potatoes as a health food.

The Advantages and Disadvantages of Different Media

Magazines

Primary Demand or Generic Advertising The total demand for a product or service can be increased by using **primary-demand** or **generic advertising**. This type of advertising does not distinguish between brands. Such advertising can help products that are losing market share. "Crafted with pride in the USA" is the key line in the advertising campaign sponsored by the Crafted with Pride in the U.S.A. Council, which is made up of American apparel and textile manufacturers.[5]

When consumers began to buy less beef in response to reports indicating that red meat was unhealthful, the Beef Industry Council responded with a $10-million campaign. Television and print ads emphasized that beef is now leaner and less cholesterol-laden than it was once. The council supplied stores with charts to be placed next to their meat counters comparing the calorie and cholesterol levels of various meat products.[6]

Institutional Advertising Firms use **institutional advertising** to generate good will or enhance their image rather than to sell a specific product. Such advertising often promotes an idea or philosophy.

For more than a decade, the Mobil Oil Company has offered its political views in advertisements in leading newspapers. Mobil recognized that a great advantage of advertising is its ability to reach a large target market quickly, something that is most important to firms that market throughout the nation. The R. J. Reynolds Tobacco Company, one of the leading cigarette manufacturers, initiated a campaign to encourage everyone to "lower their voices" about smoking in public places. In the face of antismoking campaigns initiated in both the public and the private sectors, Reynolds emphasized the rights of smokers.

Advertising Media

Procter & Gamble, the nation's largest advertiser, and your local hardware store have at least one thing in common: they must decide what advertising medium to use. **Advertising media** are the means of communication used by major advertisers, including magazines, newspapers, direct mail, radio, television, and outdoor advertising.

Magazines Using magazines, advertisers can reach either a national audience through, say, *People* or *Sports Illustrated* or a specialized audience through trade magazines like *Beverage World* or *Lodging Hospitality*. Unlike newspapers, magazines may remain around the home or in a doctor's waiting room for months. They are thus more likely to be read and reread than are newspapers. Their high quality reproduction of photographs and art gives them a notable advantage over newspapers. Advertisers can target markets not only by choosing the type of magazine in which they advertise but also by picking the regional or demographic editions of major publications. *Time* has 220 editions, including one that reaches 550,000 persons affiliated with educational institutions, a business edition reaching 1.6 million, and 115 test-market editions.

Magazines have some major disadvantages as an advertising medium. Because magazines often require copy months in advance, they lack time flexibility. Preparing the copy also takes considerable time and is quite expensive. Small retail and service businesses usually find magazine advertising beyond their reach.

FIGURE 14-3

Advertising Expenditures since
1970

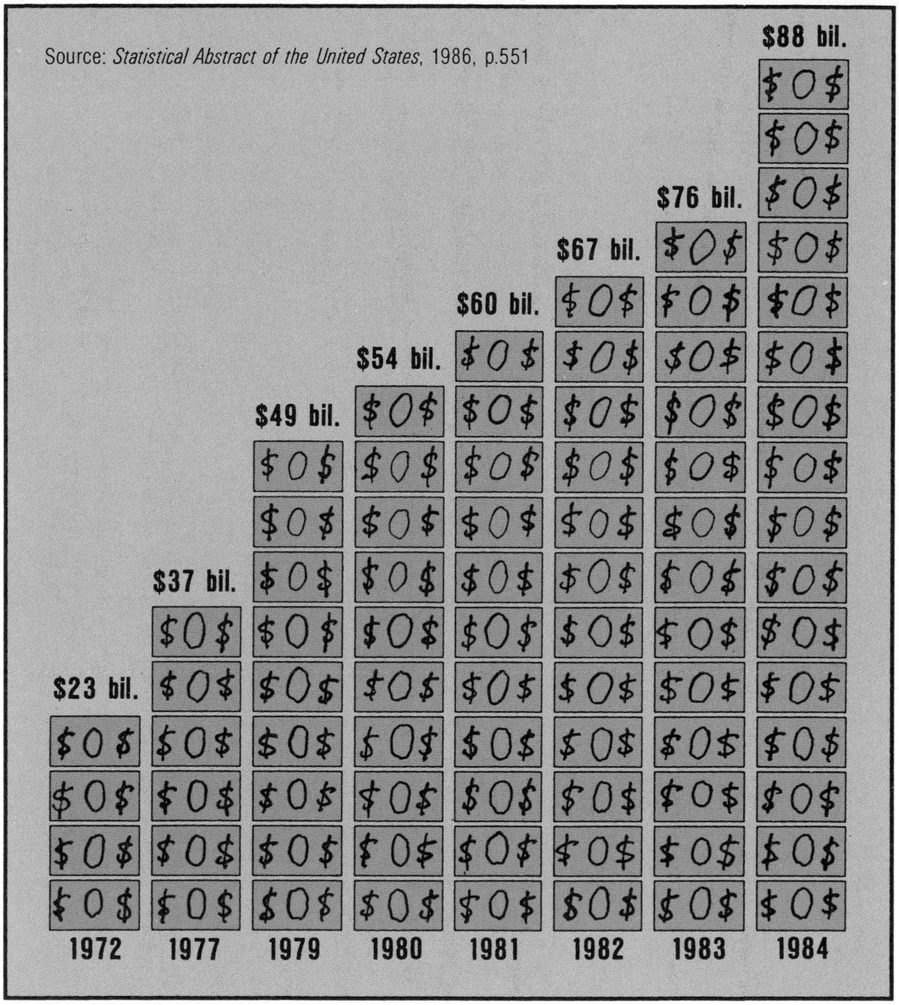

Source: *Statistical Abstract of the United States*, 1986, p.551

							$88 bil.
						$76 bil.	
					$67 bil.		
				$60 bil.			
			$54 bil.				
		$49 bil.					
	$37 bil.						
$23 bil.							
1972	**1977**	**1979**	**1980**	**1981**	**1982**	**1983**	**1984**

Newspapers Newspaper advertising attracts approximately 27 percent of all advertising dollars and is the most popular advertising medium. Almost everyone buys them, so they meet the needs of both large and small advertisers. Readers can save newspapers to refer to the ads later. For example, local retail groceries know that 80 percent of all food shoppers check the newspaper ads before going to the market.[7] Next to the local ads, readers may find such national ads as those for the Nestlé Foods Corporation or the Campbell Soup Company's products.

Advertisers can target particular newspaper readers who are likely to buy their products by using a **preferred position**: a section of the paper that is more likely to be read by the target market, such as sports enthusiasts, moviegoers, or do-it-yourselfers. However, advertising rates are higher for preferred positions than for **run-of-the-press placement**, which allows the newspaper to put an ad wherever space is available.

Newspapers have some disadvantages for advertisers. An ad may be "lost" in a large metropolitan newspaper where it must compete with hundreds of other ads for reader attention. Also, newspapers do not reproduce photographs as well

Newspapers

TABLE 14.1

The Advantages and Disadvantages of the Major Media

Medium	Advantages	Disadvantages
Magazines	Selectivity; long life; good reproduction of pictures and art	Lack of flexibility; long lead time; cost
Newspapers	Wide readership; preferred positioning; flexibility	"Lost" ads; poor reproduction of photos and color; brief ad life
Direct mail	Selectivity	Difficulty of maintaining lists; expense
Radio	Selectivity; flexibility	Ads not available for later examination; limited only to hearing
Television	Vast audience; appeals to both sight and hearing; flexibility	Cost; clutter; control lost to videocassette recorders
Outdoor advertising	Visibility; reinforcement value	Brevity of messages; unpopularity of medium

as magazines do, though newspaper quality has improved over the last few years. Finally, a newspaper ad has little impact the day after it is published.

Direct Mail Any advertising sent through the mail directly to a target market is **direct-mail advertising**. This term has become a catchall that includes everything from post cards to leaflets to sales letters to booklets to elaborate catalogs.[8]

Direct Mail

Direct mail's major advantage is its selectivity. An advertiser can target precisely the market it wishes to tap. For example, L. L. Bean, Inc., a leading direct-mail advertiser, issues different catalogs to fit its target markets. Hunters and serious outdoor enthusiasts receive one type, whereas more recreation-oriented people receive quite a different type. Direct mail's success depends on how current and of how high a quality the advertiser's mailing list is. It would do little good for Harry & David, which sells gourmet foods by mail, to mail to a Dairy Queen list. After all, each brochure or catalog may cost one dollar or more to print and mail. Their mailing list must therefore contain a very high proportion of people who will at least be qualified to buy from the catalog. The difficulty and expense of maintaining sound lists and the common practice of throwing away direct-mail advertising without reading it are the major disadvantages of this medium.

Radio Like direct mail, radio advertising offers the advertiser selectivity. Commercial radio stations develop programing targeted for particular audiences: rock, easy listening, classical, all-news, and the like. The cost of radio ads tends to be lower than direct-mail ads, particularly at smaller, local stations. Radio advertising is also extremely flexible. An advertiser can change messages, if need be, in just a few hours. And radio reaches vast numbers of people. There are more than 470 million radios in the country — two for every person, which is an average of nearly six per household. With Walkman units and car radios, radio is the most mobile medium.

Nonetheless, radio has disadvantages. Listeners may forget radio messages because they are not available for relistening. (Repetition can sometimes compensate for this problem.) And some people can "tune out" commercials or grow adept at changing stations when ads intrude. Also, radio appeals to only one sense — hearing.

Television Television advertising can have considerable impact because it appeals to two senses — sight and hearing. More than 20 percent of the nation's total advertising expenditures goes for television. Large companies like television advertising because it offers mass coverage. When General Foods introduced new flavors to its Post Fruit and Fibre cereal line, the company's marketers chose television commercials to reach the public. Television is also a flexible medium. Advertisers can target geographic regions and to some degree particular types of viewers. Here, too, they can change ad content quickly.

A great disadvantage to television is its high cost. A thirty-second prime-time spot on a national network can cost $120,000, or $550,000 for the same spot during the Super Bowl.[9] Local rates vary widely, depending on the size of the market and the type of station. The television industry and advertisers are growing increasingly concerned about **clutter**, an industry term for everything that is broadcast that is not part of a program: commercials, station identifications, public-service messages, and program promotional ads.[10] Particularly with the increasing use of fifteen-second spots, clutter may cause people to pay attention to fewer commercials. Already, advertisers face a serious problem in the form of remote control "commercial zappers," which allow the more than 30 million owners of videocassette recorders to fast-forward through commercials in programs they tape.[11]

Outdoor Advertising Posters, billboards, signs, and the like comprise **outdoor advertising**. Despite the amount of it we see each day, outdoor advertising accounts for only 1 percent of total advertising expenditures. By necessity, a typical message is simple, easy to comprehend, and usually just six to eight words longs. Outdoor advertisements are often quite effective in reaching customers who live close to the point where the products advertised are being offered for sale. Repetition is a major advantage of outdoor advertising; members of a target audience may pass by a particular sign several times a day. Also, advertisers often use the outdoor medium to reinforce other campaigns.

Outdoor advertising's major disadvantages are the brevity of its messages and the controversy surrounding them. Because of billboards' unattractiveness, many areas restrict them, and some have even banned them.

Other Media Although newspapers, television, radio, and direct mail absorb most advertising expenditures, advertisers commonly use other media to reach specific audiences. Firms often use alternative media, such as the examples discussed below, to reinforce campaigns in the major advertising media.

Today's Ads: Trying Harder

TV commercials and advertisements of all kinds so fill our world that many people can just ignore them like the hum of a refrigerator. This growing ability to turn our eyes and ears off to commercials is producing major changes in the ads themselves, in the media through which they're presented, and in the way people respond to them. While some analysts fear the proliferation of ads will some day destroy the effectiveness of all advertising, others see the current changes leading to an era of more creativity and ingenuity in the field.

Although people are not abandoning their television sets, new technology is allowing more and more viewers to tune out anything they don't want to hear. Many Americans have found ways to quiet the voice of TV commercials. With a remote "zapper" you can cut the sound of a commercial without leaving your easy chair. Many others now pay for their TV directly, so they don't have to sit through the commercials that have traditionally paid for the shows we watched for "free."

But most ad agency executives worry less about technology than about "clutter." While the total time devoted to television commercials, about 6–8 minutes per prime time hour, has remained virtually constant for the last 20 years, the *number* of commercials has risen tremendously. One study found that the number of advertising messages put out by all media doubled in the years between 1967 and 1982. Another showed that network television now broadcasts over 5000 advertising spots a week, compared with fewer than 3500 in 1975 and only about 1800 in 1965.

Obviously, advertisers are packing more commercials into each minute. The standard 60-second ad of the early sixties has become rarer. Many commercials are now only 30 seconds long, and in 1985 Coke, Gillette, and others began running 15-second spots. Apparently these ads work. The companies pay half the price of a 30-second spot and get more than half as much business in response. But the whole industry is paying a price in viewer overload. One gloomy ad executive said, "Proliferation might contain the seeds of the medium's destruction."

In 1974, 12 percent of TV viewers could correctly name the brand in the last commercial they'd seen. By 1981, that figure had dropped to 7 percent. Almost 90 percent of TV viewers forget the brand name within 4 minutes. The number of viewers who claim to pay "absolutely no attention" to commercials has been rising every year, and was up to 20 percent in 1984.

Those who are more optimistic about the future of advertising assert that this flood in the market will force advertisers to be more creative and come up with higher-quality commercials.

One relatively new use of advertising is to sell ideas rather than products. In magazine and newspaper ads, Mobil has tried to encourage a political outlook favorable to its business. In its ads, R. J. Reynolds has battled against evidence that non-smokers are harmed by second-hand smoke, and has lobbied against any regulation of smokers. Recently Dow Chemical Company has run a series of ads that seem to be encouraging young people to work for Dow, even though the company recently announced layoffs of 2500 people. Most analysts think that Dow put $7.5 million into the ads not to attract new employees but to change the company's image among baby-boomers who still think of Dow as the producer of Agent Orange and napalm, chemical warfare agents used in Vietnam.

There are limits to the new directions that ads are taking, and few are predicting that we will soon see the end of traditional advertising. Not all the innovations work. Two major networks recently rejected a well-produced, futuristic W. R. Grace commercial about the deficit because it was too controversial and might have obligated the networks to give equal time to opposing views. And a company that has tried to sell ad space on the doors of restroom stalls has yet to be successful.

Sources: John O'Toole, "Selling Ideas, Not Products," *U.S. News & World Report*, March 10, 1986, 54. Mark Muro, "And Now a Brief Word . . . ," *Boston Globe*, February 17, 1986, 45. Lauren R. Rublin, "Dancing in the Aisles," *Barron's*, Vol. 64, No. 22, May 28, 1984, 18.

FIGURE 14-4

Advertising Expenditures by
Medium

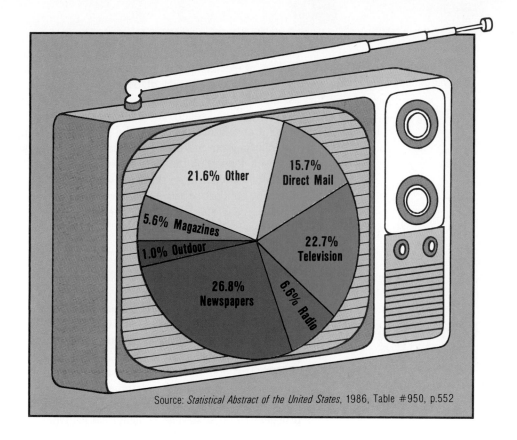

21.6% Other

15.7%
Direct Mail

5.6% Magazines

1.0% Outdoor

22.7%
Television

26.8%
Newspapers

6.6% Radio

Source: *Statistical Abstract of the United States*, 1986, Table #950, p.552

Specialty advertising usually involves producing small, inexpensive items bearing the advertiser's name, address, and occasional brief messages for free distribution. Calendars, key chains, coffee mugs, T-shirts, ball-point pens, and matchbooks are the most common items.

Display advertising consists of product exhibits in places like airports, railroad stations, billboards, and civic centers. It is often used to promote automobiles or local industries.

Targeted television advertising aimed at particular audiences is growing in popularity with the coming of cable channels specially programmed for those who enjoy sports, country or rock music, or family entertainment.

Shoppers' guides are advertising circulars featuring both display and classified ads (though they sometimes contain some nonadvertising copy) that are usually delivered door to door.

PERSONAL SELLING

Personal selling is the second of the four basic elements in the promotional mix. It offers major benefits to both sellers and buyers. The more complex the product, the greater the buyer's need for assistance from a well-trained salesperson. That is a major reason why personal selling is an increasingly important promotional method, whether its growth is measured by the number of persons employed in the field or by the total expenditures on it.

Businesses are willing to spend so much on personal selling because it offers three unique advantages. First, it permits individualized assistance to the buyer. Buyers of electronic cash registers, machine tools, computer systems, security systems, and thousands of other sophisticated products require personalized assistance. Second, personal selling provides a direct communications link between buyer and seller. The salesperson can collect information about the buyer's present and future needs for the firm's marketing information system. Finally, the salesperson can provide postsale customer service. Customer satisfaction may well depend on the salesperson's availability for product installation, on-site instruction in operation, servicing warranties, and following up on complaints and providing support services. An advertising or sales promotion department standing alone could not meet these needs.[12]

The Selling Process

Businesses spend millions of dollars annually to recruit and train people to not only sell goods and services but also serve as consultants to customers, diagnosing problems, identifying needs, and offering sound recommendations on products. For this reason, today's sales approach is often called **consultative selling**. This approach emerged at the same time as the marketing concept as a way to provide maximum customer satisfaction and repeat business. The consultative selling concept holds that a customer is a person to be served, not a prospect to be sold. The consultative salesperson does not try to manipulate a customer but instead offers information and negotiates with the customer.

Salespersons sell a vast array of goods and services to many types of businesses. Despite this diversity, salespersons all tend to use the same six-step approach.

Step 1: Preparing for the Sales Presentation The first thing a salesperson must do is called **prospecting**, developing a list of potential customers called **prospects**, who are firms or individuals who qualify as potential customers because they have the authority and the financial ability to buy the product. A salesperson should screen potential customers and eliminate anyone as a prospect who does not qualify in both regards.

All the planning that takes place before meeting with the customer is called the **preapproach**. During this stage, the salesperson attempts to learn as much as possible about the prospect, prepares a tentative sales presentation, and schedules an interview.

Step 2: The Sales Presentation Unless the selling situation simply calls for taking an order because the customer knows what he or she wants, a needs assessment should be a standard part of the sales presentation. The scope of the assessment depends mainly on the sophistication and selling price of the product and on the customer's knowledge of it. For example, most insurance salespeople sell a range of policies. They use a needs-assessment strategy to determine which policy best meets a given prospect's needs. Asking questions provides one of the best ways to assess needs. Once the customer and the salesperson have identified the customer's needs, the salesperson can recommend a product or range of products to satisfy them.

Consultative selling. *David Spark, a representative for MSD AGVET, really does go out in the field to sell his wares. Before deciding to purchase Ivomec, an injection to control parasites in cattle, a rancher needs to know about the product. Sales reps are the perfect source of that information, and they can pass on concerns and suggestions to the manufacturer.*

Step 3: The Sales Demonstration An effective sales demonstration helps verify parts of the sales story by giving customers a better understanding of the product's features. When Cuisinart, Inc., first introduced its food processors, it won many customers through its in-store demonstrations. However, demonstrations must be carefully practiced if they are to be successful.

Step 4: Handling Sales Resistance The customer's sales resistance is a normal part of any presentation. Objections like "the price is too high" or "I don't like the color" should not trouble the salesperson, since they clarify the prospect's thinking. Customer resistance often pinpoints areas that the salesperson needs to cover in more depth.

Step 5: Closing the Sale Asking the prospect to buy the product comes at the point of **closing the sale**. If the salesperson has handled the presentation well, closing is normally not difficult. When some salespeople feel the prospect is ready to buy, they use a trial closing like "May I arrange for delivery?" or "How soon will you need the tapes?" The trial close becomes an attempt to determine whether the prospect is in fact ready to buy.

"Forget the prince and the ball. Just give me exclusive marketing rights to the coach."

Step 6: Servicing the Sale   In the broadest terms, personal selling is a two-part process: closing the sale, then servicing it. Today, servicing the sale receives more attention than it did in the past because businesses have recognized that they build profits not only by attracting new accounts but also by keeping old ones active. The services provided after a sale may include supervising the delivery and installation of the item and product orientation — making sure the customer can use and maintain the product.

The General Motors Corporation established its Buick customer assistance centers to offer customers service after the sale. Buick owners receive the toll-free number of a group of specially trained advisors who can offer assistance. This service is expected to increase customer satisfaction by dealing with complaints and problems quickly and efficiently. The center can handle eleven hundred calls a day.[13]

Selling Today

The fast-talking, cigar-chewing salesman whose answer to every sales problem was more pressure on the customer is a figure of the past. Salespeople today must adopt approaches more in keeping with our market-driven economy and with a business philosophy based on customer satisfaction and repeat sales. With the modern approach to selling has come a new, well-earned status for salespeople.

The types of salespeople a firm employs depends first on where the firm is in the channel of distribution and second on its approach to sales. Also, a firm's choice of salespeople depends on its product, that is, on whether it sells primarily a good or a service.

Selling for a Retailer   Approximately 40 percent of this country's businesses are retail firms. As everyday experience indicates, the range of retailers is vast: from "mom and pop" stores to auto dealers to computer stores to boutiques and on and on. The type of salespeople needed varies with the setting. Some businesses simply require order takers. Others demand highly trained professionals who combine hands-on product knowledge with good selling skills.

Four Types of Sales Positions

Selling for a Wholesaler United States wholesalers employ over 650,000 salespeople,[14] who are normally classified as either inside or outside salespeople. **Inside salespeople** rely almost totally on telephone orders and usually follow a regular customer-contact schedule. Because of the escalating costs of personal selling, more and more wholesalers are switching to telephone sales. **Outside salespeople** or **field salespeople** typically work on the road, calling on potential buyers. Some specialize in a product niche, such as electronics or small appliances; others carry a wide range of lines. Typically, though, outside salespeople must know many products and merchandising strategies. For example, sales representatives who call on retail stores for pharmaceutical wholesalers must know dozens of different over-the-counter remedies and be able to advise their customers on advertising, display techniques, store layout, and pricing.

Selling for a Manufacturer The three most common types of salespeople employed by manufacturers are field salespeople, sales engineers, and detail salespersons.

Field salespeople for a manufacturer usually handle well-established products that require a minimum of creative selling and technical knowledge. Persons selling standard office equipment, like desks and secretarial chairs, would be classified as field salespeople. Their major concerns are price and delivery. By contrast, **sales engineers** must have precise, detailed knowledge of their products and be able to discuss technical matters. In some instances, sales engineers may

Field selling for a manufacturer. Holly Hinnenkamp is a sales representative with 3M's Commercial Office Supply Division. He's always sold products like Post-it notes and Scotch Brand Magic transparent tape, which are made by his division. Now he can serve stationery stores and his employer more effectively by providing a broad line of computer media and transparency supplies. These new items are made by sister divisions at 3M.

be needed to introduce products that mark technological breakthroughs. They must therefore be able to identify, analyze, and solve customer problems.

The third type of manufacturer's representative does not actually make sales. Instead, **detail salespersons** or **missionary salespersons** develop good will and stimulate demand for the manufacturer's products in target markets. Such salespersons are not paid on the basis of the sales they generate because their duties often focus on such different areas as training the customer's employees or advising on advertising campaigns. However, they do receive indirect recognition for increased sales they may have helped generate.

A Fourth Type of Selling Today

Selling a Service Over the last several years, the amount that consumers have spent annually on services has steadily increased. Transactions involving insurance, real estate, travel planning, finances, and business security require knowledgeable salespeople. The service sector of our economy — and with it the types of services requiring sales personnel — is likely to continue to expand.

Telemarketing

The personal selling technique that relies on the telephone to make sales as well as to schedule sales calls and follow up on orders and prospects is called **telemarketing**. The economics of telemarketing are quite convincing. The average sales call now costs more than $250, and 5.5 contacts on average are needed to close the usual sale. In contrast, telemarketing to businesses averages only $7 to $15 per contact, and consumer contacts cost only about $2.50 to $4 for each completed call. Most telemarketing campaigns aimed at customers are coordinated with direct mail or advertising campaigns to concentrate their effectiveness.[15]

SALES PROMOTION

The American Marketing Association defines **sales promotion** as "those marketing activities, other than personal selling, advertising, and publicity that stimulate consumer purchasing and dealer effectiveness."[16] Sales promotions can be as diverse as cheese sample tables in supermarkets, a one-dollar-off coupon in a newspaper, or a frequent-flier bonus offered by airlines. In effect, each of these activities serves as a bridge to connect the other three elements of the promotional mix.[17] Sales promotion can greatly increase the effectiveness of the other activities. Here are some examples of how that happens.

Sales Promotion Defined

Coupons For years, manufacturers have used **coupons**, a device that allows customers to pay a lower price for goods, to increase sales on advertised products. Several billion coupons appear in magazines, newspapers, and direct-mail packets every year. Often, coupons introduce new or improved items.

Refunds The returning of a portion of an item's purchase price is a **refund**. In recent years, many small-appliance manufacturers have used rebates from three to five dollars on everything from power tools to kitchen equipment. Manufacturers use rebates, a form of refund like coupons, both to introduce a

Billboards are a very effective medium. *Commuters and travelers pass many kinds of outdoor advertising. Although their message must be short and simple, billboards are often viewed over and over again. They make their point through repetition and through the careful coordination of image and text. Sheer size adds to their visual impact.*

new product and to build sales of an existing product. United States auto makers have used rebates successfully to build sales.

Five Techniques for Sales Promotion

Premiums Anything of value that a customer receives in addition to the purchased item or service is a **premium**. Some firms concentrate on premiums to attract and hold customers. For instance, supermarkets have used towel, record, encyclopedia, dish, and silverware giveaways to attract customers into their stores. Usually, stores hand out the items with purchases above a certain size, or they are sold to the consumer at a very low price.

Samples A free package or container of a product is a **sample**. Manufacturers often use samples to introduce new products. When Procter & Gamble introduced its Bold 3 detergent and fabric softener, it mailed a small sample to every household in the United States. The package also contained a colorful brochure that briefly described Bold 3's features.

Point-of-Purchase Displays Special racks, signs, and displays to increase consumer product awareness are sometimes supplied and set up by manufacturers or wholesalers in retail or service outlets. The continuing trend toward self-service buying has helped make these units, called **point-of-purchase displays**, a popular sales promotion device.

Trade Shows

A final type of sales promotion device is in a category by itself. The **trade show** is a large exhibit of products that are, in most cases, common to one industry. Each year, for example, the National Decorating Products Show rotates from city to city, offering suppliers of paint, wallcoverings, floor coverings, and related items an opportunity to display their wares. Large numbers of retailers and wholesalers visit the show to see its varied products. Such shows also play a key role in the fashion, furniture, toy, and automotive accessories industries.

PUBLICITY AND PUBLIC RELATIONS

Publicity

Quite simply, **publicity** is a communication in news-story form about a company or its products transmitted by a mass medium at no charge. Virtually any of the advertising media can serve as sources of publicity. The principal types of publicity mechanisms are the following:

The Principal Types of Publicity Mechanisms

- □ **News releases**: Typewritten copy, usually in the form of brief newspaper stories, circulated generally to the news media.
- □ **Feature articles**: Manuscripts longer than a news release (sometimes exceeding three thousand words), which the firm usually has prepared for a specific publication.
- □ **Captioned photographs**: Photos of a new product, a corporate officer, or something else of interest, accompanied by a brief description explaining the picture.
- □ **Press conferences**: Public meetings of corporate officials with the news media at which written and photographic materials are often supplied.
- □ **Interviews**: Private meetings of corporate officials or employees with the news media.

Publicity vs. Public Relations

What is publicized is largely under the publicity seeker's control. In many cases, the goal of publicity is to shape the image of the company and its product. Publicity is not the same as advertising. A firm does not have the control over publicity that it has over advertising. Although the firm does not pay for publicity, it is not truly free. In some situations, expensive artwork or photographs may accompany a news release or be supplied to reporters. The firm must often add a full-time employee to handle publicity. Sometimes companies avoid this cost by using the services of a public relations or advertising firm.

Public Relations

The activities designed to create and maintain favorable relations between an organization and its various publics are known as **public relations**.[18] These publics include the firm's customers, employees, and stockholders, or the government or general public. Publicity is used to inform these publics about the company's public-relations activities. For example, the 1985 Farm Aid benefit concert drew

A Yen to Trade

Breaking through traditional trade barriers in the world's most difficult markets often frustrates even the best American business people and causes problems for the country as a whole. The failure of many American companies to sell to the Japanese has helped produce the tremendous trade imbalance between the two countries. While Washington debates trade laws, many analysts feel that the secret of reducing this trade imbalance will be discovered not by government negotiators but by American corporations. Companies that have succeeded in selling to the Japanese say the key is versatility, persistence, and a new attitude towards working with the Japanese.

The crux of the issue, as American businesses see it, is that the Japanese government and bureaucracy support Japanese businesses and exports in any way they can, while making it very difficult for most foreign goods to get into Japan. The Japanese government levies high tariffs on some imported goods in order to protect small, outdated Japanese industries like tobacco growing.

American businesses must share some of the blame for not penetrating Japanese markets. While Japanese business people learn English and come to the States to do their business, few American companies have sent Japanese-speaking representatives to reside in Japan's trade centers, and American business people are often woefully ignorant of Japanese manners and culture.

Yet the stories of American businesses, that have been successful at selling to the Japanese provide lessons for all those who follow. Many American communications companies hoped they would get new business when, on April 1, 1985, Nippon Telephone & Telegraph (NTT) lost its monopoly in Japan. But at least one company, Infotron Systems Corp., didn't wait for legal changes to try to interest NTT in its products. The New Jersey manufacturer of data communications equipment proved that persistence and flexibility can work as well in Japan as they can in New York.

When the small American firm first approached the Japanese giant in 1980, NTT was uninterested, and the American executives had to be stubborn just to get a 15 minute interview. That interview stretched into 2 hours as the Americans sought to convince NTT officials what corporate promoters are always trying to show their customers: that they can supply the best product to do the job. During the negotiations that followed, the Japanese probed into every aspect of the American company, asking about engineering, quality, and delivery schedules. Infotron executives had a policy of making sure they answered every question within eight hours, an approach that apparently pleased the Japanese.

The company also ignored the conventional wisdom that recommended setting up a wholly owned subsidiary in Japan. Instead, it formed a partnership with a Japanese company, Japan Direx Corp., and agreed to share its most important technology. In return, Japan Direx gave the American company the rights to market, outside of Japan, any improvements to the technology that Direx comes up with. In effect, the Japanese company does research and development work for Infotron, gives it advice about the Japanese market, and resells some of Infotron's products. Infotron's flexibility and ability to react quickly paid off.

No doubt efforts to open Japanese markets will continue at all levels for years to come. And Japan may eventually make it easier for all American companies to sell their products on the other side of the Pacific. But for now, breaking into the Japanese markets provides a tough proving ground for creative business people who often have to establish new paths to success.

Sources: "When in Japan . . . ," Forbes, March 10, 1986, 153. Thomas Alexander, "How We Sold Japan's Toughest Customer," Fortune, January 20, 1986, 113. Lee Smith, "What the U.S. Can Sell Japan," Fortune, Vol. 111, No. 10, May 13, 1985, 92. Richard A. Phalon, "Letting Go," Forbes, Vol. 135, No. 10, May 6, 1985, 46. Leslie Helm, "Now Japan Wants to Conquer Global Finance," Business Week, No. 2889, April 8, 1985, 58. Richard Alm, "Look Who's Propping up the Dollar," U.S. News & World Report, Vol. 98, No. 20, May 27, 1985, 74. "Trade: Not Much Worse," Fortune, Vol. 111, No. 12, June 10, 1985, 49. Boyd France, Carla Anne Robbins, and Ronald Grover, "Collision Course," Business Week, No. 2889, April 8, 1985, 51.

corporate sponsors like the Chevrolet Motor Division of General Motors, Miller Brewing Company, Sears, Roebuck and Company, and the Quaker Oats Company. Their participation was a matter of public relations that garnered them much free publicity.[19] Many far smaller retailers buy space in high-school sports programs or sponsor youth athletics for their public-relations value.

PROMOTION: A PERSPECTIVE

When Melitta, Inc., developed its new coffee-maker system, it introduced not only a new product but also a new way to brew coffee — a double challenge. Its marketers decided to present the product directly to the top management of wholesalers and supermarket chains. Melitta customized a van in which its sales representatives traveled to various corporate headquarters. While Melitta's salespeople demonstrated their new product, their prospects sipped coffee fresh out of a Melitta system. The strategy worked.

As Melitta proved, few areas in business offer as many opportunities for creativity as personal selling and promotion. Sometimes a new idea comes merely from taking a fresh look at an everyday scene. An advertising company in Baltimore sells space on ten-inch meter-mounted signs to Minolta copiers, among others. Sometimes people who spend millions on advertising each year have to be sold on a great idea for publicity. That was the problem that Bantam Books, Inc., had in 1981 when it approached Chrysler president Lee Iacocca about writing his autobiography. Bantam had to spend nine months convincing him to do it. In the eighteen months after its publication, *Iacocca* was on the best-seller list for 73 weeks, sold 2.6 million hardcover copies, and became the all-time best-selling nonfiction book other than the Bible.[20] The value of the publicity that Chrysler gained from the book cannot be calculated.

No small part of the reason we are in the marketing era is that people like Lee Iacocca have recognized that marketing is both critical to any business's success and personally challenging. As the millions of Americans who work in marketing can testify, it is also rewarding and fulfilling.

Chapter Highlights

1. Define promotion and describe the two major promotional objectives.

Promotion encompasses all communication designed to stimulate consumer purchasing, acceptance, or support or to increase dealer effectiveness. Businesses use promotion to increase and manage sales. A push strategy is directed at selling goods or services to the next entity in the channel of distribution. It relies heavily on an organization's sales force. A pull strategy attempts to develop consumer demand for a product or a service, primarily through advertising or sales promotion.

2. Identify at least two promotional strategies.

Promotional strategies may include the following: providing information about the product, persuading customers to take some action, reminding the target audience about a product or organization, increasing sales of high-profit products, increasing demand during slack times, or decreasing demand.

3. List the elements of the promotional mix.

The four elements of the promotional mix are advertising, personal selling, sales promotion, and publicity.

4. Define advertising and identify the three principal types of advertising.

Advertising is any paid form of nonpersonal presentation and promotion of ideas, goods, or services by an identified sponsor. Selective or brand advertising encourages consumers to buy a certain brand of product and builds customer patronage. Primary-demand or generic advertising increases the total demand for a product or service without distinguishing between brands. Institutional advertising generates good will, enhances an organization's image, or promotes an idea or philosophy.

5. Weigh the advantages and disadvantages of the principal advertising media.

Magazines can reach selected national or specialized audiences, they may be read and reread, and they offer quality reproduction. However, they require copy far in advance and may be too expensive for smaller businesses. Newspapers attract both large and small businesses because almost everyone buys them, but ads must compete with hundreds of other ads, photographs in newspapers do not reproduce well, and their message is short-lived. Direct mail is tremendously selective, but it is expensive, maintaining sound mailing lists is difficult, and consumers can easily ignore it. Radio offers advertisers selectivity, flexibility, reasonable cost, and large audiences, but its commercials are easily forgotten. Television ads have high impact but are very expensive, although for large businesses the cost per person reached can be quite reasonable. Outdoor advertising is particularly useful for reinforcing other campaigns, but the medium is controversial and messages must be very brief.

6. List the six steps in the selling process.

The six steps are preparing for the sales presentation, the actual sales presentation, the sales demonstration, handling sales resistance, closing the sale, and servicing the sale.

7. Describe three types of sales positions typically found in manufacturing.

Inside salespeople rely almost totally on telephone orders and usually follow a regular customer-contact schedule. Outside salespeople call on customers. Outside salespeople who work for wholesalers generally must know many products and merchandising strategies. Those who work for retailers usually handle well-established products that require a minimum of creative selling and technical knowledge. Detail salespersons develop good will and stimulate demand for the manufacturer's products in target markets.

8. Define sales promotion and identify the principal means involved.

Sales promotion consists of those marketing activities — other than personal selling, advertising, and publicity — that stimulate consumer purchasing and dealer effectiveness. Its principal means are coupons, refunds, premiums, sampling, and point-of-purchase displays.

9. Distinguish between publicity and public relations.

Publicity is communication, in news-story form, about a company or its products, which is transmitted through a mass medium at no charge. Public relations is a broad set of communications activities designed to create and maintain favorable relations between an organization and its various publics.

Key Terms

Advertising	Feature article	Outdoor advertising	Press conference
Advertising media	Field salespeople	Outside salespeople	Primary-demand
Captioned photographs	Informative advertising	Persuasive advertising	advertising
Closing the sale	Inside salespeople	Point-of-purchase	Promotion
Consultative selling	Institutional advertising	displays	Promotional mix
Coupon	Interview	Preapproach planning	Prospects
Direct-mail advertising	Missionary salespeople	Preferred position	Publicity
Display advertising	News releases	Premium	Pull strategy

Push strategy	Run-of-the-press	Selective (brand)	Specialty advertising
Reminder	placement	advertising	Telemarketing
(reinforcement)	Sales engineers	Shoppers' guides	Trade show
advertising	Sample		

Review Questions

1. Define promotion and describe each of the basic elements in the promotional mix.
2. What is the primary difference between a push-oriented promotional strategy and a pull-oriented strategy?
3. Most businesses seek to achieve specific promotional objectives. What are the three most common objectives?
4. What is selective or brand advertising? How is this type of advertising different from "primary demand or generic advertising"?
5. What is institutional advertising? Give at least one example not mentioned in this book.
6. What are some of the advantages of newspapers as an advertising medium?
7. Define direct-mail advertising. What are some of the factors that contribute to effective direct-mail advertising?
8. List two advantages and two disadvantages of television advertising.
9. Why do some marketers use personal selling as a promotional strategy? Give at least three reasons.
10. What are the six steps in the selling process?
11. What are the four major employment settings for salespeople?
12. Define sales promotion. List and describe the four major sales-promotion strategies.
13. What is publicity? How is publicity different from public relations?
14. What are some of the principal publicity mechanisms a business may use?

Application Exercises

1. Develop a promotional plan for a new sporting goods store to be opened in a shopping center. This store will feature several lines of exclusive merchandise for golfers and tennis players. What elements of the promotional mix would be most effective in reaching potential consumers? Be specific as you describe promotional strategies that would be incorporated into your plan.

2. Consider the sporting goods store in Exercise 1 and answer the following questions:
   a. What role should personal selling play in the promotional mix?
   b. What steps can be taken to ensure that the sales staff is well prepared to perform their duties?

Cases

14.1 Promotion and "Demotion" at Rockport

The Rockport Company introduced its first walking shoe, the RocSport, in 1978. Walking was recommended as a cardiovascular exercise for those who cannot engage in more strenuous exercise. The RocSport is a durable, lightweight shoe that was designed specifically for comfort and support in walking.

The RocSport was well received by retailers and consumers. Another model, the ProWalker, quickly helped boost Rockport's sales to around $7 million annually, but there they remained.

To give its walking shoes a promotional boost, Rockport first redesigned and reissued a book called *The Complete Book of Exercise Walking,* selling it through stores that carried Rockport shoes. Then the firm sponsored a year-long 11,600-mile walk through the United States by Robert Sweetgall, who wore ProWalkers on his well-publicized walk. Along the way, he lectured to schools and community groups on the importance of cardiovascular health and the benefits of walking. In addition, a short documentary film, based on Sweetgall's walk, was made for distribution to the more than 2,000 U.S. walking clubs; about 100,000 copies of *Fitness Walking,* co-authored by Sweetgall, were sold through Rockport's retailers; and Rockport arranged to have its walking shoes tested by the American Podiatric Medical Association, and became the first manufacturer to be awarded that group's Seal of Acceptance.

Heavy promotion led to soaring sales, which reached $40 million in 1984. The firm could not keep up with orders from retailers. Rather than make promises of delivery that it could not keep, Rockport wrote to retailers, suggesting that they buy from competing manufacturers. This, the firm felt, was better than alienating its retailers. For a while, Rockport also stopped taking on new retailers, and stopped advertising its toll-free consumer service telephone number. The result of this "negative promotion"? Sales of $65 million in 1985, and in excess of $100 million in 1986.

Questions

1. Describe each of Rockport's promotional activities with regard to category, objective, strategy, and audience.
2. What kind of advertising would you have suggested as part of Rockport's promotional mix?

For more information see *Forbes,* June 30, 1986, pp. 67–70; *Nation's Business,* November 1985, p. 33; and *Inc.,* November 1985.

14.2 Battle of the Blimps

Goodyear Tire & Rubber Co. has been building blimps and operating them since 1911. Its four blimps provide an unusual advertising medium and an occasional aerial platform for television cameras. Goodyear considers the blimp to be its own special symbol and contends it is a registered trademark.

Now, however, several firms have encroached on that symbol. The first was the Fuji Photo Film Co., which flew its own blimp over the Summer Olympic Games in Los Angeles in 1984. Then a group of McDonald's franchise owners used a blimp to promote their products. And Resorts International used one to advertise its casino in Atlantic City, New Jersey.

A blimp is, after all, only an airship, and any firm can use one to advertise its wares. But Goodyear officials believe Fuji went too far when that firm began to use the blimp shape in its printed advertising and other promotional materials. In two lawsuits filed in the fall of 1985, the tire manufacturer contends that Fuji's use of the symbol "dilutes the distinctive quality" of the Goodyear trademark. Goodyear is suing to keep Fuji from using the blimp in its promotion; the firm is also looking into the "blimp operations" of McDonald's and Resorts International.

Questions

1. How important is a distinctive symbol to a firm's promotional effort? What can such a symbol do for the firm or its products?
2. For a time, the B. F. Goodrich Company advertised itself as the tire company *without* the blimp. Should Goodrich have done so? Should Goodyear have sued Goodrich? Explain.

For more information see *Business Week,* January 20, 1986, p. 30; *Newsweek,* January 6, 1986, p. 52; and *The Wall Street Journal,* December 27, 1985, p. 3.

Some people get tired of being told they're in the middle of the greatest personal technological revolution in history when the highest tech they've been able to afford is a watch that does multiplication and plays "Yankee Doodle" when you press the right combination of buttons. For many of us, trying to make use of a computer is like trying to "make use" of the sea — it's so overwhelmingly powerful that we don't even want to get our feet wet. If you know you're not going to be a computer programmer or a researcher in fiber optics, how is high technology really going to affect you in the near future?

Chances are you're already being affected more than you think. You may consider high tech as far from your life as the lasers of Star Wars, but if you've ever listened to a compact disk player you've heard the same laser technology in action. The laser beam bounces off the recorded surface of the disk and a microprocessor interprets the reflected beam. Laser disk technology is expected to become more and more important because the disks can store so much more information than the magnetic disks currently used in most computers. You may one day be able to have a single laser disk reader/recorder hooked up both to a computer, for information retrieval, and to a stereo to play the latest release.

The microchips that make compact disk players possible are at the heart of almost all recent developments in high technology. Such chips have been getting smaller in size while they grow in memory. So there's been steady, rapid growth in the amount of computing power available for the dollar, which has meant that more and more microprocessors are showing up in small spaces like cars.

Microprocessors give cars brains. For years some cars have been instantly calculating miles per gallon figures and letting drivers know how efficiently they're driving. Now computers are monitoring other systems in the car and either giving the information to the driver or sending it to other processors to make automatic adjustments in the car. Chips control pollution control equipment, adjust suspensions for bumpy roads or tight cornering, and in some cars tell the driver to get the brakes checked or change the oil. Cars of the future may have radar-activated brakes that will prevent head-on collisions. And they will be much more customized for individual needs. When you stick

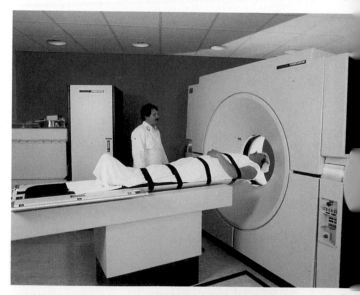

High Technology

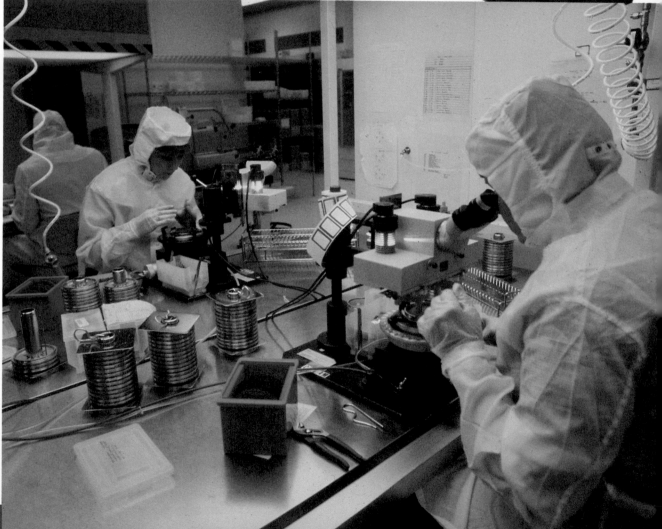

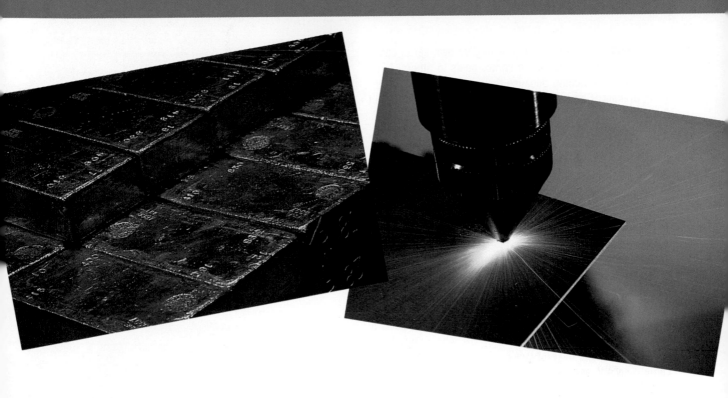

your personal key in the ignition, the car will adjust the seat, mirror, and air temperature just the way you like it.

The fear about technology that swept many work places when computers were just beginning to make their way into businesses is being gradually replaced by appreciation of what computers can do to help get the work done. People who work with the machines every day tend to see them as tools, capable of expanding and speeding up human abilities and activities, but not as alien beings. Store managers love the fact that as soon as a sale is rung up, it's entered in a central data bank, and inventory and purchasing get necessary information. Secretaries and writers have become "word processors" working on their computers. Some compare the switch from typewriters to computers to the change from a bicycle to a car — the old technology is fine if you're set on just dawdling along, but if you want to get somewhere fast and not all worn out, make use of the new machines.

Many ordinary people become fond of their computers because computers tend to do the busy work, the most tedious, repetitive *unhuman* part of the job. Instead of searching through thousands of files a researcher with a computer and a modem can find information in seconds. Instead of sending someone out to search the back room, a sales manager knows whether there are any 1981 carburetors back there. And instead of typing the same letter 100 times, secretaries can punch one button 100 times.

At the dawn of the personal computer revolution, many "experts" were predicting that soon we'd all have home computers to perform mundane household tasks like turning heat and lights on and off. That may never happen in your house, but the chances are growing each year that you will one day work in a "smart building." Such buildings do control light and heat, but they also have more specialized, unusual tasks.

One is security. A building in Lincoln Center, Dallas, was credited with apprehending an insider who was stealing from other people's offices. It identified him by noting the electronic key card that he used to get into the offices. Smart buildings also control their own elevators and can be provided with terminals in the lobby that allow people to trade on the stock market or order lunch.

If you never work on Wall Street you may never see in action the tremendous information transfer systems that brokerage houses have become part of. But you will be affected by such systems. For they are what holds the global economy together, and we are all affected by the fact that our competitors and markets now are as likely to be across the ocean as across town. In fact, technological advances are behind most of the other major trends we've looked at. High-tech business is crucial to foreign competition. Computers are responsible for many of the changes in the work place, and they will certainly be at the center of the future.

The high-tech revolution is creating its own set of characters. Hackers are heroes to some, pests to others, but always worth watching because they might turn out something brilliant. Computer criminals, hackers not for fun but for profit, force our legal system to come up with new definitions of theft and new ways of proving it. And the nation's new wizards are the programmers who spend thousands of hours meticulously piecing together the complex commands that make life easier for the rest of us.

Of course technology is progressing rapidly in many areas that may seem to have nothing to do with computers. In biology, scientists use powerful microscopes, models of individual molecules (developed by computers, of course), and new gene splicing techniques to create new drugs and even new life forms. Some of the products of this new technology could one day save your life.

Scientists are learning to discover what cells have gone wrong during a particular disease and to send chemicals to those specific cells rather than pump the whole body full of chemicals. One of the biggest steps towards this goal came a decade ago, when British researchers developed "hybridomas" by fusing antibody-secreting cells with cancer cells. These hybridomas produce large quantities of antibodies, specific proteins that the body naturally produces to deal with a particular type of foreign substance. These antibodies seek out and link up with the foreign substance. Sometimes the antibody alone will have an effect on the disease. More often, the researchers link a chemical or radioactive "payload" to the antibody, and this "magic bullet" goes directly to the offending agent and destroys it.

One of many new startup companies in the drug field, Xoma Corp. of California, is developing a magic bullet to fight melanoma, a type of skin cancer that is often fatal. The company links melanoma antibodies to ricin, a poison made from castor beans. Normally ricin is much too strong to be used as medicine, but the small quantities linked to the antibodies apparently will affect the cancer cells without harming the rest of the body.

Other scientists have developed ways to get bacteria to produce chemicals like interferon which previously were available only in minute quantities, at great expense. And new laser techniques allow researchers to isolate particular chromosomes and put together a library of human genes.

Such techniques give some sense of what the high-tech future will be like. Now that individual technologies like computers and lasers have been developed beyond the experimental stage, they become tools for research and manufacturing in a wide variety of fields. In fact, some technologies have progressed so rapidly that it may be decades before many fields of research and production learn to use fully the tools that are available today.

V

INFORMATION FOR BUSINESS DECISION MAKING

At Ford Motor Company a very large number of employees get paid for processing information, not for making cars. Ford, like most other businesses, has moved into the information age. As we move from an industrial to an information society, computers will play a more important role in the management of information. Part V begins with an introduction to the nature of accounting, then we introduce computers and management information systems.

15

ACCOUNTING

Learning Objectives

After you have completed this chapter, you will be able to do the following:

- Describe how managers, investors, and others use accounting information.
- Distinguish between the primary types of accountants.
- State the accounting equation and relate it to double-entry bookkeeping.
- List the five steps in the accounting cycle and provide a one-sentence description of each stage.
- Describe the functions of the three most common financial statements, discussed in this chapter.
- Explain briefly how analysts look at and interpret financial statements.
- Analyze accounting's role in the budget process.

At the end of their freshman year in college, instead of looking for a summer job, John and Kay organized a lawn service company in their city. To start their business on May 15, they each deposited $500 in a checking bank account in the name of their company, J and K Lawn Service. Their $1000 consisted of a $250 loan from each of their fathers and $250 each of their own money. Using the money in the checking account, they rented lawn equipment, purchased supplies, and hired fellow students to cut and trim lawns. On the 1st and 15th, they mailed statements to their customers.

On August 15, they were ready to dissolve their business and go back to college for the fall semester. Since they had been so busy, they had not kept any records other than the checkbook and a list of amounts owed to them by customers. When they brought back the rented lawn equipment, the rental manager asked them, "How did you do?" Though they thought they did quite well, they were not sure just how successful they were. What kind of information from their record-keeping system would help make it easier to tell whether they earned a profit or loss?

THE NATURE OF ACCOUNTING

The process of recording financial information, interpreting it, then communicating it is called **accounting**. Persons who provide accounting services, **accountants**, do not just compile and tabulate data. Accountants help others — managers, entrepreneurs, lenders, investors — understand what the numbers mean so that they can make informed business decisions. Accountants translate raw data into a language that businesspeople can understand and use. Thus, accounting is "the language of business." This chapter is an introduction to that language.

Who Relies on Accounting

As Figure 15.1 reveals, owners and managers use accounting information to measure a company's performance against established standards and goals. Suppose that a corporation has set a 10 percent increase in sales as its goal for a particular quarter. The raw sales data for the quarter, translated into an understandable form by an accountant, will reveal whether the goal has been met. Senior management can use this information to evaluate the sales manager's performance. In this way, accounting establishes accountability.

Accounting plays a critical role in controlling a corporation's present operations. For example, accounting provides a means of identifying expenses. This function is particularly important to new business, where every penny counts. The accountant's work also guides a company's planning for the future, because a business sets its goals by using as a base line what it has done in the past.

Creditors and investors also rely on accounting information to judge a firm. Bank-loan applications often require detailed information prepared by an accountant. Suppliers want similar information before extending trade credit. In deciding where to put their money, investors rely on **financial statements**, an organization's reports of its financial condition, which usually take the form of balance sheets, income statements, and statements of changes in financial position. (Each of these types of statement is described later in this chapter.) Shareholders and

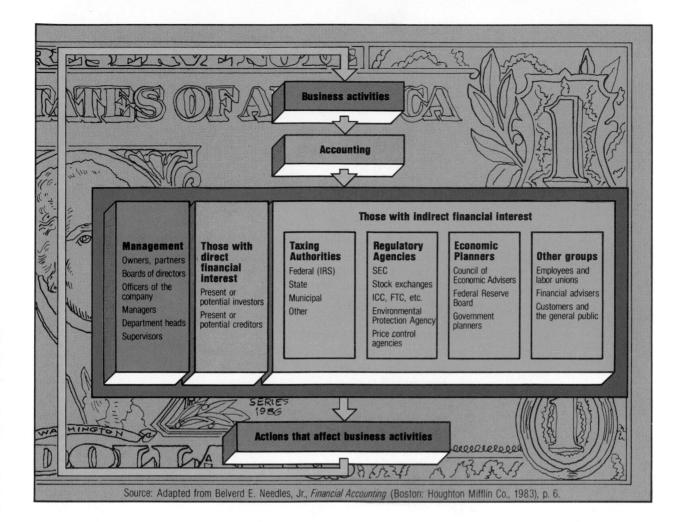

Source: Adapted from Belverd E. Needles, Jr., *Financial Accounting* (Boston: Houghton Mifflin Co., 1983), p. 6.

FIGURE 15.1

Users of Accounting

In earlier chapters, we have made dozens of references to financial reports and to how various managers, investors, creditors, owners, government agencies, and others rely on them. As this figure indicates, what we were talking about were people and entities who made use of a firm's accounting.

boards of directors judge a company's management by reference to these statements. And if a company's financial statements are available, unions analyze them before wage negotiations with management begin. Finally, a host of government agencies demand detailed financial information. The Internal Revenue Service and the various state and local taxing authorities have complex reporting requirements, with accountants on staff to verify the reports they receive.

A business's system of reporting financial data, its **accounting system,** clearly must be equipped to record data accurately, be organized so that an accountant can readily translate the data, and be flexible so the data can be used for different purposes.

Accounting's Relationship to Bookkeeping

"Accountants are just glorified bookkeepers." This common opinion could not be more wrong. A **bookkeeper** is a clerical employee who records day-to-day business transactions. A bookkeeper's thoroughness and accuracy are critically important to a good accounting system. But entry level bookkeepers generally have only a year's in-house or comparable training. On the other hand, accountants are professionals who design and oversee an entire system of recording and reporting financial data. Bookkeepers work within that system. Accountants take the raw information that bookkeepers record, then summarize it, make adjustments to it, and interpret it for others. Figure 15.2 shows how accountants transform raw data about business activities into useful information for decision makers.

Types of Accountants

There are two basic classes of accountants: public and private.

Public Accountants An independent professional whom individuals or companies may hire to perform specific accounting services is a **public accountant**. Some public accountants practice as sole practitioners, that is, as individuals. Others form partnerships of from two to hundreds of accountants. The largest of these, "the Big Eight" listed in Table 15.1, serve primarily the nation's large corporations.

Besides the functions identified in the previous section, public accountants perform **audits,** formal examinations of a firm's financial records. An accountant then prepares financial statements based on the audit. Many lenders and government agencies require certification that the financial statements were properly prepared and fairly present the company's condition. Only a **certified public accountant** (CPA) can make that certification. A CPA is an accountant who has passed an examination prepared by the American Institute of Certified Public Accountants (AICPA) and satisfied a state's educational and experience requirements. Most states require a degree in accounting plus a period of practical training. Fewer than one-quarter of the nation's accountants are CPAs.

Those interested in a corporation's financial statements, like lenders and shareholders, rely on the independence of a CPA's certification. As have the members of other professions, accountants have found people increasingly willing to sue

The Primary Types of Accountants

FIGURE 15.2

Accounting as an Information System

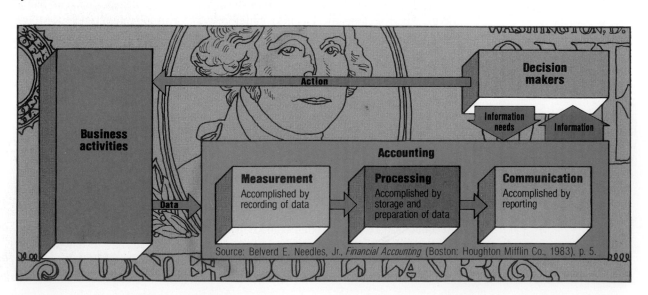

Source: Belverd E. Needles, Jr., *Financial Accounting* (Boston: Houghton Mifflin Co., 1983), p. 5.

TABLE 15.1	Arthur Andersen & Co.	Peat Marwick Mitchell & Co.
The "Big Eight" Accounting Firms	Coopers & Lybrand	Price Waterhouse & Co.
	Deloitte Haskins & Sells	Touche Ross & Co.
	Ernst & Whinney	Arthur Young & Co.

Source: Adapted from Belverd E. Needles, Jr., *Financial Accounting* (Boston: Houghton Mifflin Co., 1983), p. 6.

when they believe they have been misled. For example, some members of the Los Angeles Raiders who invested in Technical Equities Corporation sued the firm's accountants when it went bankrupt.[1]

Private Accountants It is important to keep in mind that the client prepares the data and financial reports that the CPA examines and tests in the course of an audit. The larger the firm, the more likely it is to have one or more accountants as employees. Accountants who are employees of companies or government agencies are called **private accountants** or **management accountants**. Management accountants can become **certified management accountants** by passing the National Association of Accountants' test and satisfying its educational and professional criteria.

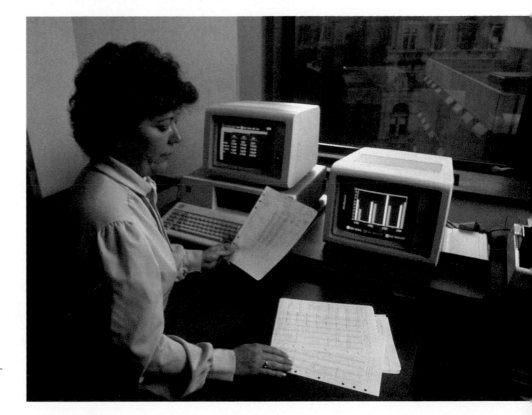

Private accounting. Most mid- to large size businesses employ accountants. Their services can be critical when it comes to controlling costs, analyzing performance, budgeting, and planning for the future.

The Accounting Process

How do accountants create financial statements? What do they work from? What is the accounting process? The easiest way to answer these questions is to look at the operations of a hypothetical company. Suppose that two friends, Margot and Dave, decide to open a sporting goods store specializing in equipment for joggers and amateur runners. They lease a store, buy inventory, and open their new business, which they decided to call Pacesetters. They quickly find, especially when the first wave of tax forms arrives, that they cannot keep track of their business just by using the company checkbook. They immediately seek out an accountant who can tell them how to cope. We will look now at what the accountant might tell Margot and Dave about recording, classifying, and summarizing their business transactions.

The Accounting Equation

An organization's economic resources — everything of value that it owns — are its **assets**. Cash, inventory, useful machinery and equipment, and real estate are all assets. On the other hand, the amounts that a firm owes to others are its **liabilities**. Subtracting a firm's total liabilities from its total assets produces a figure called **owners' equity**, the amount the owners would have left if they used the firm's assets to pay all its liabilities. Thus:

$$\text{Assets} - \text{Liabilities} = \text{Owners' Equity}$$

Accountants regard both liabilities and owners' equity as claims against the firm's assets, so normally the formula, which is called the **accounting equation**, appears in this order:

$$\text{Assets} = \text{Liabilities} + \text{Owners' Equity}$$

Double-Entry Bookkeeping

The accounting equation is the basis of **double-entry bookkeeping**, a system of recording business transactions in which each transaction is recorded in at least two separate accounts. One side of an equation must always equal the other, whether in algebra or accounting. An increase or decrease on one side of an equation requires a corresponding change on the other. This principle applies in recording business transactions, too.

How the Accounting Equation Relates to Double-Entry Bookkeeping

Let's return to the hypothetical Pacesetters company. Suppose that it owes a jogging-suit maker $500. Margot writes a check for that sum. That transaction — paying the bill — not only reduces Pacesetters' assets by $500 in cash but also decreases its liabilities by the same amount. The equation therefore remains in balance:

$$-\$500 = -\$500$$

$$\text{Assets} = \text{Liabilities} + \text{Owners' Equity}$$

FIGURE 15.3

The Accounting Equation
Illustrated

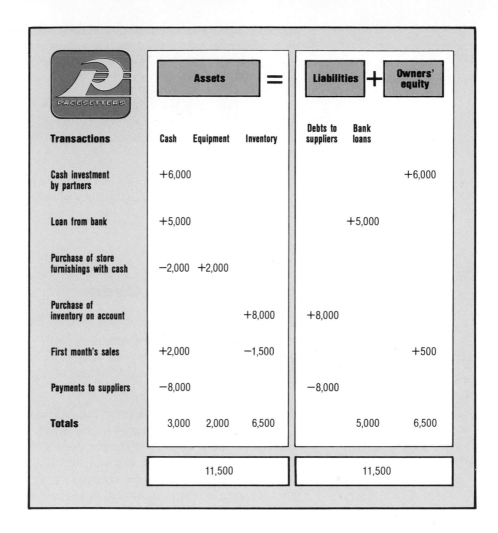

| Transactions | Assets = | | | Liabilities + | | Owners' equity |
	Cash	Equipment	Inventory	Debts to suppliers	Bank loans	
Cash investment by partners	+6,000					+6,000
Loan from bank	+5,000				+5,000	
Purchase of store furnishings with cash	−2,000	+2,000				
Purchase of inventory on account			+8,000	+8,000		
First month's sales	+2,000		−1,500			+500
Payments to suppliers	−8,000			−8,000		
Totals	3,000	2,000	6,500		5,000	6,500
	11,500			11,500		

Every business transaction can be thought of in this way. Figure 15.3 illustrates how several types of transactions fit into the equation.

1. Suppose that Margot and Dave invest a total of $6,000 to start Pacesetters. That amount appears on the books as both a cash asset and owners' equity.
2. When they decide to borrow $5,000, it becomes both a cash asset and a liability — they must repay the bank.
3. Pacesetters' purchase of furnishings affects only the left side of the equation. It is simply an exchange of one type of asset — cash — for another — equipment.
4. When Pacesetters needs more shoes and T-shirts, it makes a **purchase on account**, or a purchase on credit. The inventory becomes an asset, the obligation to pay a liability.
5. In Pacesetters' first month, it brings in $2,000 by selling $1,500 in inventory. This sales performance adds $500 to the left side of the equation. As a result, $500 must go on the right side, too — in this case under owners' equity, because it is "owed" to Margot and Dave.

TABLE 15.2

The Accounting Cycle

Step 1.	Examining the source documents that identify transactions.
Step 2.	Entering the transactions in a journal.
Step 3.	Posting the transactions in a ledger.
Step 4.	Calculating a trial balance.
Step 5.	Preparing financial statements.

6. When Pacesetters pays its suppliers for the inventory purchased on account, its liabilities decrease, but so do its cash assets.

As the last line of Figure 15.3 shows, after all these transactions the equation still remains in balance.

The Accounting Cycle

Accounting systems typically consist of the five steps listed in Table 15.2. These steps are called the **accounting cycle** because they describe the process that takes a transaction from being mere raw data to its being summarized in the financial statements, a process repeated over and over again during a firm's life.

Step 1: Examining Source Documents Accounting's **source documents** are the papers or computer entries which prove that a transaction actually took place. These documents include memos, checks, credit-card receipts, invoices, and purchase orders. Before entering a transaction on the books, bookkeepers look at the source documents to determine what occurred and which accounts were affected. An **account** is a record of the increases, decreases, and balance of an item reported in financial statements.[2]

The Five Steps in the Accounting Cycle

Step 2: Entering Transactions in a Journal A **journal** or **book of original entry** is a chronological list of transactions each assigned to a particular account. A journal should include sufficient detail so that someone examining it can understand each transaction's nature. Journals are kept either by hand or on a computer, but the entry process is the same for both.

Figure 15.4 includes a page from the Pacesetters' journal. The titles of the two columns on the right are often confusing. In everyday usage, a credit is something positive and a debit something negative. When you deal with accounting, you must forget the term's everyday meanings. In accounting, a **debit** is an entry on the left side of an account; a **credit** is an entry on the right side. A bookkeeper credits an account by making an entry on the right side of an account and debits it with an entry on the left.[3]

The Second Step in the Accounting Cycle

Every transaction has two entries: a debit to one account and a credit to another. Where the entry affects an asset or expense account:

☐ An *increase* in the account is a *debit*.
☐ A *decrease* in the account is a *credit*.

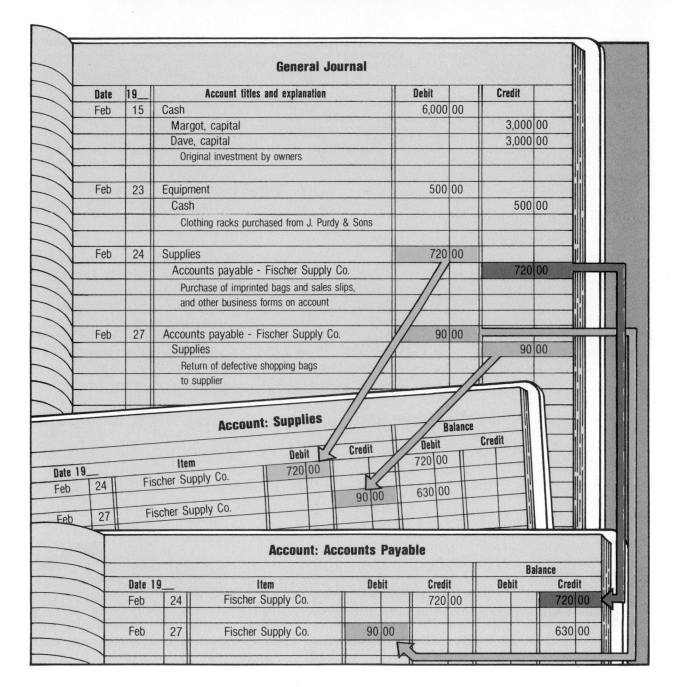

General Journal

Date	19__	Account titles and explanation	Debit		Credit	
Feb	15	Cash	6,000	00		
		Margot, capital			3,000	00
		Dave, capital			3,000	00
		Original investment by owners				
Feb	23	Equipment	500	00		
		Cash			500	00
		Clothing racks purchased from J. Purdy & Sons				
Feb	24	Supplies	720	00		
		Accounts payable - Fischer Supply Co.			720	00
		Purchase of imprinted bags and sales slips,				
		and other business forms on account				
Feb	27	Accounts payable - Fischer Supply Co.	90	00		
		Supplies			90	00
		Return of defective shopping bags				
		to supplier				

Account: Supplies

Date 19__		Item	Debit		Credit		Balance Debit		Credit	
Feb	24	Fischer Supply Co.	720	00			720	00		
Feb	27	Fischer Supply Co.			90	00	630	00		

Account: Accounts Payable

Date 19__		Item	Debit		Credit		Balance Debit		Credit	
Feb	24	Fischer Supply Co.			720	00			720	00
Feb	27	Fischer Supply Co.	90	00					630	00

FIGURE 15.4

Sample Page from Pacesetters' Journal

Where the entry affects a liability, owners' equity, or revenue account:

☐ An *increase* in the account is a *credit*.
☐ A *decrease* in the account is a *debit*.

These sets of rules mirror each other because they deal with the opposite halves of the accounting equation. The two sides have opposite rules of entry so that the equation will always balance.

In Figure 15.4, the entry for February 15 deals with the owners' original in-

The Computerized Accountant

To many outside the profession, an accountant is someone who permanently rests one hand on the keys of an adding machine. But in an age where computer enthusiasts encourage people to use computers just to balance their checkbooks, you can be sure that a lot of work has gone into creating software to keep track of companies' numbers.

For most businesses, the question is not "Will a computerized system save us money?" but "How soon will a computerized system pay for itself?" Computers can search continuously for trends in sales figures and can warn a company when changes are beginning to occur. Computers can keep so much better track of inventory and accounts receivable than can traditional accounting methods that businesses using computerized systems can often see improvements of 35 to 40 percent in the ratio of sales to average inventory or sales to average accounts receivable. Keeping inventory to a minimum and collecting on accounts may not raise a company's sales, but they lower the amount a company has to borrow and make it appear more financially healthy.

Many businesses that long ago purchased programs to handle their accounts payable and order processing are now purchasing *integrated* accounting programs. These more sophisticated programs combine what used to be separately purchased functions like general ledger, accounts receivable, and accounts payable. By allowing the accountant to move data quickly to and between these various functions, this new breed of software cuts down

considerably the amount of time the software user needs to spend in front of the screen.

The next step, for accounting as for many computer applications, is the expert system. These systems codify the methods experts in a given field use to make judgments in that field. With enough input from experts, the system can establish rules and relationships that underlie a decision. With these relationships the system can draw inferences or make judgments.

Such systems, still mostly in the developmental stages, will help human accountants in a number of areas. An expert system will be able to keep track of the changes in accounting standards and requirements. Then it can help the accountant make important decisions about reporting and disclosure. Best of all, the program will explain how it reached a particular conclusion so a user can follow the computer's path of logic.

Systems are now in the works that will help auditors assess whether a company has made enough allowance for bad debts. Others will help auditors analyze a company's books, deciding which errors or unusual practices are important or cause for alarm.

Sources: Sheldon Needle, "A Hard Look at Accounting Software," *Nation's Business*, May 1985, 42. Software Digest, Inc., "How Do Integrated Accounting Programs Compare?" *Journal of Accountancy*, March 1986, 96. Jon A. Booker, Russell C. Kick, Jr., and John C. Gardner, "Expert Systems in Accounting: The Next Generation of Computer Technology," *Journal of Accountancy*, March 1986, 96.

vestment. It shows an increase in cash of $6,000. Cash is an asset, so the increase appears as a debit. The $6,000 also increases the owners' capital accounts and therefore appears as a credit to those accounts. The entry dated February 23 records a cash purchase of equipment. The increase in the equipment account appears as a debit, the decrease in cash as a credit. The February 24 entry records a purchase of supplies on account. Supplies is an asset, so the bookkeeper debited that account. **Accounts payable** — amounts due others — is a liability, so the bookkeeper credited that account. When Dave returns the defective shopping bags to the supplier, the bookkeeper will debit accounts payable and credit inventory.

FIGURE 15.5

Pacesetters' Balance Sheet

Pacesetters, Inc.
Balance Sheet
December 31, 19___

Assets

Current assets			
Cash		$39,000	
Marketable securities		8,000	
Accounts receivable	$8,000		
Less allowance for doubtful accounts	200	7,800	
Notes receivable		2,000	
Inventory		38,000	
Prepaid expenses		8,200	
Total current assets			$103,000
Fixed assets			
Store equipment and fixtures	76,200		
Less accumulated depreciation	10,200	66,000	
Office furniture and equipment	27,000		
Less accumulated depreciation	4,200	22,800	
Total fixed assets			88,800
Intangible assets			
Leasehold	6,000		
Less amortization	600	5,400	
Total intangible assets			5,400
Total assets			$197,200

Liabilities and owners' equity

Current liabilities			
Accounts payable	$41,800		
Notes payable	10,000		
Accrued expenses	4,200		
Total current liabilities		$56,000	
Long-term liabilities			
Long-term notes payable	10,000		
Total long-term liabilities		10,000	
Total liabilities			$66,000
Owners' equity			
Common stock (14,000 shares at $5.00 per share)		70,000	
Retained earnings		61,200	
Total owners' equity			131,200
Total liabilities and owners' equity			$197,200

Step 3: Posting Transactions in a Ledger The third step in the accounting cycle involves transferring data from the journal — a chronological listing of transactions — to an appropriate account in a **ledger,** a book or computer file in which each account appears separately. The process of transferring information from the journal to the ledger is called **posting.** Figure 15.5 indicates how the last two journal entries in Figure 15.4 might appear in a ledger. Note that each transaction will still result in a debit to one account and a credit to another, even though the corresponding entries may be pages apart. In the columns at the far right, the bookkeeper maintains a running balance on the account.

Step 4: Calculating a Trial Balance If the bookkeeper has kept the **books** — the journal, ledger, and other accounting records — accurately, the ledger accounts should balance. The total debits across all ledger accounts should equal the total credits.

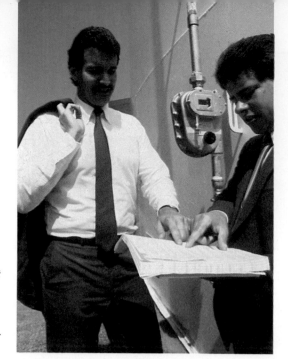

Before preparing the financial statements, an accountant will calculate a **trial balance** to make sure that a credit offsets every debit and that the arithmetic was done correctly. First, he or she brings individual accounts up to date by making adjustments to certain accounts like Supplies and Prepaid Insurance. People use papers, pencils, paperclips, typewriter ribbons, and other supplies every day. It would normally be too expensive to change the accounting records every time a secretary took out a new notepad. Therefore, at the end of the accounting period, someone counts the supplies to determine what has been used up during the period. That amount is then recorded in a journal entry. The same logic explains adjustments made to the prepaid insurance account. The firm pays the premium at the beginning of the insurance's term, which is usually a year. Each day, a portion of that benefit is used up, however. Whenever the financial statements are prepared, the prepaid insurance account is brought up to date by posting appropriate adjusting entries — entries made to apply accrual accounting to transactions that span more than one accounting period. [4]

After bringing the accounts up to date, the accountant sums up all accounts with debit balances and all with credit balances. Finally, the accountant checks one against the other. If the two are not equal, he or she looks for mistakes and corrects errors in accounts. Note, however, that a trial balance will not reveal all kinds of errors. If the bookkeeper reversed certain credit and debit entries or even failed to enter a transaction, the accounts would still balance.

The Final Step in the Accounting Cycle

Step 5: Preparing Financial Statements An accountant prepares financial statements at the end of every accounting period. The three most common statements are:

☐ The balance sheet
☐ The income statement
☐ The statement of changes in financial position

The remainder of this chapter examines these three types of statement in detail.

An **accounting period** is any regular period of one year or less for which a business decides to have financial statements prepared. Many firms have them prepared quarterly or monthly as well as annually. Almost always, firms prepare statements for the same period each year, which allows users to compare the company's performance from period to period and to identify trends. In other words, a company that one year prepares financial statements for the quarter ending March 31 can be expected to prepare financials for the same quarter the next year.

After the accountant has completed the financial statements, the accounts are closed for the accounting period the statements cover. Revenue and expense accounts are returned to zero by transferring their balances to owners' equity. By the time the accountant finishes this work, a new accounting period will be under way and bookkeepers will have started entering transactions in the journal and posting them to the ledger.

THE BALANCE SHEET

The First of the Three Most Common Financial Statements

The **balance sheet,** or **statement of financial position,** summarizes an organization's financial status at the end of an accounting period. Figure 15.5 shows the hypothetical Pacesetters' year-end balance sheet after the business has been operating for some years. By now, Margot and Dave have incorporated and brought in new investors. They have also diversified into other sporting goods lines.

As the headings on Figure 15.5 clearly reveal, the balance sheet is another expression of the accounting equation. Like a photograph, a balance sheet freezes a firm's financial condition at a particular moment. By law, shareholders must receive these "snapshots" at least annually.

Assets

The left side of a balance sheet lists the asset accounts in order of their decreasing **liquidity,** the ease with which the actual assets they represent can be turned into cash.

Current Assets   Cash and any other assets that are likely to be used up or be converted into cash, usually within a year, are included in **current assets. Cash** includes both money on hand, as in the cash box, and money in bank demand accounts. **Marketable securities** are securities the holder can turn into cash in only a few days. Any security traded on an exchange is marketable.

The Types of Current Assets

Accounts receivable are any amounts owed to an organization by its customers or clients. Pacesetters' customers pay primarily with credit cards or cash, so its $8,000 in accounts receivable is quite small. Some accounts receivable may become **doubtful accounts,** accounts receivable that appear uncollectable. For this reason, accountants make an allowance, based on the company's experience, for doubtful accounts. **Notes receivable** are formal, signed promises to pay a certain amount on a certain date. Generally, notes are paid over a somewhat longer period than accounts receivable, which are usually due within thirty days. In some cases, a debtor issues a note receivable to settle a past-due account.

Inventory is a general term used to describe certain classes of goods that are assets of a business. Inventory may represent the merchandise a company holds for sale. Pacesetters' $38,000 in inventory consists of finished products — shoes, jogging outfits, and the like. By contrast, the manufacturers who sold it these goods would include in their inventory raw materials and goods used in the process of manufacturing, too. The final type of current asset account is **prepaid expenses**, the services and supplies an organization has paid for but has not yet used. Insurance premiums are a common example. Office supplies, like paper and pens, are another.

The Main Types of Assets

Fixed Assets   The tangible assets called **fixed assets**, or **plant and equipment assets**, are those that a firm expects to use for more than a year. Except for land, fixed assets tend to wear out with time. An automobile or a lathe or a computer has a limited period of usefulness before it wears out or becomes obsolete. In financial reports, companies deal with this fact through **depreciation**, the process of distributing the original value of a long-term asset over the years of its useful life. Each year, a portion of an asset's value is considered to be spent and is entered on the books as an expense. The asset's value is at the same time reduced by an equal amount. Both the accounting profession and the Internal Revenue Service have elaborate procedures for calculating depreciation. In the Pacesetters case, its office furniture and equipment originally cost $27,000. Over the period that the property has been in use, the accountant has reduced its value, or depreciated it, by $4,200.

Intangible Assets   Long-term assets that have no physical substance but have a value based on rights or privileges that belong to the owner are **intangible assets**.[5] A trademark, like Pepsi-Cola's logo, has a real value to the company, but, unlike a bottling machine, it cannot be touched. Patents, copyrights, leaseholds (ownership of a lease), and franchises are also intangible assets. When an intangible asset has a limited life, like a patent or a leasehold, accountants show its decline in value over time by **amortization**, a process much like depreciation. Pacesetters' ten-year leasehold on its new store is carried at its original value. Each year, a portion of the original value is converted into an expense until at its expiration the leasehold disappears from the balance sheet.

An asset that appears on many balance sheets, though not on Pacesetters', is **goodwill**, a firm's extra earning power compared to other firms in the same industry. Goodwill is more than just a good reputation or a warm relationship with customers. It may come from a good location or excellent management. Goodwill does not appear on Pacesetters' balance sheet because it is not listed as long as a firm remains in the hands of its original owners. When a firm is sold, buyers will often pay a premium above the value of the company's assets. That premium is said to pay for the firm's goodwill, so the premium is assigned to that account.

Liabilities

The balance sheet lists liabilities according to the dates when they must be paid.

Current Liabilities   Debts that will fall due within the next twelve months are **current liabilities. Accounts payable** consist primarily of debts owed suppliers

Determining the value of intangible assets. Winning exclusive broadcasting rights to the Celtic's away games was quite a plum for Gannett's WLVI-TV. People like Larry Bird and interviewer Bob Cousy understand the importance of the broadcast rights to the station and to the team, but putting an exact value on intangible assets is often the responsibility of accountants.

of goods and services that are due during the next accounting period. Essentially, they are the reverse of accounts receivable. Thus, a customer's debt to Pacesetters for a pair of shoes is an account receivable; Pacesetters' debt to the manufacturer for the same shoes is an account payable. **Notes payable** are notes that will fall due during the next twelve months. They are the opposite of notes receivable.

The **accrued expenses** category lumps together various kinds of obligations that were incurred during the accounting period but are not yet actually due or owing. Accrued expenses include wages that an employee has earned but are not yet due to be paid; taxes that will be due a taxing authority; interest on bank loans, and the like. If a firm takes delivery of a filing cabinet during the accounting period but has not yet been billed for it, its obligation to pay is an accrued expense. All such expenses must appear on the balance sheet in order to present a true picture of the firm's position.

The Main Types of Liabilities

Long-Term Liabilities Debts that will fall due more than a year after the date of the balance sheet are **long-term liabilities**. Mortgages, bonds, and long-term notes fall in this category. Pacesetters' balance sheet shows that it has a $10,000 note due to the bank.

Owners' Equity

The owners'-equity section of the balance sheet varies with the type of business it describes. A sole proprietorship's reflects simply the difference between the assets and the liabilities. Generally, its balance sheet does not distinguish the owner's original investment from later profits. The same is true of partnerships' owners'-equity sections except that the equity is divided among the partners. A corporation's balance sheet, does distinguish between what the corporation has received for its stock since its founding and its **retained earnings**, profits kept in the business after any dividends are paid. Quite often, retained earnings are used to fund plant expansion and other long-term capital investments.

THE INCOME STATEMENT

The balance sheet, as noted, records a company as though frozen at a particular moment. The **income statement** summarizes what an organization has earned and spent over a given period. It first totals a firm's **revenue**, the cash and accounts receivable a firm generates from its operations. Then it deducts expenses. The result is the firm's profit or loss for the period. The basic formula is as follows:

Revenues − (Cost of goods sold + Operating expenses) = Net income

Businesses can record revenues and expenses on one of two bases. On an **accrual basis**, the bookkeeper lists sales on the dates they take place and expenses on the dates they are incurred, regardless of whether any money actually changed hands. If Pacesetters sold new warm-ups to a college track team in December but the college did not pay for them until February, on an accrual basis it would treat the revenue as December's and therefore as the prior year's. Alternatively, on a **cash basis**, sales and expenses are listed according to the dates when money changes hands. The accounting profession and the Internal Revenue Service agree that the accrual basis more accurately reflects a company's true income. Only certain types of relatively simple businesses may use a cash basis.

Revenues

Generally, revenues come from sales of goods and services. However, items in this category may also include income from the sale or rental of property; royalties earned on patents, copyrights, or trademarks; and interest or dividends on investments.

Let's assume that Pacesetters' annual revenues come entirely from the sale of sporting goods. The first category in the revenue category on its income statement (Figure 15.6) is **gross sales**, the total value of all goods or services sold during the accounting period. However, Pacesetters did not actually receive $294,000 for its merchandise because not all its customers paid full price and some returned the goods. The categories listed below gross sales adjust it to reality. **Sales returns** are the refunds allowed customers when they return something. **Allowances** are price reductions granted if merchandise is slightly damaged

Harmonizing with the World

If you've ever looked closely at a company's financial statement or tried to make sense of the intricacies of accounting rules, you've probably developed a respect for the people who take the thousands of figures a company generates each year and put them into a few pages of comprehensible tables and balance sheets. But have you ever considered what that job would be like for a multinational corporation that has to make financial reports to scores of different governments?

Just as the countries of the world speak hundreds of different languages and use hundreds of different monetary systems, so too they use scores of different accounting methods. Multinational corporations aren't the only ones affected. Anyone trying to invest in a company based in another country must be aware that the company's bottom line reflects the accounting principles of that country, principles that could inflate or depress earnings. In Europe, for instance, companies tend to make profits look smaller to avoid taxes, while most American companies try to show high profits to attract investors.

For these reasons, accountants worldwide are under a great deal of pressure to develop international accounting standards — a process known as "harmonization." As we move closer to a global economy, such harmonization becomes ever more crucial, and people who are involved in the process become more important to governments and corporations.

A number of international groups are at work on the problem. The International Accounting Standards Committee, which has members in 65 nations, has developed more than 20 international accounting guidelines.

The root of the problem is that there are at least five different historical bases for accounting: British, American, Germanic-Dutch, Franco-Spanish-Portuguese, and communist. While most nations agree that harmonization would help international business, some resist giving up their own standards. French finance officials, for instance, say that each country "should be free to use the methods best suited to it and its traditions"; "there's a danger in trying to apply in France standards hammered out for a different country — that is, America."

Such resistance may prevent international organizations from achieving accounting harmony in the near future, but some analysts think that the international marketplace itself will lead to standardization. Foreign companies that list stock in the U.S. must comply with some American standards, and for many foreign companies a stock listing in the U.S. is an important step in the company's growth and prestige. The amount of such stock sold on U.S. markets has grown from $2 billion in 1970 to over $30 billion today. Some companies may not like meeting the guidelines set down by the Financial Accounting Standards Board of the U.S., but they realize it's an economic necessity.

Sources: Paul Hemp, "Where Boards and Governments Have Failed, The Market Could Internationalize Accounting," *The Wall Street Journal*, May 8, 1985, 34. Adolf J. H. Enthoven, "U.S. Accounting and the Third World," *Journal of Accountancy*, June 1983, 110. Lee Berton, "International Congress of Accountants Focuses on Harmonized Standards," *Journal of Accountancy*, January 1983, 48.

or defective. **Cash discounts** are given when customers are charged less than the full amount if they pay their bills promptly. Discount terms usually appear on invoices. For example, "2/10 net 30" means that the buyer may deduct 2 percent from the sale price if the invoice is paid within ten days. Otherwise, the total amount, the net, is due in thirty days.

After subtracting the adjustments from gross sales, the figure that results is **net sales**, the amount the firm added to its assets by selling goods during the accounting period. Net sales is not, however, a synonym for profit.

FIGURE 15.6

Pacesetters' Income Statement

Pacesetters, Inc.
Income Statement
For the year ended December 31, 19___

Revenues

Gross sales		$294,000	
Less sales returns, and cash discounts		9,000	
Net sales			$285,000

Cost of goods sold

Beginning inventory (January 1)		30,000	
Purchases	$170,000		
Less purchase discounts	6,000		
Net purchases		164,000	
Cost of goods available for sale		194,000	
Less ending inventory (December 31)		38,000	
Cost of goods sold			156,000
Gross profit			$129,000

Operating expenses

Selling expenses

Sales salaries	46,000		
Advertising	5,300		
Depreciation of store equipment and fixtures	1,700		
Miscellaneous	1,000		
Total selling expenses		54,000	

Administrative expenses

Office salaries	20,600		
Office supplies	1,000		
Rent	15,500		
Utilities	2,000		
Depreciation of office furniture and equipment	800		
Miscellaneous	600		
Total administrative expenses		40,500	
Total operating expenses			94,500

Net income before taxes			$34,500
Less income taxes			6,500
Net income after taxes			$28,000

The Cost of Goods Sold

The amount that an organization spent to buy or produce the goods it sold during an accounting period is its **cost of goods sold.** Calculating the cost of goods sold varies according to which of the two basic inventory systems a firm uses. The **perpetual inventory system** records every change in inventory as soon as it happens. By contrast, the **periodic inventory method** calculates the effect of sales on inventory only at the end of an accounting period.

Perpetual Inventory The main advantage of a perpetual inventory is that it tells managers immediately the precise value of merchandise on hand. Suppose that an automobile dealership sells a car on March 8. If it uses a perpetual inventory system, as of that date its inventory account is reduced by the cost of the car. Because managers will know exactly what inventory is on hand, they

How the Two Basic Types of
Inventory Systems Affect the
Cost of Goods Sold

Accountants in many arenas. *What was Norm Pasas, a partner with Ernst & Whinney, doing at the Los Angeles Olympics? He was in charge of the firm's Olympic Group. Today's Games rely on almost instantaneous calculation of scores and transmittal of those results without error to officials, competitors, and 8,000 representatives of the media. Large accounting firms have the staff and the expertise to develop the reporting systems; they have the reputation for honesty and reliability that gives them credibility.*

can maintain smaller inventories. Against this obvious benefit is the significantly greater cost of maintaining a perpetual inventory system. Businesses that sell comparatively few but relatively high-cost units find that perpetual inventory systems work well. These systems also simplify preparation of the income statement. A perpetual inventory firm will have a continuous ledger account for the cost of goods sold and can simply enter the total for the accounting period. Today, universal product codes and electronic scanners attached to computers have made perpetual inventory systems attractive to high-volume businesses like supermarkets, which could not use them before.

Periodic Inventory Firms using the periodic inventory method calculate their inventories by looking at the change in inventory during an accounting period. Pacesetters is such a firm. The first line under the cost of goods sold heading on its income statement is its **beginning inventory** — what it carried over from the prior accounting period. To that $30,000, it adds its **purchases,** the value of what it bought for inventory during the accounting period. Pacesetters received some volume discounts and some prompt-payment discounts, so their total is subtracted from the figure for purchases to produce **net purchases.** The total of beginning inventory plus net purchases equals the **cost of goods available for sale** during the accounting period. Of course, not all the goods available for sale were sold. To find the value of the unsold inventory, Pacesetters subtracts the inventory remaining at the end of the year from the cost of goods available for sale. The result is the cost of goods sold: $156,000.

Pacesetters' income statement calculations are typical of retailers'. A manufacturer's would be somewhat different, though. Its cost of goods sold would include raw materials or parts, labor, and factory overhead. Still, if the manufacturer used a periodic inventory system, the basic calculation would be the same.

Gross Profit   Subtracting the cost of goods sold from the net sales produces a company's **gross profit** or **gross margin.** Managers use this important figure to compare the company's current sales performance with it in prior accounting periods. Also, the gross profit figure offers a good standard of comparison with the performance of other companies in the industry.

FIFO and LIFO   The gross profit calculation seems simple, but it conceals a difficult question: How do you put a value on the ending inventory if the prices of the goods making it up change during the accounting period? Consider Pacesetters' situation when on March 1 it orders 100 pairs of running shoes at $18 apiece and then, three weeks later, orders 50 more pairs of the same shoe at a new price of $18.95. By the year's end, Pacesetters has sold 90 of the 150 pairs. In calculating its income, what value should it assign to the 90 pairs it sold?

Companies with perpetual inventory systems assign a value to each item brought into inventory and therefore do not have this problem. However, firms with relatively fast inventory turnover must choose among somewhat arbitrary methods of assigning inventory costs. The two most common are called FIFO and LIFO. The *FIFO* — **First In, First Out** — system assumes that the first items brought into inventory are also the first sold. Thus, it would treat the 90 pairs of shoes Pacesetters sold as coming entirely from the $18 shipment. In times of rising prices, FIFO minimizes the cost of goods sold and maximizes the gross profit, so the firm seems more successful. By inflating profits, though, it also increases the firm's taxes. More importantly, it distorts the financial picture of the firm by understating the cost of goods sold, presenting a misleading picture of what it will cost to replace inventory.

For these reasons, most accountants prefer the *LIFO* — **Last In, First Out** — system, which assumes that the last items taken into inventory are the first sold. Thus, Pacesetters would treat 50 of the 90 pairs as $18.95 shoes and 40 as $18 shoes. In times of rising prices, LIFO understates profits and minimizes taxes but, far more importantly, it better reflects the current cost of replacing the inventory. In times of falling prices, LIFO overstates profits, understates the cost of goods sold, and maximizes taxes.

Operating Expenses

The income statement's third section, **operating expenses,** includes all costs of running the business except the cost of goods sold. Normally, an income statement divides these expenses into two general categories. **Selling expenses** are all costs directly associated with selling products or services to customers. **Administrative expenses,** also called **general expenses,** are the overall costs of operating the firm, excluding selling expenses and the cost of goods sold. Figure 15.6, Pacesetters' income statement, lists examples of both types of expenses.

Net Income

Subtracting the total operating expenses from the gross profit produces the figure known as **net income,** the amount of profit or loss the organization has generated during the accounting period. Normally, the amount of income taxes due reduces the net income figure. The last line of the income statement is the famous "bottom line," net income after taxes.

THE STATEMENT OF CHANGES IN FINANCIAL POSITION

The Third Common Type of Financial Statement

In addition to the balance sheet and the income statement, many firms provide a **statement of changes in financial position**, which summarizes changes in the firm's generation and use of cash that have taken place during the accounting period being analyzed. Generally, it lists the resources provided, where they came from, and how they were used. If, for example, a firm issued bonds to acquire new plant and equipment, those figures would appear on a statement of changes in financial position. This type of statement thus shows the flow of assets into and out of the organization. The Securities and Exchange Commission regards this information as critically important to investors and requires all companies subject to its regulation to provide these statements.

INTERPRETING FINANCIAL STATEMENTS

Financial statements are not particularly valuable for their own sakes. They are important only for what they can tell about a business.

Financial Ratios

Accountants, managers, owners, and investors analyze financial statements by applying **financial ratios,** certain mathematical relationships between numbers, to the components of the financial statements. In algebra, ratios always involve dividing one number by another, but there are other calculations, too, among financial ratios. Financial ratios provide important clues to the meaning of a company's reports. Table 15.3 includes the most significant financial ratios and computes them for Pacesetters, using the numbers shown in Figures 15.5 and 15.6.

Percentage of Net Sales   Managers and other analysts often examine the elements of an income statement to determine the percentage of net sales that each element accounts for. Such an analysis quickly points up costs that are unusually high or low. Management then knows where problems may be developing and can concentrate on those areas. Bankers, auditors, and investors know where they should look to see if problems exist or to determine whether this firm is set for growth and expansion. Figure 15.7 illustrates the percentage of net sales breakdown for Pacesetters.

Profitability Ratios   Although the bottom line of the income statement shows the actual amount of **profit** — the excess of revenues over expenses —

TABLE 15.3

Common Financial Ratios

Name of Ratio	Ratio	Standard of Comparison
Profitability Ratios		
Net Profit Margin (Return on Sales)	$= \dfrac{\text{Net income after taxes}}{\text{Net sales}}$ $= \dfrac{\$28,000}{\$285,000} = 0.098 = 9.8\%$	5% for retailers
Return on Equity	$= \dfrac{\text{Net income after taxes}}{\text{Owners' equity}}$ $= \dfrac{\$28,000}{\$131,000} = 0.213 = 21.3\%$	Very good, but young businesses often retain earnings
Earnings per Share	$= \dfrac{\text{Net income after taxes}}{\text{Common shares outstanding}}$ $= \dfrac{\$28,000}{\$14,000} = \$2.00$	Fair; IBM earns more than $11
Short-Term Financial Ratios		Ability to repay short-term debts
Working Capital	$= \text{Current assets} - \text{Current liabilities}$ $= \$103,000 - \$56,000 = \$47,000$	Not a true ratio; hard to use for comparison
Current Ratio	$= \dfrac{\text{Current assets}}{\text{Current liabilities}}$ $= \dfrac{\$103,000}{\$56,000} = 1.84$	2:1 the usual minimum; weak
Acid-Test Ratio (Quick Ratio)	$= \dfrac{\text{Cash} + \text{Marketable securities} + \text{accounts receivable} + \text{notes receivable}}{\text{Current liabilities}}$ $= \dfrac{\$39,000 + \$8,000 + \$7,800 + \$2,000}{\$56,000} = 1.01$	1.0 is standard; quick assets should cover liabilities
Activity Ratios		
Inventory Turnover	$= \dfrac{\text{Cost of goods sold}}{\text{Average inventory per period}}$ $= \dfrac{\$156,000}{((\$30,000 + \$38,000) : 2)} = 4.6$	Variable with industry; e.g., supermarkets in high teens

Part V INFORMATION FOR BUSINESS DECISION MAKING

TABLE 15.3

(continued)

Name of Ratio	Ratio	Standard of Comparison
Long-Term-Debt Ratios		
Debt-to-Assets Ratio	$= \dfrac{\text{Total liabilities}}{\text{Total assets}}$	Normal; the lower the better for lenders
	$= \dfrac{\$\ 66{,}000}{\$197{,}200} = 0.33$	
Debt-to-Equity Ratio	$= \dfrac{\text{Total liabilities}}{\text{Owners' equity}}$	Normal; the lower the better for lenders
	$= \dfrac{\$\ 66{,}000}{\$131{,}200} = 0.50$	

it does not reveal whether the profit level is appropriate for a given firm. Larger firms usually make larger total profits, but they should. And some industries earn very high profits, whereas others have difficulty showing any profit at all. To determine whether a firm is earning a reasonable profit, most people use data from its financial statements to calculate several profitability ratios. The most commonly used are the following:

☐ Net profit margin, also known as return on sales
☐ Return on equity
☐ Earnings per share

The Three Most Common Profitability Ratios

The net profit margin ratio, or return on sales, measures how much profit each dollar of sales generates. The return on equity ratio shows how much the firm earns on every dollar the owners or shareholders have invested. Earnings per share states the profits realized for each share of stock the company has issued. As Chapter 19, Securities Markets, will show, those profits can either be distributed as dividends to shareholders or kept in the firm as retained earnings.

Short-Term Financial Ratios These types of ratios let managers, lenders, and investors judge the liquidity of a firm. They also give the analyst important information about a company's ability to pay its debts. Even very profitable firms can fail if they do not have enough money to pay their debts when they fall due. The most common short-term financial ratios are:

The Three Most Common Short-Term Financial Ratios

☐ Working capital
☐ Current ratio
☐ Acid-test ratio (quick ratio)

Working capital — the difference between current assets and current liabilities — is not, strictly speaking, a ratio. It is, nevertheless, an important indicator of

Accounting for a Big Mistake

Accountants and their work seldom make the headlines. Few people outside the profession fully understand the procedures that make accounting news, and most stockholders and customers blindly put their faith in a company's accountants and auditors. But when, in 1986, Cigna Corp., a giant insurance company, announced that it had made an accounting estimate that was $1.2 *billion* off, a lot of people took notice.

The error occurred because of the unusual and complex accounting procedures followed by the insurance industry. An accident that happens today may not lead to an insurance payment for years. But insurance companies try to include the cost of that accident in this year's accounting statement. Because the company may not know for a long time exactly what it will pay on a given claim, it estimates what the final cost will be. It then puts the estimated amount into a "reserve." Ideally, the amount a company puts into a reserve every year will exactly equal the total amount that the company has to pay on that year's claims.

Of course, real claims seldom follow this ideal scenario, and companies often have to adjust their reserves to make up for changes in claim patterns. Companies may be tempted to underestimate the amount they put into reserves because reserves are paid out of profit. A company that underestimates reserves for a particular year will appear to be more profitable for that year than one that overestimates them.

Apparently what happened at Cigna, the nation's largest commercial property and casualty insurer, was that the company underestimated future claims payments for a number of years in a row, putting less into reserves than needed. Then at the end of 1985, the company looked at its figures and realized that claims for 1984 and before were costing much more than expected. The unanticipated costs meant that reserves were low — $1.2 billion low.

Cigna came under a lot of scrutiny because of the huge error, but that scrutiny didn't seem to inhibit its accounting techniques or financial performance. Soon after the company made the error public, it announced that it was actually going to put only half the $1.2 billion into reserves. It planned to raise the other $600 million from interest on the new cash reserves. State regulators looked suspiciously at the arrangement.

You would think that such a blunder would hurt a company's stock value, and in fact the price of Cigna stock did plummet briefly. But soon it was back near a 12-month high. Investors seemed to be telling Cigna what many other executives need to hear: a company that looks strong for the future — that has a lot of reserves — often inspires more investor confidence than one that simply has a profitable year to show on its financial statement.

Sources: Carol J. Loomis, "How Cigna Took a $1.2-Billion Bath," *Fortune*, March 17, 1986, 46. Steve Swartz and David B. Hilder, "Cigna Is Setting Aside in Cash Only Half of $1.2 Billion Addition to Its Reserves," *The Wall Street Journal*, February 10, 1986, 1a. James Nolan, "Commissioner Questions Cigna Corp. Accounting," *Journal of Commerce*, February 14, 1986, 2.

a company's short-term financial strength. Working capital shows how much of its assets the company would have left if it used its current assets to pay off its current debts. The "current ratio" uses the same amounts, but under this situation the current assets are divided by the current liabilities, as seen in Table 15.3. Investors generally look for a current ratio of 2 to 1 or better. Finally, because current assets include items like inventory as well as prepaid expenses that cannot be easily turned into cash, some analysts prefer the acid-test ratio over the current ratio. Because this ratio excludes all assets that are not quickly convertible into cash, the analyst using it gets a much better picture of how the company would survive a short-term crisis.

FIGURE 15.7

Pacesetters' Percentage of Net Sales

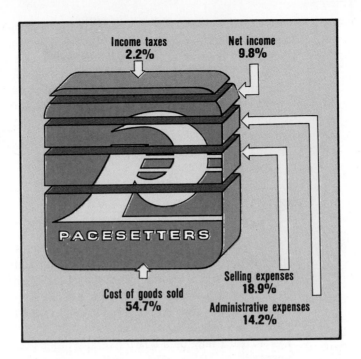

Income taxes 2.2%

Net income 9.8%

PACESETTERS

Cost of goods sold 54.7%

Selling expenses 18.9%

Administrative expenses 14.2%

The Uses of Financial Ratios

Activity Ratios How efficiently an organization is using its resources is shown in its activity ratios. The most commonly used activity ratio measures inventory turnover, the number of times during an accounting period that inventories are sold and replaced. Analysts use this ratio to determine how long it takes the firm to convert the inventory into cash or receivables.

Long-Term-Debt Ratios A company's financial health depends not only on its profitability and its power to repay short-term debts but also on how it stands with respect to long-term obligations. Bankers in particular pay heed to these ratios, the most common of which are these:

□ Debt-to-assets ratio
□ Debt-to-equity ratio

The debt-to-assets ratio shows the proportion of a firm's assets that would be used up if the firm were to eliminate its debt. This ratio also reveals how much of the firm is financed by its creditors and how much by its owners. Firms that owe a large proportion of their assets to creditors are riskier investments. The debt-to-equity ratio, which divides total liabilities by owners' equity, as shown in Table 15.3, also shows how much of the firm's activity is financed by creditors. Lenders generally look for low debt-to-equity ratios.

Applying the Financial Ratios

Financial ratios are not particularly useful in isolation. Analysts want to know if a firm is doing better or worse than average and if it is more or less efficient than other firms of the same size in the same industry. They also want to know if a firm has enough cash to fund expansion and growth or whether lack of cash might cause the business to fail.

To get information of this sort, analysts compare financial ratios — either against the firm's own past performance or against similar firms' performance. A firm that is growing more profitable every year and using its resources more and more efficiently is likely to be a good candidate either as a creditor or as an investment. Another yardstick that financial analysts commonly use is the performance of comparable firms. A number of sources offer this information. Dun & Bradstreet publishes industry averages for operating ratios of over 150 different industries, and many trade groups and specialized publications publish similar information for particular industries.

BUDGETING

The financial statements we have analyzed describe a company's present position or its performance during a prior period. Accounting principles also play an important role in preparing a firm's **budget**, an organization's financial plan for the future in which it describes how it will use its resources to meet its goals. Normally, firms draw up budgets for a given **operating period**, the length of time it takes to complete a manufacturing or sales cycle. An operating period is usually a year, but it may be a quarter or any other length of time appropriate for the business.

Types of Budgets

Budgets are based on the income statement's two basic items: revenue and expenses. A large corporation will have a **master budget**, which is an overall financial plan for the entire firm, and a number of subsidiary budgets for the units that make up the whole. A large corporation will also develop specialized budgets. For instance, an operating budget would project sales revenues, the cost of goods sold, and operating expenses. A cash budget would anticipate the flow of cash into and out of the firm. A capital budget would project expenditures on buildings and equipment over a period of years.

In addition to giving an organization a financial plan, a budget helps managers head off problems. For example, the process of developing a cash budget might reveal that in certain months the firm would not generate sufficient cash to meet operating expenses. Our hypothetical company, Pacesetters, might identify January and February as months in which cash-flow problems might arise because of a low interest in running in their area during that time of year. Margot and Dave might either set up a reserve for that period or arrange with a bank for a line of credit. July and August might, in contrast, be Pacesetters' biggest months, and its managers might want to arrange for some short-term investments to soak up the cash.

The Responsibility for Budgeting

In large corporations, the accounting department will do most of the budgeting, but every department will contribute its own projections. The overall budget

"Say! What a nice office!"

lists what each department hopes to spend in the next operating period, so it tends to contain some fat, because no manager wants to be unduly restricted.

Traditionally, one year's budget is built on the prior year's. In the last fifteen years, though, another method has become popular. **Zero-based budgeting** requires managers to justify their programs — and therefore all their expenditures — each time a new budget is prepared. Instead of starting from old figures, managers start from zero to show why they need to spend what they are requesting and explain how these expenditures will produce revenues.

Budgets as Controls

When a new operating period begins with the budget in place, managers can begin to use it as a controlling device. If a particular department is selling less or spending more than the budget predicted, higher levels of management will want to know why and how those in charge plan to solve their problems. This function of budgeting returns us to a concept discussed at the beginning of this chapter. Without adequate accounting procedures, starting with bookkeeping and proceeding through the development and analysis of the financial statements to end with budgeting, no manager can accurately tell where the reasons for success or failure lie. Managers will be confused about the effectiveness of their methods, and the firm's prospects will become doubtful at best.

A good accounting system makes people and programs accountable. It puts managers, owners, and investors in control of their businesses by giving them the information they need to improve their firm's present performance and to plan the company's future.

Chapter Highlights

1. Describe how managers, investors, and others use accounting information.

Accounting information is useful to owners, managers, creditors, investors, and others. Owners and managers use the information to see how the business is doing and to identify its strengths and weaknesses. Bankers and creditors use financial statements and other accounting information to judge whether a business can be expected to pay its debts. Investors are most interested in determining whether a firm is likely to grow. Union employees want to know what they can reasonably expect from contract negotiations.

2. Distinguish between the primary types of accountants.

A public accountant is an independent professional who is hired by individuals or companies to perform specific accounting services. Certified Public Accountants (CPAs) must pass an exam prepared by the American Institute of Certified Public Accountants and satisfy a state's educational and experience requirements. Only CPAs may certify an organization's financial statements. Private accountants, or management accountant, are employed by businesses or government agencies. Certified management accountants have passed the National Association of Accountants' test and satisfied its educational and professional criteria.

3. State the accounting equation and relate it to double-entry bookkeeping.

The accounting equation is:

Assets = Liabilities + Owners' Equity

Double-entry bookkeeping is a system of recording business transactions that requires an entry in at least two separate accounts for each transaction. Accounts on the left-hand side of the equals sign (assets) record an increase as debits and a decrease as credits. Accounts on the right-hand side of the equals sign (liabilities and owners' equity) show increases as credits and decreases as debits. Any transaction that is recorded correctly leaves the accounting equation in balance.

4. List the five steps in the accounting cycle and provide a one-sentence description of each stage.

First, examine source documents to make certain that a transaction has in fact occurred. Next, enter the transaction in a journal, a chronological list of all the transactions that occur. Transactions are then posted in a ledger. After all the accounts have been posted and brought up to date, a trial balance is taken to make sure that credits equal debits and that the equation is still in balance. Mistakes and errors are corrected at this point. Finally, financial statements are prepared and accounts are closed for the period covered by the statements.

5. Describe the functions of the three most common financial statements, discussed in this chapter.

The balance sheet, or statement of financial position, provides a snapshot of a firm's financial condition at a particular moment. Analysts use it to assess a firm's liquidity and to determine what proportion of the business is financed by creditors and what by owners. The income statement gives a picture of a business's performance over time. In it, expenses are subtracted from revenues to show a firm's net income for the period. The statement of changes in financial position summarizes changes that have taken place during the accounting period in the firm's generation and use of cash. It shows the flow of assets into and out of the organization. The Securities and Exchange Commission requires all companies subject to its regulation to provide these statements to their shareholders and to the commission.

6. Explain briefly how analysts look at and interpret financial statements.

Analysts (including owners, managers, creditors, and investors) examine financial statements to identify trends in a firm's performance or to see how a business is doing in comparison with similar firms. An analyst usually compares financial ratios for the business with industry averages or with ratios calculated on the basis of the firm's statements for the preceding two or three years.

7. Analyze accounting's role in the budget process.

Budgets show what a business intends to achieve over the planning period and the resources it expects to use in reaching its goals. The accounting department of a large corporation usually has the major responsibility for preparing the budget as well as the responsibility to collect and interpret the raw data that allow actual performance to be compared with planned performance.

Key Terms

Accounting cycle
Accounting equation
Accounting period
Assets
Balance sheet
  (statement of
  financial position)
Budget
Credit
Debit
Depreciation

Double-entry
  bookkeeping
FIFO (First In, First
  Out) inventory
  accounting
Financial ratios
Financial statements
Gross profit
Income statement
Journal
Liabilities

LIFO (Last In, First
  Out) inventory
  accounting
Liquidity
Master budget
Net income
Net sales
Operating expenses
Periodic inventory
  method
Perpetual inventory
  system

Posting
Profit
Purchases
Retained earnings
Revenue
Source documents
Statement of changes
  in financial position
Trial balance
Zero-based budgeting

Review Questions

1. It has been said that accountants do not just compile and tabulate data. What other duties do they perform?
2. In what ways are the duties of a bookkeeper different from those of an accountant? What is the difference between a public accountant and a private accountant?
3. Define owner's equity. How would the owner of a hardware store determine his owner's equity?
4. List and briefly describe the major steps in the accounting cycle.
5. Explain the function of the balance sheet. In what ways is the balance sheet like a photograph?

6. What is the major function of the income statement? What are the major components of the income statement?
7. In what ways does a perpetual inventory differ from a periodic inventory? What are the major advantages of a perpetual inventory?
8. What is a financial ratio? List and describe at least two common financial ratios.
9. Why do business firms develop budgets? What types of specialized budgets do firms develop?
10. Owners of small business firms can utilize the services of an accountant, or compile, tabulate, and interpret their own data. What would be the advantages of employing an accountant?

Application Exercises

1. Use the financial data in the income statement for Anton's Fashions Ltd. on the following page. Determine the net profit margin. What additional information would be needed to determine if this business is earning a reasonable profit?

2. Use the balance sheet on the next page for Anton's Fashions Ltd. Review the financial data and calculate the Return on Equity. Also determine the Debt to Assets ratio.

ANTON'S FASHIONS LTD.
Income Statement
For Year Ending December 31, 198x

Revenues

Gross Sales		$264,000	
Less Sales Returns and Allowances	$ 4,200		
Less Sales Discounts	2,150	6,350	
Net Sales			$257,650
Cost of Goods Sold		$ 38,000	
Beginning Inventory, January 1, 198x			
Purchases	$134,000		
Less Purchase Discounts	4,000		
Net Purchases		130,000	
Cost of Goods Available for Sale		$168,000	
Less Ending Inventory, December 31, 198x		36,000	
Cost of Goods Sold			132,000
Gross Profit on Sales			$125,650

Operating Expenses

Selling Expenses			
Advertising	$ 3,450		
Sales Salaries	18,200		
Sales Promotion	3,100		
Depreciation — Store Equipment	1,400		
Miscellaneous Selling Expenses	720		
Total Selling Expenses		$ 26,870	
General Expenses			
Office Salaries	$ 9,200		
Rent	18,300		
Depreciation — Office Equipment	1,800		
Utilities	1,350		
Insurance	600		
Miscellaneous Expenses	250		
Total General Expenses		$ 31,500	
Total Operating Expenses			$ 58,370
Net Income from Operations			67,280
Less Interest Expenses			2,100
Net Income Before Taxes			$ 65,180
Less Federal Income Taxes			9,500
Net Income After Taxes			$ 55,680

ANTON'S FASHIONS LTD.
Balance Sheet
July 31, 198x

Assets

Current Assets		
Cash	$ 3,700	
Accounts Receivable	4,500	
Inventory	36,000	
Total Current Assets		$44,200
Fixed Assets		
Equipment		16,000
Total Assets		$60,200

Liabilities

Current Liabilities		
Accounts Payable	$ 4,400	
Notes Payable	8,500	
Payroll Taxes Payable	2,200	
Total Current Liabilities		$15,100
Long-Term Liabilities		
Long-Term Notes Payable		21,000
Total Liabilities		$36,100
Owner's Equity		24,100
Total Liabilities and Owner's Equity		$60,200

Cases

15.1 Generally Accepted Principles

CPAs put their reputation on the line every time they certify a firm's financial statements. For that reason, they tend to be very conservative in their audits and their certifications. The notation that financial statements were prepared "in conformity with generally accepted accounting principles applied during the period" is close to a rave review.

That was the certification given to the 1982 financial reports of Stauffer Chemical Company by Deloitte Haskins & Sells, its Big Eight auditors — with one small caveat. The caveat was additional language which read, "except for a change, with which we concur, in the method of accounting for inventories."

That change must have worried the Securities and Exchange Commission (SEC), because it performed its own audit of Stauffer. The SEC audit resulted in charges that Stauffer fraudulently overstated its 1982 earnings in two ways: (1) through an inventory accounting change that liquidated LIFO (last in, first out) inventory that had been carried at a lower prior-year cost, and (2) by including in its 1982 financial reports, revenues and earnings from goods that might not be billed or paid for until 1983. (These goods were, however, shipped in 1982.)

According to the SEC, the overstated earnings totaled approximately $31 million, making this one of the largest financial fraud cases it had ever filed.

Stauffer officials maintained that no fraud was involved, but rather a disagreement between the firm and the SEC over "highly technical accounting issues." The charges were dropped when Stauffer agreed to restate its 1982 and 1983 earnings. Stauffer believed that the restatements would decrease its 1982 profits by 17% to $102 million. It would also cut its 1983 operating losses to $4 million from $22.5 million.

No penalty was levied against Stauffer by the SEC, but on news of the SEC's action Stauffer's shares fell 75 cents to $17.375 a share. Deloitte Haskins & Sells was not named in the suit.

Questions

1. Which of the three common financial statements are affected by a change in inventory value? By shifting revenues from one year to another?
2. Good accounting practice allows a firm to use any accepted inventory valuation method, but not to arbitrarily change methods. Why should this be so?

3. Why do most companies prefer the LIFO method of accounting?

For more information see *Business Week*, August 27, 1984, p. 38; *Chemical Week*, August 22, 1984, pp. 10–11; *Chemical & Engineering News*, August 20, 1984, p. 8; and *Forbes*, October 8, 1984, p. 82.

15.2 Investigative Accounting

The Price Waterhouse accountants were appointed as examiners in bankruptcy proceedings involving the DeLorean Motor Company. But soon they and other investigators were following a paper trail in the United States and abroad, searching for a missing $12.5 million. The money had been raised in 1978 by the DeLorean Research Limited Partnership, for development work on a new car for DeLorean Motor Company. It was paid to GPD Services, Inc., a mysterious Panamanian firm that was supposed to do the work.

The investigators allegedly found that, in October 1978, GPD and John DeLorean, head of the short-lived DeLorean Motor Company, set up an $8.5 million escrow account in an Amsterdam bank. Then, in June 1979, DeLorean purchased Logan Manufacturing Company with a $6 million loan from the Continental Illinois Bank. In September of that year, DeLorean authorized Swiss bankers, Rothschild A.G., to obtain the $8.5 million, plus accrued interest. The money, $9.3 million in all, was transferred to a Rothschild account at New York's Chase Manhattan Bank.

The following month, the $9.3 million was again transferred, this time to the account of the Pierson Bank (a Dutch bank) at New York's Mellon Bank. The same day the money was transferred, DeLorean got a loan of $8.9 million from the Rothschild bank. The loan allegedly was effected via a transfer of $8.9 million from the Pierson account at the Mellon Bank to DeLorean's checking account at Citibank.

The investigators believe that DeLorean used $7.5 million of that money to pay off the Continental Illinois loan and other loans. The remaining $1.4 million was supposedly used for personal expenses. Still missing is $4 million of the money originally paid to GPD by the DeLorean Research Limited Partnership.

During the time of the alleged wrongdoing, DeLorean lived a glamorous life with his wife, the model Cristina Ferrare, replete with a 25-room Bedminster, New Jersey mansion, a 48-acre San Diego County, California ranch, and a 20-room apartment on Manhattan's Fifth Avenue overlooking Central Park.

DeLorean was no stranger to controversy. When his DeLorean car debuted in 1981 for $25,000, sales were disappointing. DeLorean allegedly tried to raise cash to keep his company going by participating in a cocaine deal. The dealers turned out to be FBI agents, but DeLorean was ultimately acquitted of charges because a jury deemed that the agents had entrapped him. Just before the trial ended, Cristina Ferrare, who had steadfastly stood by him throughout the trial, told DeLorean she was leaving him.

In September 1985, as one result of the investigation in which Price Waterhouse participated, a federal grand jury indicted John DeLorean on charges of fraud, interstate transportation of stolen money, and income tax evasion. DeLorean maintained his innocence. In his autobiography published that year, DeLorean wrote:

"When all the documents and facts are presented, I expect to be fully vindicated."

Questions

1. Why would CPAs be needed in what seemed at first to be ordinary bankruptcy proceedings?
2. What made up the "paper trail" that the investigators followed? What made it useful to them?

For more information see *Time*, September 30, 1985, p. 66; *Automotive News*, September 23, 1985, p. 3; *Automotive News*, October 31, 1983, pp. 1, 8; *Automotive News*, November 21, 1983, p. 6; *Automotive News*, June 13, 1983, pp. 2, 14; *Automotive News*, August 1, 1983, pp. 1, 38; *Automotive News*, October 29, 1984, pp. 1, 61; and John DeLorean's *DeLorean*, Zondervan, 1985.

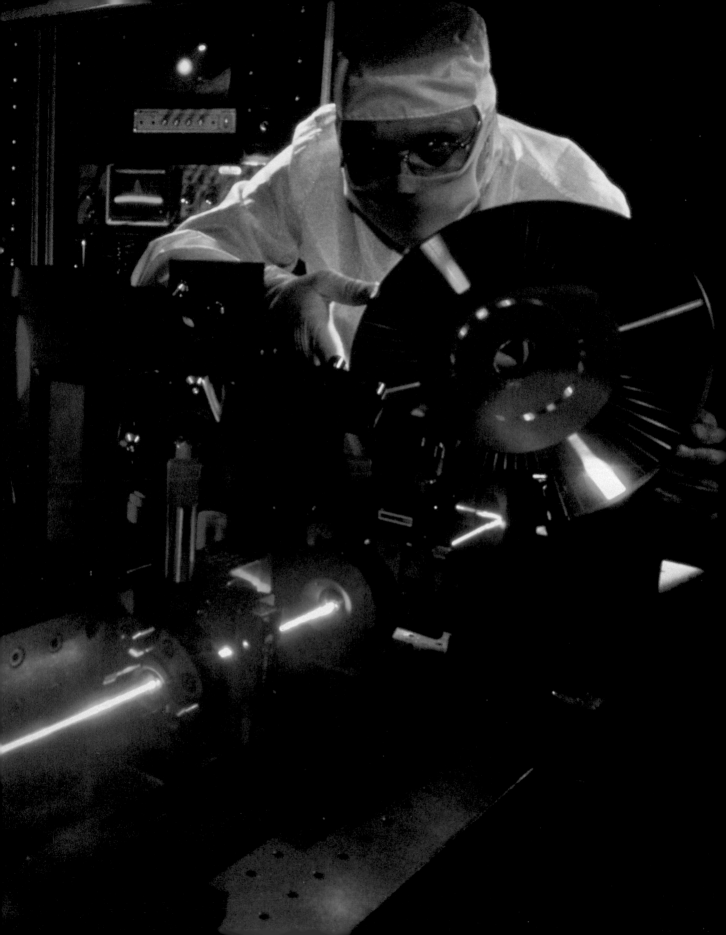

16

COMPUTERS AND MANAGEMENT INFORMATION SYSTEMS

Learning Objectives

After you have completed this chapter, you will be able to do the following:

- Explain how data differs from information.
- Describe the various components of a computer system.
- Classify the various types of computers used by business firms.
- Discuss the role of management information systems in a modern business.
- List and describe the four functions of a management information system.
- Explain the role of descriptive statistics in a management information system.

I n 1975, a pair of computer hackers put together a small computer in a garage. They tried to sell it to both Hewlett-Packard and Atari, which wanted nothing to do with it. So the two young entrepreneurs marketed it themselves. They sold $2.5 million worth of computers in their first year (1977), and the Apple became the first successful personal computer.

Apple Computers is the example that first comes to many minds when they think of technological breakthroughs. Another pioneer in information processing was the Computer-Tabulating-Recording Company. It earned $1.2 million in its first year, 1911. That company today pays its shareholders more than two thousand times that amount in dividends. In 1924 the Computer-Tabulating-Recording Company changed its name to the more familiar one of the International Business Machines Corporation (IBM).[1]

The push toward the technology we call computers began at approximately the same time the automobile graduated from being a toy to becoming a means of transportation. The two technologies — cars and computers — that have revolutionized American life in this century matured together and are not new. Learning to use computers is in fact much like learning to drive a car. It requires familiarity with what the machines can and cannot do and with how they respond

ENIAC — forerunner of a revolution. In 1946, J. Presper Eckert, Jr., and John W. Mauchly, shown here with their machine, completed the Electronic Numerical Integrator and Computer, the first large-scale electronic digital computer. ENIAC cost its inventors $400,000 to build, contained 18,000 vacuum tubes and 70,000 resistors, weighed 30 tons, and filled an entire room. Each time the program was changed, ENIAC had to be completely rewired.

to various commands. However, just as safe driving does not require any knowledge of automotive engineering, the effective use of computers in the work place does not require any conceptual understanding of computer science. This chapter is an introduction to how one goes about "driving" computers. We will introduce the terms that describe computers and give you some feel for the roads they can take you down.

DATA AND INFORMATION

When people talk about computers, they tend to use the words *data* and *information* as though they meant the same thing, but they do not. For example, the numbers and letters 77, DE, 75, 260, 14, YANKTON are data. When we learn that they have some relation to the Los Angeles Raiders football team, the data can take on some meaning. Number 77 was Lyle Alzado, a defensive end who is six feet two inches (seventy-five inches) tall and weighs 260 pounds. He was a fourteen-year veteran who played for Yankton College. Thus, **data** are numbers, letters, facts, and figures that usually come from measurements or observations but have little or no meaning by themselves. (*Data* is the plural of *datum*.) The telephone book is packed with data. When you find a particular person's address and phone number, you have **information**, data that have been extracted or summarized so that they have meaning to the person who will use them.

A computer's ability to calculate, extract, and summarize turns meaningless numbers, letters, facts, and figures into meaningful information. As Figure 16.2 indicates, the data put into a computer are called **input**. The functions that a computer performs on the data are called **data processing**. The information that comes out of the computer system after processing is called its **output**. Suppose that a certain corporation sells widgets. Each month, its salespeople report their sales and a computer operator enters the data from their reports into the computer. The instructions given to the computer may be to turn the data into a sales report that presents such information as the following:

☐ Sales by each salesperson
☐ Sales by each sales office
☐ Sales by each region
☐ Sales for the current month compared to the same month last year
☐ Sales for the year to date as compared with original projections

These categories are common types of computer output. Later we will look at many more. First, let us examine the mechanics of computing.

THE MACHINERY OF COMPUTING

Strictly speaking, a **computer system** is a mechanical means of transforming data into information consisting of **hardware** (the electronic and mechanical components of a computer system) and **software** (the commands that make the machinery run). It has also been argued by many people that computer systems in addition include data, personnel, and procedures. Hardware and software are of course important, but the type of data the system will process and how much it can

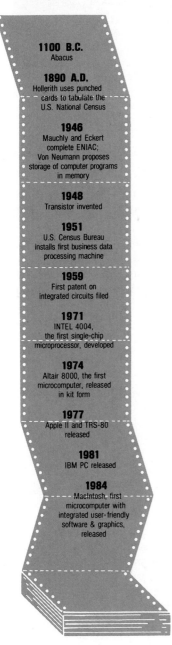

FIGURE 16.1

Time Line of Computer Development

1100 B.C.
Abacus

1890 A.D.
Hollerith uses punched cards to tabulate the U.S. National Census

1946
Mauchly and Eckert complete ENIAC; Von Neumann proposes storage of computer programs in memory

1948
Transistor invented

1951
U.S. Census Bureau installs first business data processing machine

1959
First patent on integrated circuits filed

1971
INTEL 4004, the first single-chip microprocessor, developed

1974
Altair 8000, the first microcomputer, released in kit form

1977
Apple II and TRS-80 released

1981
IBM PC released

1984
Macintosh, first microcomputer with integrated user-friendly software & graphics, released

FIGURE 16.2

Information Processing System

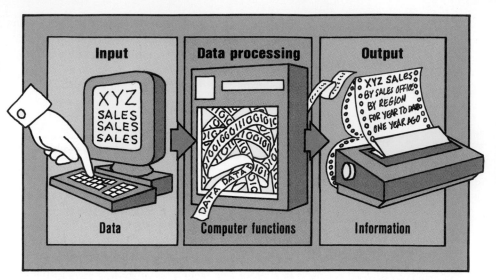

handle are crucial factors in any decision about buying computer equipment. Even more critical is the people who operate and rely on the system as well as the procedures a business establishes for its use.

In short, the easiest and final element in a decision about choosing a computer system is what software and hardware to buy.[2] Evaluating the data demands, personnel usage, and procedures to be followed requires management decisions that are beyond our present scope. Our focus here is on what one can walk into a store and buy: hardware and software.

Hardware

The machinery of a computer system is its hardware. The three main types of hardware are

☐ The central processing unit (CPU)
☐ Input devices
☐ Output devices

All hardware devices other than the CPU are referred to as **peripherals**, because they are attached to but are not part of the CPU.

The Central Processing Unit   A computer system's brains, the place where the data processing actually occurs, is the **central processing unit (CPU)**. A CPU has three main parts:

☐ The main memory
☐ The control unit
☐ The arithmetic-logic unit

The **main memory** holds data and programs (discussed below) while the computer is manipulating them. The main memory consists of memory cells that hold numbers expressed in a **binary** or base-two notation. Each digit in a binary number

Main Parts of a CPU

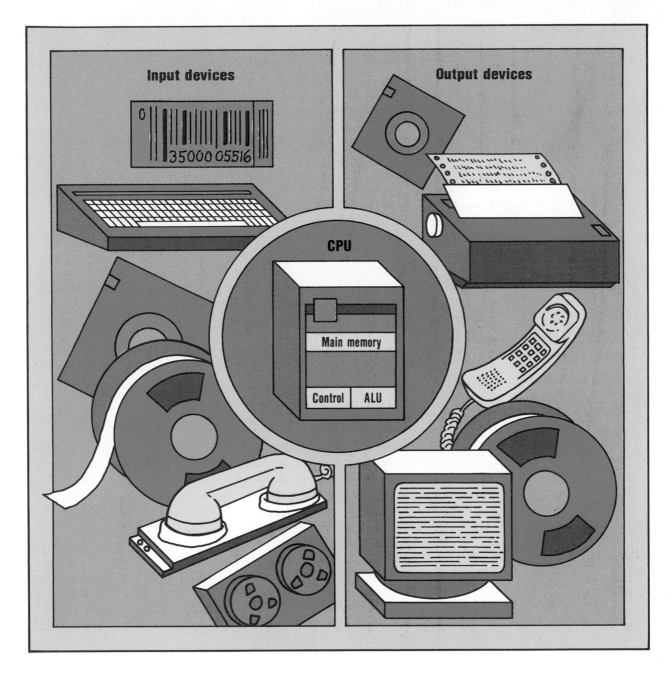

FIGURE 16.3

Computer Hardware

is either a 0 or a 1 and is called a **binary digit**, or **bit** for short. Eight bits make up a **byte**.

The memory cells used to store changeable data or instructions are called the **RAM**, for **random access memory**. Depending on the power of a computer, its RAM may contain thousands, millions, or even billions of memory cells. For that reason, computer memories are usually described in terms of **kilobytes (K)**, each of which represents 1,000 bytes (actually, 1,024 bytes) of memory. Thus, a computer with 256 K of internal memory has approximately 256,000 bytes (actually, 262,144 bytes) of memory. Less common terms are **megabyte (M)**,

1,024 K, or about 1 million bytes of computer memory, and **gigabyte (G)**, 1,024 M, or about a billion bytes of memory.

The main part of the CPU, the **control unit**, tells the computer what to do and where to find or put data. The control unit interprets the computer's instructions by means of permanently stored programs. These instructions are stored in an area called the **Read-Only Memory (ROM)**. The **arithmetic-logic unit (ALU)** handles arithmetic computations.

In addition to these three main units, the CPUs in most computers also have **auxiliary storage devices**, units in a computer system that supplement the main memory storage. The most common of these devices comes as either a floppy-disk drive or a hard-disk drive. Auxiliary storage devices store data far more cheaply and permanently than can the internal memory.

Once a computer has processed the data in its main memory, the user can store those data in an auxiliary storage device and bring new data into the main memory. A computer's main memory is much faster to run and more costly to store data in than is auxiliary storage. It is also considered volatile, because data and programs in the main memory will disappear if there is a power failure or a major operator error. In general, auxiliary storage devices are less volatile than the main memory, though in some circumstances they, too, can lose data.

Input Devices   That part of a computer system which transmits data from a source to the computer is an **input device**. Today, the most common input device is a keyboard. Other such devices include optical scanners like the ones used at grocery store checkouts, magnetic tapes, magnetic disks, light pens, some appliances, and readers.

Output Devices   That part of a computer system which receives data from the computer and presents it to the user is its **output device**. The most common output devices is the typewriterlike printer, along with a televisionlike screen that displays the data being typed in. The screen has cathode-ray tubes, so the device is referred to as a **CRT**. Magnetic tape and magnetic disks are also used. Output devices designed to produce graphics, either on a CRT or on a printer, are especially important in the computer-aided design/computer-aided manufacturing (CAD/CAM) systems discussed in Chapter 10.

An exciting recent development is voice output. Some auto manufacturers have installed such devices to warn drivers that, for instance, it is time to buy gas. Some schools have used voice output for instructing special-needs students. And some telephone sales and canvassing operations have relied on it, to the great annoyance of many consumers.

Classifying Computers

Classes of Computers

The basic criteria for classifying computers relate to their cost, speed, size, and the number of users who can work on them at the same time.

Supercomputers   As their name suggests, the largest, most powerful computers made today are the **supercomputers**. Used primarily for scientific, government, and military purposes, these giants do extensive computations with massive quantities of data. They have huge memories and often have multiple

Supercomputers. This Cray I supercomputer is about the biggest computer around today. It is used primarily for defense and advanced scientific purposes. Supercomputers are extremely expensive, often costing over $5 million, but their phenomenal speed makes their cost per calculation quite reasonable for applications that demand tremendous numbers of calculations.

CPUs designed to operate in parallel on different parts of the same program simultaneously. Some examples include the Cray I and the Cyber 203.

Mainframes The workhorses of the computer industry are the **mainframe computers**, like the IBM 4381 and the Cyber 175. These large computers handle government and business data processing and extensive scientific projects. Mainframe systems have enormous memories that can support hundreds of **terminals**, the input devices usually consisting of a keyboard and a CRT linked to a central computer. Walt Disney Productions runs its U.S. theme parks, hotels, cable television channel, and television and movie productions by relying primarily on five mainframe computers and 1,200 terminals.[3]

Minicomputers Originally, **minicomputers** were designed to be connected directly to scientific and medical instruments to control their operation and analyze the data they produced. Later, they were connected in networks of terminals to provide computing and word-processing services for the individual departments of corporations. Large minicomputers now rival the mainframes in their size and sophistication. Also, they use operating systems, like A T & T's UNIX, that are particularly suited to research and development. A few examples include Digital Equipment Corporation's VAX series and Data General's MV series.

Microcomputers Originally designed for the hobbyist, **microcomputers** are now the backbone of many small businesses, ranging from accounting firms to architectural design companies. More than 3 million of these machines are sold each year. The best known are the IBM PC line and all of Apple's computers. Microcomputers are ideally suited for applications requiring moderate speed and

The Superchips Are Coming!

Imagine 4500 transistors on a human hair. Impossible? Not if you're dealing in the submicron world of the superchip. A micron is a unit of length equal to 1/1000 of a millimeter, or .000039 inches. This seems like an impossibly small size, yet already chip-makers have produced circuits that are only half a micron wide, and the quarter-micron circuit is only a few years away. At that stage, 4500 transistors will *fit* on a human hair, and tens of millions will fit on a quarter-inch square computer chip.

If the very concept makes you squint and shake your head, you're not alone. But these unbelievably tiny circuits are the key to the next phase of the continuing computer revolution. Though you may never see the chips, and you certainly won't see those infinitesimal circuits, your life will be changed by them within the next decade.

You've already been affected by the shrinking of the circuit size. In 1980, the smallest circuits were 4 microns wide, and they made digital watches, video games, and personal computers possible. In 1985, the size was down to 2 microns, and a single chip could hold over 256,000 (256K) bits of information, making possible lap computers and programmable appliances. The one-micron circuit is expected in 1987, with a memory capacity of 1,024K; the half-micron circuit should follow 3 or 4 years later, making possible a supercomputer on a chip, with 4,096K. By the middle of the 1990s, the quarter-micron circuit should usher in the age of the ultracomputer, with 16,384K of memory available on a single chip.

As the circuits get smaller, manufacturing the chips becomes more difficult and costly, and soon there will be no room for humans in the process. Already, the air in semiconductor manufacturing plants has to be 1000 times cleaner than that in a hospital operating room, because a tiny speck of dust could ruin a chip. But to manufacture submicron chips, the air will have to be much cleaner, with a limit of one two-tenths-of-a-micron speck in each cubic foot. Even in those strange white "bunny suits" and with surgical masks, humans are too dirty to work in such an atmosphere, so robots will have to do the job. Laying out the millions of devices on a tiny piece of silicon would blow a human engineer's circuits, so computers will do that job too. A single manufacturing plant will be very expensive — about $200 million. Already, because of the difficulty and cost, formerly competing companies and universities are banding together to work on the new technology, and in the future only a handful of the largest chip-makers will have the facilities to make the smallest chips.

Luckily, most of us won't have to worry about making the chips; we can just enjoy their benefits. Besides making more computer power available in a smaller area, new chips tend to bring down the price of the power. The price per unit of memory has been dropping about 35 percent a year, meaning that today a $1000 computer is at least twice as powerful as a comparably priced model just 3 or 4 years ago.

We can expect innovations in a wide variety of areas. Automakers are talking about radar-controlled brakes that will prevent head-on collisions. The Pentagon is counting on the superchips for Star Wars and for more down-to-earth purposes like pocket radar for soldiers. The superchips may first enter your home in your television. Your superchip TV will pick up digital transmission signals, enabling it to produce a much sharper picture. It will also allow you to freeze a frame, store the image, and print it out, as well as receive teletext data and even split the screen and watch two channels at the same time. Movie makers are even talking about creating computerized simulations of well-known actors, so that at least an image of Charlie Chaplin could make another film.

You may have laughed at someone who, upon first watching a computer work, declared it magic. But when something that's practically invisible can prevent a car accident or bring Charlie Chaplin back from the dead, with what other word would you describe it?

Sources: Philip Elmer-DeWitt, "The New Breeds of Software," *Time*, Vol. 125, No. 11, March 18, 1985, 71. Kenneth Dreyfack, "Zenith Wants to Give the Boob Tube a Brain," *Business Week*, No. 2893, May 6, 1985, 69. John W. Wilson, "Superchips: The New Frontier," *Business Week*, No. 2898, June 10, 1985, 82. John W. Wilson and Jonathan B. Levine, "Making Submicron Chips: Only Computers Are up to the Job," *Business Week*, No. 2898, June 10, 1985, 88.

No bigger than a brief-case. Portable computers have been a boon to salespeople and others who are often away from their office. Customers do not have to wait to find out what material is in stock and how soon it can be delivered. Complex cost calculations can be carried out on the spot, and information on sales and scheduling is immediately available to the main management information system.

memory capacity, like word processing and office management. However, in terms of operating speed and memory capacity, the microcomputers are rapidly moving up to where minicomputers were just a few years ago.

Microcomputers come in many sizes. The most familiar is the desktop model with a separate CRT, a CPU with built-in disk drives, and a keyboard. Another group, called **portable computers**, takes in a great range of machines, all the way from hand-held programmable calculators to lap-sized computers that can perform any function that the larger and heavier microcomputers can. Most portables have special or limited functions, however.

Computer Networks

Large mainframe computers usually have a number of terminals linked to them by various means of communication, including direct wiring or telephone lines. For example, airline reservation systems consist of terminals in airports, downtown ticket offices, and travel agents' offices in many locations, all linked by telephone lines to the airline's mainframe. From any one of those terminals an agent can add, retrieve, and alter information about a passenger booked on a flight — even if the terminal is in Phoenix, the mainframe in Bangor, and the flight is from Pittsburgh to Honolulu.

Mainframes have had this multiuser capacity for many years, but one of the major advances in the past decade was the development of the technology to link several minicomputers or microcomputers together into networks. A **network** is a communication system that links computers so that they can either operate independently or can communicate with and share the resources of other devices linked to them. A common type of network is the **local area network (LAN)**, a network linking computers in a small geographical area or a particular building. The great advantage of a LAN is that it allows computers to send messages to other computers and to share peripherals, like printers and hard-disk drives, thus increasing the peripherals' cost efficiency. However, while the user is not communicating with another machine or using a peripheral device, the machine acts alone.

In Japan, computer networks have gone several steps farther than local area networks. There, such American and Japanese computer companies as IBM, A T & T, and NEC, among others, have developed the **value added network (VAN)**, a computer network that links customers' computers to middlemen's and the middlemen's to manufacturers' computers or distributors'. These networks hold the promise of integrated computer communications among five or more levels of businesses. One auto maker is even working on a system that would link its dealers into a system that ultimately would instruct factory-floor robots to make any car a customer has ordered.[4]

Other network applications of computers involve the use of a modem, a device to transmit computer signals over ordinary telephone lines. With this device an individual microcomputer user can access (read) databanks, like the Dow Jones News Service, and use electronic bulletin boards, like the Source.

Software

We can best describe **software** as a set of intangible commands that instruct a computer to read data into its memory from a peripheral device, perform operations on the data, store it in the main memory or in some form of auxiliary storage unit, and output the information to the user in some form. When people talk about software, they usually talk in terms of a **program**, "a list of instructions that the computer hardware follows."[5] Without software programs to tell it how to behave, computer hardware could not function.

Stored Programs   All modern computers are **stored-program computers**, machines "controlled by software stored within the hardware." A program is said to be stored because it sits in a computer's main memory while telling the computer what to do with the data that are also in the main memory.[6]

Speaking to a Computer   The computer's native language, its **machine language**, is built into it. Machine language is in a binary format and is very difficult for humans to read. A close relative of machine language is **assembly language**, mnemonic instructions or memory codes that are more comprehensible to humans than machine language.

Operating Systems   A program that does the detailed work of running hardware is called an **operating system**. In the early days of computers, the user had to specify everything a program was to do. Modern operating systems have eliminated much of this drudgery of **programing**, the designing and writing of computer programs. An operating system may perform the following tasks, among others:

1. Store and protect data in files, on peripheral devices like tape drives, hard disks, and floppy-disk drives.
2. Control the CRT, keyboard, and printer.
3. Switch the computer's resources around among multiple users.
4. Interact with other computers by means of local area network (LAN) hardware.
5. Provide informative error messages and **menus,** displays of available programs to help the computer user carry out tasks.

*"The good news is that we've designed a computer no bigger than a doughnut...
the bad news is that Hungerford dunked it in his coffee."*

An operating system is usually written in a computer language that people also can read. A small program written in machine language loads the operating system's software into the computer's memory from a disk drive or magnetic tape. This program is said to "pull the operating system up by its bootstraps," so the process is referred to as **booting.** On some computers, like the Apple Macintosh, the machine is preprogramed with the operating system, which becomes available to the user as soon as the machine is turned on.

A **utility program** is a program provided by the manufacturer of the operating system that runs below the operating system. Such programs are often used to create files, edit and change files, compare them with each other, copy one file into another, and erase files.

Software Applications Packages

The program with which a user tells the CPU what to do with the data entered is called a **software applications package.** Such packages are generally written in a high-level language and call up utility programs to do file handling, input, and output.

Modes A computer user carries out tasks in either an interactive or a batch mode. Most software applications packages are interactive.

The Interactive Mode

In the **interactive mode,** the software displays instructions called prompts to the user, which appear on either a CRT or other display device. In some programs, the user responds to prompts by typing in command lines. In others, the user directs a mobile spot on the CRT, called a **cursor,** to choices on a menu. In most cases, the user can specify the input and output files wanted and instruct the interactive software to get data from them.

In the **batch mode,** the software runs from the operating system just like a utility program. The user creates an input file and calls up the program with this file, perhaps along with the name of an output file. A batch program will then ordinarily run without further human intervention. It will produce its results in an output file, on a CRT, or on any other specified output device. The user can print the new output file or merely look at it. Until quite recently, all software ran in this fashion.

Business Applications   Software packagers have written programs for almost every aspect of a business's data-processing needs. The most common types of packages are the following:

- ☐ Accounting
- ☐ Word processing
- ☐ Decision support
- ☐ Spreadsheets
- ☐ Database managers

- ☐ Computer-aided Design (CAD)
- ☐ Computer-aided Manufacturing (CAM)
- ☐ Computer-aided Engineering (CAE)
- ☐ Computer-aided Instruction (CAI)
- ☐ Desktop publishing

We will discuss a number of these packages in the next section.

Choosing Software and Hardware

Only when a firm knows what kind of management information system it needs, what types of demands will be made on the system, and which people will use the system and make it run is it ready to look into software and hardware. A business should look first for software that does everything it needs done, then — and only then — look for hardware to run it. Relatively speaking, hardware is the least important of the elements of a computer system.

MANAGEMENT'S NEED FOR INFORMATION

Managers are paid to make decisions. Whatever their functional areas, managers require relevant information on which to base these decisions. This information may come from data collected by their companies, from information built upon their business and personal lives, or from external sources such as friends, news reports, television, and magazine articles. Our focus in this chapter is on the management information systems that companies develop. These systems may or may not be computerized, though today it is difficult to find any but the smallest businesses that are not at least partially computerized.

Information Requirements by Functional Area

A firm's information needs depend on the nature of its business. Managers, too, have different needs, depending on their functional area. And even within a given area, managers on different levels have distinct information needs. Table 16.1 shows the four areas of managerial decision making.

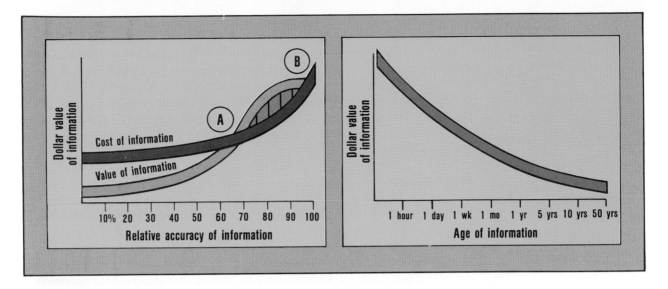

FIGURE 16.4a

Relation of Cost Value to Accuracy

FIGURE 16.4b

Value as Related to Age

Human Resources The increasing complexity of hiring, training, and terminating employees makes information on recruitment, salaries, benefits, employee compensation, employee skills, absenteeism, and staffing patterns a necessity for human-resource managers. Companies affected by government employment regulations need reports showing the number of employees with various sex, age, race, salary, and job characteristics. Producing this information is the responsibility of human-resources managers. To do so, they must maintain detailed data on the company's employees.

Operations Operations managers are concerned with the materials required to manufacture their products or provide their services, the cost of production (labor and material), the cost of inventory, the efficiency of their machinery, and many other matters. Information systems can address all these needs. A materials-requirement planning (MRP) system such as those discussed in Chapter 10 provides the information necessary to manage the materials used in production. A cost-accounting system assists operations managers to deter-

TABLE 16.1

Information Needs by Functional Area

Functional Area	Information Needs
Human Resources	Compensation data; job openings; benefit packages; employee skills
Operations	Cost of materials; inventory flow; labor costs; machine use
Marketing	Customer profiles; survey research; sales; transportation availability
Finance	Cost of funds; amount needed for capital improvements; comparative investment benefits

mine the cost of producing their goods. Mathematical tools of various sorts help operations managers schedule the machines used in the production process.

Many other software packages assist in operations management. For example, some packages are designed to facilitate planning, using the Program Evaluation and Review Technique (PERT) discussed in Chapter 10. Computer-aided design (CAD), computer-aided engineering (CAE), and computer-aided manufacturing (CAM) are widely used in many industries, especially automobile manufacturing. Walt Disney Productions uses computer graphics to create backgrounds for its animated features.[7]

Information Systems

Marketing   Two broad categories of information systems assist marketing managers. The first type of information system in the marketing area, the **operational system,** is the management information system designed to handle all customer orders, whether placed by mail, in person, or through a salesperson. Operational systems record what was sold and where, and by whom and to whom it was sold. Such systems can perform credit checks on customers and can help in marketing by, for example, processing lists for direct-mail operations.

The second type of information system to assist marketing managers, the **managerial marketing system,** is the management information system that can develop answers to questions regarding customer profiles, product penetration, and sales effectiveness. These systems tell managers who sold what to whom, and when and where the sale took place.

Finance   Financial managers need information to determine, first, how much money their companies need; second, how best to obtain the money; and third — given competing alternatives — how best to spend the money. These managers often face a series of complex "what if" questions: What if sales increase by 8 percent? What if interest rates increase in the same period by 1 percent? What if new tax laws alter the depreciation allowance on the business's equipment — should that change affect the company's new equipment purchases? Financial managers can develop answers to these questions by using complicated formulas that would take considerable time to work by hand. Spreadsheet programs like Lotus 1-2-3 permit managers to change the variables in these formulas, then perform calculations far faster than any human could.

Financial managers rely on accounting data, of course. Many software makers have developed a range of off-the-shelf packages suitable for all save the largest or most complex organizations. General ledger systems, accounts payable systems, and accounts receivable and cash applications systems are among those that have taken some of the repetitiveness and drudgery out of the daily routine of accounting departments.

Information Requirements by Management Level

The three levels of management — top management, middle management, and supervisory or first-line management — each have different information requirements. Consider a hypothetical organization with these three levels of management. Tex is the top manager and owner. Tom is the middle-level manager and, in this case, the head coach. Drew is a line manager, called the receiving coach. We'll call the organization the Dallas Cowboys.

Humanizing the Computer

Some people take to computers the way others take to horses or skis. But for many Americans, computers are still an alien, menacing presence. Most of us still harbor some fear that computers will turn out to be modern Frankenstein monsters which will turn on and destroy their human inventors. Computer companies and those who make computer accessories have recognized this widespread feeling and are busy marketing products designed to make the owner feel that the computer will adapt to the human, rather than the other way around. With so many different computers on the market, manufacturers feel pressured to respond to buyers' demands that their machines work well and are comfortable to use.

Ergonomists — scientists who adapt machines to people — have kept busy adjusting machines to eliminate the minor problems encountered by almost all computer users. They have experimented with the "feel" of the keyboard and made the keys themselves somewhat concave for a light but sure touch. The keyboard has become more independent of the computer, attached only with a long cord, or, in some cases, not attached at all. The height and angle of the monitor have also become more adjustable, giving workers the chance to develop their own comfortable alternatives to sitting in the same position, staring straight ahead all day. The layout of the keys undergoes constant scrutiny, in part because a "good idea" may have unforeseen consequences. For instance, the "reset" key on some keyboards is located close to the "return" key. This makes it easy to reset the machine, but also too easy to hit the reset key accidentally and lose part of a file.

The ways to move around the screen have also changed. Apple introduced the "mouse," a device that allows the user to move the cursor (a blinking space that shows the user where the next character will appear) without pressing keys at all. Some current screens are touch-sensitive, allowing the user to get information simply by touching the appropriate part of the screen.

The ultimate keyboard — that is, no keyboard at all, but a computer that will respond to voice commands — already exists in crude form. At Chicago's O'Hare Airport, some baggage handlers call out the name of a bag's destination as they heave it onto a conveyor belt. A computer recognizes the name and directs the belt to take the bag to an appropriate tray. Some cars now "talk" to the driver, and in a few years car makers expect to have voice-activated locks and windshield wipers. The Air Force is testing a jet with voice-controlled equipment that will allow the pilot to concentrate on flying the plane with both hands while giving voice commands to prepare for attack. Advances in this area will be of tremendous use to paralyzed people who even now can use voice-activated computers to dial telephones and, slowly, to write.

The ability of people to work at home on computers, sometimes hooked up to company machines, also has advantages and disadvantages. For the right people — self-paced, responsible workers who don't relish office life — working at home with a computer increases productivity and makes work more pleasurable. Many consultants and freelance writers can't imagine how they lived without their machines. But other home workers worry about getting out of touch with the office, being passed up for promotions because they're not visible, or losing social contacts. Labor unions fear that home computer work may allow companies to bypass employment laws, lower benefits, and bring back the kind of exploitation common in turn-of-the-century sweatshops.

Still, there's no question that computers have found a permanent place in many offices and homes — as many as 10 million people may be working at home on computers by the end of the century. And by that time, it seems fairly certain that computers will be almost as easy to use as radios, and people will feel as comfortable with them. But many people will still be questioning whether we want this mechanical brain to play such a big part in our lives.

Sources: Walter McQuade, "Easing Tensions Between Man and Machine," *Fortune*, Vol. 109, No. 6, March 19, 1984, 58–66. "Kid-friendly Keys," *Fortune*, Vol. 111, No. 3, February 4, 1985, 10. Philip Elmer-DeWitt, "His Master's (Digital) Voice," *Time*, Vol. 125, No. 13, April 1, 1985, 83. John Greenwald, "How Does This #%$@! Thing Work?" *Time*, Vol. 123, No. 25, June 18, 1984, 64. Robert T. Grieves, "Telecommuting from a Flexiplace," *Time*, Vol. 123, No. 5, January 30, 1984, 63.

As the top manager, Tex works within a budget and will be quite interested, for instance, in how the total funds available for salaries compare with the total amount committed to salaries. The difference will tell him what he has available to offer to a free agent. For Tom, the total salary figure will have little relevance to his coaching efforts. This number will not affect his game plan for the coming week. Tom's plans depend instead on careful study of his opponent's play selections and defensive sets under particular circumstances and on the players Tom has available for the game. However, none of the information that absorbs Tom is of any direct interest to Tex or Drew. As receiving coach, Drew's job consists primarily in training the receivers, preparing them to go up against the defensive backs they will have to beat, and monitoring his players' physical condition. In short, Drew's interest in salaries is probably limited to the size of his own.

Tex, Tom, and Drew are all managers in the same organization — yet their information needs are vastly different. What Tex wants is something that is far more comprehensive than what Tom and Drew work with. Conversely, what Drew uses is far more detailed than what Tom wants. In other words, the lower the level of management, the more specialized its needs will be. And the higher the level of management, the more general will be the information it requires for decision making. A good top manager is a facilitator, a manager who makes other managers' jobs easier by providing the tools and information they need to do their jobs. However, they all require information from each of the functional areas in order to make their decisions.

Sources of Data

Internal and External Sources of Data

Much of the data a firm requires will come from internal sources like the functional divisions. Other data will originate outside the firm. Internal data sources provide past and present data that managers can use as a basis for making predictions about the future. Company records, customer records, employment data, reports, conference minutes, memoranda, and the like will supply the bulk of the data in a firm's information system.

The external sources of data are almost limitless. Today's manager must be well informed, which means keeping up with newspapers, radio, television, journals, and the like. General business publications, such as *The Wall Street Journal, Business Week,* and *Forbes,* often contain necessary information on industry and competitive conditions. Most importantly, industry-specific publications, often referred to as trade journals, are must reading. For example, athletic administrators might be expected to read *Athletic Administration, Athletic Journal,* and *Interscholastic Athletic Administration.* The general media usually provide low-cost sources of data. The free sources tend to be the informal ones, like customers, bankers, suppliers, and friends. High-priced sources might include market research provided by outside consultants.

MANAGEMENT INFORMATION SYSTEMS

As the hypothetical experience of the Dallas Cowboys' management indicates, the transformation of data into information has different meanings at different

Computers making computers. *Robotics keyboard assembly at Burroughs' Flemington, New Jersey, plant helps ensure a steady supply of goods. Robots, which are essentially computer-controlled machines, are invaluable for performing dangerous or highly repetitive operations.*

levels of an organization. J. W. Marriott, Jr., the chief executive officer of the Marriott Corporation, once recalled, "I asked for some information on a specific problem, and in response [some subordinates] brought in a computer runout several inches high. I threw them out of the office. I said, 'You're not running a business when you bring in something like that. You're not contributing.'"[8]

A **management information system (MIS)** is a collection of tools that provides information to a manager to facilitate that person's decision-making processes. Specifically, an MIS should help a manager either make a better decision or make a decision more easily than he or she would have otherwise.

Types of MIS

We have already seen that an information system may be either manual or computerized, informal or formal. Historically, well-defined reports produced on a regular basis have characterized the formal MIS. They still play an important role in it today. Such reports must be both accurate and timely if managers are to use the information properly to assist in their decision making. If the information is too old, managers either cannot or should not use it. That is why an MIS today must not only produce the regular reports it has always been expected to generate but must also respond quickly to unscheduled requests for information. A modern MIS answers "what ifs" rapidly on a CRT or else produces a

Improving white-collar productivity. *When Allied Stores computerized the collections department at Bonwit Teller, productivity doubled. Terminals were installed in 1982, and at the end of a year staffing requirements were down by 25 percent. It took longer than that to see how changing the work flow could enhance the computer's efficiency. By the end of 1985, staffing was half what it had been in the days of paper and pencil.*

printed report. The format of the MIS response is up to the manager who asks for it. For example, a sales manager might use a computer terminal to determine the projected or actual annual sales for the products sold in each of the regions under his or her direction.

Decision Support Systems (DSS)

Closely related to the MIS is the **decision support system (DSS)**, a computer system that permits managers to call up whatever specific information they need whenever they need it. These systems allow managers to gain information in a less structured manner than from a traditional MIS. They assist a manager in formulating questions and gathering answers rather than in generating formal reports to answer the same questions for each period.

The ever-increasing number of personal computers with decision-support software has proved a mixed blessing. In some cases, managers have made huge errors in projections because they forgot to enter some element or did not check their work. The computer cannot compensate for human error, a fact people who rely on computers are liable to learn the hard way.[9]

FUNCTIONS OF A MANAGEMENT INFORMATION SYSTEM

Four Functions of an MIS

A management information system must efficiently perform four functions:

☐ Collect data
☐ Store data
☐ Update data
☐ Process data

The value of an MIS lies in its ability to accumulate data so that it can be manipulated or processed into information. Computer programs process data by summarizing, merging, selecting, and sorting them according to the needs of an MIS user. Once the computer has performed these functions, the information is ready for circulation to managers.

Collecting Data

Before an MIS can produce information, someone must feed it data. In determining whether data belong in an MIS, three questions have to be asked:

1. Are the data accurate?
2. Are the data timely?
3. Are the data too expensive?

Inaccurate or dated data are valueless. And some data that are both accurate and timely may simply not be worth the cost of collection. Identifying such data requires a cost-benefit analysis.

Storing Data

Two Ways to Store Data

Storing data simply means saving it for later use. Once collected, MIS data are entered into the computer for later processing into information. Computer systems may store data in two places: in the main memory, or on auxiliary storage devices, such as magnetic tapes, hard disks, or floppy disks. As noted earlier, the main memory holds programs and data that the computer is currently using. For permanent storage, users should rely on auxiliary storage devices like backup disks.

The anticipated use of the data determines the type of auxiliary storage device to use in storing them. Data that will rarely be accessed, read or written, will frequently be stored on magnetic tape rather like the tape in an audio or videocassette. Magnetic tape is also used when data must be retrieved by **sequential access**. In other words, if a user wants to locate a particular file, the computer must read all the entries preceding the file before it can access the file. A typical 2,400-foot reel of magnetic tape can store up to 150 million characters.

A hard disk can store hundreds of millions of characters and you can randomly access them. **Random access** means that a computer can retrieve any piece of data from the source in the same amount of time as any other piece and that the

Selling Computers Abroad

Most international news about computers seems to involve American computer companies' and chip-makers' battles to keep Japanese computer makers from taking over the domestic American computer market. But there are other markets for computers around the world, and American companies from the giants to small start-ups are beginning to turn their attention to those countries for which computers are still largely alien, futuristic devices.

One of the largest and most unlikely markets opened up in 1985, when Western companies began competing to sell low-power computers to the Soviet school system. All Western sales to the Soviet Union are controlled by the Coordinating Committee for Multilateral Export Controls (Cocom) and by individual governments. The U.S. government has been reluctant to do "anything that increases computer literacy in the Soviet Union," as one American official put it. But the Reagan administration has gradually softened its stance, and recently the Commerce Department has even been encouraging American computer companies to sell across the iron curtain. So when the Cocom eased restrictions, allowing computer makers to sell eight-bit microcomputers to the Soviets without a license, many companies jumped at the chance.

The potential market is huge. The Soviet school system is one of the largest in the world. The Soviets talk of eventually purchasing one million micros for the classroom, and in 1985 the country's 60,000 high schools began training students in computer science. Western companies are counting on the backwardness of the Russian computer industry to ensure that all those high school students learn on Western computers. The market is particularly tempting because the low-power, eight-bit machines the companies are allowed to sell the Soviets have been largely outmoded in the U.S. Companies like Commodore that make these smaller machines are hoping the Russian market might create a boom for the eight-bit machines similar to the great growth period of the early 1980s. British companies are so eager to get the Soviets' business that one produced free trial software for the Russians, while another painted its sample computers red. (The Russians "thought the color was a bit harsh.")

Besides new iron-curtain markets, computer companies are hoping to find the next generation of computer buyers in the Third World. A couple of immigrant entrepreneurs in California have come up with an enterprising way to break into these new markets without the backing of a huge computer company like Apple or IBM. With just over $100,000 they founded Proven Technology in 1984. Their business? Used computers.

"The old technology is new technology in South America," says Benito Giovo, one of Proven Tech's owners. The company figures to ship most of its products to Central and South America, though so far some of its best business has come from the developed West.

The company's biggest problem so far has been coming up with a product to sell. Computer prices have been dropping so steadily that computer owners are appalled at how little they can get for their used computers. A standard IBM PC set-up cost over $5000 in 1981 but only $1900 today. Proven Technology will give the used PC owner $1000 of credit towards a new computer purchase, but many computer owners balk at getting back only a fifth of what they paid, and decide instead to give the old computer to a child or friend. Proven Technology has agreed to buy used trade-ins from almost 100 Computerland franchisees, but in its first year the company was able to ship only 250 computers overseas.

With American computer sales leveling off and competition among suppliers growing ever fiercer, more and more computer companies are likely to look overseas for new markets. For clever entrepreneurs with an international bent, the possibilities seem endless. As Giovo says, "In China there are a billion people with no computers."

Sources: Marc Beauchamp, "¿Como está computer?" *Forbes*, January 27, 1986, 44. George Anders and Richard L. Hudson, "Computer Firms Rush to Sell the Soviet Union Low-Power Units After West Eases Restraints," *The Wall Street Journal*, July 19, 1985, 24. David E. Sanger, "Computer Makers Eye Soviet School Market," *The New York Times*, April 4, 1985, A11.

time required to access the last record will be no greater than that required for the first. Thus, random access is the opposite of sequential access. For some years, a floppy or flexible disk, with random-access capability, has been the most common type of auxiliary storage device. A floppy disk can hold up to 1.2 megabytes and is quite cheap.

Updating Data

Data would be of little value if they could not be updated and refined. Updates are of three types: adds, changes, and deletes. For example, a store's MIS will include its inventory. The store will add to that inventory new classes of merchandise. It may also have to change existing entries to reflect replacements of or additions to existing data. And, finally, the store may delete items dropped from stock.

Manual updating of an MIS occurs when a person does something that alters the existing data, like transfering new data to the appropriate storage device or deleting entries. Manual updating can occur on a daily, weekly, or monthly basis, as needed, depending on a firm's business. Manual-updating systems are often referred to as **batch systems,** because the data are first collected, then stored in a batch until time to process them.

Automatic updating of an MIS occurs when computer hardware and software interact to make changes to the data as new data become available. People do not have to intervene, because the data to be accessed, the changes, and the programs are all permanently stored on an auxiliary storage device permanently attached to the computer. For example, as items pass over a supermarket's optical scanners at the checkout counters, messages go to the computer about the items each customer is buying. The computer adjusts the inventory and transmits the price to the cash register. An optical scanner that operates under the direct, immediate control of a computer is said to be **on line.**[10]

PERSPECTIVE: CHANGES IN THE WORK PLACE

Traditionally, managers have seen automation as a means of improving employee productivity in terms of the net profit to be derived per wage and benefit dollar. As artificial intelligence begins to realize its promise, these benefits will travel up into the professional and managerial ranks, too.

Some students of the issue claim that the new technology that computers represent will cause the work force to partition itself between an elite who can work with the new machines and those who cannot. As computers become increasingly "user-friendly" word workers will have access to the new technology.

Another fear is that of possible job loss. In one sense, computerization will cause none. Rarely will a business be able to lay off people because of computerizing its information system. On the contrary, a business will be unlikely to hire the additional staff it might have hired without computers. In the bigger picture, experts expect that a quarter of a million new computer jobs will be created by the year 1990. Where the computer is having its most noticeable

When the drawing board is a computer. *Computer-aided design (CAD) has revolutionized the way engineers and designers develop and test new product ideas. Firestone, like many other manufacturers, uses computers to design tire treads.*

effect is in the types of workers that large corporations are beginning to feel necessary to their operations. Firms like the Exxon Corporation have eliminated whole layers of middle managers, in part because computers have forced redefinition of the duties performed by these persons. What is happening is a change far beyond a simple improvement in technology; the change is in our work place.

Computers can have a subtle effect in the work place. Because of the computer's capacity to recall what has been entered into it during a given period, it is possible to evaluate the efficiency of a word-processing operator, say, by the number of characters he or she enters during a set period. Some have claimed that this form of supervision increases job stress. Others insist that it increases individuals' productivity by identifying the truly productive ones to be rewarded.

Another effect of computerization is the development of the electronic cottage, the home work place that depends on computers. Working at home has its pluses and minuses. For some, the flexibility of setting one's own hours and working in the informal comfort of one's home outweighs any disadvantages of such an arrangement, like the loss of the social life surrounding work. For one type of worker, though, the handicapped or disabled, the development of the electronic cottage can be an almost unqualified blessing. Such previously disadvantaged workers can now find employment in a much wider range of occupations.

SUPPLEMENT: STATISTICS AS SUMMARIES

A **statistic** is a number that is "calculated as a summary of data."[11] It describes certain characteristics of that group of numbers. The raw materials of statistics are thus numbers that represent counts and measurements of occurrences.

WHAT STATISTICS DESCRIBE

Data do not become information until they are presented in a meaningful way. Statistics give us a vocabulary for describing numbers and turning data into information. For instance, when we list the hourly temperatures for each day in July, we have data. However, once we say that the temperature in July averaged 68 degrees or that this July was 3 degrees cooler than average, we have transformed the data into information that almost everyone can understand.

The numbers that a business is concerned with describing come from primary and secondary data collected and stored in its management information system (MIS). Businesses have such data as figures on costs, on the time it takes to make each product, the hours it takes to perform specific processes, and the average time it takes to collect bills. Sometimes internal records do not contain sufficient data, so outside sources of data must be located. Research companies will often provide such data for a fee.

Samples

Types of Samples

Because collecting and storing many kinds of data are expensive, researchers often rely on a **sample**, a small group of representative units selected from a much larger group, to answer their questions.[12] Samples are also important in quality control. For many products, the only way to test them is to destroy them. The firm will therefore test only a certain number of items, to get an idea of the number of problems or failures it can expect in the entire production run.

Market research often relies on the use of samples, because it would be prohibitively expensive to ask, say, all persons between eighteen and twenty-five living in the Detroit metropolitan area what they were looking for in a soft drink. Many, but not all, surveys use **random samples** in which "all units in a population have an equal chance of appearing in the sample."[13] Random samples are also known as probability samples. The results achieved with a sample should be representative of the results that would have been reached if the entire population had responded. The data provided by the sampling are obtained by either observations or surveys.

Observations   Observations are used to record overt behavior or physical characteristics. In many instances, a business's ordinary records supply these data. For example, a business should know how long it takes, on average, to collect its bills. The data to calculate the average would take into account the payment time on every bill that had been sent out. A restaurant might also use observation to determine how many customers ordered dinner every half hour, say, between five and eleven o'clock on weeknights. Such information could help managers determine the appropriate number of employees to schedule during those hours.

Survey Methods

Surveys When a company wants to know why people act as they do, surveys are important. Often it is not enough to know that 30 percent of the homeowners in a test market bought a company's new product. A company may decide to commission a survey of an entire population, called a **census.** Virtually all surveys done for businesses use only a sample of the population, however. The most common ways of carrying out a survey are by mail, personal interviews, and telephone interviews.

Mail surveys are the lowest-cost option, but they present a number of drawbacks. This method takes time to implement and offers little flexibility, and the questionnaire must be short and fairly simple. Also, the number of people who will return a questionnaire is usually low, often less than 30 percent. In addition, people who answer mail surveys may not be representative of the whole population. After all, it is unusual for many to take the time to complete a survey.

Personal interviews consume the most time and cost the most money. However, they are also the most flexible technique and offer the best opportunity to ask probing questions. Many companies conduct surveys in supermarkets or at malls or conduct panel interviews, called focus groups, to reduce the cost of personal interviews.

Telephone interviews, the most common survey method, are relatively inexpensive when compared to personal interviews, but they do not necessarily produce a representative sample. Many people have unlisted numbers or do not have a telephone at all. Eliminating these categories from the survey distorts the results. Dialing random numbers makes the surveys more representative, but many people refuse to answer survey questions over the phone. Even so, telephone surveys have a higher response rate than mail surveys and can be conducted quickly.

TYPES OF STATISTICS

Statistics are either inferential or descriptive. **Descriptive statistics** portray the characteristics of a larger set of data. A study of the payment patterns in a company's accounts receivable would produce descriptive statistics. **Inferential statistics** describe the behavior of a small group, from which the user may be able to predict the behavior of a larger group. Market research usually develops inferential statistics. Our main concern here is descriptive statistics.

Table CS16.1 lists the number of onion-ring orders served in West Shore Community College's snack bar during a ten-day period. Firms commonly deal with data that contain hundreds or thousands of observations, but these ten days will serve our purposes here.

A **frequency distribution** summarizes data by reducing the size of the listing or the number of items in the data set. With large quantities of data, this usually means grouping data into ranges. One first establishes reasonable ranges, then records the number of times actual observations occurred within each of them.

Day of the Week	Number of Orders Sold
Sunday	15
Monday	30
Tuesday	18
Wednesday	35
Thursday	18
Friday	32
Saturday	37
Sunday	17
Monday	21
Tuesday	24
Total	247

Table CS16.2 shows the onion-ring sales data transformed into ranges. Note that frequency distributions can be shown without grouping. For example, Table CS16.1 shows that the snack bar twice served eighteen-onion-ring orders but all other numbers just once.

Measures of Size and Dispersion

Arithmetic Mean The best-known statistical form is the **average,** technically referred to as the **arithmetic mean,** which is the total number of observation values divided by the number of occurrences of them. In our example, West Shore's Community College's snack bar served a total of 247 orders over the ten-day period. The arithmetic mean or average daily sale is arrived at by dividing 247 by 10, for a figure of 24.7. Of course, the snack bar never sold 0.7 orders of onion rings. The closest we can get is to say that the snack bar sold approximately 25 orders each day.

TABLE CS16.2

Onion-Ring Sales
Frequency Distribution

Number of Onion Ring Orders	Frequency
10–15	1
16–20	3
21–25	2
26–30	1
31–35	2
36–40	1

Median The figure called the **median** is the value that appears in the middle of the data when the observations are arranged in order from the lowest to the highest. This arrangement for the onion-ring sales in our sample is 15, 17, 18, 18, 21, 24, 30, 32, 35, 37. This particular series of numbers has no middle value. The two values closest to the middle are 21 and 24. Adding these two values and dividing by 2 produces 22.5 as the median value. An odd number of days would have a middle value that would become the median value, without any computation.

Mode The **mode** of a collection of data is that value which occurs most frequently. In our example, 18 occurred twice. When no one value occurs more often than any other, there is no mode.

Range Arithmetic means, medians, and modes are **measures of central tendency,** indications of how data will cluster about a central point. Frequently, however, a business will also want to look at what is called the **measure of dispersion,** an indication of how widely spread the data are. The principal measure of dispersion is the data's **range,** the difference between the highest and lowest observed values. In our example, we would calculate the range by subtracting the minimum value of 15 from the maximum value of 37.

Variance and Standard Deviation Two sets of data may have the same arithmetic mean, yet have ranges that are vastly different. When the range of a set of data is small, the measures of central tendency will more accurately represent what actually occurred in each collection of observations. Of course, the arithmetic mean — a statistic — may or may not match an actual recorded event. The snack bar never sold 24.7 orders of onion rings in any day. The range is a rough notion of dispersion, but it is not usually relevant for analytical purposes.

Two more reliable indications of dispersion that describe the variability within data are its **variance** and **standard deviation.** Both measure the difference between each observed value and the arithmetic mean of the entire set of data. Computing variances and standard deviations is more complicated than calculating a range, and there is no need to explore such calculations here. The point to remember is that the greater the standard deviation or the variance, the greater the spread of the data. Measures of central tendency alone can deceive the user, so the acute manager will question the meaning of such statistics.

Time Series Analysis

Managers will want explanations for any fluctuations in the recorded observations over time. **Time series analysis** or **trend analysis** is a statistical technique for examining the ways that observations of a variable move over time and then basing forecasts on the observations. Always keep in mind that trend analyses provide information that a manager must still test against his or her experience. Predicting the future is far from an exact science. Figure CS16.1 represents in a line chart our snack bar's daily onion-ring sales over a ten-day period. A chart like this one, if based on many more observations, could help a business compare demand on weekdays and weekends, for instance.

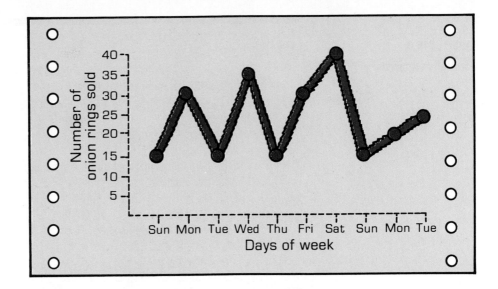

Trend, Cyclical, and Seasonal Variations   The first of the three recognized types of fluctuations, the **secular trend,** refers to a smooth upward or downward movement over a long period. For example, the number of home entertainment systems and the cost of housing would both reveal secular trends over the last twenty years. The second type, **cyclical fluctuations,** is business-cycle movements over periods ranging from two to fifteen years. No simple rationale can explain these movements. They result from widespread changes in economic activity, such as boom periods and recessions. The third type of fluctuation, **seasonal trends,** is patterns that complete themselves within one year or less and then begin to repeat themselves. Weather and such customs as the celebration of major holidays produce seasonal trends. Summer sees an upswing in ice-cream purchases, and Thanksgiving and Christmas mark the high points of the year for the turkey industry.

Correlation Analysis   The arithmetic mean, median, and mode measure the central tendency and summarize the larger set of data into a single statistic. Trend analysis, coupled with a manager's judgment, permits certain predictions about the future.

Correlation analysis is a statistical technique to measure the association between two or more variables. It helps managers identify the factors that can be used to predict fluctuations in one variable when changes in another are known. This ability can be especially valuable for products that depend on derived demand (see Chapter 13), as, for example, prehung doors. Sales of such doors go up when housing starts go up and drop when housing starts drop. Sales of doors and housing starts therefore exhibit positive correlation. Other factors may demonstrate negative correlation, like the value of a car, which drops as its age goes up. (See Table CS16.3). And sometimes two factors show no correlation at all. The number of baseball bats sold in Oregon is unlikely to have any association with the amount of nail polish sold in Mississippi.

One caution is very important. Correlation analysis does *not* prove that changes in one variable cause changes in another. A drop in the sale of lobster may in

TABLE CS16.3

Correlation Analysis

Variables	Correlation
Age of runner and time recorded in 40-yard dash	+
Community disposable income and $ value of food stamps issued	−
Population of college and number of basketball games won	0
Number of complimentary pizza coupons issued and number of pizzas ordered	+
Age of automobile and value of automobile	−
Number of Madonna albums displayed in store window and number of albums sold	0

fact positively correlate with a rise in the number of past-due car payments in a given community, but one cannot be said to have caused the other. Both changes probably resulted from an unfavorable change in the economy.

PRESENTING INFORMATION

Proper presentation is the key to successfully conveying information. "A picture is worth a thousand words" is particularly true of statistical information in visual and tabular displays.

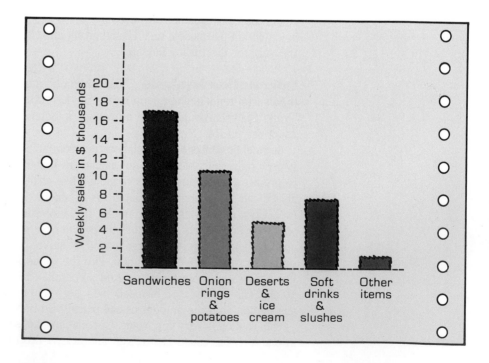

FIGURE CS16.2

Bar Chart

Visual Display

A picture that portrays information items in a way that makes them easy to compare with one another or reflects trends among the items is a **visual display**. Some of the more popular forms include graphs, bar charts, and pie charts.

Graphs are particularly effective in showing how a situation changed over time. We saw this in Figure CS16.1, the graph or line chart of onion-ring sales over a ten-day period. **Graphs** indicate upward and downward movements of the values of a variable over a specified period. They are constructed with a vertical X axis (typically used to show the quantity or relative quantity of an item) and a horizontal Y axis, which usually represents time or some other variable, such as cost.

A **bar chart** presents a comparison of several values at a stationary point in time. Either horizontal or vertical bars are used to show the quantity of an item, with the largest bar representing the greatest value. Figure CS16.2 is a bar chart. Often symbols, called pictographs, are used rather than bars to convey information in a bar chart, as in Figure CS16.3.

A **pie chart** is a circle that, like a pie, has been divided into pieces, with each piece used to portray the kind and proportion of the data it represents. Figure CS16.4 is a pie chart.

Tabular Displays

An array or matrix of information in vertical columns and horizontal rows is a **tabular display.** Such a display shows the relationship between two or more variables and may contain either numeric or verbal data. Figure CS16.5 is a two-column tabular display with numeric information about a single variable, the

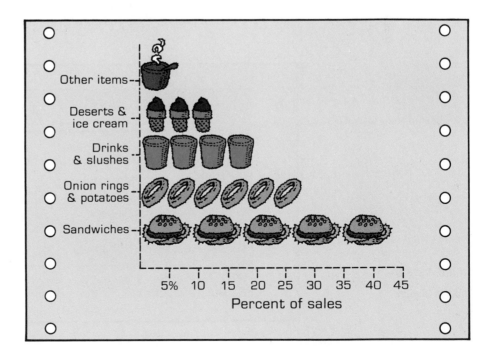

FIGURE CS16.3

Pictographs

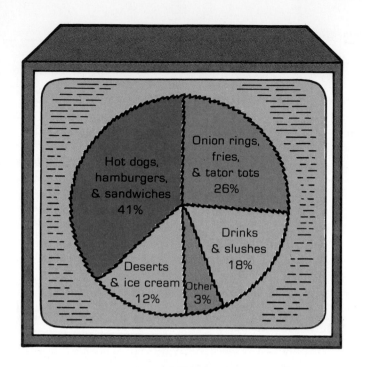

percent of sales. By contrast, Table 16.1, Informational Needs by Functional Area, which we saw earlier, describes four variables, the four functional areas, and compares verbal information about each.

Pie charts can be used to convey the same information as a tabular display. However, the more complex the visual display in terms of the number of its columns, the greater the need to put its information into the form of a pie chart. In general, tabular displays can convey more information in a smaller space, but they have less impact on their audience than do visual displays.

Food group	Percent of sales
Burgers, hot dogs, sandwiches	41%
Onion rings, fries, tator tots	26%
Deserts, ice cream	12%
Soft drinks, slushes	18%
Other items	3%

FIGURE CS16.5

Tabular Display

Chapter Highlights

1. Explain how data differs from information.

Data are numbers, letters, facts, and figures that usually come from measurements or observations but have little or no meaning by themselves. Once data has been extracted or summarized so that it has meaning to the person who will use it, it becomes information.

2. Describe the various components of a computer system.

A computer system is a mechanical means of transforming data into information. It consists of hardware and software. Hardware refers to the electronic and mechanical components of a computer system. The three main types of hardware are the central processing unit (CPU), input devices, and output devices. Software is usually descibed in terms of programs which are lists of instructions that tell the hardware how to behave.

3. Classify the various types of computers used by business firms.

We usually classify computers according to their cost, speed, size, and the number of users who can work on them at the same time. Supercomputers, used primarily for scientific, government, and military purposes, are the largest and most powerful computers made today. Mainframe computers represent the workhorses of modern business. These computers have enormous memories and can support hundreds of terminals. Minicomputers are connected to networks of terminals to provide computing and word processing services for individual departments in large companies. Microcomputers are suited for applications requiring moderate speed and memory capacity, like word processing and office management. Most are desktop models.

4. Discuss the role of management information systems in a modern business.

A management information system (MIS) is a collection of tools that provide information to a manager that facilitates that person's decision-making process. An MIS should help a manager make either a better decision or to make a decision more easily than he or she would without the system.

5. List and describe the four functions of a management information system.

A management information system must efficiently perform four functions: collect data; store data; update data; and process data. The value of an MIS lies in its ability to accumulate data so that it can be manipulated or processed into information.

6. Explain the role of descriptive statistics in a management information system.

Data do not become information until they are presented in a meaningful way. Statistics gives employees a vocabulary for describing numbers and turning data into information. For example, researchers often rely on a sample (a small group of representative units selected from a much larger group) to answer questions about products or services. A random sample of all persons who own motorhomes, for example, can give us information about the total population of motorhome owners. This statistical technique can save large amounts of time and money.

Key Terms

Arithmetic-logic unit (ALU)	Batch mode	Control unit	Inferential statistics
Assembly language	Batch system	Correlation analysis	Input
Automatic updating	Binary	Cyclical fluctuation	Input device
Auxiliary storage device	Byte	Data	Kilobyte
Average	Census	Data processing	Machine language
Bar chart	Central processing unit (CPU)	Descriptive statistics	Main memory
	Computer system	Frequency distribution	Mainframe computers
		Hardware	

Management	Minicomputer	Programming	Seasonal trend
information system	Network	Random access	Secular trend analysis
(MIS)	Operating system	Random access	Software
Managerial marketing	Output	memory (RAM)	Standard deviation
system	Output device	Random sample	Statistic
Manual updating	Peripherals	Range	Terminal
Measures of central	Pie chart	Read-Only Memory	Time series analysis
tendency	Program	(ROM)	Variance
Microcomputer			

Review Questions

1. Distinguish between data and information. Give examples of each.
2. In basic terms, what is a computer system?
3. What is the function of the central processing unit? What are the three main parts of the CPU?
4. What is the major difference between a super-computer and a minicomputer?
5. Describe the role of computer networks in the travel industry. How do travel agents benefit from this form of electronic data processing?
6. What is the role of software in modern computer systems? List and describe at least three software packages that are currently used to meet the data processing needs of business.

7. What is a management information system? What are the four functions of a management information system?
8. How do the information requirements of top management differ from first line management?
9. What is automatic updating? Give an example of an application of this procedure.
10. What is the difference between inferential and descriptive statistics? Describe how each might be used in a business setting.
11. How do managers use time series analysis?

Application Exercises

1. In the near future you will open a book store near the campus of a large university. You have decided to develop a management information system. As the owner of a book store, what type of data would you collect? How might this data be classified? How long would you store the various types of data? Would you use manual or automatic updating?
2. Assume the following monthly sales for your book store which opened in January:

Month	Sales	Month	Sales
January	42,000	July	50,000

February	40,000	August	52,000
March	43,000	September	54,000
April	45,000	October	56,000
May	48,000	November	60,000
June	48,500	December	66,000

What is the arithmetic mean for monthly sales figures? What is the median sales figure for the one-year period? What are the limitations of these two figures when assessing sales figures for the first year of the store's operation?

Cases

16.1 Computers in Business

There is no doubt that computers are great labor-saving devices. In business, computers should also represent a cost-effective investment that enhances the operation and profit-making ability of the firm. To a growing number of CEOs, that means a firm's computer system should be administered by someone who knows the industry and understands people and productivity as well as systems.

Merrill Lynch, like all investment firms, must store and update information on each account held by each of its customers. A customer can have several types of accounts, including checking and savings accounts, several types of securities accounts, and a credit card account. Merrill Lynch simply used its computer-based information system to do two things that had not been done before: (1) produce a single monthly statement covering all of a customer's accounts and (2) automatically invest unused dollars in a money market fund. All the necessary information and capability were available. But by combining it Merrill Lynch was able to create an extremely successful product — its Cash Management Account — which has brought billions of investment dollars into the firm.

Allied Stores owns a number of department and specialty stores. In 1982, Allied began using computers in some of its collection departments. The computers eliminated a lot of paper handling, since the information needed for most calls appears on the caller's monitor screen.

Productivity rose slowly after the computers were installed, and by the end of a year it had increased by about 25 percent. Then the director of credit operations made a work-oriented change: He provided clerical support for the callers. Now those people who do well at calling stick with the phones and computers, while others obtain information for them from the files. The result has been a doubling of productivity in the computerized departments.

Questions

1. More than a few firms have discovered that their new computers have not increased productivity and show no signs of paying off their hefty investments. What are some possible explanations for this unexpected outcome?
2. Why did the productivity of Allied's collection personnel jump after the callers were given clerical help?

For more information see *Fortune*, May 26, 1986, pp. 20–24; *Business Week*, October 14, 1985, pp. 108–114; and *Management Technology*, July 1984, p. 43.

16.2 That's Using Your MIS

Westinghouse Electric has had a traditional MIS for years. The system is capable of storing, updating, and processing data on a variety of company activities. Operations managers use it to keep tabs on production levels and on the flow of materials and work in process. It is used by the personnel department; by accounting and financial managers, and by administrators throughout the company. Recently Westinghouse instituted a program to extend its information management effort to less traditional areas.

Perhaps the most revolutionary approach to information management at Westinghouse was taken by the firm's Construction Group in Pittsburgh. Every Construction Group typewriter except one has been removed. The exception was a machine that was left close to the office of the group president, for making minor corrections.

A computer terminal was issued to every secretary and every boss. The terminals give them direct access to the MIS for immediate input or retrieval of information. This computerized system extends the usefulness of the system and eliminates some annoying chores.

Executives who are away from their desks often return to find a small stack of memos about telephone calls they missed. Now, people who call the Construction Group can record their messages in the information system. Whenever an executive has a few minutes of free time, he or she simply dials the message center. All messages addressed to that executive are then displayed on his or her own screen. The executive can, in turn, use the system to respond or to transmit additional messages.

The Construction Group also eliminated the standard dictation equipment. Now managers dictate their letters and reports into a central word-processing system. A clerical pool then performs any necessary editing and routes the communication to the appropriate person.

The expanded system seems to be working well. Managers report that they now have more time for substantive matters. And after clerical employees realized that the changes were not made to eliminate jobs, they took to the system enthusiastically.

Questions

1. Are message transmission and dictation really legitimate functions of an MIS? Was Westinghouse justified in adding them to the Construction Group MIS? Explain.
2. What problems might arise when all administrative employees have access to a firm's MIS?

For more information see *Fortune*, June 15, 1981, pp. 74–93; *Fortune*, June 28, 1982, pp. 58–65.

The Global Economy

If you want to get a sense of current world economic relations, walk around your house some time looking at labels. Chances are, besides the stereo equipment made in Japan and the wiffle-ball bat made in Taiwan, you'll find shirts made in Korea or Sri Lanka, baskets made in China, and coffee imported from Colombia. Even the honey label says "Product of Canada, Argentina, and the United States." Those bees get around!

Of course it's not the bees but the products of the world's labor that move around so quickly. We may take that situation for granted, but it's a relatively recent phenomenon. To our grandparents, anything from across the sea was rare and exotic. In the first half of this century, you might have seen someone's best *Chinese* China at a fancy tea, but generally the only products you'd see from foreign lands would be souvenirs that world traveler Uncle Mert brought back from India. The limits of the average consumer's reach were the limits of the Sears or Montgomery Ward catalogues, and something that came from far-off California or Florida was likely to provoke more excitement than a modern Christmas where a good portion of the United Nations might be represented under the tree.

What has brought on these changes? How did this global economy come about? Among the answers are two of the forces that have helped make the American domestic economy grow — speed and efficiency. There have always been workers on the other side of the world willing to labor for less pay than their American counterparts, but when their products were months of oxcart, rail, and boat travel away from our shores, the cheap labor meant little to our economy. Perhaps even more important, in the past American importers had little control over what they could buy from other countries. A boatload of goods from India did the importer little good if it was full of the madras that everyone had declared out of fashion the year before.

Changes in transportation have played a major role in shrinking the globe. You can fly or ship a product from virtually anywhere in the world in days rather than months. Especially in the last three decades, the kind of mechanical improvements that have streamlined transportation have improved overseas industrial production as well. While some of the unique, hand-made character of foreign goods has been lost, the predictability and reliability of overseas production has greatly increased. Goods from Taiwan are

almost as easy to get as those from Houston — they still take a little longer, but they're likely to cost much less.

Information transfer, necessary for any business transaction, has been improved even more than transportation. Already, the only limit to an American businessperson's talking to a supplier on the other side of the world is the cost of the call. Now over those same phone lines data can be electronically transferred, so that information that once took weeks to send through the mail can now cross the globe in seconds. We're within a few years of having a truly global market in which brokers can buy and sell stocks and commodities twenty-four hours a day. There will always be a market open somewhere.

Probably the biggest single force in the development of a truly global economy has been the growth of corporations and trading agreements. Giant companies like IBM and ITT have subsidiaries in scores of countries and can therefore directly profit from low labor rates or the valuable natural resources of another country, without having to buy goods from another company. Some people worry about the tendency of American corporations to become giant octopuses with tentacles reaching around the earth. The fear is that "network" corporations will become "hollow," not manufacturing goods themselves but simply acting as information and marketing centers, shifting goods and services from one place to another.

Another way large corporations have made their way into foreign countries is through international cooperative agreements and joint ventures that allow one company to supply certain elements of a successful business venture — technology and capital, for instance — while its partner supplies the labor and other resources. Such agreements allow companies to get a foothold in countries, particularly communist countries, where U.S. subsidiaries are not yet always welcome.

The car, that most American of industrial products, stands today as the perfect symbol of the global economy. Half the parts in many American cars come from outside the U.S. Less than a century after Henry Ford's assembly line cars became the model for U.S. industrial production, a Ford coming out of Detroit might have parts made or assembled in Mexico, Brazil, Germany, Korea, and Japan.

The difficulties involved in selling cars overseas show why the true global economy is still years in the future. Cultural differences and government regulations can still cause problems for international traders. General Motors couldn't figure out why it was having trouble selling its Nova car in Spanish-speaking countries until someone pointed out that in Spanish "no va" means "no go." And Americans who try to buy a Mercedes or a BMW in Europe

or on the gray market discover that there are a lot of differences between cars made for Europe and those made for America. Bringing a European car up to American standards can be time consuming and costly.

So we're still some years away from an international economy that pays no more attention to boundaries between nations than it does to boundaries between states. Accounting practices and financial disclosure rules differ from country to country. Such practices are often tied to long cultural tradition and will not change overnight just to please multinational corporations. In some instances American multinationals have taken advantage of different — often laxer — laws in foreign countries to make a profit. These companies have been under a great deal of criticism lately for "dumping" on foreign markets products that were banned in the U.S. because of their hazardous effects. Some people point to the disaster at Bhopal as an example of how American companies are moving the most dangerous parts of their operations overseas where they won't be so closely scrutinized by U.S. regulators. Such attempts to escape U.S. laws are likely to lead to a further development of the global economy, global standards, and regulations.

However the global economy may end up changing nations economically, it seems certain to affect us all socially and politically. With luck most of those effects will be positive. We come to know other nations and cultures through trading with them, and we may be less likely to go to war with countries with whom we have been exchanging microchips or textiles. Our economic links with the Soviet Union, particularly our grain sales, have been some of our most important international bonds in recent years. They can even act as a weapon — when we want to "punish" the Soviet Union, we can do it by selling them less food rather than with troops and bombs. Perhaps as the world becomes smaller economically, nations will grow closer together politically as well, and our differences will be worked out in the marketplace rather than with guns.

VI

FINANCIAL MANAGEMENT

The once staid banking industry has taken on a new look in recent years. New services are being offered and traditional services such as checking accounts and loans have become more competitive. Since the deregulation of banking services, some of the changes have been quite dramatic. Citicorp, for example, chose to function as a national distribution company, with a full line of products and emphasis on new services and price tradeoffs. In Part VI we examine money, banking, and credit. Financial management, securities markets, and risk management are also covered in this section.

17

MONEY, BANKING, AND CREDIT

Learning Objectives

After you have completed this chapter, you will be able to do the following:

- Define *money* and list five of its characteristics.
- Explain what financial intermediaries are and distinguish the two major categories of them.
- Describe the principal organizational elements in the Federal Reserve System.
- Define *monetary policy* and explain the three principal ways the Federal Reserve has of implementing it.
- Define the five *C*'s of credit and explain the function of credit bureaus in relation to them.
- Outline the collection process.

As soon as Edgar Miranda, a schoolteacher in La Paz, Bolivia, receives his month's pay of 25 million pesos, he races home. He hands his wife some of the money, then they rush off. She buys rice and noodles for the next month, and he exchanges the remainder of his pay on the black market for American dollars.

The Mirandas repeat this drill every month, because Bolivia's inflation rate tops 7000 percent per year. The peso's value declines and prices increase dramatically from moment to moment. For example, on the day Edgar Miranda received his 25 million pesos, a dollar cost 500,000 pesos. A few days later, the price was 900,000. The Mirandas change into dollars all the pesos they do not need immediately, for the dollar is among the world's most stable currencies. When Bolivians need pesos, for daily purchases like fresh fruits and vegetables, they change on the black market only the dollars they need. Like street vendors, currency traders shout competing offers for dollars, and the value of a dollar can vary within a block up to 6 percent or more, from perhaps 800,000 to 850,000 pesos.[1]

The Mirandas' experience is not one that many Americans have had — or is it? If we ignore the fact that buying and selling dollars is illegal under Bolivian law, what the Mirandas do is little different from what good managers may well do with the money entrusted to them. They convert their cash into safe, profitable investments like certificates of deposit (CDs). The Mirandas must go to the lengths they do because their government lacks the will and the resources to cope with inflation. By contrast, the U.S. government has made a low inflation rate its principal economic goal for almost twenty years. (During this period, our inflation rate has varied between 2 and 13.5 percent per year.) Bolivia also lacks the strong public and private financial institutions that form the backbone of our economic system.

This chapter is about the nature of our money. It also describes the function of credit, or how to get more money when it is needed. We also survey our financial institutions. The next two chapters explore how managers use these institutions to manage their financial resources.

THE FUNCTION OF MONEY

Before money existed, the only way to acquire something was to **barter**, to trade or exchange what one person owns for something another owns without using money. The problem with barter as a system of exchange is that every transaction is unique. If one shepherd trades three lambs and some wool for a new coat, this exchange offers little guidance to another shepherd who might want to make a similar transaction, because the second shepherd's lambs, wool, and coat may be of a different quality.

Money Defined

Money solves the barter problem. **Money** is anything that is generally accepted in exchange for goods or in payment of debts, not necessarily valued for itself but because it can be used for the same purposes repeatedly. Money includes not only bills and coins but anything commonly accepted in place of cash, like checks or credit cards.

The Purposes of Money

Money serves three essential purposes. It is

☐ A measure of value
☐ A medium of exchange
☐ A store of value

As a **measure of value**, money is a readily accepted means of relating or comparing the worth of different things. Money permits people to identify the relative value of two items, say a blank audiocassette at $1.49 and a blank videocassette at $4.49.

Money is also a **medium of exchange**, anything that people are willing to accept in return for goods or services and that they in turn can exchange for other goods or services. For example, when a consumer buys a new car stereo, the dealership may use the money it receives either to buy more inventory or to pay salaries.

The Three Essential Purposes of Money

The kind of money most commonly used in exchanges is currency. Strictly speaking, **currency** refers only to coins and bills, but it may also refer to a nation's money. So when you see mention of, say, "British currency," look at the context to see whether it means "British coins and bills" or "British money."

Money is also a **store of value**, a means of holding and collecting wealth. A farmer could not amass wealth by keeping milk that his or her cows produce over the years. Instead, the farmer exchanges the milk, which would spoil in a few weeks, for money, which he or she can hold indefinitely without risk of spoilage.

The Characteristics of Money

Money should have the following characteristics:

☐ Stability of value
☐ Divisibility
☐ Portability
☐ Durability
☐ Not easily counterfeited

Marketing banking services. For many consumers, choosing a bank used to be as easy as walking into the only bank in town. Today all states allow banks to own more than one branch and many allow interstate banking. To succeed in the fierce competition for deposits, banks must adopt a marketing orientation and offer a distinctive range of services.

The Five Characteristics of Money

Stability of Value   The value of money should not change significantly over the short run. An item valued at $100 today should be worth the same amount tomorrow or next month and approximately the same next year and the year after. Of course, inflation erodes the value of all currencies. The dollar has decreased in value over the last half century. For example, based on the **Consumer Price Index (CPI)**, the monthly governmental index of inflation, $1 today buys about what 37 cents bought in 1967. Countries like Brazil and Israel have even had inflation rates more than two hundred times ours. Their people, like the Mirandas in Bolivia, protect themselves against rapid declines in value by exchanging their currencies for something of predictable value, either goods or a stable currency.

Divisibility   For a currency to work efficiently, its units of measure must permit precise valuation. The units should range from quite small to quite large and be divisible by the smallest unit. Goods and services in the United States can be precisely valued, and we can make exchanges in exactly the right amounts. It is no trick to buy a $1.19 bag of potato chips with two $1 bills and get back 81 cents in coins. But in the Yap Islands of the South Pacific, at the beginning of the twentieth century great stone wheels were still used as money. In east Africa, until very recently cows were money.[2] To arrive at an exchange that matched whole stones or cows required an infinitely more complicated process than our monetary exchanges. Today, virtually all currencies use a decimal system like ours.

Portability The holders of a currency must be able to move it easily to wherever a transaction is to take place. In facilitating exchanges, the advantage of a decimal currency over stone wheels and cows is obvious.

Durability Any currency must be able to survive many transactions without wearing out. When it does need replacement, people must know that they can exchange it for new currency without its suffering any loss of value. The average one-dollar bill lasts one and a half years. It is equally a dollar for both its first and its last holder.

Not Easily Counterfeited A currency's users must have confidence that what is in circulation is genuine. The federal government therefore goes to great lengths to make the design of bills difficult to counterfeit. Since 1985, the government has also extended its protective efforts to the principal currency substitute, checks, by changing the kind of paper government checks are printed on, to prevent their being copied.

The Concept of Liquidity

One could summarize the nature of money by saying that it must be liquid. **Liquidity** is the capacity of an asset to be turned into currency. As Figure 17.1 shows, assets can be classified according to their liquidity. A **liquid asset** is one that can routinely be turned into cash at its market value within thirty days. Neither real estate nor an antique rocker, for instance, is a liquid asset, because liquidating them within thirty days would normally require the seller to take a lower-than-market price.

Bank accounts are indeed liquid assets, but their degree of liquidity depends on whether they are classified as demand deposits or time deposits. **Deposit** has two meanings. First, it may refer to currency, checks, or drafts given to a financial institution for crediting to a customer's account. Second, deposit may be a synonym for *account*. The most liquid assets other than currency are **demand deposits**, individual and business accounts from which depositors can withdraw funds at any time without prior notice to the bank. The **depositor**, a person or business in whose name funds have been put in a bank, can make withdrawals by check, automated bank machine, or the like.

A somewhat less liquid asset is a **time deposit**, funds deposited with a bank either in the form of a savings account or a certificate of deposit under an agreement that the bank will pay interest on the funds and the depositor must give notice to the bank a specified time before withdrawing funds. For instance, banks may require up to thirty days' notice before permitting a withdrawal from a savings account.

FINANCIAL INTERMEDIARIES

Just as marketing requires intermediaries to match producers and retailers, as we have seen, the financial system needs intermediaries to put together those

FIGURE 17.1

The Concept of Liquidity

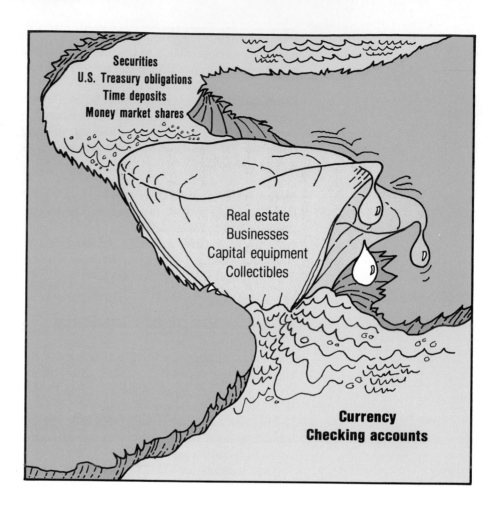

Securities
U.S. Treasury obligations
Time deposits
Money market shares

Real estate
Businesses
Capital equipment
Collectibles

Currency
Checking accounts

who have funds with those who require funds. **Financial intermediaries** are institutions that take in funds, then loan them at a price (an interest charge) sufficient to reward the supplier adequately and make a profit for the intermediary.[3] Figure 17.2 illustrates the relationships among the suppliers and requirers of funds and financial intermediaries.

Financial Intermediaries Defined

Suppliers and Users of Funds

The cash flow of people and organizations rarely matches their cash needs. From time to time, individuals, businesses, and units of government supply excess cash to financial intermediaries and borrow from them.

Individuals   Individuals invest money that they do not need immediately into life insurance, pension plans, and bank accounts. Many open Keogh plans or Individual Retirement Accounts (IRAs). They use funds that financial intermediaries make available to them in the form of, say, home mortgage loans, bill-consolidation loans, and student loans.

FIGURE 17.2

How Financial Intermediaries Work.

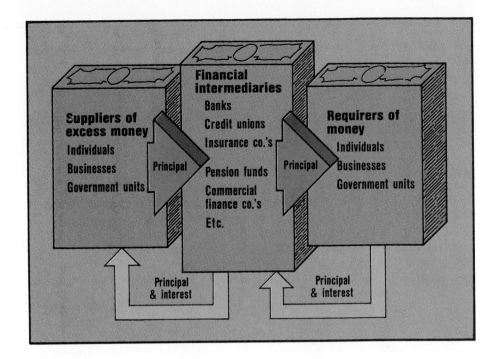

Businesses As Chapter 18 discusses, a combination of financially perilous times and increasingly sophisticated communications has made money management a key managerial function. Businesses can now shop worldwide for the best interest rates on short-term investments. Businesses supply their financial intermediaries with cash when, for example, they pay life-insurance premiums on their employees and officers or make contributions to pension funds. Of course, businesses are also major requirers of funds, whether to solve a brief cash-flow problem or for something like a long-term mortgage loan.

Government Units Government units are also suppliers and users of funds. For instance, a town collects property taxes only once or twice a year, but it must meet payrolls every week. At times, towns must borrow for the short term in anticipation of receiving revenues. Towns borrow for the long term by issuing **bonds,** promises to pay interest and repay principal on a loan. Chapters 18 and 19 will look more closely at government bonds.

Nondepository Institutions

The First Type of Financial Intermediary: Nondepository Institutions

There are two types of financial intermediaries: nondepository institutions and depository institutions. **Nondepository institutions** are, as the name suggests, financial intermediaries that do not accept deposits. The six most common types are insurance companies, pension funds, commercial finance companies, consumer finance companies, mutual funds, and money-market mutual funds. We will examine the first four of these in this section and the others in the following two chapters.

Panic at the Savings and Loan

"Thrift" institutions — the generic name given to savings banks and savings and loan associations — have long been seen as the friendly local cousin of larger, more impersonal commercial banks. For many young Americans, being taken down to the local savings and loan to establish a first savings account has been a significant rite of passage into the adult world. Growing with consumer confidence and a friendly image, thrifts currently hold $1.1 trillion in 146 million accounts.

In 1985, however, the image of the local savings and loan as a safe, friendly place to deposit your money crumbled. Driven by stories of banks' mismanagement and fears of their failure, thousands of people in Ohio and Maryland acted out scenes from the Great Depression, camping outside savings and loan offices to withdraw their money before the bank closed its doors. As a result of the anger and confusion, other thrifts moved to improve their deposit insurance, but some observers worried about the strength of the whole banking system.

It all started in March, in Ohio, with the failure of Home State Savings Bank of Cincinnati. The failure was precipitated by the collapse of E.S.M., a shady government-securities dealership, which left Home State with $146 million in losses. Depositors, worried that other thrifts would close, withdrew $200 million in a week, leading Governor Celeste to close the doors of 70 Ohio savings institutions, the most widespread closure in the industry since President Roosevelt declared a week-long national bank holiday in 1933. For a week, half a million Ohio depositors couldn't get at their $4 billion in savings.

Two months later, a similar panic spread across Maryland when the state's insurance fund removed the president of Old Court Savings & Loan in Baltimore because of mismanagement. Maryland depositors, who had already withdrawn $630 million in the time since the Ohio crisis, suddenly feared the worst and began lining up to get their cash.

What connects Ohio and Maryland is not that they have the most paranoid citizenry in the country, but that a relatively high proportion of their thrifts were insured by private rather than federal companies. Over 80 percent of the country's 3700 thrifts are covered by one of two federal insurance corporations. Because of the size of these corporations, if a member bank fails, the insuring corporation can easily cover all the depositors' withdrawal demands. But the private insurance funds in Ohio and Maryland contained only a few hundred million dollars, enough to cover one failure perhaps, but not a whole series. Thus depositors who knew about the insurance situation were justifiably wary when they heard of one bank failure, figuring that if their bank was next, the insurance pool might not be big enough to pay off all the depositors.

Swift moves by the governors of the states involved, assurances of financial backing from Federal Reserve Board Chairman Paul Volcker, and rapid processing of thrifts' applications for federal insurance protection soon ended the panic at most thrifts in both states. Some of the weaker banks will remain closed until they are taken over by larger commercial banks, and a host of changes in the regulating system may result from the crisis. Washington committees pondered legislation that would force all banks to be federally insured, though some in the industry say that such legislation will be unnecessary — many thrifts have learned their lesson, and are signing up voluntarily.

It may be that the panic of '85 was unwarranted, and that people were just overreacting to a consolidation in the thrift industry, a weeding out of weaker institutions that has been going on since 1975, when there were almost 50 percent more savings institutions than there are today. But the high rate of failures — among businesses as well as banks — is troublesome, and some people are now casting a wary eye on the 15 percent of credit unions that are privately insured.

Sources: Stephen Koepp, "Another Time Bomb Goes Off," *Time*, Vol. 125, No. 21, May 27, 1985, 56. Susan Dentzger, "The Ohio Thrift Panic," *Newsweek*, Vol. 105, No. 13, April 1, 1985, 24. Blanca Riemer, "Washington Wrangles as the Thrift Crisis Deepens," *Business Week*, No. 2896, May 27, 1985, 128. Sidney Lens, "Will It Be the Crash Next Time?" *The Nation*, Vol. 240, No. 24, June 22, 1985, 764.

Insurance Companies An insurance company takes in funds, called **premiums,** from its policyholders. In return, the firm promises to pay the insured if a specific event occurs while its contract, the **policy,** is in force. For example, a life-insurance company promises to pay if the person insured dies. Insurance companies make money by generating more premiums at higher rates than they must pay in claims and by earning interest on loans. They make short-term loans to policyholders and long-term loans to corporations, real-estate developers, and governments.

Pension Funds The second type of nondepository institution, **pension funds,** accumulates funds intended to generate retirement income for persons who belong to the pension plan. These plans take money, called **contributions,** from employees or employers (or both) and invest it so they can pay retirees the benefits promised. Pension funds make very conservative investments and usually focus on blue-chip stocks and bonds, high-quality mortgages on commercial property, and government bonds.

Four Types of Nondepository Institutions

Commercial Finance Companies The third category of institution under discussion, **commercial finance companies,** consists of nondepository financial intermediaries that make business loans. Because commercial finance companies do not take deposits, they are not subject to the banking regulations discussed below. They fund their operations by borrowing large sums, then making loans to smaller businesses that cannot obtain bank financing. Such borrowers are not the best credit risks, so they must pay commercial finance institutions a higher rate of interest than they would a bank.

Consumer Finance Companies The fourth type of institution, **consumer finance companies,** is nondepository financial intermediaries that lend to individuals. They operate much like commercial finance companies, making loans to individuals who cannot get bank loans and are thus willing to pay higher interest rates.

Depository Institutions

The Second Type of Financial Intermediary: Depository Institutions

A financial intermediary that accepts deposits is a **depository institution.** Lines once clearly divided the types of depository institutions, but the deregulation of financial services has largely erased the traditional boundaries, which existed until the 1970s.

Commercial Banks Originally, **commercial banks** served primarily business customers. They concentrated on attracting demand deposits, which paid no interest, and making loans to businesses. Commercial banks have broadened their services recently to penetrate the consumer-banking market. They now offer virtually all the different forms of customer services, including automatic teller machines, credit cards, and brokerage services.

Some commercial banks are **national banks,** financial institutions organized with the approval of the Comptroller of the Currency, who issues them a charter, and operated subject to federal banking regulations. National banks must be members of the Federal Reserve System. Other types of commercial banks, called **state**

Safety of the banking system. Depositors in federally insured banks can be certain their funds are safe, but not all banks carry the same guarantees. Many state-chartered banks are insured by state and private insurance programs. Other state-chartered thrifts and commercial banks choose not to insure their accounts. It's not easy to get money out of a bank once depositors start a run on it.

Three Types of Depository Institutions

banks, are chartered by the state in which they operate. Many state banks also join the Federal Reserve System, but they do not have to.

All members of the Federal Reserve System must insure their deposits against loss if the institution fails, through the **Federal Deposit Insurance Corporation (FDIC),** a corporation established by the Banking Act of 1933. Other financial institutions that meet the FDIC's requirements may also apply for insurance. The FDIC insures each account in a member bank for up to $100,000 per account. State insurance programs may or may not apply to accounts in institutions not covered by federal insurance. Unfortunately, as depositors in Ohio and Maryland banks learned recently, some institutions have no insurance at all, and some state programs are not sufficient to protect depositors.

Thrift Institutions   Originally, **thrift institutions,** such as savings banks and savings-and-loan associations, were the ones that served individuals by providing safe, interest-bearing accounts for savings mortgages and other local, long-term loans. However, with the entry of commercial banks into arenas previously restricted to the thrifts, any difference in the services offered by these two types of depository institutions has almost disappeared. Nevertheless, the thrifts' organizational structure still distinguishes them from commercial banks. **Savings-and-loan associations (S & Ls),** also known as building-and-loan associations, are thrift institutions that are usually owned by their depositors. They offer a wide variety of services, including checking accounts, and still invest primarily in mortgages, within their communities. **Mutual savings banks,** a class of thrift institutions found mainly in the Northeast, are also owned by their depositors. They have investment policies similar to those of the savings and loans. An increasing number of thrifts are turning themselves into shareholder-owned institutions the way commercial banks have.

The thrifts have a number of options when it comes to deposit insurance. They may participate in the FDIC or in the **Federal Savings and Loan Insurance Corporation (FSLIC),** a corporation established by federal law to insure the deposits of thrift institutions. Like the FDIC, the FSLIC has a current maximum per account of $100,000. A variety of other state and private insurance programs exist. And like state-chartered commercial banks, thrifts also have the option of simply not insuring their accounts.

Credit Unions A nonprofit savings-and-loan organization operated specifically for the benefit of its members (all of whom must have some common link, such as employment or ethnic background) is a **credit union**. For example, state employees in Ohio may join the Ohio State Employees' Credit Union. Credit unions primarily make automobile, student, and consumer loans. Because they operate as cooperatives, they channel their earnings back to their members in the form of higher interest rates while at the same time charging as much as 6 percent less than commercial rates to their members on loans and credit-card purchases. Credit unions may insure their deposits, most commonly through the **National Credit Union Administration,** an agency of the federal government. The coverage is similar to that of the other federal deposit insurance programs. Table 17.1 shows how the total assets of credit unions relate to those of the other depository institutions we have discussed.

TABLE 17.1

Selected Financial Institutions — Number and Assets, by Type of Institution and Asset Size [As of December, 1984]

ASSET SIZE	NUMBER OF INSTITUTIONS				ASSETS (bil. dol.)			
	Insured commercial banks[1]	Savings and loan associations[2]	Mutual savings banks[1] [3]	Credit unions[4]	Insured commercial banks[1] [5]	Savings and loan associations[2]	Mutual savings banks[1] [3]	Credit unions[4]
Total	**14,481**	**3,391**	**267**	**15,144**	**2,108.0**	**902.4**	**135.6**	**99.0**
Less than $250,000	2	70	—	2,902	(z)	(z)	—	.3
$250,000–$999,000	9		—	4,444	(z)		—	2.5
$1.0 million–$4.9 million	320	130	—	4,688	1.1	.4	—	11.0
$5.0 million–$9.9 million	1,150	135	1	1,284	8.8	1.1	(z)	9.1
$10.0 million–$24.9 million	4,064	422	7	1,051	69.3	7.4	.1	16.3
$25.0 million–$49.9 million	3,761	600	3	403	135.1	22.6	.1	14.3
$50.0 million–$99.9 million	2,741	671	57	226	190.1	49.6	4.3	15.5
$100.0 million–$499.9 million	1,956	1,034	136	139	371.2	224.2	32.2	23.9
$500.0 million or more	478	329	63	7	1,332.4	597.2	98.9	6.1
PERCENT DISTRIBUTION								
Total	**100.0**	**100.0**	**100.0**	**100.0**	**100.0**	**100.0**	**100.0**	**100.0**
Less than $250,000	(z)	2.1	—	19.2	(z)	(z)	—	.3
$250,000–$999,000	.1		—	29.3	(z)		—	2.5
$1.0 million–$4.9 million	2.2	3.8	—	31.0	.1	(z)	—	11.1
$5.0 million–$9.9 million	7.9	4.0	.4	8.5	.4	.1	(z)	9.2
$10.0 million–$24.9 million	28.1	12.4	2.6	6.9	3.3	.8	.1	16.5
$25.0 million–$49.9 million	26.0	17.7	1.1	2.7	6.4	2.5	.1	14.4
$50.0 million–$99.9 million	18.9	19.8	21.4	1.5	9.0	5.5	3.2	15.7
$100.0 million–$499.9 million	13.5	30.5	50.9	.9	17.6	24.8	23.7	24.1
$500.0 million or more	3.3	9.7	23.6	(z)	63.2	66.2	72.9	6.2

— Represents zero. Z Less than $50 million or .05 percent.
[1]Source: U.S. Federal Deposit Insurance Corporation, *Statistics on Banking*, annual.
[2]Source: U.S. League of Savings Institutions, Washington, DC, *The Savings and Loan Source Book*, annual.
[3]Excludes federally chartered mutual savings banks.
[4]Source: National Credit Union Administration. *National Credit Union Administration Yearend Statistics 1984*. Excludes nonfederally insured State chartered credit unions and federally insured corporate credit unions.
[5]Covers domestic assets only.
Source: U.S. Bureau of the Census, *Statistical Abstract of the United States*: 1986 (106th edition) Washington, DC, 1985.

THE FEDERAL RESERVE SYSTEM

From 1837 to 1907, panics marked by unstable currency and runs on banks punctuated American history. With the lesson of the Panic of 1907 fresh in their minds, Congress began to fashion a mechanism to stabilize the banking system. In 1913, President Woodrow Wilson signed the Federal Reserve Act, which created the **Federal Reserve System** as the United States' central bank. A **central bank** is the government agency responsible for acting as a government's bank, managing its monetary policy, serving as the primary bank of the banking system, and overseeing the nation's international financial relationships.

Its Structure

As Figure 17.3 indicates, the Federal Reserve's structure is somewhat complex. Although we will examine the functions of each component in more detail later, an overview of the system here will be helpful.

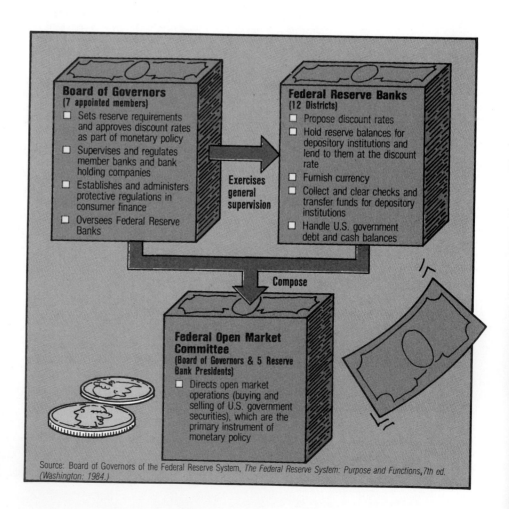

FIGURE 17.3

Organization of the Federal Reserve System

Board of Governors
(7 appointed members)
- Sets reserve requirements and approves discount rates as part of monetary policy
- Supervises and regulates member banks and bank holding companies
- Establishes and administers protective regulations in consumer finance
- Oversees Federal Reserve Banks

Exercises general supervision

Federal Reserve Banks
(12 Districts)
- Propose discount rates
- Hold reserve balances for depository institutions and lend to them at the discount rate
- Furnish currency
- Collect and clear checks and transfer funds for depository institutions
- Handle U.S. government debt and cash balances

Compose

Federal Open Market Committee
(Board of Governors & 5 Reserve Bank Presidents)
- Directs open market operations (buying and selling of U.S. government securities), which are the primary instrument of monetary policy

Source: Board of Governors of the Federal Reserve System, *The Federal Reserve System: Purpose and Functions,* 7th ed. (Washington: 1984.)

The Board of Governors   The board of governors of the Federal Reserve System oversees the entire system. Its seven members are appointed by the president, and its chair serves as a principal government spokesperson on economic and monetary policy.

The Federal Reserve Banks   The daily routine of ensuring the financial system's smooth operation falls to the twelve **Federal Reserve Banks**. Every day, these banks oversee the transfer of billions of dollars in currency and checks. Figure 17.4 shows the boundaries of each Federal Reserve District and of their branch territories, with the locations of their branches and other facilities. The twelve Federal Reserve Banks provide a number of services in addition to the ones discussed below. For instance, they issue **Federal Reserve Notes,** the nation's currency. They disburse funds and provide accounts for federal agencies. They also issue, service, and redeem U.S. Savings Bonds.

The **members** or shareholders of the Federal Reserve System in each district own its Federal Reserve Bank. As noted earlier, all national banks must belong to the Federal Reserve System, and many state-chartered commercial banks also elect to join. As one condition of membership, a member bank must maintain a certain percentage of its deposits as a **reserve,** which is the liquid assets — usually currency — that are set aside in a bank's vault or on deposit with the Federal Reserve Bank to which a commercial bank belongs.

Member banks are not the only institutions that use the Federal Reserve

FIGURE 17.4

Federal Reserve District Boudnaries

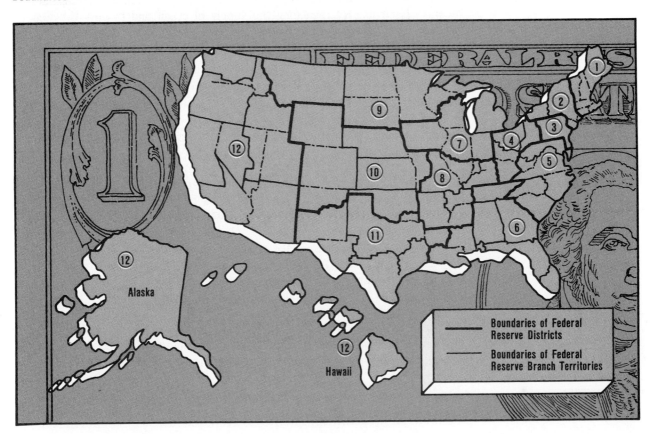

Boundaries of Federal
Reserve Districts

Boundaries of Federal
Reserve Branch Territories

System's services. The Depository Institutions Deregulation and Monetary Control Act of 1980 gave all depository financial institutions the right to use Federal Reserve services. Today member banks make up less than one-sixth of the more than 39,000 financial institutions subject to Federal Reserve System requirements. However, these approximately 6,000 member banks hold about 70 percent of the deposits in commercial banks and 40 percent of all bank deposits.[4]

Federal Open Market Committee   The third major element in the Federal Reserve System's structure is the **Federal Open Market Committee.** This twelve-member committee consists of the board of governors, the president of the New York Federal Reserve Bank, and the presidents of four other Federal Reserve Banks. The Open Market Committee's principal function is to carry out the Federal Reserve Board's monetary policy. This body directs the Federal Reserve System's buying and selling of U.S. government securities on the open market in order to increase or decrease the funds available for lending by member banks.

Monetary Policy Responsibilities

The Federal Reserve's most publicized duties involve its control over the nation's **monetary policy,** the Federal Reserve System's management of available credit and the money supply. The level of credit and currency available strongly affects economic activity. By regulating the supply of credit and money, the Federal Reserve tries to stabilize fluctuations in the economy.

Measuring the Money Supply   Every week, the Federal Reserve Board measures the **money supply,** the total amount of currency in circulation, deposits in checking and savings accounts, and other liquid assets. It uses four measures of the money supply.

The narrowest money measure, called M_1, primarily includes money held for the purpose of completing exchanges. Its components are either currency or currency equivalents, like travelers' checks, and demand deposits. One major component, in the currency equivalents or "other checkable deposits" category, is **NOW (negotiable order of withdrawal) accounts,** individual checking accounts that earn interest until the bank receives an order of withdrawal, a check drawn on the account.

The second classification in the money supply, M_2, expands M_1 by including also all time deposits. Although time deposits are supposed to remain in an account for its entire term, in practice they are quite liquid, subject to withdrawal with or without notice. The measure called M_3 then expands M_2 by including large time deposits and investments in less liquid investment vehicles. Finally, the measure known as L expands M_3 by including all remaining liquid assets.[5]

Once the Federal Reserve knows how much money is available in the system, it has three principal tools it can use to adjust the supply to meet its goals:

☐ Open-market operations
☐ The reserve requirement
☐ The discount rate

The Cashless Society

Our language, songs, and slang are full of images that spring from the use of cash. When you hear of someone "rolling in the green stuff," or when someone asks you for a "ten," you know what they're talking about. But as vital as "greenbacks" and "cold, hard cash" may seem to our way of life, they may one day be obsolete. Plastic and microchips are the currency of modern banking, and even those who now relish the feel of change in their pockets may one day be just as attached to a "smart card."

The automatic teller machine (ATM) has come a fixture of American life. Many banks give their customers ATM cards when they open an account, and some card users find the service so convenient that they almost never see the inside of the bank. All you do is insert your card into a slot and punch in your personal identification number and your transaction. The machine makes sure you have enough in your account to cover your present request, then spits out the cash. Customers like the service because it's available at off-hours and because the machines tend to be faster than going inside and waiting for a human teller. Banks like the machines because they often save money.

When ATMs first appeared, they were set up by individual banks to serve just that bank's customers. Now, however, most ATMs are part of networks. Instead of driving to the ATM at their home branch, most people can now use their cards at ATMs in shopping malls and supermarkets, or in the machines of other banks. Small banks join together to create regional shared networks, so cardholders can do business anywhere within their region. And though the concept is relatively new, two major *national* networks, Cirrus Systems and Plus Systems, have already made their 30,000 ATMs available to 100 million cardholders.

If being able to get money anywhere in the country just with a card seems like the ultimate in convenience, just wait. They're improving the card, making the machines more convenient, and even bringing the bank into your home.

Already banks are test-marketing "smart" cards that have a tiny microchip imbedded in them. This computer-on-a-card helps maintain records of multiple accounts and can communicate with the bank's computer when the card is used. Experts expect that by the end of the century, one of every two or three bank cards will be "smart."

If you get irritated by the two steps involved in getting cash at an ATM and spending it at the supermarket, you're ready for point-of-sale (POS) transactions. A POS terminal works much like an ATM. You put in your card and punch in your ID. But you'll find the POS terminal in a retail outlet, and instead of asking the machine for cash, you punch in the amount you've just rung up at the supermarket or gas station. The computer makes sure you have enough money, then transfers the funds electronically.

If you want to keep track of your accounts at home, all you need these days is a computer hooked up to a phone line. Banking giants like Bank of America, Chemical Bank, and Citibank already have thousands of customers who do their banking on their home Apples or Ataris. While customers like the up-to-date information and the ability to transfer money from one account to another, the banks are happy to note that the typical bank-at-home customer opens new accounts within a few months of starting the service, and that some customers switch banks just to be able to use the service.

These technological innovations are not without their drawbacks, of course. Criminals can steal a lot of money just by getting access to numbers and IDs. But on occasion a high-tech bank can be your best friend. In 1985 when panic closed Ohio savings and loans, those clever enough to use machines found that their faithful friends the ATMs doled out cash for hours after the banks had closed their doors.

Sources: R. A. Blake, "Money Grows on Machines," *New Hampshire Times*, July 11, 1986, 7. Robert M. Garsson, "Chemical's Pronto Seems Good Bet for Success, Analyst Says," *American Banker*, July 27, 1983, 12. "Pocket Terminal Used for Secured Banking," *The New York Times*, August 24, 1985, 32.

Open-market Operations   The Federal Reserve's third tool for carrying out its monetary policy is its **open-market operations**, the buying and selling of government securities on the open market, which are supervised by the Federal Open Market Committee discussed earlier. The securities are ones issued by the United States Treasury and federal or federally sponsored agencies. (We will discuss these securities in detail in Chapter 19.) When the Federal Reserve purchases securities, it issues a check on itself, which is deposited in the seller's bank. When the bank presents that check for payment, the Federal Reserve increases the amount in the bank's reserve account. Just the opposite happens when the Federal Reserve sells securities to member banks.

The Federal Reserve is interested in open-market operations because when financial intermediaries buy government securities, they have less money to loan to businesses and individuals. Conversely, when the Federal Reserve buys government securities, the financial intermediaries have more money to loan out. If conditions indicate that the economy needs a boost, the Federal Reserve will buy up government obligations, thus loosening credit. However, if inflation seems to be on the rise, the Open Market Committee will begin selling government obligations.

The Federal Reserve's Three
Main Controls over the Money
Supply

The Reserve Requirement   As we have seen, the Federal Reserve's money supply measures include not just available currency but also bank deposits. Banks of course make loans against their deposits. They must also maintain some liquidity, however, in order to meet customer demands. The Federal Reserve sets a **reserve requirement**, a specified percentage of deposits that a member must either deposit with the Federal Reserve or hold in its own vaults as cash and may not lend.

The reserve requirement in effect defines how much of a bank's deposits it may loan. If, as in Figure 17.5, the reserve requirement happens to be 10 percent, a bank can lend as much as $1,000 for every $100 it has in deposits, as long as it maintains $100 in reserve. Thus, a financial intermediary in effect creates money through lending several times the amount of its deposits.

If the Federal Reserve increases the reserve requirement, it decreases the amount that commercial banks under its regulation can lend. The supply of credit available then shrinks and the money supply therefore contracts. Lowering the reserve requirement has the opposite effect. Adjustments to the reserve requirement do take some time, though, before they ripple through the financial system and have any major effect on the economy.

Further Federal Reserve
Controls over the Money Supply

The Discount Rate   A more sensitive and faster acting economic lever is the **discount rate**, the amount the Federal Reserve charges on loans to all banks subject to its reserve requirements. In effect, the discount rate establishes a floor for interest rates charged by banks, because banks tie the interest that they charge their customers to what the Federal Reserve is charging them. When the discount rate is lower than the rates charged banks by their other sources of funds, they tend to borrow from the Federal Reserve and use that money to make their own loans. This loan activity stimulates the economy by encouraging businesses and individuals to spend. When the Federal Reserve determines that too much money is available, it raises the discount rate and, at least theoretically, the process reverses itself.

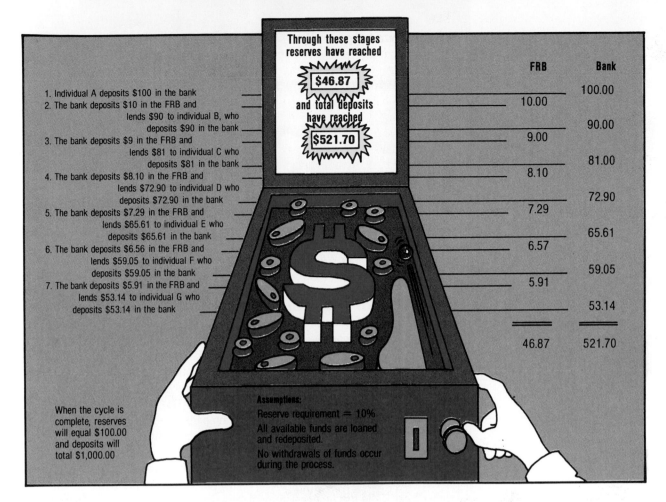

1. Individual A deposits $100 in the bank
2. The bank deposits $10 in the FRB and
   lends $90 to individual B, who
   deposits $90 in the bank
3. The bank deposits $9 in the FRB and
   lends $81 to individual C who
   deposits $81 in the bank
4. The bank deposits $8.10 in the FRB and
   lends $72.90 to individual D who
   deposits $72.90 in the bank
5. The bank deposits $7.29 in the FRB and
   lends $65.61 to individual E who
   deposits $65.61 in the bank
6. The bank deposits $6.56 in the FRB and
   lends $59.05 to individual F who
   deposits $59.05 in the bank
7. The bank deposits $5.91 in the FRB and
   lends $53.14 to individual G who
   deposits $53.14 in the bank

Through these stages
reserves have reached
$46.87
and total deposits
have reached
$521.70

FRB	Bank
	100.00
10.00	
	90.00
9.00	
	81.00
8.10	
	72.90
7.29	
	65.61
6.57	
	59.05
5.91	
	53.14
46.87	521.70

When the cycle is
complete, reserves
will equal $100.00
and deposits will
total $1,000.00

Assumptions:
Reserve requirement = 10%
All available funds are loaned
and redeposited.
No withdrawals of funds occur
during the process.

FIGURE 17.5

The Creation of Money

Selective Credit Controls The Federal Reserve has a number of other, more specifically targeted tools that it uses to fine tune the monetary system. These techniques are lumped into the category of **selective credit controls**. The most important one is the Federal Reserve's ability to set **margin requirements**, the minimum amount that a purchaser of securities must deposit with a broker in order to be able to buy securities on credit. Like the reserve requirement, the margin requirement specifies how much securities dealers may lend to investors. (We will discuss margin requirements in detail in Chapter 19.)

The Banking System's Bank

As the banks' bank, the Federal Reserve provides many of the same services to its members as banks provide their own customers. It makes loans, particularly when banks have liquidity problems, and it holds deposits.

Check Clearing The function of the Federal Reserve Banks that undoubtedly affects the most people and businesses every day is its check clearing. The Reserve Banks direct millions of transfers every day between districts and between banks.

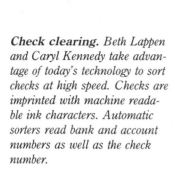

Check clearing. Beth Lappen and Caryl Kennedy take advantage of today's technology to sort checks at high speed. Checks are imprinted with machine readable ink characters. Automatic sorters read bank and account numbers as well as the check number.

Other Means of Transferring Funds   Checks remain the most common means of transferring funds, but new means that are also regulated by the Federal Reserve are gaining rapid acceptance. For example, the **debit card**, a machine-readable plastic card, creates a receipt that authorizes a bank to transfer funds immediately from the debit-card holder's account to the business presenting the receipt. In effect, a debit card allows its holder to buy now and pay now without using cash. An **automated teller machine (ATM) card** is a form of debit card that allows the card holder to make certain bank transactions with a machine instead of having to see a teller. ATMs are often located in busy areas like supermarkets or shopping centers, far from the banks with which they are associated. **Point-of-sale terminals** also provide a direct link between a bank and computers at a place where consumers pay for goods or services. Using the customer's card, the machine will immediately transfer funds from the customer's account to the seller's.

Today, many transfers between distant parties are accomplished directly by computer in a process called **electronic funds transfer (EFT).** Consumers often authorize mortgage companies or insurance companies to make automatic withdrawals from their accounts for their regular monthly payments. The pay-by-phone services offered by some banks also fall into this category. Using EFT, employers deposit wages and the government deposits Social Security and pension payments directly to the recipients' accounts. EFT significantly reduces paperwork and the delays inherent in the check-clearing process. It also minimizes the risk of theft or loss as documents pass from hand to hand.

Deregulation and the New Financial Services Companies

Just as the computer began revolutionizing banking, the federal government began dismantling the regulatory structure that had governed the industry since the 1930s. As noted earlier, the lines that used to exist between the types of financial intermediaries began to disappear. Deregulation opened banking to other businesses that began to invade the banks' territory. For instance, Sears, Roebuck and Company, the nation's largest retailer, entered the marketplace by offering financial counseling, insurance, and a general-purpose credit card it called the Discover Card. Such developments have placed the Federal Reserve System in a difficult position. Its authority to regulate these new financial intermediaries is not at all clear. Meanwhile, the intermediaries already subject to its regulations complain about the difficulties these regulations create for them in competing.

The course of banking and financial services regulation is difficult to predict. In the early 1980s, it seemed certain that banking regulation would die rather quickly. However, record numbers of bank failures, including those of the Penn Square Bank and the first National Bank & Trust Company of Oklahoma City, and the near failure of Continental Illinois in Chicago, made further deregulation unlikely and even led to calls for reregulation.

CREDIT

Let us examine the nature of **credit,** the ability of a business or a person to obtain money or property and to defer repayment or payment because the lender makes a favorable appraisal of the debtor's ability to repay.

The Five *C*'s of Credit

The five criteria most commonly applied by those evaluating credit applications can each be described by words beginning with the letter *C*. These criteria apply whether the borrower is applying for consumer or **commercial** (that is, business) **credit** or for **trade credit** (the sale of goods or services on the promise of payment in the future) or **debt financing**, the lending of money at interest.

The Five Criteria in Assessing Credit Applications

Character   The reputation for honesty and integrity of the person or organization seeking credit is known as its **character.** As with many of the *C*'s of credit, character is difficult to evaluate, but it may be the most important of the five. Many lenders assess character by looking at a potential borrower's history of loan repayments. If the lender and the borrower are new to each other, the lender may do a credit check (described below). The lender may also ask for a list of **references,** firms or banks with whom the borrower has done business in the past.

Capacity   The measure of a borrower's ability to live up to the terms of a credit agreement and to pay off an obligation as promised is known as its **capacity.** Financial managers measure the capacity of individuals by evaluating their statements of assets and liabilities on the credit application. In the case of businesses, lenders review and analyze financial statements and historical trends and try to project historical performance.

Collateral   The security for a loan — usually an asset with enough value that it could be sold to satisfy the obligation — is called **collateral.** The collateral for a mortgage loan, for example, is the real estate on which the borrower gives the lender the mortgage. When collateral **secures** or assures the repayment of a loan, the borrower **assigns** or transfers ownership rights in the collateral to the lender in the event that the borrower defaults. An **unsecured loan,** one for which the borrower does not provide collateral, usually carries a higher interest rate than a secured loan. For example, unsecured credit extended on bank-issued credit cards routinely carries a much higher interest rate than secured loans granted by the same bank.

Capital   In the context of a credit application, **capital** means the financial resources that a borrower has available to assure the lender that the credit is secure. In this context, capital reflects the borrower's **net worth,** the amount by which assets exceed obligations. In making this calculation, a creditor looks at a business's financial statements or an individual's credit application.

Conditions   The final one of the five *C*'s, **conditions**, refers to the current economic environment. The ways in which it might affect the particular borrower's ability to repay the obligation must be calculated as another element in a credit application.

Consumer Credit

The credit extended to individuals for nonbusiness personal, family, or household purposes is **consumer credit.** Such transactions may be either secured or unsecured, long-term or short-term. A consumer may obtain credit from many sources, including banks, credit unions, stores, gasoline companies, or national credit-card companies like Diners Club.

The Function of Credit Bureaus

Before extending credit, a financial institution will as lender carefully investigate the borrower and verify the information on the credit application. Lenders can check on consumer credit applicants by using **credit bureaus,** businesses that keep records on the credit and payment practices of individuals and firms. Credit bureaus also maintain data on consumers' employment and marital histories, as well as other information that a lender might find relevant. Federal Reserve regulations restrict access to the information that credit bureaus maintain, to protect the consumers from possible misuse of the data. Persons on whom a credit bureau maintains information also have a right to see their files and to correct or add explanatory information to them.

Credit Cards

A **credit card** is a card, usually made of plastic, which may represent two types of agreements. One agreement is between the card issuer and the merchant, to affirm that the merchant will honor the card and the issuer will pay the charge slips. The second is between the card issuer and the card holder, saying that the issuer will extend a certain amount of credit to the holder and that the holder will make payments in accordance with the contract. If a business, like Neiman Marcus, issues a credit card good only in its own stores, then the first element of the agreement in this definition would not of course apply.

Applicants for credit cards must fill out an application, which the issuer then checks the information on, as any lender would. Note that a business accepting a national credit card, like Visa, does not extend credit to the patron using the card. Rather, the business is extending credit to Visa, which has itself extended

A retail entry in the battle of the cards. Today Americans can get all kinds of credit cards — bank cards, dining and entertainment cards, and cards from new financial services conglomerates. The competition is a lot stiffer than Sears estimated at first, but the giant retailer has plenty of clout with customers. It's going after customers by offering free cards, dividends based on purchases, and incentives to use the company's other financial services.

credit to the card holder. The business's payment by Visa does not depend on the card holder's paying Visa. Visa assumes the risk that its card holders will not pay. Visa and the other national card issuers make money both by discounting each sale before paying the merchant and also by charging card holders an annual fee as well as interest on bills not paid in full or on time.

Credit cards are big business today. More than 125 million Visa and MasterCards are in use, along with tens of millions of other cards. These cards represent billions of dollars' worth of purchases each year and are a major reason why relatively little currency is needed in an economy the size of ours.

Commercial Credit

Businesses apply for credit in much the same way consumers do. For a credit check, a lender can turn to a special credit investigative service or to a commercial rating firm like Dun & Bradstreet or TRW Information Services. Such firms provide relatively detailed reports on business borrowers. If sufficient information is available, they rate the potential borrower's financial strength and payment history. The services publish their ratings in reference volumes that they sell to credit managers.

In determining whether to extend trade credit to a new customer, a credit manager uses the rating firms and contacts the customer's trade and bank references to evaluate its creditworthiness. With this evaluation in hand, the credit manager can decide whether to extend credit and, if so, how much. Generally, the amount of credit extended is small at the beginning of a relationship, often equaling just one or two orders. If the invoices covering this amount are paid promptly, the credit manager may increase the customer's line of credit.

Over time, a credit manager evaluates the customer's payment practices and adjusts the borrower's credit limits as circumstances dictate. Quite often, credit managers share information with credit bureaus.

Collection Practices

The Collection Process

Most firms and individuals pay their bills on time or at least meet the partial payment terms of their credit agreements. When payments are not made, however, a credit manager or his or her staff initiates **collection procedures**, a system used to collect past-due accounts. Normally, the full process includes the following steps, in increasing urgency:

1. A series of computer-generated reminder letters
2. A strong personal letter
3. A telephone call or series of calls
4. Legal action

INTERNATIONAL BUSINESS

The Swiss Keep Their Secrets

For years, anyone with reason to hide large amounts of money from the inquisitive eyes of government or banking officials has turned to one safe haven: Swiss banks. A Swiss bank employee who reveals information about a customer's account faces six months in jail or $22,000 in fines. The safety and secrecy of a Swiss bank account have helped make tiny Switzerland one of the world's leading banking centers. But the often shady sources of that money have become an increasing concern for many Swiss citizens and politicians. A national referendum on the issue in 1984 produced a clash between those who wanted to preserve Switzerland's financial status, and those who were more interested in ridding Switzerland of its image as "a pension fund for Third World dictators," as one proponent of the referendum put it.

The bankers, forced out of their usual secrecy by the referendum on the issue, argued that changing Swiss banking laws would be disastrous for the entire country. Nervous depositors would withdraw their money, the bankers warned, leading to a collapse in stock prices, a jump in interest rates, the loss of thousands of jobs, and general economic ruin. Just before what some called the

"socialist challenge" of the referendum, Switzerland's three biggest banks boosted dividends, trying to show the strength of the banking industry and its importance to the Swiss economy.

In response to the concerns about the kinds of people who benefit from the secrecy laws, the Swiss government and banks have made some concessions. A 1978 treaty opened the way for the Swiss to cooperate in American investigations into organized crime leaders. And in 1982 the Swiss agreed to help the Securities and Exchange Commission track down insider-information schemes.

The bankers and tradition appear to have won this round — 70% of Swiss voters cast their ballots against the referendum. But proponents of the measure have not given up, and hope that within the next decade, "a Swiss bank account" will have a very different meaning.

Sources: Alexander L. Taylor III, "Swiss Secrets Are Put to a Vote," *Time*, Vol. 123, No. 22, May 28, 1984, 69. Alfred Zanker, "Days Numbered for Secret Swiss Accounts?" *U.S. News & World Report*, Vol. 96, No. 20, May 21, 1984, p. 40. "The Banks Aren't Flinching from a Socialist Challenge," *Business Week*, No. 2838, March 19, 1984, 39. John Parry.

It is important to note that federal regulations limit how collection practices on consumer debts can be carried out. For example, a bill collector cannot call a consumer debtor after 9:00 P.M. or if the debtor has requested that no more phone calls be made.

CREDIT: A PERSPECTIVE

The restrictions mentioned on credit bureau reports and on collection activities became law as a result of one of the consumer movement's greatest triumphs. Four federal laws passed during one decade completely changed the face of consumer credit. The first of these laws, the Truth in Lending Act, was passed in 1969 and amended in 1980. In essence, this act requires lenders to present prospective borrowers with standard statements of all credit costs so that borrowers can compare prices. The act also limits consumer liability on a lost or stolen credit card to fifty dollars.

The next important consumer credit act was the Fair Credit Reporting Act of 1970, whose provisions relating to credit bureaus were discussed above. This act applies not only to consumer credit applications but also to credit reports supplied for decisions on hiring or retention in employment or for insurance applications.

In 1974, Congress enacted the Equal Credit Opportunity Act, which prohibited discrimination in evaluating and granting credit because of an applicant's race, color, sex, age, religion, marital status, or national origin. Finally, in 1978 came the Fair Debt Collection Practices Act, which restricted abuses that had occurred in collection practices.

The irony of this new regulatory program lies in its timing. Just as deregulation was becoming the watchword in financial services, this new structured credit environment arrived. Yet, in all the fervor for deregulation, no one seriously proposed abolishing the new credit practices acts.

Chapter Highlights

1. Define *money* and list five of its characteristics.

Money is a measure of value, a medium of exchange, and a store of value. Five characteristics important for money to have are stability of value, divisibility, portability, durability, and resistance to counterfeiting.

2. Explain what financial intermediaries are and distinguish the two major categories of them.

Financial intermediaries are middlemen that take in funds from various sources on a temporary basis and provide those funds to temporary users of funds at a price (the interest charge) that adequately rewards the suppliers and users of funds and also satisfies the intermediary's own

earnings requirements. The major categories of financial intermediaries include insurance companies, pension funds, commercial and consumer finance companies, commercial banks, thrift institutions, and credit unions.

3. Describe the principal organizational elements in the Federal Reserve System.

The principal organizational elements in the Federal Reserve System are the board of governors, a seven-member board appointed by the president; twelve Federal Reserve Banks; and the Federal Open Market Committee, made up of the board of governors and five other presidents of Federal Reserve Banks, one of whom must head the New York bank.

4. Define *monetary policy* and explain the three principal ways the Federal Reserve has of implementing it.

Monetary policy is the management of available credit and the money supply to regulate economic activity. The Federal Reserve uses three primary tools to implement its monetary policy: the reserve requirement, the discount rate, and open-market operations. All three tools affect the amount of money that is available for lending.

5. Define the five *C*'s of credit and explain the function of credit bureaus in relation to them.

The five *C*'s of credit are character, the honesty and integrity of the loan applicant; capacity, the ability of the borrower to repay a loan; collateral, the security available for a loan; capital, the financial resources of the borrower; and conditions, the general economic environment. Credit bureaus keep records on the credit histories and payment practices of individuals and firms. The information they provide helps lenders evaluate an applicant's past payment history (character) and ability to repay (capacity).

6. Outline the collection process.

The collection process generally consists of four steps: (1) A series of computer-generated reminder letters; (2) A strong personal letter; (3) A telephone call or series of calls; and (4) Legal action.

Key Terms

Capital
Collateral
Commercial bank
Commercial credit
Conditions
Consumer credit
Credit bureau
Credit card
Credit union
Currency
Debit card
Demand deposit
Depository institution

Discount rate
Federal Deposit
  Insurance
  Corporation (FDIC)
Federal Open Market
  Committee (FOMC)
Federal Reserve Bank
Federal Reserve
  System
Federal Savings and
  Loan Insurance
  Corporation (FSLIC)
Financial intermediaries

Liquid asset
Margin requirements
Medium of exchange
Monetary policy
Money supply
National Credit Union
  Administration
Nondepository
  institution
NOW (negotiable order
  of withdrawal)
  account

References
Reserve requirement
Savings-and-loan
  association (S&L)
State bank
Thrift institution
Time deposit
Unsecured loan

Review Questions

1. What is the function of money? Before money existed, how did we acquire things?
2. What are the five important characteristics of money?
3. Describe the concept of liquidity. Give some examples of liquid assets.
4. What is a financial intermediary? Describe the two types of financial intermediaries.
5. What is the difference between a thrift institution and a credit union?
6. What is the Federal Reserve System? In what ways does the Federal Reserve System stabilize the banking system?
7. Describe the open market operations of the Federal Reserve System.
8. What are the five Cs of credit?
9. Describe consumer credit. How do lenders check on consumer credit applications?
10. What has been the impact of deregulation in the financial services community?

Application Exercises

1. At some time in the future you will very likely seek credit for the purchase of an automobile, a home loan, educational needs, or the establishment of a small business. The lender will very likely apply the five C's when evaluating your credit application. How will you measure up? For each of the five C's of credit, circle one of the four criteria provided. Upon completion of this self-assessment, what are your chances of obtaining a substantial loan?

	Poor	Fair	Good	Excellent
Character	1	2	3	4
Capacity	1	2	3	4
Collateral	1	2	3	4
Capital	1	2	3	4
Conditions	1	2	3	4

2. Using the yellow pages of your local phone directory, prepare a list of nondepository and a list of depository institutions that serve your community.

Cases

17.1 Credit-Card Capers

The federal government was careful to build protections into the currency it created, but credit-card issuers were not. That has made credit-card fraud almost too simple, and very lucrative for those who care to practice it.

A lost or stolen wallet may contain hundreds of dollars of cash, but each credit card it holds is good for an average $3000 in fraudulent purchases before it is reported lost or the real cardholder complains about the billing. Counterfeit cards can net much more.

Only three bits of information — name, number, and expiration date — are required to use a credit card. That can be taken from copies of charge slips or charge-slip carbons. It can be used to buy a wide range of products by phone, or to submit phony charges. Fraud artists have been able to extract that information from great numbers of unsuspecting individuals.

Credit-card fraud accounts for only about 0.2 percent of all credit-card transactions, but that represents close to $1 billion which banks and credit-card companies would rather not lose. The major companies are working to make their cards less easily counterfeited. But the fraud problem will likely remain as long as there is a time lag between card use and cardholder billing.

Questions

1. How are credit-card purchases like consumer bank loans?
2. Would the extensive use of debit cards help to reduce card fraud? Explain.

For more information see *Forbes*, September 9, 1985, pp. 88–91; *American Banker*, April 30, 1985, p. 12; and *American Banker*, June 13, 1983, p. 3.

17.2 The New American Eagle

In 1933 the U.S. government stopped minting its eagle ($10) and double-eagle ($20) gold coins. Those coins are now *numismatic* coins — valuable for their rarity as well as their gold content. In 1986 the government began minting and selling new American Eagle gold coins with contents of one-tenth, one-quarter, one-half, and one ounce of gold. Those are *bullion* coins — valuable primarily for their gold content. The prices of the coins will vary with the market price of gold; that price was $426 per ounce the day the first new coins were sold.

Are the new American Eagle coins a good investment? Many people must think so, because the initial minting of 558,000 ounces was sold out almost as soon as selling began. The U.S. Mint had no choice but to halt sales for a week until it could catch up. Officials promised they would make available more than 100,000 ounces of gold coins each week after that, to satisfy the demand.

Gold is among the best defenses against inflation, so gold coins are a favored investment for those who see inflation on the horizon. Experts note that the merit of bullion coins as investments also depends on the size of the premium, the liquidity of the coins, and the nation backing them. The purity of bullion coins must also be taken into account in the purchase price.

Questions

1. What makes gold a good investment in times of inflation?
2. American Eagles are being minted as investments, not as currency. Why?

For more information see *The Boston Globe*, November 1, 1986, p. 102; *The Wall Street Journal*, October 22, 1986, p. 35; and *The Wall Street Journal*, January 20, 1986, p. 19.

18

FINANCIAL MANAGEMENT

Learning Objectives

After you have completed this chapter, you will be able to do the following:

- Describe the financial management function and distinguish it from the other finance-related activities within a business.
- List the elements of a financial plan.
- Describe the two major sources of funds for a financial plan.
- Identify the major sources of short-term financing.
- Describe the types of equity financing used by businesses.
- List and describe the principal types of long-term-debt financing.

I t takes more than a good idea and hard work to succeed in business. It also takes money. In 1979, Paul Hawken had a good idea. He and a friend, David Smith, spotted a coming boom in home gardening. They decided that a mail-order company offering the best English gardening tools and excellent customer service would succeed. Hawken and Smith lacked the cash to start their business, however, so they borrowed $50,000 from friends and private investors. Today, after several years of hard work, Smith & Hawken Ltd. has sales exceeding $12 million. The problem that now confronts the company centers on how to structure the company's growth so that the firm continues to be an enterprise that its owners can enjoy being involved with.[1]

This chapter is about **financial management**, the process of obtaining money and using it effectively to achieve an organization's goals. Financial management may serve goals that may range from wanting to become the next IBM to maintaining a slow growth pattern such as that of Smith & Hawken Ltd.

THE NATURE OF FINANCIAL MANAGEMENT

The Financial Management Function

Without exception, every business has a person who manages its finances. The smallest firms, like a sandwich shop, may not have anyone who spends full time on financial management. In other words, the owner may wear all the hats. Or the firm may have someone like Mrs. J. Willard Marriott, Sr., who kept the Marriott Corporation's books on a yellow legal pad when it started in the 1920s.[2]

The Financial Managers

The best way to analyze the financial management function is in terms of how it functions in large corporations, because of the high degree of specialization in these firms. Figure 18.1 charts the typical finance activity within a large firm. At the top, the **vice president of finance** is the officer in a corporation with overall responsibility for its financial functions. The **controller,** who reports to the vice president of finance, has responsibility for accounting, data processing, and taxes. Chapters 15 and 16 focused primarily on the controller's areas of responsibility. The **treasurer,** who also reports to the vice president of finance, has responsibility for overseeing and planning for the firm's expenditures and income.[3] The discussion that follows centers on the treasurer's areas of responsibility. Clearly, the controller and the treasurer must work together closely. In effect, the controller is the firm's scorekeeper. The treasurer will need up-to-the-minute reports before making important decisions.

We will refer to those making decisions in the treasurer's areas of responsibility as financial managers or financial management. Financial management performs three crucial functions:

1. Planning for a company's financial needs and reevaluating the plan after it is put into action.
2. Acquiring enough funds at the right times to keep the company moving.
3. Deciding how and when to spend the funds on hand.

FIGURE 18.1

Finance Activity Within a Firm

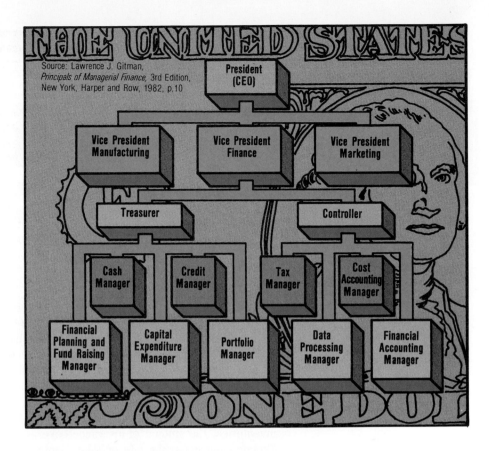

Developing a Financial Plan

To create a sound financial plan, financial managers must have a firm grasp of the company's aims for both the short and the long term. Once they know what these are, managers can draw up budgets and identify where the cash flow may exceed or fall short of the company's needs. With this information, managers can arrange in advance to invest any surplus or to acquire additional funds as needed.

Establishing Objectives The objectives of a financial plan must be precise enough so that managers can translate them into numbers. Then, if one objective conflicts with another, someone in management must establish priorities for these objectives. Suppose that a clothing manufacturer plans to introduce a new line of men's sportswear. The firm of course wants to see the new line launched successfully, but it also wants its line of business clothes to continue to do well. In such a situation, management may have to decide which of these objectives is the more important to the company and allocate the firm's resources accordingly.

Budgeting Financial plans for the future, **budgets,** are detailed projections of income and expenses over a specified period. The budgeting process requires financial managers to predict a company's needs at various points. For example, a ski shop's cash budget would show high income during December and January but quite low income in July and August. Yet the pattern of the shop's cash needs

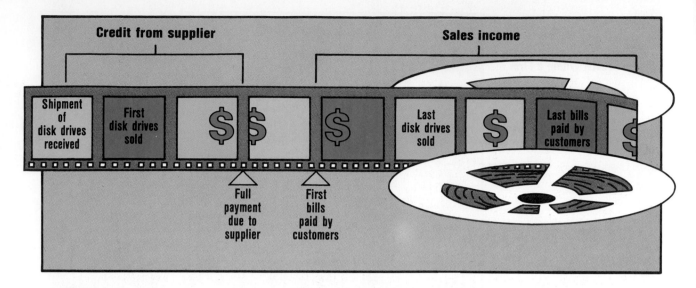

FIGURE 18.2

The Time Gap Between
Expenses and Income

may well be precisely the reverse of its income pattern, because it may have to order and pay for inventory for the next season during the summer.

The budget process can sometimes lead financial managers into involvement in matters of company policy. For instance, if **cash flow**, the movement of money into and out of a firm, is slow and accounts receivable are high, they may argue that the firm is extending too much trade credit (discussed later in this chapter). Other issues that may attract the attention of financial managers include the size of inventories, the amount of insurance coverage that is desirable, the costs of marketing campaigns, the fate of older plants, and the value of automation and computerization.

Financing the Plan

The Need for Financing

From the financial manager's standpoint, implementing a plan consists primarily of financing it. The first option is **internal financing**, money generated from cash flow or retained earnings. This choice is often not available, for liquidity reasons or simply because the company has not yet begun to turn a profit. It might seem that a healthy business would not need the second option, **outside financing**, which is money generated by borrowing from or selling ownership interests to sources outside the business for its use. Most firms do require outside financing at one time or another, however.

Short-term Needs Most firms discover that there is a gap between the time they must pay for inventory and the time when they can expect to receive income. To bridge this gap, a firm will usually obtain a loan. This type of loan is described as **short-term financing**, money that a firm will borrow for a year or less. Virtually every firm must resort to short-term financing at one point or another.

The need for short-term financing is clear in Figure 18.2, which shows what happens when a computer store orders some disk drives. Even if sales of the

Seasonal sales and the need for funds. *It's a long wait from one Christmas tree season to the next. Growers and their employees need money to live on and capital to invest in the operation. Taxes and other bills must be paid. Most businesses in seasonal industries — even the successful ones — depend on short-term financing.*

drives are brisk, the store will probably have to pay its supplier before it can sell all the merchandise. If the store sells the drives on credit, it will have to wait thirty to sixty days for its money. In the meantime, the firm must meet its overhead of rent, salaries, utility bills, and the like.

In seasonal industries, like Christmas tree farms, the time gap between expenses and income can prove especially troublesome. To prepare for the holiday season, such industries must build up their inventories in advance and often pay for them before their season begins.

The Types of Financing

The need for short-term financing can also arise unexpectedly, as in emergencies. For instance, the roof on a warehouse may spring a major leak and require immediate replacement.

Long-term Needs   A business's stability depends on secure **long-term financing,** money that will not be repaid within one year. Generally, long-term financing is used for buying such assets as real property, plants, equipment, and the like. It may also be used to fund the purchase of another company.

As we will see later in this chapter, short-term and long-term financing meet very different needs. Nevertheless, the decision to use either should flow out of a detailed, systematic approach to financial management.

Managing growth. Paul Hawken started Smith & Hawken, Ltd. with his partner David Smith in 1979. This successful company imports and markets high-quality garden tools and has increased its revenues annually ever since by paying attention to quality and to the needs of its customers.

THE USES OF FUNDS

Once a business has raised money, other than to bridge an expense–income gap, its managers must put it to work.

The Nature of Investments

The Uses of Financing

The means of using funds now in order to achieve financial goals in the future is called **investments.** Every investment decision requires weighing three factors: safety, income, and growth.

Safety   The **safety** or security of an investment or its **risk** is judged by the likelihood that the investor will be able to get his or her money back. Given two investment choices with equal returns, an investor will choose the one thought to be safer. The less safe investment will thus always have to offer a higher return to attract investors. As a result, there is a direct relationship between perceived risk and return.

The Three Factors in an Investment Decision

Safety relates to liquidity, too. If you can get your money back whenever you want it, an investment is both safe and liquid. Liquidity minimizes the chances of having a cash-flow problem, which is why every financial manager keeps a portion of a company's assets in cash. However, when an investor demands liquidity, as with a bank account, the financial institution cannot count on having this money for its long-term purposes. And because an institution has transactional costs every time cash comes in or goes out, the more liquid an investment is, the less likely it is to provide a high return. A savings account is the safest, most liquid form of investment, so it pays a very low rate of return.

Income The return that an investment provides is its **income**. To get higher income, an investor must give up either safety or liquidity — or both. If two investments look equally risky, an investor will choose the one offering the higher income.

Growth The measure of increase in the value of an investment is its **growth**. A business grows by reinvesting its earnings in itself, which is to say by compounding its returns rather than by paying them out. Investors may thus trade off income for growth, because an investment that pays out cash to the investor is not using it for reinvestment and growth. There is a corresponding relationship between growth and risk. Investments with high growth potential also have an equal potential for failure.

Acquiring Current Assets

Current assets are the most liquid form of assets, because they are to be used or converted into cash within one year. Cash is a current, but nonproductive, asset.

Inventory The most obvious productive current asset is inventory. A business must have sufficient inventory to fill its orders, but not have so much that its cash is unnecessarily tied up. An automobile dealer's inventory of cars, for instance, usually consists of current assets, because the dealer normally sells the cars within one year. Should sales slow down, though, the cars in stock will be much less useful to the dealer than would cash. By weighing the advantages of inventory against their business's need for liquidity, financial managers influence a firm's purchasing policy.

Marketable Securities To maintain a desired level of liquidity, businesses often keep a certain amount of money in **marketable securities,** securities that can be easily converted into cash without being significantly discounted from market value. Besides the publicly traded stocks and bonds issued by corporations, businesses most commonly purchase commercial paper (discussed under the next section), treasury bills, and certificates of deposit. All three of these securities are **promissory notes,** written contracts involving a promise to pay money.

The Liquidity and Safety of
Various Types of Current Assets

Treasury bills (T-bills) are short-term promissory notes issued weekly by the U.S. Treasury to finance the government's day-to-day cash requirements. The federal government's taxing power backs these obligations.

Certificates of deposit (CDs) are time deposits evidenced by promissory notes issued by a bank. These deposits may be in amounts as small as five hundred dollars and for periods from just days to years. Banks change their interest rates on CDs daily or weekly to reflect changes in the marketplace. Generally, banks pay higher rates for larger deposits and for those to be held for longer terms. Banks impose what is referred to as a penalty for cashing in a CD before the end of its term, but this penalty involves only a reduction in the interest paid. In some cases, holders of large-denomination CDs can sell them directly to a private investor and turn them into cash to avoid this penalty.

Acquiring Fixed Assets

The assets that an organization will use for more than one year are called **fixed assets**. Accountants normally divide such assets into three classes: property, plant, and equipment. **Property**, in the context of fixed assets, refers to land, **plant** applies to buildings, and **equipment** means machinery and tools.

The financial manager plays an especially critical role in acquiring fixed assets. The expenditures for doing so are sizable — a mainframe computer system can

---

BUSINESS ISSUES

Investment Scams

Most of us know better than to pay someone who says he's selling a certain bridge in Brooklyn. Yet every year thousands of investors are lured into putting their money into equally dubious schemes, often with only a slick-talker's guarantee of a return. Greed makes people do strange things, and it doesn't seem to be going away.

Although recent losers thought they were investing in oil exploration or foreign currency trading, rather than in the salad oil scheme of the 1960s or the postal coupon scheme of the 1920s, today's investors and swindlers are familiar to anyone who has followed the history of con artists. The swindlers are usually very smooth, like-able people who take a personal interest in an investor's problems. Such people quickly develop a sense of trust, and often fierce loyalty, among those whom they have persuaded.

Word of mouth is often the swindler's biggest ally. Once three or four investors are sold on a scheme, they tend to talk about it at gatherings of the rich and soon all their friends are buying in, not wanting to be left behind when the big profits start to roll. Although most scams are backed by assets that appear only on paper and by promises of profits around the next corner, some early investors generally do make money, and of course they enthusiastically spread the word. Even seasoned, knowledgeable investors ask few questions when someone who has been highly recommended promises to double their money in a matter of months.

The scene for one of the most widely publicized recent frauds was San Diego, and the villain was J. David Dominelli, formerly known by enthusiastic investors as "the

Genius." The investors were many of Southern California's most respected citizens, including San Diego Mayor Roger Hedgecock.

Dominelli built a reputation as a trader in international currency, and he promised yearly returns of up to 40 percent. "A master at making people believe him," as one investor put it, Dominelli made friends with the right people in the social and political world of San Diego. He attracted investors with glowing reports of how well his company was doing. And, as his own wealth increased, he gave lavishly to charities.

Things began unraveling for Dominelli in 1984, when investors' withdrawal checks started to bounce. Dominelli finally fled to the Caribbean but was brought back to the United States. He took the Fifth Amendment many times as the court probed into what had happened to $112 million that belonged to 1500 investors. In 1985 a federal judge sentenced Dominelli to 20 years in prison.

Con men today may be more sophisticated than those of the eighteenth century who solicited investments in perpetual motion machines and boards made out of saw-dust. But many of their methods are similar, and the results are almost always the same — everyone loses. If they're lucky, the investors are a little wiser the next time.

Sources: "Bunco Artists Are Waiting in the Wings," *U.S. News & World Report*, Vol. 96, No. 22, June 4, 1984, 67. Allan Sloan, "Drilling for Suckers," *Forbes*, Vol. 133, No. 13, June 4, 1984, 36–38. "Where's That $112 Million?" *Newsweek*, Vol. 103, No. 20, May 14, 1984, 53. Robert Lindsey, "The Dominelli Affair," *The New York Times Magazine*, June 3, 1984, 53. "20-Year Term for Dominelli," *The New York Times*, June 25, 1985, D23.

---

easily cost $1 million or more. To finance such assets can require a sophisticated approach. A commercial jet liner, for instance, costs over $20 million and is typically acquired through a commercial credit company like G.E. Credit. In evaluating such commitments, financial managers consider not only the effect such expenditures will have on cash flow and potential profitability but also the degree of risk involved.

SOURCES OF SHORT-TERM FINANCING

As we have seen, short-term financing refers to funds that a firm will use for a year or less. Short-term financing is normally unsecured, not backed by collateral.

Unsecured Short-term Financing

Some of the most common sources of unsecured short-term financing are trade credit, promissory notes to suppliers, bank loans, and commercial paper. These are discussed below.

Common Sources of Short-term Financing: Unsecured Loans

Trade Credit   Many suppliers will grant buyers financing in the form of **trade credit,** an agreement whereby a supplier sells goods or services to a buyer but does not require immediate payment. In some cases, payment is not due for a specific period, such as thirty, sixty, or ninety days. In other arrangements, the buyer makes periodic installments. Trade credit is the most available form of credit. It is also the cheapest form, because the supplier usually spreads the cost of trade credit among its customers by building these costs into its own cost of goods sold.

Promissory Notes to Suppliers   In some cases, a supplier may have reason enough not to grant trade credit to a customer. A poor credit rating, a history of slow payment, and a large order in relation to the customer's ability to repay are common reasons. In these situations, the supplier may insist that the customer sign a promissory note as a condition for extending credit.

One advantage of a promissory note is that it clearly specifies the customer's obligation, usually including the interest to be paid. Another advantage is that if the supplier needs cash before the note comes due, it may be able to sell the note to a bank. This process is called **discounting,** the sale of a promissory note to a bank for the amount of the note less a discount for the bank's services. The bank then assumes the responsibility for collecting from the customer when the note comes due.

Bank Loans   Aside from suppliers, the most common sources of short-term financing are financial institutions. Companies with good credit ratings can often arrange unsecured short-term bank loans. However, in place of collateral, banks often require what is called a **compensation balance,** an amount that a firm must keep on deposit with a financial institution during the term of a loan or the period covered by a line of credit (discussed below). For example, a firm might have to maintain a $10,000 compensating balance in order to borrow $50,000.

The cost of borrowing from a bank is usually described in terms of the **prime rate** (or simply "the prime"), the interest rate a bank charges the largest and most reliable customers that borrow from it regularly. Other customers must pay from 2 to 4 percent above the prime, depending on the bank's evaluation of their creditworthiness. The prime fluctuates with the Federal Reserve Board's discount rate. A financial manager must therefore regularly monitor the economy to try to time borrowings when the prime is relatively low.

Bank loans take three forms: promissory notes, lines of credit, and revolving credit agreements. A promissory note to a bank is the same as a promissory note to a supplier. A **line of credit** results from an agreement with a bank that over a specified period it will lend up to a certain amount at a set rate of interest, as the borrower needs the funds. The borrower pays interest only on what it borrows. Note that the bank is not legally obligated to honor the line of credit. By contrast, a **revolving credit agreement** is a line of credit backed by a bank's legally enforceable guarantee that the money will be available whenever the borrower wants it. The bank will charge a **commitment fee** for its guarantee and may also require a compensating balance.

Commercial Paper   Large corporations often acquire short-term financing by selling **commercial paper,** unsecured promissory notes issued by a corporation that mature in from 3 to 270 days. Such notes typically have a face value of $100,000 or more. This form of financing usually carries a lower rate of interest than a bank loan, and the issuer, the seller of the note, does not have to maintain a compensating balance. Commercial paper is normally sold at a discount from its face value. The difference between its actual price and its face value represents what the purchases will earn on the loan. Typical buyers of commercial paper include banks, pension funds, and mutual funds.

Secured Short-term Financing

Both commercial banks and commercial finance companies grant secured short-term loans. Small companies or new ones, companies with mediocre credit ratings, and firms that already owe a good deal of money are among the poorer candidates for unsecured financing. To minimize the lender's risk, such firms often have to put up collateral that may exceed the value of the loan by as much as 20 to 30 percent. Any relatively liquid asset will do, but lenders tend to look to inventory and accounts receivable to secure such loans. Often, lenders to such firms demand that the firm's owners cosign the note. The interest rates on such loans tend to be higher than on unsecured loans because of the borrower's lack of creditworthiness and the expenses of obtaining and liquidating collateral.

Inventory as Collateral   Companies that sell goods often have much of their capital tied up in inventory. Lenders prefer security in the form of finished, readily salable goods, but they will sometimes accept raw materials, parts, or components.

Accounts Receivable as Collateral   Accounts receivable are usually created when trade credit is extended. Normally, these accounts are due in not more than sixty days. However, if a firm needs cash more quickly than it

"Before I read the financial report I suggest a moment of prayer . . . . !"

Common Sources of Short-term Financing: Secured Loans

The Tale of the Kited Checks

The technologies of the modern financial world — computers and instant information transfer systems — have led to a new kind of crime and a new breed of criminal. Computer experts have programmed bank computers to send money to their own secret accounts. But one of the most famous of recent high-tech crimes resulted not from any overtly illegal act. Instead, the people involved profited from their knowledge of the technologies of money and information transfer. It was their timing that got them in trouble.

Have you ever written a check on Thursday, knowing that you didn't really have enough money in your account, but hoping you could deposit your pay on Friday before the check bounced? If so, what you did, in effect, was get a free one-day loan from your bank for the amount you were technically overdrawn. But if no one asked any questions and you did deposit your paycheck on Friday, you probably didn't get into any trouble.

In the spring of 1985 E. F. Hutton, the nation's fifth-largest brokerage firm, was fined $2 million for doing on a much larger and more complicated scale what you did when you stretched your bank account at the end of the week. In a scheme known as "check-kiting," branch offices of the firm would write checks that they could not at that moment cover, transfer the checks to other Hutton branches or use the money to pay Hutton's bills, and then later deposit money to cover the checks before they "bounced." Such schemes work because it takes a check a few days to get cleared and to return to the bank it was drawn on and because many banks routinely allow big corporations to draw on deposited checks before they clear. By using instant money transfers Hutton could catch up with its bad checks before they bounced. In essence, the company was getting interest-free loans for the 2 or 3 days until the check was cleared.

Until you start looking at the figures involved, "borrowing" money for so short a period of time may not seem like "a swindle of stunning proportions," as one observer called it. Over 100 Hutton branches participated, using money in 400 commercial bank accounts, in effect getting as much as a quarter-million dollars a day in interest-free loans. The banks involved ranged from giants like Chase Manhattan to tiny Cape Cod Bank & Trust of Hyannis, Massachusetts. Over a year-and-a-half period between 1980 and 1982, when short-term interest rates were as high as 20 percent, the scheme may have involved as much as $10 billion.

The company pleaded guilty to 2000 separate criminal charges of mail and wire fraud, and a Federal judge in Pennsylvania imposed the maximum penalty of $1000 per charge. But that was only the beginning of the problems Hutton created for itself. The company also agreed to pay the government's costs for the investigation — $750,000 — and it may have to pay up to $20 million to the banks now making claims for the interest they weren't paid years ago.

Sources: Spencer Davidson, "A $2 Million Fine for Kited Checks," *Time*, Vol. 125, No. 19, May 13, 1985, 51. Susan Dentzger, "E. F. Hutton: It's Not Over Yet," *Newsweek*, Vol. 105, No. 20, May 20, 1985, 52. "They Shouldn't Have Listened," *Fortune*, Vol. 111, No. 11, May 27, 1985, 8. "Black Day for a Wall Street Giant," *U.S. News & World Report*, Vol. 98, No. 18, May 13, 1985, 12. William B. Glaberson, "The Punishment of Hutton Doesn't Fit the Crime," *Business Week*, No. 2897, June 3, 1985, 40.

can collect these debts, it can pledge them as security for a loan. As it collects the accounts receivable, it repays the lender.

A related, but quite different practice, is called **factoring,** the selling of a firm's accounts receivable to another firm called a **factor,** which then owns and collects the debts. Customers are often told to pay the factor directly. Because a factor assumes all risk of bad debts, it pays considerably less than the face value of accounts receivable. A factor is thus an expensive source of short-term financing.

EQUITY FINANCING

Long-term financing provides stability so that a company can expand, buy new equipment, develop products, acquire other companies, and make other capital expenditures. Long-term financing takes two forms. **Equity** represents the value of the owner's investments in a firm. A company can raise money by selling additional equity. **Debt**, discussed in the next section, represents borrowed money. Table 18.1 summarizes the growth of a hypothetical company and the ways it might meet its long-term financing needs.

The Nature of Equity

All businesses start with some equity capital, which is the assets that the owners invest to get the business off the ground. The monetary value of those assets stays in the business and forms the basis for the company's long-term financing. The owners of a small business may dig into their own pockets for these assets or seek partners to supply the cash. A business with seemingly great potential may attract a **venture capitalist**, an investor willing to put money into a business in exchange for a substantial block of stock.

Generally, when we speak of equity financing, we mean the issuing of additional stock by a corporation. **Stock** is a security in the form of an ownership interest in a corporation. In the next chapter, we will examine what a security is and what it means to have this designation. For now, the basic idea can be summed up in the following equation:

$$\text{Equity} = \text{Ownership} = \text{Stock}$$

By definition, shares of stock represent ownership interests in a corporation, but not all ownership rights are equal. Ownership brings with it a right to share in any distributions of profits, but again this right varies among the various classes and types of stock.

Common Stock

By law, every corporation must have common stock. A corporation may in fact have several classes of it, as General Motors and Wang Laboratories do, but one class of common stock must come with **voting rights**, the right to vote for directors and on extraordinary transactions, like a merger, that will affect the nature of the company. In other words, common shareholders (or one class of them) exercise the essential rights of ownership of the corporation.

Share Valuation   A share of common stock, as depicted by the certificate in Figure 18.3, represents ownership of a portion of the net worth of a company. **Net worth** is determined by subtracting the value of a company's liabilities and preferred stock from the assets reflected on its balance sheet. Net worth is a relatively uncommon way to value shares, though.

The Types of Equity Financing: Common Stock

Year 1	
Start-up Capital	To begin, Marcie and Jim each contribute their savings to the business. Marcie has $2,000 and Jim has $142.12. This $2,142.12 is their initial equity financing.
Trade Credit	When they order company stationery, their printer sends a thirty-day invoice. They plan to take advantage of this credit by waiting to pay until the full month expires.
Promissory Note to Supplier	When MJ Associates fails to pay for the stationery on time, the printer becomes impatient. Jim signs a note promising to pay within twenty additional days.
Unsecured Bank Loan	On the strength of the company's first large contract, a deal to adapt inventory-control software for a lumber-supply house, Marcie negotiates a small, short-term unsecured bank loan. With this, MJ Associates can cover its expenses until the contract begins to pay off.
Year 2	
Commercial Draft	MJ purchases new computer equipment, signing a time draft that obligates the company to pay the supplier on a certain date.
Secured Bank Loan	Jim and Marcie convince the bank to supply additional funding, but this time the bank requires a written pledge of monies due from the lumber-supply house and other clients.
Year 3	
Stock Issue	Incorporating their business, Marcie and Jim sell shares of the company — common stock — to relatives, friends, and other investors.
Long-term Bank Loan	With several employees and a multitude of contracts, MJ needs a bigger office. Jim and Marcie decide to buy a building that the company can grow into. A bank puts up a mortgage loan, which is secured by the building and land.
Years 4–5	
Retained Earnings	Because the company's rapid growth demands plenty of cash, most of its earnings are retained rather than being distributed to the stockholders.
Year 10	
Commercial Paper, Bonds	Now a major corporation, MJ can finance many of its short-term needs with commercial paper and its long-term needs with bonds. Because the firm's reputation is soaring, these securities are snapped up by corporate investors.

TABLE 18.1

Financing Arrangements for a Hypothetical Company

Scenario: Marcie and Jim meet and realize that Marcie has ideas for new types of software that Jim might be able to develop. They decide to go into business together as MJ Associates.

The three most common ways to value shares are

☐ Par value
☐ Book value
☐ Market value

The **par value** of a security is its stated or face value. Today, par value has virtually no meaning *as applied to common stocks.* Most states now permit corporations to issue **no-par shares,** or shares that are not assigned a dollar value.

Book value is the value of a company's net worth as represented by a common share. It can be calculated as follows:

FIGURE 18.3

A Stock Certificate

$$\text{Book Value} = \frac{\text{Assets} - (\text{Liabilities} + \text{Preferred Stock})}{\text{Common Shares Outstanding}}$$

Book value gives a very conservative value to shares, because it does not reflect their potential for appreciation. It merely shows what the shares would bring if the company were to be liquidated.

One stock valuation method that does indicate a company's potential is called **market value**, the current price that a willing buyer will pay a willing seller. This price is the one published in newspapers if the stock is publicly traded and is the price one must pay in a private transaction. The market price may be affected not only by a company's performance but also by its competitors' performance, the market's mood, the economy's general condition, and other factors having nothing to do with the company itself. A stock whose book value exceeds its market value is termed **undervalued**.

Stock Splits   Individual investors today prefer to buy stocks in the $15 to $35 range because they can then afford to buy 100-share lots and thus save on brokerage commissions. When a stock's market price is so high that many investors do not want to buy it, a company may decide to "split" its stock. When a **stock split** takes place, a company issues to shareholders one or more additional shares for each share currently held. A split increases the number of shares outstanding and reduces their market price proportionately, but it does not change the percentage that a shareholder owns.

When the share price is too low to be attractive, the company's directors may implement a **reverse split,** reducing the number of shares outstanding and raising their market price.

Preemptive Rights   Under some states' laws, shareholders may have a **preemptive right,** the right to buy additional shares to preserve their ownership

Equity financing. Debbi and Randy Fields built their small business into a big operation with over 345 outlets. Mrs. Fields Cookies needed more money than it could get from cash flow to fund its continued growth. The Fields offered stock in the company on the London exchange.

positions if the company issues additional shares to the public. Not all states recognize this right. Even where it is recognized, the articles of incorporation may deny it to shareholders.

Dividends   Ownership brings with it a right to share in **dividends,** that portion of a company's earnings that the board of directors votes to distribute to stockholders on a per-share basis in either cash or stock. The directors have no legal obligation to vote a dividend, much less one of a certain amount.

Most growing companies do not declare cash dividends, preferring to retain any earnings in the business. Even some multibillion-dollar companies like the Tandy Corporation with its $2.8 billion in sales do not pay dividends. It might seem that retaining earnings is unfair to shareholders, but most shareholders are more concerned with appreciation in the value of their shares than they are with quarterly dividend checks. Still, some investors do look for a steady, high dividend. Table 18.2 lists some companies with extraordinary dividend records.

Cash dividends are dividends voted by the directors to be paid by the company to its shareholders. These dividends are expressed in terms of so many cents or dollars per share. Shareholders who owned their shares as of a specified date, the **record date,** receive dividends. Even if the shareholder sells the shares between the record date and the payment date, payment will still be made to the shareholder of record. Sales of the shares after the record date are sold **ex-dividend,** that is, without the dividend.

Sometimes a company wishes to reward its shareholders but still conserve cash. In such a situation it may issue a **stock dividend,** a dividend in the form of shares in the corporation's stock. For example, a corporation might issue one

TABLE 18.2

Annual Dividend Payments Since before 1900

Began in	Stock	Began in	Stock
1784	Bank of New York Co., Inc.	1881	Corning Glass Works
1784	First National Boston Corp.	1882	Bell Canada*
1791	Fleet Financial Group, Inc.	1883	Carter-Wallace, Inc.
1813	Citicorp	1883	Chesebrough-Pond's Inc.
1813	First Nat'l State Bancorporation	1883	Exxon Corp.
1827	Chemical New York Corp.*	1885	Consolidated Edison Co.
1848	Chase Manhattan Corp.	1885	Eli Lilly and Co.
1850	Connecticut Energy Corp.	1885	UGI Corp.
1851	Connecticut Natural Gas Corp.*	1886	Hackensack Water Co.
1851	Manhattan National Corp.	1890	American Brands, Inc.
1852	Manufacturers Hanover Corp.	1890	Boston Edison Co.*
1852	Washington Gas Light Co.*	1890	Commonwealth Edison Co.*
1853	Cincinnati Gas & Electric Co.	1890	Hydraulic Co.
1853	Continental Corp.	1890	Procter & Gamble Co.*
1856	Scovill Inc.	1891	Southern New England Tel. Co.*
1863	Pennwalt Corp.	1892	Times Mirror Co.
1863	Singer Company	1893	Coca-Cola Co.
1865	Irving Bank Corp.*	1894	Standard Oil Co. (Indiana)
1866	Travelers Corp.	1895	Colgate-Palmolive Co.
1867	CIGNA Corp.	1895	Mellon National Corp.*
1868	American Express Co.	1898	General Mills, Inc.
1877	Stanley Works*	1898	Springs Industries, Inc.
1879	Cincinnati Bell Inc.*	1899	Borden, Inc.
1881	American Tel. & Tel. Co.*	1899	General Electric Co.*

*Unbroken quarterly record since the nineteenth century.

Source: From New York Stock Exchange, *1983 Yearbook* (New York: N.Y. Stock Exchange, 1983), p. 30. Used by permission.

new share for every ten already held, thus increasing the number of shares outstanding by 10 percent. The shareholders would then have the same percentage of ownership, but each share would be worth proportionately less.

Preferred Stock

In addition to raising money through common stock, some companies attract capital by issuing preferred stock. **Preferred stock** is a class of stock "that pays dividends at a specified rate and that has preference over common stock in the payment of dividends and the liquidation of assets."[4] Like a loan, preferred stock pays a specified dividend, stated either as a percentage of the par value or, more commonly, as a specific amount. The company must pay this preferred dividend before it can pay any dividend on its common stock. In addition, should the company be liquidated, the preferred shares are **redeemed** (paid at par) in full before anything is paid on the common stock. Frequently, a preferred stock's

TABLE 18.3

Types of Preferred Stock

Type of Preferred	Description
Cumulative	If the corporation fails to make a dividend payment to preferred of this type, it must pay all accumulated unpaid dividends before it can pay any dividends on the common.
Noncumulative	If the corporation omits a dividend, the shareholders have no claim against the corporation for it; the opposite of cumulative.
Participating	In years when the corporation does well, shareholders receive a fixed dividend and, perhaps, after the common dividend is paid, a bonus.
Callable or redeemable	Stock that a corporation has a right to repurchase at its option; usually, the higher the dividend, the more rapidly it is called or redeemed.
Convertible	Stock that can be exchanged for common at a certain fixed ratio of preferred to common; this feature often allows a corporation to offer a lower dividend rate.

indenture, a formal legal agreement between the issuer and the holder, contains a **call feature,** a provision allowing the company itself to redeem it.

Purposes   Companies usually issue preferred stock when they need funds and either cannot or do not wish to increase their debt levels or stockholder bases. The preferred's dividend, which is paid out of after-tax profits, has the advantage of being an identifiable expense that companies can plan for.

Sometimes a company issues preferred stock to pay for an acquisition when it wishes to limit the dilution of its existing shareholders' ownership while making the transaction attractive to the acquired company's shareholders. In addition, if the acquiring company's financial planning is sound, the earnings of the acquired company will do three things:

☐ Pay for the preferred dividends.
☐ Generate a **sinking fund,** a fund set aside by the company, generally according to a formula based on profits or time, to redeem particular issues of preferred stock or debt.
☐ Produce income or an improved marketplace opportunity for the acquiring company so that the common shareholders benefit further.

Cumulative and Noncumulative Dividends   Preferred stock pays dividends rather than interest, and a company has no legal obligation to pay dividends. If dividends are to be paid, then, a company's preferred shareholders must receive theirs before the common shareholders do. However, the indenture may specify that the dividends are **cumulative**, meaning that the company must pay all preferred dividends for past periods before paying any common stock dividends. A noncumulative issue's dividend will be higher than a cumulative one's on equivalent stock, to make up for the risk of its being skipped.

Suppose that a company **passed its dividend** (did not pay it) on its cumulative preferred in 1986. If the directors want to pay dividends on either preferred or common stock in 1987, they must first authorize payment of the 1986 preferred dividend. Then if they wish to pay a dividend on the common stock for 1987, they must pay the 1987 preferred dividend first.

The indenture will sometimes provide that if the dividends are passed for a certain period — often, three consecutive years — the preferred shareholders can then determine the composition of the board of directors and vote on the other decisions normally reserved for the common shareholders.

Participating and Nonparticipating Stock   The type of stock called **participating preferred stock** is preferred stock that may, under circumstances specified in the indenture, participate in the dividend distributions on the common shares. Participating preferred stock is unusual. Most preferred stock is **nonparticipating**, meaning that it receives only the stated dividend.

Convertibility   Another way that companies limit their dividend and redemption obligations is by issuing **convertible preferred stock,** preferred stock whose indenture includes the right to convert a share into some number of common shares. Typically, investors forego a certain amount of interest as payment for convertibility. For a start-up company that expects to grow, offering investors convertible preferred stock provides the firm the advantage of debt in its early years and, after conversion, the advantage of capital appreciation.

DEBT FINANCING

Debt appeals to financial managers because it is a predictable, stable source of long-term financing. The advantage that debt financing has over equity is its fixed rather than open end. Shares last forever, but debt expires when it is paid off. Also, debt tends to carry a fixed interest rate, so companies like to use it when they think that inflation and interest rates are likely to climb over the loan's term. They gamble that they can pay off the debt with cheaper dollars than they originally borrowed. Debt takes two basic forms: loans and bonds. Again, though, as with equities, there are many variations on the forms.

Loans

Long-Term-Debt Financing: Loans

Long-term loans are often used to finance the purchase of new equipment or other major expenditures. Although repayment periods vary widely, they average between three and five years. The borrower signs a promissory note and makes payments on a regular schedule, just like an individual with an auto or a mortgage loan. The goods purchased with the proceeds of the loan usually secure the repayment of it, though the lender may demand other collateral, too. Common lenders include financial institutions, insurance companies, commercial credit companies, and pension funds. In some instances, manufacturers of heavy equipment will make the loans themselves, but on terms that resemble those of a bank loan rather than trade credit.

INTERNATIONAL BUSINESS

We Owe the World

The United States is a debtor nation. We owe more money to foreigners than foreigners owe us. We may already be the greatest debtor nation in the world. For years, economists will be discussing how we got here, and what effect our debtor status has. Most are worried.

The situation is not entirely new for the U.S. We were a debtor nation until the First World War. But in the second half of the 19th century, the money we were borrowing from other countries financed tremendous expansion as America industrialized and moved west. Now, much of our borrowed money goes to pay for our high-consumption society and the interest on our government's debt. We are living beyond our means.

The roots of the situation are numerous and complex. A strong dollar and high interest rates lure foreign money into the U.S. When foreigners can make more by investing in American companies than in their own, the money floods in. Without foreign capital, the government would have to raise its interest rates in order to attract money from investors. Such high interest rates could spur inflation and would make it difficult for businesses to find investors.

Our trade deficit also contributes to the problem. We buy more things abroad than we sell to other countries. That leaves our biggest trading partners, like Japan, with a surplus of dollars which they often, in turn, invest in the U.S. In fact, as the U.S. has become the world's biggest debtor, Japan has become its biggest creditor.

The 1981 tax cut must take some of the blame for the current situation. Our account balance with the world slipped some in the late 1970s but has gotten radically worse since 1982. The tax cut put more money in the pockets of Americans and was expected to increase savings. Instead, most Americans spent. This increased spending helped pull both the U.S. and the rest of the world out of a recession. A healthier American economy made investment in America more attractive, and Americans with money in their pockets often bought goods from Japan and Western Europe.

So what does our debtor status mean for our future? Gloomy economists note that Britain lost its international stature at about the same time it lost its creditor status. Without a sudden balancing of the Federal budget or our trade deficit, we seem destined to borrow more and more just to pay the interest on our debts.

On the bright side, foreign investment in the U.S. produces jobs, and stimulates the economy. And we do have some control over the situation. Shifts in Federal fiscal policy could turn the tide of cash, as could future business cycles. If the value of the dollar falls, foreign goods will be more expensive for Americans and American goods cheaper for foreigners, changing the cash flow. Another recession could leave Americans with less to spend on overseas goods and could make American companies less attractive to foreign investors.

The problem will not go away instantly, and it may plague future generations of Americans. But unlike a number of Third World countries, we're not likely to soon find ourselves drowning in our debt.

Sources: George P. Brockway, "Becoming a Debtor Nation," *The New Leader*, February 24, 1986, 11. David Hale, "U.S. as Debtor: A Threat to World Trade," *The New York Times*, September 27, 1985, F2. "Uncle Sam Could Soon Be One of the World's Biggest Debtors," *Business Week*, February 27, 1984, 106.

One place to start looking for funds. A loan and some good advice from a bank can make all the difference in the world. Nancy Stow opened a retail store with four friends. None of the five had much experience. They give part of the credit for their success — they now have four stores and plan for more — to the bank that had faith in a fledgling business and explained what could be done to get it off the ground.

Bonds

Long-term-Debt Instruments: Bonds

You have probably heard the expression "his word is his bond." A bond in this context is an obligation to perform. A **corporate bond** is a long-term obligation to pay, usually represented by a certificate of indebtedness, as in Figure 18.4. By issuing such bonds a corporation promises to pay the investor a specified rate of interest (the **coupon rate**) on set dates until the bond's **maturity date,** the date on which the corporation will redeem the bond by paying its par value. The maturity date can be as far as forty years in the future. Bonds are normally issued in par-value multiples of $1,000 and may reach $50,000 for a single bond. Public offerings of bonds work like those of stocks.

Bonds do not bring with them an ownership interest in the **issuer,** an entity with the power to authorize the sale and distribution of securities on its behalf. Rather, the bondholder is entitled only to the payment of interest and principal in accordance with the terms of the bond's indenture. Should the issuer fail to make the payments on schedule, it can be forced into bankruptcy. The federal Trust Indenture Act of 1939 requires that each bond issue have an independent **trustee,** a person or (usually) a firm that protects the bondholders' interests by making sure that the issuer meets its obligations under the indenture.

The Advantages and Disadvantages of Bonds

Secured and Unsecured Debt Like all loans, bonds are either secured or unsecured, and the security can take various forms. Mortgage bonds, for instance, are secured by fixed assets like land and buildings, just as an individual's home mortgage loan is. Collateral trust bonds are secured by other securities that the issuer owns. Equipment bonds are secured by equipment and machinery used in the business, like railroad cars or an assembly line. In contrast, only the issuer's good faith and good reputation guarantee an unsecured bond, which is called a **debenture.**

Redemption Bond issues can pose a major problem for an issuer that does not plan ahead. Normally, all the bonds in a particular issue mature on the same date. If a corporation sold, say, $400 million in one issue, it would have to repay the entire amount all at once. To avoid this problem, an issuer may choose to sell **serial bonds,** bonds of one issue but that mature on different dates. Another common method is to establish a sinking fund. Often this fund is in the hands of an outside trustee, who is charged with ensuring that the company lives up to its obligations.

Quite commonly, the indenture will require the issuer to call bonds for redemption periodically. Before buying a bond, an investor should check to determine when and under what circumstances it is callable. Making a bond callable is a device designed to protect the issuer, not the holder. For example, in early 1985, Minstar, Inc., issued $300 million in 14⅞ percent bonds to finance its acquisition of AMF, Inc. With interest rates running at about 9 percent, the bonds were trading at 112 percent of their par value, $1,000. Because of an obscure provision in the indenture, Minstar a year later began calling the bonds for redemption at par. Thus, the bondholders faced the prospect of losing the benefit of an excellent interest rate. What's more, those who paid a **premium,** more than par, for the bonds would lose it. However, from the company's point of view, for every $30 million it called, Minstar would save $4.5 million annually in interest.[5]

Convertibility Some corporate bonds are convertible into shares of common stock. As with preferred stock, the indenture will specify a conversion rate, that is, the number of shares available for each $1,000 bond.

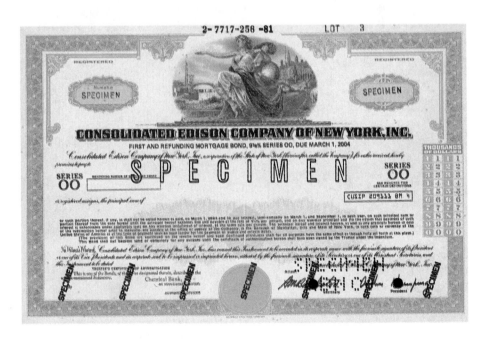

FIGURE 18.4

A Bond

FINANCIAL MANAGEMENT: A PERSPECTIVE

As we have seen, financial management has responsibility for

☐ Performing financial analysis and planning
☐ Managing a firm's asset structure
☐ Managing a firm's financial structure

The balance sheet is financial management's report card. A firm's overall condition reflects the quality of the financial analysis and planning. The left side of the balance sheet reveals the firm's asset structure, and the right side shows its financial structure.[6]

The way in which many people appraise financial management's report card has changed, because companies have come to use long-term debt instead of equity to finance expansion. An important financial ratio, **long-term debt to equity,** measures the relationship between bonds and shareholders' equity, as in this formula:

$$\frac{\text{Bonds}}{\text{Shareholders' Equity}} = \text{leverage ratio}$$

The resulting percentage represents the firm's **leverage,** its use of debt to improve the return on its shareholders' equity.[7]

Since the 1960s, managers have tended to operate with high degrees of leverage. They have done so because if they can use borrowed money to raise profits, the shareholders earn more for each dollar invested. Also, long-term debt eliminates the need to dilute the current shareholders' equity. Another major reason for borrowing is that the interest paid on either bonds or bank

FIGURE 18.5

Leverage

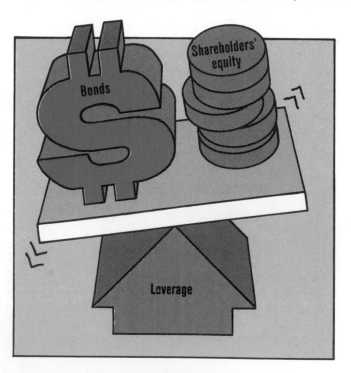

loans is tax deductible. Dividends paid to shareholders are not. Finally, when inflation dominates the economy, borrowing appears wise because the debt is repaid with cheaper dollars.

Traditionally, a 55 percent debt–equity ratio was regarded as the top percentage a first-quality firm could have[8] and, from a potential lender's standpoint, the lower the better. Today, a number of firms' debt–equity ratios exceed 70 percent. For instance, Minstar's debt equaled 77 percent of total equity in early 1986.[9] Highly leveraged balance sheets are now regarded with more skepticism. An old saying goes, "There's no such thing as a free lunch," and those who once bet that inflation would last forever found that it at least paused in the mid-1980s. The drop in the inflation rate proved quite painful for those financial managers who had not recognized the risks of a potential change in the economic weather and taken cover under equity financing.

Chapter Highlights

1. Describe the financial management function and distinguish it from the other finance-related activities within a business.

Financial management is the process of obtaining money and using it effectively to achieve an organization's goals. In a small business, the owner may manage the finances. In a large corporation, the finance manager is often given the title of vice-president of finance. The controller reports to the vice-president of finance and has responsibility for accounting, data processing, and taxes. The treasurer also reports to the vice-president of finance and has responsibility for overseeing and planning for the firm's expenditures and income.

2. List the elements of a financial plan.

To create a sound financial plan, financial managers must have a firm grasp of the company's objectives for the short- and long-term. Once the company's objectives are identified, the managers can draw up budgets and identify where cash flow may exceed or fall short of the company's needs. Budgets are detailed projections of income and expenses over a specified period.

3. Describe the two major sources of funds for a financial plan.

From the financial manager's standpoint, implementing a financial plan consists primarily of financing it. The first option is internal financing, money generated from cash flow or retained earnings. The second option is outside financing, money generated by borrowing from or selling ownership interests to sources outside of the business.

4. Identify the major sources of short-term financing.

In most cases, short-term financing is unsecured, not backed by collateral. The most common sources of unsecured short-term financing are: trade credit, promissory notes to suppliers, bank loans, commercial paper, and commercial drafts. The most common form of secured short-term financing is the use of inventory or accounts receivable as collateral.

5. Describe the types of equity financing used by businesses.

Most business firms start with some equity capital, such as the assets the owners invest to get the business off the ground. Generally, when we speak of equity financing, we mean the issuing of stock by a corporation. Stock is a security in the form of an ownership interest in the corporation. This ownership can be represented in the form of common or preferred stock.

6. List and describe the principal types of long-term debt financing.

Debt is a predictable, stable source of long-term financing. Long-term loans represent one form of debt financing. The repayment periods average between three and five years. Corporate bonds, a long-term obligation to pay usually represented by a certificate of indebtedness, represents another form of debt financing. Bonds do not bring with them an ownership interest in the issuer.

Key Terms

Book value
Call feature
Cash dividend
Cash flow
Certificates of deposit (CDs)
Commercial paper
Commitment fee
Compensating balance
Corporate bond
Coupon rate
Debenture
Debt

Discounting
Dividends
Equity
Ex-dividend
Factoring
Financial management
Fixed assets
Indenture
Investment
Issuer
Leverage
Long-term debt to equity

Long-term financing
Market value
Marketable securities
Maturity date
Net worth
Par value
Preemptive right
Premium
Prime rate
Promissory note
Reverse split
Revolving credit agreement

Serial bonds
Short-term financing
Sinking fund
Stock
Stock dividend
Stock split
Trade credit
Treasury bills (T-bills)
Trustee
Unsecured
Voting rights

Review Questions

1. What is the major role of financial management in a modern business?
2. In what ways do the controller and the treasurer assist the vice-president of finance in a corporate setting?
3. What is a budget? What is involved in the budgeting process?
4. What are current assets? Describe some common forms of current assets.
5. Distinguish between internal financing and outside financing.
6. When a company decides to make investments, what three decisions must be weighed?
7. List and describe four sources of unsecured short-term financing.
8. What is equity financing? What are the advantages of financing through the sale of stock?
9. How does preferred stock differ from common stock? Why do companies issue preferred stock?
10. What is debt financing? What are the two basic forms of debt financing?

Application Exercises

1. Obtain an annual report from a corporation. Study the report and obtain the following information: a. List the name and title of the officers involved in financial management; b. Identify the types of long-term financing used by the company.

2. You are planning to purchase a home for investment purposes. The home will be rented and rental income will be applied to monthly payments. Establish a budget showing your projected income and expenses for the first year.

Cases

18.1 Profit Down, Stock Up

Cigna Corporation has subsidiaries that sell just about every kind of insurance there is. Like other insurance companies, Cigna must show, in the same accounting period, both the premium earned on each policy and the costs associated with that policy. This means that Cigna must estimate future claims costs on every policy and immediately take those costs out of earnings. The future claims costs, which are called *reserves*, become balance-sheet liabilities (money owed to policyholders). The pay-out of a claim reduces the firm's reserves.

The process of estimating future claims is far from exact; for that reason, reserves are reviewed periodically. When an insurer decides its reserves are too low, it takes extra money out of current earnings to bolster them. In 1984, Cigna decided its reserves had to be increased by $224 million to reflect increasing claims on its older policies. That left the firm with a profit of $103 million for the year. Investors weren't especially happy about the two-thirds reduction in earnings, but probably felt it was necessary. Now, at least, reserves were realistic.

Then, in January 1986, Cigna announced that it was increasing its reserves by an additional $1.2 billion. That took everyone by surprise — investors and analysts alike. Instead of an expected 1985 profit of perhaps $300 million, the firm ended up with $733 million loss. Again, increased claims were blamed.

As you might expect, the market price of Cigna's stock dropped sharply — by about 7 percent in one day. But as you might not expect, that price began to rise the very next day; and it continued to increase until it came near to its high for the previous twelve-month period. Why the increase? It's hard to tell, but perhaps investors agreed with Cigna's chairman when he said the huge addition to reserve "improves our outlook for 1986 and beyond."

Questions

1. In what ways could Cigna finance its $1.2 billion addition to reserves?
2. Which sources of financing would you recommend to Cigna, and why?

For more information see *Fortune*, March 17, 1986, pp. 46–47; *National Underwriter*, February 8, 1986, pp. 3, 38; and *The Wall Street Journal*, January 31, 1986, p. 3.

18.2 Investing in Junk

Standard & Poor's Corporation assigns ratings to corporate bonds, based on the corporation's ability to pay interest and to repay the face amount. The ratings, in descending order, are: AAA (extremely strong); AA (very strong); A (strong); BBB (adequate); BB, B, CCC, CC (increasingly speculative); C, D (no longer paying dividends). The lower the rating, the riskier the bond and generally the higher the interest rate it carries. Bonds rated BB or lower are termed "junk bonds" by financial analysts.

Junk bonds are often favored by speculators — investors who are willing to accept the risk along with the chance of high earnings. They played an important role in the financing of many mergers during the 1980s, and have helped save a number of firms that were on shaky financial ground. Junk bonds are also the staple of the so-called "high yield" mutual funds.

There are now an estimated $100 billion worth of junk bonds outstanding. Because of the risk involved, the market for those bonds is highly sensitive to corporate goings-on. That was the case when LTV Corporation, the nation's second largest steel company, declared bankruptcy in July 1986. LTV had, at the time, $2.2 billion in long-term debt; its Standard and Poor's rating was CCC, which placed its bonds squarely in the "junk" category.

There were three immediate results of LTV's filing. First, its own bonds shot down in price to as low as 18 (meaning that a $1000 bond could be purchased for $180). Second, the prices of many other low-rated bonds, especially those of steel and energy firms, dropped by smaller (but still significant) amounts, as did the prices of shares of high-yield funds. And third, the interest paid on new junk-bond issues tended to increase somewhat. (A predictable fourth consequence was the immediate reduction of LTV's bond rating to D.)

Some analysts believe this is the beginning of a major change in the junk-bond market. Yet others see it as only a ripple, one that has increased the stakes for those who are willing to take the risk.

Questions

1. What are investors actually saying about a bond and its issuer when the market price of that bond drops to 18?
2. Who do you think is better off right now: LTV's shareholders or its bondholders? Why?

For more information see *The Wall Street Journal*, July 31, 1986, p. 53; *The Wall Street Journal*, July 21, 1986, pp. 2, 10; and *The New York Times*, July 18, 1986, p. A1.

19
SECURITIES MARKETS

Learning Objectives

After you have completed this chapter, you will be able to do the following:

- List the attributes of a security.
- Describe the three basic processes by which securities change hands.
- Identify the principal secondary markets for securities and describe each.
- List the principal sources of financial information and give an example of each.
- Identify the principal federal securities statutes.
- Describe the process by which commodities contracts are traded.

Adams was a rabbit breeder. For $7,200, he sold a "rabbit kit" consisting of 12 female and 2 male rabbits to buyers who wanted to go into the rabbit-pelt business. Those 14 rabbits would produce an estimated 720 breeding females within a year. Adams promoted these rabbit kits by offering seminars on rabbit breeding across Florida. Part of his pitch — not included with the rabbit kit — was membership in a marketing association that he owned, which promised to find markets for the pelts. The state of Florida indicted him for selling an unregistered security, and a jury found him guilty.

When Adams appealed his conviction, the court had to decide whether or not a rabbit kit was a security. Most people think of securities as just stocks and bonds, so a rabbit kit seems a poor candidate for one. However, the term *securities* takes in a host of investments — so many types, in fact, that no one has been able to develop a completely adequate definition of the term. For instance, the courts have held both a distributorship in a cosmetics firm and an ownership interest in an orange grove to be securities. State and federal securities laws, which require registration of securities in order to ensure that investors have sufficient information to evaluate investments, resort to listing dozens of examples of securities instead of attempting to define the word.

The Attributes of a Security

The U.S. Supreme Court eventually devised a solution to the problem. It created a three-part test, which the Florida District Court of Appeals applied in Adams's case. To be a **security,** there must be

☐ An investment of money
☐ A common enterprise
☐ An expectation of profit solely from the efforts of others

The rabbit kits did not satisfy the second test, because the buyers were not putting their money into a company or partnership — they were buying actual animals.[1] The rabbit kits failed the third test, too, so Adams's conviction was overturned. People who bought the kits had to turn the kits into marketable pelts.

Our focus here is on why and how people invest in the most common securities, stocks and bonds. In fact, we will focus even more narrowly on the stocks and bonds of the ten thousand or so corporations whose securities change hands on the national stock exchanges. This figure represents only .3 percent of all U.S. corporations, but transactions involving billions of dollars' worth of their securities occur every working day.

HOW SECURITIES CHANGE HANDS

A publicly traded stock can be transferred in three ways: in a private transaction between two parties, in a transaction on a primary market, or in a transaction on a secondary market.

Private Transactions

Suppose for a moment Adams's rabbit kits were in fact a security. The contract, for that is what a security is, would be between Adams and the buyer. No broker

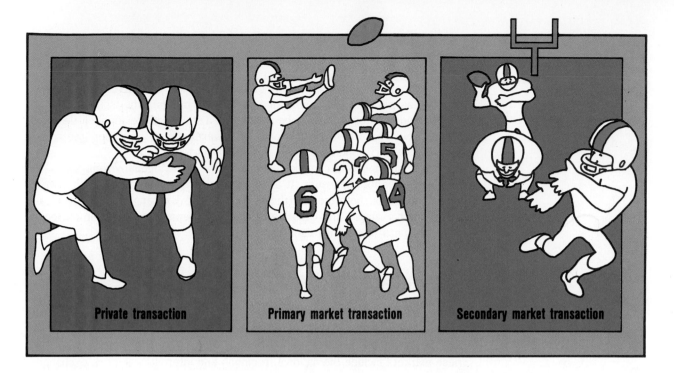

FIGURE 19.1

How Securities Change Hands

The Three Ways Securities
Change Hands

or other intermediary would have been involved. It is important to note that unless transfer of a security is somehow restricted, two persons can simply agree to the transfer. All that the holder must do to transfer the shares is to fill out the form on the back of the stock certificate and hand it to the **transferee**, the person to whom something is transferred. Transactions of this sort occur every day of the year. After all, 2.95 million corporations' stocks and debts are not publicly traded.

The publicly traded securities, the ones we are focusing on, are also transferred by executing the transfer form on the back of the certificates. However, in such cases the buyer and seller are brought together by intermediaries who make money by performing this service. The two contexts in which these transfers occur are called either primary markets or secondary markets.

Primary Markets

Those markets in which the issuer of a security receives some or all of the funds paid for the security are known as **primary markets.** Primary markets exist to market new issues of securities. In contrast, on the secondary market the issuer does not benefit from transactions, because they involve securities issued in the past, unless the issuer is selling its own stock.

One type of primary market transaction is **private placement,** the direct sale of stock by an issuer to investors. Securities and Exchange Commission regulations restrict the types of investors who may buy stock in private placements and limit how much money can be involved in any one issue.

More commonly, a primary market transaction is an indirect sale arranged through the efforts of an **underwriter,** an investment banker who agrees to buy a new issue and distribute it to the public. The process of initially selling a new issue of securities to the public is called a **public offering.** Generally, the issuer and the underwriter negotiate the amount that the issuer will receive and the price to be offered the investing public. The difference between the amount paid to the issuer and the amount paid by the public is called the **spread**. The spread goes to the underwriter or group of underwriters, collectively known as a **syndicate,** as payment for their taking the risk in bringing the issue to market. When an underwriter expects to be able to sell a stock with relatively little effort, as when a well-known strong company or government is the issuer, the spread is small. As the risk increases, the spread grows too.

A public offering is a complicated procedure involving numerous steps and heavy expenses for the issuer. It also requires formal registration with governmental regulators, both federal (the Securities and Exchange Commission) and state, as, for example, the Ohio Department of Commerce's Division of Securities, for issuers who want to sell in Ohio.

Secondary Markets

Those markets in which the sale of a security ordinarily does not involve any proceeds going to the issuer are **secondary markets.** When people refer to the stock market, they usually mean the various secondary markets for securities. These markets include the national, regional, and international stock exchanges, the over-the-counter market (discussed below), and the bond exchanges. The **exchanges** are the actual markets where stocks and bonds are traded. They serve as continuous markets for the securities of the companies listed on them. On an average day, 300 million shares of common stock change hands on U.S. exchanges and $50 million worth of bonds are traded on the bond exchanges.

Trading Securities on an Exchange

Let's take a look at how shares actually change hands on a secondary market.

How Secondary Exchanges Function

A Trade   Suppose that an investor wants to buy 100 shares of Exxon Corporation common stock, which is traded on the New York Stock Exchange (NYSE). First, an investor who wishes to buy or sell stocks on an exchange must place an order with a stockbroker. This **broker,** sometimes called an account executive or a registered representative, works for a brokerage firm or a broker-dealer. Table 19.1 identifies several players who are important in the process of buying and selling stocks on an exchange. If the broker is not a member of the exchange on which the stock is traded, the broker must process the order through a member. (We will discuss membership on an exchange below.)

An exchange processes each transaction in sequence, according to certain preestablished rules. After taking the order, the broker immediately notifies the **floor broker,** a member of the firm who is on the floor of the exchange and whose job it is to execute customers' orders. The floor broker goes to the trading post on the floor of the exchange where Exxon is traded and tells the specialist there that he or she has a **market order,** an order at the market price, for 100 shares of Exxon. A **specialist** is a member of an exchange who is responsible for matching buy and sell orders or, if there is an imbalance of orders, for using his or her own portfolio to balance the buy and sell orders. The specialist may be holding

TABLE 19.1

The Key Players in Stock
Transactions

Investor	The individual seeking to buy or sell a security.
Account executive	Also known as a stockbroker or registered representative. Serves as the intermediary between the investor and market professionals.
Floor broker	The professional on the floor of an exchange who carries out an investor's order.
Specialist	A member of an exchange who, on the floor of the exchange, maintains a fair and orderly market by matching orders and by buying and selling as needed to balance the market.

an order to sell at market 100 shares of Exxon and will then match up the two orders at the price of the most recent transaction in Exxon stock.

After the transaction at the trading post has been completed and the exchange has been properly recorded, the floor broker then notifies the broker about the transaction's being executed. At this point the broker notifies the investor, usually by phone, and follows up that notice with a written record detailing the transaction. The sale is manually recorded at the time of execution and is almost immediately displayed on the **ticker,** the electronic system that provides the public with notice of each transaction on the exchange. Investors can remain current by watching the ticker in any brokerage office around the country.

Other Types of Orders   Instead of requesting a market order, our imaginary investor might have made the order more explicit. "Buy 100 shares of Exxon at 58" represents a **limit order,** an order specifying the maximum price acceptable to the investor. If 58 is lower than the market price, the transaction will not be executed until and unless the price reaches 58. The broker will hold the order until it can be completed or until the end of the day. An **open order** extends beyond the day's end and runs until it is cancelled. A **stop order** is an explicitly priced sell order triggered when a stock price falls to or below a specified level. An investor can also place a **discretionary order,** which puts the decision about whether to act or to wait into the broker's hands.

Commissions   Brokers make money by charging fees, called **commissions,** on the transactions they facilitate. Commission rates vary from one brokerage house to another and with the size of the order. For example, the commission on 100 shares of stock can vary all the way from thirty-five dollars to ninety dollars. In part, this variation occurs because brokerages offer different levels of service. **Full-service brokers** charge the highest commissions, because they provide advice, reports, research and analysis, portfolio management, and other services. **Discount brokers** charge the lowest commissions, because they merely execute their customers' instructions.

Generally, the commission per share drops as the number of shares in the transaction increases. An especially steep price break comes at the 100-share level. One hundred shares is a **round lot;** less than 100 shares is generally

Electronic Trading

When most of us think of stock trading, we picture the floor of the New York Stock Exchange looking like a cross between a three-ring circus and recess at an old-fashioned madhouse. Frantic people scurry around yelling at each other, holding dozens of slips of paper, talking on two or three telephones, chewing antacids and aspirin. While this image may still bear some resemblance to reality, it is fast being replaced by the cool calm glow of the computer screen as information services compete to make electronic trading ever more efficient and useful.

Five years ago, many computer experts predicted that we would all soon be getting the bulk of our information through our computers. For most individuals, the speed and efficiency of such electronic information transfer is not yet worth the high price of the service. But for brokers, traders, and big-time investors, instant information can sometimes mean instant profits. So Wall Street has become the proving ground for the latest in information services.

The first step in computerized information delivery was the "dumb" terminal that provided brokers with the latest in stock prices. Quotron Systems has been the leading marketer of such terminals, which generate revenues of almost half a billion dollars a year. Most brokerages can afford the terminal's $200 a month price tag.

The new generation of systems does a lot more and, naturally, costs a lot more. Rather than just deliver information, the new systems monitor, analyze, and sort the information. They can call attention to major news events that may affect a company's stock prices and list for the broker the clients that hold stock in that company.

Sure to be a leader in this new generation of information systems is International MarketNet (Imnet), a joint venture of IBM and Merrill Lynch & Co. that uses special IBM Personal Computers. But Imnet has plenty of competition. E. F. Hutton & Co. is spending $40 million on its own system of Data General computers and market data supplied by Bunker Ramo Information Systems.

While Imnet is aimed primarily at brokers and large investors, other companies are taking their services directly to consumers and small investors. Apple Computer is selling specially equipped Macintosh computers that will receive information via satellites and FM radio signals. McGraw-Hill publishing company has linked up with Tele-Communications, Inc., the nation's largest cable-TV company, to deliver financial information on cable for around $20 a month.

While brokers have generally welcomed the speed and efficiency of their own information transfer systems, they look at these latest developments with some anxiety. For the day may yet come when investors can do all their trading from a home terminal, leaving brokers to find a new role in the stock market of the future.

Sources: John Marcom, Jr., "Electronic Market-Data Delivery Expands Beyond Simple Stock-Quote Terminals," *The Wall Street Journal*, June 19, 1985, 33. "Stock Quotes via Macintosh," *The New York Times*, August 6, 1985, D4. "Instinet and Amex to Offer Overseas Trading Hookup," *The Wall Street Journal*, December 10, 1985, 6.

considered an **odd lot.** Odd-lot commissions are charged a premium because the transaction involves one extra step. Before an odd-lot order can be executed, one odd lot must be matched with another, either one ordered by another investor or one filled by a specialist. This extra effort that is necessary explains why individual investors prefer to trade round lots and why companies split stock to keep prices low. In contrast, on very large orders the investor may negotiate an especially low commission.

Margin   A brokerage will extend credit to its individual customers to enable them to buy securities. These credit arrangements are called **margin accounts**.

An era of computerized trading. Not only have computers changed the way exchanges operate, they have radically altered the information available to individual investors and specialists. Gold specialist Melvin Lazarus has instant access to data on market activity.

The Federal Reserve Board requires that the customer put up collateral, usually in the form of securities, to secure a brokerage's loan. The brokerage customer's margin is expressed as a percentage of the market value of the collateral plus the purchased securities, which remain in the brokerage's possession until the customer pays off the loan. The percentage has varied between 50 and 100 percent, depending on existing credit conditions.[2]

The customer's margin may go below the required percentage, if there is a decline in the market value of either the collateral or the purchased securities. In such a case, the brokerage issues a **margin call**, which demands additional collateral from the customer. If the customer fails to supply it, the brokerage will liquidate enough of the securities it holds for this customer to bring the margin up to the required level.

The New York Stock Exchange

The Principal Secondary Markets for Securities: The NYSE

The New York Stock Exchange (NYSE) is the largest of the U.S. secondary markets. The first recorded exchange of stocks in New York dates to 1792. Today, the daily average trading volume exceeds 120 million shares, up from less than 50 million in 1981. Figure 19.2 is a New York Stock Exchange listing.

The New York Stock Exchange is a national exchange. The more than 2,325 issues of common and preferred stocks traded on it are those of over 1,550 national and international companies. Only the stocks of companies that can meet certain specific criteria for size and breadth of ownership can qualify for listing on the NYSE. Table 19.2 identifies the criteria.

Membership in the New York Stock Exchange is limited to individuals, although the brokerage house for which a member works often pays for the membership and advertises itself as a Member of the New York Stock Exchange. The 1,336 regular members are said to have seats on the exchange, which are bought and sold. Their price has ranged from $35,000 in 1979 to $500,000 or more today.

Other Stock Exchanges

Virtually all stock exchanges function like the New York Stock Exchange, and their rules and regulations governing their members' conduct also resemble the NYSE's.

American Stock Exchange (Amex)   The American Stock Exchange, also located in New York, is the second of the national exchanges. Because different issues trade on the New York Stock Exchange and the Amex, most brokerage houses also employ Amex members. Only about 930 issues trade on the Amex. It is regarded, somewhat inaccurately, as the appropriate exchange for newer, smaller, and more speculative companies. Table 19.3 presents the Amex's listing requirements.

Regional Exchanges   The several regional exchanges are similar in structure to the major exchanges but are much smaller in size and scope. They primarily serve the demand for stocks of regional companies, but the stocks of national companies trade on them, too. For example, the Boston Edison Company, an electric utility, is listed on both the New York and Boston stock exchanges.

In recent years, the number and importance of the regional exchanges has declined. In 1930 there were more than thirty regionals; today there are eight. The Midwest, Pacific, and Philadelphia regional exchanges are significantly larger

Wall Street. *This street at the southern tip of Manhattan has long symbolized the world of high finance and investments. Clustered along its length are exchanges, brokerage firms, and investment banks.*

TABLE 19.2

NYSE Listing Requirements Domestic companies, 1961–1985 (Shares and dollars in thousands)

Prior Year Pretax Income	$ 2,500
Pretax Income, Two Previous Years	2,000
Net Tangible Assets	18,000
Publicly Held Shares	1,100
Market Value of Publicly Held Shares (may be less under certain circumstances): Maximum	18,000
: Minimum	9,000
Number of Holders of 100 Shares or More	2,000

Note: These listing requirements are reviewed regularly by the exchange and are changed as circumstances warrant. They apply only to companies seeking a new listing, although failure to maintain a broad distribution of shares will result in the delisting of shares. Delisting may also occur for failure to conform to regulatory requirements, for creation of nonvoting common shares, or for any other activity that detracts from an orderly market or injures the rights of shareholders.

Source: New York Stock Exchange Fact Book 1986, New York Stock Exchange, Inc., p. 37. Used with permission.

FIGURE 19.2

New York Stock Exchange
Listing

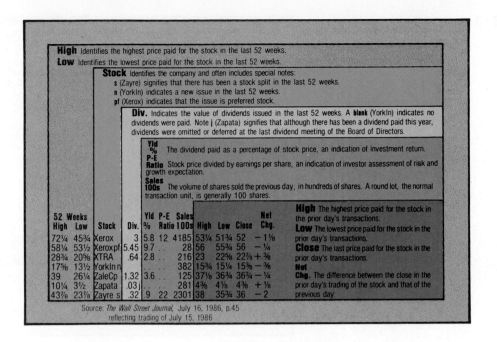

Source: *The Wall Street Journal*, July 16, 1986, p.45
reflecting trading of July 15, 1986

than the others. The Cincinnati exchange functions quite differently from the others. Since 1978 it has operated a computerized exchange — without a trading floor. Brokers transmit orders to a central computer, which receives, stores, displays, matches, and executes the orders. It functions on a first come, first served basis. Whether this new method of handling orders will succeed over the long run remains to be seen.

The Over-the-Counter Market (OTC)   The telecommunications network linking broker-dealers for transactions in securities not listed on exchanges is called the **over-the-counter market (OTC)**. Some 4,700 stocks, issued primarily by smaller and newer companies, trade over the counter. See Figure 19.3. Some trade frequently, others only occasionally. The annual OTC transaction volume is about the same as the NYSE's, however.

TABLE 19.3

**The Amex's Listing
Requirements**

Last Fiscal Year Pretax Income	$ 750,000
Last Fiscal Year Net Income	400,000
Net Tangible Worth	4,000,000
Publicly Held Shares (of which 150,000 shares must be in 100–1,000-share lots	500,000
Market Value of Publicly Held Shares (3,000,000/$5 Price Per Share)	3,000,000
Number of Stockholders (1,000 including 800 holders of round lots, of which 500 must be holders of 100–1,000-share lots)	1,000

Source: Taken from *1985 Amex Fact Book* (N.Y. American Stock Exchange, p. 8).

FIGURE 19.3

Over the Counter Listing

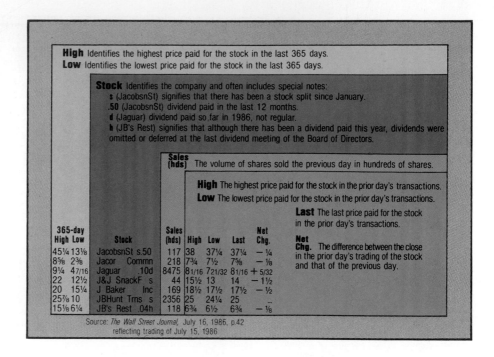

| | **High** Identifies the highest price paid for the stock in the last 365 days. |
| | **Low** Identifies the lowest price paid for the stock in the last 365 days. |

The OTC is not an exchange like the NYSE or the Amex. It functions through the members of the **National Association of Securities Dealers (NASD).** This organization has set up **NASDAQ** (National Association of Securities Dealers Automatic Quotations), a computerized system enabling dealers to determine instantly the current market price for the more popular OTC shares and see who is making a market in them. A transaction occurs only when another party of a dealer acting as a market maker agrees to buy or sell. In essence, the investor using NASDAQ negotiates the transaction through the broker.[3] For issues not included in NASDAQ, brokers must call dealers to find a participant willing to complete the transaction.

The Bond Markets

In Chapter 18, we discussed corporate bonds as certificates of indebtedness offered to the public. It is important to note that anyone — individuals, partnerships, or governments — can issue such certificates. However, we are concerned here only with those issued by larger corporations and the different units of local, state, federal, and foreign governments, because they trade on secondary markets. The bond markets are separate from the stock markets. Corporations whose stock trades on the NYSE may thus list their bonds on the AMEX, and OTC markets exist for government bonds. Figure 19.4 is a typical bond listing.

Secondary Markets: Bonds

Government Bonds The debt certificates issued by federal, state, and local governments and their agencies are called **government bonds.** Government bonds are classified as **U.S. government issues,** which includes all bonds issued by any unit of the federal government or issued as municipal bonds.

FIGURE 19.4
Bond Listing

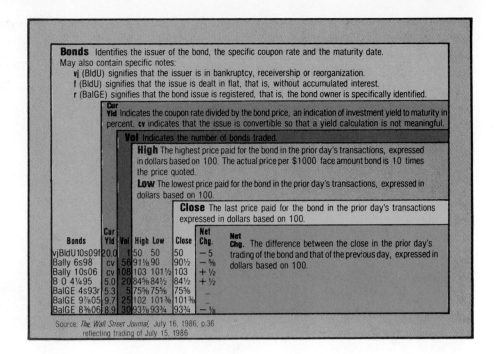

Bonds Identifies the issuer of the bond, the specific coupon rate and the maturity date. May also contain specific notes:
  vj (BldU) signifies that the issuer is in bankruptcy, receivership or reorganization.
  f (BldU) signifies that the issue is dealt in flat, that is, without accumulated interest.
  r (BalGE) signifies that the bond issue is registered, that is, the bond owner is specifically identified.

Cur Yld Indicates the coupon rate divided by the bond price, an indication of investment yield to maturity in percent. **cv** indicates that the issue is convertible so that a yield calculation is not meaningful.

Vol Indicates the number of bonds traded.

High The highest price paid for the bond in the prior day's transactions, expressed in dollars based on 100. The actual price per $1000 face amount bond is 10 times the price quoted.

Low The lowest price paid for the bond in the prior day's transactions, expressed in dollars based on 100.

Close The last price paid for the bond in the prior day's transactions expressed in dollars based on 100.

Net Chg. The difference between the close in the prior day's trading of the bond and that of the previous day, expressed in dollars based on 100.

Bonds	Cur Yld	Vol	High	Low	Close	Net Chg.
vjBldU 10s09f	20.0	1	50	50	50	− 5
Bally 6s98	cv	56	91⅛	90	90½	− ⅝
Bally 10s06	cv	108	103	101½	103	+ ½
B 0 4¼95	5.0	20	84⅝	84½	84½	+ ½
BalGE 4s93r	5.3	5	75⅝	75⅝	75⅝	...
BalGE 9⅞05	9.7	25	102	101⅜	101⅜	...
BalGE 8⅜06	8.9	30	93⅞	93¾	93¾	− ⅛

Source: *The Wall Street Journal,* July 16, 1986, p.36 reflecting trading of July 15, 1986

Bonds issued by the U.S. Treasury are considered the safest investment available in the United States and perhaps in the world. Because the taxing power of the U.S. government backs them, they carry the lowest net interest rate of any bond. Treasury issues provide operating funds for the federal government. Also, as we saw in Chapter 17, the Federal Reserve buys and sells U.S. bonds as part of its monetary policy.

Other federal bonds are generally considered somewhat more risky, even though neither the federal government nor any federal agency has defaulted on an obligation in this century. The most active markets are for the bonds of the Federal National Mortgage Association (FNMA, "Fannie Mae") and the Government National Mortgage Association (GNMA, "Ginnie Mae"). The FNMA purchases and sells residential mortgages as part of its effort to stabilize the availability of mortgages and promote residential construction. The GNMA, a part of the Department of Housing and Urban Development, guarantees mortgages and buys and sells mortgages in the same way the FNMA does.[4]

Municipal bonds are debt obligations of state and local governments and their agencies. In other words, a government bond that is not issued by the federal government, a federal agency, or a foreign government is a municipal bond. The interest these bonds pay is not taxed by either the federal government or the state that benefits from their being issued. What this means is that the interest on a bond issued by the city of Buffalo, for example, is not subject to the New York state income tax. However, an Ohio resident, let's say, would have to pay Ohio state income taxes on this bond's interest.

Once the tax benefits are factored back in, it becomes clear that municipal bonds carry a higher interest rate than do federal bonds. The reason is simply that municipals are riskier. In 1983, for instance, the Washington Public Power Supply System defaulted on over $2 billion in bonds. In the mid-1970s, New York City nearly defaulted on its bonds.

Mutual Funds

Mutual funds are not secondary markets themselves. Rather, they are major participants in the secondary markets. **Mutual funds** are poolings of various people's investments that are managed for a fee by professional investment managers toward a particular goal or with a particular philosophy. Individual investors may thus invest a modest sum and participate in a portfolio that they could not otherwise afford to create by themselves. The mutual-fund investor spreads the risk of loss across a whole portfolio and can take advantage of professional management.

The Role of Mutual Funds in Secondary Markets

Investment Objectives   Mutual funds are not all alike. Each has a different philosophy and set of principles that guide its investments. And even within a particular type of mutual fund, philosophies and performance may vary widely.

Mutual funds may choose to invest in common stocks, corporate bonds, government bonds, or combinations of these securities. They may invest principally in just certain types of investments, such as energy stocks, aerospace stocks, high-technology stocks, or other specialized categories. Mutuals may characterize themselves as **growth funds** (offering limited dividends and investing in more speculative stocks), as **income funds** (concentrating on a high-yield portfolio with limited growth and risk), or as **balanced funds** (seeking to provide modest income and growth from a generally conservative portfolio).

Loads, No-Loads, and Management Fees   A sales charge, usually ranging from 2½ to 8½ percent, assessed on the purchase of a share in a mutual fund is a **load**. A fund salesperson or, more commonly, a stockbroker markets load funds, and the load goes principally to them. In other words, for a fund to break even in its first year on an 8½ percent load, the fund must yield more

"Well, yes, we've put your money to work. As for what it's doing at this very moment, I have no idea."

than 8½ percent to the investor — after taxes. The investor then can start to actually earn something on the investment.

A **no-load fund** has no sales charge, so all of the purchaser's money is invested. Investors buy no-load fund shares directly from the fund itself. The studies made thus far have been inconclusive as to whether load or no-load funds perform better.

All funds charge a management fee to compensate the funds' managers and pay administrative costs. Generally, the fee is based on a percentage of the assets and is often on a sliding scale. At present, management fees are highly controversial. Many investors have questioned whether 2½ percent of earnings, a typical charge, is too much to pay for these services.

SOURCES OF FINANCIAL INFORMATION

In years past, investors had to seek out the business and financial news on their own. Today, television and radio include stock summaries in their daily newscasts. Special programs also deal exclusively with business and financial news. There is even a cable television service, Financial News Network, that covers business news exclusively throughout the day. Even with all this electronic coverage, though, the major sources of business and financial news remain the magazines and newspapers.

The Principal Sources of Financial Information

Magazines

Many weekly magazines cover different aspects of business. Among the most popular are *Business Week, Industry Week,* and *Fortune. Barron's* is a weekly securities-oriented tabloid owned by Dow Jones, the publisher of the *Wall Street*

Journal. And *Forbes,* a biweekly, offers an assortment of stories about business and investing but does not try to cover current events. Hundreds of other publications each cover a particular market or subject, like *Aviation Week, Sheep & Goat Ranchers Magazine,* and *Publishers Weekly.*

Newspaper Coverage

Some industries have their own newspapers. The women's apparel industry, for one, now has *W,* formerly called *Women's Wear Daily.* In the past, only the *Wall Street Journal* covered the securities markets extensively. Today, many papers

---

INTERNATIONAL BUSINESS

The All-Night Market

In April 1985, Stephen Raven checked a stock price on his computer screen, then bought 1000 shares of Electrolux from a New York dealer. Big deal? It was if you consider that Raven was in London, and the trade was made with the help of a new transatlantic computer link, part of a growing network of international connections between securities brokers. As a result of such new technology and trading patterns, investors will soon be able to buy any stock, any time.

Raven made his trade with the help of a new link between the U.S. National Association of Securities Dealers (NASD) and the London Stock Exchange. London traders get the latest prices for nearly 200 stocks that the NASD trades over-the-counter, while NASD members get current quotes on almost 300 London stocks. American investors can now get up at 4:30 A.M., New York time, and get the latest quotations from the London market. Such an early bird investor can take advantage of the effects of a major overnight development on a particular stock's value and can make major trades hours before the New York Stock Exchange opens.

Although an important step in the development of a global market, the NASD link is far from the first. Toronto's exchange is already linked with the American Stock Exchange, and Montreal's with Boston's. An Institutional Networks Corporation installation in late 1985 allowed London brokers to trade any time in 8000 stocks available on American exchanges.

The growing ability of investors to trade stocks where and when they want poses a major threat to the less efficient stock exchanges of the world. Exchanges in Paris and Frankfurt conduct business for only two hours a day, which means a lot of Continental European trading actually takes place in London. Other exchanges in Europe are expanding their hours and working on a computerized network that will link them all.

These developments are a result of, and contribute to, a tremendous explosion in the amount of investment capital that has crossed international borders in recent years. In 1980, U.S. institutional investors held $3 billion in foreign stocks. By 1985, that figure had risen to $16 billion, in part because statistics show that British stocks have been growing better than American, and Japanese stocks have outperformed them both. At the same time foreign investment in U.S. firms has also increased, from $69 billion in 1983 to $135 billion in 1985.

Computers and high-tech information transfer systems can do a lot to make the world smaller, but they can't erase hundreds of years of cultural differences — yet.

Sources: "Distant Stocks, Instant Trades," *Time,* May 5, 1986, 55. Richard A. Melcher, Amy Borrus, John Rossant, "The Electronic Threat to the World's Stock Exchange," *Business Week,* December 2, 1985, 44. Jill Andresky, "Ready or Not," *Forbes,* February 10, 1986, 94.

---

devote a whole section or part of one to business news several times a week. Most newspapers carry complete NYSE and Amex listings and selected listings from other markets. Recall, for instance, Figure 19.2, an excerpt from a NYSE listing; Figure 19.3, from an over-the-counter listing; and Figure 19.4, from a bond market listing.

The source of the data in these listings is the computerized record of the daily transactions in each market. It is this same record that produces the ticker data described earlier. At the end of each trading day, this information is transmitted electronically to newspapers and any others who order it. It is also available to subscribers, like brokerages, who have the proper microcomputer equipment. Some individual investors use these computerized listings to manage their own portfolios.

Other Sources

An investor seeking specific information on a firm can go directly to a particular company's shareholder or investor-information department. Public companies will provide annual reports, SEC Form 10-K reports, and many other reports.

The key investor protection offered by the securities regulations discussed in the next section is their requirement that the issuer fully and fairly disclose the nature of the investment to all prospective buyers. This disclosure comes in the form of two documents. All issuers must file a **registration statement** with the Securities and Exchange Commission and state securities regulators that fully describes the investment and the issuer. The second document, the **prospectus**, summarizes the information contained in the registration statement. Full-service brokerages or the companies themselves are the best sources for these documents.

Full-service brokerages also provide detailed reports on investments, prepared by their own in-house analysts. Often, brokerages' larger branches have libraries with financial information services like *Value Line, Moody's Industrial Directories, Moody's Million Dollar Directory,* and *Standard & Poor's Reports.* Public libraries, which often have substantial collections in business and finance, usually also subscribe to some of these information services.

Stock Averages

Several statistical averages measure the activity of the New York Stock Exchange and the stock market in general. These include

☐ The Dow Jones Averages (NYSE)
    30 Industrials
    20 Transportation stocks
    15 Utilities
    The Composite (the 65 stocks of the other three averages)
☐ The Standard & Poor's 500 stock average (NYSE)
☐ The NYSE average price of all issues traded
☐ The Amex average price of all issues traded
☐ The NASDAQ index

FIGURE 19.5

Dow Jones Average

These closely watched averages are computed constantly during the trading day. Over time, they should reflect trends in the markets. The charts shown in Figure 19.5 depict the movement over six months of the three most important Dow Jones averages. Also shown are the stocks included in the computations, which change from time to time, because of mergers, bankruptcies, and other factors.

The Standard & Poor's Corporation prepares a broader set of averages similar to the Dow Jones averages. The NYSE, Amex, and NASDAQ averages are broader still, since they include all the stocks traded each day.

REGULATION OF SECURITIES TRADING

Before World War I, most securities trading involved a few knowledgeable investors and some highly sophisticated speculators. Then, during the postwar boom of the 1920s, ordinary people increasingly became involved in the market. At the same time, many investors and speculators overextended themselves, bidding the market up to record levels. When the bubble burst, on "Black Tuesday," October 29, 1929, the stock market crashed. At its lowest point, on July 1, 1932, the values of the stocks on the New York Stock Exchange had declined more than 82.5 percent from their pre-crash highs.[5] The time line shown in Figure 19.6 identifies the major securities legislation that followed the election of Franklin D. Roosevelt in 1932.

The success of this sequence of regulations is beyond question. Since 1929, this country has not suffered from a crash that even slightly resembles that of 1929–1932. Before 1929, however, such crashes had occurred about once a generation. The **Securities and Exchange Commission,** the federal agency created in 1934 charged with enforcing the federal securities laws as well as designing regulations for the securities markets, was the most highly regarded federal agency for more than forty years. However, budget cuts and an official policy of deregulation have led many to question whether the agency can effectively monitor the rapidly expanding national and international markets for securities.

Federal Securities Legislation

The Securities Act of 1933   The first major piece of legislation on our timeline, the **Securities Act of 1933,** is a disclosure act requiring that the issuer of a public offering file a registration statement providing   specific   information about the issuer, its financial condition, management, properties, and general operation. This act also prohibits false and misleading statements in registration statements or in connection with public offerings.

The Principal Federal Securities Statutes

The Securities Exchange Act of 1934   The Securities and Exchange Commission was established by the **Securities Exchange Act of 1934.** This act requires periodic disclosures in the form of reports to the SEC by companies whose securities are publicly held. It also greatly strengthens the government's hand in regulating the ways in which securities change hands in public transactions. Later amendments to the act provided for the registration of brokers and dealers and established periodic reporting requirements for the issuers of listed securities.

The key point to remember about the 1933 and 1934 acts is that they mandate disclosure of relevant financial information to the public so that investors can make up their own minds about the merits of an investment. It must be emphasized that these acts do not try to keep people from making bad investments.

The Public Utility Holding Company Act of 1935   The SEC is empowered by the **Public Utility Holding Company Act of 1935** to regulate the companies that control public utilities, notably the electric utilities, natural-gas pipeline companies, and their subsidiaries. Because utility companies usually have legal monopolies, utility holding companies exercise enormous power over their customers and markets.

The Maloney Act of 1938 The present self-regulation of the OTC market was authorized by the **Maloney Act of 1938**. It led to the creation of the National Association of Securities Dealers, which now regulates the market.

The Trust Indenture Act of 1939 The next important regulatory act, the **Trust Indenture Act of 1939**, requires that any corporate debt offered to the public be registered with the SEC and conform to certain requirements relating to maturity, interest, and financial backing. As noted in Chapter 18, this act also requires the appointment of an independent trustee for each issue of long-term debt.

The Investment Company Act of 1940 The **Investment Company Act of 1940** made mutual funds subject to SEC registration and reporting requirements.

The Investment Advisers Act of 1940 Those who advise investors, whether or not they actually handle investor funds, must register with the SEC, as required by the **Investment Advisers Act of 1940**. This act provides penalties for improper actions, fraud, and conflict of interest.

The Securities Act of 1964 Companies whose securities trade over the counter were brought under SEC jurisdiction by the **Securities Act of 1964**, if the company and its stockholders met certain criteria. This act broadened the SEC's jurisdiction to include companies that had avoided regulation by staying off the exchanges. After the passage of this act, many of the larger OTC companies applied to the national exchanges for listing.

The Securities Investors Protection Act of 1970 Until 1970, such legislation of the Roosevelt era as that just described provided most of the regulatory structure in the securities marketplace. Market activity grew rapidly in the late 1960s, however, and a number of brokerage houses that could not cope with those changes failed, bringing great losses to their customers.

The **Securities Investors Protection Act of 1970** created the **Securities Investors Protection Corporation (SIPC),** which oversees the liquidation of failed broker-dealers and insures investors when the assets of a failed firm are insufficient to cover its obligations to its customers. The SIPC insures investor accounts held by the brokerage houses for up to $500,000 in total and $100,000 in cash deposits. Like the FDIC and FSLIC in the banking industry, members of the securities exchanges, who are required to join, and other brokers, dealers, and fund managers, who may elect to join, fund the SIPC.

The Insider Trading Sanctions Act of 1984 One of the results of deregulation was a drastic cutback in the enforcement of the antitrust laws. The 1980s became the era of the megamerger, as giant oil companies merged, conglomerates like Beatrice Foods merged with other conglomerates and then

FIGURE 19.6

Securities Regulation Time Line

July 1, 1932
Stock market
bottoms out

1933
Securities Act

1934
Securities
Exchange Act

1935
Public Utility
Holding Company
Act

1938
Maloney Act

1939
Trust
Indenture Act

1940
Investment
Company Act

1970
Investment
Advisers Act

1984
Insider Trading
Sanctions Act

An "Insider" on the *Journal*

Some on Wall Street say that the market is controlled by two emotions: greed and fear. When the greed wins out, people can make millions, lose their shirts, or (sometimes) go to jail. Even those in the Wall Street community occasionally succumb to greed and use information illegally to trade on the market and make easy money. The recent case of a scandal at Wall Street's most influential paper shows what happens when insiders' greed overcomes their fear.

R. Foster Winans was one of the writers of the "Heard on the Street" column for *The Wall Street Journal*. The column contains tips, information, and gossip about companies and Wall Street activities. Because the *Journal* is so widely respected, a favorable word about a company in the column can cause the value of that company's stock to rise. Therefore, anyone who could find out what was going to be in that column before everyone else in New York found out could buy the stock before everyone else did and make a handy profit.

That's exactly what five Wall Street veterans were accused of doing in the spring of 1984. The SEC charged that Winans would call a friend, Peter Brant, and tell him about the next day's column in the *Journal*. Brant and three others then used the information to trade on the market. They reaped a reported $900,000 in profits over the next 6 months before their scheme began to unravel.

Employees of a corporation, as well as lawyers, brokers, and others with special information, are prohibited by law from profiting from nonpublic information about a company. These "insiders" can't use such privileged information unless it's made available to the general public; otherwise, public confidence in the fairness of stock trading would fall.

The Winans scandal made the headlines largely because it sullied, if only slightly, the reputation of his paper, *The Wall Street Journal*, the most respected and influential source of information about the nation's business and financial dealings.

Winans was sentenced to 18 months in prison and three years probation and fined $1000 — a relatively stiff penalty for insider trading. Tougher penalties are needed, many argue, because the whole system suffers from insider trading.

A positive point raised by the scandal concerns Wall Street's ability to detect such illegal trading. Less than a month after the scheme began, the internal surveillance system at the brokerage firm that employed some of the accused men noticed the pattern of trading. And within four months, the American Stock Exchange reported trading irregularities to the SEC.

One effect of this scandal may be to make future insider trading more dangerous. Another is to bring to light one of the most difficult questions facing many who work in the world of securities: How much am I allowed to use the information I have?

Sources: Ann Reilly, "Insider Crackdown," *Fortune*, Vol. 109, No. 10, May 14, 1984, 143–144. "'Heard on the Street': A $900,000 Windfall," *Newsweek*, Vol. 103, No. 22, May 28, 1984, 63. "Opening up the *Journal* Scandal," *Time*, Vol. 123, No. 22, May 28, 1984, 68. "A Get-Tough Mood on Insider Trading," *Business Week*, No. 2844, May 28, 1984, 16. "Winans Gets 18-Month Term in Trading Case," *The Wall Street Journal*, August 7, 1985, 2.

went private, and diversified giants like R. J. Reynolds swallowed related companies like Nabisco. Information about merger plans became valuable to stock-market speculators, whose activities brought into serious question the fairness of the market. Trading on **insider information,** information available only to persons who owe a fiduciary duty to a corporation's shareholders, had long been illegal under the 1934 SEC Act, but many believed the penalties to be inadequate. The **Insider Trading Act of 1984** subjected those guilty of insider trading to forfeiture of up to three times their gain on the illegal trades and expanded the SEC's powers to investigate such trading.

Commodities. Investors buy and sell contracts for sugar long before it is harvested and ready to be sold. For some investors commodities trading is a way to assume an adequate supply of necessary raw materials. For others, commodities offer a convenient vehicle for speculation.

How Commodities Contracts Are Traded

COMMODITIES

Gold, silver, wheat, cotton, pork bellies, and orange juice — in other words, our basic resources and agricultural products — are **commodities. Commodities contracts** — commitments to buy a quantity of a commodity at a particular time — are bought and sold on secondary markets. Investors may purchase a contract up to eighteen months before it is due to expire. Most investors do not actually want the commodity itself. They expect to sell the contract before it matures and hope to make money by doing so.

Most investors purchase on margin, which the industry margin requirement of 5 percent encourages. They speculate that the price of a contract will rise so that the contract can be sold at a profit before it expires. Buyers bet that, by putting a small amount down, they will make a very high return on their investment and not have to take title to the goods. The risk of loss is at least as great as the chance for gain, though.

For example, say that a contract in sugar is for 112,000 pounds of it. Its price is, perhaps, 20.88 cents per pound. On margin, a speculator is able to buy a sugar contract for only $1,169.28 plus the commission. An increase in the sugar's market price of only 1 cent per pound would result in a profit of $1,120.00, or 95.8 percent, less commission. A drop of 1 cent would result in a loss of the same $1,120.00, however. Because an investor needs only to put down 5 percent, very small price movements have large impacts. A failure to sell before maturity will result in the delivery of 112,000 pounds of sugar and a demand by the seller for $22,216.32. Furthermore, speculators usually magnify these consequences by buying or selling several contracts at once.

Let us be clear that the commodities market is not only for speculation. Often, businesses that expect to require certain quantities of the commodities will contract for delivery through the exchanges, assuring themselves of a supply when needed and at a predictable cost.

SPECULATING AND INVESTING: A PERSPECTIVE

When we discussed commodities, we used the term *speculate*. This word, often associated with both commodities and stocks, implies the kind of gambling that knowledgeable football bettors engage in. It is true that early information about crop reports, long-range weather forecasts, and political changes could make a knowledgeable investor's fortune, but the speculative nature of commodities trading is easily exaggerated.

Commodities market regulators have taken a tolerant view of insider trading. In fact, unlike securities issuers, the issuers of commodities contracts are not subject to reporting requirements. Ever since the Securities Act of 1933, though, the watchword for all issuers has been *disclosure*. In recent years, insider-trading scandals have rocked Wall Street. These cases mainly involved people who had access to confidential information about coming takeover attempts or mergers. Some cases, however, simply involved passing on information that would affect a stock's price. For example, a Deputy Secretary of Defense in the Reagan administration went to jail for four years for obstructing an SEC investigation into tips he had given friends.[6]

Why is a certain type of conduct with respect to securities a crime when the same conduct with respect to commodities is simply sound trading? More and more people are asking this question. The philosophy behind the securities laws is that securities are investments and all investors should have equal access to relevant information. Is this really possible, since markets always operate on information?

The regulatory philosophy seems to be that an investment somehow has positive qualities that a speculation does not. It is difficult to feel sorry for those convicted of insider trading. Almost without exception, they knew that what they were doing was wrong. Still, it is worth considering whether the law as it stands makes sense and whether people who buy and sell commodities or stocks are in fact engaged in the same types of transactions and should thus be treated the same way.

Chapter Highlights

1. List the attributes of a security.

To qualify as a security, there must be (1) an investment of money; (2) a common enterprise; and (3) an expectation of profit solely from the efforts of others.

2. Describe the three basic processes by which securities change hands.

A publicly traded stock's transfer can occur in three ways: (1) In a private transaction between two parties. Unless transfer of a security is somehow restricted, two persons can simply agree to the transfer. (2) In a transaction on a primary market. Primary markets are those in which the issuer of a security receives some or all of the funds paid for the security. Primary markets are markets for new issues of securities. (3) In a transaction on a secondary market. When people refer to "the stock market," they usually mean the secondary markets for securities. Secondary markets are those markets in which the sale of a security ordinarily does not involve any proceeds going to the issuer.

3. Identify the principal secondary markets for securities and describe each.

Secondary markets for securities include the national,

regional, and international stock exchanges, the over-the-counter market and the bond exchanges. The New York Stock Exchange is the oldest and largest of the U.S. secondary markets. The NYSE is a national exchange. The American Stock Exchange, also located in New York, is the second of the national exchanges. Regional exchanges are similar in structure to the major exchange but are much smaller in size and scope. The over-the-counter market refers to a telecommunications network linking broker-dealers for transactions in securities not listed on exchanges. The bond markets are separate from the stock markets. Government bonds and municipal bonds are common bond listings.

4. List the principal sources of financial information and give an example of each.

The major sources of business and financial news remains magazines and newspapers. Several magazines, *Business Week, Industry Week,* and *Fortune* feature financial information. Newspaper coverage of financial information is provided in the *Wall Street Journal* and the financial section of many daily papers. Full service brokerages also provide detailed reports on investments prepared by in-house analysts. Some investors go directly to the company's shareholder or investor information department.

5. Identify the principal federal securities statutes.

The regulation of securities trading was triggered by the stock market crash of 1929. The Securities Act of 1933 is a disclosure act requiring that the issuer of a public offering file a registration statement providing specific information about the issuer. The Securities Exchange Act of 1934 established the SEC. This act requires periodic disclosures in the form of reports to the SEC by companies whose securities are publicly held. It also greatly strengthened the governments' hand in regulating the ways in which securities changed hands in public transactions.

6. Describe the process by which commodities contracts are traded.

Commodities are basic resources and agricultural products such as gold, silver, wheat, cotton, pork bellies, and orange juice. A commodity contract is a commitment to buy at a particular time a quantity of a commodity that is bought and sold on secondary markets. Investors purchase the contract up to 18 months before it is due to expire. In most cases, the investor does not want the commodity. They expect the price of the contract will rise and that the contract may be sold at a profit before expiration.

Key Terms

Balanced funds	Income funds	Mutual funds	Secondary markets
Broker	Limit order	No-load fund	Security
Commodities	Load	Open order	Specialist
Commodities contracts	Margin account	Primary markets	Spread
Discretionary order	Margin call	Prospectus	Syndicate
Government bonds	Market order	Public offering	Ticker
Growth funds	Municipal bonds	Registration statement	Underwriter

Review Questions

1. Describe the major ways a publicly traded stock transfer can occur.
2. What is the function of a secondary market?
3. Describe how shares change hands on a secondary market.
4. How does the New York Stock Exchange operate? How does this exchange differ from the over-the-counter market?
5. What is a government bond? How do U.S. government bonds differ from municipal bonds?
6. If you want to begin investing in stocks or bonds, what sources of financial information are

7. Describe the role of the Securities and Exchange Commission. Why was it established?

8. By law, the issuer of stock must provide investors with two disclosure documents. List and describe each one.

Application Exercises

1. Select two companies listed on the New York Stock Exchange. Throughout a two-week period, review newspaper stock quotations and chart the following information: annual dividend; closing price; net change.

   At the end of the two-week period, decide which stock is most attractive in terms of an investment plan that stresses growth. Explain.

2. You are preparing to give a brief oral report on the concept of stock averages. Prepare an outline that focuses on these questions: What does the term stock average mean? What is the value of stock averages to investors? Describe one major stock average.

Cases

19.1 Damson's Gamble

Damson Oil sold limited-partnership units in oil- and gas-producing properties it owned. The partnerships, useful as tax shelters, sold briskly.

In 1983, Damson purchased all of the outstanding shares of Dorchester Oil Corp., an independent oil firm, for $22.50 per share. Dorchester owned 1900 producing wells, large oil and natural gas reserves, and other assets. The purchase cost Damson about $400 million, but it got the equivalent of 50 million barrels of oil at $7.70 per barrel — dirt cheap in early 1984.

Unfortunately, the purchase exhausted Damson's cash and its ability to borrow, just when partnership sales began to decline. Dorchester's assets had to be sold to existing partnership funds rather than to new ones. Then declining oil prices and uncertainty about proposed tax laws hit Damson's partnerships. In mid-1985, trying to maintain their value, Damson consolidated 16 of its 17 funds into Damson Energy, issuing share-like partnership units traded on the American Exchange. Units were issued at $20. They soon dropped to around $13. By the end of 1986 their market price was only about $1.50.

Questions

1. What factors caused Damson to have difficulty with its newly acquired Dorchester Oil?
2. What factors affected Damson Energy's market price?

For more information see *Financial Planning*, August 1985, pp. 67–78; *The Wall Street Journal*, April 11, 1985, p. 6; and *Business Week*, March 5, 1984, p. 40.

19.2 The Takeover Game

Individuals and investment firms, trying to cash in on the rash of corporate takeovers in the 1980s, used money and accurate information that a takeover attempt was in the works to buy the stock of target firms before the company attempting the takeover bid up the stock's price.

The SEC prohibits using insider information before it is made public. At least a few players have been unable to resist the temptation to profit from what they know.

One was Dennis Levine, a young investment banker. The SEC charged him with using inside knowledge of potential takeover attempts. Levine supposedly profited (allegedly $12.6 million worth) by secretly buying stocks of 54 target firms through a Bahamian subsidiary of a Swiss bank.

He pled guilty to four felony counts, for which he could receive twenty years in prison and fines up to $610,000. By agreeing to help the SEC investigation of insider fraud, he will likely receive a lighter sentence. Levine turned his entire wealth — $11.5 million — over to the court along with this $100,000 red Ferrari.

He was barred from the securities business for life.

Questions

1. How can insider trading affect securities markets?
2. How could Levine's insider trading affect firms attempting takeovers? What can they do about it?

For more information see *Time*, June 23, 1986, p. 61; *Fortune*, June 9, 1986, p. 101; and *The New York Times*, June 6, 1986, p. A1.

20

RISK MANAGEMENT AND INSURANCE

Learning Objectives

After you have completed this chapter, you will be able to do the following:

■ Define the types of risk and describe the four main ways of handling risk.

■ Define *insurance* and explain how insurance reduces risk.

■ Outline the four principles of insurance.

■ List the major forms of public insurance and the primary categories of private insurance coverage.

■ Describe the applications of insurance to business risks.

■ Compare term life insurance with whole-life insurance.

During the first three months of 1986, it was hard to escape news about space. A space probe sent back the first pictures of the planet Uranus and its mysterious moons. As Halley's Comet passed close to Earth, five space probes visited it. And, tragically, the space shuttle Challenger blew up just after it was launched. The great successes of humans in space tend to make us forget that space flight is a risky business. In fact, all ventures — particularly the entrepreneurial ones — pose risks. The problem is how to manage them.

Edmund Halley (1656–1742), who identified the seventy-six-year cycle of the comet that bears his name, was a great student of natural phenomena. One of his projects was to examine data on the sex and age of every person who had died in the German city of Breslau in 1692. From these data, Halley devised mortality tables, figures indicating the percentage of people who live to a given age. His study, called the *Breslau Table of Mortality,* proved that it was possible to study life and death (and, incidentally, risk) statistically, thus laying the foundation for the modern insurance industry.[1]

Insurance is not the only — or necessarily the best — way to cope with risk. At one extreme, a firm might simply take its chances that the risk will not occur. At the other, the company might avoid an activity because of its potential risk. Between those two extremes lie the options that this chapter examines.

THE NATURE OF RISK

The uncertainty about whether an event will or will not occur is **risk**. Note that risk is not the same as the odds that an event will occur.

An event that has a 95 percent chance of occurring is highly certain and is therefore of low risk. Facing such a likely occurrence, a business will either avoid activities that might lead to the event or plan how to deal with it when it happens. For example, Federal Express knows that accidents involving its thousands of delivery vans are inevitable. Its strategy for dealing with this risk is both to put a premium on accident-free records for its drivers and also to maintain stores of replacement parts and vehicles. Federal Express is in a high certainty, low risk situation. The contrary is also true, however: a "one in a billion" event is also a low risk, because there is a high degree of certainty that it will not happen. Normally, businesses assume the risk of such events. The greatest risk occurs when the level of certainty is neither extremely high nor extremely low. These risks are the ones a business must focus on.

The Two General Types of Risk

There are two categories of risk. **Speculative risks** offer the potential for gain as well as loss. Starting a new business or buying securities involves speculative risk. **Pure risks,** the second type, offer only the potential for loss. Fires, automobile accidents, and illnesses are pure risks. Firms can buy insurance to protect against pure risks, but not against speculative risks. Figure 20.1 outlines the classifications of risk.

Risk Management

In a business, **risk management** is the process of identifying exposures to risk, choosing the best method for handling each exposure, and implementing it.

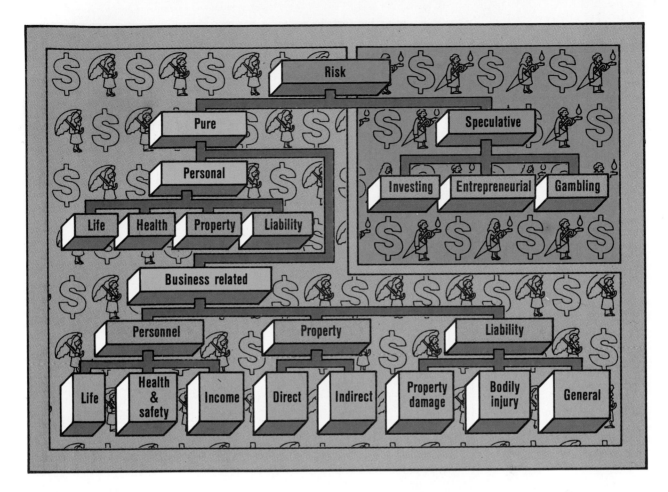

FIGURE 20.1

A Classification of Risk

The Two Business-Related Types of Risk

The managing of speculative risks is a general responsibility of the overall management team. Managing pure risks, though, is in many firms the job of a **risk manager,** a person whose job it is to preserve company assets and a business's earning power against pure risks. Among the risk manager's most common concerns are **property risks,** the potential direct loss of the firm's property due to fire or similar causes. Indirectly, property losses can cause revenue losses if, say, fire destroyed an automobile dealership's paint shop. A risk manager's other major area of concern is **liability risks,** those risks that involve the potential that a firm might be held legally responsible for losses suffered by a person or another firm. Personal injury liability for automobile accidents is the most common type. For manufacturers, another critically important type of risk management is product liability insurance.

At a major corporation, the risk manager is likely to have a high rank and a large staff. One example is *Business Insurance* magazine's "Risk Manager of the Year" for 1985, Harold C. Lang of the Leaseway Corporation. Leaseway is a major transportation company with 130 subsidiaries and eighteen thousand employees. Lang and his staff of twelve oversee the expenditure of $35 million for insurance annually. He reports to a corporate vice president. In smaller businesses, risk management may be just another responsibility of the owner or a manager but that's not the case at Leaseway.[2]

FIGURE 20.2

Four Risk Management
Strategies

Risk avoidance

Risk assumption

Risk transference

Risk reduction

The Techniques of Risk Management

When deciding how to handle a particular risk, the risk manager has four basic methods from which to choose:

☐ Risk avoidance
☐ Risk assumption
☐ Risk reduction
☐ Risk transfer

**The Four Basic Methods of
Handling Risk**

Risk avoidance requires a firm not to engage in an activity or to own particular property that might lead to an exposure to risk. For example, in the mid-1980s many companies decided not to extend their operations to the Union of South Africa in order to avoid the risks of the political instability there.

By contrast, **risk assumption** requires that a firm consciously recognize a particular risk and accept it as an integral part of its activities. As mentioned, risk assumption may be in order when the odds are strongly against an event's happening or when the potential loss is low. In some instances, **insurers,** any organizations that provide insurance coverage, force their policyholders into risk assumption so that they can keep coverage affordable. They may issue a policy with a **deductible,** an amount the policyholder must pay before the insurer's

Creating a safer environment. Businesses can do a lot to promote safety. In 1985 The Times *at Gainesville, Georgia, won the Safe Driving Award from the American Newspaper Publishers Association and the International Circulation Managers Association. Independent carriers like Wanda Whitmire, who delivers* The Times, *drove over 1 million miles that year without being involved in a single accident.*

obligation to pay becomes effective. Most automobile policies require at least a $250 deductible. The other principal method that insurers have of forcing risk assumption is coinsurance, described later under "Private Insurance."

Risk reduction is the lessening of the uncertainty of financial loss in a risky situation. Many companies go to great lengths to promote worker safety so as to avoid not only the financial costs of injury but the down time and disruption of work that would accompany it.

Risk transfer shifts risk to another party. Insurance can be a prime example of risk transfer. A relatively small certain payment, the **premium**, replaces a large uncertain potential loss.

THE NATURE OF INSURANCE

Insurance **Defined**

A contract in which one party agrees to pay a specified sum to another if a certain event occurs is **insurance**. By means of an insurance contract, the **insured**, a person or firm that buys insurance, exchanges an uncertain situation for the certainty of paying an insurance premium. The contract between the insurer and the insured, the **insurance policy**, contains the terms of the insurance.

Insurance can be divided into life insurance and *all* other types. The two groups share several important characteristics, but fundamental differences distinguish them, as we will see. Insurance generally works on four principles:

☐ The law of large numbers
☐ Indemnification
☐ The concept of insurable risk
☐ The concept of insurable interest

The Law of Large Numbers

As the number of units in a group increases, predictions about the group become more accurate and therefore more certain, according to the **law of large numbers**. Insurance reduces the risk for an entire class of insured entities because the number and degree of losses are mathematically certain. Insurance giants like Allstate or State Farm, which have had tens of millions of policyholders over the years, can make extremely accurate predictions, based on their extensive research and experience.

Self-insurance The law of large numbers also works to the advantage of firms with experience running many stores, outlets, or plants. They may choose **self-insurance**, a mechanism by which a business establishes a fund to cover losses caused by particular types of events. Usually, firms assign each unit its share of the losses that are likely to occur to all the units in a given period. Suppose that a retail firm has 500 stores, each valued at $500,000. If the firm projects one fire loss per year, it could assess each store $1,000 for the year rather than buy fire insurance. If no fires occur, the fund earns interest until it is needed. However, if more than one fire occurs in the first year, the firm could find itself strapped for cash. Plainly, self-insurance is only for large firms like Safeway Stores, Inc., and the K mart Corporation. Small firms whose facilities are concentrated in only a few places should avoid self-insurance.

Indemnification

The principle of **indemnification**, which does not apply to life insurance, requires an insurer to pay no more than the financial loss actually suffered. Otherwise, the insured might be tempted to try to gain from a loss. On a property insurance claim, for example, an insurer will pay only a loss's **actual cash value**, the purchase price of an item of personal property less its depreciation. After a fire, a firm without replacement-value coverage may have to go out of business, because the insurance proceeds will not replace lost equipment. At that point, the extra cost of replacement-value coverage will look like a missed bargain.

Insurable Risk

The risks for which an insurance policy can be purchased are **insurable risks**. Emotional or sentimental values are irrelevant in respect to insurability. For all types of insurance other than life insurance, insurable risks must be financial, measurable, and predictable. A sufficiently large number of similar situations must have occurred before an insurance company can generate accurate estimates of risk. When a pianist "insures" his or her hands, what actually occurs is a transference of risk. Remember that insurance is a reduction of risk through the working of the law of large numbers. That is why insurance policies generally exclude losses from catastrophes like wars, earthquakes, or floods. Catastrophes like these are neither predictable nor isolated. Insurers base their premiums on the average of isolated losses. One can nevertheless still get policies covering some catastrophic risks.

Insurance Casualties

There is an insurance crisis in America. Insurance companies claim that huge liability suits and generous juries are driving up their costs and causing huge rate increases. Critics dispute the claim, insisting that the insurance industry has no figures to prove that its costs are rising so quickly. Whether the crisis is real or hype, it has caused rates for some kinds of insurance to shoot up and led to a lot of worry among corporate executives. Some of those executives now look at products in terms of their potential liability for the company. If that potential is high, the company may simply decide "We won't make that product any more."

That's what G. D. Searle decided about its Copper 7 intrauterine device, the most popular IUD in America. It stopped selling the Copper 7 in the U.S. in 1986, after it discovered it could no longer get insurance to cover its potential product liability. For the two million American women who rely on IUDs for birth control, Searle's decision was a shock. The Copper 7 was known as "the safest of the IUDs on the market," according to Planned Parenthood.

The company has won most of its lawsuits related to the Copper 7, but it has lost at least 2, and 300 remain outstanding. Searle's 1985 sales for IUDs amounted to only $11 million, while it spent $1.5 million in lawsuits, even though it won them all that year. The company no doubt watched the example of A. H. Robins Co. which filed for bankruptcy to try to blunt the effects of lawsuits filed against the company because of its Dalkon Shield IUD, which thousands of women say caused pelvic inflammation or sterility. The departure of Searle leaves only one IUD manufacturer in the U.S. — tiny Alza Corp, which sells 50,000 IUDs a year to Americans.

The situation is similar in a great number of American industries. But the medical casualties of high insurance costs provide good examples of what's happening in the country as a whole, and they tend to grab the headlines because the loss of a good drug or vaccine can affect us all. There is no longer an American-owned maker of anesthesia gas machines. Pregnant women were left without a prescription medicine to deal with severe nausea when Merrell Dow Pharmaceuticals stopped making the controversial drug Bendectin in 1983 because of lawsuits. Some obstetricians have simply stopped delivering babies.

Vaccines are especially endangered by liability suits and insurance costs. Only one company, Merck & Co., still manufactures a combined measles, mumps, and rubella vaccine; only two still make diphtheria, tetanus, and pertusis vaccine, and only Lederle Labs still markets an oral polio vaccine. Even though almost every American child receives these vaccines, and many doctors see them as crucial to the health of future generations, the companies can sell only 3 to 4 million doses a year. The profits are small, and can be quickly wiped out by a single successful lawsuit. The vaccine makers that have stayed in business have had to raise their prices drastically. A lawyer for Merck says, "A good businessman would not be in this business. The potential liability risk is too high. But Merck is committed to manufacturing vaccines from a social responsibility standpoint."

Many parents are understandably wary of trusting American drug manufacturers to keep making vaccines just to be socially responsible, and they have joined doctors and business people looking for a solution. One answer to liability lawsuits may be "no-fault" insurance programs that pay claims without the costly trials necessary to determine responsibility. Some businesses now train employees in how to prevent lawsuits. Congress is grappling with the problem as more and more companies get caught up in the liability panic. Meanwhile, critics of the insurance industry wait for the industry to produce figures that show their soaring rates are justified. Many view the rising rates and panic as, in Ralph Nader's words, "the greatest commercial hoax that I have ever observed in the United States." Whether Americans succumb to the panic or investigate the "hoax" will determine the course of liability insurance for years to come.

Sources: Robert Sherrill, "One Paper That Wouldn't Shut Up," *The Nation*, May 17, 1986, 688. Michael Brody, "When Products Turn into Liabilities," *Fortune*, March 3, 1986, 20. Ted Gest and Clemens P. Work, "Sky-high Damage Suits," *U.S. News & World Report*, January 27, 1986, 35.

Finding out what's standard. Business is getting more complex. So is the world. As businesses begin to operate internationally, they find that what is standard in their own country is not standard elsewhere. Some insurance companies now offer global policies to reduce the risk of the unexpected.

In general, an insurable risk is a loss that is not intentionally caused by the insured. Again, life insurance policies are an exception. Insurers will pay on a suicide's policy if it has been in effect for more than a specified period, usually two years. They will never pay the murderer of an insured, though.

Insurers also have the right to set standards for the risks they accept. They can, for instance, refuse to insure drivers who have had numerous accidents. And in terms of setting standards for financial liability, an insurable risk may be neither too big nor too small. Increasingly, insurers have begun not taking on large individual risks, particularly in the areas of medical malpractice and product liability, where a single claim can run into the millions. In contrast, insurers will not cover losses so small that the cost of processing a claim would make the premium prohibitively high. Deductibles exist specifically to bridge this gap between the costs of claim processing and premiums.

Insurable Interest

The Final Principle of Insurance

A person making a claim on a policy must have an **insurable interest**, an interest that can be protected under the law and under the terms of the policy, in the subject of the policy. This principle keeps insurance from becoming a means of gambling on another's death or misfortune. The insurable-interest principle applies in different ways to property insurance and life insurance.

With property insurance, an insurable interest must exist at the time of the loss. For instance, a person who might continue to pay the premiums on a fire insurance policy on a house he had sold could not collect if it burned down. However, a firm can obtain insurance on goods that it expects to receive, although the policy will not take effect until the risk of loss shifts over to the insured.

With life insurance, an insurable interest can arise from either family or business relationships. The insurable interest must exist at the time the policy was issued. If, for example, a wife takes out a life insurance policy on her husband and they then divorce, she can still keep it in force and collect when he dies.

Insurance Companies

Over 5,600 companies write insurance. With assets exceeding $1 trillion, the insurance industry is one of the major investors in real estate, government securities, and corporate securities. Over 2 million people work in the insurance industry.

The two major types of insurance companies are stock insurance companies and mutual insurance companies. **Stock insurance companies,** owned by stockholders, provide insurance protection for a profit. Like other for-profit corporations, stock insurance companies distribute profits to shareholders in the form of dividends. One major stock insurance company is Aetna Life & Casualty Co.

Mutual insurance companies are owned by their policyholders. Any profits they earn go to the policyholders in the form of insurance dividends. Mutual of New York (MONY) is one such leading mutual insurance company.

The Types of Coverage

Most people are familiar with the five major categories of insurance: property, liability, health, life, and income. It is not until one considers that even a medium-sized firm may require as many as three dozen types of insurance that the breadth of these categories becomes apparent, however. For the remainder of this chapter, we will examine the types and sources of coverage, as given in Figure 20.3.

PUBLIC INSURANCE

The federal government is an important source of insurance. In fact, over one-third of national government expenditures go for programs that provide insurance benefits of one kind or another.

Unemployment Insurance

The Major Forms of Public Insurance

Federal law and the laws of all fifty states make employers financially responsible when they lay off employees, and in some cases when they fire them. **Unemployment insurance** provides partial, temporary replacement income for eligible unemployed workers. A state payroll tax on employers funds the insurance

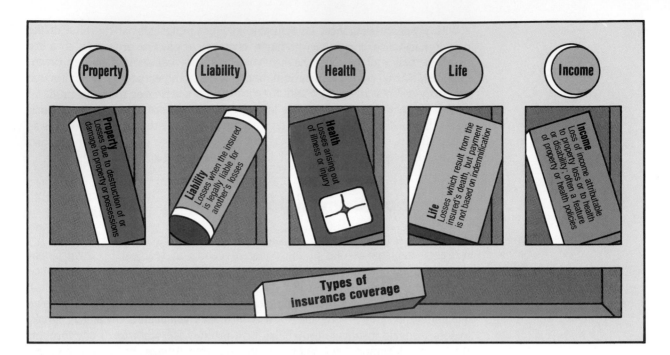

Property

Liability

Health

Life

Income

Property
Losses due to destruction of or damage to property or possessions

Liability
Losses when the insured is legally liable for another's losses

Health
Losses arising out of illness or injury

Life
Losses which result from the insured's death, but payment is not based on indemnification

Income
Loss of income attributable to property loss or to health or disability; often a feature of property or health policies

Types of insurance coverage

FIGURE 20.3

Types of Insurance Coverage

program. The level of this tax varies. Employers with high rates of claims among their employees pay more than those with low rates. The state administers the program, but during periods of high unemployment the federal government offers supplemental benefits.

Worker's Compensation

The state-administered insurance program that provides employees with protection from losses caused by injury or illness resulting from employment is called **worker's compensation.** In effect, worker's compensation is a form of **no-fault insurance,** an insurance program that compensates losses regardless of who, if anyone, is responsible for their occurrence. In the early part of this century, state legislatures devised worker's compensation systems as a means of avoiding suits against employers and as a way to see that employees received enough to live on. The program covers medical care, lost income, rehabilitation, and survivors' benefits. Worker's compensation usually covers not more than 75 percent of the worker's lost wages, but these benefits are tax free. The benefits cease when the employee returns to work.

Whether an employer must buy worker's compensation insurance from the government or from a private insurer varies from state to state. Some states allow self-insurance. Premiums vary according to the safety of the industry in question and the employer's record of claims.

Social Security

Under the **Social Security Act of 1935,** the federal **Old-Age, Survivors, Disability, and Health Insurance (OASDHI)** program provides retirement, survivors', disability, and health insurance. The federal government spends more than $200 billion each year on Social Security programs. The program is funded through a payroll tax. In 1986, employers and employees each paid in 7.15 percent of the employee's first $42,000 in wages. By 1990, the rate will have increased to 7.65 percent. Self-employed workers pay a higher rate. The maximum dollar amount to which the rate applies is adjusted for inflation each year.[3] Figure 20.4 shows some changes in Social Security.

Further Major Forms of Public Insurance

Retirement Benefits Retirement benefits are based on the covered worker's income during his or her years of employment. In 1986, the maximum benefits were $739 per month. The benefits schedule is annually adjusted for inflation. Eligible retirees can begin receiving benefits at age sixty-two, but they are permanently reduced a certain amount for each month before age sixty-five that the retiree elects to receive them. Late retirement — that is, after age sixty-five — adds 3 percent per year to benefits. Starting in the year 2000, the full-benefit retirement age will gradually increase to sixty-seven.

Survivors' Benefits Survivors of workers who paid Social Security taxes can collect these benefits if the worker dies before retirement. These benefits are a form of life insurance payable to the worker's spouse, dependent children, or dependent parents. Survivors' benefits can potentially reach $15,000 per year and last for fifteen years or more.

FIGURE 20.4

Changes in Social Security

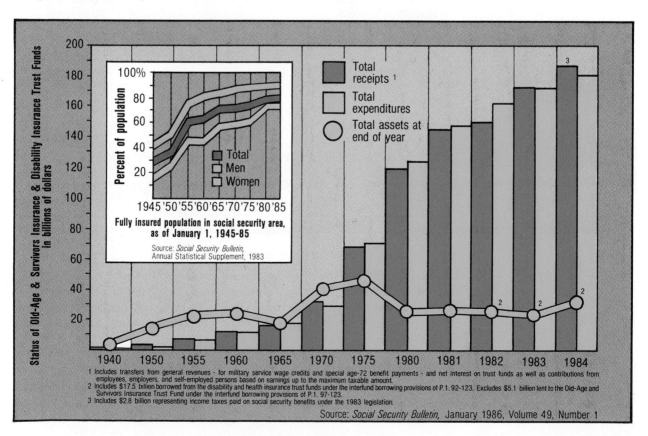

1 Includes transfers from general revenues - for military service wage credits and special age-72 benefit payments - and net interest on trust funds as well as contributions from employees, employers, and self-employed persons based on earnings up to the maximum taxable amount.
2 Includes $17.5 billion borrowed from the disability and health insurance trust funds under the interfund borrowing provisions of P.l. 92-123. Excludes $5.1 billion lent to the Old-Age and Survivors Insurance Trust Fund under the interfund borrowing provisions of P.l. 97-123.
3 Includes $2.8 billion representing income taxes paid on social security benefits under the 1983 legislation.

Source: *Social Security Bulletin*, January 1986, Volume 49, Number 1

Nuclear Insurance

The accident in the Soviet Union's Chernobyl nuclear reactor changed the focus of the debate about nuclear power. The American nuclear power industry hastened to point out how different American reactors are from Soviet ones, but more Americans now seem to fear that a disaster could happen here. Critics of nuclear power are focusing on a question that has been largely ignored in past debates: if disaster strikes here, who pays?

The current answer to that question is contained in the Price-Anderson Act, one foundation upon which the nuclear industry was built. Giving protection unheard of in other American industries, Price-Anderson sets up a fund for victims and limits the amount that the nuclear industry would have to pay in the event of an accident. This liability cap applies even if the accident is caused by gross negligence, bad faith, or willful misconduct.

At the moment, the cap is $665 million. Some experts estimate that an accident here the size of Chernobyl's could cost more than $300 billion in health and property damages. The bulk of the costs for such an accident would be borne by the victims themselves.

Some analysts feel that the act has had bad effects, creating a false sense of security in the nuclear industry. Without the fear of huge lawsuits hanging over their heads, nuclear plant builders may not have paid as much attention to safety as they should have. Ohio Representative John Seiberling, a nuclear energy supporter, says, "If the industry took the full risk, wouldn't it take every conceivable action to improve safety consciousness in order to make the risk minimal?"

Some supporters of the act acknowledge its weaknesses, but say it's better than the alternatives. Because the act eliminates the need for lawsuits and trials, it means victims can get help fast. After the Three Mile Island accident, some local residents got emergency payments within 24 hours instead of having to wait years for a court judgment. Though the cap may be too low for a worst-case scenario, it would probably cover victims' damages in a much more likely, less severe accident. If a Chernobyl-sized accident occurred in the U.S. and there wasn't a Price-Anderson act, victims would probably spend years in courts trying to get money from a company that might well declare bankruptcy.

The nuclear industry's critics point out that nuclear power's main attraction — its low cost — results at least in part from the artificial cap. In an era when a quarter of the price of every stepladder goes towards paying liability insurance, insuring nuclear power plants on the free market, without the Price-Anderson Act, would be extremely expensive. Such insurance costs almost certainly would raise the price of nuclear power, and might put the entire industry out of business. So for Congress, the question now is the same as it was in the 1950s, when Price-Anderson was created: should the government insure the survival of the nuclear power industry?

Sources: S. K. Levin, "Who'll Pay for a U.S. Chernobyl?" *The Nation*, June 14, 1986, 815. "If There's a Nuclear Disaster, Who Pays?" *The New York Times*, March 14, 1986, A34. Pete Beckmann, "Playing with Price-Anderson," *The Wall Street Journal*, February 5, 1986, 30.

Disability Benefits Totally disabled workers who have paid Social Security taxes, and their immediate families, can collect benefits if the disability is expected to last more than twelve months. Like survivors' benefits, these benefits vary according to the worker's wages, the length of time worked, and the number of dependents.

Medicare The federal health insurance program known as **Medicare** is for persons sixty-five or older, people of any age with permanent kidney failure, and certain disabled people. It provides both hospital and medical coverage.

Other Types of Public Insurance

Federal and state governments offer many other insurance programs, such as the sampling that follows.

A Sampling of Other Types of Public Insurance

Deposit Insurance   As discussed in Chapter 17, federal and state agencies insure deposits in banks, thrift institutions, and credit unions.

Mortgage Insurance   Mortgage lenders always run the risk that their borrowers will default. To protect themselves, they often require borrowers to obtain mortgage insurance. Normally, borrowers buy a policy issued by an insurance company, but the federal government also issues insurance for eligible borrowers, through the Veterans Administration (VA) and the Federal Housing Administration (FHA).

Flood Insurance   Because floods are catastrophes, insurance companies have not offered insurance against losses caused by them. To fill this need, the National Flood Insurance Act of 1968 authorized the federal government to provide such insurance at subsidized rates.

Crime Insurance   Because of the high probability of losses, insurance companies do not like to write insurance against crime covering people and businesses located in high-crime areas. The federal government will step in to fill the gap if no private insurer will take the risk.

Crop Insurance   The Federal Crop Insurance Corporation sells crop insurance through the licensed agents of private insurers.

Pension Insurance   Until 1974, employees often lost their pension benefits if their employer filed for bankruptcy, went out of business, or simply terminated its pension plan. In that year, Congress enacted the **Employee Retirement Income Security Act (ERISA)**, which created the Pension Benefit Guaranty Corporation to guarantee pension plans.

PRIVATE INSURANCE

The total spent on private insurance in the United States exceeds $286 billion each year, or more than $1,200 per person. Very little economic activity takes place without insurance to cover it. When NBC bought the rights to televise the Moscow Olympics in 1980, for instance, the network took out insurance coverage in case the United States did not field a team, which it decided not to do, in fact.

Property and Liability Insurance

The Primary Categories of Private Insurance Coverage

Property owners always run the risk that their property may be damaged or destroyed. A good-sized hurricane, for example, can easily cause $500 million in

Reducing hazards. *Insurance is not the only way to manage risk, nor is it always the best. One way to decrease the likelihood of fire is to install automatic sprinkler systems. Buildings like Seattle's Columbia Center that install such systems not only lower their risk, they lower their insurance premiums as well.*

property damage. Property owners also run the risk that someone will hold them liable for injuries that occurred on or were caused by their property. In New Jersey, for instance, a bar can be liable if a patron drinks too much and causes an auto accident in which a third person is injured. Risks like these are covered by property and liability insurance. These two forms of insurance are distinctly different types, but insurers typically sell them together. See the various types of liability insurance in Table 20.1.

Fire and Homeowner's Insurance   Fires cause more than $7 billion in damage each year. **Fire insurance** protects the insured from losses to the covered property, considered usually to be both a building and its contents, that are caused by fire and, often, other perils such as hail and windstorms. The premiums on fire insurance vary according to the property's value, the type of building it is, the use the property is put to, the value of its contents, and many other factors. Fire-insurance policies often require extensive risk-reduction efforts, such as the installation of sprinkler systems and smoke alarms.

The maximum insurance claim paid is generally the actual cash value of the loss up to the policy limits. Many fire policies contain a **coinsurance** clause, however, which requires the policyholder to pay a portion of any loss to the insured building if the policy maximum is less than a specified percentage (usually 80 percent) of the building's value at the time of the loss. For example, suppose that J & J Construction owns a garage valued at $200,000. The policy covering it has a maximum of $120,000, with $1,000 deductible and an 80 percent coin-

TABLE 20.1

Types of Liability Insurance

Types	Coverage
General liability	Basic liability coverage for a firm; other types added to it.
Owners', landlords', and tenants' (OLT)	Losses suffered by individuals other than employees as a result of the firm's use of the premises it occupies.
Manufacturers' and contractors' (M & C)	Premises coverage plus coverage for off-premises activities.
Comprehensive general liability	Umbrella liability protection, including general liability, OLT, and G & C coverage.
Product liability	Losses suffered as a result of products sold by manufacturers, wholesalers, and retailers.
Professional liability (malpractice)	Losses arising out of the rendering of services by certain professionals.

surance clause. Assume that a fire does $101,000 damage to the garage. To determine the insurer's liability to J & J, the formula is as follows:

$$\frac{\text{Policy maximum}}{(\text{Coverage \% required}) \times (\text{Property value})} \times (\text{Loss} - \text{Deductible}) = \text{Liability}$$

The insurer's liability to J & J would therefore be

$$\frac{\$120,000}{(.80) \times (\$200,000)} \times (\$101,000 - 1,000) = \text{Liability}$$

$$\frac{\$120,000}{\$160,000} \times \$100,000 = \$75,000$$

Thus, J & J will have to absorb a $26,000 loss ($101,000 − $75,000).

Many fire-insurance policies feature **business interruption insurance,** a form of income insurance that protects a firm against lost earnings as the result of a fire or similar peril. It covers expenses like taxes and payrolls, which continue even though the business may be closed. Fire policies for the home are called **homeowner's insurance,** which often covers apartments as well as houses. These package policies include both property and liability protection.

Automobile Insurance   Insurance from property and liability losses arising from the ownership or operation of motor vehicles is **automobile insurance.** This type of insurance is usually a package containing four distinct forms of coverage. Table 20.2 outlines the coverage common to personal and family automobile policies. Normally, personal auto policies have a single maximum amount that would be paid for all liability arising from any one accident. Family policies, in contrast, usually contain separate limits, often expressed as "15/40/10," or the like. In this example, in one accident any person's injuries will be covered

FIGURE 20.5

No Fault versus Fault Insurance

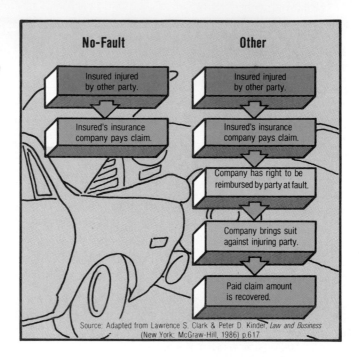

No-Fault   Other

Insured injured by other party.

Insured's insurance company pays claim.

Insured injured by other party.

Insured's insurance company pays claim.

Company has right to be reimbursed by party at fault.

Company brings suit against injuring party.

Paid claim amount is recovered.

Source: Adapted from Lawrence S. Clark & Peter D. Kinder, *Law and Business* (New York: McGraw-Hill, 1986) p.617

up to $15,000, all personal injuries will be covered up to $40,000, and all property damage liability will be covered up to $10,000.

Business auto policies are somewhat different. For one thing, liability coverage for bodily injury covers only nonemployees, because worker's compensation already covers employees. Also, a business auto policy usually has one overall limit on liability.

A major complaint about auto insurance is that it has been based on the concept of assigning fault. Suppose that parties A and B are involved in an accident caused by A in which B was seriously injured. B's insurer would pay his or her medical expenses up to its policy limits, then seek reimbursement from A's insurer. Quite often, a lawsuit will be the result. Some states have thus adopted **no-fault automobile insurance systems,** in which insurers do not have a right of reimbursement for payments to their insureds if the payments are below a specified level. Massachusetts and New Jersey have their own forms of no-fault insurance. Figure 20.5 compares no-fault systems with fault-based systems.

Business Liability Insurance   As a result of new laws and court decisions, businesses are now legally responsible for a far greater scope of losses than they were even ten years ago. As we have seen, **liability insurance** is coverage against legal responsibility for another's losses. Table 20.1 listed the most common general types. Virtually all liability policies also obligate the insurance company to provide a legal defense for the insured, up to the policy limits. If a lawsuit seeks more than the policy limits, the insured must pay for lawyers to defend against the excess liability.

Malpractice or **professional liability insurance** covers responsibility for losses arising out of professional services rendered by doctors, lawyers, accountants, and certain other professionals. A doctor who operates on a patient's left ear instead of the right or a lawyer who loses a client's money or an accountant who

Policy part	Type of coverage	Persons covered	Property covered
1.	Liability insurance	Pays when the driver of the insured car is at fault and that person is the owner of the car or is driving with the permission of the owner. The insurance company may require that some drivers be excluded, however.	——
	Bodily injury liability	Passengers of other cars and pedestrians injured as a result of the accident. Passengers of the at-fault driver will be covered only if their losses exceed that covered in Part 2 (below).	——
	Property damage liability	——	Automobiles and other property damaged through the fault of the covered driver.
2.	Medical payments insurance	The covered at-fault driver and his/her passengers.	——
3.	Property damage insurance	——	The insured automobile.
	Collision	——	The insured automobile when damaged as a result of a collision caused by a covered driver.
	Comprehensive	——	The insured automobile and its contents when damaged as a result of fire, theft, windstorm, and other perils.
4.	Uninsured motorists	Driver and passengers of insured car when bodily injuries are caused by an uninsured motorist.	The insured automobile when losses are caused by an uninsured motorist.

TABLE 20.2

Family and Personal Automobile Policies

carelessly certifies a false financial statement would all be liable for their acts, and their insurers would have to pay. An explosion of litigation in this area has resulted in malpractice insurance's becoming extremely expensive.

Product liability insurance covers a manufacturer's or seller's responsibility for losses caused by goods placed in commerce. Makers of everything from football helmets to polio vaccines need to protect themselves against liability for injuries their products may cause. Chapter 22 explores product liability in more detail.

"We're both insured by the same company
—won't they be mad."

Transportation (Marine) Insurance That form of property insurance designed to protect goods as they are moved from place to place is called **transportation insurance** or **marine insurance.** The insurance industry commonly refers to it as marine insurance, revealing its ancient function of insuring cargo shipped by sea. The first form of marine insurance appeared originally in Babylon over two thousand years ago. Today, it comes in two types. **Inland marine insurance** covers cargo carried by every form of transportation not involving water. An inland marine policy would cover cargo carried on a space shuttle, for instance. **Ocean marine insurance** covers cargo carried on any body of water.

Theft Insurance and Fidelity Bonds The general term for insurance covering losses resulting from the unlawful taking of property belonging to another is **theft insurance.** In a business context, theft insurance applies only to theft by nonemployees. Usually, but not always, theft insurance covers **robbery,** theft involving the threat or actual use of force, and **burglary,** theft from a building involving forcible entry into it. Theft insurance is often part of a property insurance package. A business can purchase robbery or burglary insurance separately or purchase an umbrella theft insurance policy that covers both kinds of loss.

Businesses that wish to insure themselves against theft by employees purchase **fidelity bonds.** For example, banks obtain fidelity bonds to cover their tellers so that the banks are protected against embezzlement.

Surety Bonds On major construction projects, particularly those under government contracts, contractors must supply **surety bonds,** insurance policies that provide for compensation to the beneficiary should a contract not be completed on time.

Title Insurance The purchaser of real property to which the seller did not have a clear or marketable title is insured against losses by **title insurance.** It protects the purchaser against the risk that he or she might not actually own the property. Banks usually require title insurance as a condition of a mortgage loan.

Credit Insurance   Insurance paid for by a borrower which compensates a lender for any losses if the borrower defaults is **credit insurance.** In theory, such insurance makes lenders willing to loan to less creditworthy borrowers or lend at lower rates. In practice, creditors often encourage or require borrowers to buy it because they receive a commission on the sale of it.

Health Insurance

As Chapter 8 noted, **health insurance,** which reimburses expenses arising from illness or accident, costs employers more than $90 billion each year. Employees consider health insurance a vital benefit, given that national health-care expenses exceed $1,700 per person per year.[4] The health insurance that employers provide is sold to employees collectively, so it is called **group health insurance.** Premiums for group insurance policies are lower than for individual policies, because the risk is spread across a wider, often healthier group. The principal types of health insurance coverage can be bought separately, but they are most commonly sold together in what is called a comprehensive health insurance plan.

The Principal Types of Health Insurance

Hospitalization   The central element in virtually all health insurance policies is **hospitalization coverage,** insurance covering all expenses of being in a hospital except doctors' charges. The covered expenses usually include charges for the room, routine laboratory tests, basic drugs, and the like. Most policies set a maximum amount covered per day for a certain number of days, with any excess paid by the insured. This type of coverage is called first-dollar coverage because it pays, for example, the first $150 per day.

Surgical Coverage   Surgeons' and anesthesiologists' fees, surgical nurses' charges, operating room charges, and similar expenses are paid through **surgical coverage.** Many insurers pay whatever is charged for surgery as long as it is "usual, customary, and reasonable." Other companies may set a maximum they will pay for particular procedures, like $1,200 for an appendectomy. In either case, it is first-dollar coverage.

Medical Expenses   Medical and doctor expenses other than those related to surgery are paid by **medical expense coverage.** These expenses may include office visits, X-rays, drugs, and the like. Medical expense coverage may be first-dollar with annual maximums, but more commonly it specifies an annual deductible or coinsurance percentage and annual per-item maximums.

Major Medical Expense   When a major illness or accident strikes, the types of health coverage we have just discussed often run out quickly. **Major medical expense coverage** reimburses a broad range of losses associated with major or catastrophic illnesses or injuries. The policy limits on this coverage can reach $100,000, and the deductible is often $5,000. Coinsurance provisions are the standard 80/20, with the insured paying 20 percent, though there is usually a cap that establishes a maximum loss beyond which coinsurance does not apply.

Dental and Vision   Some health policies include dental and vision care. Coinsurance and deductible provisions are commonly part of such coverage.

Disability Income Insurance   Income lost as a result of an illness or injury can be replaced by **disability income insurance.** This coverage is sometimes included in health policies but is routinely sold separately. Its benefits usually begin after a waiting period of from three to thirty days. The benefits replace between 50 and 70 percent of an employee's income, but they are not taxable.

Health Maintenance Organizations

Until twenty years ago, private doctors and hospitals had no real competition for patient and insurance company dollars. Also, by that time advances in medical technology had led to the introduction of extraordinarily expensive treatments like coronary bypass surgery and million-dollar diagnostic tools like the CAT scanner. These increases brought about government cost-containment programs, which largely failed, and resulted in the private efforts to cut medical costs that were discussed in Chapter 8. They also led to competition in the medical marketplace.

The most important competitor to develop was the **health maintenance organization (HMO),** a prepaid health-care provider that operates clinics and, in some cases, hospitals. HMOs provide health care, not insurance. Their members pay a monthly fee (HMOs offer both individual and group plans) and receive almost unlimited care. If the HMO cannot provide the treatment a member needs, the member is referred to an outside provider, whom the HMO pays. HMOs tend to emphasize "wellness" and attention to good health practices as a way to reduce health-care expenses. The California-based Kaiser-Permanente program is the largest HMO in the country.

LIFE INSURANCE

There are five forms of life insurance. They differ on the period of their coverage and how, if any, the cash value builds. The forms of life insurance are term, whole life, limited life, endowment, and universal life.

Upon the death of an insured, **life insurance** pays a set amount to the policy's beneficiary. A **beneficiary** is the person or organization named to receive the proceeds from a life insurance policy. The key characteristic distinguishing life insurance from the other types of insurance is that the principle of indemnification does not apply to the payment of benefits under life policies. Upon the insured's death, the insurer pays the value of the policy, no matter how long the policy has been in force. If an insured bought a two hundred thousand dollar policy six months before she died, the insurer would pay her beneficiary the full amount, even though the insured might have paid only, say, six hundred dollars in premiums. If instead she died fifty years later with the policy in force, her beneficiary would still receive the same amount.

Insurance companies base their life insurance premiums on the experience

Fallout from Bhopal

In the early hours of December 3, 1984, toxic methyl isocyanate gas leaked out of a Union Carbide pesticide manufacturing plant in Bhopal India, killing at least 2,220 and injuring 20,000 to 50,000 more in history's worst industrial disaster. The accident had political, economic, and social consequences around the globe, and its full effect won't be known for years. In the insurance world, the disaster raised two very important questions which any company engaged in overseas business must contemplate: does the value of human life depend upon the nationality of that life, and which company in which country should bear ultimate responsibility when a multinational company's subsidiary has an accident?

The lawsuits brought by the victims and their families will doubtless go on for years, watched closely by manufacturers and insurers alike. But a decision by a U.S. judge in May 1986 will probably turn out to be the key one in the case, answering at least temporarily some of the major questions. Judge John Keenan of the U.S. District Court in Charleston, West Virginia, ruled that the claims against Union Carbide should be heard in India, not the United States. The ruling was seen as a victory for Union Carbide and its insurers and a defeat for the scores of lawyers representing the Indian victims.

In sending the case to India, Judge Keenan accepted Carbide's argument that the case was, primarily, an Indian matter. Carbide lawyers emphasized that the plant belonged to Union Carbide India Ltd., an Indian company in which the American chemical giant owned only a minority share (49.1%). The Indian company made the decisions leading to the accident, Carbide lawyers argued, and the Indian government established the regulations governing the plant.

Some hailed the judge's ruling as "ingenious," respecting the rights of Third World countries. Keenan himself wrote that trying the cases in the United States would be "another situation in which an established sovereign inflicted its rules, its standards and values on a developing nation." Critics of the ruling saw it as a way to allow American companies to wash their hands of problems associated with their overseas business. The ruling, they say, permits American businesses to hide behind the guise of foreign subsidiaries.

The ruling is so important to the outcome of the lawsuits because the amount that Carbide and its insurers will ultimately pay depends upon the value placed on each human life. In America, juries consistently say that an individual life is worth hundreds of thousands — sometimes millions — of dollars. Federal agencies set up their own guidelines about the value of life based on the present value of a person's expected lifetime earnings or on how much individuals seem to think their lives are worth, as shown by their willingness to risk their lives for money. The Environmental Protection Agency puts the figure at one to seven million; the Federal Aviation Administration uses a relatively low $650,000. In India, where the average person makes about one-fortieth as much as the average American, juries are more likely to value life in three figures, rather than six or seven.

The more than fifty companies involved in insuring and reinsuring against Carbide's losses no doubt breathed a sigh of relief at Judge Keenan's ruling. If the judge had tried the cases in the U.S., and if Carbide had paid American liability rates, insurance companies would have had to raise insurance premiums for the ever increasing number of American factories moving overseas. These future insurance costs might have hurt American multinational companies in their competition with multinationals from countries that tend to be less liberal in their liability awards. As it is, industry analysts still think the case will have far-reaching effects on American companies, making insurance coverage a major part of any decision to build a plant overseas.

Sources: Stacy Shapiro, "Many Insurers Share Union Carbide Cover," *Business Insurance*, December 17, 1984, 1. James Nolan, "Insurers Bear Brunt of Bhopal," *Journal of Commerce*, January 6, 1986, 1a. Daniel Seligman, "How Much Money Is Your Life Worth?" *Fortune*, March 3, 1986, 25. Larry Everest, "More Bhopals," *The Nation*, June 21, 1986, 845.

represented by mortality tables. Thus, the price of the same amount of life insurance increases with the age of the insured. All other things being equal, a forty-year-old will pay more for fifty thousand dollars in life insurance than a thirty-year-old. Other factors that enter into the calculation of premiums include the insured's health and whether he or she smokes.

Term Life Insurance

The type of life insurance that pays the policy amount to the beneficiary only if the insured dies within the period covered by the last premium is known as **term life insurance.** It works much like automobile or health insurance in that regard. If the insured wishes to renew the policy, he or she must typically make a new contract with the insurer. Some policies guarantee renewability, however.

Whole Life Insurance

Term *vs.* Whole Life Insurance

Cash value life insurance, which is another name for **whole life insurance,** is a class of life insurance policies that requires premium payments on the insured's behalf until death or until the insured reaches a certain age. Upon the insured's death, no matter how long the policy has been in force, the insurer pays the value of the policy. Whole life insurance has two characteristics that distinguish it from term insurance. First, it has a savings aspect. The insurer uses a portion of each premium for term insurance while investing the balance. The accumulation and interest it earns is the policy's **cash value** or **surrender value.** Even if a whole life policy lapses, or ends because the premiums are not paid, the insured is entitled to its cash value. Second, a whole life policy is permanent. Once the policy is issued, it never has to be renewed and the premiums never change, unlike those for term insurance, which change with each new contract. However, its cash value and permanence features make whole life significantly more expensive than term.

Straight Life Insurance   There is a form of whole life insurance, **straight life insurance,** that is the lowest relative premium per $1000 for permanent life insurance. The premium payments take place over the lifetime of the insured. Consequently, the cash surrender value is the lowest of the whole life policies. The face value of the policy is payable to the beneficiary upon the insured's death.

Limited-Pay Life Insurance   There is a type of whole life insurance, **limited-pay life insurance,** that allows premium payments to stop at some time before death. Two common types are "twenty pay life," which requires premiums for only twenty years, and "paid at sixty-five," which requires premiums until the age of sixty-five.

Universal Life Insurance   In recent years, many candidates for insurance have regarded term life as a better buy than whole life, because the accumulations' return on whole life was less than they could obtain by investing the money themselves. Some insurers therefore began offering **universal life**

insurance, a form of whole life insurance that combines term insurance with an investment plan guaranteeing higher rates than are usually available on whole life policies. When these policies were first introduced, the advertised returns often were considerably higher than the actual returns proved to be after commissions and other fees were deducted.

Endowment Life Insurance Another form of insurance, **endowment life insurance,** that provides for payment of the face amount either at the insured's death or at some specified time before the insured's death, whichever comes first. The idea is to build up cash value so that if the insured does not die, the cash value will pay for, say, children's education or parents' retirement. Endowment policies are the most expensive policies.

Business Uses of Life Insurance

Businesses often purchase life insurance. In many cases, they buy group life insurance as a benefit for their employees. The employees, in this case, designate their beneficiaries. In other cases, businesses buy a form of term life insurance called **key person insurance** designed to protect themselves against the loss of vital employees, particularly those in upper management or ones who have crucial scientific or engineering expertise. Sometimes the coverage can be as high as $1 million.

Many partnerships and closely held corporations also buy life insurance. As Chapter 3 discussed, when a partner or shareholder in a closely held corporation dies, his or her heirs often do not want the business. What they want is the value of the decedent's interest. In anticipating this situation the partners or shareholders may agree to purchase specified amounts of life insurance on themselves so that their heirs can receive their money and the remaining partners and shareholders get the business. Such buy-sell agreements, which must appear in either the partnership agreement or the corporate articles or bylaws, should provide for regular appraisals of the business and adjustments in the amount of insurance so that the heirs do not feel cheated by what they receive.

A growing market for life insurance. More and more women are working outside the home. Both they and their families are beginning to realize that without their income — or their services — the family would suffer financially. A growing number of insurers are tailoring coverage to meet the needs of this group.

THE DEBATE OVER INSURANCE: A PERSPECTIVE

National news magazines, the television networks, and every other information medium has regularly carried major stories about the crisis in liability insurance and the legislative proposals intended to cure it. The issues can be presented in a clear-cut manner. Greedy plaintiffs with trumped-up claims, abetted by unscrupulous lawyers, have squeezed the insurance system to a point where companies and municipalities with clean records cannot afford insurance. That is one point of view. Another is that, in an effort to capture greater market shares, the insurance companies lowered their insurability standards during the late 1970s and early 1980s so that they are now facing mounting claims on the bad risks they took on.

Liability risks. Liability awards have skyrocketed, and the scope of disaster grows larger. Like all chemical manufacturers, Union Carbide must assess risks and plan for them. When gas leaked from its chemical plant in Bhopal, India, over 2,000 people were killed and hundreds of thousands were injured. The company will have to decide whether it should pursue the matter in India's courts or whether an out-of-court settlement would be wiser.

Besides reflecting badly on all concerned, such arguments conceal an extremely important and highly complex problem. Let's take a brief look at one aspect of the insurance crisis.

As we saw in Chapter 2, until the early twentieth century the principles of laissez faire put the risk of buying defective goods primarily on the user or consumer. Today, much of the burden has shifted to sellers and manufacturers. For example, Jeanne Leichtamer Samples received a $2.2 million judgment against American Motors (AMC) for injuries she suffered when the jeep in which she was a passenger flipped over. Negligence by the driver caused the accident, but a defective roll bar, and this jeep model's tendency to roll over, probably increased the severity of Ms. Sample's injuries.[5]

Given the driver's negligence, should AMC have had any responsibility to Ms. Samples? Even thirty years ago, Ms. Samples could not have collected from AMC. Also, until the 1970s the insurance laws of most states would not have allowed her, as a guest in the vehicle, to recover from the driver either, unless she could prove extreme recklessness. These factors have caused courts and juries faced with people like Ms. Samples, who at twenty-one is permanently paralyzed from the waist down, to look to manufacturers and their insurers. The logic ran that large companies could spread the costs of injuries like hers across millions of customers. Today, AMC faces claims exceeding $1.6 billion from claims arising out of over five hundred similar lawsuits.

How many times and how much should AMC have to pay for the jeep model's defective design, assuming that the design was in fact faulty and did lead to injuries and deaths? One could argue that AMC's liability should be limited only by what the courts will award. What will even $1 billion in liability mean, though, for the jobs of those working at AMC, a company that after years of losing money has just crept into the black?

At the moment, society offers no alternatives to those who are injured except to file lawsuits against the manufacturers. Aside from the very rich, no one has the financial resources to cope with such serious injuries as spinal cord damage. Without an insurance system to pay for catastrophic nonfatal injuries, victims have a choice only between accepting impoverishment or hoping to win a lawsuit.

If an insurance scheme paid for all victims' injuries, however, what mechanism would remain to force manufacturers to maintain high safety standards?

The debates raging about malpractice, automobile, and property insurance are every bit as complex as those about product liability insurance. As we have seen with product liability insurance, these debates are really about issues of responsibility, whether they are society's businesses', or individuals', in modern life.

Chapter Highlights

1. Define the types of risk and describe the four main ways of handling risk.

Speculative risks offer the potential for gain as well as loss. Pure risks, on the other hand, offer the potential for loss only. A business can handle risk through risk avoidance, risk assumption, risk reduction, and risk transfer.

2. Define *insurance* and explain how insurance reduces risk.

Insurance is a contract in which one party agrees to pay a specified sum to another if a certain event occurs. By means of an insurance contract, the insured, a person or firm that buys insurance, exchanges an uncertain situation for the certainty of paying an insurance premium.

3. Outline the four principles of insurance.

The law of large numbers holds that as the number of units in a group increases, one can make more accurate and more certain predictions about the group. The principle of indemnification requires that an insurer pay an insured no more than the financial loss actually suffered. Insurable risks, those for which an insurance policy can be purchased, must be financial, measurable, and predictable. An insurable interest is one the person making the claim must have in the property or life insured. It keeps insurance from becoming a means of gambling on someone else's misfortune.

4. List the major forms of public insurance and the primary categories of private insurance coverage.

The major forms of public insurance are unemployment insurance, worker's compensation, and Social Security (Old-Age, Survivors, Disability, and Health Insurance). The primary categories of private insurance coverage are property and liability insurance, health insurance, and life insurance. Property and liability insurance includes fire and homeowner's insurance, automobile insurance, business liability insurance, malpractice or professional insurance, and product liability insurance. It also includes transportation or marine insurance, theft insurance, and fidelity and surety bonds, as well as title and credit insurance. Health insurance generally consists of hospitalization, surgical, medical expense, and major medical expense coverage. It may also include dental and vision care coverage and disability income insurance. Life insurance may be term, whole life, limited-pay life, or universal life policies.

5. Describe the applications of insurance to business risks.

Businesses purchase property and liability insurance to protect themselves from the loss of their assets and from the loss of income produced by those assets. Liability insurance protects a business from claims against it. Public insurance offers important protection to the firm's employees. Health and life insurance, which are frequently offered as part of the employee benefits package, may be an important factor in attracting and retaining qualified workers. A business may also purchase key person insurance to protect itself from loss should a partner or a key manager die.

6. Compare term life insurance to whole life insurance.

Term life insurance will pay the beneficiary a stated sum should the insured die during the term of the policy. At the end of the term, a new policy would then have to be taken out at a new premium rate. Whole life insurance, on the other hand, lasts for the insured's entire life, unless the policy is canceled. Premiums continue until death or until a prespecified time and do not change over the life of the policy. In addition, whole life policies build up a cash value and thus have a savings dimension to them.

Key Terms

Review Questions

1. What is *risk*? How is it different from odds or probability?
2. What are the four methods of managing risk? Which of the four is most closely associated with the management of deductibles and coinsurance?
3. Define *insurance* and defend the concept that insurance reduces risk.
4. Describe one risky situation that is insurable and one that is uninsurable. Why is the uninsurable risk uninsurable?
5. Distinguish stock insurance companies from mutual insurance companies.
6. Distinguish insurance brokers from insurance agents.
7. Describe four benefits provided under the Social Security Act of 1935.
8. Discuss the liability risks faced by business firms and the insurance coverage programs available to reduce these risks.
9. What types of insurance should a business firm consider when seeking to reduce its risks from dishonest acts?
10. How does major medical insurance fit into an overall health insurance plan?
11. How is term life insurance different from whole life insurance? What are the common points between them?
12. Why should a business consider purchasing life insurance on its key employees? What special problems might life insurance solve for a small business that is not a sole proprietorship?

Application Exercises

1. You are currently living in a state that does not require persons who ride motorcycles to wear safety helmets. Recently a bill was introduced in the legislature that would require all riders to wear helmets. Given this information, respond to the following questions. What are some arguments against this type of legislation? Why would representatives of medical insurance companies support this type of legislation? How might the citizens who own group medical insurance benefit from passage of this bill?
2. In the weeks ahead you will assume ownership of a pizza restaurant. This restaurant offers food and beverage service on the premises, and delivery service to persons living in the community. What types of insurance coverage will be needed to cover the various types of risks?

Cases

20.1 Producer at Risk

Perhaps the most frightening aspect of risk management is the unknown risk. The insurer and the insured can suddenly find themselves in trouble when an unforeseen risk becomes an actuality. That is exactly what happened to the Manville Corporation.

Asbestos has been used to insulate plumbing, buildings, and ships. Because of their effectiveness and ease of application, asbestos-containing insulation materials were widely applied in schools, offices and factories. But asbestos has now been linked to two diseases that are often fatal: asbestosis, which destroys breathing capacity, and to a form of lung cancer.

More than 30,000 claims have already been filed against firms that manufactured or installed asbestos products. Manville maintains that it is the defendant in 16,000 lawsuits that seek over $2 billion in damages for individuals. Various installations are suing Manville and other producers for some $80 billion to cover the cost of removing asbestos from buildings.

By the end of 1982, about $600 million had been paid out to claimants. In that year, Manville successfully petitioned for protection from its creditors under the bankruptcy laws. The firm is now producing building materials that do not contain asbestos, under the trusteeship of the court. Disputes with its insurers over liability continue, however, and have contributed to a lack of progress in settling the thousands of outstanding claims.

Recently, Manville's board of directors agreed to set up a trust fund that would compensate those who claim they are victims of the firm's asbestos insulation. The board's decision amounts to a $3 billion product-liability settlement.

Questions

1. Is the risk involved in the asbestos suits speculative or pure? Insurable or not?
2. Assuming the asbestos firms had the usual forms of business insurance, why should there be disputes between the firms and their insurers regarding liability?

For more information see *U.S. News & World Report*, January 27, 1986, p. 36; *Business Week*, December 2, 1985, pp. 16–17; *U.S. News & World Report*, August 12, 1985, p. 14.

20.2 The Doctors' Dilemma

Business has been getting riskier year after year, as courts have expanded the meaning of liability and juries have awarded ever greater damages in increasing numbers of liability suits. As a result, the cost of liability insurance — when it is still available — has skyrocketed.

The medical profession has been especially hard hit, by both a rash of malpractice suits and ensuing increases in liability insurance premiums. The average settlement is about $330,000. Some insurers have simply refused to issue malpractice insurance to doctors in particularly hard-hit specialties.

The insurance companies tend to blame the situation on the nation's 700,000 lawyers, who, they say, are after the fat fees that are often involved. In addition, they cite a belief that no one really is hurt by a liability suit, because it is the insurance company that pays. Actually, the cost of liability suits is eventually reflected in the prices of goods and services, so in the end it is the consumer who pays. Lawyers and consumer advocates contend that the insurers are exaggerating the problem because they see a chance to increase their profits.

Physicians and surgeons have been looking for ways to protect themselves from malpractice suits and the high cost of liability insurance. Some have stopped taking on types of cases that involve a high incidence of malpractice suits. Many obstetricians who have lost their insurance have refused to deliver babies.

Another strategy is to screen out patients who have a history of filing malpractice claims. Doctors in Los Angeles can use a service called Physicians' Alert, which will identify such patients in that area. But lawyers have responded with a service that warns patients of doctors who have been sued for malpractice.

In what may be the most unique solution to the problem of malpractice suits, at least one physician has eliminated almost all of his insurance coverage. The reason? Data indicate that doctors with low insurance coverage are not exposed to awards or settlements in excess of their coverage. Unless they have large personal fortunes, there is little for a plaintiff to collect.

Questions

1. Some people claim that the increasing number and size of liability suits actually serve the public, because they warn business that it must be responsible to consumers. Do you agree or disagree? Why?
2. Discuss the technique of carrying a minimal amount of liability insurance, so as to minimize the potential award in a liability suit. What other techniques might do better for both doctor and patient?

For more information see *U.S. News & World Report*, January 27, 1986, pp. 35–43; *Newsweek*, September 30, 1985, p. 8; and *U.S. News & World Report*, October 7, 1985, pp. 56–57.

Except for readers of stars and cards, people who try to predict the future do so by looking at current trends and trying to figure out which of those trends will continue and which will change. Any prediction is at most a good guess, for even if you've got the trends figured out, you'll never be able to take into account all the factors that might radically alter the future. More heated foreign competition could lead to trade wars, tariffs, and an era of economic isolation. Desperate attempts to cut the deficit could lead to long range economic changes, as could another war.

Barring catastrophes, however, some trends that we've looked at are likely to continue on into the 1990s, while the problems of the 1980s may lead to solutions that will be the new movements of the next decade.

The United States' standing in the world economic community is likely to continue to evolve. For most of its first 200 years, America grew by constantly moving into new territories and taking advantage of new riches of the land. Our economic standing among nations of the world has depended on our growth, our resources, and our ability to flex our economic muscle in critical times.

The most profound change in the American work force is the move into the service industry. Already, two-thirds of America's jobs are service-oriented, and that figure is expected to rise. In effect, some of the jobs lost in the steel industry will turn into jobs servicing things made of imported steel. And instead of turning bolts, some assembly line workers will turn hamburgers. Currently the pay and benefits in most parts of the service industry do not match those of the jobs lost in heavy industry. But as the service sector gets more powerful, service workers may come to be more valued by our society as a whole.

On the other hand, there's no sign of a decline in the need for people who run things. People who manage personnel, money, technology, and marketing will all increase in value as the network corporation becomes more spread out, more hollow. The corporation of the future will often be simply a center of management and communications.

During the current reshuffling of personnel, one of the interesting questions being worked out in factories across the country is who will run the new machines. When a computerized robot takes the jobs of four people, should one of those people be trained as the robot's human

The Future

boss? Many experts say yes, bring the human experience skills to work with high tech — the programmers can use the help. But many companies are turning to outside specialists to run their new wonder machines, ignoring both the needs and the skills of the workers losing their jobs.

With machines handling so much of the busy work and data gathering that now keep executives busy, the managers of tomorrow will be left with a lot of decisions about how to make use of all this information and all the computerized marvels. Many of them may look for help to computer expert systems and the various approximations of artificial intelligence that are being developed. An expert system can line up the choices, report on what has happened in the past when similar choices were made, and make a recommendation.

Managerial positions of the future should draw more and more qualities that computers can't emulate — creativity, non-logical thought, interpersonal skills, verbal abilities. The executive of the year 2000 may be very different from the executive of today.

While these changes in the face of corporate America and in the use of human resources continue along present lines, we can expect new trends in the way we deal with energy, waste, and liability. These problems may not disappear by the turn of the century, but for the foreseeable future, an increasing number of people will be busy formulating and carrying out policies to cope with such problems.

For years America foresaw a nuclear future of cheap clean energy. But now the nuclear energy industry is treading water, watching the last few reactors under construction struggle to completion, waiting to see which way public opinion will turn. As the 1985–86 public hearings about an Eastern radioactive waste site showed, people tend to turn against nuclear power when they realize they may have to live near the permanently dangerous products of that power.

Unless nuclear power makes a sudden and unexpected comeback, we can expect tremendous advances in alternative energy technologies in the next few decades. So far the government has put most of its energy development money behind nuclear power, and low oil prices recently have made the search for alternative energy sources less desperate and less profitable. But there's no question that the earth's fossil fuels are finite, and that eventually we will have to turn elsewhere for our energy.

Solar energy — clean, safe, and inexhaustible — holds the greatest hope for many who wish to produce electricity without pollution. The technology of the photovoltaic (pv) cell, the primary element in the transfer of the energy from the sun's rays to electricity, has been improving slowly, though the cells still only capture a small part of the available power in sunlight. Experimental energy farms have been set up in the southwest where hundreds of mirrors focus light on a set of photovoltaic cells, and such farms may turn into power generating stations of the future. But the greatest solar successes to date have occurred at the level of individual homes and businesses which use pv cells as well as passive solar designs that take advantage of the sun's heat without using active heat transfer.

Another promising source of future energy is biomass, burning trash to produce energy. Virtually anything with a biological origin can be burned to produce energy. Some experimenters have successfully grown water hyacinths on sewage lagoons, burning the plants for energy. An enterprising New England company has developed technology that separates manure into gas, which is burned to produce heat or electricity.

An extension of biomass energy holds the greatest hope for the problem of coping with our own wastes. The 1970s saw a gradual awakening in the U.S. to the problems of air and river pollution. Though one of the most destructive effects of industrial air pollution — acid rain — is far from being solved, the government is at least starting to take the problem seriously. But we're only beginning to understand the extent of the pollution of the land and groundwater from underground gasoline tanks, illegal hazardous waste dumps, and traditional landfills.

Refuse-to-energy plants around the country provide an alternative to burying garbage, and they can burn just about anything. One in California specializes in turning old cars into energy, while Westinghouse is working on an incinerator that will burn municipal garbage and toxic PCBs at the same time. We will need many such innovations just to keep our land and groundwater in its present condition.

So the future for American business people no longer centers on the harvesting and exploitation of abundant natural resources. Many of the next generation of successful entrepreneurs and corporate executives will be like orchestra conductors, trying to keep manufacturers, suppliers, and marketers around the world in harmony. Others will be focusing their energy and inventiveness on trying to make a profit cleaning up after the industrialists of the past. Though the success stories of the future may have different plots, there will continue to be plenty of room in American business for energetic people with clever ideas.

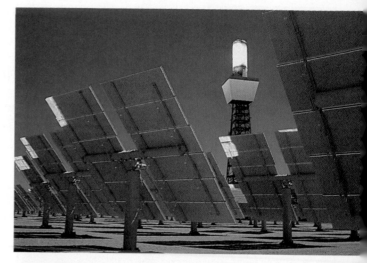

VII

BUSINESS
AND
ITS
ENVIRONMENT

Approximately 600,000 Americans are lawyers, and many of them are working for business firms. Many of the laws that influence business operations are complex, and require legal interpretation. Firms that are involved in international trade must be familiar with the laws of the countries where they do business. Lawyers are also busy helping business firms cope with many government regulations. Business law is a major topic in Part VII. We will also describe government and business, and international business in this section.

BUSINESS LAW

Learning Objectives

After you have completed this chapter, you will be able to do the following:

- Identify each of the sources of U.S. law.
- Describe the various ways we classify laws in the United States.
- Describe the dispute-resolution system and the two principal alternatives to it.
- Define tort and identify the classifications of torts.
- Describe the forms a contract may take and list the elements of a contract.
- Classify the types of property.
- Describe the Uniform Commercial Code.
- Classify the major types of bankruptcy proceedings and describe each.

People tend to think of laws as being permanent. They are by no means unchanging, however, and modifications in them have profound effects on individuals, businesses, and society. Consider the case of Lorena Weeks. In 1966 she had worked for the Southern Bell Telephone & Telegraph Company for nineteen years. Under her union's contract with the company, unionized employees had the right to bid on any job that came open. The job was to be awarded to the bidder with the most seniority who also met the job's qualifications. When a switchman's job opened, Ms. Weeks and a man with less seniority than she had both bid on it. According to the job description, a switchman had to maintain, test, and operate equipment in the telephone company's central office. Southern Bell rejected her bid solely because it had decided not to assign women to switchmen's jobs.

Ms. Weeks filed a complaint with the U.S. Civil Rights Commission. Three years, almost to the day, after she had bid on the job, a federal appeals court held that the company had unlawfully discriminated against her. The court based its decision on Title VII of the Civil Rights Act of 1964. That federal law, discussed in detail in Chapter 8, makes it unlawful for an employer to discriminate against an individual because of that person's sex.[1]

Businesspeople need to know how the law affects their operations. Ideally, once they know what the law requires, they can structure their operations to achieve their goals and avoid legal problems. Business-law courses stress this perspective, which is called **preventive law**. For example, human resources personnel must be careful during hiring interviews to avoid questions about a woman's marital status and child-bearing plans. Under most circumstances, such questions violate Title VII.

Businesspeople rightly understand that what they need to know about law is its practical aspects. Yet in order to make sense of what the law requires and to apply it to their affairs, they also need a working knowledge of how law develops.

Preventive Law Defined and Applied

THE SOURCES OF AMERICAN LAW

American law originates not only in each branch of government — legislative, executive, and judicial — but also at each level of government — federal, state, and local. Ultimately, of course, all laws must meet the test of the United States Constitution.

The U.S. Constitution

It would be easy, but a misunderstanding, to think of Title VII as being just another business regulation. Title VII also represents Congress's interpretation of its duties under the Fifth and Fourteenth Amendments to the Constitution.[2] The **U.S. Constitution**, dating from 1789, states in rather specific terms how the federal government is to be organized and what its legal relationships to the states and the people are to be. It lists in general terms the fundamental principles on which our society is based.

FIGURE 21.1

Classification of Law

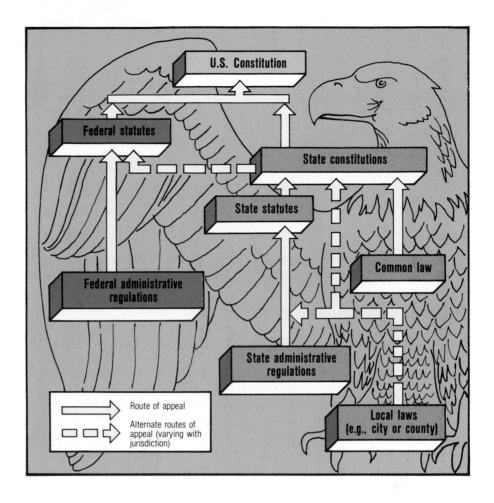

Ms. Weeks's case was one of the first decided under the Civil Rights Act of 1964. Today, cases like hers rarely come up. Society has largely accepted and incorporated the Civil Rights Act's goals into everyday life. Before the law changed in 1964, however, the courts would have rejected Ms. Weeks's claim of discrimination. Until that time, businesses and government agencies routinely barred women and minorities from certain types of jobs. Title VII of the Civil Rights Act forced all employers — at no little cost — to change their hiring practices. Against that cost, though, must be balanced the benefits to society of opening up jobs to new pools of talented individuals. Perhaps more importantly, the Civil Rights Act brought the nation closer to the ideal of equal protection under the law for all citizens. These considerations are typical of those that Congress, state legislatures, county commissioners, and city councils must routinely weigh before making new laws within the context of already existing principles.

Our system works because our Constitution and the system of government it defines facilitate the interaction between our deeply held principles and the constantly changing circumstances of American life. In this chapter and the next, we will survey the major areas of American law that affect business.

Statutes and the Common Law

The Sources of American Law

Few people deal on a daily basis with matters directly touching on the U.S. Constitution. Outside of government, the people who do so most often work in the media. They live constantly with the question of what speech the Constitution protects and what it does not. Likewise, few people have daily contact with their state constitutions, either.

For most of us, the law is **statutes**, laws passed by Congress or state legislatures and signed by, respectively, the president or a state governor. Businesses routinely deal with statutes. The federal and state laws governing securities discussed in Chapter 17 are **statutory**. All tax laws are statutory, as are the laws permitting incorporation and those regulating environmental hazards. Statutes also authorize government agencies to issue **administrative regulations**, legally binding requirements designed by a government agency to accomplish the purposes of a specific statute. For example, Congress authorized the Occupational Safety & Health Administration (OSHA) to issue regulations covering work-place hazards. In the next chapter, we will take a close look at administrative regulations.

Another familiar form of the law is **common law**, a body of legal principles developed over centuries by judges in deciding cases. Some people refer to the common law as unwritten law, because it originated in cultural customs and practices, not statutes. However, written common-law case reports and digests line miles of law-library shelves.

Common law evolved in England from the thirteenth century onward and came to this continent with British colonists. Common law exists only at the state level, because the U.S. Constitution effectively limits federal laws to statutes and administrative regulations. Every state has its own body of common law, which consists primarily of the law relating to contracts, torts, and property. (Louisiana is the sole exception, because of its legal roots in the French tradition.) It is important to note that constitutional amendments and statutes supersede common-law principles. As you will see, the Uniform Commercial Code, a statute, has replaced much of the common law of contracts as it applies to businesses.

The Classification of Laws

How U.S. Laws Are Classified

There are several ways to classify laws, but the divisions that follow are the most common.

Public Law and Private Law   Duties imposed by governments to protect the rights of individuals or preserve social order are termed **public law**. In this country, public law is found in constitutions, statutes, and administrative regulations. It is never found in common law. By contrast, **private law** is law that defines the relationships between and among individuals and other nongovernmental entities like corporations. Private law comes mainly in the form of statutes and common law.

Criminal Law and Civil Law   Statutes that specify the duties owed to society and that prescribe penalties like fines, imprisonment, or loss of life for

Raiders of the High Tech

Computer "pirates" and "hackers," virtually unheard of ten years ago, are now frequently making headlines, operating in moral and legal grey areas, seemingly daring the law to come find them. Some people commit outright robbery with a computer, but others engage in shady behavior that raises difficult ethical questions.

First there was the question of "pirates," people who illegally copy computer discs. Anyone who has done more with a computer than play games knows that the ability to copy information is essential to the safe use of computers. The electronics world is so subject to minor disasters that most people don't want to have only a single copy of their novel or tax figures. Direct sunlight, a sudden electrical surge, or a careless foot can destroy hundreds of hours of work. Therefore, any prudent person makes copies, or "backups," of important discs.

The situation gets more complicated when people start copying software, the programs which come on discs and turn your computer from a box with circuit boards into something approaching a brain. This software can be extremely time-consuming, difficult, and costly to develop. After a computer user has paid $500 for a software program, he or she will logically want to make a copy of it, a practice the software companies encourage. The problem is, what's to keep Jane Doe from making a copy of the program for her three friends who have computers, thus saving them $500 each (and effectively costing the software company $900 in lost sales)?

Since 1978 software manufacturers have been working on "copy protection," trying to stay one step ahead of those who make it their business or their hobby to duplicate copyrighted programs. The manufacturers can store information on the software disc in unusual ways that will confuse a computer trying to copy it. They can leave blank spots on the disc that will shut the computer down. Or they can construct the program to work only with the unique operating system and serial number of the first computer it's put into.

One recent scheme involves instructing the software to "crash," or stop working, hours after it has been introduced into a "pirate's" computer. This kind of time bomb effect is much harder for the pirate to deal with than if the program simply won't run the first time it is put into a new computer. Other software makers have simply given up on copy protection, and some have found that advertising their software as unprotected increases their sales. Programmers like to alter the programs that they buy, something that is much easier to do if the software is unprotected. Like the makers of pre-taped videocassettes, however, most software makers simply grumble about the ineffectiveness of copyright laws and look for better protection.

While "pirates" primarily hurt software makers, computer "trespassers" can hurt everyone. With a home computer, a telephone line, skill, and some luck, a computer trespasser can break into almost any other computer that's hooked up to a phone line. Sometimes, these trespassers are just "hackers," often kids who simply want to see what they can do with their computers. Increasingly, however, these trespassers are serious thieves. They can break into data banks to change grades or credit balances. Or they can copy information and use other people's credit cards or phone numbers. They can steal valuable oil-drilling data, or simply convince a bank computer to transfer money to their account, often in a Swiss bank. An American Bar Association study found that 27 percent of the businesses and public agencies polled had been victims of computer crime in the previous year. Total losses were estimated at half a billion dollars.

Keep your eye open for further developments. "Privacy" and "privileged information" are going to take on entirely new meanings in the computer age. You should know the latest developments before you hook your computer up to a phone line or give a bank information that you don't want the whole world to know.

Sources: Gina Kolata, "Playing Hardball with Software," *Science 83* Vol. 4 No. 4, May 1983, pp. 67–69. Philip Elmer-DeWitt, "Cracking Down," *Time* Vol. 123 No. 20, May 14, 1984. "Computing the Risks," *The Progressive*, Vol. 47 No. 10, October 1983, p. 11. "When Thieves Sit Down at Computers," *U.S. News & World Report*, Vol. 96 No. 25, June 25, 1984, p. 8.

violating them are called the **criminal law**. Of these laws, those involving white-collar crime, like embezzlement or theft by computer, affect business the most. Still, criminal law has relatively little impact on business when compared to **civil law**, which simply is all law that is not classified as criminal law.

Substantive Law and Procedural Law All laws are either substantive or procedural. **Substantive law** describes rights or duties. A seller's obligation to deliver goods that conform to his or her contract with a buyer is a matter of substantive law.

By contrast, **procedural laws** are the provisions in constitutions or statutes that describe how something is to be done by, or in relation to, government. If, for instance, a seller fails to deliver conforming goods, procedural laws define how — not on what grounds — the buyer might take the seller to court. As another example, when you apply for a driver's license, procedural laws list the steps that you and the Department of Motor Vehicles must each follow in filing and acting on the application. And when the legislature adopts a state budget, it must follow procedural laws. These three examples hint at the importance of procedural laws. In short, the "mere technicalities" that unsuccessful **litigants** — persons involved in lawsuits — often complain about are the procedural laws. Without these laws, we would have chaos, not a legal or a social system.

Procedural laws are virtually always written, so the law presumes that people have been given adequate notice of the requirements in them. Ignorance of the law is, in fact, no excuse. When it comes to getting a dog license or a title transferred on a car, an ordinary person can deal quite effectively with procedural requirements. For more complicated matters, coping with the procedural laws probably requires a lawyer's help. It is impossible to say precisely when someone should call in a lawyer. For instance, in some parts of the country getting approval for a two- or three-house subdivision or obtaining a liquor license means involving a lawyer, but not necessarily in other areas.

THE DISPUTE-RESOLUTION SYSTEM

No society could function without a peaceful means for resolving disputes. The formal system must be regarded as a last resort, however. Preventive law principles dictate that everything that can be done to avoid disputes should be done. If a dispute arises, the **parties** — the people involved — should first do everything they can to resolve it themselves. Failing that, the parties may enter the **dispute-resolution system**, the structure that society has established for resolving differences. The idea of disputes immediately brings to mind the courts as a means of resolving them. The costs associated with litigation, or lawsuits, have soared over the last thirty years, however, and much effort has gone into devising alternatives to lengthy court actions.

The State and Federal Court Systems

The federal government and each state as well have court systems. Figure 21.2 is a much-simplified diagram of the federal and state court systems. As it reveals, their structures are roughly parallel.

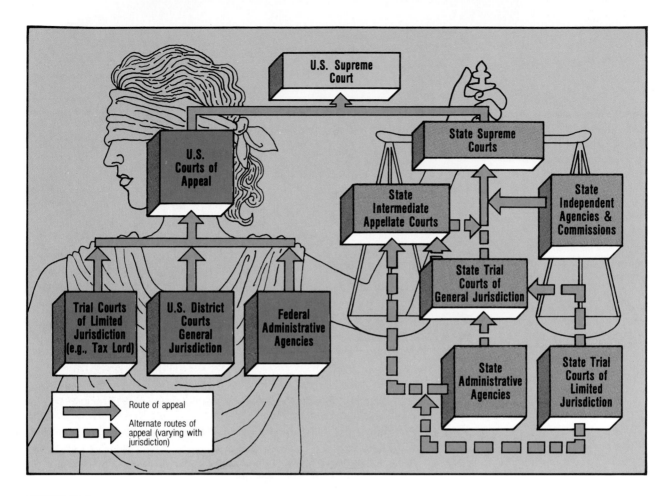

FIGURE 21.2

The Court System

Dispute Resolution in
Trial Courts

Trial Courts All litigation that does not begin in administrative agencies or commissions starts in the trial courts. Like our economic system, our system of dispute resolution rests on competition. If the two sides are allowed the chance to present their own version of the facts aggressively but in a neutral forum, we believe that the truth will emerge. Because of this characteristic, our dispute-resolution institutions are called an adversary system.

In a trial court, the facts of a case are established through evidence and testimony. Sometimes both a judge and a jury **hear**, that is, decide, a case. The judge determines what law applies to the case and instructs the jury on the law. The jury then applies the law to what it determines to be the facts and gives its **verdict**, the jury's finding. If a judge alone hears a case, he or she makes both the findings of fact and the conclusions of law.

There are two types of trial courts. **Trial courts of general jurisdiction** can hear any matters that a trial court in its system has authority or **jurisdiction** to hear. In the federal system, such courts are called U.S. District Courts. In state systems, they have many names, including superior courts, courts of common pleas, and district courts. The state and federal systems both also have **trial courts of limited jurisdiction**, courts with authority to hear only particular types of cases or cases involving less than a certain dollar amount. In the state systems, the courts of this type that have the most impact on business are the small-claims courts — like Judge Wappner's "People's Court" — and the courts with

Resolving disputes through the courts. Pennzoil's attorney Joseph Jamail was elated when he spoke with reporters in the Harris County Civil Courts Building after Judge Solomon Casseb upheld a jury's $10.5 billion judgment against Texaco on December 23, 1985. Texaco could pay the award, negotiate an out-of-court settlement, or appeal the case all the way up to the U.S. Supreme Court. Appeals take time, however, and interest on $10.5 billion is about $3 million a day.

names like *county court, municipal court,* or *district court,* which hear only cases involving less than $10,000. In the federal system, these courts include the tax court and the bankruptcy courts.

In an important sense, all federal trial courts have limited jurisdiction. They are allowed to hear only the cases involving substantial questions of federal law or cases in which the parties on the two sides live in different states and the amount at issue exceeds $10,000. By contrast, state courts have the power to resolve any dispute, including those that a federal court might decide, unless the U.S. Constitution or a federal statute assigns jurisdiction exclusively to the federal courts. For this reason, state courts regularly decide questions of federal statutory and constitutional law and disputes involving more than $10,000 between residents of different states. The Constitution assigns all cases involving treaties to the federal courts, however.

Intermediate Appellate Courts   In virtually all cases, the losing party in a trial-court case has a right to **appeal**, to ask a higher court to review the record of the case for errors in the trial court's interpretation and application of law. Which court an **appellant**, a person who appeals an adverse judgment by a court, may choose to appeal to depends on the court system. Some less populated states, like Nebraska, have only one appellate court, the supreme court. The federal court system and more than thirty states have **intermediate appellate courts**, courts that hear appeals of trial-court decisions but that are not the supreme court of their particular jurisdiction.

Appellate courts never listen to witnesses or accept new evidence. Rather, they look at what happened in the trial court, read the written arguments, called **briefs**, and listen to lawyers' oral presentations. Possibly weeks or months later, the judges will issue a written decision. Unless the trial court made an error of law that could have materially affected the case's outcome, the appellate court will normally approve or **affirm** the trial court's judgment. However, if the trial court made an error of law that might have materially affected the case's outcome, the appellate court will **reverse** or overturn the trial court's judgment. Only in the most extreme circumstances will an appellate court reverse a trial court's decision because of errors in its findings of fact. When an appellate court reverses a trial court's judgment, it returns the case to the trial court with instructions about what to do with the case. The trial court will often have to hold a new trial on some or all of the issues in the original trial.

Dispute Resolution in Supreme Courts

Supreme Courts   Every court system has a **supreme court**, the highest appellate court in an American court system. A state's supreme court is the ultimate authority on the state's law and constitution. As long as a state supreme court's decision does not touch on matters of federal law or the U.S. Constitution, the U.S. Supreme Court lacks jurisdiction to review the state decision. In every system with intermediate appellate courts except New York's, the supreme court chooses the cases it will review. In the others, the supreme court hears all the cases appealed to it. The U.S. Supreme Court reviews only about 180 of the more than 3,000 cases appealed to it annually. In effect, in cases that a supreme court declines to review, the judgments are affirmed.

The Importance of Judicial Review

The courts have the last word on the interpretation of a constitutional provision or a statute. When faced with a question of law, courts seek guidance in **precedents**, earlier decisions on similar or identical questions of law. Precedents are of two types. A persuasive precedent is a case decided by a court in any other judicial system except the U.S. Supreme Court. It is important to note that a court does not have to follow a persuasive precedent. By contrast, a binding precedent is a case decided by a higher court in the same system. Under the rule of **stare decisis**, a Latin term meaning literally "to stand by decisions," a court must follow a decision by a higher court in its own system or by the U.S. Supreme Court. *Stare decisis* is among the most important stabilizing factors in our legal system.

Alternative Dispute-Resolution Mechanisms

Perhaps the most common alternative to litigation is arbitration, a procedure in which the parties agree to submit a dispute to a third party and to be bound by that party's decision. Normally, a contract provision will require the submission of disputes involving it to the arbitration process. Construction contracts for the complicated projects often have arbitration clauses, for example. And the sports pages regularly report the arbitration of salary disputes between professional athletes and their teams. Note that even if a contract does not require arbitration, the parties can agree to it.

Three Alternative Dispute-Resolution Techniques

Another alternative in dispute resolution is mediation, the procedure in which the parties agree to submit a dispute to a third party, the **mediator**, but are not bound by his or her recommendations. A mediator's role is more one of trying to bring the parties together.

Finally, entrepreneurs are entering the dispute resolution business, competing in price with the judicial system. The wheel of retailing, discussed in Chapter

The Hong Kong Gamble

In 1997, one of the world's greatest centers of capitalism will become part of the world's most populous communist country, The People's Republic of China. No one knows exactly what will happen, which makes living — and especially investing — in Hong Kong a risky business. Negotiations are underway between the British (Hong Kong has been a British colony since 1841) and Chinese to figure out exactly what will happen when Britain's 99 year lease on 90% of the colony runs out. The Chinese agreed in 1984 to allow capitalism to exist in Hong Kong for at least 50 years, which will create a unique legal situation: "one country, two systems."

Hong Kong is crucial to the rest of the world for a number of reasons. For a century and a half it has been one of the major links between China and the rest of the world. Early in its history, the Colony established a reputation for having the most reliable banking, insurance, and shipping services in South East Asia. It has been efficiently governed, and after 1950, when the Communists temporarily cut off most of Hong Kong's trade with the People's Republic, it developed light industry, primarily textiles. For the last quarter century, although the Communists have restricted immigration to Hong Kong, they have used it as a key commercial and foreign exchange link to the rest of the world. Despite limited natural resources of all kinds, Hong Kong has prospered.

But when the Chinese take over, will they try to make Hong Kong over in a communist mold? No one knows. It is becoming clearer that the Chinese, and not the British, legal system will usher in the new century, a fact that upsets wary British investors. China, however, is unlikely to try to change Hong Kong drastically. Because of the constant immigration of Chinese, Hong Kong's urban areas are the most densely populated in the world, and any major economic upheaval could lead to chaos. Chinese spokespeople have tried to calm the financial community by pledging that Hong Kong will remain a free port, and that economic interests will be guaranteed. Despite China's movements towards free enterprise, however, will the communist government really be willing to absorb such a symbol of capitalism without putting it through major changes?

U.S. firms (which have invested a total of $3 billion in Hong Kong) don't seem too upset. They view the Chinese takeover of Hong Kong has a chance to open further trade with one billion mainland Chinese. Many British companies, on the other hand, are worried. The colony was shocked in 1984 when Jardine, Matheson & Co., Hong Kong's largest and oldest trading company, changed its legal domicile to Bermuda. Jardine had helped found the Colony in 1842, but the current chairman, a fourth-generation nephew of the company's founder, has made no secret of his worries about Hong Kong's future.

His company's announcement caused a big drop in the stock market, and observers wonder how many other companies will follow suit in the next decade, gradually reducing their holdings in Hong Kong so they won't be devastated by whatever changes occur in 1997. Chinese leader Deng Xiaoping tried in June 1984 to allay such fears by repeating the pledge that Hong Kong won't change, and by promising that the Chinese troops stationed on the island would not "interfere in the internal affairs of Hong Kong." But the announcement that Chinese troops would be there at all shocked the community.

Companies that stay in Hong Kong are gambling on the outlook of a future Chinese government that may differ as much from today's government as the current one differs from that under Mao. No one can yet tell to what extent Chinese decisions about Hong Kong will be ideological, and to what extent they will be practical. The legal problems involved in doing businesses with Hong Kong in the next century may be enormous. All the people and companies of Hong Kong can do is wait . . . and gamble.

Sources: "HongKong Land: Battered and Still Bleeding from the Real Estate Collapse," *Business Week*, No. 2843, May 21, 1984, p. 96. "Will Other Companies Follow Jardine out of Town?" *Business Week*, No. 2838, April 16, 1984, p. 62. "Communist Rule for Hong Kong," *U.S. News & World Report* Vol. 96 No. 18, May 7, 1984, p. 45. "Looking Ahead," *Time*, Vol. 123, No. 5, January 30, 1984, p. 24. UPI, "Deng Says Troops Won't Interfere with Hong Kong Administration," *The Boston Globe*, July 1, 1984, p. 6.

13, seems to work here, too! Some firms offer services in which they supply a retired judge to hear and decide a dispute that the parties have agreed to submit. Similarly, some corporations have staged private minitrials in front of their executives to resolve disputes.

THE LAW OF TORTS

Torts Defined

A **tort** is a legal wrong as defined by the common law. A legal wrong is one that causes an injury for which society has determined that the injured party deserves compensation from the party responsible for the injury. Suppose that Jane invites Ben for dinner at 7:00 P.M. sharp. He shows up at 8:00 P.M. and the dinner is ruined. Ben has indeed wronged Jane, but the law does not consider mere bad manners to be a legal wrong.

Over the last eight centuries or so, the common law has come to define the rights of people with which others may not interfere without being responsible, or **liable**, in **damages**, money paid to an injured party to compensate for the injury. The law of torts grew out of the need to prevent violence between parties and to compensate the injured party.

Intentional Torts

The First Type of Torts

The clearest indication of these ancient purposes comes in the class of torts called **intentional torts**, acts for which the **plaintiff**, the person who starts a lawsuit, does not have to prove a monetary loss in order to collect damages. These acts are ones the law regards as so serious that once the plaintiff proves that the act did in fact occur, the **defendant**, the party against whom the lawsuit is brought, is presumed to have intended its consequences. **Intent** here simply refers to a voluntary act or omission that is reasonably likely to bring about a particular consequence.

Types of Intentional Torts

Retailers who arrest suspected shoplifters sometimes find themselves subjected to large damage awards for **false arrest**, the wrongful confinement or restraint of freedom of movement of someone. By contrast, a business could sue an employee who wrongfully took for personal use office supplies for **conversion**, the use of a person's property inconsistent with that person's ownership rights. Another common intentional tort is **fraud**, the intentional misrepresentation of the truth to convince someone to give up something of value. One of the largest jury verdicts in history came in a recent suit based on the intentional tort of **inducing breach of contract**, the act of convincing a person to violate an existing contractual duty. A Houston jury awarded Pennzoil over $11 billion because it decided that Texaco had convinced Getty Oil to abandon its agreement to sell to Pennzoil and to sell to Texaco instead.

Negligence

The Second Major Type of Torts

There is a broad range of torts known as *negligence torts*, which do not require the plaintiff to prove that the defendant intended to commit them. Instead, the plaintiff must prove that the defendant had a duty to act with a certain degree of care but failed to do so. Suppose that a customer in a grocery store drops a jar of pickles that breaks. An employee cleans up the mess and mops the floor. Before the floor can dry, the plaintiff comes along, starts across the wet floor, slips, and falls. For the plaintiff to recover damages, he or she must prove that the store had a duty to keep patrons off the wet floor and that the store employees' conduct fell below the requirements of that duty. The plaintiff must also prove that actual harm occurred that can be calculated in terms of a dollar amount of damages.

Types of Negligence Torts

Strict Liability   Certain types of negligence torts involving abnormally dangerous activities or dangerous animals impose **strict liability** on the defendant even if he or she acted with due care. This standard applies, for instance, to people who keep poisonous snakes or use explosives on construction projects.

Product Liability   The law takes a similar view of **product liability**, a commercial seller's responsibility for products it puts into someone else's hands. Product liability is not in the category of strict liability, however. Rather, the term describes a class of lawsuits in which the defendant's responsibility for the plaintiff's injuries may be based on an intentional tort or on negligence, strict liability, or breach of contract.

THE LAW OF CONTRACTS

The word *contract* may bring to mind the familiar multipage, single-spaced documents that no ordinary person seems able to read. There are, of course, contracts like that, but the contracts that fuel our economy are the ones we make every day in buying groceries, clothes, or a fast-food chain's hamburger.

Contracts — an important part of doing business. A lease is a very common type of contract, one that can spell life or death to a business. A contract for a lease generally runs for a specified period of time. If the lease is not renewed or if the rent is raised, a business may be forced to close.

A **contract** is simply a promise or promises that the courts will enforce. Fortunately, the courts have to enforce only a minuscule percentage of the huge number of contracts made each year in the United States. Nonetheless, the principles of preventive law dictate that businesspeople should put all important contracts into a form that courts will readily enforce.

The Form of Contracts

In theory, all contracts are oral, and oral contracts are usually enforceable. A written contract just lists what the parties to the oral contract have promised. The promises and not the writing form the contract.

Oral contracts are definitely enforceable, but written contracts are preferable. They reduce the possibility of disagreement and the courts give them great weight in a lawsuit. A written contract can consist of a sales slip, a notation on a check, or any other writing that evidences the promises that the parties made.

The Elements of a Contract

The elements of a contract are the signs that a court looks for in deciding whether a contract is enforceable. The five elements are:

1. Mutual assent
2. Consideration
3. Contractual capacity
4. Legal purposes
5. In writing, if required by law

Mutual Assent   All contracts must satisfy this equation:

$$\text{Offer} + \text{Acceptance} = \text{Mutual Assent}$$

The Five Elements of a Contract

An **offer** is a proposal of what one party will or will not do in exchange for the other party's act or promise. The party making the offer is the **offeror**, the party receiving the offer, the **offeree**. An **acceptance** is the offeree's agreement to the terms of the offer. **Mutual assent** is the parties' agreement on the contract's terms as expressed in the offer and acceptance. Normally, mutual assent consists of an exchange of promises. The offer may be, "I'll give you five dollars for your calculator." The acceptance may be simply, "Okay." Mutual assent is present; therefore, the contract is valid if the other elements of a contract are present too.

Consideration   In our example, note that each party's promise involved **consideration**, something of legal value that each party agrees to exchange. For a contract to be enforceable, one party's consideration need not be even approximately equal in value to the other's. However, if the considerations are grossly or absurdly unequal, a court may question whether mutual assent was really present.

Contractual Capacity   A party has **contractual capacity** if he or she has the ability to understand the nature of a contract. The mentally retarded and the infirm are among those presumed to lack this capacity. Some persons under eighteen lack contractual capacity in certain circumstances, but it is wrong to assume that they lack it in all situations.

Legal Purposes   Just as the law will not enforce a contract in which one of the parties lacks contractual capacity, the law will not enforce a contract that has an illegal purpose. For example, contracts for the sale of illegal drugs or agreements to pay gambling debts (even in Nevada) are not enforceable.

Relation to the Law of Agency

The law of agency, discussed in Chapter 3, is an outgrowth of contract law. An **agent**, you may recall, is an individual who represents another. The other, the **principal**, can be another individual, a partnership, or a corporation. Agency relationships — and therefore an agent's authority — are always defined by contract. The law of partnerships, also discussed in Chapter 3, developed from the concept of agency. The relations between partners are thus also a matter of contract. By contrast, corporations are created under statutes. There is no such thing as a common-law corporation. A corporate charter or certificate of incorporation is a contract between the corporation and the state issuing it. However, a corporation's relationships with employees, vendors, and customers are matters of contract negotiated on its behalf by its agents.

THE LAW OF PROPERTY

When parties make a contract, the subject is usually property. Property takes two forms. **Real property** is land and everything attached to it. A tree is part of real property; a condominium is real property; a garage or a barn is real property; built-in bookshelves are real property. Technically, the bookshelves are **fixtures**, personal property that becomes permanently attached to real property.

The Two Types of Property

Personal property is all property that is not either a fixture or real property. Personal property is also of two types. **Tangible personal property** is property that one can touch, like a baseball, a book, furniture, jewelry, or a blouse. **Intangible personal property** is property that one cannot touch, like a share of stock or a bank account. In both these cases, the owner has something — a certificate or a bankbook — that represents the property but is not the property itself. Trademarks (discussed in Chapter 12), patents, and copyrights are other forms of intangible personal property. A **patent** is a seventeen-year monopoly granted by the federal government to exploit new processes, machines, or manufactured goods, or significant improvements to existing processes. A **copyright** is a monopoly granted by the federal government on the exploitation of literary or artistic works. The creator of the works holds the monopoly for his or her lifetime plus fifty years.

Property takes many forms. *Many different kinds of property are shown here. The buildings and the land they sit on are real property. The signs attached to the buildings are fixtures. Trucks and cars are tangible personal property, and the Nike trademark shown on the billboard is an example of intangible personal property.*

THE UNIFORM COMMERCIAL CODE

Any list of the great developments in American law would have near its top the adoption of the **Uniform Commercial Code (UCC)**, a body of statutes that replaces several areas of business law formerly covered individually by each state's common law of contracts. Every state except Louisiana has adopted most or all of the UCC. Doing business across state lines has thus now become quite stabilized. Table 21.1 lists the subject areas covered in the UCC. We are able to identify here only a few of the many topics the UCC covers.

Sales

Provisions of the Uniform Commercial Code

Despite its name, the law of sales contained in UCC Article 2 covers only the sale of **goods**, personal property that is both tangible and movable. It does not affect the sale of real property or of services, which are covered by common law or other statutes. Article 2 does not fundamentally alter the common-law contract concepts, but it does bring the details associated with those concepts into line with modern commercial practice.

Warranties In one particular area, the UCC significantly changes the common law. Under this provision, a seller of goods makes certain **warranties**, guarantees or assurances. These warranties relate to the seller's title to the goods and to the satisfactory performance of the goods. Before the introduction of warranties, a buyer's only remedy for defective goods, if the seller would not voluntarily offer to make good, was a lawsuit for breach of contract. In such a suit, the buyer would have to prove precisely what representations the seller had made about the goods and establish that he or she had relied on these representations. Under the UCC, however, it is often the seller who must prove that he or she did not make the warranty in question.

The Types of Warranties

As its name implies, a **warranty of title** guarantees that the seller has the right to transfer to the buyer the title to the goods. When you buy a stereo, the store **warrants** its right to sell it. As to this warranty alone, courts virtually never allow a seller to protect itself against liability by means of a **disclaimer**, a refusal to make a warranty. A seller can disclaim almost all other warranties, though.

Warranties of performance guarantee that the goods will conform to certain standards. These warranties are of two sorts. An **express warranty** is an oral or written promise that the seller makes to the buyer. If a seller represents a certain car as being a 1985 Mustang, that is an express warranty. Suppose that instead the buyer plainly says, "This is a 1985 Mustang, isn't it?" If the seller does not contradict the statement, the buyer can accept the buyer's silence as being an express warranty.

The second type of warranties of performance is **implied warranties**, or warranties imposed by Article 2 of the UCC rather than those created by a seller's representations. Implied warranties themselves fall into two classes. **Warranties of merchantability** are warranties, made only by merchants, that a product is fit for the ordinary purposes for which it is sold. A merchant who sells microwave ovens warrants them to be fit for use in cooking. It does not warrant that the oven is safe for drying pottery or clay statues.

The second class of implied warranties relates to **warranties of fitness for a particular purpose**, warranties made when a seller knows that a buyer is purchasing goods to be used in a certain way. Suppose that the sole proprietor of a small business describes the business's bookkeeping and word-processing needs to a salesperson. Then the proprietor buys the hardware and software that the salesperson recommends. If the goods are not sufficient for the business's needs, the computer store has breached its warranty of fitness for a particular purpose.

The Law of Negotiable Instruments

Negotiable Instruments Defined

The UCC Article 2 law of sales probably has the greatest day-to-day impact on a business. Article 3 is in second place. Article 3 covers the law of **negotiable instruments**, written contracts containing a promise to pay money to one person

The Court Changes the Business of Law

Two recent Supreme Court decisions are likely to have profound effects on the way lawyers form partnerships and find clients. In a society in which every business dealing seems to involve "I'll ask my lawyer about it," these changes could affect us all.

In 1984 the Court dealt a stunning blow to exclusive, male-dominated professional partnerships. In a unanimous ruling, the Court said that the opportunity to become a partner is a "benefit of employment" and therefore covered under Title VII of the Civil Rights act of 1964, which prohibits discrimination in employment by firms with more than fifteen employees.

Elizabeth Anderson Hishon sued a prestigious Atlanta law firm when she was twice considered for partnership in the firm and twice rejected. Although record numbers of women and members of minority groups have been making it through law schools and into entry-level positions in law firms, many, like Hishon, are denied the important final step up to "partner." Women make up 30 percent of the associates in this country's largest law firms, but only five percent of the partners.

The firm Hishon sued, King and Spalding, argued that its right to choose new partners in its own way was protected by the constitutional right to free association. The court disagreed.

The ruling will probably affect other organizations set up as partnerships, including accounting and investment banking firms. It will not assure anyone of getting a job, but it will give individuals grounds for lawsuits if they feel they've been denied a position as a partner because of some kind of discrimination.

The target of the suit, the most powerful law firm in Atlanta, boasts Jimmy Carter's Attorney General, Griffin Bell, among its partners. Some people, however, compare it to a Southern men's club. The firm has no black partners, did not accept its first Jewish partner until 1976, and accepted its first female partner only in 1980, after the law suit was filed.

But even partnerships with better hiring and promotion records will now have to be more careful about the way they select partners. The ruling says, in effect, that a partnership cannot accept a new male simply because he is "one of the boys." Nor can it reject a female because she doesn't go to the Thursday night poker games. Though some people question whether the ruling can really force partnerships to change their ways, it was the Court's clearest support recently of equal opportunity.

A May 1985 Court decision will probably have a more immediate effect on the ways the rest of us view lawyers. The Court reaffirmed and broadened a 1977 decision that legalized advertising by attorneys. Some see the ruling as a long-overdue step in making lawyers' services easily available. Others view it as an insult to an ancient profession that has always valued credibility and dignity.

Some areas have already seen the kind of ads that the whole country can soon expect from lawyers. A firm in Milwaukee has been running TV ads inviting injured skiers to sue, and a Minneapolis firm ran an ad in *The Wall Street Journal* asking investors, "Have You Lost Money Because You Were Misled?" 300-pound Ken Hur, the "clown prince of attorneys," appears as a condemned prisoner in his own ads, giving as his last words "I should have called the Legal Clinic."

Attorney advertising has its critics, among them retired Chief Justice Warren E. Burger, who calls some advertising by lawyers "sheer shysterism" and says he would dig ditches before he took out an ad for himself. Banks complain that lawyers have fueled the growing number of personal bankruptcies by advertising with headlines like "Wipe Out Debt." However, at least one law firm that advertises heavily figures it gets eight times its money back in increased business as a result of its ads. With results like that, lawyers will sue to keep the practice alive.

Sources: Michael S. Serrill, "Less Dignity, More Hustle," *Time*, Vol. 125, No. 23, June 10, 1985, 66. Daniel B. Moskowitz, "Lawyers Learn the Hard Sell — And Companies Shudder," *Business Week*, No. 2898, June 10, 1985, 70. David Margolick, "Burger Criticism Prompts Defense of Lawyer Ads," *The New York Times*, July 9, 1985, A10. "Getting a Piece of the Power," *Time*, Vol. 123, No. 23, June 4, 1984, 63. "Red-Letter Day for Working Women," *U.S. News & World Report*, Vol. 96, No. 22, June 4, 1984, 16. "With Justice for Some," *Newsweek*, Vol. 103, No. 23, June 4, 1984, 85.

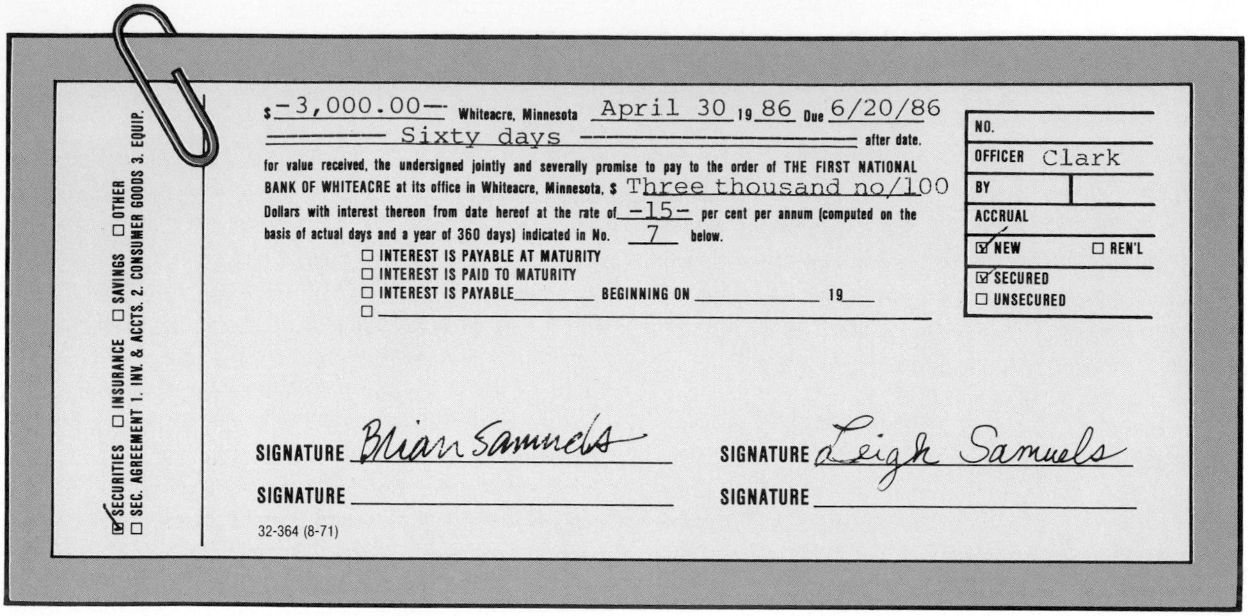

SECURITIES ☐ INSURANCE ☐ SAVINGS ☐ OTHER
☐ SEC. AGREEMENT 1. INV. & ACCTS. 2. CONSUMER GOODS 3. EQUIP.

$ -3,000.00- Whiteacre, Minnesota April 30 19 86 Due 6/20/86
Sixty days after date.
for value received, the undersigned jointly and severally promise to pay to the order of THE FIRST NATIONAL BANK OF WHITEACRE at its office in Whiteacre, Minnesota, $ Three thousand no/100 Dollars with interest thereon from date hereof at the rate of -15- per cent per annum (computed on the basis of actual days and a year of 360 days) indicated in No. 7 below.
☐ INTEREST IS PAYABLE AT MATURITY
☐ INTEREST IS PAID TO MATURITY
☐ INTEREST IS PAYABLE ________ BEGINNING ON ____________ 19___
☐

NO.
OFFICER Clark
BY
ACCRUAL
☑ NEW ☐ REN'L
☑ SECURED
☐ UNSECURED

SIGNATURE Brian Samuels SIGNATURE Leigh Samuels
SIGNATURE SIGNATURE
32-364 (8-71)

FIGURE 21.3

A Note

who may then assign this right to another. Negotiable instruments function in effect as another form of currency. For this reason, the Federal Reserve includes them in its counting of the money supply, as we saw in Chapter 15.

Types of Negotiable Instruments Negotiable instruments include promissory notes, checks, and certain types of warehouse receipts and bills of lading. Clearly, the most important of these are notes and checks.

Requirements for Negotiability UCC Article 3 requires that an instrument meet six criteria to be negotiable. These criteria are designed to ensure that negotiable instruments can change hands almost as freely as money.

The Six Requirements for Instruments to Be Negotiable

First, a negotiable instrument must of course be an **instrument**, that is, something in writing. Second, the person making the note or instructing his or her bank to pay the check must himself sign the instrument. Third, the instrument must contain an unconditional promise or order to pay a certain sum in money.

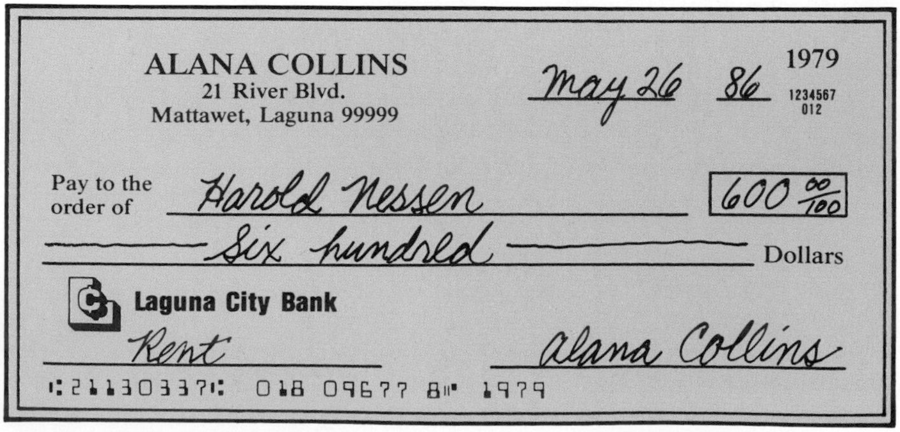

ALANA COLLINS
21 River Blvd.
Mattawet, Laguna 99999
May 26 86
1979
1234567
012
Pay to the order of Harold Nessen 600 00/100
Six hundred Dollars
Laguna City Bank
Rent Alana Collins
⑆211303371⑆ 018 09677 8⑈ 1979

FIGURE 21.4

A Check

A check would not be a negotiable instrument if it said, "Pay to the order of ABC Office Supplies only if the postage meter works." A note for a certain dollar amount plus interest at a set rate is negotiable even if the dollar amount of the interest is not expressly stated. A very simple calculation can put a value on the interest.

Fourth, the instrument must be payable either on demand or at a specified time. **Payable on demand** means that the maker of an instrument will pay it when it is presented to him or her for payment. Fifth, the instrument must state that it is "payable to order" or "payable to bearer." **Payable to order** on an instrument signifies that it can be transferred by means of an indorsement, discussed below. An **indorsee**, the person to whom an instrument is indorsed, may demand payment. **Payable to bearer** means that anyone who has possession of the instrument may demand payment. Sixth, the front of the instrument must plainly show that it satisfies the five previous criteria.

An instrument that does not satisfy these criteria is not negotiable, but that does not mean it is worthless. Rather, it means that the rights that UCC Article 3 grants to persons to whom the instrument may be transferred do not apply. The instrument still remains a contract and may be enforced under either the common law or the law of sales.

Indorsements Whatever appears on the back of an instrument has no effect on its negotiability. The front establishes that. However, what's on the back does affect how an instrument can be transferred. All instruments, except those payable to bearer, called bearer instruments, are transferred by **indorsement**, a notation, usually on the back of an instrument. Bearer instruments can be transferred simply through a change of who is in possession of them.[3]

All indorsements are made either "in blank" or "specially," as they are com-

TABLE 21.2

A Classification of Indorsements

Note: The symbol |s| means "signed."

Indorsement	In blank	Special	Restrictive	Nonrestrictive	Qualified	Unqualified
|s| Michael Manson	X			X		X
Pay Susan Gray |s| Michael Manson		X		X		X
Pay Susan Gray only |s| Michael Manson		X	X			X
For deposit only |s| Michael Manson	X		X			X
Pay Susan Gray for account of Robert Gray |s| Michael Manson		X	X			X
To Susan Gray, without recourse |s| Michael Manson		X		X	X	

Source: Lawrence S. Clark and Peter D. Kinder, *Law and Business* (New York: McGraw-Hill Book Co., Inc., 1986), p. 652.

monly described. A **blank indorsement** is an indorsement that does not name a specific indorsee. Like indorsement 1 in Table 21.2, a blank indorsement turns an order instrument into bearer paper. Thus, an **indorser**, a person who indorses an instrument, should use a **special indorsement**, an indorsement that names a specific indorsee. Indorsements 2, 3, 5, and 6 are special indorsements.

All indorsements are what is called either nonrestrictive or restrictive. A **nonrestrictive indorsement** does not limit the indorsee's ability to transfer the instrument. Indorsements 1, 2, and 6 in Table 21.2 are nonrestrictive. In contrast, a **restrictive indorsement** tries to limit the indorsee's ability to transfer the instrument. Indorsements 3, 4, and 5 are common restrictive indorsements.

Finally, all indorsements are either qualified or unqualified. A **qualified indorsement** indicates that the indorser denies all liability under the rights of subsequent holders of the instrument in the event that the instrument is not accepted or paid. Indorsement 6 in Table 21.2 is a qualified indorsement.

THE LAW OF BANKRUPTCY

Bankruptcy, whether your own or someone else's, is an ordinary risk of doing business. UCC Article 9, "Secured Transactions," provides a first line of defense for creditors. A second line of defense commonly used by creditors of small businesses is to require the businesses' owners to cosign notes with their businesses. In the event of bankruptcy, the creditor therefore has a claim on the individual cosigner's personal assets as well as the business's.

The cosigner strategy is perfectly legal, but it defeats one of the goals of a bankruptcy proceeding: to give the **bankrupt**, the person or business in a bankruptcy proceeding, a clean slate to start over with. The other principal purpose is to give the creditors as much of what is due them as possible.

TABLE 21.3

Bankruptcy Filings: 1975–1984

[For years ending June 30]

ITEM	1975	1976	1977	1978	1979	1980[1]	1981	1982	1983	1984
Total	254,484	246,549	214,399	202,951	226,476	277,880	360,329	367,866	374,734	344,275
Business	30,130	35,201	32,189	30,528	29,500	36,449	47,415	56,423	69,818	62,170
Non-business	224,354	211,348	182,210	172,423	196,976	241,431	312,914	311,443	304,916	282,105
Voluntary	253,198	245,383	213,257	201,944	255,549	276,691	358,997	366,331	373,064	342,828
Involuntary	1,286	1,166	1,142	1,007	927	1,189	1,332	1,535	1,670	1,447
Chapter 7[3]	209,330	209,067	181,194	168,771	183,259	214,357	265,721	255,098	251,322	232,994
Chapter 9[4]	—	2	1	2	1	—	1	4	3	4
Chapter 11[5]	3,506	3,235	3,046	3,266	3,042	5,302	7,828	14,059	21,207	19,913
Chapter 13[6]	41,178	33,579	29,422	30,185	39,442	58,216	86,778	98,705	102,201	91,358
Section 304[7]	(x)	(x)	(x)	(x)	(x)	5	1	—	1	6

— Represents zero.   X Not applicable.   [1]For the first three months of 1980 the judiciary operated under the Bankruptcy Act and for the last nine months under the new bankruptcy code established by the Bankruptcy Reform Act of 1978. Includes only those petitions filed under the new bankruptcy code.   [2]Includes five Section 304 cases filed under the Reform Act in 1980 and 1 in 1981 which are not included in the subcategories of voluntary/involuntary.   [3]Chapter 7, liquidation of non-exempt assets of businesses or individuals.   [4]Chapter 9, adjustment of debts of a muncipality.   [5]Chapter 11, individual or business reorganization.   [6]Chapter 13, adjustment of debts of an individual with regular income.   [7]11 U.S.C., Section 304, cases ancillary to foreign proceedings.

Source: Administrative Office of the U.S. Courts, *Annual Report of the Director*, in *Statistical Abstract of the United States* (1986), Table 888, p. 522.

FIGURE 21.5

Resolving a Bankruptcy

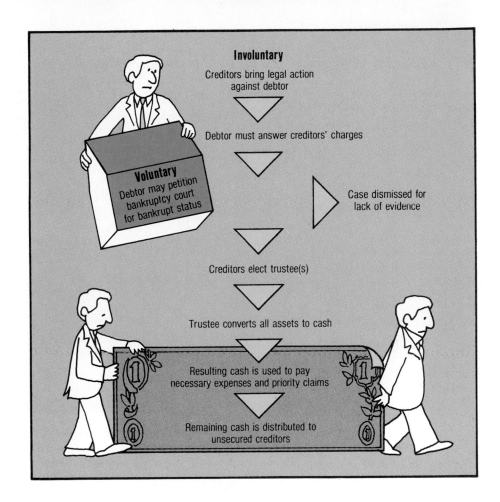

Involuntary

Creditors bring legal action against debtor

Debtor must answer creditors' charges

Voluntary
Debtor may petition bankruptcy court for bankrupt status

Case dismissed for lack of evidence

Creditors elect trustee(s)

Trustee converts all assets to cash

Resulting cash is used to pay necessary expenses and priority claims

Remaining cash is distributed to unsecured creditors

The Bankruptcy Code

Bankruptcy is a matter of federal law. The most recent revisions of the Bankruptcy Code, the Bankruptcy Reform Act of 1978 and the Bankruptcy Amendments of 1984, almost totally rewrote the law. Special bankruptcy courts hear such cases.

Proceedings under the bankruptcy statutes are commonly referred to by their chapter numbers in the Bankruptcy Code. The three common types of proceedings are

Chapter 7: Straight bankruptcy or liquidation
Chapter 11: Reorganization (mainly used for businesses)
Chapter 13: Regular income plans (individuals only)

In Chapter 7 proceedings, the most common type, businesses are dissolved, their assets liquidated, and their debts **discharged** or terminated. Individuals emerge from Chapter 7 with a minimal amount of assets. Everything else is liquidated and paid to their creditors. Proceedings in Chapter 11 and Chapter 13 shield businesses and individuals from their creditors while they work out payment arrangements. The famous bankruptcy cases of the 1980s — the Manville Corporation, Continental Air Lines, and the A. H. Robins Manufacturing Company — were Chapter 11 proceedings.

Protection and heartache. *Bankruptcy can be a personal tragedy, as many of the people attending this farm auction know. In Bloomfield, Missouri, and throughout much of America's heartland, farmers have been forced into bankruptcy by rising debts and falling farm prices. While it can be very painful, bankruptcy is designed to protect both the bankrupt and his or her creditors.*

Bankruptcy Proceedings

The Two Major Types of Bankruptcy Proceedings

Bankruptcy proceedings are either voluntary or involuntary. The bankrupt initiates voluntary proceedings, and creditors initiate involuntary proceedings. Normally, Chapter 13 proceedings are voluntary.

Once bankruptcy papers are filed, all bankruptcy proceedings follow essentially the same pattern. The court will grant the bankrupt relief from the creditors' collection efforts, appoint an interim trustee to protect the bankrupt's assets, and order the creditors' committee to meet. The **creditors' committee** is simply all of the bankrupt's creditors called together by the court to review the bankrupt's documentation of his or her debts and assets and to elect a permanent trustee in bankruptcy. The permanent trustee's job is to protect the existing assets, sort out the liabilities, and rule on the validity of claims. If the bankrupt is an individual, the trustee segregates the assets that he or she may keep. Depending on the bankrupt's state of residence, for example, he or she may keep a vehicle worth up to $1,200, plus household goods, furnishings, and clothing totaling up to $4,000. What remains is distributed to creditors in the order of their priority as established by the Bankruptcy Code. Once the distributions are completed, the court discharges the debtor.

The court's discharge order ends the proceeding and the bankrupt's liability on all debts covered in it. The bankrupt's financial slate may still be far from clean, though. Some debts are **nondischargable**, meaning not releasable in a bankruptcy proceeding. These debts include those that may be owed to the government in the form of taxes, fines, penalties, or — in most circumstances — educational loans. Judgments in tort actions based on a claim other than negligence are not dischargable, either, nor are alimony, separate maintenance, and child-support payments.

BUSINESS LAW: A PERSPECTIVE

"Just say we're reorganizing under Chapter 11, not 'we've gone belly-up'!"

It is often said that ours is a government of laws, not people. This saying accurately reflects the respect we share for the principles that govern us. However, those principles and the laws that express them apply to people and are applied by people. Therefore, our political laws cannot be as inflexible as the physical laws, like $E=MC^2$. For the businessperson, preventive law is one more planning tool. The law makes predicting or structuring the outcome of transactions significantly easier. Still, the prudent businessperson will keep in mind the famous saying of our most practical philosopher, Benjamin Franklin, "In this world nothing is certain but death and taxes."

Chapter Highlights

1. Identify each of the sources of U.S. Law.

U.S. law originates in each branch of government — legislative, executive, and judicial, and at each level of government — federal, state, and local.

2. Describe the various ways we classify laws in the United States.

There are several ways to classify laws. The three major divisions include public law and private law, criminal law and civil law, and substantive law and procedural law.

3. Describe the dispute-resolution system and the two principal alternatives to it.

The structure society has established for resolving differences is called the dispute-resolution system. This system includes trial courts, intermediate appellate courts, and supreme courts. The two major alternative dispute resolution mechanisms include *arbitration* and *mediation*.

4. Define tort and identify the classifications of torts.

A tort is a legal wrong defined by the common law. A legal wrong is one that causes an injury for which society

has determined the injured party deserves compensation from the party responsible for the injury. Torts are classified as *intentional torts, negligence, strict liabililty*, and *product liability*.

5. Describe the forms a contract may take and list the elements of a contract.

In simple terms, a contract is a promise or promises that the courts will enforce. Contracts may be in written or oral form. While oral contracts are enforceable, written contracts are often preferable because they reduce the possibility of disagreement. In case of lawsuit, the courts give a written contract greater weight in most instances. The elements of a contract are mutual assent, consideration, contractual capacity, legal purposes, and a writing, if required by law.

6. Classify the types of property.

Property takes two forms. *Real property* is land and everything attached to it. A home, and the trees surrounding the house, are examples of real property. *Personal property* is all property that is not a fixture or real property. The suit you wear to work, the boat you take to the lake on weekends, and your bank account represent types of personal property.

7. Describe the Uniform Commercial Code.

The Uniform Commercial Code is a body of statutes that replaces several areas of business law formerly covered by each states' common law contracts. It has been adopted by nearly every state, so doing business across state lines is now quite predictable.

8. Classify the types of bankruptcy proceedings and describe each.

Proceedings under the bankruptcy statutes are commonly referred to by their chapter numbers in the Bankruptcy Code. The three common proceedings are:
Chapter 7: Straight bankruptcy or liquidation
Chapter 11: Reorganization (mainly businesses)
Chapter 13: Regular income plans (individuals only)

Key Terms

Affirm	Disclaimer	Jurisdiction	Procedural laws
Appeal	Dispute-resolution	Liable	Product liability
Appellant	system	Litigant	Real property
Bankrupt	Fraud	Litigation	*Stare decisis*
Blank indorsement	Goods	Negotiable instrument	Statutes
Civil law	Indorsee	Patent	Statutory
Common law	Indorsement	Payable on demand	Tort
Contract	Indorser	Payable to bearer	Uniform Commercial
Copyright	Instrument	Payable to order	Code (UCC)
Criminal law	Intermediate appellate	Plaintiff	Warrant
Defendant	court	Precedent	Warranties

Review Questions

1. What is *preventive law*?
2. Identify the sources of U.S. law. How do we classify U.S. law?
3. Describe the dispute-resolution system.
4. What is a tort? An intentional tort?
5. What is the Uniform Commercial Code? What are some of the topics it covers?
6. Describe the law of property.
7. Describe the law of negotiable instruments. What are the six requirements for their negotiability?
8. What are the goals of a bankruptcy proceeding? List and describe three common chapter numbers in the Bankruptcy Code.

Application Exercises

1. As the owner of a small auto agency, you have decided to expand the service department. The new construction will cost approximately $75,000, according to a local building contractor who happens to be a close friend. Your lawyer has suggested that the details of the construction project be outlined in a contract. Should you follow the lawyer's advice? If a contract is to be prepared, what information will be required for a valid contract?

Cases

21.1 The Triple Ripple Contract

An oral contract is fine when both parties are happy with the performance of the contract. But when there is disagreement, the courts may not honor it. Civil court judges will not routinely uphold an oral contract unless (1) it involves $500 or less; (2) it covers a period of one year or less; and (3) both parties are available to testify about it. Even then, the judge has to decide whether there really was a contract and what its terms were.

Ray Kroc, the founder of McDonald's Corp., occasionally contracted with suppliers via handshake. In 1970, he got the idea of selling combination vanilla, chocolate, and strawberry ice cream cones in McDonald's fast-food outlets. He got in touch with Tom Cummings, the son of a friend, who owned Central Ice Cream Co. in Chicago. According to Cummings, the two men agreed orally that Cummings would design the "Triple Ripple" cone for McDonald's; if it passed a taste test, McDonald's would carry the cone exclusively for twenty years. They sealed the bargain with a handshake.

Cummings developed the cone, and it was accepted by McDonald's. Cummings then borrowed heavily to upgrade his equipment, and began production. McDonald's added the Triple Ripple cone to its menu, but it turned out to be a dud. After three years, McDonald's gave up on the cone and stopped buying it from Central. Cummings was unable to meet his loan obligations, and Central went into Chapter 11 bankruptcy.

Cummings sued McDonald's for breach of contract, on behalf of himself, his wife, and Central. McDonald's maintained that there had been no long-term contract. In 1984, a jury awarded Cummings and Central Ice Cream $52 million in damages. McDonald's immediately appealed and, at the same time, offered to settle for a smaller amount. One year later, Central and McDonald's agreed to a settlement of $15.5 million.

Ray Kroc became seriously ill during the trial and died before it was over. His successors at McDonald's maintain that, in spite of the decision, they still believe in doing business by handshake.

Questions

1. What does a written contract provide, that an oral contract may not provide?

2. Assuming Kroc was unable to testify, none of the three conditions for upholding an oral contract were met. Yet the jury obviously believed there had been a contract. Why?

For more information see *Forbes*, August 25, 1986, p. 82; *Inc.*, June 1986, pp. 131–132; and United Press International, June 21, 1985, BC cycle.

21.2 Fighting the Doughboy

In 1984, Vermont-based Ben & Jerry's Ice Cream brought suit against Häagen-Dazs, which by then had been acquired by the Pillsbury Corporation. The complaint alleged that Häagen-Dazs had tried to coerce Boston and Connecticut distributors into dropping Ben & Jerry's products.

The suit was based on the word of two distributors and was entirely serious. But Ben Cohen and Jerry Greenfield, Ben & Jerry's owners, thought it also should produce some fun and some publicity for their firm. They placed an ad in *Rolling Stone*, asking readers to buy "What's the Doughboy Afraid Of?" bumper stickers to help them fight the giant corporation. They also printed that slogan on T-shirts and on advertising signs on Boston busses.

Ben & Jerry's established a toll-free Doughboy hotline. The firm also made available special "Doughboy kits" that explained their suit and contained two form letters which could be sent to Pillsbury's board chairman. Both ended with the postscript "Why don't you pick on someone your own size?" And Greenfield spent a day on a one-man picket line in front of Pillsbury's Minneapolis headquarters.

The result of the campaign was thousands of letters to both Pillsbury and Ben & Jerry's, along with heavy press coverage of the battle. The result of the suit was an out-of-court agreement — a promise by Pillsbury that it would not seek exclusive distribution contracts in Massachusetts and Connecticut for two years.

Questions

1. Which body of law was involved in the Ben & Jerry's suit?
2. State and explain your opinion of the Ben & Jerry's "Doughboy campaign."

For more information see *The New Yorker*, July 8, 1985, pp. 31–45; *Fortune*, September 3, 1984, p. 9; and *Dairy Record*, June 1984, p. 14.

22

GOVERNMENT AND BUSINESS

Learning Objectives

After you have completed this chapter, you will be able to do the following:

■ Describe the three principal areas of government's relations with business.

■ Explain the origins and purposes of the antitrust laws.

■ Identify the two major prohibitions included in the Sherman Act.

■ Define the three restraints on trade forbidden by the Clayton Act.

■ List and describe the three forms of mergers.

■ Outline the Federal Trade Commission's role in policing the marketplace.

■ Describe the theory underlying environmental, health, and safety regulations.

■ Explain the various meanings of the term deregulation.

The great humorist Will Rogers once noted, "The business of government is to keep the government out of business — that is, unless business needs government aid."[1] This saying no doubt has a familiar ring to persons associated with the American textile industry. In the early 1970s, the federal government aggressively implemented occupational health standards, which had a serious economic impact on many textile mills. One of these health standards limited the concentration of cotton dust allowable in the air because this contaminant had been associated with lung disease among textile workers.[2] To reduce the concentration of cotton dust in the air required remodeling plants and installing expensive equipment. Needless to say, this type of government involvement in business was not welcomed.

In the early 1980s, the American textile industry was struggling to compete with low-cost imports from many foreign countries. Some companies were able to reduce the size of their labor forces, but others had to close plants. Many textile executives voiced the need for government action to save the industry. They recommended, among other things, a series of tariffs on imported textiles. These tariffs would raise the price of imports, thus making them less attractive to consumers, the argument ran.

GOVERNMENT'S ROLES

One can describe government's relations with business in terms of three S's: subsidy, support, and supervision. As we look at each of these activities, keep in mind that they occur at all three levels of government: local, state, and federal.

Subsidy

Imagine what our country would be like if private companies owned the highways and bridges. Suppose that each five-mile segment belonged to a different company, which would make money by charging tolls on vehicles using its road segment or bridge. This system may sound ridiculous, but it existed in France until the 1880s and in parts of New England even until the 1920s. In this country, the question of whether government should fund the railroads, canals, and highways dominated the political agenda between 1789 and about 1850. Only the coming of railroads resolved the question in favor of government subsidy. In fact, government money and other assistance led to the construction of virtually all the railroads built west of the Appalachian Mountains.

Today, relatively few highways still have tolls, and government agencies oversee the maintenance of these roads. State and local governments assist business with financing and by giving tax breaks for new plants, like General Motors' Saturn auto plant in Tennessee. The federal government also subsidizes commercial space ventures by using NASA rockets and space shuttles. In addition, electric and gas companies receive special privileges to enable them to bring their services to homes and businesses. The list of subsidies seems endless.

FIGURE 22.1

A Government's Role in
Business

Subsidy   Support   Supervision

Support

Government at all its levels offers tangible support to business. One important way in which government supports business is in its purchasing of private-sector goods and services. The government produces only a tiny proportion of the goods it uses, so it buys tons of paper, for example, from private suppliers. And in order to keep public payrolls lean, government units contract with businesses for a whole array of services ranging from computer maintenance to prison management.

Many of government's support services to business are less obvious than the financial subsidies. For instance, no major business does any long-term planning or market research that is not in some way influenced by data from the U.S. Department of Commerce and the U.S. Department of Labor. Likewise, in the mineral-producing states, federal and state agencies supply invaluable information about promising geological formations. And businesses that develop goods for the government can often apply the same technology to other, private-sector, products. Commercial jet aviation began with the Boeing 707, a modified version of a cargo plane that Boeing had developed for the Air Force. Farmers, the commercial fishing industry, and amusement parks, among many others, rely on weather forecasts supplied by the Department of Commerce that are based on NASA satellite photos.

Perhaps the most important support that government provides business — and, indeed, all citizens — is a stable system of laws and justice. For instance, the value to business of the predictability in the commercial climate supplied by the Uniform Commercial Code (discussed in Chapter 21) is beyond calculation. Commerce as we know it simply could not exist without the laws and constitutional amendments permitting incorporation (discussed in Chapter 3). And a

FIGURE 22.2

Laws the EPA Enforces

Air pollution

Off-shore exploration for oil and gas

Surface mining

Water pollution

system of courts and regulations (discussed in Chapter 21) protects American businesses from unfair competition by foreign companies.

Supervision

It is far easier to complain about the burdens that government imposes in the form of regulation and taxation than it is to acknowledge the benefits that government provides. As any other member of society, business finds its freedom of action limited by laws and regulations. Unlike the average citizen, however, businesses, and large ones in particular, have the ability to make their complaints heard. For the past fifteen years, business has complained about the heavy hand of government regulation. What is government regulation, and does it really harm business? These questions do not have simple answers.

The government regulation of business takes three forms. First, business must observe the same laws that all other members of society must obey. The criminal laws apply to businesses and individuals alike. Corporations obviously cannot serve jail terms or suffer the death penalty, but their managers can. Prosecutors have become increasingly aggressive in their efforts to convict errant executives and managers. In one highly publicized recent case, a jury found certain executives of the Film Recovery Systems Corporation guilty of manslaughter in the death of a worker from cyanide poisoning on the job.[3]

The second type of government regulation is designed to encourage competition and keep the marketplace free of abusive practices. These laws and regulations fall into the two broad categories of antitrust and consumer protection, discussed below.

The third type includes all the government regulations designed to achieve the results that an unfettered free market will not produce. Under free enterprise,

The Third Area of Government–Business Relations: Supervision

The Three Forms of Government Regulation

Information — the basis for sound planning. Census workers collect information on all Americans, even those in the most inaccessible regions, for publication in the national census every 10 years. Businesses rely on accurate data to plan for the future.

the market mechanism works wonderfully in meeting consumer and social needs in many areas. In areas like worker safety, however, the market mechanism does not provide enough encouragement to guarantee that there will be at least minimally safe conditions in all work places. Virtually all occupational health and safety, equal employment, labor, environmental, and public-health regulations fall into this category. The first three of these areas were covered in Parts 2 and 3. We will discuss environmental and public-health regulations later in this chapter.

THE ANTITRUST LAWS: REGULATIONS PROMOTING COMPETITION

One of the most important governmental regulatory functions is the encouragment of fair and open competition. The marketplace would seem not to need this help, but, as the free market's great apostle Adam Smith noted, "People of the same trade seldom meet together, even for merriment and diversion, but the conversation ends in a conspiracy against the public, or in some contrivance to raise prices."[4] What Smith observed in England in 1776 proved prophetic of late nineteenth- and early twentieth-century America. Society's response took the form of what are now called the antitrust laws.

The Nature of the Antitrust Laws

The Origins and Purposes of the Antitrust Laws

The antitrust laws are misnamed — they should be called the procompetition laws. Most states have their own antitrust laws, but they are of limited scope and for the most part, they duplicate the federal laws. We will therefore discuss only the federal statutes.

Antitrust means literally "against trust." In the context of the late nineteenth century, a trust was a legal device designed to get around certain restrictions on the ownership of corporations. These restrictions disappeared in the 1880s and 1890s, but the name *trust* remained as a term to describe giant industrial and natural-resource consortiums that attempted to absorb or destroy all other companies in their markets. Once a trust controlled a market, it was free to charge what it wanted for its goods, as John D. Rockefeller's Standard Oil Company did. What was worse, it could use its economic power to make or break businesses that relied on its commodity. Sometimes one trust even had enough power to break another.

The Sherman Act

The first federal legislation aimed at controlling trusts was the **Sherman Act** of 1890, named for its sponsor in the U.S. Senate. The Sherman Act contains two broad prohibitions. Section 1 declares illegal "every contract, combination in the form of trust or otherwise, or conspiracy in restraint of trade or commerce. . . ." Section 2 prohibits the wrongful acquiring of a monopoly, attempting to monopolize, and conspiring to monopolize.

Restraints of Trade   The restraints of trade and commerce targeted by the Sherman Act include price fixing, allocation of markets among competitors, boycotts, and certain types of monopolies.

Price fixing is an agreement between two parties as to the prices to be charged for goods. Such agreements, whether explicit or implicit, can have no other purpose but to limit competition. The government has only to prove that the forbidden conduct actually occurred; there is no defense for the conduct. Such antitrust violations are called **per se violations.** The agreements to fix prices may be between competitors or between a buyer and a seller. If a seller requires a buyer to agree to charge not less than a certain amount for a product when it is resold, the seller has violated the Sherman Act.

Market allocations are agreements to divide markets among potential competitors. **Horizontal market allocation** is the division of a market among independent competitors. It is a per se violation of the Sherman Act. Suppose, for example, that the Widget Corporation, International Widgets, and Widgets, Ltd., agree to divide the California market for industrial widgets. Their agreement would limit the number of sellers from which buyers could choose, leaving buyers with only a "take it or leave it" option.

By contrast, **vertical market allocation** is the division of a market among related entities, like franchisees or subsidiaries. Such allocations may or may not be violations of the Sherman Act. The courts apply to these allocations what is called a **rule-of-reason standard**, meaning that the defendant in an antitrust case is given the opportunity to prove that the conduct does not unreasonably restrict trade. For example, if our widget companies were all franchisees of Worldwide Widgets, which had divided California among them, a court would probably not find a violation. There would be no horizontal market allocation because the franchisees would still have to compete against other businesses selling widgets.

A **boycott** is an agreement among competitors not to sell to or buy from a particular entity. It is a per se violation of the Sherman Act.

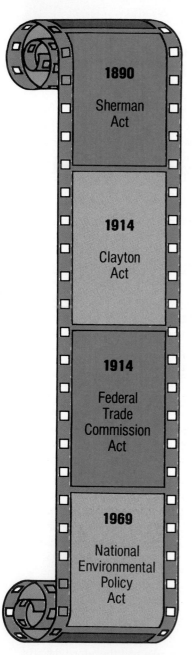

FIGURE 22.3

Government Regulation of Business

1890

Sherman Act

1914

Clayton Act

1914

Federal Trade Commission Act

1969

National Environmental Policy Act

Monopolies "A **monopoly** is the power to control prices and exclude competition."[5] Monopoly violations are particularly hard to prove. They are rule-of-reason offenses, which require highly sophisticated economic and demographic analyses. One type of monopoly violation is relatively easy to prove, though. **Predatory pricing** is an abuse of monopoly power involving the pricing of products in such a way as to eliminate competition. Suppose that B. C. Bowling Balls has been the only source of balls for miniature bowling, until A. D. Bowling Balls

INTERNATIONAL BUSINESS

Is the U.N. in the U.S.'s Future?

The United Nations Educational, Scientific, and Cultural Organization (UNESCO), founded in 1945, seeks to promote world peace by improving education, creating an open interchange of ideas and scientific and cultural information, and lessening social, religious, and racial tensions. Despite these worthy goals, the United States left the organization at the end of 1984, in part because it saw UNESCO turning into a forum for criticism of American policies, in part because the organization was allegedly being run like a corrupt business. The move left many wondering about the future relationship of the U.S. and the world's most powerful international organization. The position of the U.S. in the U.N. and other international organizations is likely to take on even greater importance as American businesses become increasingly enmeshed in the global economy.

The pullout from UNESCO was seen by many as a victory for conservatives suspicious of any world governing body. "Get the U.S. out of the U.N.!" has long been a rallying cry for conservatives who see the whole concept of a single world government as communistic and who don't like the idea of sitting down at the bargaining table with the Russians any time or any place. Such critics point to the tendency of the U.N.'s debates and conferences to give those angry with U.S. policies a chance to sound off to an international audience. They see no reason to subject the U.S. to such criticism.

Economic considerations were important in the administration's decision to pull out of UNESCO. The organization is badly run, and, many say, corrupt. And it has been running on American dollars. The U.S. has been paying one-quarter of UNESCO's bills, which help to bring the entire American tab for the U.N. up to $1.5 billion each year. The U.N. is becoming, some say, too expensive for the U.S.

Among the opponents of the American pullout were many in the American business community who acknowledged UNESCO's problems but contended that leaving the organization was not the proper solution. Supporters of the U.N. see the U.S. as increasingly isolating itself from the rest of the world, cutting off the dialogue that is crucial both to peaceful coexistence and to international economic cooperation.

Such supporters feel that it is worth funding an inefficient organization in order to maintain the symbolic status of America as the chief champion of international cooperation and harmony. They view with alarm the Reagan administration's refusal to accept the jurisdiction of the U.N.'s International Court of Justice, or World Court.

The rest of the world must be getting mixed signals about how the U.S. wants to relate to other countries. On the one hand our leaders call for free and open access to foreign markets, and they support the multinational corporations that are helping to move us rapidly closer to a truly global economy. On the other hand, the administration has been trying to cut down on the free international exchange of ideas and information and withdrawing its support from international agencies. The direction chosen by the next administration may well have a profound effect on the future of international business.

Sources: "Death of a Pipe Dream," *The Wall Street Journal*, October 8, 1985, 30. Steven W. Colford, "Businessmen Can't Halt UNESCO Pullout," *Advertising Age*, December 13, 1984, 3. Sol W. Sanders, "Jeane Kirkpatrick's Two-Fisted Style Is Paying Off," *Business Week*, December 31, 1984, 59.

decides to enter the market. When B. C. hears the news, it drops its prices to below its costs, to prevent A. D. from successfully entering the market. A company that has a legal monopoly violates the Sherman Act by trying to keep its monopoly by preventing another company from entering the market.

Some monopolies are completely legal and even socially desirable. Suppose that B. C. Bowling Balls again had acquired its monopoly as a result of simply staying in the field after its competitors had dropped out, for one reason or another. B. C. would then have acquired a **natural monopoly,** a monopoly acquired as a result of market forces, without violating the antitrust laws. In some instances, statutes and even the U.S. Constitution allow the granting of monopolies. As noted in Chapter 3, public utilities have monopolies in their service areas because having, say, natural-gas companies compete for residential service would be inefficient. As another example of allowed monopolies, copyrights and patents, which are authorized by the U.S. Constitution, give their holders monopolies on the benefits derived from creative works or inventions. Without such monopolies, people would have little incentive to create or innovate.

The Clayton Act

The **Clayton Act** (1914) broadened the scope of the Sherman Act by trying to prevent anticompetitive behavior rather than by dealing with its consequences.

Preventing Restraints on Trade   The Clayton Act focuses on three devices — tying arrangements, reciprocal-dealing arrangements, and exclusive-dealing arrangements — that can lessen competition or lead to the gaining of monopoly power.

A **tying arrangement** results when the seller agrees to sell a product that the buyer wants (the tying product) only if the buyer also purchases another product that the buyer does not want (the tied product). Suppose that the Nadir Corporation is the sole source for left-handed sky hooks. Nadir decides to sell sky hooks only to buyers who also agree to buy certain quantities of widgets. Nadir has thus committed a per se violation of the Clayton Act. Note that a tying arrangement violates the Clayton Act only if the seller has so much power in the market that the buyer will buy the tying product without regard for what else it must buy to get what it wants. If the buyer has the choice of an adequate substitute elsewhere, the seller's conduct does not violate the Clayton Act.

A **reciprocal-dealing arrangement** occurs when a buyer can force a seller to buy something from it as a condition of the buyer's making the purchase. A reciprocal-dealing arrangement is, of course, the opposite of a tying arrangement. Now it is the buyer's market power that forces a seller to buy what it does not want.

An **exclusive-dealing arrangement** is an agreement by one party to sell all its output of a certain product to the other party, or to buy all it requires of a product from that party, in exchange for that party's promise not to engage in similar transactions with anyone else. These cases are enormously technical and complicated, and there are many exceptions to the general rule against exclusive-dealing arrangements.

Regulating Mergers   Section 7 of the Clayton Act prohibits mergers that "substantially lessen competition." A **merger** is one company's acquisition and absorption of another.

One way to destroy the competition. Many governments take part in the battle against knock-offs — cheap imitations of well-known items. Such illegal copies infringe on the patent and trademark laws of many nations. Here imitation Cartier watches are being destroyed in a most dramatic fashion.

Protecting patents. Kodak took some shortcuts when it decided to compete with Polaroid in the lucrative instant photography market. After the courts found that Kodak had violated 7 Polaroid patents, the company's problems started piling up. Dealers and consumers began returning their cameras. Kodak had to figure out how to dispose of its mammoth headache.

The Three Forms of Mergers

Mergers take one of three forms. A **vertical merger** is a merger of two companies in the same chain of supply. For instance, if Coca-Cola acquires an independently owned Coca-Cola bottler, a vertical merger has occurred. A **horizontal merger** occurs when two competitors merge. Horizontal mergers are of special concern to regulators. By contrast, **conglomerate mergers** are of little concern to government regulators, because they involve the acquisition of companies in different markets. For example, the nation's leading seller of bathroom fixtures, American Standard, once owned American Bank Stationery and Mosler Safe, two businesses unrelated to its main business.

The government regulates mergers because they may remove competitors, or at least potential competitors, from the marketplace. In recent years, the government has taken a very relaxed attitude toward mergers. Because lawsuits can often take a decade or more to resolve, the Clayton Act authorizes the government to issue merger guidelines specifying the permissible boundaries. The law also requires that the acquiring firms with assets exceeding $100 million must submit proposed mergers for government clearance before they take place.

Interlocking Directorates The Clayton Act prohibits **interlocking directorates**, the presence of the same individual on the boards of two companies

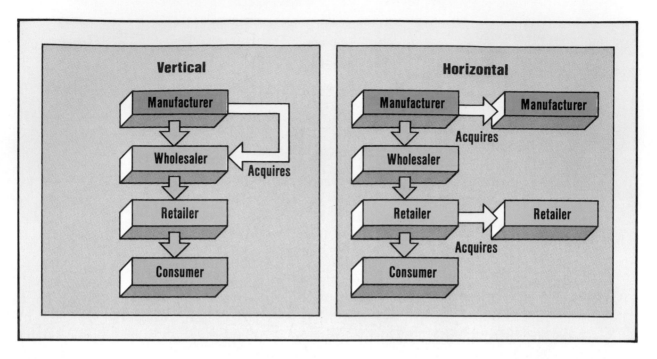

FIGURE 22.4

Forms of Mergers

that are in similar product markets if the combined total capital of the two companies exceeds $1 million. A person sitting on the boards of two competing companies could easily give information about one to the other, with serious anticompetitive results.

The Robinson-Patman Act

The Robinson-Patman Act bans **price discrimination,** the sale of goods at different prices by a commercial seller to two or more nonretail buyers. The law's goal is to prevent large buyers from obtaining price advantages over small ones. Thus, a shaving-cream manufacturer must sell its product to both a giant chain and a corner drugstore at the same price. If volume discounts are available they must be offered to all buyers. The Robinson-Patman Act does not apply to retail sales, so it still permits the corner drugstore to sell the same product at different prices to two customers. (Other laws may affect the drugstore's pricing, of course.) The workings of this act are extremely complicated and go beyond our scope here.

The Federal Trade Commission Act

The **Federal Trade Commission Act** of 1914 created the **Federal Trade Commission (FTC)** and gave it extremely broad authority to police the marketplace. Its authority includes not only jurisdiction over some antitrust cases but also the power to act against unfair trade practices, as we will see in the next section. The act gives the Federal Trade Commission the power to regulate any "unfair methods of competition," which includes any anticompetitive behavior that falls short of being a violation of the other acts discussed above.

"The trouble with a merger like this is that our people who know computers don't know a thing about bubble gum, the people who know bubble gum don't know a thing about hats, the people who know hats . . ."

FIGURE 22.5
Interlocking Directorates

Enforcing the Antitrust Laws

The federal and state governments have the duty to enforce the antitrust laws. However, private entities, whether individuals or businesses, also have the right to enforce any antitrust laws except the Federal Trade Commission Act by means of lawsuits if they are injured by anticompetitive behavior. The law provides a strong incentive for private antitrust actions: triple damages for a successful plaintiff. Big business has mounted a serious attack on the triple damages remedy, claiming that it has created a "bounty hunter" mentality among greedy lawyers. Thus far, smaller businesses and lawyers have had the better of the argument. They have noted that the extreme length and complexity of antitrust cases makes successful claims expensive, as well as the fact that many victims of anticompetitive practices are bankrupted, so they could not sustain the costs of a suit if all that they were to recover was what they had originally lost.

POLICING THE MARKETPLACE

As noted earlier, the antitrust laws are really procompetition laws designed to ensure that the heart of our capitalist system, competition, flourishes in the marketplace. Market competition is not like war. Laws and regulations define what society regards as fair, and competitors must observe them.

In Chapter 19, we encountered the Securities and Exchange Commission (SEC), which has the responsibility for maintaining a fair market for securities. Various other federal and state agencies are responsible for policing other markets. The beneficiaries of these regulations are businesses and consumers alike.

The Federal Trade Commission

The Federal Trade
Commission's Pole

The Federal Trade Commission's enabling act charges it to prevent "unfair or deceptive acts or practices in commerce." We have already seen the effect of that provision in the antitrust area, but this provision also gives the FTC powers over the marketplace that go well beyond antitrust's narrow limits. In general, unfair or deceptive practices include any that tend to fool the consumer. For example, a sign over a tape deck in Looney Louie's Stereo Store may advertise that the price is "$250 off!" If the sign means "$250 off the manufacturer's list price," it probably is deceptive, since almost no stereo retailers sell at that deep a discount. In order to avoid being deceptive, Louie must either indicate on the sign what the discount really means or else sell the tape deck at $250 below his normal prices.

Sellers can also make deceptive presentations about the quality of their goods. If Louis claims that the tape deck has four recording heads when it has only two, his representation is deceptive. A celebrity who endorses a product must actually use the product, unless he or she obviously would not be expected to use it. The classic example of the exception to this rule was All-Pro quarterback Joe Namath's endorsement of a certain brand of pantyhose. Another important area of marketplace regulation concerns consumer credit. If a credit card issuer advertises a specific rate, for example, it is obligated to charge that rate.

The Federal Trade Commission's rules do not inhibit tough competition, like advertisements comparing competing products. They do, however, enforce minimum fairness standards.

State Regulations

Almost all states have consumer-protection laws similar to the provisions of the Federal Trade Commission Act. Virtually any case involving deceptive practices can be brought by a state as well as the FTC.

The states enforce many other laws that ensure honest dealings. For instance, all cities and counties have laws regulating the weights and measures used in trade. Inspectors check scales in supermarkets, pumps in gas stations, and the like to make sure that customers receive what they are charged for. The states also set and enforce standards for the practice of the professions: doctors, lawyers, accountants, engineers, and others.

ENVIRONMENTAL, HEALTH, AND SAFETY REGULATIONS

Our country's experience has convinced most Americans of the superiority of a market-based economy and social system. The market mechanism is not perfect, however. It cannot achieve some goals that we as a society need and want. These social aims are expressed primarily in environmental, health, and safety regulations.

Toxic spills. *EPA workers, agents of the federal government, clean up a dioxin-contaminated street in Newark, New Jersey. Although businesses often complain about government regulations, they depend on government agencies to provide help in emergencies. Dioxin is one of the most toxic chemicals known. When it is accidentally discharged into the environment, everyone appreciates government intervention.*

When Market Incentives Do Not Work

Theoretically, the invisible hand working through the marketplace described by Adam Smith should guide businesses toward producing the greatest good for the greatest number. Unfortunately, though, doing the right thing sometimes lessens a firm's ability to compete. In these cases, the government must supply incentives before a business will take action. Let's look at an example.

The Theory Behind Environmental, Health, and Safety Regulations

When firms discharge pollutants into the air or water, they may create a serious danger to human health. No firm has a direct incentive to stop, however — particularly when stopping costs money. Success in a competitive marketplace requires companies to keep costs to a minimum and maintain a healthy profit margin. If three competing manufacturing firms each discharge pollutants into the same river from identical plants, let's say that it will cost each one $2 million

Choking on Debts and Bad Advice

The government has been involved in the business of agriculture for most of this century. Government decisions about land and water rights have largely shaped the way America grows its food, government advice helped create the crisis of the 1980s, and now everyone is turning to the government to try to solve the problem. The business of agriculture concerns us as taxpayers as well as consumers and perhaps parents. It is worth trying to understand some of the tangle of forces that resulted in the present situation.

Put yourself in the shoes of a farmer in 1971. In that year, President Nixon froze wages and prices and devalued the dollar; coincidentally, the Soviet Union and other countries suffered from major crop failures. The devaluation meant that American crops were cheaper for foreigners to buy and the crop failures meant that many nations needed American food. Grain exports increased dramatically, by 70 percent between 1970 and 1973. Due to this demand, the price of corn doubled and the price of wheat tripled, and American farmers suddenly had cash in their pockets.

At the same time, the government changed its farm policies. For years, the government had tried to prevent crop surpluses by encouraging farmers to cut production. But in the early 1970s, Earl Butz, Richard Nixon's Secretary of Agriculture, toured the country saying that the government would no longer limit farm production, encouraging farmers to grow food for a hungry world.

Farmers who accepted this patriotic call to grow more bought land, driving land prices up at a rate of 15 percent per year in many areas. Convinced that their land would continue to become more valuable, farmers borrowed money to buy more. Some worried about going into debt, but if you were paying 8 percent on a loan and the value of your land was going up 15 percent a year, how could you lose?

The new bigger farms led to changes in the way many farmers did business. Farmers used more technology, chemical fertilizers, and pesticides, they often switched to growing just one crop, and went further into debt buying expensive machinery to take care of that crop.

Before they even had time to enjoy their prosperity, farmers began to watch it crumble. The oil embargo made all high-tech farming techniques suddenly more expensive — the prices of fuel, fertilizer, pesticides, and herbicides all shot up. When the profit-per-acre began to fall, the first reaction of many farmers, again encouraged by government agencies, was to buy more acres, going even further into debt.

By 1980, almost everything had gone wrong for farmers. The Soviet invasion of Afghanistan led President Carter to cut off grain sales to the Soviet Union. Other countries were beginning to feel the effects of the worldwide economic recession, and because of high U.S. budget deficits and interest rates, the dollar continued to grow stronger, making American goods more expensive for other countries. So while the supply of food continued to be high, demand dropped, and the constant growth that farmers, bankers, and the government had counted on came to a halt.

Some huge farms are still making money, but most farmers can no longer borrow money to get this year's crop planted, much less buy more land. So they turn to the government for help, feeling, justifiably, that the government had a big part in getting them into this fix. But the government, despite spending more every year supporting farmers, seems unable to come up with a program that will do any good.

Although everyone agrees that agriculture shouldn't be so dependent on the government, the choice between these alternatives will probably be made, again, by the government, as it decides who gets everything from loans to export treaties to federal irrigation projects. And government funding of small farm research has been dropping almost as fast as farm profits.

Sources: George J. Church, "Real Trouble on the Farm," *Time*, Vol. 125, No. 7, February 18, 1985, 24. John N. Frank, "The Farm Rut Gets Deeper," *Business Week*, No. 2899, June 17, 1985, 32. Daniel Zwerdling, "Down on the Farm," *The Progressive*, Vol. 47, No. 9, September, 1983, 18. Kenneth R. Sheets, "Few Hopes Blossom for Farmers in Spring of '85," *U.S. News & World Report*, Vol. 98, No. 19, May 20, 1985, 74. Barbara H. Seeber, "The Producer," *Science 84*, Vol. 5, No. 6, July/August, 1984, 40. John McCormick, "A Bumper Crop of Problems," *Newsweek*, Vol. 106, No. 3, July 15, 1985, 60.

to install pollution-control systems to eliminate the problem. It might also cost $1 million per year to operate each system. Clearly, if one of the three firms refuses to install such a system, that company will have a continuing cost advantage over its two competitors. In this case, open competition provides an incentive *not* to solve the environmental problem. Thus, society must step in, acting through government. At the very least, it must remove the disincentive to meet the public's needs.

Air, Water, and Conservation Regulations

The most recent regulations designed to meet societal needs are the environmental ones. Although some American water-pollution regulations date from the early 1900s, comprehensive regulation dates only to the mid-1960s. Air-pollution regulation began about the same time. The National Environmental Policy Act of 1969 provided a framework for the expression of environmental concerns and for the inclusion of such considerations in national decision making. In 1970, the Environmental Protection Agency came into existence to take charge of most air and water regulations. The 1970s saw water and air legislation dominating the national agenda.

Perhaps the most remarkable aspect of these regulatory programs was the national consensus that developed around them. When the Reagan administration set out to abolish the environmental programs created in the 1970s, the public offered no support for its efforts. The administration did weaken or eliminate enforcement to a degree, but it abandoned its push to eliminate the programs.

Other programs affecting natural resources and conservation were adopted in the 1970s. For instance, the first comprehensive federal regulation of surface mining began in 1977. Regulation of the offshore exploration for oil and gas was revised, for the first time in twenty-five years. The federal Coastal Zone Management Act encouraged the first comprehensive examination of our coasts as national and state resources.

Regulation of Food and Drugs

Every state has a department of agriculture and a department of health, which share responsibility for policing the quality of the food produced and consumed within the state. On the federal level, the United States Department of Agriculture and the Food and Drug Administration (FDA) share these duties in regard to goods in interstate commerce. The FDA is responsible for enforcing the Pure Food and Drug Act, one of the earliest efforts to regulate the marketplace. Under this act the FDA evaluates new drugs coming onto the American market, for instance, and develops standards for food additives.

Regulation of the Work Place

As we saw in Parts 2 and 3, government regulation of the work place has a long history. These regulations, on the federal, state, and local levels, have not always kept pace with modern technology. Ironically, the consensus that developed

Capitalizing on the State of Vermont. Caroline Longe never meant to get into the food business. She just canned good food for her farm family and the hired hands. When neighbors and local stores began ordering her products, she contacted the Vermont Department of Agriculture to find out if she needed a license. Not only did that agency test her products and explain how to meet state standards, it helped Longe design the label Clearview Farms Cannery uses today.

around the environmental legislation of the 1970s never formed for the Occupational Safety and Health Act enacted by Congress during the same era. The Reagan administration has had a significantly easier time not enforcing these laws than the environmental laws.

Contemporary Regulatory Issues

Two major regulatory issues have dominated the news for much of this decade and seem likely to continue to do so well into the next. These issues are the questions of what to do about hazardous wastes and acid rain. Both problems are phenomenally complicated, no less for having been with us for so long.

Hazardous Waste   Even seemingly clean industries like semiconductor manufacturing produce hazardous wastes. Older disposal methods once thought safe, like burial and injection into deep wells, have proven inadequate — or worse. Ignoring for a moment the companies that did not act responsibly, we must still ask if it is fair to pursue, years later, the companies that acted in good faith from the beginning in disposing of their wastes. Congress has answered this question in part by creating the so-called Superfund to finance the cleanup of old dumps, like California's Stringfellow acid pits and New York's Love Canal. However, the cleanup costs have exceeded even the highest early estimates. And worse still is that we have no assurances yet that current technologies will ultimately work any better than the older ones did.

Acid Rain   Acid rain is gradually destroying biological life in lakes and botanical life in forests from New York to Maine and in southeastern Canada. Most experts believe the major culprits to be sulfur particles that are released when coal is burned in midwestern power plants. This sulfur combines with water in the atmosphere to form low concentrations of deadly sulfuric acid, which returns to earth in the form of rain, often hundreds of miles away.

Fitting all power plants with pollution-control devices to minimize sulfur emissions would cost billions. And if the plants chose instead to burn low-sulfur western coal, the eastern coal industry would collapse. Neither alternative appeals to the public utilities that own the plants or to the residents of the states that would have to pay higher electric bills, lose mining jobs, or both. A contributing problem is that in the 1960s a number of midwestern utilities constructed major coal-fired stations employing "high stack" technology. These huge smokestacks were designed to reduce air pollution near the plants by sending the smoke into the upper atmosphere and dispersing it over a wide area. It is generally believed that this early solution to air pollution led to a great acceleration in the acidification of rainfall.

The Dilemma   The great progress made in just the last twenty years to clean up the environment seems easy compared to solving the problems that remain. As open sewers have been capped and industrial discharges ended, salmon have returned to rivers like the Connecticut, in which only carp swam twenty years ago. Smokestacks pouring out soot and ash have largely disappeared. The remaining tasks are the relatively more difficult ones that involve attacking largely invisible hazards at costs that are staggering.

Much the same problem exists in the field of health and safety regulation. Cars have become much safer in the twenty years since the publication of Ralph Nader's indictment of automobile quality, *Unsafe at Any Speed*. How to assess the social cost of safety still focuses on whether the number of lives saved and injuries prevented warrants the extra expense to society of more and more costly safety devices.

DEREGULATION

As discussed in Chapter 1, the pace of business regulation began to accelerate in the 1930s and reached its high point in the early 1970s. At that time, a reaction set in and deregulation became the watchword. The impact of deregulation on financial services was discussed in Chapter 17.

The Two Types of Deregulation

Deregulation has two meanings. This term originally referred to the stripping away of regulations restricting competition in entire industries, particularly in regard to railroads, airlines, and trucking. The second meaning has the sense of nonregulation, the elimination or avoidance of regulation, particularly in the environmental, health, and safety areas where it cannot be readily justified on a strict cost–benefit basis.

The Various Senses of Deregulation

Industry Deregulation   The process of industry deregulation, begun under the Carter administration, has proven an enormous success.

Beginning in the nineteenth century, the transportation sector in particular came under close government regulation. The railroads were the first to trigger regulation, by abusing their hold over national transportation. The Depression then saw a surge of regulation. The Roosevelt administration felt that it not only had to protect the public interest against industry abuses but also had to protect jobs. These often conflicting goals led to **featherbedding**, the requiring of more workers than needed to do a job and transportation rules and routes that make little sense now. Perhaps the greatest achievement of the Carter administration was its dismantling of these regulatory structures. Changes in technology, the economy, and the nation's shifting population patterns dictated the end of these regulations. For instance, at the start of the 1970s, the railroads were known for their bankruptcies and aged equipment. Today, the rail industry carries 35 percent more tonnage than it did in the 1940s, but it is using less than 25 percent of its 1940s work force.[6]

Nonregulation   Deregulation also became synonymous with not regulating, particularly in the areas of the environment, health, and safety. After failing to convince Congress to repeal much of the legislation in this area, administrators simply stopped enforcing the parts of laws with which they disagreed. This approach led to scandals in the Environmental Protection Agency and Department of the Interior — the two principal environmental agencies — and the Department of Labor. Nonregulation remains highly controversial and lacks the broad support that true deregulation has. Still, nonregulation has succeeded in drastically reducing what its advocates regard as an unjustifiable intrusion into the marketplace by the government.

TAXATION

"The power to tax involves the power to destroy," wrote U.S. Chief Justice John Marshall in 1819.[7] The argument about how much deregulation is appropriate centers on whether tax dollars are being used to destroy businesses. There can be little doubt that President Reagan aimed his aggressive domestic budget cutting at preventing such an abuse of power.

Taxes today are of course a far more complicated matter than they were in Chief Justice Marshall's day. Now they are instruments of social and economic

The Arms Business — High- and Low-Tech

American defense contractors have made a lot of news in the past few years. The Defense Department's budget has climbed to record levels, and the Reagan administration has been eager to use arms sales as part of its foreign policy. Both the sale of high-tech arms to foreign countries and the outrageous charges for low-tech defense parts make the news regularly. They present a contrast in the way the military services and their suppliers handle the technology of war.

The defense budget has climbed since Ronald Reagan took office, although often not as quickly as the President had hoped. Defense contractors have welcomed the build-up; in the fiscal 1985 budget alone, over $100 billion was earmarked to buy new planes, ships, and other equipment. Even some members of Congress who are often critical of defense appropriations encourage military buying that will affect their own states.

The U.S. vies with the Soviet Union to be the largest supplier of arms to the rest of the world. Jimmy Carter tried to slow the exporting of American arms, but President Reagan regards arms sales as an "essential element of [America's] global defense posture and an indispensable component of its foreign policy." Sales to the rest of the world have dropped since their peak in 1982, but U.S. high-tech weapons continue to be world favorites.

The sale of "support" to foreign countries is just as big a story. The rest of the world needs spare parts, modifications, training, and ammunition to keep the marvels of the past working. So arms sales produce income long after the furors die. Of America's $3.1 billion in military sales to Saudi Arabia in 1984, 96 percent was support.

Amid this good news for defense contractors, however, comes increasing criticism of cost overruns and outrageously inflated spare parts costs. The spare parts controversy has been particularly damaging to the image of defense contractors because the markups have been so large and because the costs of nuts and bolts are easier to understand than those associated with major weapons systems like the MX missile. Most people don't have much sense of what a missile *should* cost, but we know

that an ordinary Allen wrench should not sell for the $9606 that the Air Force paid. The overcharges outraged the public: the Navy paid over $2000 for a $.13 nut; the Air Force spent $1118 for plastic caps for the bottoms of stool legs, available for $.31 in bulk; the Navy bought electronic diodes for $110 each when it could have gotten them for $.04 from its own supply system.

A new wrinkle was added to the spare parts controversy when, in July 1984, Defense Department officials admitted that Armed Services policies have been responsible for the routine junking of perfectly good parts. Any parts that hadn't been called for in 12 months were removed, often sold to scrap dealers for a fraction of their worth. When the parts were needed again, the scrap dealers often sold them back to the Army or Air Force. One Air Force official estimated that the practice cost the Air Force $700 million in 1983 alone.

Critics charge that the Pentagon's expensive and sometimes absurd way of paying for its arms could be improved simply by following normal business practices. It might help, for instance, if purchasing agents knew what they were paying for, not just the item number. A $37 charge won't seem excessive unless you know it's for a single screw.

So far the pricing scandals and even some legal judgments against defense contractors have not substantially affected their business. But because of the headlines, more people around the country have become curious about the wonderful and deadly machines we're selling overseas and are wondering what the latest price for a Pentagon cotter pin is. Defense contractors may find in the future that the contracts and the profits of the past won't come so easily.

Sources: Robert A. Kittle, "Pentagon Bogs Down in Its War on Waste," *U.S. News and World Report*, Vol. 96, No. 22, June 4, 1984, 73–76. "U.S. Again World's No. 1 Arms Merchant," *U.S. News and World Report*, Vol. 96, No. 21, May 28, 1984, 59. "Waste Is Charged in Military Work," *The New York Times*, Feb. 22, 1984, A15. Fred Hiatt, "$700 Million in Parts Junked by Air Force in '83, Aide Testifies," The *Boston Globe*, July 7, 1984, 3. Wayne Biddle, "The Big Business in Arms and Add-Ons," *The New York Times*, September 29, 1985, E5.

The Baltimore Metro System — an example of government buying power. One *of the most important — and least obvious — ways for government to support a business is to buy its products. Federal, state, and local governments have tremendous purchasing power. Expenditures cover a wide spectrum, ranging from small, everyday items like paper clips and paper to huge construction projects like this subway system, which moves 40,000 commuters a day.*

The Major Types of Taxation

policy, which is why federal and state tax legislation has dominated the news since 1980. The power to tax involves the power to foster and protect as well as to destroy.

Federal Taxation

The tax that first comes to mind is of course the federal income tax. This tax applies to both corporations and individuals and is the government's principal source of revenue. A special tax funds the Old Age, Survivors, Disability, and Health Insurance (OASDHI) program, better known as Social Security. **Excise taxes** have the effect of raising prices of liquor, jewelry, and cigarettes. Liquor and cigarette taxes are often called "sin taxes." Some justify them as a way to discourage consumption, even though there is no evidence that these imports have done anything but increase government revenues. A **sales tax** on gasoline supports the so-called highway trust fund, which collects money for highway and mass-transit improvements. The federal government also taxes any decedents' estates that have a value exceeding $500,000.

Tariffs, which we will discuss in the next chapter, are taxes on goods imported into the United States. Tariffs can be selectively raised on particular goods so that imported goods become more expensive than the same type of goods made in the United States.

Another type of government charge is **user fees,** charges to the public designed to compensate the government for services it performs. Fees for the use of national parks and campgrounds, for power-boat inspections, and the issuing of water-fowl hunting stamps are among the thousands of charges that are not called taxes but still feed the public treasury.

State and Local Taxes

State governments impose many of the same types of taxes as the federal government. However, the U.S. Constitution forbids states to impose tariffs either on foreign goods or on goods made in another state.

The two principal sources of state revenues directly affect business. The first is the **property tax,** a tax imposed by a state or local government on real property. Real property includes land, buildings, and fixtures, discussed in detail in Chapter 21. Normally, businesses and individuals pay different rates on their property taxes, with the higher rates being charged to businesses. The second major source of government income is sales and gross receipts taxes. Both taxes are collected by business for government. Figure 22.5 presents a breakdown of state tax receipts.

FIGURE 22.6

State Tax Receipts

Many states have income taxes, and all have estate taxes. States also impose "sin" taxes and other excise taxes. And their repertoire of user fees probably exceeds the federal government's. For instance, any business constructing a new plant must pay a sewer-connection fee. Building-inspection departments often charge significant fees.

GOVERNMENT AND BUSINESS: A PERSPECTIVE

Regulation and taxation are issues that generate great emotion among business people. Not a few have questioned whether they are getting their money's worth from government. Of course, given the many considerations we have examined in this chapter, it is impossible to answer this question in any concrete way.

For all the negative factors surrounding government control, consider how much a bureaucrat like Jerome Kelley could accomplish. In 1982, Kelley became the director of development for the Vermont Department of Agriculture. His goal was to re-create the farm economy that Vermont had had fifty years before, when 23,000 farms had covered the tiny state. With only a $100,000 budget, Kelley embarked on a campaign to persuade Vermont food producers to take advantage of their state's image. He encouraged them to use the word *Vermont* on their labels and package their goods to capitalize on the state's "down home" image. For instance, maple syrup that used to be packaged in nondescript tins now comes in reusable Mason jars. Today, Vermont has a vibrant specialty food industry that knows how to market itself.[8]

Chapter Highlights

1. Describe the three principal areas of government's relations with business.

The government's relations with business can be described in terms of the three S's: (1) *subsidy,* the use of government money and other assistance to build highways, subsidize commercial space ventures, and help develop other projects deemed beneficial for the general public; (2) *support* in the form of purchases of private sector goods, weather forecasts supplied by the Department of Commerce, and other forms of assistance; (3) *supervision,* in the form of various government regulations.

2. Explain the origins and purposes of the antitrust laws.

Antitrust laws support a series of regulatory functions that encourage fair and open competition. Antitrust means literally "against trust." The term was used in the 1880's and 1890's to describe giant industrial and natural resource combinations that attempted to absorb or destroy all other companies in their markets. When Standard Oil Company controlled the petroleum market, it was free to charge what it wanted.

3. Identify the two major prohibitions included in the Sherman Act.

The Sherman Act was the first federal legislation aimed at controlling trusts. Section one declares illegal "every contract, combination in the form of trust or otherwise, or conspiracy in restraint of trade or commerce. . . ." Section 2 prohibits wrongfully acquiring a monopoly; attempting to monopolize; conspiring to monopolize.

4. Define the three restraints on trade forbidden by the Clayton Act.

The Clayton Act broadened the effect of the Sherman Act. It was designed to prevent anticompetitive behavior rather than deal with its consequences. The act focused on three devices that restrain trade: (1) tying arrangements which result when the seller only agrees to sell a product the buyer wants (the tying product) if the buyer also purchases another product the buyer does not want (the tied product); (2) a reciprocal dealing arrangement occurs when a buyer can force a seller to buy something from it as a condition of the buyer's original purchase. It is the opposite of a tying arrangement; (3) exclusive dealing arrangements arise out of an agreement by one party to sell all of its output of a product to, or to buy all it requires of a product from the other party in exchange for the party's promise not to engage in similar transactions with anyone else. Each of these three arrangements can lessen competition.

5. List and describe the three forms of mergers.

A *vertical merger* is a merger of two companies in the same chain of supply. If Piedmont Airlines purchases a small independently owned regional airline, a vertical merger has occurred. A *horizontal merger* occurs when two competitors merge as when People Express purchased Frontier Airlines. *Conglomerate* mergers involve the acquisition of companies in different markets. If Miller Brewing Company purchases B.E.L.-Tronics Limited, a manufacturer of radar detection equipment, then a conglomerate merger has taken place.

6. Outline the Federal Trade Commission's role in policing the marketplace.

The Federal Trade Commission, created in 1914, has been given broad authority to police the marketplace. The Federal Trade Commission Act gave the FTC the power to pursue "unfair methods of competition" which include any anti-competitive behavior that falls short of violation of the other acts. Federal and state governments have the duty to enforce the antitrust laws.

7. Describe the theory underlying environmental, health, and safety regulations.

Theoretically, the marketplace should guide businesses toward producing the greatest good for the greatest number. But sometimes doing the right thing (such as spending large sums of money to improve safety in a coal mine) lessens a firm's ability to compete. In these cases, the government must supply the incentives for a business to take action. A firm is less likely to discharge pollutants into a nearby body of water if they know such an action may result in a large fine.

8. Explain the various meanings of the term deregulation.

Deregulation has two meanings. In the past it referred to the stripping away of regulations that restricted competition in entire industries such as railroads, airlines, and trucking. The second meaning is nonregulation, the elimination or avoidance of regulations particularly in the environmental, health, and safety areas that cannot be justified on a strict cost-benefit basis.

Key Terms

Boycott	Horizontal market allocation	Per se violation	Sales tax
Clayton Act		Predatory pricing	Sherman Act
Conglomerate merger	Horizontal merger	Price discrimination	Tariff
Deregulation	Interlocking directorates	Price fixing	Tying arrangement
Excise taxes		Property tax	Vertical market allocation
Exclusive-dealing arrangement	Market allocation	Reciprocal-dealing arrangement	
Featherbedding	Merger	Rule-of-reason standard	Vertical merger
Federal Trade Commission (FTC)	Monopoly		
	Natural monopoly		

Review Questions

1. Describe the three principal areas of government's relations with business.
2. Government regulation of business takes three forms. Discuss how these regulations apply to the production and distribution of agriculture products.
3. What are the major purposes of the antitrust laws?
4. Name and describe the first federal legislation aimed at controlling trusts.
5. Why is it difficult to prove monopoly violations?
6. What are the three major restraints of trade forbidden by the Clayton Act?
7. What is a merger? What are the three major forms of mergers?
8. Describe the Robinson-Patman Act.
9. Describe the Federal Trade Commission's role in policing the marketplace.
10. Explain why it is necessary for government agencies to establish environmental, health, and safety regulations.
11. What are two of the most important contemporary regulatory issues?
12. What are the two types of deregulation?
13. What are the major types of taxation?

Application Exercises

1. The deregulation of the airlines has created major changes in this industry. How have consumers benefited from deregulation? What problems have consumers faced since this industry was deregulated? What has been the impact of deregulation on commercial airlines?
2. In recent years, you have, let's say, operated a small women's apparel store in a county that enforces a blue law. This law prohibits the operation of certain types of business firms on Sundays. With only a few exceptions—service stations, food stores, drugstores, and the like — most stores cannot open for business on Sundays. The Chamber of Commerce decides to seek repeal of the blue law and wants every business owner to sign a petition requesting that the law be put before the voters at the next election. Would you sign the petition? What are some of the common arguments in favor of this form of government regulation? What are some of the major arguments against blue laws?

Case

22.1 Legislating Safety and Quality

Since the mid-1960s, Congress has prodded and legislated American auto manufacturers toward a concern for the safety of their customers. Mandatory standards have led to the development of shoulder-and-lap belts, collapsible steering columns, increased side protection for passengers, stronger door latches, and less dangerous dashboards and windshields. As a result of these standards the frequency of highway fatalities has been cut in half.

But even with increased attention to safety and quality, machines as complex as automobiles and trucks are almost sure to be sold with occasional defects. New-car warranty periods allow time for individual owners to discover such problems and have them removed at the manufacturer's expense. Government-mandated recalls do the same for larger-scale safety defects.

Yet many consumers continue to find that they have purchased a "lemon" — a vehicle with a defect that resists repair, or one with so many defects that repairs just don't help. Purchasers of lemons are protected by the federal Magnuson-Moss Act, passed in 1975. That act increased consumer access to the courts in product-defect cases. However, it requires the car buyer to first try to obtain satisfaction through the manufacturer's arbitration program — if there is one that has been approved by the FTC. The manufacturer must accept the arbitrator's decision, but the consumer need not.

Forty-one states have their own "lemon laws." These laws are intended to define a lemon, amplify the Magnuson-Moss Act, and provide for speedy arbitration.

The primary objective of the lemon laws is to eliminate court suits — to settle disputes quickly and at minimal cost. For that reason, a number of states have recently toughened their laws. Massachusetts has removed loopholes that previously allowed manufacturers to get around the arbitration process, and has set up its own arbitration centers, which will rule on each case within forty-five days of the hearing. The consumer and the manufacturer can both appeal the arbitrator's decision; however, a manufacturer that appeals must post a $2500 bond to cover the consumer's legal fees. It may be that the most effective provision of the new law is the requirement that stickers explaining the law be placed on all new cars sold in Massachusetts. Those stickers will be lemon yellow.

Questions

1. Which federal laws (other than the Magnuson-Moss Act) protect American consumers in their relations with motor vehicle manufacturers, and in what ways?
2. What motivates federal and state governments to pass laws aimed at specific industries, such as the automobile industry?

For more information see *The Wall Street Journal,* October 21, 1986, p. 35; *The Boston Globe,* April 24, 1986, p. 61; and *The New York Times,* December 29, 1985, p. E15.

22.2 Texas Air and Eastern

Eastern Air Lines was in trouble. They had just about broken even in 1985, but had lost $110 million in the first three months of 1986. At the same time Eastern was battling the Federal Aviation Administration over a $9.5 million fine for safety violations.

Texas Air Corporation was willing to purchase Eastern, and Eastern was willing to be purchased. Texas Air's chairman, Frank Lorenzo, felt that he could deal with Eastern's problems and make that firm profitable. And Texas Air would get Eastern's New York-Washington, D.C., and New York-Boston routes. Moreover, the merger would make Texas Air the nation's largest airline company.

The purchase had to be approved by the U.S. Transportation Department. However, the U.S. Justice Department intervened first, noting that the merger would tend to create a monopoly for Texas Air on the Boston-New York-Washington routes. Texas Air had previously purchased New York Air, which was already servicing that heavily traveled corridor. the merger would eliminate existing competition between Eastern and New York Air.

Texas Air responded by offering to sell some of its passenger loading gates and slots in the three cities to a competing airline. The sale of the slots and gates would ensure continued competition on the routes. That satisfied the Justice Department. In May 1986 Texas Air agreed to sell Pan American World Airways enough slots and gates to provide twelve round-trip flights on each of the two routes. Pan Am expected to offer hourly service on those routes, as did New York Air and Eastern.

The Transportation Department was not satisfied. Officials doubted that Pan Am could provide hourly service with the gates and slots it owned; they worried about service during peak morning and evening hours.

In August 1986, the Transportation Department rejected the Eastern-Texas Air merger on the ground that it would reduce competition on the Boston-New York-Washington routes. However, the department implied that the merger would be approved if Texas Air sold additional slots to Pan Am — enough so that Pan Am could fly a total of fifteen flights each day on each of the two routes. On October 1, 1986, the Transportation Department approved the purchase of Eastern Airlines by Texas Air; on that same day, Pan Am began flying the Boston-New York-Washington routes, and Frank Lorenzo became chief of Eastern's board of directors.

Questions

1. What could Texas Air have done to exclude competition and gain the power to control prices if it had purchased Eastern without selling slots and gates?
2. For whom is monopoly a bad thing? Why?

For more information see *The New York Times,* August 27, 1986, p. 1A; *The Wall Street Journal,* July 10, 1986, p. 5; *Business Week,* May 26, 1986, p. 48; and *The Wall Street Journal,* May 14, 1986, p. 23.

23

INTERNATIONAL BUSINESS

Learning Objectives

After you have completed this chapter, you will be able to do the following:

■ Describe the importance of foreign trade in our global economy.

■ Identify two major types of trade advantages.

■ Explain how a nation's balance of trade and balance of payments influence economic stability.

■ Discuss three common types of trade barriers.

■ Describe those factors that have created a global marketplace.

■ Explain the different ways a purely domestic business can become an international operation.

When milk is poured on it, what famous breakfast cereal goes "patchy, pitchy, putchy"? If Kellogg's Rice Krispies does not come to mind, it is probably that you are used to hearing them go "snap, crackle, pop." Because the Japanese have trouble pronouncing these words, the M. W. Kellogg Company changed its advertising for the Japanese market.[1]

Like Kellogg's, American firms entering international markets must be prepared to adapt their ways of doing business if the foreign culture demands it. Today, the ability of American businesses to sell their goods overseas has become critical to our national economic survival. This chapter introduces the principles of doing business across national boundaries.

THE ELEMENTS OF TRADE

The word *business* in this chapter will have a broader meaning than the more usual sense of just commercial transactions between individuals or business entities. *Business* can also mean **trade**, the buying or selling of goods or services among companies, states, or countries. **International trade** is trade that involves the crossing of national boundaries.

Types of Trade

Trade develops when two entities, called **trading partners**, recognize that there are mutual benefits in a transaction or series of transactions and decide to undertake them. **Foreign trade** is thus trade between partners of different nationalities. A nation can gain by specializing in those goods or services that it can produce with relative efficiency and trade for what it cannot produce efficiently. For example, Brazil has a large, unskilled labor force. This factor, along with its climate and soil, makes Brazil an ideal producer of oranges and coffee. In contrast, West Germany has a large, highly skilled, well-educated work force that allows it to produce goods requiring intensive capital investment. These conditions make West Germany an ideal producer of technologically sophisticated equipment, appliances, and chemicals.

Specialization

Two countries with different work forces and different levels of capital investment will have different production costs if they both produce the same product. This fact argues for **specialization**, the concentration of economic activity in those areas in which the country, the individual, or the business has either natural or acquired advantages.[2]

Two Types of Trade Advantages

Absolute Advantages   In general, economic theory recognizes two main types of advantages: absolute and comparative. An **absolute advantage** exists when one country can produce a product more efficiently than any other country. South Africa has an absolute advantage in the production of diamonds, for example. No other country has such extensive deposits of these gems; therefore, no other country can produce them as cheaply. Absolute advantages are rare.

FIGURE 23.1

Balance of payments

Comparative Advantages   More commonly, a country will have a **comparative advantage**, which is the ability to produce a product at a lower cost than a competitor can. Suppose that the United States can produce a ton of aluminum for one hundred dollars while Brazil's costs are two hundred dollars. In this instance, the United States has a comparative advantage in aluminum and should specialize in producing it. Let's assume also that Brazil can produce a ton of orange concentrate for juice at one hundred dollars per ton when that ton of concentrate costs two hundred dollars to produce in the United States. In this case, Brazil is the country with the comparative advantage and should specialize in orange concentrate. According to the principle of comparative advantage, such specialization by these two countries should result in more efficient use of both countries' resources.

Exporting and Importing

Economic theory holds that, as a consequence of specialization, countries will produce more of the products in which they have a comparative advantage than they need for their own consumption. The excess quantities thus become available for foreign trade. There are two sides to foreign trade. An **export** is a good or service that is produced in one country and sold for consumption in another.[3] An **import** is a good or service consumed in one country that was bought in another.[4] PepsiCo manufactures cola concentrate for Pepsi-Cola in the United States. When it sells the concentrate to the Soviet Union, the concentrate becomes an American export. Conversely, when PepsiCo buys Stolichnaya vodka from the Soviet Union and resells it here, this liquor becomes an import.[5]

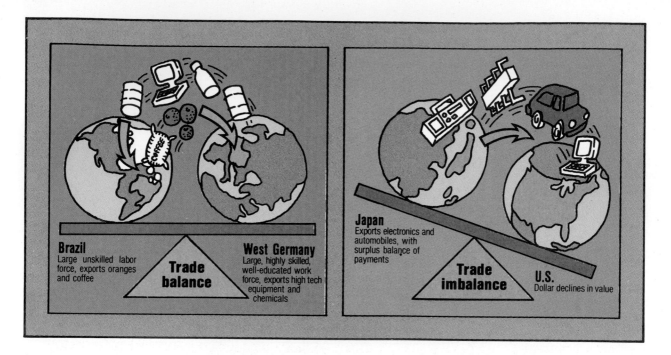

FIGURE 23.2

Balance of Trade

Balance of Trade   Nations watch very closely their **balance of trade**, the relationship between the value of goods imported and goods exported during a particular period. A favorable balance of trade exists when the value of exports exceeds that of imports. When imports exceed exports, there is an unfavorable balance of trade.

The Balance of Payments

Balance of Payments   A country's balance of trade is only one element in a much more important economic index, its balance of payments. The **balance of payments** measures the relationship between payments coming into and going out of a country during a particular period. In this context, *payments* includes all transfers of assets across the nation's boundaries. For example, a calculation of payments leaving the United States would include foreign aid, military assistance, private overseas investment, and tourist spending abroad. It is possible for a nation to have a favorable balance of payments but an unfavorable balance of trade, or vice versa.

The Valuation of Currency

The condition of a nation's balance of payments directly affects the value of its currency. Currency can be a synonym for money, which is how we will use the term in this chapter. Currency includes not only coins and bills but everything commonly accepted in place of cash. As we saw in Chapter 17, a nation's currency serves three purposes. It is a measure of value, a store of value, and a medium of exchange. (Chapter 17 contains a full discussion of money and currency.)

Exchange Rates   In international trade, a currency's value is its **exchange rate**, the value of a currency expressed in terms of another currency. For

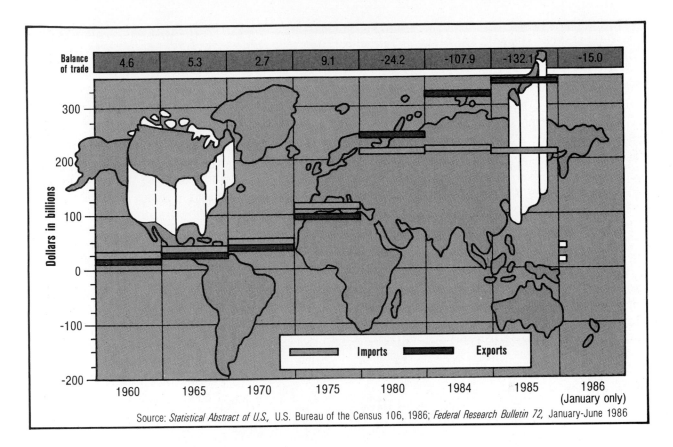

| Balance of trade | 4.6 | 5.3 | 2.7 | 9.1 | -24.2 | -107.9 | -132.1 | -15.0 |

Dollars in billions

300

200

100

0

-100

-200

Imports   Exports

| 1960 | 1965 | 1970 | 1975 | 1980 | 1984 | 1985 | 1986 (January only) |

Source: *Statistical Abstract of U.S.,* U.S. Bureau of the Census 106, 1986; *Federal Research Bulletin 72,* January-June 1986

FIGURE 23.3

Balance of Trade Deficits

example, on a particular day the price of a U.S. dollar might be 12 Indian rupees, 1,500 Italian lira, or .8 Argentine australs. In most of the free world, the law of supply and demand establishes the prevailing exchange rates, at least to some degree.

If a country has a balance of payments deficit, it is sending out more currency than it is taking in. The supply of its currency among its trading partners will rise as a result, and its value against other currencies should decline. In short, its exchange rate will drop. That is precisely what happened to the value of the U.S. dollar in relation to Japanese yen, starting in the mid-1970s. Americans overwhelmingly came to prefer Japanese electronics at the same time that a large segment of the U.S. population began buying Japanese cars. The Japanese did import more goods from America than from any of their other trading partners at this time, but their balance of payments with the United States still showed a huge surplus.

The Problem of Imbalance This persistent imbalance caused the dollar to decline in value in terms of the yen. There are two standard remedies to this problem. The artificial solution is to institute either devaluation or revaluation. **Devaluation** is an arbitrary downward adjustment of one country's currency in terms of another country's. The converse of devaluation is **revaluation**, an arbitrary upward adjustment of one country's currency in terms of another country's. In essence, a country sets a fixed rate of exchange for its currency, which it hopes will then accomplish the desired result in terms of the balance of payments.

The IMF — Everybody's Scapegoat

The International Monetary Fund (IMF) was set up in 1944 to keep order in the international monetary system. As its role has evolved over the past 40 years, it has become the bank of last resort, the only source of funds for nations whose economies are in deep trouble. After spending years in obscurity, the IMF has now taken center stage in the continuing drama of ballooning Third World debt. Because of its power to make or break economies and its insistence that borrowers institute certain economic reforms, the IMF has become a scapegoat for many politicians in countries with shaky economies. With criticism coming from a number of different sides, the IMF is likely to undergo ever greater scrutiny, as it has become a symbol of the West's relationship with developing countries.

The Fund has often successfully served the purpose it was created to serve — helping countries through balance of payments difficulties. It lent Great Britain $3 billion in the 1960s to deal with just such difficulties. In 1976 in Italy and again in 1981 in India, the IMF's loans and the economic conditions that came with the loans helped pull those countries out of financial holes.

The controversy surrounding the Fund and its loans to the Third World started in the 1970s. Much of the money that OPEC nations made after the Arab oil embargo ended up in American banks. These banks found that Third World countries were eager to borrow money, even at high interest rates, so nations like Brazil and Mexico went far into debt to finance their growing economies. When the growth did not meet expectations and the loans came due, many nations turned to the IMF for loans to pay the interest on the earlier loans.

Before it will lend a country money, the IMF insists that the country institute austerity measures like raising taxes, reducing government spending, and devaluing currency. These measures are supposed to ensure that the debtor country's economy will improve so that it will be able to pay back the loans. But when such measures are instituted overnight, as happened in the Dominican Republic in 1983, prices at the consumer level can double, leading to widespread unrest and often riots. Therefore government officials, caught between needing the loans and not wanting to get the blame for austerity measures, often blame the IMF.

Some critics look at the entire cycle of loans and wonder who the IMF is really serving. American banks made many questionable loans to Third World countries that used the money to begin projects they couldn't afford. If the IMF hadn't been around, some of these countries would probably have defaulted on their loans, hurting the big American banks and perhaps teaching everyone a lesson about living within their means and growing at a more moderate pace. Instead, the IMF stepped in, making more loans, putting the Third World even further into debt, so that those countries could pay back American banks. Some see the only winners in the situation as the banks that collect huge interest payments while the people in the Third World countries suffer and the American taxpayer pays.

Sources: John Nielsen, "Third World Lightning Rod," *Time*, July 2, 1984, 49. Jeff Faux, "Bankers Go Bananas," *Mother Jones*, February-March 1984, 40. Kai Bird and Max Holland, "I.M.F.: Reagan's Reliable Soldier," *The Nation*, June 30, 1984, 791.

The government enforces the new fixed exchange rate by imposing civil and criminal penalties on people and businesses that exchange currency at other rates.

Until 1971, most of the free world operated on a fixed rate of exchange. In that year, most of the major industrial countries abandoned fixed rates of exchange because they no longer reflected economic realities. Today, only the less developed nations and the Communist countries rely on them. For example, Bolivia has a fixed rate of exchange in terms of the dollar, which bears little

Changing exchange rates and changing prices. Theoretically at least, when the dollar falls against another country's currency, the price of goods imported from that country should go up. American manufacturers are discovering, however, that foreign companies like Honda are willing to cut profit margins to maintain their market share. When American consumers compare prices, they see little indication of the dollar's drop in value.

relationship to the free market rate. As we saw at the beginning of Chapter 17, the result there has been a massive black market in currency.

The free market solution for an imbalance in payments is to increase exports to the nation enjoying the favorable balance of payments. In other words, the United States should sell Japan more of the goods and services in which it enjoys a comparative advantage, to reduce its trade deficit with that country. The solution to payment imbalances may thus be seen to lie in specialization and in the removal of artificial barriers to free trade between nations, as Adam Smith urged in 1776 in *The Wealth of Nations*.

Trade Barriers

No one has ever effectively rebutted the logic of Smith's argument. The problem lies in the domestic politics of trade. Consider these examples. For more than ten years, American clothing manufacturers have waged a highly publicized fight for government protection from low-priced foreign competition. On the other hand, for two generations French farmers have toppled governments that have dared to suggest opening the country to less expensive imports, primarily from the United States. And Japan pays two to three times the world price for rice because, to preserve a key element in its culture, it insists on producing its own rice instead of importing it from its neighbors.[6] It is clear that, from a domestic standpoint, free trade can cost jobs or a way of life.

For many reasons, nations protect their domestic industries by means of **trade barriers**, factors that place imports at a disadvantage in their competition with domestic goods. The most common of these restrictions are tariffs, import quotas, and embargoes.

Trademarks recognized around the world. Pepsi is sold in the Soviet Union and in the People's Republic of China, as well as other countries around the world, but its logo is always unmistakable.

Three Types of Trade Barriers

Tariffs Historically, nations have protected themselves against imports by using **tariffs** or **duties**, taxes imposed by a country on imported goods. These taxes take two forms. **Revenue tariffs** are ones imposed solely to generate income for a government. For example, the United States imposes a duty on Scotch whisky solely for revenue purposes. Those who favor free trade have less trouble with revenue tariffs than they do with the other form of import duty, the **protective tariff**, one imposed to protect a domestic industry from competition by keeping the price of competing imports level with or higher than the price of domestic products. The French and Japanese agricultural sectors would both shrink drastically if their nations abolished the protective tariffs that keep the price of imported farm products high.

Import Quotas A limit on the quantity of a particular good that can be brought into a country is an **import quota**. The most important quota imposed by the United States in recent years was one on Japanese cars in response to Japanese dominance in the economy car market. Japanese auto makers responded to the import quota in classic free-market style simply by exporting more-expensive cars. Such cars provided them with greater per-car profit margins, thus making up for the lost volume.

Embargoes A law or government order forbidding either the importing or exporting of certain specified goods is an **embargo**. More often than not, countries impose embargoes not to protect a domestic industry but to punish another country. In 1961, the United States placed an embargo on Cuban cigars that it has never lifted. In 1973, a number of Arab oil-exporting countries imposed an embargo on the United States and certain Western European countries that supported Israel.

Trade Agreements

The type of understanding between nations that regulates the commerce between them is called a **trade agreement**. Since 1947, the United States has relied far more heavily on trade agreements than on protective tariffs. By that time, many historians and economists had concluded that the Smoot-Hawley Tariff Act of 1930 had greatly increased the severity of the Depression by setting off a tariff war with our trading partners and ourselves. The effect on our exports was disastrous.

In 1947, the United States and twenty-two other nations signed the **General Agreement on Tariffs and Trade (GATT)**, which established an international mechanism for mutual adjustments of trade barriers and regulations. GATT expresses the principal concept on which the United States has based its trade policy ever since. This concept is called **reciprocity**, the belief that one country's markets can be only as free as its trading partners'.[7] Each year, the GATT nations meet to review recommendations, settle disputes, and devise ways to reduce trade barriers between countries.

The United States has not relied solely on GATT to implement its free trade philosophy. Representatives from the United States and its six major trading partners also hold an annual economic summit meeting to resolve trade problems.

TRADE IN A SHRINKING WORLD

International trade existed even before there really were nations. From records and the wreckage of ancient ships, we know that trade crossed certain boundaries at least five thousand years ago. In some ways, particularly in transportation, little changed for thousands of years. For instance, in the 1830s it still took as long for a message to go from London to Rome as it had eighteen hundred years earlier.[8] In only another forty years, however, trains had replaced horse-drawn coaches, and steamships had outmoded sailing vessels. The transatlantic telegraph cable ultimately linked the United States and Europe with instantaneous communications.

A Global Marketplace

Factors That Have Created a Global Marketplace

The pace at which the world had grown smaller in the nineteenth century accelerated in the twentieth. Automobiles, jet planes, and satellites that could handle routine telephone calls completely revitalized transportation and communications. Most recently, the computer and the microchip have again revolutionized communications and information processing.

Since the dawn of this phenomenal era, optimists have persisted in predicting the disappearance of national boundaries and identifications in the face of the accelerating speed of transportation and the homogenizing effect of mass communications. We find ourselves instead living in a "global village" with quite distinct neighborhoods whose residents trade in a global marketplace. Even as recently as fifty years ago, the world's principal financial centers were New York and London. Today the centers are spread across the globe.

FIGURE 23.4A

The Size of the Market

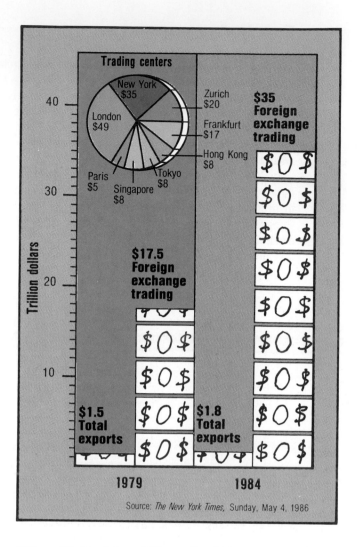

Trading centers

New York $35
London $49
Zurich $20
Frankfurt $17
Hong Kong $8
Paris $5
Singapore $8
Tokyo $8

$35 Foreign exchange trading

$17.5 Foreign exchange trading

$1.5 Total exports

$1.8 Total exports

1979

1984

Source: *The New York Times,* Sunday, May 4, 1986

The U.S. Position in World Trade

The position of the United States in world trade has gone through four distinct phases. Until about 1873, the United States had a chronic deficit in its balance of payments. The country borrowed heavily from Europe to build its transportation and industrial base. In the second phase, from 1873 until the beginning of World War I, in 1914, the nation's balance of trade was in surplus, but payments on what we owed foreign creditors kept the balance of payments in deficit. World War I marked the emergence of the United States as the world's premier economic power. Its exports boomed, and it became Europe's principal creditor. World War II and the great era of postwar prosperity confirmed the United States in its role as the world's banker. However, in this last period its balance of trade became solidly negative, as can be seen in Table 23.1.

The cause of this trade imbalance was an overall rise of the dollar against the currencies of its trading partners. The dollar's value soared by nearly 50 percent between 1979 and 1985. In other words, the prices of U.S. products rose in relation to similar foreign products.[9] The irony is that during this period the dollar was declining against the yen. The United States found itself in the worst possible

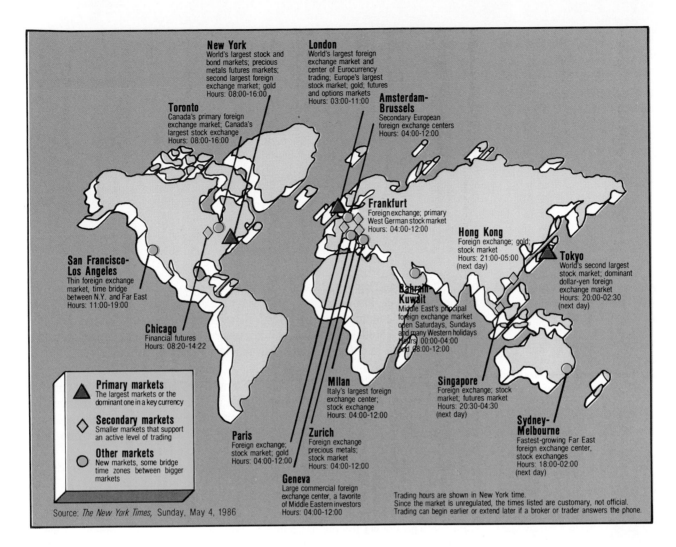

New York
World's largest stock and bond markets; precious metals futures markets; second largest foreign exchange market; gold
Hours: 08:00-16:00

London
World's largest foreign exchange market and center of Eurocurrency trading; Europe's largest stock market; gold; futures and options markets
Hours: 03:00-11:00

Toronto
Canada's primary foreign exchange market; Canada's largest stock exchange
Hours: 08:00-16:00

Amsterdam-Brussels
Secondary European foreign exchange centers
Hours: 04:00-12:00

Frankfurt
Foreign exchange; primary West German stock market
Hours: 04:00-12:00

Hong Kong
Foreign exchange; gold; stock market
Hours: 21:00-05:00 (next day)

Tokyo
World's second largest stock market; dominant dollar-yen foreign exchange market
Hours: 20:00-02:30 (next day)

San Francisco-Los Angeles
Thin foreign exchange market, time bridge between N.Y. and Far East
Hours: 11:00-19:00

Bahrain-Kuwait
Middle East's principal foreign exchange market open Saturdays, Sundays and many Western holidays
Hours: 00:00-04:00 and 08:00-12:00

Chicago
Financial futures
Hours: 08:20-14:22

Primary markets
The largest markets or the dominant one in a key currency

Secondary markets
Smaller markets that support an active level of trading

Other markets
New markets, some bridge time zones between bigger markets

Milan
Italy's largest foreign exchange center; stock exchange
Hours: 04:00-12:00

Singapore
Foreign exchange; stock market; futures market
Hours: 20:30-04:30 (next day)

Sydney-Melbourne
Fastest-growing Far East foreign exchange center, stock exchanges
Hours: 18:00-02:00 (next day)

Paris
Foreign exchange; stock market; gold
Hours: 04:00-12:00

Zurich
Foreign exchange precious metals; stock market
Hours: 04:00-12:00

Geneva
Large commercial foreign exchange center, a favorite of Middle Eastern investors
Hours: 04:00-12:00

Source: *The New York Times,* Sunday, May 4, 1986

Trading hours are shown in New York time.
Since the market is unregulated, the times listed are customary, not official.
Trading can begin earlier or extend later if a broker or trader answers the phone.

FIGURE 23.4B

World Financial Centers

trading situation. Its currency value made its exports noncompetitive in Europe and the Third World, where the United States should have had a trade surplus. However, because the dollar was rising in value against the currencies of almost all of its other major trading partners, U.S. industries were not in a position to take advantage of the weaker dollar in Japan.

If you find all this quite complicated, be assured that prominent economists, top government officials, and leading businesspeople do too. There is an obvious lesson here, though: neither the United States nor any other country can deal with its economic problems in isolation. Whether we like it or not, we are all in the same marketplace.

Thinking Internationally

Americans have rightly been criticized for knowing, and caring, too little about the rest of the world. The tiny number of people born in this country who can speak more than one language fluently testifies to the truth of this criticism. (Europeans, among others, routinely master at least two languages besides their

TABLE 23.1

U.S. Exports and Imports for Selected Product Groups

Product Group	Exports (millions)	Imports (millions)
Motor vehicles and car bodies	$6,388	$25,579
Motor vehicle parts and accessories	$6,844	$ 6,045
Petroleum refinery products	$5,957	$15,590
Industrial inorganic chemicals	$2,497	$ 1,896
Photographic equipment and supplies	$2,390	$ 2,107
General industrial machinery	$2,350	$ 1,527

Note: Imports are valued on a customs basis.
Source: *U.S. International Trade Administration*, 1984 U.S. Industrial Outlook.

Challenges of operating multinationally. About 30 percent of Kellogg's sales come from foreign countries. Getting those sales in a new market can be a major challenge since not everyone is used to an American style breakfast.

own.) It is ironic that Americans, who have done so much to make the world smaller, are quite ill prepared to deal with those from different cultures. It is also ironic that a nation like ours, which is based on immigrants, should fall into having narrow attitudes about the way foreigners live. These preconceptions are attitudes that we as a nation of businesspeople simply cannot afford.

Ethnocentrism   The belief in the superiority of one's own race or culture is **ethnocentrism**. Ethnocentric businesspeople believe that the way something is done in their country is the only way to do it. They cannot admit that another nation or culture might have devised a better approach, or at least one that works better for it, from which they themselves could learn.

Often, U.S. managers assigned to foreign countries will not entrust residents of that country with significant decision-making power, because they can't believe that foreigners are capable of making decisions. As a result, an American or someone from the home office will make decisions that would be better made by someone who knows the culture and the country. Sophisticated companies have recognized this reality for years and have made this understanding the foundation of their international successes.

Ethnocentrism is, as we have suggested, an irrational, unthinking reaction to different peoples and cultures. However, it is not necessarily true that a company with a policy or technique that does not fit a local culture is ethnocentric. In fact, such a firm may be smart. For example, in Japan the concept of a commitment to equal job opportunities for women is not as generally accepted as it is in the United States. IBM is committed to this concept world-wide, however. As a result, women students in Japan rank IBM as their most desirable employer.[10] Thus, IBM gets its pick of the brightest women graduates.

Avoiding the Trap   A successful international manager must acknowledge that deep differences separate cultures but that each culture has undeniable merits and works for those belonging to it. Only those who have lived in a culture for a considerable time can understand it sufficiently to function effectively in it. Managers taking this view will strongly favor hiring local personnel to run foreign operations and give them considerable discretion in decision making. Such managers will also favor intensive training for their American employees going overseas. A number of sound training strategies exist to prepare managers and

International Amateurs

Amateur sports have become a big business. Millions of people around the world watch amateur events from marathons to tennis at Wimbledon to the Olympics, and promoters and advertisers make a lot of money from the interest that good amateur athletes generate. Increasingly, amateur athletes, who must devote themselves virtually full-time to their sports to remain competitive, have been demanding — and getting — support from the sports industry built around them. Around the world, the line between amateur and professional is becoming further blurred.

The 1984 Olympics provided the most publicized recent showing of professional amateurs. In the winter games, every time the cameras focused on America's elated skiers like Bill Johnson and Debbie Armstrong, the manufacturers of the equipment they were wearing could count on a few more seconds of mass exposure and many more sales in the months to come. It took the manufacturer of the boots Johnson was wearing less than 24 hours after his history-making victory in a pre-Olympic downhill to start working on a new series of ads featuring Johnson. Said the company's president, "We get a boost in sales every time a top name is seen wearing our brand."

Many sports fans and older athletes complain about this commercialization and look back to a time when an amateur's sport was more of a hobby than a profession, when athletes would have scorned the idea of accepting money for racing or wearing a particular kind of shoes. They yearn for the kind of athletic world portrayed in the movie *Chariots of Fire*. Most of today's athletes argue that the current competition, athletes who look on their sport as a hobby can't compete. Becoming a top-notch wrestler or skater takes as much time as a full-time job. And, they point out, the central characters in *Chariots of Fire* were all independently rich gentlemen.

Amateurs get money for practicing their sport in three major ways — by being consultants for sporting goods companies, by doing advertisements, and by competing in races. The International Amateur Athletics Federation, which oversees track and field competition, has recently changed its rules to allow athletes to accept such money

legally. The money goes into trust funds from which the athletes can withdraw cash to cover training and cost of living expenses. Although the living expenses are limited to $5900 a year, training expenses are loosely defined, and top amateurs can lead a fairly comfortable life legally under the present system.

Although most amateurs are not eager to talk about how much they're paid, record-holding hurdler Edwin Moses made almost $500,000 a year before the last Olympics, and Olympic star Carl Lewis, still in his early twenties, may earn as much. Some runners get bonuses from their sponsors for setting new records. Steve Ovett and Sebastian Coe, two of Britain's brilliant milers, reportedly get $25,000 just to appear.

Although the committees which set rules for track are known to be liberal in their definition of "amateur," most sports' governing bodies have similar rules. The International Olympic Committee leaves most rules about money up to member nations and the sports governing bodies. Some sports have even bigger payoffs than track.

To those who see international athletic competition as a matter of national pride, the strongest argument for allowing amateurs to make money off their sport is that competing with countries like East Germany and the Soviet Union would otherwise be next to impossible. Eastern block countries openly support their athletes, acknowledging, in effect, that such athletes perform a service for their country. For years American athletes complained that they were victims of a double standard, expected to be amateurs in the traditional sense while their competitors received direct state support. Apparently the governing bodies of most sports have heard their complaints and are gradually allowing sports equipment manufacturers, and the free enterprise system, to give athletes the support they don't always receive from their governments.

Sources: Stephen Koepp, "Waxing Sales with a Downhill Race," *Time*, Vol. 123, No. 6, 49. "Professional Amateurs," *Health*, April 1984, 37. David Goddy, "Dispute Over the Amateur Ideal," *Scholastic Update*, Vol. 116, No. 17, April 27, 1984, 19. Allan Fotheringham, "Challenging the Purity of Sports," *Maclean's*, Vol. 19, No. 12, March 19, 1984, 68.

employees to respond to intercultural problems. One technique involves teaching human resources managers how to interview foreign applicants. Others attempt to give trainees a sense of the culture they will be entering.[11] For example, employees heading for Saudi Arabia should know that Muslim law authorizes stiff penalties for those who consume alcohol and allows the death penalty for any non-Muslim caught in certain sacred areas like parts of Mecca.

In some ways, employees of an American corporation cannot adapt their practices to fit local customs. The most important of these differences is bribery. The federal **Foreign Corrupt Practices Act** forbids the bribing of foreign officials by U.S. companies or their employees to obtain favorable treatment.

ENTERING THE INTERNATIONAL MARKETPLACE

Four Types of Venture

When a firm decides to expand from being a purely domestic business to an international operation, it can choose to become one of several types of venture. Among these are the following kinds of firms:

- ☐ Exporting
- ☐ Licensing
- ☐ Joint ventures
- ☐ Direct foreign investment

Exporting

As we have seen, exporting occurs when goods are produced in one country for consumption in another. For example, Komatsu Ltd., a Japanese heavy-equipment maker, exports its construction equipment worldwide, as does the Caterpillar Tractor Company, of Illinois. The Swedish firms Begus Inter and Faluhus export prefabricated modular homes to the United States.[12]

Licensing

In international business, a **license** is a privilege to manufacture or sell a product in all or part of a country or to extract a natural resource from a particular location. Coca-Cola, for example, has had to obtain licenses to produce and sell its soft drinks in the over 155 countries in which it does business.[13] And the Anaconda Company, a subsidiary of Arco, has received licenses to mine copper in Chile.[14]

A license is a contract, and its provisions are therefore subject to negotiation. A license can require a company to pay the issuing government

- ☐ A one-time fee
- ☐ A percentage of annual receipts
- ☐ A **royalty** or share, usually of the gross output, from the extraction of a natural resource

Entertainment industries go international. Walt Disney's famous mouse is practically a symbol of America, but offshoots of the Disneyland Park have broad appeal. Japan already has its version, Tokyo Disneyland. Euro Disneyland will bring visitors from many countries to Marne-La-Vallee, a new town about 20 miles from Paris.

Licenses often have a limited duration. Some licenses grant monopolies, whereas others simply allow their holders to compete for business within the country issuing the license.

Joint Ventures

As we saw in Chapter 3, a **joint venture** is simply an agreement between two businesses to combine their resources to accomplish a particular objective. They may agree to produce a product jointly or just market it, store it, or transport it. The financial arrangements between **coventurers**, the parties in a joint venture, can vary as much as in a partnership. For small firms, joint ventures can provide entry into international business that they could not otherwise afford. In other instances, companies must form joint ventures with foreign corporations to crack a foreign market. Since 1980, A T & T, for example, has formed joint ventures with Dutch, Italian, Spanish, South Korean, Taiwanese, and Japanese coventurers.[15]

Direct Foreign Investment

Direct foreign investment describes the situation in which a corporation forms a subsidiary in another country to produce a product and market it in that country. Volkswagen, for instance, is a West German company. Its subsidiary, Volkswagen of America, manufactures and markets cars in this country. Similarly, the Ford Motor Company has subsidiaries across Europe. A corporation does not have to be especially large to have a foreign subsidiary. However, as we will see below, ownership of a foreign subsidiary is an essential requirement if a company is to become a multinational corporation.

Franchises make their presence felt around the world. What works in America can be just as successful elsewhere. The United Kingdom licensee opened 7-Eleven convenience stores in this London suburb and 14 other locations in its first year of operation.

THE MULTINATIONAL CORPORATION

A large firm with a home base in one country operating wholly or partially owned subsidiaries in other countries is a **multinational corporation**.[16] The point at which a company engaged in international business becomes a true multinational is a subject of debate. Most people would agree that a company with subsidiaries in several countries is a multinational. However, a firm need not operate in all — or even most — industrial countries to be considered a multinational.

Characteristics

Multinationals come in many types. Exxon, McDonald's, Phillip Morris, General Electric, and American Express are some of the better known U.S.-based multinationals. Phillips NAV, Mitsubishi Heavy Industries, British Petroleum, and Nestle are some well-known foreign multinationals. As these examples illustrate, multinationals typically control vast assets. They generally tend to be conglomerates, though many, like the Royal Dutch/Shell Group, are not.

The Scale of Multinationalism Multinational businesses are by no means new. They have existed since the thirteenth century, and one noted economic historian has argued that capitalism as we know it could never have developed without them.[17]

As transportation and communication improvements shrank the world, multinational businesses increased in number and size. It is no coincidence, then, that multinationals grew rapidly following World War II and explosively after about 1970. By the early 1980s, the 100 largest American multinationals, ranked by their foreign revenues, had $590 billion in foreign assets. However impressive this number, it does not reveal that American multinationals had lost the domination of the global marketplace that they had enjoyed well into the 1960s. Of the world's 100 largest industrial firms in 1963, fully two-thirds were American. Today, fewer than half are.[18] Japan, West Germany, and France are fully engaged in multinational competition. It is fair to say that every industrial country, from Sweden to South Korea, is actively engaged in devising ways to compete on a multinational level.

Free Flow of Resources As with domestic companies, profit — not national boundaries — determines the business strategies that these corporate giants develop. In a fully developed multinational, capital, technology, personnel, information, goods, and services flow freely from one country and one subsidiary to another. If you buy an IBM PC, you will own a video monitor made in Korea; floppy disk drives made in Singapore, semiconductors made in Japan, and a product that was assembled in the United States. Often, managing this type of flow is the multinational's biggest operational problem.

Political Influence

Many critics claim that the intense concentrations of power that multinationals can bring to bear corrupt the political processes of the countries in which they operate. These complaints have centered most often on the mineral extraction and oil companies, though ITT also was a major focal point for critics in the 1970s because of allegations of illicit meddling in U.S. and Chilean politics.[19]

It is a mistake, however, to view the multinationals as flukes. Instead, they are the visible proof of our shrinking world. Without question, the managers of multinational corporations are constantly confronted by decisions that have large political and economic consequences. They know that they are in a global marketplace and that their actions can affect several neighborhoods.

"Have Jensen find out what effect, if any, the collapse of the economies of the Western industrial nations would have on sales."

Cooperating for a High-Tech Future

For at least the last decade, the key word in the world of international technology has been competition. The United States, once the undisputed leader in most areas of technology, has been struggling to keep up with the fast pace of technological innovation overseas, particularly in Japan. You've read about the widespread effects such competition has had on American business and life, and any business magazine you pick up these days is likely to carry a story on how a particular American company is "fighting back." But now, as the result of a number of forces in the national and international marketplace, a new era may be beginning in which cooperation becomes as important as competition.

One major reason for international cooperation lies in the nature of the technology itself. As the technology becomes more sophisticated, it generally becomes more difficult and expensive to develop. When companies find themselves spending millions of dollars on research and development that they know is being duplicated somewhere else, they're likely to look for ways that both companies can benefit from just one research investment. In the world of microchips, for instance, scores of companies around the world have been competing to manufacture cheaper, more powerful chips.

The desire to retain the rights — and profits — to a high-tech product also can lead to international cooperation, most often in the form of joint ventures. The high-tech world often echoes with the cries of companies that spent millions in developing a product — computer software, for instance — only to find that it is being copied and sold overseas. This situation leads some companies to guard their secrets ever more closely, but others have formed joint ventures with overseas firms. Generally the overseas partner acquires the right to market the technology in a particular country, returning some of the profits to the company that paid for the research and development.

Cooperation across national boundaries often provides an alternative to trying to batter down trade barriers and walls of protectionism. Both communist countries and some capitalist countries like Japan and Taiwan make it difficult for foreign companies — particularly American ones — to sell products within their borders. But if the American company sets up a joint venture or some form of international cooperative agreement with a company in the host country, both the outside firm and the host benefit.

Ironically, the United States has become the host country to some such ventures. A number of foreign car manufacturers, bothered by American quotas on imported cars and by protectionist rhetoric in Washington, have begun to build plants in the United States. Sometimes these plants are wholly owned by the foreign company but employ American workers, bringing some of the profit to America. In other cases a foreign and an American company are working together, as are Toyota and General Motors.

One of the most ambitious international cooperative agreements is Europe's Eureka project. European countries have been frustrated by spending so much on high-tech research — double what the Japanese spend — yet steadily losing ground to foreign competitors. European companies supply only about 40 percent of the computers and one-third of the computer chips used in their region. So now the governments and companies of Europe are banding together to compete against the rest of the world and save money by ending research duplication. They are defining cooperative goals, entering into joint ventures, funding cooperative research, and calling for less local, and more region-wide control over technological development.

Given the historical difficulties faced by cooperative agreements in the European economic community, many observers are skeptical about the success of Eureka. But as national boundaries become less and less important in the global economy, we're sure to see more such ventures springing up, and cooperation may one day be the norm, not the exception.

Sources: "Europe's Desperate Try for High-Tech Teamwork," *Business Week*, May 30, 1983, 45. Paul Lewis, "Europe's Eureka Project Aims to Narrow U.S. Lead," *The New York Times*, March 23, 1986, Sec. 12, 8. Philip L. Sunshine, "Joint Ventures, an Alternative to Protectionism," *Journal of Commerce*, January 13, 1984, 4a.

INTERNATIONAL BUSINESS: A PERSPECTIVE

One of the most controversial issues surrounding American multinationals is whether or not they export American jobs. In recent bargaining with the Big 3 domestic car makers, the United Auto Workers (UAW) expressed great concern about Ford, General Motors, and Chrysler's moves toward foreign plants to save on labor costs. The UAW has sought restrictions in their contracts on the number of cars the Big 3 can produce overseas. It has also pushed **domestic content legislation** that would require a certain percentage of a car's parts to be made in this country. Neither effort has succeeded so far.

Organized labor as a whole shares the UAW's concerns. After all, the link between a multinational's closing of an American plant and its opening of a foreign plant manufacturing the same product seems too obvious for debate. The American jobs lost are usually high-paying unionized positions in industries like textiles, shoes, and consumer electronics. Unionized workers are also losing jobs, though, in industries like steel, aluminum, and oil and gas production, where it is not easy to find a multinational villain.

The villain is modern times. Fifty years ago, you would have gotten a laugh by suggesting that Pittsburgh steel companies would someday compete with Japanese and German companies for the domestic market, much less that South Korea would also enter the fray. You would have had your sanity challenged if you had also suggested that the efficiency of these countries' plants and their lower labor costs would not be offset by their higher transportation costs. Yet this is precisely the situation today.

How will the United States respond to this loss of jobs and industry? Can the country devise solutions that do not require a lowering of the national standard of living? These are the kinds of questions business will have to answer. If the last two hundred years have proven nothing else, it is that where the questions relate to competition in world markets, the answers must come from the innovation and ingenuity of American businesspeople.

Chapter Highlights

1. Describe the importance of foreign trade in our global economy.

Foreign trade is one of the most important factors that contributes to the economic development of a nation. When Korea began exporting the Hyundai automobile to the United States, the production of this car created many new jobs. The currency received from the sale of these autos could be used by Korea to purchase goods and services from the United States and other nations. The end result should be an increase in the standard of living for the citizens of Korea.

2. Identify two major types of trade advantages.

Economic theory recognizes two major types of advan-tages. An absolute advantage exists when a country can produce a product more efficiently than any other coun-try. This type of advantage is quite rare. A comparative advantage exists when a country can produce a product at a lower cost than a competitor can.

3. Explain how a nation's balance of trade and bal-ance of payments influence economic stability.

Balance of trade is the relationship between the value of goods imported and the value of goods exported during a particular period. A favorable balance of trade exists when the value of exports exceeds that of imports. The balance of payments measures the relationship between payments coming into and payments going out of a country during a particular period. Payments include all transfers of assets across the nation's boundaries. When American tourists spend money in England, they are transferring assets (cash) overseas.

4. Discuss three common types of trade barriers.

Nations often attempt to protect their domestic industries by means of trade barriers. Tariffs represent one method of placing imports at a disadvantage in their competition with domestic goods. A tariff is a tax imposed by a country on imported goods. A second barrier to imports is the import quota, a limit on the quantity of a particular good that may be brought into a country. An embargo is a law or government order forbidding either the importing or the exporting of specified goods.

5. Describe those factors that have created a global marketplace.

In many ways the world has grown smaller in the Twentieth Century. Jet planes permit faster business travel between nations, satellites now permit us to make international phone calls with ease, and ships are now bigger and faster. Most importantly, Americans and people from many other nations are beginning to think internationally.

6. Explain the different ways a purely domestic business can become an international operation.

When an American business decides to move from a purely domestic business to an international operation, it can choose from several types of ventures. One option is exporting. Exporting occurs when goods are produced in one country for consumption in another. A second option is licensing. A license is a privilege to manufacture or sell a product in all or part of a country or to extract a natural resource from a particular location. The third option is the joint venture, an agreement between two businesses to combine their resources to accomplish a particular objective. Direct foreign investment, a fourth option, describes a situation in which a company forms a subsidiary in another country for the purpose of producing a product and marketing it in that country.

Key Terms

Absolute advantage	Ethnocentrism	Import	Revaluation
Balance of payments	Exchange rate	Import quota	Revenue tariff
Balance of trade	Export	International trade	Specialization
Comparative advantage	Foreign Corrupt	Joint venture	Tariffs *or* duty
Coventurers	Practices Act	License	Trade
Devaluation	Foreign trade	Multinational	Trade agreement
Domestic content	General Agreement on	corporation	Trade barrier
legislation	Tariffs and Trade	Protective tariff	Trading partners
Embargo	(GATT)	Reciprocity	

Review Questions

1. Provide a definition of foreign trade. What are some of the common reasons countries engage in foreign trade?

2. Distinguish between absolute advantages in foreign trade and comparative advantages.

3. Why do nations seek to achieve a favorable balance of trade?

4. A nation can have a favorable balance of payments and an unfavorable balance of trade, or vice versa. Why?

5. What is meant by the term exchange rate?

6. In recent years, Japan's balance of payments with the United States has showed a huge surplus. What is the free market solution to this imbalance in payments?

7. List and describe three of the most common trade barriers used by nations wishing to establish barriers to imports.

8. How does a trade barrier differ from a trade agreement?
9. What factors have contributed to the creation of a global marketplace?
10. The United States' position in world trade has gone through four distinct phases. Briefly describe each phase.
11. What is ethnocentrism? How does ethnocentrism serve as a barrier to cooperation between nations?

Application Exercises

1. In recent years America has used import quotas to reduce the number of automobiles imported from Japan. Prepare a list of the arguments for and against this practice using concepts taken from this chapter. Then indicate what your position would be regarding future import quotas for Japan, Korea, or any other country that is providing strong competition for the American auto industry.
2. Assume the position of vice president of marketing for a small manufacturing company. This company manufactures a series of high-quality tools used by cabinet makers. Research indicates that a market for these tools exists in several European countries including Germany, France, and Italy. You are considering the direct export of these tools which will require setting up a sales and marketing network in these countries. Another option under consideration is a joint venture with a manufacturing firm in Europe that also makes woodworking tools. What are the advantages and disadvantages of each option?

Cases

23.1 Competing Together — Internationally

Today's electronics industry is characterized by stiff competition in terms of both price and technological innovation. A firm's profitability — and sometimes its existence — depends on its ability to combine the latest technology with low-cost production and effective marketing. And that has led to some seemingly strange international partnerships.

American firms have complained, often bitterly, about unfair competition from Japanese firms. Yet a number of U.S. electronics firms are working closely with Japanese firms. RCA Corporation, for example, has an agreement to share design and process technology with Japan's Sharp Corporation. Motorola has signed production agreements with at least three Japanese electronics firms, including one — Hitachi, Ltd. — that is expected to begin marketing in the United States under its own brand. Hitachi also supplies video cassette recorders to RCA.

Many American companies have turned to South Korean firms for low-cost production of electronics equipment and parts. The Koreans, remembering four decades of Japanese occupation, were quite willing to compete with Japan's electronics industry. But here too, the exigencies of the electronics business seem to override other factors. A number of Korean producers have agreed to work with Japanese firms. Among those firms are Sony (many of whose Walkman products are built in Korea), Sanyo, and Hitachi (again).

There are also three-way arrangements. Perhaps typical is one that involves a low-cost IBM-compatible computer. The computer was designed and is assembled by Korea's Daewoo Telecom Company. Its floppy disks, keyboard, power supply, and about one-third of its integrated circuits are purchased from Japan. And the completed unit is marketed by Leading Edge Hardware Products of Canton, Massachusetts.

Questions

1. How does the concept of comparative advantage enter into the agreements among American, Japanese, and Korean electronics firms?
2. Is Daewoo a multinational firm? Is Leading Edge? Why, or why not?

For more information see *Forbes*, September 22, 1986, p. 85; *Electronics*, November 25, 1985, pp. 62–63; and *Electronics Week*, May 6, 1985, p. 34.

23.2 Made in America

Textiles and clothing can be produced overseas at much lower cost than in the United States, primarily because of lower wage rates. Thus, many American firms now either own foreign plants or purchase goods made by foreign manufacturers. About 50 percent of the textiles and clothing sold here is now produced abroad. The foreign-made textiles and clothing carry lower retail prices and often provide larger margins for retailers. However, the shift to overseas production has cost more than 600,000 American jobs and contributed over $16 billion to the U.S. trade deficit.

In an attempt to convince Americans to buy American, some 250 U.S. textile and apparel producers, labor unions, farm groups, and others have formed the Crafted With Pride in U.S.A. Council. Through television ads featuring such celebrities as Bob Hope, Cathy Lee Crosby, and O. J. Simpson, they have been urging consumers to look for the "Made in the USA" label on clothing and textiles. The ads imply that American-made goods are of higher quality. They also tell viewers that "it matters" when they buy American.

The television ads are planned to run for at least three years. So far, their effect on sales has been difficult to ascertain. Their effort on foreign producers is another story: A spokesman for the Hong Kong Trade Development Council noted that they were unfair and discriminatory. (Hong Kong is one of the three largest exporters of clothing to the United States.) And a representative of the Italian Trade Commission said the ads would not affect U.S. sales of Italian-made clothing, because of the higher quality of Italian clothing.

Questions

1. Evaluate the Council's campaign, its "fairness," and the use of patriotism in international marketing.
2. What other weapons can America's textile and clothing industries use in their international competitive battle?

For more information see *U.S. News & World Report*, January 27, 1986, p. 52; *Marketing & Media Decisions*, November 1985, pp. 68–74, 132; and *Daily News Record*, July 3, 1985, p. 4.

APPENDIX

Work and Careers in Business: 1987–2025

by S. Norman Feingold*

I. INTRODUCTION

The last decade of the 20th Century and the first quarter of the 21st Century is the time frame in which this book's readers will be active labor market participants. The pace of change in jobs and careers that provide employment opportunities may well accelerate from today's rapid tempo. The education, training, and personal requirements for these jobs will change equally as quickly. Thus, gaining a grasp of upcoming work/career trends and of future employment trends becomes necessary for today's college freshmen and sophomores, returnees to the labor force, and displaced workers. The total number of employed women will soon surpass the total number of employed men.

Farmer, laborer, clerk, professional are occupational titles that briefly elucidate the work history of the United States. Knowledge and how it transforms the tasks of farmer, laborer, clerk, and professional is the critical new ingredient of the information or post-industrial age.

Job opportunities for certain classes of "white collar" workers are changing dramatically; the number may be decreasing, also because of information technology. There is less need for middle management and clerical workers in Government and large private concerns.

Professional workers today, as they have been in the past, are almost always information workers (lawyers, teachers, engineers, accountants, librarians, psychologists, reporters, etc.). Microprocessors speed the manipulation, storage and use of numbers, words, ideas, and information. Carried another step, information that is properly manipulated, stored, and used is lessening the need for human beings as the operators of farm equipment, auto assembly lines, mining excavators, typewriters, or cash registers.

*Dr. Feingold is President of the National Career & Counseling Services in Washington, D.C. 20005.

Eighty percent of workers in the year 2000 will probably be employed in the information industry or will use the tools of the information industry in heavy industry. Many, if not most of those in farming and manufacturing will be using machines made possible by the information industry.

Some occupations and careers become obsolete but new ones are emerging all the time. Milk man, elevator operator, and bowling pin setter are three job titles that have disappeared. At the same time, new emerging careers such as information specialist, thanatologist, and divorce mediator are growing in number and influence.

The U.S. Bureau of Labor Statistics estimates that in 1984 the civilian labor force, i.e., those with jobs and those looking for jobs, totaled approximately 114 million people, or 44% of the total United States population of 237 million. BLS projections for 1995 are a total population of about 260 million with a civilian work force of about 129 million or 50%.

BLS further expects that continuing population growth will cause greater demand for workers in many industries and occupations.

From earliest times America has been the land of the entrepreneur. Our founding fathers patronized and created businesses, some of which are still around today.

President George Washington gave a gift of Number 6 cologne to the Marquis de Lafayette. The scent is still on sale at the nation's oldest apothecary, Caswell Massey Company, started in 1752. The Dexter Corporation was started in 1767. Located in Windsor Locks, Connecticut, it is the oldest company listed on the New York Stock Exchange. It started as a sawmill. Today, it makes products for the aerospace, biotechnology, and electronics industries. President Reagan works on his exercise treadmill and jogs on belting from the nation's oldest business, J. E. Rhoads and Sons, Inc., which was founded in Delaware in 1702.

Which of today's new business ventures will still be viable in the year 2270?

The economy of America has always been driven by entrepreneurs both in large and small concerns. Today many young people with vitality and vision are leaving king-sized corporations and making it on their own. Their thrust probably will help the United States regain its competitive clout in new areas. Entrepreneurship may provide the big push for the decades ahead.

II. JOBS AND CAREERS. HOW DO THEY DIFFER? HOW DO THEY MESH?

There is a big difference between a job and a career. A job for many workers is something they do to earn a living. They may or may not enjoy what they do from day to day. The job may provide important other benefits to the individual. The job does not, however, hold a central focus for the person's overall view of the world and its impact on the worker as a person.

A career is much more than a job. It is not only a source of financial income but also provides psychic income as well. A career is usually an important part of the person's concept of himself or herself and the world about her or him. A career means one has to keep up with new developments. It means facing changing information and many technological advances in order to function effectively. A career means more in-depth involvement than is true usually for a job. Jobs may change but a career receives much more commitment including preparation, time, and continuing education. It is expected of a person who is pursuing a career, not just a job, to continue to make contributions and life-long learning in his or her chosen field of endeavor.

We have been talking about jobs and careers. What is the main difference? The Random House Dictionary provides the following definitions. A job is "a piece of work done as part of the routine of one's occupation." It is "anything one has to do, as a task." It is "a post of employment." A career is the "progress of a person through life, as in some profession." It is "an occupation followed as one's life work."

One's life work may be followed either in industry, social services, or farming as well as in a profession. There are some people who make their careers in the insurance industry, the building trades, retail trade, health, or philanthropy. There are others who make their careers in accounting, law, or biochemistry. A significant difference between having a career as an accountant or having a job as an accountant is determined by the degree of personal commitment to educational, personal and skill growth, and tasks at work as well as to identification with and contributions to accounting.

After determining their job/career choices, some people reach their career goals by obtaining training on the job. They start at an entry level job. Motivation, employer-assisted on-the-job training, and self-paid education and training enable them to obtain the required skills, education, and training to enter and progress in the career of their choice. Some careers, of course, require extended and extensive training before even an entry level job can be obtained.

For some workers a job may lead to interest and skills in a certain career. This option may not have occurred to the person in the midst of early career choice and change. For many employees their early work experiences are in a job. Later on as they advance in the world of work or gain further education and training they move on to careers.

Let's take the work history of one individual to explain the difference between a job and a career and to illustrate how jobs are a part of career development.

Career change as well as job change occurs at many life stages because of the experiences of living. Let's see how job and career experiences and planned educational steps led to changing career choices for a female baby boomer.

Undergraduate degree: A.B., psychology major
Job: Part time during undergraduate years: selling in a specialty shop and assisting store owner with his community and business activities, particularly when they required record keeping.
Graduate Degree: M.A., rehabilitation counseling
Reason for choice: Determined to continue education through doctorate in psychology; this plan offered continuing education in psychology and provided financial benefits of paid tuition by a grant and a small stipend.
Job: Continued working in the specialty shop and for the owner.
Decision Choice: Upon finishing course work for the master's degree decided that a break from formal education was needed.
Job: Moved away from college town but obtained a job in a large department store based on experience in specialty shop. Moved up to buyer. Used some of skills learned in psychology and rehabilitation counseling to train new employees. While in high school, summer jobs as a life guard and swim instructor had provided an awareness of how to teach and train.
Career Choices: Enjoyed business and started taking courses at night that ultimately led to obtaining an M.B.A.
Job assignment change at department store while studying for M.B.A.: Developed communication beween the computer user staff and the buyers so that each could understand the needs of the other.

She maintained Association memberships and active involvement in local groups relating to buying, computer use in retail trade, business and professional women.

One of her professors was a highly successful business mentor who provided invaluable assistance in her career development.

Post M.B.A. Job/Career Choices: 1. Continued as buyer for department store. 2. Moved to small human relations/training concern; decision based on past experience as a trainer and working in a specialty shop. After a year she found this kind of job was not what she wanted.

Career Decision: Whether to be a consultant using her past experience and contacts or to work for someone else. Based on her personality and psychic needs, she chose to go into consulting work.

Her career remains in business particularly in those areas where her experience and contacts can be used to assist small retail companies that need professional help in going from manual systems to computerized systems.

The above example provides insight into the difference between a job and a career and how experiences can lead to career choices that originally were not considered.

III. JOB/CAREER SEEKING METHODS

Even when employment conditions are favorable, the job/career seeking techniques listed below will maximize the number of job and career offers you'll receive.

The following list of *35 Ways to Get the Job and/or Career of Your Choice* is not in any priority order. Use as many techniques as you can.

1. Place and answer ads in newspapers, magazines, and newsletters.
2. Use computerized placement services.
3. Use "head hunters" (executive search).
4. Utilize college alumni and placement services.
5. Attend job and career fairs.
6. Apply in person to an employer.
7. Use community counseling and placement services.
8. Use free services of your state Employment Service.
9. Use commercial employment agencies.
10. Initiate a direct job and career mail campaign.
11. Start your own business.
12. Attend career days.
13. Make cold telephone calls to possible employers.
14. Use job banks.
15. Use job clearinghouses.
16. Let your hobby network know of your job and career search and let them help.
17. Find a part-time job or career in your general area of interest that may lead to full time work.
18. Use local and national directories and other books and resources of your college or local public or private library. Many libraries have a job information center located in a specific section.
19. Obtain civil service job opening lists published by local, county, state, and federal governments.
20. Join a job or career club.
21. Let as many relatives, friends, and acquaintances as possible know of your career and job search, and let them help.
22. Be in contact with people who work in a company where you would like to be an employee.
23. Get job and career help from trade and professional associations and unions where you are a member or can become one.
24. Job and career network with people in everything you do.
25. Try to get a qualified mentor, sponsor, or advisor who will take a special interest in you.
26. Listen to public service announcements of job and career openings on radio and TV.
27. Visit and utilize resources of your local Chamber of Commerce.
28. Volunteer in a job or career so that when a job or career opening becomes available you are the one chosen.
29. Apply for internships that offer visibility and access to job and career opportunities.
30. Use cooperative education programs as experience and entrance into specific jobs and careers.
31. Read national, local, or regional newspapers that list primarily job and career openings and read articles that are job and career oriented.
32. Have an outstanding résumé and/or portfolio that helps you present yourself in the best possible way.
33. Use job or career hotlines for job and career information including openings.
34. Check in-house job and career vacancy lists. Many companies post vacancies at the work site or mail printed job and career announcements to appropriate organizations and people.
35. Use employment registries. One of those most used is that for nurses.

IV. THE RÉSUMÉ

Before you start the job/career search, but certainly while you are conducting it, start preparing a résumé. *Résumé writing takes lots of time and many rewrites.* Allow yourself periods of time during which you do not look at the résumé so that you can return to it with a fresh look.

The résumé needs to be:
- ☐ Organized
- ☐ Coherent
- ☐ Persuasive
- ☐ Concise
- ☐ Visually pleasing

For the effective magnetic résumé, you will want to:
- ☐ Organize your thoughts for maximum efficiency
- ☐ Use action verbs and nouns
- ☐ Be certain that grammar and spelling are perfect

- Inform, persuade, and appeal all at the same time
- Grab the reader's attention; then allow his or her eye to follow the flow
- Ruthlessly edit unnecessary verbiage
- Use one page; never more than two
- Do not crowd the page; use margins and white space for eye appeal

Your résumé has only about 45 seconds to attract the attention of the reader.

The efficient résumé has a goal: to obtain an interview, which, if skillfully handled, may result in a job or career. Write in a clear, concise manner. Focus on your career objective and the job/career you are seeking.

Résumés generally follow one of three formats. The chronological résumé is the most common and most familiar to employers. It is a time ordered form with the most recent education or work experience first. It is the easiest to write. It usually is the best to use if you have had continuous employment. It is still the most widely accepted format.

The functional résumé is most often used by those career candidates who wish to stress special qualifications without putting emphasis on dates. It is also used by career changers, older workers, and people leaving one work field for a very different one. Details are grouped by the skill or task they illustrate.

The combination chronological-functional résumé allows stressing special skills. It also provides past employment dates. This format also helps highlight pertinent volunteer experiences in addition to salaried employment. Many personnel directors prefer the combination functional-chronological to the purely functional résumé.

Two pages are usually more than enough to highlight accomplishments. A properly pruned page and a half may help establish the writer as a disciplined, organized person. Sprinkle adjectives as carefully as garlic in your cooking — a little will add spice; a lot may spoil the dish. Business-oriented nouns and action-oriented verbs will serve you well. Eliminate wordiness.

All résumés must contain name, address, telephone numbers (home and work); job/career objective; work experience; education; honors, awards, affiliations and/or community activities; references (usually available upon request).

V. THE INTERVIEW

Interviews are the final screening process. They may be conducted by one person or by a committee. Be prepared. Get as much information as you can about the organization, and if it's a conglomerate, about the company and the company within the company at which you will be interviewed.

The library can provide a great deal of important information, such as the size of the company, total sales, and its business, etc. An annual report can be helpful. College placement offices have a great deal of critical job and career information about businesses and industry throughout the United States.

For most interviews you will not know in advance the exact questions you will be asked. Choose a friend to role play the interview process with you. Have fun selling yourself. Embellish a little but do not stray far from the truth. Believe in yourself. There are problem questions that can arise in an interview.

- What do you know about our company?
- Where would you like to be five years from now?
- Tell me about yourself.
- Why do you want to work for us?
- Why should I hire you?
- What did you like most and least about your present job?
- What two or three achievements have given you the most satisfaction?
- What are three of your greatest assets?
- What are three of your greatest limitations? When answering a question like this, couch your response in positive terms.
- What are your salary requirements?
- What was your salary in your previous position?
- What kind of work situation irritates you?
- Why did you leave your last job?
- How much responsibility do you like?
- Do you work well under pressure?
- Would you mind moving away from this area?
- When you are annoyed or angry, what do you do?
- What features of prior jobs have you liked or disliked?
- How do you evaluate your present supervisor?
- How do you describe yourself?

All of these questions frequently have been asked in interviews.

The interviewee is expected to have questions and to ask them. Be sure yours are legitimate ones. You won't need or want to make all of the following inquiries. Some questions may be asked safely only after the job offer. Check out answers to these questions before the interview. See whether or not the interviewer confirms the facts you have already gathered. Asterisk (*) indicates questions to be asked only if the job appears to be yours.

What are the special job duties or responsibilities of the position?

Is this a newly created position or is someone being replaced? If the latter, why did the person leave? How long was she or he on the job?

Is there a probationary period?

* Do you have to join a union after a certain period of time?

* What are the fringe benefits?

* Who will be my immediate supervisor? Where does she or he stand in the organizational picture?

* Are there parking facilities at the work site? If not, is there public transportation or the possibility of car pools?

Does the job require travel? How often?

* What are the chances for advancement on this particular job?

* Does the organization have a day care center for employees'children?

Does this organization have branches or subsidiaries? If so, how many and where are they located?

Is it possible for me to have a tour of the physical plant?

* Have there been recent employee lay-offs?

* What expenses do you pay for moving home items and family?

* Can a husband and wife both work for the company?

* If moving to a new community, do you help the spouse find a position?

* When will I begin?

What is the first challenge requiring my attention?

* Do I get a letter or contract confirming my hiring?

* Is there a profit sharing or pension plan?

VI. FORCED CAREER CHOICE

Once you have obtained a job or career offer, you then must choose whether or not to accept it.

The forced career choice process helps people decide whether or not to take a job offer or whether or not they should change their present job or career.

First list in no particular sequence positive factors of the job or career offer. List them all. No time limit is imposed.

Then list in no particular order negative aspects of the job or career offer. List them all. No time limit is imposed.

Assign a plus (+) or plus plus (++) to each item on your list of positive indicators.

Assign a minus (−) or minus minus (−−) to each item of your list of negative indicators.

Each + or ++ item and each − or −− item may be discussed in some depth with a career counselor. After a complete discussion, if one item is decided to be of unusual importance or has a very high priority (positively or negatively), three +s or three −s may be assigned to that factor.

Should I Accept the Job or Career Offer?

Status +	High risk for failure −−
Good salary ++	Need to make an early
Psychic satisfaction ++	decision −
Some travel +	Lots of company turnover −−
Congenial peers +	Supervisor at a plateau −−
Executive office +	Don't know any of staff −

Chance for advancement ++			
Favorable fringe benefits +			
Interesting company & product +			
Learn new skills +			
Office near home ++			
Size of company +			
Total	15	*Total*	8

The odds are in favor of taking the position. Full speed ahead.

VII. EMERGING, CHANGING, AND GROWTH BUSINESS OPPORTUNITIES

(Find a need of consumers, whether they be businesses or individuals, and fill them.)

A sample listing of about 330 emerging, changing, and growth business careers and jobs for the balance of the 20th century and the first quarter of the 21st century follows:

accounting services
actuary services
acupuncture clinic
adaptive clothing designer shop
adult day care center
advertising and public relations services
ambulatory medical care center
androgynous clothing manufacturer
animal care and grooming services
antique store
apparel store
appliance repair shop
aquaculture farm
aquarium supplies and services
artist supplies and services
astronaut meals restaurant
audio-visual equipment supplies & repairs
automobile leasing service
automobile parts and services
automobile towing service

baby sitting services
barter shop services
bed and board hotel
bicycle & motorcycle repair services
billing services
bio-feedback health care services
bio-feedback ring and stress card services
bio-technology services
boat repair shop
book club

bookkeeping services
bookstores
bottled water services
bridal consultant shop
building material stores
burglar alarm sales and services
bus tours for college selection
business equipment sales and services

cable TV equipment manufacturer
cable TV repair services
camera repair shop
camping supplies
car and stereo sales and installation services
car wash services
career counseling agency
carpet and drapery sales and repair service
catering and fast food restaurant
catfish farm
cellular phone services
child and pet sitter
children and infants' wear shop
clearing house on new emerging careers
clock and watch shop
coin operated laundries
collection agency services
color consulting services
computer dating cards manufacturer
computer games developer
computer programming, software, and development
   services
computer rental services
computer repair and services
computer security specialist services
computer supplies store
computer systems analyst services
computer telemarketing
computer training company
computerized dating services
consulting business
convention planning services
copy services store
cosmetology supply store
crisis counseling services

database management services
day care services for adults and children
deep earth exploration services
deep sea search services
dental hygiene services
dental supply store
detective services
dialysis services
diet clinic

direct mail services
dispute resolution services
divorce mediation center services
dog training services
doll repair
doughnut and coffee shop
driving school
drug testing services
dual career family services

education and training specialist services
educational game store
electric car services station
electrical appliances store
electronic newspaper/magazine
electronic supplies store
emerging-businesses broker
employment services
energy consultant services
engine repair
engineering consultant services
environmental business assessment
ergonomic services
estate planning services
ethnic restaurants
executive protective services
executive "head hunter" services
exercise spa
exotic food restaurants
exotic welding services
experimental farmer services
express mail services

fabric care center services
farm business consultant
fast film services
fast food restaurant
fiber optics research services
film rental store
financial consultant services
financial planner services
fish farmer — salt water and fresh water
fix it shop
floating hotel
flower vending machine business
forecasting services
franchise services
freelance writer services
fundraising development services
funeral and crematorium services
furniture manufacturing
furniture rental services
furniture restoration
futuristic projections services

garden and lawn equipment and supplies
genealogy services
genetic counseling services
general contractor (building construction)
geriatric services
gift stores
gifted students school
glass sculpture
gourmet food restaurant
gourmet ice cream parlor
gourmet food store
gun repair business

hair cutting services
hair growing services center
halfway house services
handicapped placement services
handcraft business
hardware store
hazardous waste disposal services
headache care center
health clinic services for greater physical growth and athletic
   prowess
health food store
health spa
hearing aid services center
hearing dog services
heating and air conditioning services
herb farming and sales
home appliance repair shop
home cleaning services
home computer store
home health care services
home improvement services
home and industry security services
home live-in companion service
home plant care business
home recreation services
home study school
horticulture business
hospice services
house rehabilitation services
house sitting services
housekeeping and health monitoring robot companion
human parts replacements services
hypnosis service center

image consulting business
import and export services
information broker services
instant printing and copying business
instruction manual writer
interior design services
international banking specialists services
international business consultant

international food store
international law services
international product planning services
international sales and services
international video dating services
invention marketing services
invisible weaving services

janitorial services
jewelry sales and repair

landscaping and lawn services
large size men and women's apparel store
laundry and drycleaning services
lawn and snow services
leather goods repair shop
leisure agency services
learning disability services
limousine services
locksmith services
low-cal restaurant and bakery
lunar and asteroid souvenir shop
lunar mining

magazines for special interest groups
magic and fun shop
maid services
mail order services
mailing services
management consulting services
management data analysis services
management information systems specialist services
manufacturer of medical supplies
manufacturer of inexpensive and durable coffins and urns
manufacturer of equipment and supplies for swimming pools
manufacturer of ergonomic supplies and products
manufacturer of games for every purpose
manufacturer of new kinds of wine, beer, liquor
manufacturer of special plastics
manufacturer of sensory products
manufacturer of synthetic food
manufacturer of talking signs
marine ecologist services
marketing consultant services
meals-on-wheels services
media specialists services
medical and dental instrument company
medical identification card manufacturer
medical laboratories services
medical supply store
meeting coordinator services
messenger services
mid-career placement services
middle income financial planning consultants
mobile home manufacturers

mobile home parks
mobile locksmith services
modular home builders
mood altering clinic service
moving company
musical instrument (including electronic instruments) tuning and repair business

nanny and manny placement services
nationwide dial a gift business
new funeral and cremation services
new inventions and products assessment services
newsletters for specialized interest groups
new genetic vegetable and fruit grower
newsclipping services
night care services for adults and children
nuclear consultant services
nurse practitioner services
nursery business
nursing homes and convalescent hospitals
nutrition specialist services

ocean treasure hunter
office design equipment and repair services
office products store
ombudsman service
oral history services
orthodontic supplies and services
out-placement services
outer space entrepreneur
ovum and sperm bank services
oxygen services

pain clinic services
paper clothing manufacturing
paralegal training institute
personal clothing shoppers
pest control services
pet hotel, grooming services, therapy service, cemetery
phonovision installation and repair services
photo inventory services
photographic services and supplies
picture frame shop
polygraph services
poultry farmer
prison services
proposal writer services
prosthetic repair shop
public relations

ransom insurance for executives
recycling services
rehabilitation services
research services
restaurants specializing in one dish
retirement hotels

robot companion for the handicapped
robot guard services
robot rental services
robot repair shop
roommate finding services
rustproofing services

satellite saucer repair and recovery services
second hand store
security system services
self help medical diagnosis supply store
seminar and workshop services
sheltered workshops
shoe repair shop
shopping services
single club services
small business broker services
solar sales and installation services
space consultant services
space insurance services
space camp services
space manufacturer
space tourist agency
speakers bureau
stock broker services
strategic planning services
street vendor
stress services center
stuffed toy vending machines

T shirt shop
tax consultant services
technical services writer
telemarketing services
temporary employment services
terrorism protection consultant
theme amusement park
tie alteration services
training and development services
transplant registry services
treasure hunting services
truffle nursery
tutoring services
twenty-four hour snack, restaurant, and other business services

video cassette sales, services, and repairs
video year book publisher

walk-in health clinic services
waste paper collecting and recycling services
water pollution control services
weather control services
wellness consultant services
wellness employee services
workshops for top executives and particulary CEOs

VIII. CONCLUSION

As you read this book, BUSINESS, remember that you are likely to engage in many jobs and several careers over your lifetime. Most jobs and careers can occur in several areas, non-profit organizations, business organizations, government, social service organizations, etc. The choice is yours. It depends upon a number of factors such as your personality, the labor market, your skills and achievements, and your family and other responsibilities.

As an optimist by conviction and temperament, I believe the forthcoming business career challenges and opportunities will be greater than ever before. As we leave the 20th Century, we will move creatively into the 21st Century.

IX. SELECTED BIBLIOGRAPHY

In-depth review of the topics covered in this chapter, such as résumés, interviews, forced choice, etc. are covered in:

Emerging Careers: New Occupations for the Year 2000 and Beyond. S. Norman Feingold and Norma Reno Miller. Garrett Park, Maryland 20896: Garrett Park Press, 1983.

"Emerging Careers. Occupations for Post-Industrial Society." S. Norman Feingold. *The Futurist.* 1984, Vol. XVIII, No. 1, pp 9–16. World Future Society, Bethesda, Maryland 20814.

Getting Ahead. A Woman's Guide to Career Success. S. Norman Feingold and Avis Nicholson. Washington, D.C. 20009: Acropolis Books Ltd., 1983.

Making It On Your Own. S. Norman Feingold and Leonard G. Perlman. Washington, D.C. 20009: Acropolis Books Ltd., revised edition, 1985.

900,000 Plus Jobs Annually: Published Sources of Employment Listings. S. Norman Feingold and Glenda Ann Hansard-Winkler. Garrett Park, Maryland 20896: Garrett Park Press, 1982.

Occupational Outlook Handbook 1986–87 Edition. Washington, D.C.: U.S. Department of Labor Bureau of Labor Statistics, 1986.

The Professional and Trade Association Job Finder: A Directory of Employment Resources Offered by Associations and Other Organizations. S. Norman Feingold and Avis Nicholson. Garrett Park, Maryland 20896: Garrett Park Press, 1983.

"Tracking new career categories will become a preoccupation for job seekers and managers." S. Norman Feingold. pp 103–111. Alexandria, Virginia 22314: American Society for Personnel Administration. *Work in the 21st Century. An Anthology of Writing on the Changing World of Work,* 1984.

What Color Is Your Parachute? Richard Nelson Boles. Berkeley, California 94707: Ten Speed Press, 1986.

NOTES

Chapter 1

[1] Adapted from Paul A. Samuelson and William D. Nordhaus, *Economics*, 12th ed. (New York: McGraw-Hill Book Co., 1985), p. 4.

[2] "The Venture Communists Setting Up Shop in China," *Business Week*, July 7, 1986, p. 70.

[3] Karl Marx, *Critique of the Gotha Programme* (1875), as reprinted in *Karl Marx and Frederick Engels*, Selected Works, vol. 2 (London: Lawrence & Wishart, Ltd., 1962), pp. 1, 24.

[4] Adam Smith, *The Wealth of Nations*, Samuelson and Nordhaus, *Economics*, p. 760.

[5] This discussion is largely adapted from K. Davis and W. C. Frederick, *Business and Society*, 5th Ed. (New York: McGraw-Hill Book Co., 1984), pp. 101–108.

[6] "Leisure Time Drops, Poll Taker Reports," *Boston Globe*, December 26, 1985, p. 5.

[7] Lawrence M. Friedman, *A History of American Law* (New York: Simon & Schuster, 1972), p. 166.

[8] Milton Moskowitz, et al., eds., *Everybody's Business* (New York: Harper & Row, 1980), pp. 152, 153–54.

[9] Samuel Eliot Morison, *The Oxford History of the American People* (New York: Oxford Univ. Press, 1964), pp. 666–69.

Chapter 2

[1] Larry Rohter, "From 6 New Benefactors, 425 College Dreams," *New York Times*, June 21, 1986, pp. 29–30.

[2] Milton Friedman, "A Friedman Doctrine — The Social Responsibility of Business is to Increase its Profits," *New York Times Magazine*, September 13, 1970, p. 126.

[3] David Vogel, "Foreword" to Thornton Bradshaw & David Vogel, *Corporations and Their Critics* (New York: McGraw-Hill, 1982), pp. viii–ix.

[4] William L. Prosser, *The Law of Torts*, 4th ed. (St. Paul, Minn.: West Publ. Co., 1971), pp. 641–643. The example is based on *MacPhearson v. Buick Motor Co.*, 217 N.Y. 382, 111 N.E. 1050 (1916).

[5] Irving Howe, *World of Our Fathers* (New York: Harcourt Brace Jovanovitch, 1976), pp. 304-05.

[6] W. A. Haas, Jr., "Corporate Social Responsibility: A New Term for an Old Concept with New Significance," in Bradshaw & Vogel, eds. *Corporations and Their Critics*, p. 135.

[7] Amy L. Domini & Peter D. Kinder, *Ethical Investing* (Reading, Mass.: Addison-Wesley Publ. Co., 1984), p. 71.

[8] *Ibid.*, p. 190.

[9] Xerox Corporation, 800 Longridge Rd., Stamford, Ct.

[10] "The Man Who Wears the Star," *Forbes*, December 16, 1985, p. 8.

[11] L. Wayne, "American Express's Ace in the Hole," *New York Times*, June 30, 1985, p. F9.

[12] See *1985 Annual Report* (Downers Grove, Ill.: ServiceMaster Industries, Inc., 1986); Jay McCormick, "Amazing Grace," *Forbes*, June 17, 1985, p. 83.

[13] Mickey Williamson, "Phil Villers: An Equestrian Among High Tech Cowboys," *Boston Business*, Spring 1986, p. 58.

[14] Porian S. Moskal, "Corporate Responsibility: Putting Your Act Together," *Industry Week*, July 26, 1982, pp. 51–56.

[15] Karen L. Koman, "General Dynamics People Get Lessons In Ethics," *St. Louis Post-Dispatch*, March 30, 1986, pp. 1A, 8A.

[16] *Ibid.*; Allan L. Otten, "Ethics on the Job: Companies Alert Employees to Potential Dilemmas," *Wall Street Journal*, July 14, 1986, p. 21.

[17] Allen O. Otten, "Ethics on the Job," p. 21.

Chapter 3

[1] *Kielhafner* v. *Kielhafner*, 639 S.W. 2nd 228 (Mo. Ct. App. 1982).

[2] Donna Fenn, "The Family Plan," *Inc.*, April 1986, p. 119.

[3] Uniform Partnership Act, §6 (1).

[4] Model Business Corporation Act, §54 (a), (c)-(f), (h)-(j).

[5] Ibid., §55.

[6] *The Coca-Cola Company Annual Report 1985* (1986), p. 41.

[7] *General Electric Co. Annual Report 1984* (1985), p. 30.

[8] Laura Landro and Carolyn Phillips, "Pulitzer Family Feud Widens Over Bid," *The Wall Street Journal*, April 11, 1986, p. 6; Alex S. Jones, "And Now the Pulitzers Go to War," *The New York Times*, April 13, 1986, p. F4.

[9] "The 500 Largest U.S. Industrial Corporations," *Fortune*, April 28, 1986, pp. 186, 188.

[10] Model Business Corporation Act, §50.

Chapter 4

[1] Nicholas C. Siropolis, *Small Business Management*, 3rd ed. (Boston: Houghton Mifflin Co., 1986), p. 37.

[2] Quoted by Office of Economic Research, The New York Stock Exchange, *Economic Choices for the 1980s* (January 1980), p. 9, as quoted in Siropolis, op. cit., p. 37.

[3] W. L. Gore, letter to the editor, *Inc.*, December, 1985, p. 7.

[4] "The *Savvy* 60," *Savvy*, April, 1985, pp. 50, 51–52.

[5] M. Beauchamp, "Son Knows Best, for Now," *Forbes*, December 16, 1985, pp. 62, 66.

[6] M. Moskowitz, et al., eds., *Everybody's Business* (New York: Harper & Row, 1980), pp. 128–32.

[7] "The *Forbes* Market Value 500," *Forbes*, April 29, 1985, pp. 205–212.

[8] Siropolis, *op. cit.*, p. 7.

[9] *Meeting the Special Problems of Small Business* (New York: Committee on Economic Development, 1947), p. 14.

[10] "Nine Who Dare," *Forbes*, November 21, 1983, p. 123; John A. Conway, "Follow-Through," *Forbes*, January 13, 1986, p. 10.

[11] D. L. Birch, *The Job Creation Process* (Cambridge: MIT Program on Neighborhood and Regional Change, 1979), p. 8.

[12] Sheila Lukins & Julee Rosso (New York: Workman Publishing, 1981), pp. xi–xiii.

[13] Bro Uttal, "Inside the Deal that Made Bill Gates $350,000,000," *Fortune*, July 21, 1986, pp. 23–33.

[14] "Small is Beautiful," *Business Week*, May 27, 1985, pp. 88, 90.

[15] J. Bettner and C. Donahue, "Now They're Not Laughing," *Forbes*, November 21, 1983, pp. 116, 117–18.

[16] As quoted in "The *Savvy* 60," p. 50.

[17] SBA figures as quoted in R. Greene, "Do You Really Want to be Your Own Boss?" *Forbes*, October 21, 1985, p. 86.

[18] Calvin Trillin, "Competitors," *The New Yorker*, July 8, 1985, p. 31.

[19] W. Baldwin, "Too Much of a Good Thing?" *Forbes*, December 16, 1985, pp. 102–03.

[20] U.S. Department of Commerce, Bureau of Industrial Economics and the Minority Business Development Agency, *The Franchise Opportunities Handbook* (Washington: GPO, 1983), p. 24.

[21] A. Spector, "5 Franchisors Discuss Growth," *Independent Restaurants*, October, 1985, pp. 42, 45.

[22] *USA Today*, November 11, 1984.

[23] See the Automobile Dealer's Day in Court Act of 1956 and the Patroleum Marketers Practices Act of 1979.

Chapter 5

[1] Brian O'Reilly, "A Body Builder Lifts Greyhound," *Fortune*, October 28, © 1985 Time Inc. All rights reserved, pp. 124–34.

[2] *Ibid.*

[3] Robert L. Katz, "Skills of an Effective Administrator," *Harvard Business Review*, Sept.–Oct. 1974, pp. 90–102.

[4] Adapted from Henry Mintzberg, "The Manager's Job: Folklore and Fact," *Harvard Business Review*, July–Aug. 1975, pp. 49–61.

[5] Peter Petre, "The Struggle over Sperry's Future," *Fortune*, December 9, 1985, pp. 78–84.

[6] Terrence E. Deal and Allen A. Kennedy, *Corporate Cultures* (Reading, MA: Addison-Wesley Publishing Co., 1982), p. 15.

[7] Anne B. Fisher, "Glamour: Getting It — or Getting It Back," *Fortune*, May 12, 1986, pp. 18–22.

[8] Lucien Rhodes, "The Un-manager," *Inc.*, Vol. 4, August 1982, p. 34.

Chapter 6

[1] Ricky W. Griffin and Gregory Moorhead, *Organizational Behavior* (Boston: Houghton Mifflin Co., 1986), p. 20.

[2] Adapted from Jerry M. Rosenberg, *Dictionary of Business and Management*, 2nd ed. p. 92. Copyright © 1983 by John Wiley & Sons. Reprinted by permission of John Wiley & Sons, Inc.

[3] Adam Smith, *The Wealth of Nations* (Harmondsworth, Eng.: Penguin, 1982), pp. 109ff.

[4] Gene Stone and Bo Burlingham, "Workstyle," *Inc.*, January 1986, pp. 45–54.

[5] Richard E. Krafve, *Boston Sunday Globe*, May 22, 1960; as quoted in Robert W. Kent, ed., *Money Talks* (New York: Facts on File, 1985), p. 212.

[6] Tom Richman, "*Super* Market," *Inc.*, October 1985, pp. 115–20.

[7] Adapted from Robert Kreitner, *Management*, 3rd ed. (Boston: Houghton Mifflin Co., 1986), pp. 285–86.

[8] Kent, *Money Talks*, p. 214.

[9] Adapted from Rosenberg, *Dictionary of Business and Management*, p. 296. Copyright © 1983 by John Wiley & Sons. Reprinted by permission of John Wiley & Sons, Inc.

[10] Harvey F. Koloday, "Managing in a Matrix," *Business Horizons*, March–April 1981, pp. 17-24.

[11] Certo, *Principles of Modern Management*, 3rd ed. (Dubuque, Iowa: Wm. C. Brown Publishers, 1986), pp. 368, 375.

[12] Susan Mundale, "Why More CEO's Are Mandating, Listening and Writing Training," *Training*, October 1980, p. 38.

[13] © 1985 by Houghton Mifflin Company. Reprinted by permission from *The American Heritage Dictionary*, second College edition, p. 218.

[14] Colin Leinster, "Exxon's Axman Cometh," *Fortune*, April 14, 1986, p. 92.

[15] Selwyn Feinstein, "Labor Letter," *The Wall Street Journal*, May 6, 1986, p. 1.

[16] Michael Schrage and Warren Brown, "Middle Managers Find They're Becoming Expendable," *Roanoke [Va.] Times & World-News*, Sept. 8, 1985, pp. F5-6.

Chapter 7

[1] Robert Levering, et al., *The 100 Best Companies to Work for in America* (Reading, Mass.: Addison-Wesley Publishing Co., 1984), pp. 74-76, 368.

[2] Barry L. Reece and Rhonda Brandt, *Effective Human Relations in Organizations* (Boston: Houghton Mifflin Co., 1984), p. 5.

[3] Keith Davis, *Human Behavior at Work* (New York: McGraw-Hill Book Co., 1981), p. 12.

[4] Donna Fenn, "The Kids Are All Right," *Inc.*, January 1985, pp. 48-54.

[5] Levering, et al., *The 100 Best Companies to Work for in America*, p. 251.

[6] "America's Fitness Binge," *U.S. News & World Report*, May 3, 1982, p. 60.

[7] Terri Minsky, "Stride-Rite Dampers Down Smoking," *Boston Globe*, May 14, 1985, pp. 45, 47.

[8] Adapted from Ricky W. Griffin and Gregory Moorhead, *Organizational Behavior* (Boston: Houghton Mifflin Co., 1986), p. 140, and Richard M. Steers and Lyman W. Porter, *Motivation and Work Behavior*, 3rd ed. (New York: McGraw-Hill Book Co., 1983).

[9] As quoted in "Thoughts on the Business of Life," *Forbes*, October 7, 1985, p. 192.

[10] Ricky W. Griffin, *Management* (Boston: Houghton Mifflin Co., 1984), p. 571.

[11] David R. Hampton, *Contemporary Management*, 2nd ed. (New York: McGraw-Hill Book Co., 1981), pp. 15-19.

[12] Abraham H. Maslow, *Motivation and Personality* (New York: Harper & Row, 1954).

[13] Levering, et al., *The 100 Best Companies to Work for in America*, pp. 199-202.

[14] "How Bosses Get People to Work Harder," *U.S. News & World Report*, January 29, 1979, p. 63.

[15] Hampton, *Contemporary Management*, p. 52.

[16] Douglas McGregor, *The Human Side of Enterprise* (New York: McGraw-Hill Book Co., 1960).

[17] Levering, et al., *The 100 Best Companies to Work for in America*, pp. 225-28.

[18] Kenneth Blanchard and Spencer Johnson, *The One Minute Manager* (New York: William Morrow & Co., 1982), p. 40.

[19] Keith Davis, *Human Behavior at Work* (New York: McGraw- Hill Book Co., 1977), p. 61.

[20] "Idea Man," *The Wall Street Journal*, July 26, 1976, p. 1.

[21] Saul Rubinstein, "QWL [Quality of Work Life], the Union, the Specialist, and Employment Security," *Training and Development Journal*, March 1984, p. 82.

[22] *A Conference on Quality of Work Life: Issues Affecting the State-of-the-Art* (Washington, D.C.: U.S. Dept. of Labor, 1984), p. 1.

[23] Tom St. George, "Quality of Work Life: Why Things Get Tougher as You Go," *Training/HRO*, January 1984, p. 70.

[24] Paul D. Bush, "The Argument for Employee Participation," *Boston Globe*, November 12, 1985, p. 30.

[25] William G. Ouchi, *Theory Z* (Reading, Mass.: Addison-Wesley Publishing Co., 1981).

[26] Paul D. Bush, *Boston Globe*, p. 30.

[27] Sad Ingle, "How to Avoid Quality Circle Failure in Your Company," *Training and Development Journal*, March 1982, p. 54.

[28] Phillip I. Morgan and H. Kent Baker, "Taking a Look at Flexitime," *Supervisory Management*, February 1984, p. 38.

[29] Levering, et al., *The 100 Best Companies to Work for in America*, p. 104.

[30] Glenn Collins, "Many in Work Force Care for Elderly Kin," *The New York Times*, January 6, 1986, p. B5.

[31] "Telecommuting: An Idea Whose Time Has Almost Come," *Management Technology*, January 1984, p. 29.

[32] U.S. Bureau of Labor Statistics, as reported in Robert D. Hershey, Jr., "U.S. Expected to Report Creation of 10 Million New Jobs Since '82," *The New York Times*, December 6, 1985, p. B28.

[33] Karl Albrecht and Ron Zemke, *Service America* (Homewood, Ill.: Dow Jones-Irwin, 1985).

[34] Julia H. Martin and Donna J. Tolson, "Changing Job Skills in Virginia: The Employer's View," in University of Virginia Institute of Government *Newsletter*, 62: 6 (January 1986), p. 34.

[35] Robert W. Kent, ed., *Money Talks* (New York: Facts on File, 1985), p. 219.

Chapter 8

[1] W. Meyers, "Child Care Finds a Champion in the Corporation," *The New York Times*, August 4, 1985, p. F1.

[2] L. Collins, "More Firms Giving New Fathers Time Off to Share Chores and Joys of Infant Care," *The Wall Street Journal*, July 5, 1985, p. 9.

[3] ASPA-BNA Survey No. 48, *Personnel Activities, Budgets, and Staffs: 1984–85* (Wash., D.C.: Bureau of National Affairs), May 23, 1984.

[4] "Central Illinois to Be the Site of Auto Plant," *The Wall Street Journal*, October 8, 1985, p. 2.

[5] M. Schrage and W. Brown, "Middle Managers Find They're Becoming Expendable," *Roanoke [Va.] Times & World-News*, September 8, 1985, p. F5.

[6] Edwin B. Flippo, *Personnel Management* (New York: McGraw-Hill Book Co., 1984), pp. 172–73.

Chapter 9

[1] Pontiac Fiero Plant Philosophy. Developed by union and management representatives at an offsite meeting, September, 1982.

[2] Page Smith, *The Nation Comes of Age* (New York: McGraw-Hill Book Co., 1981), pp. 795–96.

[3] Paul A. Samuelson and William D. Nordhaus, *Economics*, 12th ed. (New York: McGraw-Hill Book Co., 1985), p. 635.

[4] Harold C. Livesay, *Samuel Gompers and Organized Labor in America*, Little, Brown and Company, Boston. 1978.

[5] The Clayton Act, §6.

[6] Handbook of Labor Statistics, Wages, and Industrial Relations. 1978.

[7] Bureau of Labor Statistics, Wages, and Industrial Relations, Washington, D.C.

[8] L. Bernstein, "Unions Revert to 1930s-style Organizing Tactics."

[9] Marcy Grimes, Head of Health Care Benefits, General Motors.

[10] Harold C. Livesay, *Samuel Gompers and Organized Labor in America*, Little Brown and Company, Boston. 1978.

[11] W. Serrin, "Historians See Lessons for Present in Fate of Dead Anthracite Coal Towns," *New York Times*, December 29, 1985; p. 30.

[12] "A Work Revolution in U.S. Industry," *Business Week*, May 16, 1983; p. 100.

Chapter 10

[1] Craig R. Waters, "Improved! New! Manufacturing," *Inc.*, January 1986, p. 73.

[2] See, for example, James R. Evans et al., *Applied Production and Operations Management* (St. Paul, Minn.: West Publishing Co., 1984), pp. 9–10. Used by permission.

[3] Evans et al., *Applied Production and Operations Management*, pp. 341–44.

[4] Waters, "Improved! New! Manufacturing," *Inc.*, p. 73.

[5] "Even American Knowhow Is Headed Abroad," *Business Week*, March 3, 1986, pp. 60, 63.

[6] "The Hollow Corporation," *Business Week*, March 3, 1986, p. 56.

[7] Evans et al., *Applied Production and Operations Management*, p. 618.

[8] Rux Martin, "Gourmet Foods from the Green Mountains," *Vermont Life*, Winter 1985, p. 23.

[9] Gene Bylinsky, "A Breakthrough in Automating the Assembly Line," *Fortune*, May 26, 1986, pp. 64–66.

[10] Robert Kreitner, *Management*, pp. 109–11, 614; Harry B. Thompson, "CAD/CAM and the Factory of the Future," *Management Review* 72 (May 1983), p. 28; "Special Report: High Tech to the Rescue," *Business Week*, June 16, 1986, p. 100ff.

[11] R. H. Anthony and J. S. Reese, *Management Accounting* (Homewood, Ill.: Richard D. Irwin, Inc., 1975).

[12] Adapted from Jerry M. Rosenberg, *Dictionary of Business and Management*, 2nd ed. Copyright © 1983 by John Wiley & Sons. Reprinted by permission of John Wiley & Sons, Inc., pp. 266–67.

[13] Evans et al., *Applied Production and Operations Management*, p. 572.

[14] Jack Meredith and Thomas E. Gibbs, *The Management of Operations*, 2nd ed. (New York: John Wiley and Sons, Inc., 1984), p. 539.

[15] Rifka Rosenwein, "Making Things Kosher: Passover Means Lots of Work for Many Food Processors," *The Wall Street Journal*, April 25, 1986, p. 23.

Chapter 11

[1] Fabian Linden, "Working-Women Households," *American Demographics*, August 1983; Eileen Prescott, "New Men," Ibid.; Ray Goydon, "Doing Business with Mr. Mom," *Forbes*, January 13, 1986, p. 281.

[2] "AMA Board Approves New Marketing Definition," *Marketing News*, March 1, 1985, p. 1.

[3] William M. Pride and O. C. Ferrell, *Marketing*, 4th ed. (Boston: Houghton Mifflin Co., 1985), p. 6.

[4] John Downes and Jordan E. Goodman, *Dictionary of Finance and Investment Terms* (Woodbury, N.Y.: Barron's 1985), p. 439.

[5] American Marketing Association, *Marketing Definitions* (Chicago: American Marketing Association, 1960), p. 13.

[6] *Ibid.*, p. 22.

[7] General Electric Company, *Annual Report: 1952* (New York: General Electric Co., 1953), p. 21.

[8] Gerald L. Manning and Barry L. Reece, *Selling Today* (Dubuque, Ia.: William C. Brown & Co., Publishers, 1984), p. 7.

[9]Nancy L. Croft, "Casting Stoves Upon the Waters," *Nation's Business*, February 1986, pp. 44R–45R.

[10]"Aircraft Industry Emerging from Engineering Dominance," *Marketing News*, August 2, 1985, p. 7.

[11]Lynn G. Reiling, "Wrangler Womenswear Outfits Sales Staff with Portable Computers," *Marketing News*, March 1, 1985, p. 31.

Chapter 12

[1]William M. Pride and O. C. Ferrell, *Marketing*, 4th ed. (Boston: Houghton Mifflin Co., 1985), p. 11.

[2]Kotler, "New Products Management for 1980" (New York: Booz, Allen & Hamilton, 1982), pp. 339–40.

[3]"Finding the Right Name for Brand X," *Insight*, January 27, 1986, pp. 54–55.

[4]"P & G's Rusty Marketing Machine," *Business Week*, October 21, 1985, pp. 111–12.

[5]"New? Improved?" *Business Week*, October 21, 1985, pp. 108, 109.

[6]Bill Saporito, "Ganging Up On Black & Decker," *Fortune*, December 23, 1985, pp. 63–72.

Chapter 13

[1]Data from Penny Gill, "The Joy in Toymaking," *Nation's Business*, December 1985, pp. 22–28.

[2]American Marketing Association, *Marketing Definitions* (Chicago: American Marketing Association, 1960), pp. 9, 16.

[3]Susan Buschbaum, "A Nation of Shopkeepers," *Inc.*, November 1985, p. 72.

[4]*Ibid.*, p. 66.

[5]"At Home," *Changing Times*, January 1986, p. 18.

[6]Ed Bean, "John Jay Hooker Is Betting Customers Will Put Money on His 99-Cent Burgers," *The Wall Street Journal*, November 25, 1985, p. 21.

[7]"Cadillac's Bill for Airmailing Allantes May Be $20 Million," *AutoWeek*, December 30, 1985, p. 4.

[8]Adapted from Robert A. Sigafoos, *Absolutely Positively Overnight!* (New York: Mentor Books, 1984).

Chapter 14

[1]Leo Kiley, Vice President, Marketing, Frito-Lay, Inc., Dallas, Texas.

[2]American Marketing Association, *Marketing Definitions* (Chicago: American Marketing Association, 1963), p. 9.

[3]William M. Pride and O. C. Ferrell, *Marketing*, 4th ed. (Boston: Houghton Mifflin Co., 1985), p. 352.

[4]Stephen Koepp, "All Wrapped up in Company Logos," *Time*, December 2, 1985, p. 70.

[5]Pat Sloan, "Made in America Greets Shoppers," *Advertising Age*, December 19, 1985.

[6]Edward C. Baig, "Trying to Make Beef Appetizing Again," *Fortune*, November 25, 1985, p. 64.

[7]Barry L. Reece, *Food Marketing* (New York: McGraw-Hill Book Co., 1979), p. 165.

[8]Richard L. Lynch, Herbert L. Ross, and Ralph D. Wray, *Introduction to Marketing* (New York: McGraw-Hill Book Co., 1984), p. 403.

[9]"Now We Pause for a (Very) Brief Message," *Fortune*, December 23, 1985, p. 75; "Super Bowl Offers Ad Showcase," *St. Louis Post-Dispatch*, January 26, 1986, p. 3G.

[10]John O'Toole, "Stay Tuned, America, It Could Be Fun," *U.S. News & World Report*, January 13, 1986, p. 53.

[11]Felix Kessler, "Camcorders: The New Front in the Home Video Wars," *Fortune*, March 3, 1986, p. 46.

[12]Gerald L. Manning and Barry L. Reece, *Selling Today*, 3rd ed. (Dubuque, Iowa: Wm. C. Brown Group, 1987).

[13]"Computerized Assisted Car Sales," *Personal Selling Power*, January/February 1985, p. 28.

[14]Manning and Reece, *Selling Today*, p. 57.

[15]Adapted from Ernan Roman, "Telemarketing Rings in New Business Era," *Advertising Age*, January 27, 1986.

[16]American Marketing Association, *Marketing Definitions*, (Chicago: American Marketing Association, 1963), p. 20.

[17]Lynch, Ross, and Wray, *Introduction to Marketing*, p. 40.

[18]Pride and Ferrell, *Marketing*, p. 375.

[19]"Altruistic Marketing," *Fortune*, November 25, 1985, p. 7.

[20]Kevin McManus, "If You Can Find Another Iacocca, Publish Him!" *Insight*, March 31, 1986, pp. 52–54.

Chapter 15

[1]William Nack, "Thrown for Heavy Losses," *Sports Illustrated*, March 24, 1986, pp. 40–47.

[2]Adapted from Ralph Estes, *Dictionary of Accounting*, 2nd ed. (Cambridge, Mass.: MIT Press, 1984), p. 2. Copyright © The Massachusetts Institute of Technology Press. Used by permission.

[3]Ibid., pp. 34, 38.

[4]B. Needles, Jr., Henry R. Anderson, and James C. Caldwell, *Principles of Accounting*, 2nd ed. (Boston: Houghton Mifflin Company, 1984), p. 105.

[5]Adapted from John Downes and Jordan E. Goodman, *Dictionary of Finance and Investment Terms* (Woodbury, N.Y.: Barron's, 1985), p. 184.

Chapter 16

[1]International Business Machines Corp., *Annual Report* (1986), p. 52; Bob Fenster, "Famous False Starts and Others Off the Charts," *The Wall Street Journal*, December 24, 1985, p. 8; and Milton Moskowitz et al., eds., *Everybody's Business* (New York: Harper & Row Publishers, Inc., 1980), pp. 438–42.

[2]David M. Kroenke, *Business Computer Systems: An Introduction* (Santa Cruz, Calif.: Mitchell Publishing, Inc.), p. 25.

[3] Paul B. Finney, "The Invisible Machines that Keep Disney Humming," *Management Technology*, June 1985, p. 28.

[4] Joel Dreyfuss, "Networking: Japan's Latest Computer Craze," July 7, 1986, pp. 94–96.

[5] David R. Sullivan et al., *Using Computers Today* (Boston: Houghton Mifflin Co., 1986), pp. 15–16, 33.

[6] *Ibid.*, p. 33.

[7] Paul B. Finney, "The Invisible Machines that Keep Disney Humming," p. 32.

[8] Stephanie K. Walter, "A CEO's Recipe for Mixing Management and Machines," *Management Technology*, July 1984, p. 43.

[9] "How Personal Computers Can Trip Up Executives," *Business Week*, September 24, 1984, p. 94.

[10] David R. Sullivan et al., *Using Computers Today*, p. 74.

[11] David W. Pearce, ed., *The Dictionary of Modern Economics*, rev. ed. (Cambridge, Mass.: MIT Press, 1983), p. 417.

[12] William M. Pride and O. C. Ferrell, *Marketing*, 4th ed. (Boston: Houghton Mifflin Co., 1985), p. 120.

[13] *Ibid.*

Chapter 17

[1] Everett G. Martin, "Amid Wild Inflation, Bolivians Concentrate on Swapping Currency," *The Wall Street Journal*, August 13, 1985, pp. 1, 16.

[2] Adam Smith, *The Money Game* (New York: Random House, 1967), p. 54; Arthur Fromm, *The History of Money* (New York: Archer House, 1957), p. 31.

[3] Lawrence J. Gitman, *Principles of Financial Management*, 3rd ed. (New York: Harper & Row, 1982), p. 59.

[4] Board of Governors of the Federal Reserve System, *The Federal Reserve System: Purposes and Functions*, 7th ed. (Washington, D.C.: Board of Governors of the Federal Reserve System, 1984), pp. 9–10.

[5] Board of Governors of the Federal Reserve System, *The Federal Reserve System: Purposes and Functions*, 7th ed. (Washington, D.C.: Board of Governors of the Federal Reserve System, 1984), pp. 22–23; John Downes and Jordan Elliot Goodman, *Dictionary of Finance and Investment Terms* (Woodbury, N.Y.: Barron's, 1985), pp. 117, 235–36, 336–37.

Chapter 18

[1] "A Garden-Tool Maker Who's Cultivating Slow Growth," *Business Week*, February 3, 1986, p. 54.

[2] "A CEO's Recipe for Mixing Management and Machines," *Management Technology*, July 1984, p. 43.

[3] Lawrence J. Gitman, *Principles of Managerial Finance*, 3rd ed. (New York: Harper & Row Publishers, Inc., 1982), pp. 8–10.

[4] John Downes and Jordan Elliot Goodman, *Dictionary of Finance and Investment Terms* (Woodbury, N.Y.: Barron's Educational Series, Inc., 1985), pp. 299–300.

[5] Peter Nulty, "Irwin Jacobs Stirs a Junk Bond Brawl," *Fortune*, June 9, 1986, p. 104.

[6] Lawrence J. Gitman, *Principles of Managerial Finance*, pp. 9–10.

[7] John Downes and Jordan Elliot Goodman, *Dictionary of Finance and Investment Terms*, pp. 90, 208.

[8] Benjamin Graham et al., *Security Analysis*, 4th ed. (New York: McGraw-Hill Book Co., Inc., 1962), p. 277.

[9] Peter Nulty, "Irwin Jacobs Stirs a Junk Bond Brawl," p. 104.

Chapter 19

[1] *Adams* v. *State*, 443 So. 2d 1003 (Fla. Dist. Ct. App. 1983).

[2] John Downes and Jordan Elliot Goodman, *Dictionary of Finance and Investment Terms* (Woodbury, N.Y.: Barron's Educational Series, Inc., 1985), p. 220.

[3] Frank K. Reilly, *Investments*, 2nd ed. (New York: CBS College Publishing, The Dryden Press, 1986), p. 84.

[4] David M. Darst, *The Handbook of the Bond and Money Markets* (New York: McGraw-Hill Book Company, Inc., 1981), pp. 208, 235.

[5] Frank J. Fabozzi and Frank G. Zarb, eds., *Handbook of Financial Markets: Securities, Options, Futures* (Homewood, Ill.: Dow Jones-Irwin, 1981), p. 63.

[6] Tamar Lewin, "The Dilemma of Insider Trading," *The New York Times*, July 21, 1986, p. D1.

Chapter 20

[1] Peter Gwynne, "Stargazer and Much, Much More," *Boston Globe*, March 10, 1986, pp. 45, 48.

[2] Kathryn J. McIntyre, "Risk Manager of the Year: Harold C. Lang," *Business Insurance*, April 15, 1985, p. 107.

[3] *Statistical Abstract of the United States*, 1986.

[4] *Health and Human Services News*, July 29, 1986, Department of Health Care Financing.

Chapter 21

[1] *Weeks* v. *Southern Bell Telephone & Telegraph Co.*, 408 F. 2d 228 (5th Cir. 1969).

[2] John E. Nowak et al., *Constitutional Law*, 2nd ed. (St. Paul, Minn.: West Publishing Co., 1983), pp. 718–30, 1077-78.

[3] Lawrence S. Clark and Peter D. Kinder, *Law and Business* (New York: McGraw-Hill Book Co., Inc., 1986), pp. 649–52.

Chapter 22

[1] Robert W. Kent, ed., *Money Talks* (New York: Facts on File Publications, 1985), p. 94.

[2] Ricky W. Griffin, *Management* (Boston: Houghton Mifflin Co., 1984), p. 638.

[3] David R. Spiegel, "Enforcing Safety Laws Locally," *The New York Times*, March 1986, p. 11.

[4] Adam Smith, *The Wealth of Nations* (Harmondsworth, Eng.: Penguin Books, 1982), p. 232.

[5] Lawrence S. Clark and Peter D. Kinder, *Law and Business* (New York: McGraw-Hill Book Co., Inc., 1986), p. 782.

[6] Jerry Flint, "Here Come the Truckbusters," *Forbes*, June 30, 1986, p. 87.

[7] As quoted in Kent, *Money Talks*, p. 89.

[8] Rux Martin, "Gourmet Foods from the Green Mountains," *Vermont Life*, Winter 1985, pp. 22–24.

Chapter 23

[1] Kenneth Labich, "America's International Winners," *Fortune*, April 14, 1986, p. 44.

[2] David W. Pearce, ed., *The Dictionary of Modern Economics*, rev. ed. (Cambridge, Mass.: MIT Press, 1983), p. 411.

[3] *Ibid.*, p. 147.

[4] *Ibid.*, p. 197.

[5] Milton Moskowitz, et al., eds., *Everybody's Business* (New York: Harper & Row, 1980), pp. 64–65.

[6] "Shift in Trade Policy Unlikely Despite Nakasone's Big Win," *Insight*, August 4, 1986, p. 32.

[7] "The History of Protectionism Proves the Value of Free Trade," *Insight*, June 30, 1986, p. 14.

[8] Colin Thubron, *The Ancient Mariners*, Time-Life Books, Alexandria, Virginia, 1981.

[9] Paul A. Samuelson & William D. Nordhaus, *Economics*, 12th ed. (New York: McGraw-Hill, 1985), pp. 843, 884–88.

[10] Kenneth Labich, "America's International Winners," pp. 34–35.

[11] Bob Masterson & Bob Murphy, "Internal Cross-cultural Management," *Training and Development Journal*, April 1986, p. 60.

[12] Anthony J. Yudis, "Swedish-Made Homes Rising on N.E. Lots," *Boston Globe*, July 26, 1986, p. 37.

[13] The Coca Cola Company, *1985 Annual Report* (Atlanta, 1986), p. 15.

[14] Milton Moskowitz, et al., eds., *Everybody's Business, op. cit.*, pp. 550–51.

[15] "Corporate Odd Couples," *Business Week*, July 21, 1986, p. 100.

[16] Pearce, *Dictionary of Economics*, p. 299.

[17] See generally Fernand Braudel, *The Perspective of the World* (New York: Harper & Row, 1984).

[18] "The World's 100 Largest Public Companies, *The Wall Street Journal*, September 29, 1986.

[19] Moskowitz, et al., *Everybody's Business*, pp. 825–29.

GLOSSARY

A

Absolute advantage The type of economic advantage that exists when one country can produce a product more efficiently than any other country.

Acceptance An offeree's agreement to the terms of the offer.

Account A record of the increases, decreases, and balance of an item reported in financial statements.

Accountability The mechanism that managers use to hold subordinates answerable for how they use delegated authority.

Accountants Persons who provide accounting services and help others understand what the numbers mean.

Accounting The process of recording financial information, interpreting it, and communicating it.

Accounting cycle The five steps in the process that takes a transaction from being mere raw data to its being summarized in the financial statements.

Accounting equation A formula written as follows:
Assets = Liabilities + Owners' Equity

Accounting period Any regular period of one year or less for which a business decides to have financial statements prepared.

Accounting system A business's system of reporting financial data.

Accounts payable Primarily debts owed suppliers of goods and services that are due during the next accounting period.

Accounts receivable Any amounts owed to an organization by its customers or clients.

Accrual basis The bookkeeping system that lists sales on the dates they are incurred, regardless of whether any money actually changed hands.

Accrued expenses A category that lumps together various kinds of obligations that were incurred during the accounting period but are not yet actually due or owing.

Achievement test A test that measures what a candidate can do and whether the candidate has the knowledge or skill necessary in a certain position.

Acquisition The purchase, by a conglomerate, in particular, of other companies.

Actual cash value The purchase price of an item of personal property less its depreciation.

Administered marketing system An arrangement in which one channel member dominates all the others in its channel or channels.

Administrative expenses or **general expenses** The overall costs of operating a firm, excluding selling expenses and the cost of goods sold.

Administrative regulations Legally binding requirements designed by a government agency to accomplish the purposes of a specific statute.

Advertising "Any paid form of nonpersonal presentation and promotion of ideas, goods, or services by an identified sponsor" (American Marketing Association).

Advertising media The means of communication used by major advertisers, including newspapers, direct mail, radio, television, magazines, and outdoor advertising.

Affirm For an appellate court to approve a trial court's judgment.

Affirmative action programs These programs consist of written plans to hire, train, and promote minority workers and women.

Agency The relationship between the principal and the agent, which is always voluntary.

Agency shop One in which employees may choose not to join the union.

Agent One individual who represents another.

Agent (broker) An intermediary who receives a commission for bringing together buyers and sellers for the purpose of negotiating an exchange but never takes title to property.

Alien corporation An American corporation that does business in a foreign country.

Allowances Price reductions granted if merchandise is slightly damaged or defective.

Altruism An unselfish concern for others' well-being.

American Federation of Labor (AFL) An umbrella organization for craft unions.

Amortization A process much like depreciation, in which accountants show the decline in value over time of an intangible asset with a limited life.

Antidiscrimination laws Federal, state, and local laws that forbid treating people differently — particularly in employment and housing — because of their not being the "right" religion, color, sex, race, age, or national origin.

Appeal To ask a higher court to review the record of a case for errors in the trial court's interpretation and application of law.

Appellant A person who appeals an adverse judgment by a court.

Aptitude test A test that measures whether a person has the "capacity or latent ability to learn a given job if given adequate training."

Arbitration A procedure in which the parties agree to submit a dispute to a third party and to be bound by that party's decision.

Arbitrator A neutral party who makes a decision binding on the parties who submitted the matter.

Arithmetic-logic unit (ALU) That part of the CPU that handles arithmetic computations.

Assembly language Mnemonic instructions or memory codes that are more comprehensible to humans than machine language.

Assessment center A personnel unit that carries out "a process in which individuals have the opportunity to participate

in a series of situations which resemble what they might be called on to do in an actual job."

Assets An organization's economic resources; everything of value it owns.

Assign To transfer ownership rights to collateral.

Association A voluntary organization of people with a common interest.

Atmospherics The variables that go into designing retail stores.

Atomized corporation A company that consists of smaller, task-oriented organizations subject to more local control but connected to the parent organization by computerized links and by culture.

Attrition The normal loss of employees from retirement, job changes, death, and the like.

Audit A formal examination of a firm's financial records.

Authority The power granted by an organization to control the use of its resources, direct the actions of others, act on the organization's behalf, or perform all of these functions.

Authorization cards Forms signed by employees that either authorize the union to represent them or to request a representation election, or both.

Automated teller machine (ATM) card A form of debit card that allows the card holder to make certain bank transactions with a machine instead of having to see a teller.

Automatic updating (of an MIS) The process that occurs when computer hardware and software interact to make changes to the data as new data become available.

Automation Originally, the substitution of mechanical for human labor. Now also includes the replacement of human sensory applications.

Automobile insurance The type of insurance that protects an insured from property and liability losses arising from the ownership or operation of motor vehicles.

Auxiliary storage devices Units in a computer system that supplement the main memory storage.

Average or **arithmetic mean** The total number of observation values divided by the number of occurrences of them.

B

Balanced funds Those funds that seek to provide modest income and growth from a generally conservative portfolio.

Balance of payments The measure of the relationship between payments coming into and going out of a country during a particular period.

Balance of trade The relationship between the value of goods imported and goods exported during a particular period.

Balance sheet or **statement of financial position** A summary of an organization's financial status at the end of an accounting period.

Bankrupt The person or business in a bankruptcy proceeding.

Bar chart A type of visual display that presents a comparison of several values at a stationary point in time.

Bargaining unit A group of employees who share common interests in wages and working conditions and have common skills.

Barter Trading goods for goods or services for services rather than for money.

Base pay The basic wages or salaries that workers receive.

Base wage rate The minimum paid per hour to any worker in the bargaining unit; the basis upon which everything else is calculated.

Batch mode The computer mode in which the software runs from the operating system just like a utility program. The batch program will ordinarily run without more than initial human intervention.

Batch processing or **intermittent processing** The production-to-stock process that generates lower quantities of goods than a mass-production system.

Batch system The manual updating of data collected and then stored in a batch until time to process them.

Beginning inventory The stock carried over from the prior accounting period.

Behavioral variables Lifestyle, personality, product-usage rate, and loyalty; one of the four classifications under *market segmentation*.

Beneficiary The person or organization named to receive the proceeds from a life insurance policy.

Benefits Services that employees receive that are paid for by the employer, like health insurance, pensions, and vacations.

Benefit variables Economy, convenience, and prestige; one of the four classifications under *market segmentation*.

Binary or **base two notation** The form in which numbers are expressed in the main memory.

Binary digit or **bit** Each digit in a binary number, either a 0 or a 1.

Blank indorsement An indorsement that does not name a specific indorsee.

Board of directors A group of individuals elected by the shareholders to oversee the operation of corporation.

Bond A long-term promise by a municipality to pay interest and repay the principal on a loan.

Bonus A payment beyond the employees' base pay or commissions.

Bookkeeper A clerical employee who records day-to-day business transactions.

Books The journal, ledger, and other accounting records.

Book value The value of a company's net worth as represented by a common share.

Booting The process of having a small program written in machine language load the operating system software into a computer's memory from a disk drive or magnetic tape, said to "pull the operating system up by its bootstraps."

Boycott An agreement among competitors not to sell to or buy from a particular entity; a per se violation of the Sherman Act.

Brand A name, term, symbol, design, or any combination of these elements used to identify a specific product and distinguish it from its competition.

Brand name That part of a brand that can be spoken.

Brand symbol A graphic portrayal of an element that identifies a product or firm.

Breakeven analysis A method used to determine the demand or sales volume required at a given price for a firm to break even.

Briefs Written arguments.

Broker Someone who may be called an account executive or registered representative who works for a brokerage firm or a broker-dealer.

Budget An organization's financial plan for the future in which it describes how it will use its resources to meet its goals.

Budgets Financial plans for the future, detailed projections of income and expenses over a specified period.

Bureaucracy Another term to describe the administrative structure of a departmentalized, hierarchical organization.

Bureaucrat Someone who works in a bureaucracy.

Burglary Theft from a building, involving forcible entry into it.

Business ethics   The study of the moral problems that confront members of business organizations and others who engage in business transactions.

Business interruption insurance   A form of income insurance that protects a firm against lost earnings as the result of a fire or similar peril.

Business plan   A meticulous step-by-step statement of the rationale for a business and how it will achieve its goals.

Business representative or **business agent**   A person employed by a union to represent it in matters with management.

Business unionism   The philosophy which emphasizes that American unions exist primarily for the economic improvement of workers, not to engage in a class struggle to alter the American form of government or to promote socialism.

Bylaws   Rules adopted for a corporation's internal operations.

Byte   Eight bits of memory.

C

Call feature   A provision allowing a company to redeem an indenture.

Capacity   The rate at which an operation can produce output over a given period.

Capital   Assets that are exchanged for an ownership interest in a business; also the factor of production that includes the property, plant, and equipment required to produce goods. In the context of a credit application, the financial resources that a borrower has available to assure the lender that the credit is secure.

Capital contribution   A partner's investment, whether in cash or property, in the business.

Captioned photographs   Photos of a new product, a corporate officer, or something else of interest, accompanied by a brief description explaining the picture.

Carriers   Firms that offer transportation services.

Carrying costs   Expenses incurred because an item is held in inventory.

Case studies   Training devices that require students to evaluate situations that have actually occurred in business organizations.

Cash   Both money on hand, say in the cash box, and money in bank *demand accounts*.

Cash basis   The bookkeeping system that lists sales and expenses according to the dates when money changes hands.

Cash discounts   A discount allowed customers if they pay their bills promptly.

Cash dividends   Dividends voted by the directors to be paid by the company to its shareholders.

Cash flow   The movement of money into and out of a firm.

Cash value or **surrender value**   The accumulation and interest an insurance policy earns.

Catalog showroom   A special type of discount store in which only one unit of each product the store carries is on display. The customer selects the product he or she wants and it is brought to a pickup area from an adjacent warehouse.

Caveat emptor   A Latin phrase meaning "let the buyer beware."

Census   A survey of an entire population.

Central bank   The government agency responsible for acting as a government's bank, managing its monetary policy, serving as the primary bank of the banking system, and overseeing the nation's international financial relationships.

Centralization   An organizational arrangement in which all decisions are passed along to top management before being implemented.

Central processing unit (CPU)   A computer system's brains, the place where data processing actually occurs.

Certificate of incorporation or **corporate charter**   A document that a secretary of state issues certifying that a corporation has come into existence and is authorized to do business.

Certificates of deposit (CDs)   Time deposits evidenced by promissory notes issued by a bank.

Certified management accountant   A management accountant who has passed the National Association of Accountants' test and satisfied its educational and professional criteria.

Certified public accountant (CPA)   An accountant who has passed an examination prepared by the American Institute of Certified Public Accountants (AICPA) and satisfied a state's educational and experience requirements.

Chain of command   The organizational design to ensure the flow of communications toward authority, equals, and subordinates.

Chain stores   Groups of retail outlets under common (usually corporate) ownership and management.

Channels of distribution   A group of intermediaries or middlemen that direct products to customers.

Character The reputation for honesty and integrity of the person or organization seeking credit.

Chief steward An elected union official for the employee's department or plant who represents the members in grievances and oversees the execution of the collective bargaining agreement.

Civil law All law that is not classified as criminal law.

Civil Rights Act of 1964 Commonly referred to as *Title VII*, after its key section. That part declares it to be illegal to discriminate in employment against any individual in respect to his or her compensation, terms and conditions or privileges of employment because of that individual's race, color, religion, sex, or national origin.

Clayton Act The 1914 act that broadened the scope of the Sherman Act by trying to prevent anticompetitive behavior rather than by dealing with its consequences.

Closed shop One that requires workers to belong to the union before they can be hired.

Closely held corporation A firm with fifty or fewer shareholders.

Closing the sale Asking the prospect to buy the product.

Clutter Anything broadcast in television that is not part of a program.

Coinsurance A clause in many fire policies that requires a policyholder to pay a portion of any loss to the insured building if the policy maximum is less than a specified percentage (usually 80 percent) of the building's value at the time of the loss.

Collateral The security for a loan — usually an asset with enough value that it could be sold to satisfy the obligation.

Collection procedures A system used to collect past-due accounts.

Collective bargaining Negotiation of the terms and conditions of employment between management and an organization representing its employees.

Commercial bank A type of bank that originally served primarily business customers but now offers much broader services.

Commercial credit Credit designed to be used for business purposes.

Commercial finance company A nondepository financial intermediary that makes business loans.

Commercial paper Unsecured promissory notes issued by a corporation that mature in from 3 to 270 days.

Commission basis Either a fixed amount or a percentage of the value of the sales that sales employees make.

Commissions Fees that brokers charge on the transactions they facilitate.

Commitment fee The fee that a bank will charge to guarantee a revolving credit agreement.

Commodities Basic resources and agricultural products such as gold, wheat, silver, cotton, pork bellies, and orange juice.

Commodities contracts Commitments to buy a quantity of a commodity at a particular time.

Common carrier A firm that offers transportation services to the public.

Common law A body of legal principles developed over centuries by judges in deciding cases.

Communism A classless, propertyless society based on the slogan "From each according to his ability, to each according to his need."

Comparative advantage The ability to produce a product at a lower cost than a competitor can.

Compensating balance An amount that a firm must keep on deposit with a financial institution during the term of a loan or the period covered by a line of credit.

Compensation The money or benefits or both for which an employee exchanges work.

Competition The situation that occurs when two or more businesses offering similar goods or services go after the same customers.

Competition-based pricing Pricing based on competitive price levels.

Computer-integrated manufacturing (CIM) A manufacturing system that, linked with computer-assisted design and computer-assisted manufacturing (CAD/CAM), manages data flow while directing the movement and processing of materials.

Computer system A mechanical means of transforming data into information consisting of hardware (computer machinery) and software (the commands that make the machinery run).

Concentrated marketing A single strategy aimed at one specific market segment.

Conceptual skills The ability to understand all the organization's activities, how its various parts fit together, and how the organization relates to others.

Conditions The current economic environment and the ways in which it might affect a particular borrower's ability to repay an obligation.

Conglomerate A corporation that owns several other corporations that are in different industries.

Conglomerate merger A merger that involves the acquisition of companies in different markets.

Congress of Industrial Organizations (CIO) An umbrella organization for industrial unions.

Consent election A representation election agreed on by union and management.

Consideration Something of legal value that each party agrees to exchange.

Consultative selling The concept that holds that a customer is a person to be served, not a prospect to be sold.

Consumer credit The credit extended to individuals for non-business personal, family, or household purposes.

Consumer finance company A nondepository financial intermediary that lends to individuals.

Consumer Price Index The government's monthly measure of the inflation level for goods and services.

Consumer products Goods and services purchased in the consumer market.

Consumer-oriented layout An operational layout designed to make easy the customer's interactions with the firm's services.

Continuous-flow system or **continuous-process system** The production-to-stock process that produces large quantities of a single standardized product.

Contract An agreement between two or more parties that the law will enforce.

Contract carrier A carrier that provides service to one shipper or a limited number of shippers.

Contractual capacity A function that a party is said to be able to perform if he or she has the ability to understand the nature of a contract.

Contractual vertical-marketing system A contractual relationship formalizing the dominance of the channel leader.

Contributions Monies accumulated from employees or employers or both and invested to pay retirees a pension.

Control The process of measuring an organization's performance against its plans to make certain that the actual operations conform with the plans.

Controller The corporate officer who reports to the vice president of finance and has responsibility for accounting, data processing, and taxes.

Controlling The process of measuring an organization's performance against its plans to determine whether operations conform to its expectations.

Control unit The main part of the CPU, which tells the computer what to do and where to find or put data.

Convenience goods Products consumers purchase frequently, generally at low prices, and for which they are willing to spend only a minimum of effort in completing the exchange.

Convenience store A food store of considerably smaller size than supermarkets that offers a limited range of staples and snack foods at prices considerably higher than those at supermarkets.

Conversion The use of a person's property inconsistent with that person's ownership rights.

Convertible preferred stock Preferred stock whose indenture includes the right to convert a share into some number of common shares.

Cooperative A corporation or association formed to perform services so that its owners or members can make a profit — but without making any profit itself.

Co-owner Joint owner, not equal owner.

Copyright A monopoly granted by the federal government on the exploitation of literary or artistic works.

Corporate bond A long-term obligation to pay, usually represented by a certificate of indebtedness.

Corporate culture A system of informal rules that spells out how people are to behave most of the time.

Corporate officers Officials elected by a board of directors; a president, one or more vice presidents as specified in the bylaws, a secretary, and a treasurer.

Corporate vertical-marketing system An arrangement in which companies perform all the channel functions themselves.

Corporation A form of business organization authorized by state law that comes into existence when the secretary of state issues a certificate of incorporation.

Correlation analysis A statistical technique to measure the association between two or more variables. It helps managers identify the factors that can be used to predict fluctuations in one variable when changes in another are known.

Cosign To guarantee a loan.

Cosmetic change   An alteration in a product that has little or no effect on its basic function.

Cost of goods available for sale   The total of beginning inventory plus net purchases.

Cost of goods sold   The amount that an organization spent to buy or produce the goods it sold during an accounting period.

Cost of living adjustments (COLAs)   Charges to the base wage rate, up to an established maximum, to reflect increases in the inflation rate for the preceding quarter or year.

Cost-based pricing   An approach to pricing that starts with production or purchasing costs to establish a *markup* that is added on.

Council bargaining   The collective bargaining process in which several locals join to negotiate together.

Coupon   A device that allows customers to pay a lower price for goods.

Coupon rate   A specified rate of interest.

Coventurers   The parties in a joint venture.

Credit   The ability of a business or a person to obtain money or property and to defer payment or repayment because the lender makes a favorable appraisal of the debtor's ability to repay; also a bookkeeping entry on the right side.

Credit bureaus   Businesses that keep records on the credit and payment practices of individuals and firms.

Credit card   A card, usually made of plastic, which may represent two types of agreements, either between the card issuer and the merchant that the merchant will honor the card and the issuer will pay the charge slips, or between the card issuer and the card holder that the issuer will extend a certain amount of credit to the holder and that the holder will make payments in accordance with the contract.

Credit insurance   Insurance paid for by a borrower which compensates a lender for any losses if the borrower defaults.

Creditors' committee   All of the bankrupt's creditors called together by the court to review the bankrupt's documentation of his or her debts and assets and to elect a permanent trustee in bankruptcy.

Credit union   A nonprofit savings-and-loan organization operated specifically for the benefit of its members, all of whom must have some common link.

Criminal laws   Statutes that specify the duties owed to society and that prescribe penalties like fines, imprisonment, or loss of life for violating them.

Critical path   The path with the longest total time from start to finish.

CRT   The computer monitor screen that has cathode ray tubes and so is thus abbreviated.

Cumulative   The specification in an indenture that a company must pay all preferred dividends for past periods before paying any common stock dividends.

Currency   Refers only to coins and bills, but may also include more generally a nation's money.

Current assets   Cash and any other assets that are likely to be used up or be converted into cash, usually within a year.

Current liabilities   Debts that will fall due within the next twelve months.

Cursor   A mobile spot on a CRT screen that is directed to choices on a menu.

Customer orientation   Basing a firm's marketing decisions on its customers' wants.

Customer satisfaction   The goal of firms that try to remove all potential dissatisfaction that might be associated with what they sell.

Cyclical fluctuation   Business-cycle movement over periods ranging from two to fifteen years.

D

Damages   Money paid to an injured party to compensate for the injury.

Data (singular, **datum**)   Numbers, letters, facts, and figures that usually come from measurements or observations but have little or no meaning by themselves.

Data processing   The functions that a computer performs on data.

Debenture   An unsecured bond.

Debit   An entry on the left side of an account. A bookkeeper debits an account by making an entry on the left side of an account.

Debit card   A machine-readable plastic card that creates a receipt authorizing a bank to transfer funds immediately from the debit card holder's account to the business presenting the receipt.

Debt   Borrowed money.

Debt financing   The lending of money at interest.

Decentralization   An arrangement in which decisions are pushed down the organization to the level where the functional expertise lies.

Decision A choice of actions by means of which a manager seeks to achieve the organization's goals.

Decision support system (DSS) A computer system that permits managers to call up whatever specific information they need whenever they need it.

Decline stage This phase of the product life cycle begins when sales begin to decrease and normally ends when the firm abandons the product.

Defendant The party against whom a lawsuit is brought.

Delegate To assign authority and responsibility for day-to-day management.

Delegation The assignment of authority to perform a duty.

Demand The willingness of purchasers to buy specific quantities of a good or service at a particular price at a particular time.

Demand curve A graphed line reflecting a relationship between the price of goods and the quantities demanded.

Demand deposit An individual or business account from which depositors can withdraw funds at any time without prior notice to the bank.

Demographic variables Age, sex, family size, income, occupation, education, religion, race, nationality, and social class; one of the four classifications under *market segmentation.*

Departmentalization The arranging of divided tasks into meaningful groups.

Departmentalization by customer The process of arranging employees according to the particular group of customers they serve.

Departmentalization by function The process in which tasks are grouped according to the basic business functions with which they are associated.

Departmentalization by location The process of arranging employees into groups according to the physical location of where they work.

Departmentalization by product or service The process in which tasks are grouped according to the product or service with which they are involved.

Department store A retail outlet that carries a diverse assortment of merchandise grouped into departments.

Deposit First, currency, checks, or drafts given to a financial institution for crediting to a customer's account; second, a synonym for *account.*

Depositor A person or business in whose name funds have been put in a bank.

Depository institution A financial intermediary that accepts deposits.

Depreciation The process of distributing the original value of a long-term asset over the years of its useful life.

Deregulation Originally, the stripping away of regulations restricting competition in entire industries, particularly railroads, airlines, and trucking. Now also nonregulation, the elimination or avoidance of regulation, particularly in the environmental, health, and safety areas.

Derived demand Products the demand for which is created by the demand for other products, as car radios and cars.

Descriptive statistics The type of statistics that portrays the characteristics of a usually large set of data.

Detail salespeople or **missionary salespeople** Sales staff who develop good will and stimulate demand for the manufacturer's products in target markets.

Devaluation The arbitrary downward adjustment of one country's currency in terms of another country's.

Development "Learning activities that increase the competence and ability of employees to progress with the organization as it changes and grows."

Differentiated marketing Individualized appeals aimed at particular market segments.

Directing The process of guiding, leading, persuading, influencing, and motivating people to accomplish an organization's objectives.

Direct inventory In manufacturing, raw materials, work in process, and finished products. In retail and service operations, all goods bought for resale.

Direct-mail advertising Any advertising sent through the mail directly to a target market.

Disability income insurance A type of insurance that replaces income lost as a result of an illness or injury.

Discharge or **termination** A permanent separation initiated by the employer, usually for a cause, such as absenteeism or poor job performance.

Disclaimer A refusal to make a warranty.

Discount brokers Those brokers who charge the lowest commissions, because they merely execute their customers' instructions.

Discounting The sale of a promissory note to a bank for the amount of the note less a discount for the bank's services.

Discount rate The amount the Federal Reserve charges on loans to all banks subject to its reserve requirements. It in effect establishes a floor for interest rates charged by banks.

Discount store A retail outlet that competes primarily on the basis of price.

Discretionary income More income than what is required to obtain the necessities of life.

Discretionary order An order that puts the decision about whether to act or to wait into the broker's hands.

Display advertising Product exhibits in places like airports and civic centers.

Dispute-resolution system The structure that society has established for resolving differences.

Disseminator A person who spreads information.

Dissolution An act, like dying or saying "I quit," which indicates that a partner has ended the partnership relationship.

Disturbance handler A manager who makes decisions to keep his or her group operating in the face of circumstances that are out of the ordinary.

Dividends That portion of a company's earnings that the board of directors votes to distribute to stockholders on a per-share basis in either cash or stock.

Domestic content legislation Federal regulations that would require a certain percentage of, say, a car's parts to be made in this country.

Domestic corporation The term for a corporation in the state in which it receives its articles of incorporation.

Double-entry bookkeeping A system of recording business transactions in which each transaction is recorded in at least two separate accounts.

Doubtful accounts Accounts receivable that appear uncollectable.

E

Economics The study of how individuals and society choose to employ resources that could have other uses in order to produce goods or services and also an analysis of how to distribute those goods and services for consumption to the various groups of people within the society.

Economic strike A strike called because of failure to reach agreement on wages and benefits.

Economic system How a society produces and distributes goods and services.

Education Learning activities that prepare an employee for a higher position in the organization.

Electronic funds transfer (EFT) The process of transferring funds between distant parties directly by computer.

Embargo A law or government order forbidding either the importing or exporting of certain specified goods.

Emotional buying motives The wish for social approval, a desire to be different, and a need to be free of fear.

Employ To put to work.

Employee A general term for anyone who works for a business but does not own it; a technical term for a person who works for a business but does not have authority to make contracts on behalf of the business.

Employee Retirement Income Security Act (ERISA) The 1974 federal rules designed to correct serious abuses in private pension plans.

Employment process The procedure by which a firm matches its hiring needs with the available human resources.

Employment tests Standardized tests of various types designed to help an employer predict whether a job applicant will perform successfully.

Enlightened self-interest The conscious policy of pursuing long-term rather than short-term interests.

Entrepreneur A person who organizes, operates, and assumes the risk of a business venture in the hope of making a profit.

Entrepreneurship The capacity for innovation, investment, and expansion in new markets, products, and techniques.

Environmental analysis A study of conditions in the marketplace and the world that might affect an organization.

Equal Employment Opportunity Act The 1972 amendment by Congress of Title VII of the Civil Rights Act.

Equal Employment Opportunity Commission (EEOC) The federal agency that enforces the employment-related aspects of the antidiscrimination laws. This independent board consists of five members appointed by the president.

Equilibrium The point at which demand and supply are in balance. It is there that the intentions of the seller and buyers coincide.

Equipment Machinery and tools as fixed assets.

Equity Ownership interest, as in a home or life insurance policy.

Esteem How a person is regarded by others and by himself or herself.

Ethics The study of moral, as contrasted with legal, obligations.

Ethnocentrism The belief in the superiority of one's own race or culture.

Event The finishing of a major activity required to complete a project.

Exchange process The transfer of money or its equivalent for goods, services, or labor.

Exchange rate The value of a currency expressed in terms of another currency.

Exchanges The actual markets where stocks and bonds are traded.

Excise taxes Federal taxes that have the effect of raising the prices of liquor, jewelry, and cigarettes.

Exclusive-dealing arrangement The anticompetitive agreement of one party to sell all its output of a certain product to the other party, or to buy all it requires of a product from that party, in exchange for that party's promise not to engage in similar transactions.

Exclusive distribution strategy The distribution system that relies on a single retail outlet or a very few outlets in a given market area.

Ex-dividend Sale of shares without the dividend.

Export A good or service that is produced in one country and sold for consumption in another.

Express warranty An oral or written promise that the seller makes to the buyer.

External motivators Usually rewards or other types of positive reinforcement provided to someone by another person.

F

Facilitating agent A person or firm, like a warehouse or a freight carrier, that does not take title to goods but assists in distributing them.

Factfinding The process by which an outside factfinder narrows the issues that are before the negotiating parties.

Factor A firm that buys up another's accounts receivable, then owns and collects the debts.

Factoring The selling of a firm's accounts receivable to another firm.

Factors of production The three ways in which people can make money from their property.

Fair Labor Standards Act Also known as the minimum wage law or the wages and hours law.

False arrest The wrongful confinement or restraint of freedom of movement of someone.

Family brand or **blanket brand strategy** A branding approach based on the use of one brand name for all of a firm's products.

Featherbedding The requiring of more workers than needed to do a job.

Feature article A manuscript longer than a news release (sometimes exceeding three thousand words), which the firm usually has prepared for a specific publication.

Federal Deposit Insurance Corporation (FDIC) A corporation established by the Banking Act of 1933 to insure all members of the Federal Reserve System against loss if the institutions should fail.

Federal Open Market Committee The twelve-member committee consisting of the board of governors, the president of the New York Federal Reserve Bank, and the presidents of four other Federal Reserve Banks, that directs the Federal Reserve System's buying and selling of U.S. government securities on the open market, to increase or decrease the funds available for lending by member banks.

Federal Reserve Banks The twelve national banks that are responsible for the smooth daily operation of the financial system.

Federal Reserve Notes The nation's currency.

Federal Reserve System The United States' central bank.

Federal Savings and Loan Insurance Corporation (FSLIC) A corporation established by federal law to insure the deposits of thrift institutions.

Federal Trade Commission (FTC) The federal commission with extremely broad authority to police the marketplace.

Federal Trade Commission Act The 1914 act that created the Federal Trade Commission (FTC).

Fidelity bonds The type of bonds purchased by businesses that wish to insure themselves against theft by employees.

Fiduciary duties or **duties of trust** The unique responsibilities that apply to a person who acts on another's behalf.

Field salespeople (for a manufacturer) Usually handle well-established products that require a minimum of creative selling and technical knowledge.

FIFO (First In, First Out) An accounting system which assumes that the first items brought into inventory are also the first sold.

Figurehead role An interpersonal managerial role in which the manager engages in symbolic activities.

Financial intermediaries Institutions that take in funds, then loan them out at a price (an interest rate) sufficient to reward the suppliers and make a profit for the intermediary.

Financial management   The process of obtaining money and using it effectively to achieve an organization's goals.

Financial ratios   Certain mathematical relationships between numbers.

Financial resources   Intangible personal property that may with more or less difficulty be converted into cash.

Financial statements   An organization's report of its financial condition, which usually takes the form of balance sheets, income statements, and statements of changes in financial position.

Fire insurance   The type of insurance that protects the insured from losses to the covered property caused by fire and often other perils such as hail and windstorms.

Fixed assets   Those assets that an organization will use for more than one year.

Fixed costs   Expenses that do not vary with the level of production.

Fixed-position layout   An operational arrangement in which workers and equipment come to the product.

Fixtures   Personal property that becomes permanently attached to real property.

Flexible-benefit programs (also known as **cafeteria-style benefit programs)**   Plans that permit employees to choose from an array of benefit programs, up to a preset limit.

Flexitime   The policy of replacing traditional fixed work hours with a more flexible schedule set by employees within the company's guidelines.

Floor broker   A member of a brokerage firm who is on the floor of the exchange and whose job it is to execute customers' orders.

Foreign corporation   The term for a corporation outside the state in which it receives its articles of incorporation.

Foreign Corrupt Practices Act   The federal regulation that forbids the bribing of foreign officials by U.S. companies or their employees to obtain favorable treatment.

Foreign trade   Trade between partners of different nationalities.

Formal group   An element of the organization that exists within an organization because of management's decision to create it to perform certain tasks.

For-profit corporation   A corporation created to make profits for its owners.

Franchise   A license to sell another's products or to use another's name in business, or both.

Franchisee   The person who buys a franchise.

Franchiser   The company that sells a franchise.

Franchise tax   A state fee for the privilege of doing business as a corporation.

Fraud   An intentional misrepresentation of the truth to convince someone to give up something of value.

Free-enterprise or **free-market system**   The economic system based on the ideal of privately owned businesses competing freely; an economy based on the principle of voluntary association and exchange.

Freight forwarder   A common carrier that will often lease space from other carriers and combine small individual shipments into economical lot sizes.

Frequency distribution   A statistical summarizing of data by reducing the size of the listing or the number of items in the data set.

Full-service brokers   Those brokers who charge the highest commissions, because they provide advice, reports, research and analysis, portfolio management, and other services.

Full-service wholesalers   The type of wholesaling that offers the widest variety of services to its customers, including maintaining inventories, promotional activities, gathering and interpreting market information, extending credit, and distributing goods.

Functional organization   A system in which the various functions involved in supervising a worker are divided into separate tasks performed by specialists.

G

General agent   A person hired by a principal to conduct a series of transactions over time.

General Agreement on Tariffs and Trade (GATT)   The 1947 agreement between the United States and twenty-two other nations which established an international mechanism for mutual adjustments of trade barriers and regulations.

General partnership   The usual form of partnership, an ongoing business involved in a series of transactions.

Generic term   One that has passed into common, everyday language.

Geographic variables   Regions, counties, cities, and climate areas; one of the four classifications under *market segmentation*.

Gigabyte (G)   A quantity of 1,024 M, or about a billion bytes of computer memory.

Givebacks   A union's foregoing of wages or benefits or working conditions won in earlier bargaining.

Goal   A condition a manager wishes to achieve in the end.

Going rate   The average pay for a particular position among comparable firms.

Good   A tangible item of personal property.

Goods   Personal property that is both tangible and movable.

Goodwill   A firm's extra earning power compared to other firms in the same industry.

Government bonds   The debt certificates issued by federal, state, and local governments and their agencies.

Grading   The assignment of "predetermined standards of quality classifications to individual units or lots of a commodity" (as defined by the American Marketing Association).

Graph   A type of visual display that indicates upward and downward movement of the values of a variable over a specified period.

Grievance   An employee complaint about wages, hours, working conditions, or disciplinary action for which the collective bargaining agreement provides a procedure to resolve it.

Grievance committee   A union committee that meets with management to resolve matters relating to the contract that the stewards are unable to resolve.

Gross national product (GNP)   The current market value of all final goods and services that a nation produces within a particular period.

Gross profit or **gross margin**   Net sales less the cost of goods sold.

Gross sales   The total value of all goods or services sold during the accounting period.

Group health insurance   The health insurance that employers provide, sold to employees collectively.

Growth   The measure of increase in the value of an investment.

Growth funds   Those funds that offer limited dividends and invest in more speculative stocks.

Growth stage   This stage begins when sales start to increase rapidly and ends when sales begin to level off.

H

Hardware   The electronic and mechanical components of a computer system.

Health insurance   The type of insurance that reimburses expenses arising from illness or accident.

Health maintenance organization (HMO)   A prepaid healthcare provider that operates clinics and, in some cases, hospitals.

Hear   To decide a case.

High technology   A broad term for the new and innovative types of businesses that depend heavily on advanced scientific and engineering knowledge.

Homeowner's insurance   Fire policies for the home, often covering apartments as well as houses.

Horizontal market allocation   The division of a market among independent competitors; a per se violation of the Sherman Act.

Horizontal merger   A merger that occurs when two competitors merge.

Hospitalization coverage   Insurance covering all expenses of being in a hospital except doctors' charges.

Human relations   All the types of interactions among people: conflicts, cooperative efforts, and group relationships.

Human resource development   The activities involved in acquiring, developing, and using people effectively in a business.

Human resource planning   The systematic process of forecasting the future demand for employees and estimating the supply available to meet that demand.

Human resources   Those people who actually make the organization's product or provide its service, as well as its other employees, outside vendors, and suppliers.

Human skills   The ability to work with and for people, to communicate with others, and to understand others' needs.

I

Idea   A concept, a philosophy, an image, or an issue.

Ideology   A set of aspirations or ideals on how society should run.

Implied warranty   A warranty imposed by Article 2 of the Uniform Commercial Code rather than being created by a seller's representations.

Import   A good or service consumed in one country that was bought in another.

Import quota   A limit on the quantity of a particular good that can be brought into a country.

Incentive rate formulas   Pay increments awarded for increased productivity.

Incentives Bonuses and other plans designed to encourage employees to produce work beyond the minimum acceptable levels.

Incentive systems Compensation systems that pay employees according to their productivity.

Income funds Those funds that concentrate on a high-yield portfolio with limited growth and risk.

Income statement A summary of what an organization has earned and spent over a given period.

Incorporator Someone who signs and files two copies of proposed articles of incorporation with the secretary of state.

Indemnification The principle that requires an insurer to pay no more than the financial loss actually suffered.

Indenture A formal legal agreement between the issuer and the holder of a loan.

Independent bargaining The collective bargaining process in which the local negotiates for itself, without any help from the national or other local unions.

Independent retailer One store that is often a sole proprietorship or partnership.

Indirect inventory The supplies a business uses that are not purchased with the intention of reselling them.

Individual brand strategy A strategy that calls for a different brand name for each product.

Indorsee The person to whom an instrument is indorsed.

Indorsement A notation, usually on the back of an instrument.

Indorser A person who indorses an instrument.

Inducing breach of contract The act of convincing a person to violate an existing contractual duty.

Industrial products Goods used in the production of another good or service. Essentially, any product not for personal or household consumption.

Industrial unions Unions whose membership includes all the workers in an industry, regardless of the tasks they perform.

Inferential statistics The type of statistics usually used in market research to describe the behavior of a small group, from which the user may be able to predict the behavior of a larger group.

Informal group An element of an organization that develops naturally as a result of people within an organization interacting.

Information Data that have been extracted or summarized so that they have meaning to the person who will use them.

Information resources The knowledge and data necessary to the business, such as market research, legal advice, scientific or technical materials, and economic reports.

Information sector That portion of our economy that produces computers and related equipment and instructions.

Informative advertising Provides the consumer with product information and is generally used to build demand for new products or to let consumers know about improvements to mature products.

Infringement Violation of a brand name or symbol.

In-home retailer Someone who sells directly to customers in their homes.

Injunction A court order forbidding certain actions.

Inland marine insurance That type of insurance which covers cargo carried by every form of transportation not involving water.

Input The data put into a computer.

Input device That part of a computer system which transmits data from a source to the computer.

Insider information Information available only to persons who owe a fiduciary duty to a corporation's shareholders.

Insider Trading Act of 1984 The act that subjected those guilty of insider trading to forfeiture of up to three times their gain on the illegal trades and expanded the SEC's powers to investigate such trading.

Inside salespeople Sales personnel who rely almost totally on telephone orders and usually follow a regular customer-contact schedule.

Institutional advertising Used to generate good will or to enhance a firm's image rather than to sell a specific product.

Instrument Something in writing.

Insurable interest An interest that can be protected under the law and under the terms of a policy.

Insurable risk A risk for which an insurance policy can be purchased.

Insurance A contract in which one party agrees to pay a specified sum to another if a certain event occurs.

Insurance policy A contract between the insurer and the insured.

Insured The person or firm that buys insurance.

Insurer Any organization that provides insurance coverage.

Intangible personal property Property that one cannot touch.

Integrated marketing The concept that marketing is the responsibility of everyone in a company because each employee can influence the firm's ability to gain and retain customers.

Intelligence tests Standardized tests that measure such general mental abilities as reasoning, comprehension, verbal fluency, memory, spatial relations, and numerical ability.

Intensive distribution strategy The distribution system in which a producer saturates the market to guarantee purchasers that the product will be available wherever they are.

Intent A voluntary act or omission that is reasonably likely to bring about a particular consequence.

Intentional tort An act for which the plaintiff does not have to prove a monetary loss in order to collect damages.

Interactive mode The more common computer mode, in which the software displays instructions called prompts to the user, which appear on either a CRT or other display device.

Interest tests Standardized tests that measure an individual's likes and dislikes.

Interlocking directorates The presence of the same individual on the boards of two companies.

Intermediaries, or **middlemen** Firms between the manufacturer and the ultimate user that take title or directly assist others to take title to goods.

Intermediate appellate court A court that hears appeals of trial-court decisions but that is not the supreme court of its jurisdiction.

Internal financing Money generated from cash flow or retained earnings.

Internal motivator An intrinsic reward that occurs when a duty or task is performed.

International trade Trade that involves the crossing of national boundaries.

Interpersonal roles The roles that primarily require a manager to deal with people.

Interview Private meeting of corporate officials or employees with the news media.

Inventory A general term to describe certain classes of goods that are assets of a business.

Inventory control A physical distribution activity whose purpose is to develop and maintain levels and assortments of products appropriate for a firm's target markets.

Investment Advisers Act of 1940 The act that requires those who advise investors, whether or not they actually handle investor funds, to register with the SEC.

Investment Company Act of 1940 The act that made mutual funds subject to SEC registration and reporting requirements.

Investments A means of using funds now in order to achieve financial goals in the future.

Issuer An entity with the power to authorize the sale and distribution of securities on its behalf.

J

Job analysis A systematic study of an employee's duties, tasks, and work environment.

Job description A written summary of the duties, tasks, and responsibilities associated with a job.

Job enlargement The adding to a worker's basic responsibilities of more responsibilities on the same skill and job level.

Job enrichment Programs whose major goal is to make routine jobs more challenging and interesting by giving employees more independence and responsibility.

Job rotation A system in which workers switch for a time from one job to another.

Job sharing A program in which two people share one job.

Job-shop processing or **job-order processing** The production-to-order process in which the producer makes a quantity of goods to the customer's satisfaction.

Job specification A listing of the key qualifications a person needs to perform a job successfully.

Joint venture An association of individuals for a limited, specific, for-profit business purpose.

Journal or **book of original entry** A chronological list of transactions each assigned to a particular account.

Jurisdiction The authority to hear trials.

Just-in-time inventory system A program designed to ensure a continuous flow of manufacturing input from suppliers while minimizing the amount of goods held in inventory.

K

Key person insurance The form of term life insurance that businesses buy to protect themselves against the loss of vital employees, particularly those in upper management or ones who have crucial scientific or engineering expertise.

Kilobyte (K) A standard measure of computer memory, each representing 1,000 bytes (actually, 1,024 bytes) of memory.

Knights of Labor The post–Civil War umbrella union that tried for the first time to organize all workers into one union.

L

L The largest classification of the money supply, which expands M_3 by including all the remaining liquid assets.

Label That part of the package or product that contains information.

Labeling The presentation of information on a package or product.

Labor The factor of production that is the work supplied by humans.

Labor theory of value The Marxist tenet which holds that labor is what gives value to goods and services and that labor therefore deserves to be rewarded for this production.

Laissez faire A French phrase meaning roughly "to let people do as they choose"; a term used to describe the concept of marketplace nonregulation.

Land The factor of production that includes real estate and all natural resources, including minerals, timber, and agricultural products.

Landrum-Griffin Act The 1959 Congressional act guaranteeing union members the right to vote in union elections, speak at union meetings, receive union financial reports, and be treated like other members.

Lapse For a policy to end.

Law of large numbers The mathematical law which holds that as the number of units in a group increases, predictions about the group become more accurate and therefore more certain.

Layoffs Separations caused by the employer's lack of work, which may become permanent.

Layout The physical arrangement of an operational facility.

Leadership The ongoing process of influencing others' behavior toward certain goals.

Lead time The period that elapses between the time of placing an order and its receipt.

Ledger A book or computer file in which each account appears separately.

Leverage The use of debt to improve the return on shareholders' equity.

Liabilities The amounts a firm owes to others.

Liability insurance Coverage against legal responsibility for another's losses.

Liability risk Risks that involve the potential that a firm might be held legally responsible for losses suffered by a person or another firm.

Liable Legally responsible.

Liaison A role in which the manager serves as a communications link between people and groups.

License In international business, a privilege to manufacture or sell a product in all or part of a country or to extract a natural resource from a particular location.

Life insurance Insurance that upon the death of the insured pays a set amount to the policy's beneficiary.

LIFO (Last In, First Out) An accounting system which assumes that the last items taken into inventory are the first sold.

Limit order An order specifying the maximum price acceptable to the investor.

Limited partner An investor in a limited partnership whose liability is limited to the amount he or she invests.

Limited partnership A form of business in which the general partners have essentially the same rights and liabilities as partners in a general partnership while the limited partners have virtually no management rights.

Limited pay life insurance The type of whole life insurance that allows premium payments to stop at some time before death.

Limited-service wholesalers A type of wholesalers who offer a narrower range of services than do full-service wholesalers and often tend to specialize.

Line authority The power to make decisions that directly affect a firm's output.

Line employees Everyone involved in actually producing or distributing what a firm sells.

Line managers Those responsible for line employees and through them the firm's productivity.

Line of credit An agreement that over a specified period a bank will lend up to a certain amount at a set rate of interest, as the borrower needs the funds.

Line organization The structure in which top management has total, direct control and each subordinate reports to a single supervisor.

Liquid asset An asset that can routinely be turned into cash at its market value within thirty days.

Liquidity   The capacity of an asset to be turned into currency.

Litigant   A person involved in a lawsuit.

Litigation   Lawsuits.

Local area network (LAN)   A network linking computers in a small geographical area or a particular building.

Lockout   The tactic that occurs when management puts economic pressure on a union by closing its doors to the unionized workers.

Long-term debt to equity   The financial ratio that measures the relationship between bonds and shareholders' equity.

Long-term financing   Money that will not be repaid for at least one year.

Long-term liabilities   Debts that will fall due more than a year after the date of the balance sheet.

M

M₁   The narrowest money measure, which includes primarily money held for the purpose of completing exchanges.

M₂   The second classification in the money supply, which expands M_1 by including time deposits.

M₃   The third division of the money supply, which expands M_2 by including large time deposits and investments in less liquid investment vehicles.

Machine language   A computer's native language, built into it. Machine language is in a binary format and is very difficult for humans to read.

Mail-order retailer   A retailer who issues a catalog from which consumers can choose items and place their orders by mail or telephone.

Mainframe computers   The workhorses of the computer industry, like the IBM 4381 and the Cyber 175.

Main memory   The part of a computer that holds data and programs while the computer is manipulating them.

Maintenance (or hygiene) factors   The elements that form the work environment. They take their name from Frederick Herzberg's view that keeping them in good order was necessary to avoid the discontent that would reduce everyday levels of performance.

Maintenance shop   A shop in which an employee who joins a union must remain in it only so long as he or she works in that bargaining unit.

Major medical expense coverage   The type of insurance that reimburses a broad range of losses associated with major or catastrophic illnesses or injuries.

Maloney Act of 1938   The act that authorized self-regulation of the OTC market.

Malpractice or **professional liability insurance**   That type of insurance which covers responsibility for losses arising out of professional services rendered by doctors, lawyers, accountants, and certain other professionals.

Management   The process of coordinating human, informational, physical, and financial resources to accomplish organizational goals.

Management by objectives (MBO)   An employee performance appraisal technique based on objectives established jointly by the employee and his or her supervisor.

Management information system (MIS)   A collection of tools that provides information to a manager to facilitate that person's decision-making processes.

Manager   A person who coordinates an organization's resources.

Managerial marketing system   The management information system that can develop answers to questions regarding customer profiles, product penetration, and sales effectiveness.

Managing partner   Someone who tends to have managerial skills and to whom is delegated the day-to-day management of the firm.

Manual updating (of an MIS)   The process that occurs when someone does something to alter the existing data, like transferring new data to the appropriate storage device or deleting affected entries.

Manufacturing   The management of the resources necessary to convert raw materials into finished goods.

Margin accounts   The credit arrangements that a broker makes to customers to allow them to buy securities.

Margin call   A brokerage's demand for additional collateral.

Margin requirements   The minimum amount that a purchaser of securities must deposit with a broker in order to be able to buy securities on credit.

Market   A group of people or firms who currently demand or might potentially require a product or service and who are, or might be, willing and able to pay for it.

Market allocation   An agreement to divide markets among potential competitors.

Market coverage   The number and types of outlets a producer wants for its product.

Market niche   The area in which a firm specializes or holds a special position.

Market order   An order at the market price.

Market price (of goods or services)   The point of equilibrium between supply and demand.

Market research   The systematic gathering and analyzing of data on a particular marketing problem.

Market segmentation   The division of a total market into smaller groups of consumers based on identifiable common characteristics called segmentation variables.

Market value   The current price that a willing buyer will pay a willing seller.

Marketable securities   Securities that can be easily converted into cash without being significantly discounted from market value.

Marketers   The people who work in marketing.

Marketing   The process of planning and executing the conception, pricing, promotion, and distribution of ideas, goods, and services to create exchanges that satisfy individual and organizational objectives.

Marketing concept   The idea that "the ultimate purpose of every business should be to satisfy the customer."

Marketing information systems (MIS)   A combination of people, equipment, and procedures organized to gather, process, and disperse information needed for making marketing decisions.

Marketing intermediaries (middlemen)   Firms between the manufacturer and the ultimate user or consumer that take title or directly assist others to take title to goods or that assist in physically moving or storing goods while they are in the channel.

Marketing mix   The combination of the Four P's in any strategy.

Marketplace   The forum where individuals and businesses exchange money for goods and services.

Markup   A predetermined percentage of a product's cost that is added to its cost to arrive at its selling price.

Mass production or **assembly-line production**   The production-to-stock process that produces large quantities of a small number of products.

Master budget   An overall financial plan for an entire firm.

Materials handling   The physical handling of items during transportation and warehousing.

Materials requirements planning (MRP)   The computerized technique used to plan and control manufacturing inventories.

Matrix organizational structure   A form of organization that combines horizontal and vertical lines of authority and also functional and product departments. Sometimes it is referred to as *project management,* because it brings together personnel drawn from different departments to focus on a particular project.

Maturity date   The date on which a corporation will redeem a bond by paying its par value.

Maturity stage   This stage of the product life cycle begins when sales start to level off and ends when they eventually begin to decline.

Means of production   The factories in which workers toil and the capital it takes to organize and build them.

Measure of dispersion   An indication of how widely spread data are.

Measure of value   A readily accepted means of relating or comparing the worth of different things.

Measures of central tendency   Indications of how data will cluster about a central point.

Median   The value that appears in the middle of the data when observations are arranged in order from the lowest to the highest.

Mediation   The process in which an impartial third party helps the parties settle unresolved issues.

Mediator   The person in the mediation process who suggests nonbinding alternatives for the two parties' consideration.

Medical expense coverage   The type of medical insurance that pays for medical and doctor expenses other than those related to surgery.

Medicare   A federal health insurance program for persons sixty-five or older, people of any age with permanent kidney failure, and certain disabled people.

Medium of exchange   Something that people are willing to accept in return for goods or services and that they in turn can exchange for other goods or services.

Megabyte (M)   A quantity of 1,024 K, or about 1 million bytes of computer memory.

Members or **shareholders** (Federal Reserve System)   The individuals or organizations in each district that own its Federal Reserve Bank.

Menu   A display of available programs to help the computer user carry out tasks.

Merchant   An intermediary — a wholesaler, distributor, or retailer — who takes title to goods and resells them.

Merger One company's acquisition and absorption of another.

Microcomputer Smaller than a minicomputer but rapidly gaining on it in terms of operating speed and memory capacity; ideally suited for applications requiring moderate speed and memory capacity.

Minicomputer Smaller-capacity computers originally designed to be connected to scientific and medical instruments to control them, but later connected in networks of terminals to provide computing and word-processing services for the individual departments of corporations.

Minutes The official records of corporate meetings.

Mission A statement of the reason an organization exists.

Mixed economies or **democratic socialist systems** Economic systems in which there is both government and private ownership of businesses and resources.

Mode (of a collection of data) The value that occurs most frequently.

Monetary policy The Federal Reserve System's management of available credit and the money supply.

Money Something that is generally accepted in exchange for goods or in payment of debts, not necessarily valued for itself but because it can be used for the same purposes repeatedly.

Money supply The total amount of currency in circulation, deposits in checking and savings accounts, and other liquid assets.

Monitor A manager who gathers information.

Monopolistic competition The situation that occurs when a relatively large number of sellers market similar but not identical products.

Monopoly The situation that occurs when one company alone offers a particular good or service and therefore controls the market and price for it.

Morale The state of psychological well-being based on such factors as a sense of organizational purpose and confidence in the future; the enthusiasm workers display toward their jobs, fellow employees, and employers.

Mortality tables Figures indicating the percentage of people who live to a given age.

Mortgage A security interest in real property.

Motivation The factors that cause people to behave in a certain way.

Multinational corporation A large firm with a home base in one country operating wholly or partially owned subsidiaries in other countries.

Multiple bases of departmentalization The mixture in one firm of two or more forms of departmentalization.

Multiple-unit pricing The practice of providing discounts for purchases of two or more units.

Municipal bonds Debt obligations of state and local governments and their agencies.

Mutual agency The authority of each partner to act on behalf of the other partners and the partnership as a whole.

Mutual assent The parties' agreement on a contract's terms as expressed in the offer and acceptance.

Mutual funds Poolings of various people's investments that are managed by professional investment managers toward a particular goal or with a particular philosophy.

Mutual insurance companies Companies owned by their policyholders.

Mutual savings banks A class of thrift institutions, found mainly in the Northeast, that are owned by their depositors and have investment policies similar to those of the savings and loans.

N

National Association of Securities Dealers Automatic Quotations (NASDAQ) A computerized system enabling dealers to determine instantly the current market price for the more popular OTC shares and to see who is making a market in them.

National Association of Securities Dealers (NASD) The organization through which the OTC functions.

National bank A financial institution organized with the approval of the Comptroller of the Currency, who issues them a charter and operates subject to federal banking regulations.

National brand or **manufacturer's brand** A brand owned by a manufacturer.

National Credit Union Administration An agency of the federal government that insures the deposits of credit unions.

National Labor Relations Act (NLRA) The 1935 act, popularly called the Wagner Act, that made labor–management relations a federal matter and established the National Labor Relations Board to regulate them.

National Labor Relations Board (NLRB) A five-member board appointed by the president to carry out the federal labor laws.

National negotiation The collective bargaining process in which the national union negotiates wages and benefits on an industry- or company-wide basis and the local unions negotiate working conditions.

Natural laws The unchanging laws of nature that govern economic life just as they control the physical world.

Natural monopoly A monopoly acquired as a result of market forces, without violating the antitrust laws.

Need Something that disturbs our satisfied physical or psychological state.

Negligence torts A broad range of torts that do not require the plaintiff to prove that the defendant intended to commit them.

Negotiable instrument A written contract containing a promise to pay money to one person who may then assign this right to another.

Net income The amount of profit or loss the organization has generated during the accounting period.

Net purchases Purchases less volume discounts, prompt-payment discounts, and the like.

Net sales The amount a firm adds to its assets by selling goods during the accounting period.

Network A communication system that links computers so that they can either operate independently or can communicate with and share the resources of other devices linked to them.

Net worth The amount by which assets exceed obligations.

News releases Typewritten copy, usually in the form of brief newspaper stories, circulated generally to the news media.

No-fault insurance An insurance program that compensates losses regardless of who, if anyone, is responsible for their occurrence.

No-fault insurance system The system in some states that gives insurers a right of reimbursement for payments to their insureds if the payments are below a certain specified level.

No-load fund A fund with no sales charge, so that all of the purchaser's money is invested.

No-par shares Shares of securities that are not assigned a dollar value.

Nondepository institution A financial institution that does not accept deposits.

Nondischargable Not releasable in a bankruptcy proceeding.

Nonparticipating stock Stock that receives only the stated dividend.

Nonprofit corporation or **not-for-profit corporation** A corporation set up for charitable, educational, or fraternal purposes.

Nonrestrictive indorsement An indorsement that does not limit the indorsee's ability to transfer the instrument.

Nonstore retailer A retailer who does not operate in conventional store facilities.

Notes payable Notes that will fall due during the next twelve months.

Notes receivable Formal, signed promises to pay a certain amount on a certain date.

Not publicly traded A designation meaning that a corporation's stock is not traded on a stock exchange.

NOW (negotiable order of withdrawal) accounts Individual checking accounts that earn interest until the bank receives an order of withdrawal, a check drawn on the account.

O

Ocean marine insurance That type of insurance which covers cargo carried on any body of water.

Odd lot Less than 100 shares.

Odd/even pricing The popular psychological pricing strategy in which prices ending in an odd number are meant to give the customer an impression of low prices and convey the idea that the firm has cut prices to the last possible penny. Even prices, usually given in round dollar amounts, are meant to give the opposite impression.

Off-price retailer A distributor that carries high-quality, name-brand merchandise priced usually 20 to 70 percent lower than department stores.

Offer A proposal of what one party will or will not do in exchange for the other party's act or promise.

Offeree The party receiving an offer.

Offeror The party making an offer.

Old-Age, Survivors, Disability, and Health Insurance (OASDHI) The federal program that provides retirement, survivors', disability, and health insurance.

Oligopoly A market dominated by a few large sellers, usually in industries that require huge initial investments in plant and equipment.

On line A device, like an optical scanner, that operates under the direct, immediate control of a computer.

Open-market operations   The buying and selling of government securities on the open market, which are supervised by the Federal Open Market Committee.

Open order   An order that extends beyond the day's end and runs until it is cancelled.

Open shop   One in which union membership is not a condition of employment.

Operating expenses   All costs of running a business except the cost of goods sold.

Operating period   The length of time it takes to complete a manufacturing or sales cycle. Usually a year, but it may be a quarter or any other appropriate length of time.

Operating system   A program that does the detailed work of running hardware.

Operational planning   The scheduling of an organization's day-to-day needs and the designing of how to meet them.

Operational system   The management information system in the marketing area designed to handle all customers' orders, whether placed by mail, in person, or through a salesperson.

Operations   All activities associated with the production of goods and services.

Operations management   The process of coordinating the production of goods and services with all the activities associated with production.

Order processing   A physical distribution activity whose purpose is the receiving and filling of customers' orders.

Ordering costs   Expenses incurred whenever a business places an order for inventory goods with a vendor.

Organization   Two or more people working together to achieve a common goal.

Organization chart   A diagram of the positions and reporting relationships within an organization.

Organizational goals   The long-range objectives of a firm.

Organizational structure   A pattern of task groupings, reporting relationships, and authority in an organization.

Organized labor   Workers represented by unions.

Organizing   The process of assigning to the appropriate position the tasks required to achieve the organization's objectives, along with the authority and responsibility for accomplishing those tasks.

Organizing drive   The collective steps toward unionization.

Orientation   The systematic introduction of new employees to their organization, job, and coworkers.

Outdoor advertising   Posters, billboards, signs, and the like.

Output (noun)   The information that comes out of a computer system after data processing.

Output device   That part of a computer system which receives data from the computer and presents it to the user.

Outside financing   Money generated by borrowing from or selling ownership interests to sources outside the business for its use.

Outside salespeople or **field salespeople** (for a wholesaler)   Typically work on the road calling on potential buyers.

Over-the-counter market (OTC)   A telecommunications network linking broker-dealers for transactions in securities not listed on exchanges.

P

Packaging   The development of a container and a graphic design for a product.

Par value (of a security)   The stated or face value.

Participating preferred stock   Preferred stock that may, under circumstances specified in an indenture, participate in the dividend distributions on common shares.

Parties   The people involved in a dispute.

Partner   A co-owner of a business.

Partnership   "An association of two or more persons to carry on as co-owners a business for profit."

Partnership agreement   A contract between two persons stating the terms on which they agree to be partners.

Patent   A seventeen-year monopoly granted by the federal government to exploit new processes, machines, or manufactured goods, or significant improvements to existing processes.

Path   A series of sequential events in the production process.

Pattern bargaining   The collective bargaining process in which the local unions in a single company or industry negotiate on their own under the supervision of the national union.

Pay structure   The relationship among the rates of pay for various jobs within the company.

Payable on demand   A recognition that the maker of an instrument will pay it when it is presented to him or her for payment.

Payable to bearer   A recognition that anyone who has possession of the instrument may demand payment.

Payable to order   Acknowledgment that an instrument may be transferred by means of an indorsement.

Penetration pricing strategy The practice of introducing a new product at a low price to attain a sizable market share.

Pension fund The second type of nondepository institution, which accepts funds intended to generate retirement income for persons who belong to the pension plan.

Performance appraisal A formal assessment of how well employees are doing their jobs, then communicating the results of the assessment to the employees.

Periodic inventory method The inventory procedure that calculates the effect of sales on inventory only at the end of an accounting period.

Peripherals All computer hardware devices other than the CPU, referred to thus because they are attached to but not part of the CPU.

Perpetual inventory system The method of inventory control that records every change in inventory as soon as it happens.

Per se violations Antitrust violations in which the government has only to prove that the forbidden conduct actually occurred; there is no defense for the conduct.

Personal property All property that is not either a fixture or real property.

Personality test A test that assesses a candidate's mental make-up.

Persuasive advertising Influences the target market's beliefs, attitudes, or behavior.

Physical distribution The process of moving goods.

Picketing The patrolling of the entrances to an employer's facilities by members of a labor union often carrying signs to inform other employees and the public that a strike is in progress and to persuade them not to enter.

Pie chart A circle that, like a pie, has been divided into pieces, with each piece used to portray the kind and proportion of the data it represents.

Piece-rate system An incentive system that compensates a worker according to the number of units of a product he or she produces.

Piece-work rates Pay to employees according to what they produce, not by the time they work.

Plaintiff The person who starts a lawsuit.

Planned economies or **authoritarian socialist systems** The economic system in which the government owns or controls virtually all of a nation's land and industrial capacity. The government plays a large role in determining what will be produced, who will produce it, and to whom the products will be distributed.

Planning The process of determining the objectives of an organization, whether it is a large corporation, an individual department, or a small sole proprietorship, and deciding how to achieve them.

Plant Buildings as fixed assets.

Point-of-purchase displays Special racks, signs, and displays to increase consumer product awareness that are supplied and set up by manufacturers or wholesalers in retail or service outlets.

Police powers The state and local governments' powers to protect the health, safety, and welfare of their citizens.

Policy A contract between an insurance company and a policyholder.

Portable computer A great range of computers for handheld programable calculators of lap-sized computers that can perform any function that the larger and heavier microcomputers can.

Posting The process of transferring information from a journal to a ledger.

Preapproach All the planning that takes place before a meeting with the customer.

Precedent An earlier legal decision on similar or identical questions of law.

Predatory pricing An abuse of monopoly power involving the pricing of products in such a way as to eliminate competition.

Preemptive right The right to buy additional shares to preserve shareholders' ownership positions if a company issues additional shares to the public.

Preferred position A section of a newspaper that is more likely to be read by a target market.

Preferred stock A class of stock that pays dividends at a specified rate and that has preference over common stock in the payment of dividends and the liquidation of assets.

Premium Anything of value that a customer receives in addition to the purchased item or service; a relatively small insurance payment that replaces a large uncertain potential loss.

Premiums Funds that an insurance company takes in from its policyholders.

Prepaid expenses Services and supplies an organization has paid for but not yet used.

Press conference A public meeting of corporate officials with the news media at which written and photographic materials are often supplied.

Prestige pricing Setting a very high price on an item to give the impression of high quality.

Preventive law The management approach of structuring operations to achieve a firm's goals and avoid legal problems.

Price discrimination The sale of goods at different prices by a commercial seller to two or more nonretail buyers.

Price fixing An agreement between two parties as to the prices to be charged for goods.

Price lining A pricing strategy used primarily by retailers in which the firm selects a limited number of key prices for certain classes of products.

Price points Key prices used to establish *price lining.*

Price–quality relationship The implication that a high price implies high quality.

Primary boycott An action by a union to try to persuade others not to deal with an employer against whom it has a grievance.

Primary markets Those markets in which the issuer of a security receives some or all of the funds paid for the security.

Primary-demand or **generic advertising** Used to increase the total demand for a product or service and does not distinguish between brands.

Prime rate; "the prime" The interest rate a bank charges the largest and most reliable customers that borrow from it regularly.

Principal A person represented by an agent; it can be another individual, a partnership, or a corporation.

Private accountant or **management accountant** An accountant who is an employee of a company or government agency.

Private carrier A carrier owned and operated by a shipper.

Private corporation A corporation organized by private individuals or companies for some purpose other than for providing utility service.

Private label brand A brand owned by a retailer or wholesaler.

Private law Law that defines the relationships between and among individuals and other nongovernmental entities like corporations.

Private placement The direct sale of stock by an issuer to investors.

Private sector The part of the economy not controlled by the government.

Private warehouse A warehouse owned by a firm that has sole access to it.

Proactive In favor of action.

Procedural law The provisions in constitutions or statutes that describe how something is to be done by, or in relation to, government.

Process layout The grouping of machinery or activities according to their purposes.

Product Any good or service that may be the subject of an exchange for money.

Product differentiation strategy A program designed to give a product distinctive characteristics that can serve as competitive advantages over similar products in the maturity stage of the product life cycle.

Product layout The equipment arrangement relating to the sequence of operations performed in manufacturing a product.

Product liability A commercial seller's responsibility for products it puts into someone else's hands.

Product liability insurance The type of insurance that covers a manufacturer's or seller's responsibility for losses caused by goods placed in commerce.

Product life cycle Products have lives with four identifiable stages: introduction, growth, maturity, and decline.

Production The process of transforming resources into the goods or services that an organization sells.

Production planning and control The management function involving the scheduling of operations relating to the production of goods or services.

Production-to-order system The type of inventory system that produces only what customers or clients demand, as the order comes in.

Production-to-stock system The type of inventory system that produces goods to be held in inventory.

Productivity The level of output of goods and services achieved by the resources of an organization.

Professional corporation The newest form of corporation, a firm whose shareholders offer such professional services as medical, legal, and engineering work.

Profit The excess of revenues over expenses.

Profit-sharing program A plan that distributes a set portion of a company's profits to its employees, according to a standard formula.

Profits　The compensation awarded a capitalist for the efforts and risk assumed in establishing or operating a venture.

Program　"A list of instructions that the computer hardware follows."

Program Evaluation and Review Technique (PERT)　One of the most popular scheduling techniques for production control.

Programing　The designing and writing of computer programs.

Project processing　The production-to-order system in which the manufacturer produces a one-of-a-kind item.

Promissory notes　Written contracts involving a promise to pay money.

Promotion　The communications that an entity uses to inform, persuade, or remind a target market about its product, its services, its message, or itself; an advancement granted to an employee to a higher position, greater responsibility, or more prestige.

Promotional mix　The combination of advertising, personal selling, sales promotion, publicity and public relations in a firm's promotion strategy.

Property　When used in the context of fixed assets, a term that refers to land.

Property risk　The potential direct loss of a firm's property due to fire or similar causes.

Property tax　A tax imposed by a state or local government on real property.

Prospecting　The process of developing a list of potential customers.

Prospects　Firms or individuals who qualify as potential customers because they have the authority and the financial ability to buy the product.

Prospectus　A document that summarizes the information contained in a registration statement.

Protective tariff　A duty imposed to protect a domestic industry from competition by keeping the price of competing imports level with or higher than the price of domestic products.

Public Utility Holding Company Act of 1935　The act that empowers the SEC to regulate the companies that control public utilities, notably electric utilities, natural-gas pipeline companies, and their subsidiaries.

Public accountant　An independent professional whom individuals or companies may hire to perform specific accounting services.

Public corporation　A corporation set up by Congress or a state legislature for a specific public purpose.

Public law　Duties imposed by government to protect the rights of individuals or preserve social order.

Public offering　The process of initially selling a new issue of securities to the public.

Public warehouse　A warehouse that can be used by the general public to store goods for a fee.

Publicity　A communication about a company or its products that a mass medium transmits at no charge.

Publicly traded　Shares that are bought and sold on stock exchanges.

Pull strategy　Attempts to develop consumer demand for a product or service primarily through advertising or sales promotion.

Purchase on account　A purchase on credit.

Purchases　The value of what a firm bought for inventory during the accounting period.

Purchasing　The operational function by which a business obtains the goods and services it requires.

Pure competition or **perfect competition**　The situation that occurs when no single seller can control the price of a particular good or service.

Pure risk　The type of risk that offers only the potential for loss.

Push strategy　Directed at selling goods or services directly to the next entity down the channel of distribution.

Q

Qualified indorsement　One that indicates that the indorser denies all liability under the rights of subsequent holders of the instrument in the event that the instrument is not accepted or paid.

Quality circles　Groups of volunteer employees who meet regularly on company time to discuss ways to improve work procedures, eliminate defects, and perform their work more efficiently.

Quality control　The operations management function meant to ensure that output meets the planned standards.

Quality of Work Life (QWL) movement　The drive to achieve a better work-place environment for employees while increasing profitability for the employer.

Quasi-public corporation or **public utility**　A corporation granted a monopoly by a government unit on providing certain kinds of services to the public.

R

Random access The opposite of sequential access; the retrieval by a computer of any piece of data from the source in the same amount of time as any other piece and with the time required to access the last record being no greater than that required to access the first.

Random access memory (RAM) The memory cells used to store changeable data or instructions.

Random sample or **probability sample** A survey in which "all units in a population have an equal chance of appearing in the sample."

Range The principal measure of data's dispersion; the difference between the highest and lowest observed values.

Rank-order technique A type of performance appraisal that requires the supervisor to rank all employees under his or her supervision from the best to the worst on a global performance scale.

Rational buying motives The desire for dependability, durability, efficiency, financial gain, and the like.

Read-Only Memory (ROM) An area that permanently stores programs from the control unit interpreting the computer's instructions.

Real property Land and everything attached to it.

Reciprocal-dealing arrangement The anticompetitive situation that occurs when a buyer can force a seller to buy something from it as a condition of the buyer's making his purchase. It is the opposite of a tying arrangement.

Reciprocity The belief that one country's markets can be only as free as its trading partners'.

Record date The specified date by which shareholders must have owned their shares to receive dividends.

Recruitment The process of attracting qualified people to apply for jobs.

Redeemed Paid at par.

References Firms or banks with whom the borrower has done business in the past.

Refund The returning of a portion of an item's purchase price.

Registration statement A form that issuers must file with the Securities and Exchange Commission and state securities regulators that fully describes the investment and the issuer.

Reminder or **reinforcement advertising** Reminds the target market about something.

Reporting relationship The responsibility of a person to report information to his or her superior and vice versa.

Representation election An election to determine whether a union will represent a particular group of workers.

Reserve The liquid assets, usually currency, that are set aside in a bank's vault or on deposit with the Federal Reserve Bank to which a commercial bank belongs.

Reserve requirement A specified percentage of deposits that a member must either deposit with the Federal Reserve or hold in its own vaults as cash and may not lend.

Responsibility A person's obligation to accomplish a task.

Restrictive indorsement One that tries to limit the indorsee's ability to transfer the instrument.

Retailer One who acquires goods from manufacturers, producers, or wholesalers, then sells them to consumers.

Retained earnings Profits kept in the business after any dividends are paid.

Revaluation An arbitrary upward adjustment of one country's currency in terms of another country's.

Revenue tariff A duty imposed solely to generate income for the government.

Reverse For an appellate court to overturn a trial court's judgment.

Reverse split The process of reducing the number of shares outstanding and raising their market price.

Revolving credit agreement A line of credit backed by a bank's legally enforceable guarantee that the money will be available whenever the borrower wants it.

Right to employment The methods by which promotions, transfers, and layoffs are determined within a bargaining unit.

Right-to-work laws Laws that forbid union shops or work places.

Risk The uncertainty about whether an event will or will not occur.

Risk assumption The strategy that requires a firm to consciously recognize a particular risk and accept it as an integral part of its activities.

Risk avoidance The strategy that requires a firm not to engage in an activity or own particular property that might lead to an exposure to risk.

Risk management The process of identifying exposures to risk, choosing the best method for handling each exposure, and implementing it.

Risk manager   A person whose job it is to preserve assets and a business's earning power against pure risks.

Risk reduction   The lessening of the uncertainty of financial loss in a risky situation.

Risk transfer   The strategy that shifts risk to another party.

Robbery   Theft involving the threat or actual use of force.

Robot   A reprogramable machine capable of performing a variety of tasks requiring programed manipulations of tools and materials.

Role playing   A training device that requires students to resolve a situation in which they play the parts of people who were actually involved.

Round lot   One hundred shares.

Royalty   A share, usually of gross output, from the extraction of a natural resource.

Rule-of-reason standard   Giving the defendant in an antitrust case the opportunity to prove that the conduct in question does not unreasonably restrict trade.

Run-of-the-press placement   Allows a newspaper to put an ad wherever space is available.

S

Safety or **security** or **risk**   The likelihood that the investor will be able to get his or her money back.

Salary   Compensation, usually calculated on a weekly, monthly, or yearly basis and not normally related to the number of hours actually worked.

Sales engineers   Representatives who have precise, detailed knowledge of their products and are able to discuss technical matters.

Sales returns   The refunds allowed customers when they return something.

Sales tax   The federal tax on gasoline that supports the highway trust fund.

Sample   A small group of representative units selected from a much larger group.

Savings-and-loan associations (S & Ls)   Thrift institutions usually owned by their depositors; also known as building-and-loan associations.

Scheduling   The function of production control that sets the time for and duration of tasks.

Seasonal trends   Patterns that complete themselves within one year or less and then begin to repeat themselves.

Secondary boycott   A refusal to work for, purchase from, or handle the products of another company with which the union has no dispute in order to force that company to stop doing business with the company with which the union does have a dispute.

Secondary markets   Those markets in which the sale of a security ordinarily does not involve any proceeds going to the issuer.

Secular trend   A smooth upward or downward statistical movement over a long period.

Secure   To assure repayment of a loan.

Securities Act of 1933   A disclosure act requiring that the issuer of a public offering file a registration statement providing specific information about the issuer, its financial condition, management, properties, and general operation.

Securities Act of 1964   The act that brought companies whose securities traded over the counter under SEC jurisdiction, if the company and its stockholders met certain criteria.

Securities Exchange Act of 1934   The act requiring periodic disclosure in the form of reports to the SEC by companies whose securities are publicly held.

Securities Investors Protection Act of 1970   The act that created the *Securities Investors Protection Corporation.*

Securities Investors Protection Corporation (SIPC)   The agency that oversees the liquidation of failed broker-dealers and insures investors when the assets of a failed firm are insufficient to cover its obligations to its customers.

Securities and Exchange Commission   The federal agency created in 1934 charged with enforcing the federal securities laws as well as designing regulations for the securities markets.

Security   One of a wide range of investment vehicles that requires an investment of money, a common enterprise, and an expectation of profit solely from the efforts of others.

Security interest   A financial interest in personal property or fixtures that secures the payment of a debt or obligation.

Selection   The identification of appropriate candidates for a position.

Selective credit controls   The category of specifically targeted tools that the Federal Reserve uses to fine tune the monetary system.

Selective distribution strategy   A distribution approach that centers on a moderate proportion of the retailers likely to carry a particular product in a given market area.

Selective or **brand advertising** Promotion materials designed to encourage a consumer to buy a certain brand of product and thereby build customer patronage.

Self-actualization Self-fulfillment, or the tapping of one's potential to one's own satisfaction.

Self-esteem How a person feels about himself or herself.

Self-insurance A mechanism by which a business establishes a fund to cover losses caused by particular types of events.

Selling expenses All costs directly associated with selling products or services to customers.

Seniority A system in which the order of hiring determines the order of promotions, layoffs, rehirings, and the exercise of all other employment rights.

Seniority differential An incremental pay increase determined by the length of the worker's service with the employer.

Separation The ending of the employment relationship.

Sequential access The reading of all preceding files on a magnetic tape before accessing the file wanted.

Serial bonds Bonds of one issue but that mature on different dates.

Service The term to describe work that is done for others that does not involve the production of goods.

Service sector That portion of the economy consisting of businesses that perform work for others that does not involve producing goods.

Setups Modifications of a process or a machine to meet the specifications for a new order.

Shareholder A person who owns shares in a corporation and is thus part owner of the corporation.

Shares Units into which ownership of a corporation is divided.

Sherman Act The first federal legislation (1890) aimed at controlling trusts.

Shift differential An incremental pay increase for working specified time periods.

Shop Simply a work place.

Shop steward A union member elected to represent the other members employed in a particular work unit in their day-to-day dealings with the employer.

Shoppers' guides Advertising circulars featuring both display and classified ads.

Shopping goods Products that are purchased infrequently, have a relatively high unit price, and are bought only after comparison with other product alternatives.

Short-term financing Money that a firm will borrow for a year or less.

Sinking fund A fund set aside by a company, generally according to a formula based on profits or time, to redeem particular issues of preferred stock or debt.

Skills inventory A data bank containing a list of each employee's employment history, skills, interests, and performance that can be used to match personnel with new jobs or to select candidates for promotion, transfer, or added responsibilities.

Skimming price strategy A technique that charges a high price when the product is introduced.

Small Business Administration (SBA) An agency of the federal government that offers both managerial and financial assistance to small businesses.

Small business Any business that is independently owned and operated, is not dominant in its field, and does not employ more than five hundred persons.

Social audit An annual assessment of a company's effects on society and the environment.

Social responsibility Business's obligation to consider the consequences of a decision it makes for society as a whole, for various groups within society, and for particular individuals.

Socialism An economic system in which the state owns the principal means of production but private property of some sort does exist.

Social Security Act of 1935 A wide-ranging federal program of health and retirement benefits.

Software A set of intangible commands that instruct a computer to read data into its memory from a peripheral device, perform operations on the data, store it in the main memory or in some form of auxiliary storage unit, and output the information to the user in some form.

Software applications package The program with which a user tells the CPU what to do with the data entered.

Sole proprietorship A form of business in which one individual (the *sole proprietor*) owns all the assets of the business and is alone responsible for its debts.

Source documents Papers or computer entries which prove that a transaction actually took place.

Span of management The number of people who report directly to a manager.

Special agent An agent for one transaction or a limited series of them.

Special indorsement An indorsement that names a specific indorsee.

Specialist A member of an exchange who is responsible for matching buy and sell orders or, if there is an imbalance of orders, for using his or her own portfolio to balance the buy and sell orders.

Specialization The concentration of economic activity in those areas in which the country, the individual, or the business has either natural or acquired advantages.

Specialty advertising Usually involves producing small, inexpensive items bearing the advertiser's name, address, and occasional brief messages for free distribution.

Specialty goods Products for which consumers develop a strong preference and loyalty.

Specialty store A store carrying a limited line of merchandise, such as computers, records and tapes, auto parts, and so on.

Speculative risk The type of risk that offers the potential for gain as well as loss.

Spread The difference between what is paid to an issuer of a security and the amount paid by the public.

Staff The many employees and managers in a modern organization not directly producing or distributing the goods and services it sells.

Staffing The process of locating, selecting, and assigning people to the tasks designed to achieve an organization's objectives.

Standardization "The determination of basic limits or grade ranges in the form of uniform specifications to which particular manufactured goods may conform and uniform classes into which the products of agriculture and [mineral extraction] industries may or must be sorted or assigned" (as defined by the American Marketing Association).

Stare decisis A Latin term meaning literally "to stand by decisions."

State bank A type of commercial bank chartered in the state within which it operates.

Statement of changes in financial position A summary of the changes in a firm's generation and use of cash that have taken place during the accounting period.

Statistic A number that is "calculated as a summary of data."

Statutes Laws passed by Congress or state legislatures and signed by, respectively, the president or a state governor.

Statutory Certain federal and state laws governing securities.

Stock A security in the form of an ownership interest in a corporation.

Stock dividend A dividend in the form of shares in a corporation's stock.

Stock insurance companies Companies owned by their stockholders and that provide insurance protection for a profit.

Stock split That which takes place when a company issues to shareholders one or more additional shares for each share currently held.

Stop order An explicitly priced sell order triggered when a stock price falls to or below a specified level.

Store of value A means of holding and collecting wealth.

Stored-program computer A machine that is "controlled by software stored within the hardware."

Strategic planning The determination of where an organization wants to go in the long run and how it plans to get there.

Stress interview A selection interview in which the interviewer deliberately annoys, embarrasses, or frustrates the applicant to determine his or her reaction.

Strict liability Certain types of negligence torts involving abnormally dangerous activities or dangerous animals that impose this liability on the defendant even if he or she acted with due care.

Strike The bargaining tactic that occurs when a union, in an effort to put economic pressure on management, calls on its members not to work.

Strikebreakers or **scabs** Persons hired to replace striking employees, either in an effort to force the union to come to terms or to destroy its effectiveness by minimizing the strike's effect on the employer's operations.

Structured interview An employment interview in which the interviewer asks a series of prepared questions based on the job specifications.

Subchapter S corporation or **S corporation** A corporation with thirty-five or fewer shareholders that elects under Subchapter S of the Internal Revenue Code to be treated for federal tax purposes essentially as a partnership.

Substantive law The type of law that describes rights or duties.

Supercomputers The largest, most powerful computers made today.

Supermarket The familiar large food store that offers relatively low prices and carries many nationally recognized brands displayed in various departments, most of which are self-service.

Superstore and **hypermarket** Large type of store that has evolved from the supermarket; it often includes such services as florists, pharmacists, bakeries, and banking.

Supply The willingness of sellers or producers to provide goods or services at a particular price and particular time.

Supply curve A graphed line reflecting the relationship between price and quantity.

Supreme court The highest appellate court in an American court system.

Surety or **guarantor** A person who promises to repay a debt if the debtor does not pay it.

Surety bonds Insurance policies that provide for compensation to the beneficiary should a contract not be completed on time.

Surgical coverage The type of insurance that pays surgeons' and anesthesiologists' fees, surgical nurses' charges, operating room charges, and similar expenses.

Syndicate A temporary association formed to carry out a specific, usually short-term investment.

T

Tabular display An array or matrix of information in vertical columns and horizontal rows to show the relationship between two or more variables in either numeric or verbal data.

Taft-Hartley Labor Act The 1947 act that abolished the closed shop and authorized right-to-work laws.

Tangible personal property Property that one can touch.

Target marketing Choosing the particular markets on which a firm will focus its marketing activities.

Targeted television advertising Advertising aimed at particular audiences, such as sports fans and those interested in particular types of entertainment.

Tariffs or **duty** A tax imposed by a country on imported goods.

Technical skills The ability to use the tools, equipment, procedures, and techniques of a specialized field.

Telecommuters Persons "who work at home or in a satellite office and electronically transfer the information needed to do their job between home/satellite and headquarters."

Telemarketing A personal selling technique that relies on the telephone to make sales as well as to schedule sales calls and follow up on orders and prospects.

Term life insurance The type of life insurance that pays the policy amount to the beneficiary only if the insured dies within the period covered by the last premium.

Terminals An input device usually consisting of a keyboard and a CRT linked to a central computer.

Termination Simply recognition of the fact that the winding up is complete and the partnership has therefore ended.

Test markets Selected areas with cooperative media and retailers, the necessary audit and research facilities, and a track record of providing marketers with an insight into the behavior of the entire market.

The wheel of retailing A concept used to describe the effect of new entrants into a retail market.

Theft insurance The general term for insurance covering losses resulting from the unlawful taking of property belonging to another.

Theory X Douglas McGregor's theory which holds that people really do not want to work and will avoid it if possible. To make people productive, they have to be pushed, closely supervised, and threatened with some type of punishment.

Theory Y Douglas McGregor's theory which holds that work is as natural to people as recreation and rest. Employees do not want to be rigidly controlled or threatened with punishment.

Thrift institution Originally, a type of institution that offered mortgages and other local long-term loans through savings banks and savings-and-loan associations; now less clearly differentiated from commercial banks.

Ticker The electronic system that provides the public with notice of each transaction on the exchange.

Time deposit Funds deposited with a bank either in the form of a savings account or a certificate of deposit under an agreement that the bank will pay interest on the funds and the depositor must give notice to the bank a specified time before withdrawing funds.

Time series analysis or **trend analysis** A statistical technique for examining the ways that observations of a variable move over time, then basing forecasts on the observations.

Title The right to own property that usually (but not always) comes with physical possession of tangible personal property or real property. A better way to think of title is as the right to sell or otherwise transfer property, whether or not the seller has actual possession of the property or has paid for it.

Title insurance Insurance against losses resulting from the purchase of real property to which the seller did not have a clear or marketable title.

To pass a dividend To forego paying a dividend.

Tort A legal wrong as defined by the common law.

Total costs The sum of the *fixed* and *variable costs*.

Trade The buying or selling of goods or services among companies, states, or countries.

Trade or **craft union** A union made up of skilled workers of the same or related vocations.

Trade agreement The type of understanding between nations that regulates the commerce between them.

Trade barriers Factors that place imports at a disadvantage in their competition with domestic goods.

Trade credit An agreement whereby a supplier sells goods or services to a buyer but does not require immediate payment.

Trade show A large exhibit of products that are, in most cases, common to one industry.

Trademark A legally protected name or design used to identify a product.

Trademark A symbol registered with the U.S. Patent and Trademark Office. Indicated by the symbol ® at the end of a brand name or ™ beside a symbol.

Trading partners Two entities that recognize the mutual benefits in a transaction or series of transactions and decide to undertake them.

Training "Learning activities designed to improve current job performance. Its objectives can be stated in specific behavioral terms."

Transfer A shift from one job to another in an organization that may or may not require a change in the employee's place of work.

Transferee The person to whom something is transferred.

Transformation The conversion of input (resources) into output (goods or services).

Transportation The process of actually moving goods from one location to another.

Transportation or **marine insurance** That form of property insurance designed to protect goods as they are moved from place to place.

Treasurer The corporate officer who reports to the vice president of finance and has responsibility for overseeing and planning for the firm's expenditures and income.

Treasury bills (T-bills) Short-term promissory notes issued weekly by the U.S. Treasury to finance the government's day-to-day cash requirements.

Trial balance An accountant's calculations before preparing the financial statements, to make sure that a credit offsets every debit and that the arithmetic was done correctly.

Trial courts of general jurisdiction One of the two types of trial courts; it can hear any matters that a trial court in its system has authority to hear.

Trial courts of limited jurisdiction Courts with authority to hear only particular types of cases or cases involving less than a certain dollar amount.

Trust Indenture Act of 1939 The act that requires that any corporate debt offered to the public be registered with the SEC and conform to requirements relating to maturity, interest, and financial backing.

Trustee A person or (usually) a firm that protects the bondholders' interests by making sure that the issuer meets its obligations under the indenture.

Tying arrangement The anticompetitive situation that results when the seller agrees to sell a product that the buyer wants (the tying product) only if the buyer also purchases another product that the buyer does not want (the tied product).

U

Undercapitalization The lack of sufficient funds to operate a business normally.

Undervalued A stock whose book value exceeds its market value.

Underwriter An investment banker who agrees to buy a new issue and distribute it to the public.

Undifferentiated marketing A loosely conceived form of target marketing that consists of a single strategy aimed at everyone.

Unemployment compensation A state program, sometimes supplemented by federal funds, that for a set period pays allowances to workers who are out of work and actively looking for a job.

Unemployment insurance The state-sponsored insurance that provides partial, temporary replacement income for eligible unemployed workers.

Unfair labor practices Violations of the laws the NLRB enforces.

Uniform Commercial Code (UCC) A body of statutes that replaces several areas of business law formerly covered individually by each state's common law of contracts.

Union shop One in which workers do not have to be union members when hired but must later join, usually within thirty days.

Unions Organizations, like the United Auto Workers, through which employees combine their strength to advance their common interests.

Universal life insurance That form of whole life insurance that combines term insurance with an investment plan guaranteeing higher rates than are usually available on whole life policies.

Unsecured Not backed by collateral.

Unsecured loan A loan for which the borrower does not provide collateral.

Unstructured interview An employment interview in which the interviewer does not have a firmly set structure for the interview and the interviewee does most of the talking.

U.S. Constitution The 1789 formulation in rather specific terms of how the federal government is to be organized and what its legal relationships to the states and the people are to be.

U.S. government issues All bonds issued by any unit of the federal government.

User fees Charges to the public designed to compensate the government for services it performs.

Utility The satisfaction that goods and services yield to their buyers.

Utility program A computer program provided by the manufacturer of an operating system that runs below the operating system.

V

Value added network (VAN) A computer network that links customers' computers to middlemen's and middlemen's to manufacturers' computers or distributors'.

Variable costs Costs that depend on the number of units produced and sold.

Variance and **standard deviation** Two reliable indications of dispersion that measure the difference between the observed data and the arithmetic mean of the entire set of data.

Variances Departures from zoning regulations that may be granted for different land use.

Variety store A relatively small store that offers a wide range of small items.

Vending machine An electromechanical device that dispenses something when a customer inserts the appropriate amount of money, a credit card, or a code.

Venture capitalist An investor willing to put money into a business in exchange for a substantial block of stock.

Verdict A jury's finding.

Vertical market allocation The division of a market among related entities, like franchisees or subsidiaries; may or may not be a violation of the Sherman Act.

Vertical merger A merger of two companies in the same chain of supply.

Vertical-channel integration The process that occurs when a firm either acquires another firm in its channel or sets up a division to carry out other channel functions.

Vice president of finance The officer in a corporation with overall responsibility for its financial functions.

Visual display A picture that portrays information items in a way that makes them easy to compare with one another or reflects trends among the items.

Voting rights The right to vote for directors and on extraordinary transactions, like a merger, that will affect the nature of a company.

W

Wage/salary survey A review of pay rates at companies within comparable industries in a particular region.

Wages Compensation, usually calculated according to the number of hours an employee actually worked.

Warehouse receipt The record that a public warehouseman gives a person who is storing goods.

Warehouse store Essentially a discount or off-price food store that offers approximately the same merchandise as supermarkets but has virtually no ambience or services.

Warehousing A set of activities designed to ensure that goods are available when they are needed.

Warrant In the retail context, a store's guarantee of its right to sell specific goods.

Warranty A guarantee or assurance.

Warranty of fitness for a particular purpose A warranty made when a seller knows that a buyer is purchasing goods to be used in a certain way.

Warranty of merchantability A warranty, made only by merchants, that a product is fit for the ordinary purposes for which it is sold.

Warranty of performance A guarantee that goods will conform to certain standards.

Warranty of title A guarantee that the seller has the right to transfer to the buyer title to the goods.

Whistle blowers Employees who report unethical or illegal conduct to their superiors or to a government agency.

Whole life or **cash value life insurance** A class of life insurance policies that requires premium payments on the insured's behalf until death or until the insured reaches a certain age.

Wholesaler A merchant who buys and resells products to such other merchants as retailers and other wholesalers and larger industrial users, but not to consumers.

Winding up The liquidation of a partnership's assets, payment of its debts, repayment of the partners' capital contributions, and division of the remaining funds.

Work ethic The generally held belief that work is good for both the individual and society.

Workers' compensation A program established under state law that provides compensation for workers who suffer on-the-job injuries.

Working capital The money necessary to fund a business's regular operations.

Working conditions A catch-all term to describe all aspects of the relationship between employer and employee that are not related to the area of compensation.

Z

Zero-based budgeting The type of accounting that requires managers to justify their programs — and therefore all their expenditures — each time a new budget is prepared.

Zoning regulations Local rules that specify the uses to which land and buildings on it may be put.

p. 26, © 1982 Arnold Zann/Black Star; p. 27, by Mike Keefe; © by and permission of News America Syndicate, 1986.

Chapter 2   P. 35, © Glenn Moody; p. 41, © Gary Gladstone; p. 46, courtesy of Detroit Edison; p. 48, courtesy of IBM; ad published in 1986; p. 51, courtesy of Kraft, Inc.; p. 52, by permission of Johnny Hart and News America Syndicate.

Chapter 3   P. 62, © Andrée Abecassis; p. 68, Lowe's Companies, Inc. 1984 Annual Report; photo by Dana L. Duke; p. 72, © Robb Kendrick; p. 77, James Mitchell/Ebony Magazine; p. 81, drawing by Joe Mirachi; © 1985 The New Yorker Magazine, Inc.; p. 82, courtesy of Chevrolet Motor Division.

Chapter 4   P. 90, Wide World Photos; p. 96, © Wm. Franklin McMahon; p. 98, drawing by H. Martin; © 1985 The New Yorker Magazine, Inc.; p. 103, photo by Nancy Bundt; printed courtesy of Leeann Chin; p. 106, © Cindy Charles; p. 108, photo courtesy of International Multifoods Corporation.

Chapter 5   P. 128, © John Reis; p. 132, photo courtesy of Kellogg Company; p. 135, courtesy of First Wisconsin Corporation; photographer Tim Bieber; p. 137, courtesy of Scott Paper Company; p. 139, © 1986 Time Inc.; p. 142, © 1986, Singer Communications, Inc., Anaheim, CA 92801; p. 144, photo courtesy of Hilton Hotels Corporation.

Chapter 6   P. 153, © Mark Hanauer/Onyx; p. 155, © 1986, Singer Communications, Inc., Anaheim, CA 92801; p. 160, American Airlines photo; p. 168, BankAmerica Corporation 1984 Annual Report; p. 168, © 1985 NCR Corporation; p. 171, © K. Lambert/Black Star.

Chapter 7   P. 179, Peter Dupré/Colorado Outward Bound School; p. 180, © Roman Sapecki; p. 189, drawing by C. Barsotti; © 1985 The New Yorker Magazine, Inc.; p. 190, courtesy of Bethlehem Steel Corporation; p. 194, courtesy of Burlington Industries.

Chapter 8   P. 215, courtesy of Lockheed Corporation; p. 217, © 1986 Singer Communications, Inc., Anaheim, CA 92801; p. 218, courtesy of AT&T; designed by UniWorld Group, Inc.; p. 230, courtesy of The Firestone Tire & Rubber Company; p. 236, © Robert Knowles/Black Star.

Chapter 9   P. 247, UPI/Bettmann Newsphotos; p. 250, © 1985 Roger Sandler/Black Star; p. 254, © Steven Burr Williams; p. 258, © 1986 Singer Communications, Inc., Anaheim, CA 92801; p. 261, © 1984 Jim Mendenhall/Gamma-Liaison; p. 267, © Richard Olsenius/Black Star.

Chapter 10   P. 277, courtesy of Moore's Food Products; p. 280, drawing by Weber; © 1983 The New Yorker Magazine, Inc.; p. 281, courtesy of Alcoa; p. 284, © Arlene Gottfried; p. 287, © Steve Dunwell; p. 289, © Jed Wilcox; p. 291, photo courtesy of Goodyear Tire & Rubber Co.

Chapter 11   P. 308, © Lou Jones; p. 322, drawing by Saxon; © 1985 The New Yorker Magazine, Inc.; p. 313, advertising courtesy of AT&T; p. 319, courtesy of Coca-Cola U.S.A.; p. 320, courtesy of Campbell Soup Company; p. 323, J. Walter Thompson/San Francisco: Copywriter, Michael Gallagher; Art Director, Rory Phoenix.

Chapter 12   P. 332, courtesy of Burroughs Corporation; p. 334, Yamaha International; p. 337, compliments of Danskin; p. 339, reprinted by permission of Tribune Media Services; p. 340, courtesy of Campbell Soup Company; p. 343, courtesy of Brockway, Inc (NY); p. 348, courtesy of Yugo America, Inc.

Chapter 13   P. 362, © 1985 by Sidney Harris - Management Review; p. 363, © 1985 Bob Colton/Black Star; p. 367, photo courtesy of Fleming Companies, Inc.; p. 371, © Steve Liss/Gamma-Liaison; p. 373, Emery Air Freight — photographed by Skip Perry; p. 374, Tenneco Inc. — photo by Carlos Carpenter; p. 376, photo courtesy of Staley Continental, Inc., Chicago.

Chapter 14   P. 389, The Coleman Company, Inc.; p. 390, courtesy of The Potato Board; p. 397, Merck & Co., Inc.; p. 398, © 1986 Singer Communications, Inc., Anaheim, CA 92801; p. 399, © Mark Joseph; p. 401, © 1982 Will McIntyre/Photo Researchers.

Chapter 15   P. 421, © 1984 Richard Howard; p. 428, photo courtesy of Arthur Young & Company; p. 431, Scott Maclay/Gannett Co., Inc.; p. 435, © 1984 Black Star, courtesy of Ernst & Whinney; p. 443, © 1985 M. Twohy, Datamation.

Chapter 16   P. 452, UPI/Bettmann Newsphotos; p. 457, courtesy of Cray Research, Inc.; p. 459, courtesy of Radio Shack, a division of Tandy Corporation; p. 461, © 1986 Singer Communications, Inc., Anaheim, CA 92801; p. 467, courtesy of Burroughs Corporation; p. 440, © Jan Staller; p. 472, courtesy of The Firestone Tire & Rubber Company.

Chapter 17   P. 495, "Sally Forth" by Greg Howard; © by and permission of News America Syndicate, 1985; p. 496, Barnett Banks of Florida, Inc./McElwee & McElwee; p. 502, Wide World Photos; p. 510, photo courtesy of Bank of Boston; p. 513, courtesy of Discover Card Services Inc.

Chapter 18   P. 523, © 1983 Richard Howard/Black Star; p. 524, © Cindy Charles; p. 528, © 1986 Singer Communications, Inc., Anaheim, CA 92801; p. 533, © Patrick McDowell/Park Photo; p. 538, courtesy of Indian Head Bank.

Chapter 19   P. 551, © Gallie-Figaro/Gamma-Liaison; p. 552, © 1986 Naoki Okamoto/Black Star; p. 556, courtesy of Skip Hine; p. 557, drawing by Levin; © 1985 The New Yorker Magazine, Inc.; p. 564, © P. Bosio/Gamma-Liaison.

Chapter 20   P. 573, Johnny Bailey/The Times; p. 576, permission granted by CIGNA Corporation; p. 583, courtesy of Figgie International Inc.; p. 586, © 1986 Singer Communications, Inc., Anaheim, CA 92801; p. 591, © 1986 Metropolitan Life Insurance Company, N.Y., NY; Peanuts Characters © 1952, 1966, 1971 United Feature Syndicate, Inc.; p. 593, © Dilip Mehta/Contact.

Chapter 21   P. 612, © 1985 Dan Ford Connolly/Gamma-Liaison; p. 576, © 1986 Paul Light; p. 579, © Pierre Perrin/Gamma-Liaison; p. 626, © J. P. Laffont/Sygma; p. 627, © 1986 Singer Communications, Inc., Anaheim, CA 92801.

Chapter 22   P. 635, © D. Walker/Gamma-Liaison; p. 638, © L. Maous/Gamma-Liaison; p. 639, © Gordon/Traub - Wayfarer; p. 640, © 1985 by Sidney Harris - Management Review; p. 643, © George Ott/Gamma-Liaison; p. 646, © Didier Delmas; p. 650, courtesy of Ashland Oil, Inc.

Chapter 23   P. 663, © Joseph Kugielsky; p. 664, © Henoch/Gamma-Liaison; p. 668, photo courtesy of Kellogg Company; *Kellogg's Zucaritas*® is a registered trademark of Kellogg Company; p. 671, © The Walt Disney Company; p. 673, courtesy of The Southland Corporation.

SUBJECT INDEX

Informal structure, 168, 170, 171

Information, 453; and computer crime, 609; and insider trading, 563, 565; in investment, 565; market, 365; presentation of, 478–480; and statistics, 473; through U.S. Census, 635. *See also* Communication; Data

Informational roles, 129

Information requirements: by functional area, 462–464; by management level, 464, 466

Information resources, 125, 126(tab); for basketball coach, 133(tab)

Information system, accounting as, 420(fig)

Information systems, *see* Management information system; Marketing information system

Informative advertising, 386

Informative (consultative) selling, 396, 397

Infringement, on brands, 338–339

In-house training programs, 231

Innovation: bureaucracy against, 170–171; international cooperation in, 674; 3M's reliance on, 19

Input devices, 456; terminals, 457

In Search of Excellence (Peters and Waterman), 143, 144(tab), 279

Insider information, 563, 565; and Swiss banks, 515

Insider Trading Sanctions Act (1984), 562–563

Inspection, in quality control, 285, 292

Institutional advertising, 390

In-store retailers, 366–367

Instrument, negotiable, 622–623

Insurable interest, 576

Insurable risk, 574, 576

Insurance, 573–577; and Bhopal disaster, 589, 592; categories of, 577; crisis in cost of, 575, 591–592; global policies for, 576; health, 587–588; liability, 575, 581–587, 591, 592–

593; life, 588, 590–591; no fault, 575, 578, 584, 584(fig); nuclear, 580; private, 500, 502, 581; property, 581–587, 593; public, 577–581; and risk, 570; in risk management, 571, 572–573; Social Security, 578–580 (*see also* Social Security); unemployment, 577–578; worker's compensation, 235, 578, 484

Insurance companies, 501, 577

Insurance policy, 539

Insurers, 572

Intangible assets, 430, 431

Intangible personal property, 618, 619

Integrated marketing, 311

Integration, vertical-channel, 360

Intensive distribution strategy, 360–361

Interactive mode (computer), 461

Interest rates: and debt financing, 536; and foreign investment in U.S., 537

Interlocking directorates, 639–640, 641(fig)

Intermediaries (middlemen), 308, 356–357; and costs, 324; financial, 497–503, 510–511; and intensive distribution, 361; retailers as, 358–359, 366–372; roles of, 356–358; wholesalers as, 358–359, 362–363, 365–366, 399

Intermediate appellate courts, 612–613

Intermittent processing, 277

Internal data sources, 466

Internal financing, 522

Internal motivators, 188–189

Internal Revenue Service, reporting requirements of, 419

Internal sources of employees, 224(tab)

International Accounting Standards Committee, 433

International Amateur Athletics Federation, 669

International business: and ethnocentrism, 226, 668; insurance for, 576; and job loss, 675; multina-

tional corporations, 433, 589, 637, 672–673; and network corporations, 159; training for, 668, 670; types of venture in, 670–671; and U.S. policy, 637

International Monetary Fund (IMF), 662

International trade, 658

International Workers of the World, 245

Interpersonal skills, of managers, 128, 133

Interstate Commerce Commission, 23

Interview, employment, 221, 225–227

Introduction stage, of product life cycle, 334

Inventory, 288, 430, 525; calculating value of (FIFO/LIFO), 436; as collateral, 528; wholesalers' maintaining of, 363, 366

Inventory control, 288–289, 376; just-in-time approach to, 278, 285, 289, 376, 378

Inventory control system: periodic, 435; perpetual, 434–435, 436

Inventory turnover, 438(tab)

Investment, 524–525; in commodities, 564; and corporations, 75; foreign, 671; and future strength vs. current profit, 441; and information, 565; international, 558; and limited partnership, 71; and pricing, 344; in securities, 546–547 (*see also* Securities); and social responsibility, 44; by thrift institutions, 502

Investment Advisers Act (1940), 562

Investment Company Act (1940), 562

Investment objectives, and mutual funds, 556

Investment scams, 526

Investor, 549(tab)

Involvement, through QWL, 192

IRA (Individual Retirement Account), 498

Issuer of bonds, 538

Japan: auto imports from 371–372, 664; and balance of payments, 661; computer networks in, 460; as creditor, 537; doubts about practices from, 187; GM competition with, 129; just-in-time inventory system from, 264, 275, 356; quality circles in, 193; quality pursued in, 285; rice protection by, 663; and Saturn factory, 263; selling to, 403; stock performance in, 558; and technological innovation, 674; and Theory Z, 192–193; training schools in, 131; and U.S. auto companies, 342

Job analysis, 217–218

Jobbers, rack, 361(tab)

Job creation, 94(fig); in service economy, 198

Job description, 218

Job enlargement, 189; in Japanese auto plants, 195

Job enrichment, 188–189

Job-order processing, 277

Job posting, 224(tab)

Job rotation, 189, 231(tab)

Job satisfaction: and QWL programs, 182, 192; and teamwork, 198

Job security, collective bargaining over, 259

Job sharing, 196–197

Joint venture, 69, 81; international, 671, 674

Judicial review, 613

Just-in-time inventory system, 278, 285, 289, 376, 378

Keogh plans, 498

Key person insurance, 591

Kilobytes (K), 455

Knights of Labor, 245

Labeling, 341

Labor: as factor of production, 20; supply of, 216–217. *See also* Employee(s); Work force

Labor-management relations, 244; and affirmative action, 213, 214(tab), 249; government regulation of, 246–251; collective-bargaining process in,

Utility, and marketing, 315
Utility program, 461
Utopian socialists, 14

Valuation of common stock, 530–532
Valuation of currency, 660–663; stability in, 496 (*see also* Inflation); and U.S. dollar, 494, 666–667, 668(tab)
Value: labor theory of, 14; of life, 589, 647; and money, 495, 496; of various jobs, 234
Value added network (VAN), 460
Values: of organization, 142; private vs. business, 52–53
Variable costs, 346
Variables, segmentation, 318, 362
Variance (statistical), 476
Venture capitalists, 530
Vermont Department of Agriculture, 646, 652
Vertical channel integration, 360
Vertical market allocation, 636
Vertical mergers, 82, 639
Veterans Administration (VA), mortgage insurance from, 581

Vietnam War, 41, 394
Vocational Rehabilitation Act (1973–1974), 214(tab)
Voting rights, for common stock, 636

Wages, 234; collective bargaining over, 257–258; in Herzberg's motivation model, 185
Wage/salary survey, 232
Wages and hours law, 255
Wagner Act (National Labor Relations Act), 248, 248(tab), 250
Wall Street, 552. *See also* Exchanges, securities
Warehouse receipt, 375
Warehousing, 375; and handling damage, 376
Warranties, UCC on, 619–620
Warranty of fitness for a particular purpose, 620
Warranty of merchantability, 620
Warranty of performance, 620
Warranty of title, 620
Waste, hazardous, 646–647
Water transport, 374, 375(tab)
Wealth of Nations, The (Smith), 16, 663
Wheel of retailing, 369(fig), 371–372, 613

White-collar productivity: computer improvement of, 468; and office design, 187
Whole life insurance, 590
Whole person: and human relations, 178 (*see also* Human relations); and technology, 233
Wholesaler, 358–359, 362–363; and retailers, 365–366; selling for, 399. *See also* Intermediaries
Women: and Civil Rights movement, 41; equal employment for, 238; and IBM in Japan, 668; and job sharing, 196–197; life insurance for, 591; and management ladder, 136, 139; as market, 306; recruitment of, 50; and small business, 96–97; in unions and workplace, 252, 253, 253(fig)
Work, in Herzberg's motivation model, 185
Worker involvement, motivation through, 194–196
Workers, *see* Employee(s)
Worker safety: and government regulation, 635; responsiblity for, 38, 40, 41–42

Worker's compensation, 235, 578, 584
Working capital, 101–102, 438(tab), 439–440
Working conditions: alternative work patterns in, 194–197; collective bargaining over, 255; and employee health, 179; government regulation of, 41; in Hawthorne Studies, 180; in Herzberg's motivation model, 185; during Industrial Revolution, 21, 22, 244; in office, 187; and orientation, 227; and "quality of work life" programs, 182
Work place: computer's effect on, 472; home as, 465, 472; regulation of, 645–646; women in, 253, 253(fig)
Workshops, as development program, 231(tab)
World War II, 23, 40

Xerox Social Service Leave Program, 47

Zero-based budgeting, 443
Zoning regulations, 284

NAME INDEX

Strauss, Levi, 21
Strawberry's, 315
Stride-Rite Corporation, 179
Sullivan, Dianne B., 34
Sullivan, Leon, 39
Sunbeam, 350
Sun Refining & Marketing Company (Sunoco), 360
Supermarkets General, 368(tab)
Suzuki, 278, 343

Target, 367
Taylor, Frederick, 165, 166
Teets, John, 124, 125, 130, 132, 133, 144–145
Tele-Communications, Inc., 550
Texaco, 47–48, 612
Texas Instruments, 168, 348

Texas Oil Company (Texaco), 360
3M company, 19, 143, 336, 399
Times Mirror Co., 534(tab)
Touche Ross & Co., 421(tab)
Toy Go Round, 100
Toyota, 193, 342, 674
Toys "R" Us, Inc., 356
Travelers Corp., 534(tab)
Travelers Insurance Company, 197
Triumph, 312
Tupperware, 371

Ueberroth, Peter, 152
UGI Corp., 534(tab)
Union Carbide, 589, 592
Union Carbide India Ltd., 589
U.S. Steel Corporation, 344–345

Vermont Castings, 311
Villers, Phillipe, 52
Volcker, Paul, 500
Volkswagen (VW), 342, 671

Walden Book Company, 88
Wal-mart Stores, Inc., 311, 345, 368(tab)
Wang Laboratories, 50
Warehouse Foods, 367
Washington Gas Light Co., 534(tab)
Waterman, Robert H., Jr., 143, 144(tab)
Wendy's International, Inc., 358
Western Electric, 180, 231
Westinghouse Electric Corp., 49
Weyerhaeuser, Frederick, 22
Whitney, Eli, 22

Whitney National Bank, New Orleans, 104
Wilson, Woodrow, and Federal Reserve Act, 504
Winans, R. Foster, 563
Winn-Dixie Stores, 368(tab)
Witkin, Arthur, 183
Woolworth, F. W., Company, 367, 368(tab)
Wozniak, Steve, 141
Wrangler Womenswear, 320

Xerox Corporation, 47, 143, 279

Yamaha, 334
Young, Arthur, & Co., 421(tab), 428
Yugo, 348

Zemke, Ron, 198